SOCIAL PROBLEMS

SOCIAL PROBLEMS

Thirteenth Edition

WILLIAM KORNBLUM
City University of New York
Graduate School and University Center

JOSEPH JULIAN, *Emeritus*
San Francisco State University

In collaboration with
CAROLYN D. SMITH

PEARSON

Prentice
Hall

Upper Saddle River, New Jersey 07458

Library of Congress Cataloging-in-Publication Data

Kornblum, William.
  Social problems / William Kornblum, Joseph Julian ; in collaboration with
Carolyn D. Smith. — 13th ed.
      p. cm.
  Includes bibliographical references and index.
  ISBN 0-13-601648-0 (alk. paper)
  1. Social problems—United States. 2. United States—Social conditions—
1980– I. Julian, Joseph. II. Smith, Carolyn D. III. Title.
  HN59.2.K66 2008
  361.1—dc22

                                        2007048001

Editorial Director: *Leah Jewell*
Director of Marketing: *Brandy Dawson*
Marketing Manager: *Lindsey Prudhomme*
Senior Operations Supervisor: *Sherry Lewis*
Operations Specialist: *Christina Amato*
Full-Service Project Management: *Lori Hazzard/*
  ICC Macmillan Inc.
Production Liaison: *Cheryl Keenan*
Editorial Assistant: *Lee Peterson*
Marketing Assistant: *Jessica Muraviov*
Senior Art Director: *Nancy Wells*
Art Director: *Anne Bonanno Nieglos*
Interior and Cover Design: *Kathryn Foot*

Line Art Illustrations: *ICC Macmillan Inc.*
Director, Image Resource Center: *Melinda Lee Patelli*
Manager, Rights and Permissions: *Zina Arabia*
Manager, Visual Research: *Beth Brenzel*
Manager, Cover Visual Research and Permissions:
  Karen Sanatar
Senior Image Permission Coordinator: *Cynthia Vincenti*
Photo Researcher: *Teri Stratford*
Cover Photo: *Todd Davidson/Stock Illustration Source, Inc./*
  Images.com
Director, Media and Assessment: *Shannon Gattens*
Media Project Manager: *Diane Lombardo*

This book was set in 10/12 Baskerville by ICC Macmillan Inc., and was printed
and bound by Worldcolor-Taunton. The cover was printed by Phoenix Color Corp.

Pearson Education LTD.
Pearson Education Singapore, Pte. Ltd
Pearson Education, Canada, Ltd
Pearson Education–Japan
Pearson Education Australia PTY, Limited

Pearson Education North Asia Ltd
Pearson Educación de Mexico, S.A. de C.V
Pearson Education Malaysia, Pte. Ltd
Pearson Education, Upper Saddle River, New Jersey

10 9 8 7 6 5 4 3
ISBN-13: 978-0-13-601648-9
ISBN-10:   0-13-601648-0

Brief Contents

Contents

Box Features

On Further Analysis

Unintended Consequences

Current Controversies

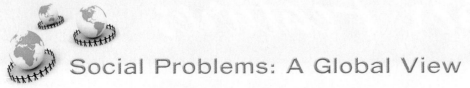

Social Problems: A Global View

Preface

This thirteenth edition of *Social Problems* appears during a period of intense political debate in the United States, a debate that is fueled, in part, by the continuing conflict in Iraq and the Middle East, by the threats of global warming, natural disasters, and food insecurity in many regions of the world, and by the rise of China, India, and Iran as new economic and political powers on the world scene. During the life of this edition, the United States will have a new president and Congress. A new federal administration will no doubt develop policies to address issues such as the crisis in health care for low-income Americans, the erosion of the United States' reputation in the Islamic world and elsewhere, and much more. Does that mean we can expect enormous progress toward solving domestic and global social problems? Not likely, because the problems discussed in this text have been with us for generations and do not admit of easy solutions. But no doubt there will be changes in policy based on trends that we can already determine.

Fortunately, for every major social problem there are groups of people dedicated to seeking a solution. Some of them are experts on particular social problems, like the members of the medical profession who each day confront the tragedy of AIDS, or the law enforcement professionals who cope with crime and violence. Others are nonprofessionals, often citizens who have decided to devote themselves to doing something about a particular situation or problem. Among these activists are people who have experienced the condition they seek to improve—women who have suffered sexual abuse, people who know what it is to be homeless, drug and alcohol abusers who want to help themselves and others, and neighbors confronted with the dumping of toxic wastes. Such groups may include elected officials and other political leaders who are expected to formulate sound social policies to address social problems. This book is written in an effort to make their work more effective and in the hope that some readers will be moved to take up their causes. We dedicate it to the citizens of the world who devote some of their precious time on earth to helping others.

ORGANIZATION OF THE BOOK

The first few chapters of this book focus on relatively individual behaviors, such as drug use and crime. The social institutions and other factors that affect these behaviors are noted and described. The middle chapters focus on inequality and discrimination, discussing such topics as poverty, prejudice, sexism, and ageism. Every attempt has been made to indicate the effects of large-scale discrimination on individuals, as well as to deal with the concept of institutionalized inequalities. Later chapters discuss problems that are common to many societies, such as those related to family life and work. The final chapters—on the problems of cities, environmental pollution, and war and terrorism—focus on matters of global significance. It seems best to discuss each subject in a separate chapter in order to deal with it comprehensively and in depth. Throughout the book, however, an attempt has been made to indicate how the different problems overlap and are interrelated.

PEDAGOGICAL DEVICES

Social Problems has been designed to be as helpful as possible to both students and teachers. Each problem is discussed in a well-organized and readable manner. As much as possible, unnecessary terminology has been avoided. The treatment of each problem is analytical as well as descriptive and includes the most up-to-date findings available.

Each chapter begins with an outline and a list of dominant trends—new in this edition—and ends with a summary that lists the important concepts presented. Important terms within the chapter are boldfaced and listed at the end of the chapter, and their definitions are included in the glossary at the end of the book. In addition, boxed discussions in each chapter deal with *Current Controversies* or *Unintended Consequences* speaking of efforts to alleviate social problems. Boxes entitled *On Further Analysis* appear in most chapters, where appropriate. Each of these boxes takes a problem that has been in the public spotlight and shows how controversies over the problem are addressed by research. An *On Further Analysis* box on racial profiling, for example, examines quantitative research on the problem of "Driving While Black" and shows how findings can have a decisive influence on how this vexing social problem is addressed. Many chapters also include a box, entitled *Social Problems: A Global View,* that discusses a particular social problem from a global perspective.

In keeping with the book's effort to achieve as much sociological objectivity as possible, there is a section at the end of each chapter called *Going Beyond Left and Right.* Its purpose is to help students think critically about the partisan debates over the problems discussed in the chapter they have just read. Each chapter also includes a pedagogical aid entitled *Social Problems Online,* which will help students use the World Wide Web to inquire more deeply into particular social problems. *Research Navigator* exercises are provided at the end of each chapter.

CHANGES IN THE THIRTEENTH EDITION

The reception given to previous editions of *Social Problems* by both colleagues and students has been encouraging, and many of their suggestions and criticisms have been incorporated in subsequent revisions. This edition represents a continuing effort to create a text that meets the needs of students and instructors and is comprehensive and up-to-date. To this end, the text has been thoroughly revised. Our aim has been to retain the book's emphasis on the sociological analysis of social problems, as well as the policies designed to alleviate or eliminate them. Although policies change continually, we have attempted to update the discussions of policy to reflect the most recent thinking about solutions to social problems.

Throughout the text, we have made numerous changes to reflect current trends in social problems or new research findings. A new section in Chapter 1 discusses the "culture war." In Chapter 2 we have added or expanded discussions of obesity, cost shifting, and the situation of Americans who are working but lack health insurance. Chapter 3 has a new *Current Controversies* box on the Virginia Tech massacre, along with expanded discussions of the effects of crowding and military duty on mental health. Chapter 5 includes an expanded discussion of gangs and violence, as well as a new section on identity theft. Chapter 6 includes a new section on the severely poor along with expanded discussions of the working poor and of welfare policies and growing inequality.

Chapter 7 offers an analysis of the social construction of minorities and a new section on political discrimination, including felony disenfranchisement and anti-voter fraud campaigns. Chapter 8 includes an expanded discussion of same-sex marriage. Chapter 10 has new sections on shelter poverty and homelessness and on abstinence-only programs. Chapter 11 has an expanded discussion of international comparisons of student achievement, along with a discussion of the recent Supreme Court ruling on segregation. Also in this chapter are new sections on Asian students and on Reading First programs.

Chapter 12 incorporates a discussion of the changing nature of jobs and the resulting economic insecurity. Chapter 14 includes a discussion of Iraqi refugees and new sections on modes of entry for illegal immigrants and on immigration reform. Chapter 15 has a new section on transhumanism and a discussion of chemical contamination of the food supply. Finally, Chapter 16 includes a new section on patterns of global terrorism.

Throughout the text, statistical material, figures, and tables have been updated wherever necessary, and recent research has been cited throughout. The *Social Policy* sections incorporate recent programs and proposals.

SUPPLEMENTS

Instructors and students who use this textbook have access to a number of materials designed to complement the classroom lectures and activities and to enhance the students' learning experience.

For the Instructor

Instructor's Resource Manual with Tests (0-13-601650-2)   For each chapter in the text, this valuable resource provides a detailed outline, a list of objectives, discussion questions, and classroom activities. In addition, test questions in multiple-choice and short-answer formats are available for each chapter; the answers to all questions are page referenced to the text.

TestGen (0-13-601651-0)   This computerized software allows instructors to create their own personalized exams, to edit any or all of the existing test questions, and to add new questions. Other special features of this program include random generation of test questions, creation of alternate versions of the same test, scrambling question sequence, and test preview before printing.

PowerPoint® Slides   These PowerPoint slides combine graphics and text for each chapter in a colorful format to help you convey the main topics covered in the text in a new and exciting way. For easy access, they are available at www.prenhall.com.

Social Problems Overhead Transparencies (0-13-111569-3)   Taken from graphs, diagrams, and tables in this text and other sources, these transparencies offer an effective way to illustrate lecture topics.

ABCNEWS ABC News/Pearson Video Library for Social Problems on DVD (0-13-601689-8)   This completely updated set includes selected video segments from award-winning ABC News programs such as *Nightline*, *ABC World News Tonight*, and *20/20* to accompany topics featured in the text. Please contact your local Pearson sales representative for more details.

Course Management   Pearson offers courses in both BlackBoard and WebCT. Each course includes the PowerPoint presentations, all of the instructor supplements, testing software, and select videos. For students, there are chapter study questions, quizzes, concept tips, and flash cards. Contact your local Pearson representative for more information on the courses and access code package ISBNs.

For the Student

Study Guide (0-13-601649-9)   This complete guide helps students to review and reflect on the material presented in *Social Problems,* 13th edition. Each of the chapters in the Study Guide provides an overview of the corresponding chapter in the student text, summarizes its major topics and concepts, offers review exercises, and features end-of-chapter tests with solutions.

Companion Website™   In tandem with the text, students can now take full advantage of the World Wide Web to enrich their study of social problems through the Kornblum Companion Website™. This resource correlates the text with related material available on the Internet. Features include chapter objectives, study questions, research projects, and links to additional material that can reinforce and enhance the content of each chapter. Address: www.prenhall.com/kornblum.

Research Navigator™   Research Navigator™ can help students complete research assignments efficiently and with confidence by providing three exclusive databases of high-quality scholarly and popular articles accessed by easy-to-use search engines.

- **EBSCO's ContentSelect™ Academic Journal Database,** organized by subject, contains the leading academic journals for sociology. Instructors and students can search the online journals by keyword, topic, or multiple topics. Articles include abstract and citation information and can be cut, pasted, e-mailed, or saved for later use.

- *The New York Times* **Search-by-Subject™ Archive** provides articles specific to sociology and is searchable by keyword or multiple keywords. Instructors and students can view full-text articles from the world's leading journalists writing for the New York Times.

- **Link Library** offers editorially selected "best of the Web" sites for sociology. Link Libraries are continually scanned and kept up-to-date, providing the most relevant and accurate links for research assignments.

Gain access to Research Navigator™ by using the access code found in the front of the brief guide called *The Prentice Hall Guide to Research Navigator™*. Please contact your Pearson representative for more information.

"10 Ways to Fight Hate" brochure (013-028146-8) Produced by the Southern Poverty Law Center, the leading hate crime and crime watch organization in the United States, this free supplement walks students through ten steps they can take on their own campus or in their own neighborhood to fight hate every day.

ACKNOWLEDGMENTS

Revising and updating a social problems textbook is a formidable task, from which the currently active authors, William Kornblum and collaborator Carolyn Smith, continue to learn a great deal. Social problems is a far-ranging field with myriad findings and concepts that accumulate rapidly and often change. This edition has benefited from the reviews of many sociologists, all of whom have contributed useful comments and suggestions. We are happy to number among them the following: Annette Schwabe, Florida State University; Greg A. Olsen, University of Wisconsin-Oshkosh; George W. Glann, Jr., Fayetteville Technical Community College; Dale Howard, Northwest Arkansas Community College; Brian C. Aldrich, Winona State University; Bobbie Brannon, Catawba Valley Community College; Theo Ekechukwu, Northwest Arkansas Community College.

To the following, whose suggestions have enriched all twelve previous editions, a special thank you: Mark Abrahamson, University of Connecticut; Lynn Anderson, Navarro College; Howard Bahr, Brigham Young University; Jeanne Ballantine, Wright State University; Nancy Bartkowski, Northern Michigan University; William Bielby, University of California—Santa Barbara; Susan L. Blackwell, Delgado Community

College; Edwin Boling, Wittenberg University; Bradley Jay Buchner, Cheyney University of Pennsylvania; Walter F. Carroll, Bridgewater State College; Carol E. Chandler, McHenry County College; Barbara K. Chesney, University of Toledo; Verghese J. Chirayath, John Carroll University; William T. Clute, University of Nebraska—Omaha; William Cockerham, University of Illinois, Urbana—Champaign; William L. Collins, Asheville–Buncombe Technical Community College; Paul L. Crook, San Diego Mesa College; William M. Cross, Illinois College; Phillip W. Davis, Georgia State University; Patrick G. Donnelly, University of Dayton; Lois Easterday, Onondaga Community College; John Farley, Southern Illinois University; Michael P. Farrell, State University of New York—Buffalo; William Feigelman, Nassau Community College; Keith R. Fernsler, Dickinson State University; James E. Floyd, Macon College; Morris A. Forslund, University of Wyoming; Sidney Forsythe, Wheaton College; John Galliher, University of Missouri; Harry Gold, Oakland University; Erich Goode, State University of New York—Stony Brook; Norman Goodman, State University of New York—Stony Brook; Marshall Graney, Wayne State University; James Greenley, University of Wisconsin; Julia Hall, Drexel University; John Hedderson, University of Texas—El Paso; John Hendricks, University of Kentucky; Simona Hill, Susquehanna University; Brenda A. Hoke, Agnes Scott College; Mary R. Holley, Montclair State College; Nils Hovik, Lehigh County Community College; Gary Jensen, University of Arizona; Richard I. Jolliff, El Camino College; Russell I. Johnson, Washington University; Daniel J. Klenow, North Dakota State University; Louis Kriesberg, Syracuse University; Patricia Lengermann, George Washington University; Betty Levine, Indiana University; and Marie Pease Lewis, Macon College.

Also, Peter Maida, University of Maryland; Wilfred Marston, University of Michigan—Flint; Edward J. McCabe, Eastern Michigan University; Richard L. Meile, Indiana University, Northwest; Steven Messner, State University of New York, Albany; Robert G. Miller, Baker University; Linda Mooney, East Carolina University; George C. Myers, Duke University; Charles Nam, Florida State University; Steven Nock, University of Virginia; Donald Noel, University of Wisconsin; Donald Olmsted, Michigan State University; Dennis L. Peck, The University of Alabama; Barry Perlman, Community College of Philadelphia; Robert Perucci, Purdue University; Edward Ponczek, William Rainey Harper College; Karen Predow, formerly of Rutgers University; Robert Rothman, University of Delaware; Nora Roy, Tennessee University; Laura Sanchez, Tulane University; Earl R. Schaeffer, Columbus State Community College; David Schulz, University of Delaware; Mary Sellers, Northampton County Area Community College; Steven C. Seyer, Lehigh Carbon Community College; John W. Shepard, Jr., Baylor University; Edward G. Stockwell, Bowling Green State University; Russell Stone, State University of New York—Buffalo; Ann Sundgren, Tacoma Community College; John Tenuto, DePaul University; Kenrick S. Thompson, Arkansas State University, Mountain Home; Kevin Thompson, North Dakota State University; Deidre Tyler, Salt Lake Community College; Miriam G. Vosburgh, Villanova University; William Waegel, Villanova University; Ruth Wallace, George Washington University; Susan J. Marnell Weaver, Miami University (Ohio); and Irving Zola, Brandeis University.

Finally, thanks are due to the many skilled publishing specialists who contributed their talents to this edition. Administrative aspects of the project were skillfully handled by Editorial Director, Leah Jewell. Kathryn Foot created a pleasing design. Lori Hazzard, the project manager, did an enormous amount of work to get the book out on time. Teri Stratford took charge of rounding up the photographs that complement the text, and Christina Amato was responsible for the manufacturing process. The book owes much to the efforts, creativity, and perseverance of each of them.

SOCIAL PROBLEMS

SOCIOLOGICAL PERSPECTIVES
on Social Problems

Dominant Trends

- *From the congressional elections of 2006 to the presidential election of 2008, terrorism and the American occupation of Iraq have been the dominant social problems cited by Americans.*

- *On the domestic front, education, health care, the environment (including the problem of global warming), and crime are the top-ranking problems—in that order—that Americans want the federal government to use their tax dollars to address.*

- *Since the 2006 congressional elections, an increasing proportion of American voters have included official corruption in their thinking about crime as a social problem.*

- *The growing disparity between the fortunes of the "haves" and the "have-nots" is increasingly cited throughout the world as the outstanding problem, along with global warming, confronting the human species.*

Although the final outcome is uncertain at this writing, it is highly unlikely that the Bush administration's initial high expectations for the Iraq war can be met. Americans face agonizing choices about how to help maintain security in Iraq while contributing to the rebuilding of a nation riven by civil strife. At home, the war on terror has strained the federal budget and made it more difficult to address longstanding social problems such as the lack of adequate health care for a very large and growing segment of the population. Have the failure of aggressive American policies in the Middle East and the devastation and delayed rebuilding of New Orleans after Hurricane Katrina caused Americans to examine their priorities and seek new directions in addressing global and domestic social problems? This is a question to which we will return in many chapters of this book.

The same need to assess the possibilities for progress versus the potential worsening of social problems also applies to the globalization of economic activities that is such a distinctive aspect of social relations in the new millennium (Stiglitz, 2002; Friedman, 2005). Globalization of economic activities provides lower-cost goods for consumers in the United States and other advanced industrial nations. It brings new jobs and more rapid economic development to developing regions of the world like the Indian subcontinent and China. The same processes of economic globalization, however, take jobs away from workers in the world's wealthier nations, including the United States. Forced to compete with lower-wage workers elsewhere, American workers and their families increasingly face the loss of pensions and other benefits that they have come to expect. Globalization, which relies on technologies such as jet travel and the Internet to "shrink the world" and speed the flow of information and commerce, also facilitates the rise of new forms of crime and other social problems, such as identity theft and the spread of relatively new diseases like AIDS.

The United States and other Western nations are experiencing far more internal conflict about how to address social problems than was true in the decades following World War II. For a few decades after the devastation and collective sacrifices of that war, there appears to have been far more consensus that governments should play an important role in providing a "social safety net" for those members of the society who lacked the means to provide an adequate level of living for themselves and their children. Today there is more debate about private versus private responsibility for addressing issues such as poverty, ill health, and environmental degradation. Americans may be divided over such issues as abortion, capital punishment, and the separation of church and state, for example, but we will also see indications that they yearn for leaders and policies that will steer them away from divisive issues toward improvements in the social safety net and the nation's responses to environmental crises.

The ongoing "culture wars," as ideological divisions and debates are often called, make it far more difficult for people to arrive at a broad consensus about which social policies are most effective for dealing with major social problems like poverty, lack of medical care, crime, and insecurity. No doubt there will be many instances in which readers of this text will want to argue strongly for one set of policies versus another, and this is perfectly legitimate and desirable. But it is the authors' task to present the basic facts and trends regarding major social problems in an objective fashion. Another main goal of this text is to show how social-scientific thinking about these problems can lead to progress in understanding their causes and arriving at policies to address them. The congressional elections of 2006 and the 2008 presidential election campaign showed that younger voters are becoming far more actively concerned about social problems than was true even a decade ago. In consequence, every chapter in this book ends with a discussion of how social policies at different levels of government and in the private sector can address specific social problems. We turn first, therefore, to the question of how social problems are defined and perceived by the public and by social scientists.

WHAT IS A SOCIAL PROBLEM?

We will see throughout this book that social problems are often closely interrelated. Crime, poverty, lack of medical care, violence, drug abuse, and many other behaviors or situations that we commonly think of as social problems rarely exist in isolation. And for any one of the problems just named or others we could cite, there are vigorous debates about causes and responsibilities. Are we responsible, some ask, for the sins of others? Are not many people with AIDS to blame for their illness, since it is often spread through casual, unprotected sex? Others might point out that the consequences of AIDS and other illnesses are problems that should concern everyone. These and similar arguments deal not only with the causes of social problems but also with what should be done about them. Most people will agree that terrorism, accounting fraud, and AIDS are problems that society must somehow address, and this is true for all the other issues mentioned earlier. Most members of society agree that they are conditions that ought to be remedied through intentional action.

Of course, agreement that remedies are necessary does not imply that people agree on what the remedies should be. Most people would like to see a reduction in rates of poverty and homelessness, but far fewer agree that welfare payments are a reasonable way of dealing with these social problems in the absence of work requirements. However, work requirements, in turn, introduce the difficulty of ensuring that there actually is work available that can be done by poor people with little education. The same controversies arise in connection with almost all social problems. Many Americans are appalled at the level of gun violence in their nation, but many others are equally appalled at the prospect of more government restrictions on their freedom to buy and use guns as they wish. Clearly, recognition that a social problem exists is far different from arriving at a consensus about a solution to the problem.

When enough people in a society agree that a condition exists that threatens the quality of their lives and their most cherished values, and they also agree that something should be done to remedy that condition, sociologists say that the society has defined that condition as a **social problem.** In other words, the society's members have reached a consensus that a condition that affects some members of the population is a problem for the entire society, not just for those who are directly affected. We will see, however, that for every social problem, there are arguments about the nature of the problem, its severity, and the best remedies—laws, social programs, or other policies—to address it. There must be enough consensus among people in a society that a problem exists for action to take place, but this does not mean that the consensus is general. In fact, we will also see that not all people count equally in defining social problems and seeking remedies.

For better or worse, even in mature democracies like those of the United States and Europe, more powerful actors have far greater influence in defining social problems than average citizens do. Rupert Murdoch, for example, is an Australian-born businessman who owns television and newspaper companies not just in the United States and Great Britain, but throughout the world. His media empire includes the Fox network and many others that adhere to his personal editorial views, which are strongly opposed to government intervention in the battle against poverty and lack of health care and very much in favor of a strong role for government in combating crime and pursuing the global "war" on terrorism.

The importance of power in the definition of social problems becomes clear if we consider one or two examples. In China, before the Communist revolution of the mid-twentieth century, opium use and addiction were widespread. In Shanghai alone there were an estimated 400,000 opium addicts in the late 1940s. Everyone knew that the condition existed, and many responsible public figures deplored it, but few outside the revolutionary parties believed society should intervene in any way. After all, many of the country's richest and most powerful members had made their fortunes in the opium trade. However, the Chinese Communists believed society should take responsibility for eradicating opium addiction, and when they took power, they did so, often through drastic and violent means. What had previously been seen as a social condition had been redefined as a social problem that had to be solved.

How does the amount of power that groups and individuals have help determine whether a situation in society is defined as a social problem?

To take an example from our own society, before 1920 women in the United States did not have the right to vote. Many women objected to this condition and opposed it whenever possible, but most men and many women valued the traditional pattern of male dominance and female subservience. To them, there was nothing unusual about women's status as second-class citizens. It took many years of painstaking organization, persuasion, and demonstration by the leaders of the woman suffrage movement to convince significant numbers of Americans that women's lack of voting rights was a social problem that society should remedy through revision of its laws. We will see later in the book, especially in Chapter 8, that the conditions affecting women's lives continue to be viewed by some members of society as natural and inevitable and by others as problems that require action by society as a whole (Lorber, 1994).

It is worth noting that the idea that a society should intervene to remedy conditions that affect the lives of its citizens is a fairly recent innovation. Until the eighteenth century, for example, most people worked at exhausting tasks under poor conditions for long hours; they suffered from severe deprivation all their lives, and they often died young, sometimes of terrible diseases. But no one thought of these things as problems to be solved. They were accepted as natural, inevitable conditions of life. It was not until the so-called "enlightenment" of the late eighteenth century that philosophers began to argue that poverty is not inevitable, but a result of an unjust social system. As such, it could be alleviated by changing the system itself through such means as redistribution of wealth and elimination of inherited social status.

The founders of the American nation applied these principles in creating a form of government that was designed to "establish justice, insure domestic tranquility . . . promote the general welfare . . . and secure the blessings of liberty." The U.S. Constitution guaranteed the rights of individual citizens and established the legal basis for remedying conditions that are harmful to society's members. Moreover, through the system of representative government that it also created, the Constitution established a means by which citizens could define a condition like poverty as one that society should attempt to remedy. Later in this chapter and at many points throughout the book, we will see how this process is carried out and the effects it has had and continues to have on American society.

We will also see many instances of the interconnections among social problems. Very often, when government leaders seek solutions to social problems, they must consider multifaceted approaches that address entire sets of problems rather than a single problem by itself, a situation that makes the formulation of effective social policy quite difficult.

PERSPECTIVES ON SOCIAL PROBLEMS

Everyone has opinions about the causes of social problems and what should be done about them. Some people will argue, for example, that the problems of a homeless single mother are her own fault. She may be morally loose or mentally unsound, not very bright, or not motivated to work hard and lift herself and her family out of poverty. These are all familiar explanations of individual misfortune. At worst, they blame the individual for his or her situation. At best, they explain individual troubles in terms of traits that the person cannot control. In fact, for this one unfortunate woman, any of these simple explanations might be true. But even if they are true for particular individuals, none of them tells us why the same pattern is repeated for entire groups of people.

Why do women become single mothers, and why do single mothers often become homeless as well? Why are women who are born into poor and minority families more likely to become single mothers, and possibly heads of homeless families, than are women who are born into middle-class families of any racial or ethnic group? And does the experience of being homeless inflict hardships on women and children that make it more difficult for them to perform productive roles in society and attain the good life?

These are sociological questions. They ask why a condition like homelessness exists. They ask how the condition is distributed in society and whether some people are more at risk than others. They are questions about the social rather than the individual aspects of a problem. And they are important not merely from an academic or social-scientific viewpoint. Answers to these questions are a prerequisite for effective action to eliminate social problems. Note, however, that research on these issues is not limited to sociology. Other social-scientific approaches to the study of social problems are described in Table 1–1.

What are the major perspectives that sociologists use to study social problems?

Contemporary sociology is founded on three basic perspectives, or sets of ideas, that offer theories about why societies hang together and how and why they change. These perspectives are not the only sociological approaches to social problems, but they can be extremely powerful tools for understanding them. Each of these perspectives—functionalism, conflict theory, and interactionism—gives rise to a number of useful and distinctive approaches to the study of social problems. (See Table 1–2.) We explore several of those approaches in the following sections, devoting special attention to how they seek to explain one of society's most pressing problems: criminal deviance.

The Functionalist Perspective

From the day we are born until the day we die, all of us hold a position—a **status**—in a variety of groups and organizations. In a hospital, for example, the patient, the nurse, the doctor, and the orderly are all members of a social group concerned with health care. Each of these individuals has a status that requires the performance of a certain set of behaviors, known as a **role.** Taken together, the statuses and roles of the members of this medical team and other teams in hospitals throughout the country make up the social institution known as the health-care system. An **institution** is a more or less stable structure of statuses and roles devoted to meeting the basic needs of people in a society. The health-care system is an institution; hospitals, insurance companies, and private medical practices are examples of organizations within this institution.

TABLE 1–1	Other Approaches to the Study of Social Problems

In addition to sociology, other disciplines in the social sciences are concerned with the analysis of human behavior, and sociologists often draw on the results of their research. The work of historians, for example, is vital to an understanding of the origins of many social problems. The research of anthropologists on nonindustrial and tribal societies offers contrasting views of how humans have learned to cope with various kinds of social problems. Perhaps the greatest overlap is between sociology and political science, both of which are concerned with the processes by which policies deal with social problems that arise in different societies. Here are brief descriptions of several social-scientific disciplines whose research findings have a bearing on the study of social problems.

HISTORY
History is the study of the past. However, historical data can be used by sociologists to understand present social problems. In studying homelessness, for example, historians would focus on changes in how people obtained shelter in a society and what groups or individuals tended to be without shelter in different historical periods.

CULTURAL ANTHROPOLOGY
Cultural anthropologists study the social organization and development of smaller, nonindustrial societies, both past and present. Because cultural anthropology is closely related to sociology, many of the same techniques can be used in both fields, and the findings of cultural anthropologists regarding primitive and traditional cultures shed light on related phenomena in more complex, modern societies. An anthropological study of homelessness would look closely at one or a few groups of homeless people. The anthropologist might be interested in how the homeless and others in their communities understand their situation and what might be done about it.

PSYCHOLOGY AND SOCIAL PSYCHOLOGY
Psychology deals with human mental and emotional processes, focusing primarily on individual experience. Rooted in biology, it is more experimental than the other social sciences. An understanding of the psychological pressures that underlie individual responses can illuminate social attitudes and behavior. Thus, a psychologist would tend to study the influences of homelessness on the individual's state of mind or, conversely, how the individual's personality and ways of looking at life might have contributed to his or her situation.

Social psychology—the study of how psychological processes, behavior, and personalities of individuals influence or are influenced by social processes and social settings—is of particular value for the study of social problems. A social psychologist would be likely to study how life on the streets damages the individual in various ways.

ECONOMICS
Economists study the levels of income in a society and the distribution of income among the society's members. To understand how the resources of society—its people and their talents, its land, and other natural resources—can be allocated for the maximum benefit of that society, economists also study the relationship between the supply of resources and the demand for them. Confronted with the problem of homelessness, an economist would tend to study how the supply of and demand for different types of housing influence the number of homeless people in a given housing market.

POLITICAL SCIENCE
Political scientists study the workings of government at every level of society. As Harold Lasswell (1941), a leading American political scientist, put it, "Politics is the study of who gets what, when, and how." A political scientist, therefore, would be likely to see homelessness as a problem that results from the relative powerlessness of the homeless to influence the larger society to respond to their needs. The political scientist would tend to focus on ways in which the homeless could mobilize other political interest groups to urge legislators to deal with the problem.

The functionalist perspective looks at the way major social institutions like the family, the military, the health care system, and the police and courts actually operate. According to this perspective, the role behavior associated with any given status has evolved as a means of allowing a particular social institution to fulfill its function in society. Thus, the nurse's role requires specific knowledge and behaviors that involve

TABLE 1–2 | Major Perspectives on Social Problems

Perspective	View of Society and Social Problems	Origins of Social Problems	Proposed Solutions
Functionalist	Views society as a vast organism whose parts are interrelated; social problems are disruptions of this system. Also holds that problems of social institutions produce patterns of deviance and that institutions must address such patterns through strategic social change.	Social expectations fail, creating normlessness, culture conflict, and breakdown. Social problems also result from the impersonal operations of existing institutions, both now and in the past.	Engage in research and active intervention to improve social institutions. Create new organizations to address social problems.
Conflict	Views society as marked by conflicts due to inequalities in class, race, ethnicity, gender, age, and other divisions that produce conflicting values. Defines social problems as conditions that do not conform to society's values.	Groups with different values and differing amounts of power meet and compete.	Build stronger social movements among groups with grievances. The conflicting groups may then engage in negotiations and reach mutual accommodations.
Interactionist	Holds that definitions of deviance or social problems are subjective; separates deviant and nondeviant people not by what they do, but by how society reacts to what they do.	Society becomes aware that certain behaviors exist and labels them as social problems.	Resocialize deviants by increasing their contacts with accepted patterns of behavior; make the social system less rigid. Change the definition of what is considered deviant.

treatment of the patient's immediate needs and administration of care according to the doctor's orders. The patient, in turn, is expected to cooperate in the administration of the treatment. When all members of the group perform their roles correctly, the group is said to be functioning well.

In a well-functioning group, there is general agreement about how roles are to be performed by each member. These expectations are reinforced by the society's basic values, from which are derived rules about how people should and should not behave toward each other in different situations. The Ten Commandments, the Golden Rule, the Bill of Rights, and the teachings of all of the world's religions are examples of sets of rules that specify how people should behave in different social roles.

But if society is made up of groups in which people know their roles and adhere to the underlying values, why do we have social problems like crime and warfare, and why does it seem so difficult to make social organizations function effectively? From the functionalist perspective, the main reason for the existence of social problems is that societies are always changing and having to adapt to new conditions; failure to adapt successfully leads to social problems.

The French social theorist Émile Durkheim observed that changes in a society can drastically alter the goals and functions of human groups and organizations. As a society undergoes a major change—say, from agricultural to industrial production—the statuses people assume and the roles they play also change, with far-reaching consequences. Thus, for example, the tendency for men and women from rural backgrounds to have many children, which was functional in agrarian societies because it produced much-needed farmhands, can become a liability in an urban-industrial society, where housing space is limited and the types of jobs available are constantly changing. From the standpoint of society's smooth functioning, it can be said that the roles of the father and mother in the rural setting, which stresses long periods of childbearing and many children, become dysfunctional in an urban setting.

Wars, colonial conquest, disease and famine, population increases, changing technologies of production, or communication, or health care—all these major social forces can change societies and thereby change the roles their members are expected to perform. As social groups strive to adapt to the new conditions, their members may feel that they are adrift—unsure of how to act or troubled by conflict over how to perform as parents or wage earners or citizens. They may question the values they learned as children and wonder what to teach their own children. This condition of social disequilibrium can lead to an increase in social problems like crime and mental illness as individuals seek their own, often antisocial, solutions to the dilemmas they face.

Criminal Deviance: A Functionalist View. From the functionalist perspective, all societies produce their own unique forms of crime and their own ways of responding to them. All sociologists recognize that there are causes within the individual that help explain why one person becomes a criminal while another, who may have experienced the same conditions, does not. But for the sociologist, especially one who applies the functionalist perspective, the question of why particular crimes are committed and punished in some societies and not in others is an important research topic. Why is it that until quite recently a black man who was suspected of making advances to a white woman was often punished more severely than one who was suspected of stealing? Why was the theft of a horse punishable by immediate death on the western frontier? Why was witchcraft considered such a heinous crime in the Puritan settlements of colonial New England? And why is it that these crimes continued to occur when those who committed them were punished so severely?

The functionalist answer is that societies fear most the crimes that seem to threaten their most cherished values, and individuals who dare to challenge those values will receive the most severe punishment. Thus, the freedom to allow one's horses to graze on common land was an essential aspect of western frontier society that was threatened by the theft of horses. The possibility that a white woman could entice a black man and that their affair could be interpreted as anything other than rape threatened the foundations of the American racial caste system, which held that blacks were inferior to whites. In both cases, immediate, sometimes brutal, punishment was used to reinforce the central values of the society.

Social Problems as Social Pathology. The functionalist perspective on problems like criminal deviance has changed considerably since the nineteenth century. In the late 1800s and early 1900s, functionalist theorists regarded such behavior as a form of "social disease," or **social pathology.** This view was rooted in the organic analogy that was popular at the time. Human society was seen as analogous to a vast organism, all of whose complex, interrelated parts function together to maintain the health and stability of the whole. Social problems arise when either individuals or social institutions fail to keep pace with changing conditions and thereby disrupt the healthy operation of the social organization; such individuals or institutions are considered "sick" (hence the term *social pathology*). In this view, for example, European immigrants who failed to adjust to American urban life were considered a source of "illness," at least insofar as they affected the health of their adopted society. Underlying this concept was a set of moral expectations; social problems violated the expectations of social order and progress.

Although many people who comment on social problems today are tempted to use the organic analogy and the disease concept, most sociologists reject this notion. The social-pathology approach is not very useful in generating empirical research; its concepts of sickness and morality are too subjective to be meaningful to many sociologists. Moreover, it attempts to apply a biological analogy to social conditions even when there is no empirical justification for doing so. More important, it is associated with the idea that the poor and other "deviant" groups are less fit to survive from an evolutionary perspective and hence should not be encouraged to reproduce. The social-pathology approach therefore has been largely discredited. Modern functionalists do not focus on the behaviors and problems of individuals; instead, they see social

How does a sociological perspective on a social problem differ from a psychological or economic perspective? Use a particular social problem to illustrate your answer.

problems as arising out of the failure of institutions like the family, the schools, and the economy to adapt to changing social conditions.

Social-Disorganization Theory. Rates of immigration, urbanization, and industrialization increased rapidly after World War I. Many newcomers to the cities failed to adapt to urban life. European immigrants, rural whites, and southern blacks were often crowded together in degrading slums and had trouble learning the language, manners, and norms of the dominant urban culture. Many of those who managed to adjust to the city were discriminated against because of their religion or race, and others lost their jobs because technological advances made their skills obsolete. Because of these conditions, many groups formed their own subcultures or devised other means of coping. Alcoholism, drug addiction, mental illness, crime, and delinquency rates rose drastically. Some sociologists believed the social-pathology viewpoint could not adequately explain the widespread existence of these social problems. They developed a new concept that eventually became known as *social-disorganization theory.*

This theory views society as being organized by a set of expectations or rules. **Social disorganization** results when these expectations fail, and it is manifested in three major ways: (1) *normlessness*, which arises when people have no rules that tell them how to behave; (2) *culture conflict*, which occurs when people feel trapped by contradictory rules; and (3) *breakdown*, which takes place when obedience to a set of rules is not rewarded or is punished. Rapid social change, for example, might make traditional standards of behavior obsolete without providing new standards, thereby giving rise to normlessness. The children of immigrants might feel trapped between the expectations of their parents and those of their new society—an example of culture conflict. And the expectations of blacks might be frustrated when they do well in school but encounter job discrimination; their frustration, in turn, might lead to breakdown.

The stress experienced by victims of social disorganization may result in a form of personal disorganization such as drug addiction or crime. The social system as a whole also feels the force of disorganization. It may respond by changing its rules, keeping contradictory rules in force, or breaking down. Disorganization can be halted or reversed if its causes are isolated and corrected.

An example of disorganization theory appears in the seminal work of Robert Sampson and his colleagues, who study the relationships between crime and neighborhood social disorganization (Sampson, 2001; Sampson & Raudenbush, 1999). Their work figures prominently in Chapter 5.

Modern Functionalism: Building Institutions. In this book we will see many instances in which social-disorganization theory has been used to explain social problems. A more modern version of the functionalist perspective attempts to show how people reorganize their lives to cope with new conditions. Often this results in new kinds of organizations and sometimes in whole new institutions. This research focus is known as the *institutional* or **institution-building** approach (Goodin, 1995; Janowitz, 1978). Research on how to improve the organization of public schools to meet new educational demands is an example.

The Conflict Perspective

By no means do all sociologists accept the functionalist view of society and social problems. There is an alternative set of theories, often known as the **conflict perspective,** that rejects the idea that social problems can be corrected by reforming institutions that are not functioning well. The conflict perspective is based on the belief that social problems arise out of major contradictions in the way societies are organized, contradictions that lead to large-scale conflict between those who have access to the good life and those who do not. This perspective owes much to the writings of Karl Marx (1818–1883), the German social theorist who developed many of the central ideas of modern socialism.

In *The Communist Manifesto* (1848), *Capital* (1867), and other works, Marx attempted to prove that social problems like unemployment, poverty, crime, corruption, and warfare are not usually the fault of individuals or of poorly functioning organizations. Instead, he argued, their origins may be found in the way societies arrange access to wealth and power. According to Marx, the social problems of modern societies arise from capitalism. An inevitable outcome of capitalism is class conflict, especially conflict between those who own the means of production (factories, land, and the like) and those who sell their labor for wages. In such a system, workers are exploited by their bosses, for whom the desire to make a profit outweighs any humanitarian impulse to take care of their employees.

In the capitalist system as Marx described it, the capitalist is driven by the profit motive to find ways to reduce labor costs—for example, through the purchase of new machinery that can do the work of several people or by building factories in places where people will work for less money. These actions continually threaten the livelihood of workers. Often they lose their jobs, and sometimes they resort to crime or even begin revolutions to overturn the system in which they are the have-nots and the owners of capital are the haves. In sum, for Marx and modern Marxian sociologists, social problems may be attributed to the ways in which wealth and power become concentrated in the hands of a few people and to the many forms of conflict engendered by these inequalities.

Marxian conflict theory can be a powerful tool in the analysis of contemporary social problems. To illustrate this point, let us look at how this theory explains criminal deviance in societies like the United States.

Deviance: A Marxian Conflict View. Marxian students of crime and deviance believe situations such as those described at the beginning of the chapter do not occur merely because such organizations as the police and the courts function in certain ways or do not function as they were intended to. Instead, Marxian theorists believe such situations are a result of differences in the power of different groups or classes in society. For example, top organized-crime figures have the money and power to influence law enforcement officials or to hire the best attorneys when they are arrested. Street drug dealers, in contrast, are relatively powerless to resist arrest. Moreover, they serve as convenient targets for an official show of force against drug trafficking. From the Marxian perspective, the rich and powerful are able to determine what kinds of behaviors are defined as social problems because they control major institutions like the government, the schools, and the courts. They are also able to shift the blame for the conditions that produce those problems to groups that are less able to defend themselves, namely, the poor and the working class (Ehrenreich, 2001; Quinney, 1986; Robbins, 2001).

Scholars who adopt a Marxian perspective tend to be critical of proposals to reform existing institutions. Since they attribute most social problems to underlying patterns of class conflict, they do not believe existing institutions like prisons and courts can address the basic causes of those problems. Usually, therefore, their research looks at the ways in which the material conditions of society, such as inequalities of wealth and power, seem to account for the distribution of social problems in a population. Or they conduct research on social movements among the poor and the working class in an attempt to understand how those movements might mobilize large numbers of people into a force that could bring about major changes in the way society is organized (Piven & Cloward, 1977, 1982).

Value Conflict Theory. The Marxian theory of class conflict cannot explain all the kinds of conflict that occur around us every day. In families, for example, we see conflicts that may range from seemingly trivial arguments over television programs to intense disputes over issues like drinking or drug use; in neighborhoods we may see conflict between landlords and tenants, between parents and school administrators, or between groups of parents who differ on matters of educational policy such as sex education or the rights of female athletes. Such conflict often focuses not on deep-seated class antagonisms, but on differences in values. For most feminist groups, for example, abortion is a social problem if women cannot freely terminate a pregnancy within some reasonable time. In contrast, many religious groups define legal abortion as a social problem. The debate over legalization versus criminalization of abortion reflects the conflicting values of important groups in society.

Value conflict theorists define social problems as "conditions that are incompatible with group values" (Rubington & Weinberg, 1987, 1995). Such problems are normal, they add, because in a complex society there are many groups whose interests and values are bound to differ. According to value conflict theory, social problems occur when groups with different values meet and compete. To return to the example of criminal deviance, value conflict theorists would say that deviance from society's rules results from the fact that some groups do not agree with those rules and therefore feel free to break them if they can. For example, whenever a society prohibits substances like alcohol or drugs, some groups will break the rules to obtain the banned substance. This stimulates the development of criminal organizations that employ gangsters and street peddlers to supply the needs of those who deviate. The underlying cause of the problem is conflicting values concerning the use of particular substances.

From the value conflict viewpoint, many social problems need to be understood in terms of which groups hold which values and have the power to enforce them against the wishes of other groups. Once this has been determined, this approach leads to suggestions for adjustments, settlements, negotiations, and compromises that will alleviate the problem. These, in turn, may result in new policies, such as civilian review boards, arbitration of disputes, juvenile drug courts, and changes in existing laws to reflect a diversity of opinions (Larana, Johnston, & Gusfield, 1994).

A great deal of conflict revolves around the treatment of drug users. In this photo, an innovative drug court determines whether juveniles charged with drug use can receive alternative sentences, such as community service, rather than being sent to prisons or detention centers.

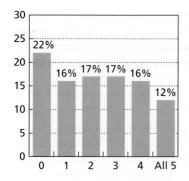

Figure 1–1 Rates of Conservatism on Social and Cultural Issues. *Number of conservative opinions expressed on five social and cultural issues.*
Source: Pew Forum on Religion & Public Life, 2006.

Is There a Culture War in the United States? When we read headlines about conflict between different religious groups or communities about gay marriage, or about pornography, school prayer, abortion, or any number of issues that arouse people's moral passions, it is easy to agree with some commentators that these conflicts are evidence of a "culture war." This supposed broad conflict over deeply held values is said to sway elections and determine the fate of many social policy issues, from gun control to "morning-after pills" and much more. Some conservative journals, and some liberal ones as well, argue that the culture war is real and must be won by their side. But in a recent national survey of Americans' attitudes on controversial issues, researchers found that Americans want their leaders to arrive at practical solutions to major problems and are impatient with ideologically extreme positions. Public attitudes across a set of five issues that have been the focus of intense political activity in recent years—gay marriage, adoption of children by gay couples, abortion, stem cell research, and the morning-after pill—show a mix of conservative and liberal majorities. On none of the five issues does more than 56 percent of the public line up on one side of the question or the other. (See Figure 1–1.)

The researchers also found that only 12 percent of respondents took a conservative position on all five issues, but only 22 percent did *not* take a conservative position on at least one of the issues. In other words, even people who may be liberal on most issues often agree with conservatives on one or more of these highly contested issues. Similar findings apply when one analyzes liberal opinions on the same issues. These results show that there is no deep and consistent division of moral values among Americans. Instead, the majority take a more practical view of these controversies and hope that wisdom rather than ideology will prevail and that eventually the government will arrive at sound social policies to address these and other social problems.

The Interactionist Perspective

Why do certain people resort to criminal deviance while the vast majority seek legitimate means to survive? A functionalist would point out that individuals who do not adhere to society's core values or have been uprooted by social change are most likely to become criminals. When they are caught, their punishment reinforces the desire of the majority to conform. But this explanation does not help us understand why a particular individual or group deviates.

Conflict theorists explain deviance as the result of conflict over access to wealth and power (in the Marxian version) or over values (in the non-Marxian version). But how is that conflict channeled into deviant behavior? Why do some groups that experience value conflict act against the larger society while others do not? Why, for example, do some homosexuals come out publicly while others hide their sexual preference? Presumably both groups know that their sexual values conflict with those of the larger society, but what explains the difference in behavior? The conflict perspective cannot provide an adequate answer to this question.

The interactionist perspective offers an explanation that gets closer to the individual level of behavior. Research based on this perspective looks at the processes whereby different people become part of a situation that the larger society defines as a social problem. The interactionist approach focuses on the ways in which people actually take on the values of the group of which they are members. It also explores how different groups define their situation and in so doing "construct" a version of life that promotes certain values and behaviors and discourages others.

A key insight of the interactionist perspective originated in the research of W. I. Thomas and his colleagues in the early decades of the twentieth century. In their classic study of the problems of immigrants in the rapidly growing and changing city of Chicago, these pioneering sociologists found that some groups of Polish immigrant men believed it would be easier to rob banks than to survive in the mills and factories, where other immigrants worked long hours under dangerous conditions. The sociologists discovered that the uneducated young immigrants often did not realize how little chance they had of carrying out a successful bank robbery. They defined their situation in a particular way and acted accordingly. "Situations people define as real," Thomas stated, "are real in their consequences" (Thomas & Znaniecki, 1922). Thus, from the interactionist perspective an individual or group's definition of the situation is central to understanding the actions of that individual or group.

Another early line of interactionist research is associated with Charles Horton Cooley and George Herbert Mead. Cooley, Mead, and others realized that although we learn our basic values and ways of behaving early in life, especially in our families, we also participate throughout our lives in groups made up of people like ourselves; these are known as *peer groups*. From these groups we draw much of our identity, our sense of who we are, and within these groups we learn many of our behaviors and values. Through our interactions in peer groups—be they teams, adolescent friendship groups, or work groups—we may be taught to act in ways that are different from those our parents taught us. Thus, when interactionists study social problems like crime, they focus on the ways in which people are recruited by criminal groups and learn to conform to the rules of those groups.

Labeling: An Interactionist View of Deviance.

Labeling theory is an application of the interactionist perspective that offers an explanation for certain kinds of social deviance. Labeling theorists feel the label "deviant" reveals more about the society applying it than about the act or person being labeled. In certain societies, for example, homosexuality is far more accepted than it is in the United States. Labeling theorists suggest there are groups and organizations in American society that benefit from labeling homosexuals deviant—religious and military institutions, for example. Similarly, deviant acts are not always judged in the same way; prison sentences for black offenders, for instance, tend to be longer than sentences for white offenders who commit the same crimes. In the view of labeling theorists, this difference has to do with the way power is distributed in our society. In short, labeling theory separates deviant and nondeviant people not by what they do, but by how society reacts to what they do.

According to labeling theorists, social problems are conditions under which certain behaviors or situations become defined as social problems. The cause of a social problem is simply society's awareness that a certain behavior or situation exists. A behavior or situation becomes a social problem when someone can profit in some way by applying the label "problematic" or "deviant" to it. Such labeling causes society to suffer in two ways. First, one group unfairly achieves power over another—"deviants" are repressed through discrimination, prejudice, or force. Second, those who are labeled deviant may accept this definition of themselves, and the label may become a self-fulfilling prophecy. The number and variety of deviant acts may be increased to reinforce the new role of deviant. A person who is labeled a drug addict, for example, may adopt elements of what is popularly viewed as a drug addict's lifestyle: resisting employment or treatment, engaging in crime, and so on. Sociologists term this behavior **secondary deviance.**

According to labeling theory, the way to solve social problems is to change the definition of what is considered deviant (Rubington & Weinberg, 1995). It is thought that the acceptance of a greater variety of acts and situations as normal would automatically

The practice of parading a crime suspect—in this case, former WorldCom CEO Bernard Ebbers—in public (sometimes called the "perp walk") often has the effect of implying guilt before a trial is held.

eliminate concern about them. Decriminalization of the possession of small amounts of marijuana for personal use is an example of this approach. Note, however, that many people would consider marijuana use a social problem even if it were decriminalized. At the same time, discouraging the tendency to impose labels for gain would reduce the prevalence of labeling and cause certain problems to become less significant. Communism, for example, was a matter of great concern to Americans in the 1950s; many people won popularity or power by applying the label "Communist" to others. When it became clear that the label was being misapplied and that the fear it generated was unjustified, the label lost its significance and the "social problem" of internal Communist influence largely disappeared.

Labeling theory is only one of numerous applications of the interactionist perspective to social problems. Another common approach focuses on the processes of socialization that occur in groups and explores the possibility of resocialization through group interaction—as occurs, for example, in groups like Alcoholics Anonymous. At many points in this book we will encounter situations in which intentional resocialization has been used in efforts to address social problems.

The Social Construction of Social Problems. The interactionist perspective also contributes to what is known as the "social construction" approach to social problems. This approach argues that some claims about social problems become dominant and others remain weak or unheeded. Our perceptions of what claims about social problems should be heeded develop through the activities of actors and institutions in society that shape our consciousness of the social world. The press, television, radio, universities and colleges, government agencies, and civic voluntary associations are examples of institutions that often have a stake in defining what social problems are. Journalists, television commentators, editorial writers, professors who take public stands on issues, scientists who appear before the cameras, and many other lobbyists and "opinion makers" are in fact involved in selecting some claims and rejecting others. In so doing, they "construct" the way we think about the issues (Griswold, 2004).

Consider an example: The issue known as global warming is extremely complex and requires knowledge that is too technical for most people to understand fully. But as members of the media and concerned, vocal scientists develop a consensus that the atmosphere is warming because of pollution, the public begins to get that message and to share the opinion that climatic change is occurring. Droughts and wildfires, which may have seemed severe but not out of the ordinary, come to be viewed as part of a social problem known as global warming, independent of whether the earth's atmosphere can actually be proven to be heating up because of the effects of carbon dioxide and other greenhouse gases.

Critics of the social construction view often argue that there are real trends and changes behind the emergence of social problems like global warming, pollution, or gun violence. Still, the influence of the media and universities does account for some tangible social construction of what we perceive as problematic in our society or in the world (Allen, 1999; Richardson & May, 1999).

THE NATURAL HISTORY OF SOCIAL PROBLEMS

To readers of daily newspapers and faithful watchers of television news, social problems may often resemble fads. We hear a great deal about a particular problem for a while, and then it fades from public attention, perhaps to reappear some time later if there are new developments in its incidence or control. With AIDS, crack cocaine, driving while intoxicated (DWI), serial killers, financial scandals, racial violence, terrorism, and so many other problems demanding attention, it is little wonder that the focus on any given subject by the press and the public tends to last only a few days or weeks.

To a large extent, the short attention span of the media can be explained by the need to attract large numbers of viewers or readers; the media can be expected to be rather fickle and to constantly pursue stories that will capture the attention of the public. However, sociologists distinguish between the nature of media coverage of a social problem and the way a problem is perceived by the public and political leaders. They have devoted considerable study to the question of how social problems develop from underlying conditions into publicly defined problems that engender social policies and sustained social movements. This subject is often referred to as the "natural history" of social problems.

Early in the twentieth century, sociologists recognized that social problems often seemed to develop in a series of phases or stages. They called the study of this process the natural history approach because their effort was analogous to the work of biologists who study the development of a great many individual organisms to chart the stages of development of a species (Edwards, 1927; Park, 1955; Shaw, 1929; Wirth, 1927). But whereas sociologists recognize that social problems often follow certain regular stages of development, they also know that there are many deviations from the usual sequence.

In a useful formulation of the natural history approach, Malcolm Spector and John Kitsuse (1987) outlined the following major stages that most social problems seem to go through:

Stage 1—Problem definition. Groups in society attempt to gain recognition by a wider population (and the press and government) that some social condition is "offensive, harmful, or otherwise undesirable." These groups publicize their claims and attempt to turn the matter into a political issue.

Stage 2—Legitimacy. When the groups pressing their claims are considered credible and their assertions are accepted by official organizations, agencies, or institutions, there may be investigations, proposals for reform, and even the creation of new agencies to respond to claims and demands.

Stage 3—Reemergence of demands. Usually, the original groups are not satisfied with the steps taken by official agencies; they demand stronger measures, more funding for enforcement, speedier handling of claims, and so on. They renew their appeals to the wider public and the press.

Stage 4—Rejection and institution building. The complainant groups usually decide that official responses to their demands are inadequate. They seek to develop their own organizations or counterinstitutions to press their claims and enact reforms.

Let us briefly apply this natural history model to the development of the idea that the easy availability of guns, especially handguns, automatic rifles and pistols, and assault weapons, contributes to higher murder rates and to sensational crimes like school shootings. In the 1980s, during the height of the crack cocaine epidemic, many teenagers and young adults were being killed in street shootings and drive-by killings. John Hinkley's shooting of President Reagan and his press secretary, James Brady, increased awareness of the problem of gun violence. At the same time, the rise of armed militia groups and an increase in the frequency of serial killings, some of which involved firearms, helped define the problem of violence as due to the easy availability of guns. Despite persistent lobbying by the National Rifle Association and other pro-gun goups, the problem definition gained credibility and legitimacy as citizen groups pressed their lawmakers for gun control legislation. The Brady Bill, which requires identity checks for gun purchasers, and the controversial ban on certain types of assault weapons resulted from this new sense of legitimacy for gun control advocates and their ideas. But the continued shootings in public schools—notably the one in Littleton, Colorado, in 1999—led to demands for more stringent gun control legislation, an issue that played an important role in the presidential campaigns of 2000.

THE MEDIA AND SOCIAL PROBLEMS

In the second half of the twentieth century, there was a communications revolution. The advent of television after World War II made far more news more immediately available to people in advanced industrial nations than had ever been possible before. In subsequent decades we have seen the advent of cable television, TV magazine shows like *60 Minutes*, the Internet, and specialized magazines catering to a wide variety of interests. This communications revolution has had a lasting impact on our perception of social problems.

One effect is the speed of communication. Information about new diseases like AIDS can be disseminated throughout the population far faster than would have been possible in the past. The rapid availability of information can help people avoid certain kinds of problems, but it can also spread fear and lead to copycat behavior. The rapid spread of crack cocaine during the 1980s and early 1990s may have been due to some extent to the power of movies and the media to produce a fad in narcotics use; some sociologists believe this also occurred in the 1960s with the spread of marijuana use among young Americans. But just as the media can accelerate the rise of social problems, they can also educate the public about how to help solve such problems as crime, delinquency, and drug abuse. Throughout this text, where appropriate, we point out the involvement of the media in social problems and in policies designed to solve or alleviate them.

Sociologist Barry Glassner (2000) argues that the media's passion for sensational stories about crime and violence and the public's ever-growing appetite for sensational coverage of violence actually mask important changes in social problems and divert public attention from problems that can be addressed through social policy. The recent killings in schools, for example, occurred as the actual rate of murder was decreasing rapidly, but the public was shocked by a few sensational crimes into overreacting to school crime and demanding measures that infringe on personal freedom and contribute to a decline in public optimism. Since the infamous murders and double suicide at Columbine High School in Littleton, Colorado, there have been several other school shootings. Sociologist Kathryn Newman studied these tragic events at the request of a congressional committee, and we will discuss this important research in the next section and in Chapter 11. It is important to note here, however, that this argument only touches on the very complex relationship between public opinion and media coverage of social problems.

Figure 1–2 shows how Americans ranked different social problems after the congressional elections of 2006. Since the terrorist attacks of 2001, the American public has consistently rated terrorism very high among its concerns, but the war in Iraq dominated responses to public opinion polls in 2006, and at this writing the war in Iraq remains the public's chief concern, followed closely by more general fears of terrorism and then by a series of important domestic issues, with corruption in government,

How can sociologists help reporters and other members of the media better understand the social conditions that cause specific social problems?

Figure 1–2 Americans' Ranking of Major Social Problems, 2007. *Percentage of Americans saying each issue is extremely important for the president and Congress to deal with this year.*

*Source: USA Today-*Gallup Poll, January 5–7, 2007. All rights reserved. Reprinted with permission.

Issue	Percentage
The situation in Iraq	62%
Terrorism	55%
Corruption in government	52%
Healthcare	50%
Social security	45%
Medicare	43%
The economy	42%
The federal budget deficit	42%
Immigration	38%
Energy policies	36%
Crime	36%
The problems caused by Hurricane Katrina	28%

health care, and Social Security highest among them. But in a similar poll taken in 1999—before the 2000 presidential election, the September 11 attacks, or the stock market crash of 2002—the top three social problems were ethics (morality and family decline), crime and violence, and education. So, do the media shape public opinion, or do the major events and social movements covered by the media determine how people rate the seriousness of social problems? The evidence in this set of data suggests that although the media play an important role in bringing information about events to the public, actual events such as rampant inflation, rising unemployment rates, the possible outbreak of war, and high rates of crime that affect people in their communities (as opposed to more sensational but isolated crimes covered on TV) shape the public's perception of how severe different social problems are.

RESEARCH ON SOCIAL PROBLEMS

Katherine Newman (1999) is a professor of anthropology and sociology at Harvard University's Kennedy School. She works closely with William Julius Wilson, the nation's leading expert on inner-city poverty. Newman has spent the last few years studying the kinds of jobs young people from ghetto neighborhoods get when they do find jobs. The majority of those jobs are in the fast-food industry. Contrary to what many critics assert, young people often learn valuable skills at these jobs. Moreover, such jobs are not easy to obtain because of the lack of alternatives in the local labor market. As a result, young people often find that they are better off staying on the job and learning the habits of the workplace, including punctuality and cleanliness. With that experience, they stand a better chance of landing other, perhaps more interesting, work in the future. Newman's research uses the methods of **ethnography,** the close observation of interactions among people in a social group or organization.

Mitchell Duneier and his students at Princeton and the City University of New York conduct research on the way people use public spaces in cities. They are particularly interested in how homeless people manage their lives in public and how they arrive at understandings with local residents and the authorities that allow them to cope with the problems and pressures of urban living even when they have access to extremely limited resources (Duneier, 2002).

Yale University sociologist Kai Erikson (1995) investigated the effects of a local bank's failure on migrant farm workers and sharecroppers in rural Florida. Erikson

The effects of natural disasters in densely populated urban areas are an increasingly important aspect of the study of social problems such as homelessness.

was asked to conduct this research by the law firm representing the people who lost their savings as a result of the bank's failure. The firm's attorneys learned about him through his famous study of the effects of the dam rupture at Buffalo Creek, West Virginia, in 1972. Erikson's book about the resulting flood, *Everything in Its Path,* won a National Book Award for social research and helped make lawmakers more sensitive to the human costs of major natural and economic disasters.

These three examples illustrate some of the ways in which sociological research is brought to bear on social problems. We could add many more. When the media seek an expert to comment on changes in crime rates from one year to the next, they often call on criminologists such as Robert Sampson, whose work we will encounter in Chapter 5. When members of Congress debate the merits of different proposals for reforming the welfare system, they often turn to the work of sociologists such as Mary Jo Bane, an expert on trends in welfare dependency, or they may consult Sheldon Danziger and his colleagues at the University of Wisconsin's Institute for Research on Poverty. In these and countless other areas, sociologists are asked to conduct empirical research and to supply information that can be referred to in debates on these issues.

In this age of rapid social change, information about social problems is in ever-increasing demand. Even if you do not go on to a career that requires expertise in social research, as an informed citizen you will benefit from the ability to evaluate its findings. In this section, therefore, we briefly introduce the most frequently used research methods: demographic studies, survey research, field observations, and social experiments.

Demographic Studies

Demography is the subfield of sociology that studies how social conditions are distributed in human populations and how those populations are changing. When we ask how many people are affected by a particular condition or problem—for example, when we want to know how many people are affected by crime or unemployment—we are asking a demographic question. The answers to such questions consist of numerical data about the people affected compared to those who are not affected. Demographers frequently supply data about the incidence of a social phenomenon—that is, how many people are affected and to what extent. Incidence can be given in absolute numbers; for example, in 2005 there were 3,254 persons under sentence of death in the United States, of whom 1,805 were white and 1,449 were nonwhite (U.S. Bureau of Justice Statistics, 2007). The incidence of a phenomenon can also be expressed as a rate. According to the National Center on Child Abuse and Neglect, for example, in 2006 the rate of reported cases of child abuse was 483 per 10,000 children in the U.S. population; in 1976 it was 101 per 10,000. Rates are often more useful than absolute numbers because they are not affected by changes in population size. Thus, in the example just given, the increase in reported cases of child abuse is not due to the growth of the population during the period covered but must have some other cause.

Whenever we see large increases in rates for a social problem, however, it is important to ask whether the changes are due to a worsening of the problem or to other factors, such as better reporting and investigation of the phenomenon, greater public awareness, or similar changes. In this case, the addition of new data from Alaska and Puerto Rico accounts for a small proportion of the change, while improved reporting systems account for a larger proportion of the change. Determining exactly how much of the increase is actually due to more abusive behavior requires further research and will be discussed in more detail in Chapter 10.

Survey Research

We often take for granted the availability of statistics about social conditions and problems. Every month we see reports on the latest unemployment figures or crime rates or trends in the cost of housing, and we are given statistics on what people think about these and other issues. Political campaigns rely heavily on measures of public opinion, both on the issues and on the popularity of the candidates. All this information, including the basic information about the U.S. population derived from the national census, is obtained through a sociological method known as **survey research.**

Survey research was developed earlier in this century as a way of gathering information from a number of people, known as a **sample,** who represent the behavior and attitudes of the larger population from which they are selected. Today survey research is a major industry in much of the world. The techniques of sampling and interviewing are used routinely by market research firms, political polling organizations, media corporations of all types, university research centers, and many other organizations, including the Census Bureau and other government agencies. Whenever we encounter statistics about what people in a society believe about a problem or how different groups within a population behave, there is a good chance those statistics are based on the results of a survey.

In a survey, people speak to interviewers—in person, on the telephone, or by mail—and provide them with information, which is aggregated and converted into numerical data. When looking at survey data, therefore, be sure to ask who was interviewed and for what reasons. You should also ask whether the survey reports the results of a set of questions asked about conditions prevailing at one time or whether matched samples of respondents were interviewed on more than one occasion. A questionnaire that is given to a sample of respondents on a single occasion yields what sociologists call **cross-sectional data** on behavior and opinion at a particular time. Comparisons of matched samples over time yield **longitudinal data,** which tell us what changes have occurred in a particular social condition over a specific period.

Field Observation

When sociologists seek to understand the processes that occur among the people who are directly involved in a social problem, they may attempt to observe social behavior as it is actually taking place. This often requires the sociologist to participate directly in the social life of the individuals or groups in question, a technique known as **participant observation** or **field research.** (The term *field* refers to the social settings in which the observed behavior occurs.) Neighborhoods, communities, and organizations like police headquarters, hospital emergency rooms, prisons, and schools are all examples of field settings. The technique of participant observation requires skill in gaining and keeping the trust of the people whose behavior is being observed; practice in careful observation and recording of the behaviors in question; and skill at conducting interviews that may range over many issues, some of which may be highly personal or controversial.

Research based on participant observation usually seeks to discover how the processes of human interaction contribute to particular social conditions or problems. Thus, field research frequently, though not always, applies the interactionist perspective. This approach is illustrated in the following example.

In a classic study of how people become drug users, sociologist Howard Becker interacted with groups of musicians and other people who were likely to use marijuana. A jazz musician himself, Becker was readily accepted in the groups whose behavior he wished to observe. As he watched first-time users take their first puffs on a joint, he noted that they often claimed not to feel any effect, even when Becker himself observed changes in their behavior. But when more experienced users explained to the novice what the "proper" feelings were, the new smokers began to feel the sensation of being high. Becker concluded that to some extent the experience of using marijuana is a social construction; the drug may have certain physiological effects on everyone, but social interaction must occur for the new smoker to define what the appropriate feelings are and then to experience them. Becker's (1963) famous article "Becoming a Marijuana User" was among the first empirical descriptions of the degree to which the experience and extent of drug use are determined by users' definitions of the situation. It is an excellent example of how sociologists can discover important aspects of behavior through observation in the field.

In the chapters to come, whenever we refer to a field research study or to participant observation research, remember that the researcher has actually observed the behavior in question. Also, since the research describes the behavior of real people, note how careful the researcher has been to disguise the identities of the individuals who were observed and interviewed.

Social Experiments

There are times when it is possible for a sociologist or other social scientist to apply experimental methods to the study of a social problem. In an experiment, the investigator attempts to systematically vary the conditions that are of interest in order to determine their effects. In a controlled experiment, the investigator applies a "treatment" to one group—that is, exposes its members to a certain condition, to which they must somehow respond—but does not apply the treatment to a second group that is identical to the first in every other way. The subjects who receive the treatment are known as the **experimental group;** those who do not are the **control group.** When the investigator compares the experiences of the experimental and control groups, it can be assumed that any differences between them are due to the effects of the treatment.

We will have occasion in later chapters to describe controlled experiments that have applied this model to human subjects to study social problems. Here we will briefly present two classic and highly influential examples of social experiments. One of them was able to use both experimental and control groups; the other could establish only an experimental group.

To study the influence of jobs on ex-offenders, the Vera Institute of Justice undertook the Wildcat experiment, in which individuals serving jail terms were allowed to take part in various forms of "supported work." Instead of being placed individually in unfamiliar jobs, Wildcat workers were assigned to jobs in groups of three to seven and received guidance and evaluation while they were working. Other prisoners were assigned to individual jobs under traditional work-release arrangements; they constituted a control group. The results of the experiment were mixed: Although the Wildcat workers earned more, had more stable jobs, and were less likely to become dependent on welfare than members of the control group, they were also more likely to be arrested and returned to prison (Friedman, 1978).

In sharp contrast to the Wildcat experiment is the famous "prison" study conducted by Philip Zimbardo and his colleagues. The researchers created a simulated prison in the basement of a building at Stanford University. Twenty-four students who had volunteered to take part in the experiment were divided into two groups: "prisoners" and "guards." The prisoners were confined to the simulated prison, and the guards were instructed in their duties and responsibilities. In this experiment it was not possible to form a control group; in fact, the experiment itself was canceled after six days. In that brief time both the guards and the prisoners had become unable to distinguish between the experiment and reality, with the result that "human values were suspended, self-concepts were challenged, and the ugliest, most base, pathological side of human nature surfaced" (Zimbardo, 1972, p. 243). When the mistreatment of Iraqi and other prisoners in Abu Ghraib prison and the American military prison in Guantanamo Bay was revealed in 2004, many commentators in the press and government cited the classic Zimbardo experiment in their efforts to understand why so many seemingly average, law-abiding young Americans could have resorted to inhumane behavior when they were assigned the task of guarding prisoners.

How does researchers' insistence on respondents' privacy, confidentiality, and informed consent help prevent ethical problems in social research?

As informative as experimental studies like these may be, they raise major questions about the ethical limits of social research. Sociologists and other social scientists realize that they must not infringe on the basic rights of human subjects. Under the rules of professional associations like the American Sociological Association and the guidelines of government agencies like the National Institute of Mental Health, people who conduct research with human subjects must guarantee the following rights:

1. *Privacy*—the right of the individual to define, with only extraordinary exceptions in the interest of society, when and on what terms his or her acts should be revealed to the general public.

2. *Confidentiality*—the assurance that information supplied by a subject or respondent will not be passed on to anyone else in a form that could be traced to that respondent.

3. *Informed consent*—the right of subjects and respondents to be informed beforehand about what they are being asked and how the information they supply will be used.

Social Policy

Much of the research conducted by sociologists is designed to provide information to be used in formulating social policies as well as in evaluating existing policies and suggesting improvements and new directions. **Social policies** are formal procedures designed to remedy a social problem. Generally they are designed by officials of government at the local, state, or federal level, but they can also be initiated by private citizens in voluntary associations, by corporations, and by nonprofit foundations.

There is generally a good deal of debate about any proposed social policy. Much of the debate consists of discussion and analysis of how well a proposed policy appears to address the problem. Such analysis tends to be considered technical in the sense that although there is general agreement on the need to address the problem, the debate hinges on the adequacy of the proposed means to achieve the agreed-upon ends. Increasingly, however, we are witnessing policy debates that are ideological rather than technical, and in the United States such debates frequently pit conservatives against liberals.

It is often difficult to involve people directly in social policy deliberations. The series of meetings in which New Yorkers evaluated plans for rebuilding the World Trade Center are an example of a successful effort to involve the public in a complex planning process.

Conservatives usually seek to limit the involvement of government in the solution of social problems. They believe private firms, governed by the need to compete in markets and make profits, are the best type of organization for coping with the problems of prisons, schools, and the like. They believe governments have a responsibility to address social problems, and oppose the dominance of the market (and, hence, the profit motive) in social-welfare institutions. However, the policies they propose may expand government bureaucracies without always delivering adequate services to the populations that need them.

Throughout the twentieth century and into the twenty-first, the government's role in attempting to solve social problems has increased steadily, despite the ideological stands of various administrations. For example, America's role as a world military power, along with new problems of terrorism, has required the continual expenditure of public funds on military goods and services. These costs have increased dramatically with every war and every major change in military technology. Similarly, the fight against drug commerce has added greatly to the cost of maintaining the society's judicial and penal institutions.

Every function of government has a similar history of escalating costs because of increases in the scale of the society or the scope of the problem. During the 1980s, for example, the Reagan administration sought to decrease the cost of government involvement in regulating economic institutions such as airlines, banks, and financial markets. Among other measures taken were those designed to decrease the regulation of the banking industry. Banks and savings and loan associations were allowed to operate in markets that had previously been barred to them because of the risks involved.

At the same time, personnel cuts were made in the federal bank regulatory agencies. The risk to depositors was held to a minimum by the continued existence of government guarantees in the form of deposit insurance. The combination of deregulation and deposit insurance, along with regional recessions in the oil-producing states, caused many savings and loan associations to become insolvent, exposing the often corrupt practices of their directors. Amid escalating costs to the government and American taxpayers—estimated in the hundreds of billions of dollars—Congress once again passed legislation designed to increase regulation of the banking industry and to prevent future financial disasters of such magnitude.

Future Prospects

In contrast to the Reagan era, when conservative critiques of governmental efforts to alleviate social problems became a dominant theme in American political life, in 2007 the trend was decidedly away from this viewpoint. Upset with the conduct of the Bush administration on a number of foreign and domestic fronts, from Iraq and the Middle East to the delayed response to rebuilding New Orleans, a frustrated American public seems again to be demanding better public policies from all levels of government. As we will see in the next chapter, there are a host of state initiatives, and proposed federal ones, that may produce significant changes in the nation's faltering health care system. At this writing, it is too soon to know whether the Democratic majority in Congress will be strengthened in 2008, and whether there will be a Republican or Democratic president, but on issues of social policy the nation's voters appear to be taking a less ideological and more pragmatic approach to social problems. For example, on the terribly thorny issue of the "right to life" versus a woman's "right to choose" abortion, there is an emerging middle ground that seeks to decrease the behaviors that lead to unwanted pregnancies while also promoting adoption. Neither of these policies directly solves the controversy, but they do point to ways in which people with different stances on the issue can co-exist as neighbors (Gibbs, 2006; Ginsburg 1998).

Policy decisions of similar scope are responsible for unemployment insurance, Social Security, community mental-health systems, and numerous other benefits that Americans have come to view as "entitlements" of citizenship. But these benefits are costly. They require the transfer (via taxation) of funds from the well-off to the less well-off. As the overall cost of government has increased, so has the tax burden on individual citizens. This increase in the cost of government comes from policies that serve specific segments of the population as well as from those designed to benefit the entire population. For example, organized labor has consistently promoted policies that regulate industry in the interests of workers, whereas industrialists claim that any regulations that increase their costs of doing business will hurt their ability to compete in domestic or world markets.

This conflict is typical of many current controversies over the best ways to handle social issues, with conservatives stressing private or market solutions and liberals calling for public or government actions. Some of the conflicting approaches to the solution of various social problems that have been proposed by conservatives, liberals, and others are discussed in the Social Policy sections that conclude each chapter of this book, as well as in boxed features that focus on particular controversies.

GOING BEYOND LEFT AND RIGHT

The tragic 2007 shooting at Virginia Tech University in Blacksburg by a deeply troubled student once again brought the issue of gun control to national attention. Predictably, opponents of gun control closed ranks against any legislation that would restrict access to guns. Proponents of gun control, led in Congress by Representative

Caroline McCarthy, whose son was killed in a similar deranged outburst, again expressed hope for passage of new gun control legislation that would enforce existing laws against the sale of firearms to potentially dangerous customers.

Rather than enter into the ideological debates around the right to own guns versus the public's need for protection against acts of violence like the Virginia Tech shooting, sociologists play an important role in providing data and interpretation of facts about the killings and about the enforcement, or lack of it, of existing gun control legislation. In the Virginia Tech case, the facts show that had Virginia's existing legislation barring the sale of guns to people with histories of mental illness been properly enforced, the tragedy might have been avoided. From a sociological perspective, therefore, there is a need for greater emphasis on enforcement of laws that people on both sides of the controversy have already agreed on. These are the kinds of issues that we will consider throughout this text.

Summary

- When many people in a society agree that a condition exists that threatens the quality of their lives and their most cherished values, and they also agree that something should be done to remedy it, sociologists say that society has defined that condition as a social problem.

- Sociologists who study social problems ask questions about the social rather than the individual aspects of a problem. The primary sociological approaches to the study of social problems are the functionalist, conflict, and interactionist perspectives.

- The functionalist perspective looks at the way major social institutions actually operate. From this perspective, the main reason for the existence of social problems is that societies are always changing; failure to adapt successfully to change leads to social problems.

- In the early 1900s, functionalist theorists saw social problems like criminal deviance as a form of social pathology. Later they tended to emphasize the effects of immigration, urbanization, and industrialization; this emphasis formed the basis of social-disorganization theory. Modern functionalists often conduct institutional research designed to show how people and societies reorganize their lives and institutions to cope with new conditions.

- The conflict perspective is based on the belief that social problems arise out of major contradictions in the way societies are organized, which lead to large-scale conflict. This perspective owes a great deal to the writings of the German social theorist Karl Marx.

- Marxian conflict theory attributes most social problems to underlying patterns of class conflict. A broader view is taken by value conflict theorists, who believe social problems occur when groups with different values meet and compete. Along these lines, it is sometimes argued that there is a "culture war" in the United States.

- Research based on the interactionist perspective looks at the processes whereby different people become part of a situation that the larger society defines as a social problem. It focuses on the ways in which people actually take on the values of the group of which they are members.

- According to labeling theory, social problems are conditions under which certain behaviors or situations become defined as problems. In this view, the cause of a social problem is simply society's awareness that a certain behavior or situation exists. The labels applied to certain behaviors act as self-fulfilling prophecies because people who are so labeled accept society's definition of themselves and behave accordingly.

- The most frequently used research methods in the study of social problems are demographic studies, survey research, field observation, and social experiments. People who conduct research with human subjects must guarantee the rights of privacy, confidentiality, and informed consent.

- Social policies are formal procedures designed to remedy a social problem. They are formulated by officials of governments at all levels as well as by voluntary associations, corporations, and nonprofit foundations. Much of the research conducted by sociologists is designed to provide information to be used in formulating and evaluating social policies.

- The natural history approach to the analysis of social problems focuses on public perception of conditions that come to be defined as problems. In this view, there are four stages in the development of a social problem: problem definition, legitimacy, reemergence of demands, and rejection and institution building.

Key Terms

Social Problems Online

The Internet provides extensive resources for researching social problems. Because sociology is the academic discipline that covers the field most comprehensively, a good place to start your search is the homepage of Princeton University's Sociology Department, **sociology.princeton.edu**. The page includes links with other sociology departments on each continent, domestic and international research institutes, data archives, and Web pages for academic journals.

The Urban Institute, one of the nation's premier think tanks for social problems, has a Web site (**www.urban.org**) that contains many of its publications on civil rights, crime, education, poverty, and government policy in a downloadable format. Current and back issues of its periodicals are also available. The site is updated regularly and has a search feature that functions much like a high-powered index.

Studying social problems requires knowledge of public opinion. The Gallup Organization, sponsor of the world-famous Gallup poll, has a homepage at **www. galluppoll.com** with reports on its weekly surveys of political developments in the United States. Besides election polls and surveys of public opinion in the United States and abroad, links are available to some of the marketing research done by the firm's foreign affiliates.

Should you be interested in analyzing public opinion research data on your own, Queens College of the City University of New York has a downloadable personal computer (PC) version of the General Social Survey (GSS) data at **www.soc.qc.edu/ QC_Software/GSS.html**. The GSS is an annual survey of approximately 30,000 families in the United States that collects data on political and social attitudes. The survey has been conducted annually since the early 1970s by the National Opinion Research Center (**www.norc.uchicago.edu**). The Queens College site also has a free and easy-to-learn downloadable statistical software package.

Research Navigator

Getting Started on Your Own

To access the full resources of Research Navigator, please find the access code printed on the inside cover of *The Prentice Hall Guide to Research Navigator.* You may have received this booklet. (If your book did not come with this printed guide, you can purchase one through your college bookstore.) Visit our Research Navigator site at **www.ResearchNavigator.com**. Once at this site, click on Register under New Users and enter your access code to create a personal Login Name and Password. (When revisiting the site, use the same Login Name and Password.) Browse the features of the Research Navigator Web site and search the databases of academic journals, newspapers, magazines, and Web links using keywords such as "social problem," "labeling theory," or "survey research."

For this chapter, go to the site for the Society for the Study of Social Problems (**www.ssspl.org/index.cfm/m/21/m/1**). At the homepage, choose the "Special Problems Division" page (see left column). On that page you will see a list of subdivisions of this research organization devoted to the study of social problems. From this list, choose the division (e.g., Crime) that you are interested in and go there. Look at the division's most recent newsletter and describe one or two of the projects discussed that interest you. Why are you interested in this area? What are social scientists who conduct research in this area doing that you feel merits further study?

2

PROBLEMS OF HEALTH
and Health Care

Dominant Trends

- Many Americans cite concerns over the cost of health care as the nation's leading social problem; in some polls, these concerns overshadow concerns about the war in Iraq, the rising cost of fuel, and global warming.

- The number of Americans without any medical insurance increased by 6 million between 2001 and 2007, when an estimated 48 million had no insurance and 32 million others were underinsured. The United States remains the only advanced industrial nation in the world without a system of universal health insurance.

- The huge "baby boom" population cohort is now in its fifties and will soon be reaching retirement age. People over age 65 utilize three times more hospital days a year on average than the general population; those over age 75 utilize over four times as many hospital days per year.

- Medical bills are the chief cause of personal bankruptcies. Americans file for bankruptcy at a rate of one every 30 seconds (1,051,200 annually) because of medical bills. More than one in four U.S. adults have not filled a prescription or have delayed a medical procedure due to expense.

- While AIDS, malaria, and tuberculosis remain urgent infectious diseases throughout the world, especially in poorer nations of Africa and Asia, chronic illnesses like diabetes, Alzheimer's, and other debilitating conditions currently account for more than half the global disease burden and are a primary challenge facing twenty-first-century health-care systems.

Sociological surveys show that Americans are increasingly worried about rising health care costs and about losing their health-care benefits (White, 2007). And compared with people in many other advanced nations, Americans pay a larger share of their incomes for health care and face greater insecurity about obtaining good health care. Little wonder that health-care issues are becoming more and more important in voters' ratings of political candidates. The problems associated with reforming the health-care system are vastly complicated by specific health problems that affect many Americans. The spread of AIDS, babies born with fetal alcohol syndrome or drug addiction, new strains of virulent diseases like tuberculosis, the moral dilemmas of prolonging or terminating life—these and other developments that we discuss in this chapter are all serious problems in themselves. From a sociological standpoint, however, the most significant problems are those that stem from the inadequacies of the existing health-care system or from the growing social inequalities that produce increasingly unequal access to health care.

HEALTH CARE AS A GLOBAL SOCIAL PROBLEM

Health care presents a variety of social problems to all of the world's societies. In more affluent regions like Western Europe, North America, and Australia, the problems associated with physical health often involve reducing inequalities in access to high-quality health care. In impoverished regions of the world, where high-quality medical care is often lacking, the social problems associated with physical health are even more profound. These problems include the spread of infectious diseases, high rates of infant and maternal death, low life expectancies, scarcities of medical personnel and equipment, and inadequate sewage and water systems. (See the Social Problems: A Global View box on page 30.)

It is true that in the past half century there have been increases in life expectancy in most regions of the world. These improvements often reflect better water and sewage systems as well as child vaccination programs. But recent reviews of the global health situation warn that continued improvements in public health systems and in the delivery of medical services will be necessary, especially in poor regions, if these gains are to continue (United Nations Development Programme, 2005).

The United Nations rates nations on the basis of a series of indicators of health, education, equality of political participation, and many other factors. The nations are then grouped into high, medium, and low levels of human development for purposes of comparison. The figures in Table 2–1 on page 31

Social Problems: A Global View

FOOD AND HEALTH IN A GLOBAL MARKETPLACE

In the summer of 2005 a dying cow was brought for slaughter to a Texas pet food producer, where it was found to be infected with bovine spongiform encephalopathy (BSE), otherwise known as "mad cow disease." This was the first case in which an animal born and bred in the United States tested positive for the deadly disease. Mad cow disease causes degeneration of brain and nerve tissue in individuals who eat meat from infected animals. In Europe and elsewhere, a number of people have died from the disease and entire herds of possibly infected animals have been slaughtered. Until recently, no diseased animals had been discovered in the United States, but in 2003 a cow in the Pacific Northwest that had been born in Canada tested positive for the disease. Many nations that buy U.S. beef, including Japan and Mexico, by far the two largest importers, banned meat from the United States pending further investigation, and with the new discovery of an infected animal in Texas, the Canadian and U.S. cattle industries risk losing additional billions of dollars in beef sales in the global market. More important, however, is that U.S. authorities claim that there is no evidence that any infected beef has entered the human food supply.

On another medical battlefront, experts in the World Health Organization and the U.S. Centers for Disease Control warn of the possible outbreak of a virulent strain of influenza. Public health officials fear that the influenza virus infecting birds in China, Vietnam, and elsewhere in Asia may mutate and become capable of infecting human populations. In 1918, an outbreak of an extremely virulent influenza, known as the "Spanish flu," killed 40 million people worldwide. Now medical researchers have the capability to produce vaccines against new stains of influenza and possibly save the lives of thousands or even millions of people, but they must have advance warnings and knowledge of outbreaks if they are to identify the new viral mutants, develop vaccines, and perhaps most difficult, work with pharmaceutical companies to produce millions of doses of vaccines. In 2004, there was a near panic in the United States when the conventional flu vaccine (not one specially developed against a new strain of virulent influenza) suddenly became unavailable. A British company producing the vaccine failed to pass inspection by U.S. authorities and had to suspend its production just before the start of the "flu season" (Garrett, 2005).

From a medical standpoint, these two cases are quite different. Sociologically, however, they raise quite similar problems of knowledge and power. Researchers and medical experts need the best possible knowledge of food and animal health inspections and all relevant data about the spread of these or any other infections into human populations. But governments and corporations often delay informing the authorities or deny that there may be a problem they are responsible for. Beef producers in the United States, for example, have lobbied Congress to prevent mandatory testing of all U.S. cattle. The existing sampling system, they claim, is effective enough, but many of those who are alarmed about BSE infection in U.S. cattle do not agree and worry that failure to institute more stringent regulations for testing cattle may be putting both the population and the industry itself at risk. In the case of a possible avian flu pandemic (i.e., a worldwide epidemic), no one knows for sure whether the virus will continue to mutate so that human-to-human infection begins to occur. So far hundreds of people have died of the virulent avian flu in China, but there and elsewhere authorities have been reluctant to share precise data about the spread of the disease. Like major corporations in the cattle industry, national governments such as those of China and Vietnam have the ability to influence policymakers who may be reluctant to criticize them (Wuethrich, 2003).

We may be fortunate enough to avoid both of these potentially devastating epidemics, but to do so we need to understand the absolute necessity of good coordination of research on a global scale so that outbreaks can be studied and controlled before they become life-threatening. And we need to realize that government regulation of foods and strict inspection of animals and processed foods is vital not just to world health, but to the economies of nations throughout the world.

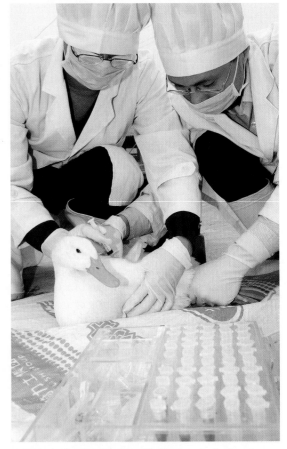

These ducks are being immunized against the avian flu virus, an immense undertaking that Chinese authorities hope will make unnecessary the killing of millions of birds if the avian flu infects their flocks.

TABLE 2–1	Health Indicators for Selected Nations

	Life Expectancy at Birth (years)		Infant Mortality Rate (per 1,000 live births)	
	1970	2005*	1970	2005*
High human development				
United States	70.7	77.7	20	6.5
Sweden	74.4	80.0	11	2.8
Argentina	66.3	75.9	59	15.9
Costa Rica	66.7	76.8	58	10.0
Medium human development				
Hungary	69.3	72.4	36	8.6
Mexico	61.1	75.2	79	20.9
China	62.0	72.3	85	24.9
India	49.1	64.4	130	56.3
Low human development				
Nepal	42.1	59.8	156	67.0
Nigeria	42.7	46.8	120	98.8
Sierra Leone	34.4	42.5	206	143.6

*Estimated.

Source: CIA World Factbook, 2005.

indicate how much or little improvement various nations have made in two key health indicators: life expectancy and infant mortality.

Life expectancy is highly correlated with the quality of health care in a society. As a population's health improves as a result of better medical care and improved living conditions, the average age to which its members live (i.e., the life expectancy of the population) rises dramatically. For example, Table 2–1 indicates that a person born in Sierra Leone in 2005 can expect to live only about 42 years; in contrast, a person born in the United States in 2005 can expect to live almost 78 years.

Differences in life expectancy between developed and less-developed nations are due largely to the increasing chance that people in the former will survive the childhood diseases and parasites that cause such high death rates in the latter. Table 2–1 shows the wide gap between the industrial and low-income countries in infant mortality rates, the most important comparative indicator of health. In Sierra Leone the infant mortality rate is 147, more than twice the rate in India, 21 times the rate in the United States, and 49 times the rate in Sweden.

Infant mortality rates are highly correlated with the number of health-care professionals in a society, which serves as a measure of the quality of the health care available to its members. However, other factors besides the availability of health-care professionals may affect the health of a population. In the poorest regions of the world, malnutrition, a decline in breast-feeding, and inadequate sanitation and health facilities are associated with high infant and child mortality. In the case of breast-feeding, companies that sell infant milk formulas have been implicated in the negative change. But poor maternal health and lack of prenatal care contribute even more to persistent high rates of infant mortality. Moreover, the emergence of new and extremely deadly epidemics, especially AIDS and other sexually transmitted diseases, diverts scarce medical resources away from basic health care and preventive public health programs. In a later section of the chapter, we return to the special crisis in world health care presented by the growing AIDS epidemic.

In the United States, our comparatively poor health is due largely to two social conditions: growing inequality and lifestyle problems. Inequality and increases in the poverty rate are associated with lack of health insurance and lack of access to high-quality medical care. Problems in the way we live, including sedentary occupations; fattening, nonnutritious foods; and lack of proper exercise, contribute to the high incidence of obesity, heart disease, and other ailments. Environmental pollution and cigarette smoking contribute to the high incidence of respiratory disease and cancer. There can be little doubt, however, that many of our health problems are aggravated by the kind of medical care that is—or is not—available.

Medical sociology is the subfield of sociology that specializes in research on the health-care system and its impact on the public, especially access to health care (Bloom, 2001; Cockerham, 2006) and the evolution of health-care institutions (Starr, 1995). In describing problems of physical health, sociologists are particularly interested in learning how a person's social class (as measured by income, education, and occupation) influences his or her access to medical care and its outcome. Sociologists also work with economists and health-care planners in assessing the costs of different types of health-care delivery systems.

Medical sociologists often point out that health-care institutions themselves are the source of many of the problems we associate with health in the United States. They emphasize that the health-care system has evolved in such a way that doctors maintain private practices while society supports the hospitals and insurance systems that allow them to function (Fox, 1997). In other words, American health care never developed as a purely competitive industry or a regulated public service. Instead, as we will see shortly, it became a complex institution comprising many private and public organizations.

As great strides were made in the ability to treat illnesses—especially through the use of antibiotics—and to prevent them through improved public health practices, doctors began to develop narrow specialties and to refer patients to hospitals with special facilities. This created a situation in which doctors and hospital personnel became highly interdependent and developed a need to "assert their long-run collective interests over their short-run individual interests" (Starr, 1982, p. 230). All efforts to change our health-care system, to make it less costly, or more efficient, or more humane, must deal with the power of insurance companies, doctors, and other health-care providers, which derives not from their wealth or their ownership of health-care facilities, but from their mode of relating to one another and to the public. This is a subject that will become clear once we have discussed some of the specific problems of health care in American society.

THE SCOPE OF HEALTH-CARE PROBLEMS IN AMERICA

The range of situations in which health care can be viewed as a social problem is extremely wide. At the micro, or individual, level, where people we know and love are affected, we think of such problems as whether to terminate life-support systems, whether the correct medical treatment is being applied, or whether an elderly parent should be placed in a nursing home. But people's experiences at the micro level are influenced by larger forces that act throughout society and touch the lives of millions. These are the macro problems of health care. At the micro level we may worry about elderly loved ones, but at the macro level the issue is how effectively health care is distributed among all people (including the elderly and the poor) and what can be done to improve the delivery of needed medical services.

In this section we explore several aspects of health care in the United States that contribute to social problems at both the micro and macro levels. Unequal access to health services, the high cost of health care, inadequate insurance coverage, the special problems faced by women and the disabled and handicapped, and ethical issues arising from medical technology are among the problems that must be addressed if more Americans are to receive more and better health care. And as we will see in the next section, these issues become even more critical in the context of the AIDS epidemic.

Unequal Access to Health Care

Health care is distributed very unevenly in the United States. We will see shortly that about 18 percent of Americans under age 65 do not currently have any health insurance, and millions more have inadequate coverage (National Coalition on Health Care, 2007). The number of uninsured Americans rose by 1.3 million between 2004 and 2005 and has increased by almost 7 million since 2000 (DeNavas-Walk, Proctor, & Lee, 2006). The poor, the near-poor, members of racial and ethnic minority groups, and residents of depressed rural areas are most likely to fall into the uninsured category. Economic class and race are also correlated with the risk of becoming seriously ill. For example, industrial workers are more likely than other population groups to contract certain forms of cancer and respiratory diseases, and lack of prenatal care is a serious problem in minority communities (Wellner, 1999). Thus, to a large extent health care as a social problem can be viewed in terms of inequality of access to health-care services.

Inequalities of Race and Ethnicity.
The use and availability of medical care are directly related to socioeconomic class, race, and ethnicity. The racial aspect is most directly illustrated by a comparison of life expectancy for whites and nonwhites: On average, the life expectancy for white males is about six years longer than that for black males; the life expectancy for white females is about four years longer than that for black females. In addition, the infant mortality rate for blacks is more than twice that for whites: 14.0 per 1,000 live births, compared to 5.7 (*Statistical Abstract,* 2007). Nonwhites suffer proportionately more from almost every illness than do whites; and because they are less likely to have been immunized, nonwhites suffer higher rates of death from infectious diseases. Such differences cannot be ascribed to income differences alone, because even in cases in which income is the same, death rates remain higher for nonwhites.

The most comprehensive recent research on inequalities in health care for U.S. minorities shows that even with equivalent insurance, racial and ethnic minorities are likely to receive less or inferior care compared to whites, especially for the following conditions:

- **Heart disease.** African Americans are less likely to receive advanced heart treatments—13 percent fewer undergo coronary angioplasty and one-third fewer undergo bypass surgery.

- **Asthma.** Among preschool children hospitalized for asthma, only 7 percent of black and 2 percent of Hispanic children, compared with 21 percent of white children, are prescribed routine medications to prevent future asthma-related hospitalizations.

- **Breast cancer.** The length of time between an abnormal screening mammogram and the follow-up diagnostic test to determine whether a woman has breast cancer is more than twice as long for Asian American, black, and Hispanic women as for white women.

- **Human immunodeficiency virus (HIV) infection.** African Americans with HIV infection are less likely to be on antiretroviral therapy and less likely to be receiving protease inhibitors than are other people with HIV.

- **Nursing home care.** Asian American, Hispanic, and African American residents of nursing homes are all far less likely than white residents to have sensory and communication aids, such as glasses and hearing aids (Agency for Healthcare Research and Quality, 2000).

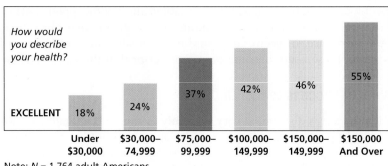

Figure 2–1 Self-Reports of Personal Health, by Income Group

Source: "Self-Reports of Personal Health, by Income Group," from *The New York Times Poll*. Copyright © 2005 by The New York Times. Reprinted by permission of The New York Times Graphics.

To be black and poor places one at the greatest risk of not receiving adequate health care or emergency treatment. In a study of patients at U.S. hospitals, medical researchers found that only 47 percent of very sick black and poor patients were put in intensive-care units, whereas 70 percent of white and poor Medicare patients were so placed. And even in federal Veterans Administration hospitals, where care is supposedly more uniformly distributed, blacks were less likely than whites to receive more costly medical procedures like catheterization of the heart for blocked arteries (Blakeslee, 1994). An outstanding reason for these disparities, which also have an enormous impact on Latinos in the United States, is the widespread lack of health insurance among minorities and the poor, a subject to which we return shortly (National Coalition on Health Care, 2007).

Inequalities of Social Class. From a socioeconomic point of view, there is a strong relationship between membership in a lower class and a higher rate of illness. The wealthier people are, the more likely they are to feel healthy. Figure 2–1 shows that only 18 percent of respondents with incomes below $30,000 rated their health as excellent, compared to 55 percent of the richest respondents. People in the lower classes also tend to be disabled more frequently and for longer periods. Moreover, mortality rates for almost all diseases are higher among the lower classes. In a classic study of social class and mortality, British researchers tracked almost 18,000 male civil service employees over a ten-year period. They found that mortality rates varied directly with the individual's job classification, a measure of social class (Marmot, Shipley, & Rose, 1984). A more recent survey of class and illness found that people who had been unemployed for a month or more were 3.8 times more susceptible to a virus than people who were not experiencing the stress of joblessness (Goode, 1999; Marmot, 1998).

Low income affects the health of the poor from birth. The high rate of infant mortality among the poor is due to a number of factors associated with poverty. Inadequate nutrition appears to account for the high death rates among the newborn children of low-income mothers. The babies most at risk are those with a low birthweight. Among the causes of low birthweight are the low nutritional value of the mother's diet, smoking or other drug use by the mother during pregnancy, and lack of prenatal care. After the neonatal period (the first three months), the higher rate of infant death among the poor is linked with a greater incidence of infectious diseases. Such diseases, in turn, are associated with poor sanitation and lack of access to high-quality medical care, as well as with drug use in some cases.

Before the creation of Medicaid, poor people who could not afford private physicians relied on a "meager combination of charity care, public hospitals and clinics, and limited public welfare-based assistance for the financing and provision of health care" (Rowland, 1994, p. 191). After the passage of Medicaid in 1965, the poor increased their consumption of medical services dramatically. Medicaid accounted for about 12 percent of the nation's health-care spending and served slightly over 30 million

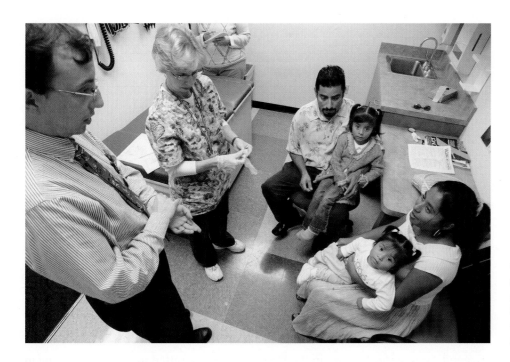

Changes in the U.S. health-care system and cuts in funding of health services are increasing the difficulty of obtaining decent health care for lower-income families.

people. Just over half of the expenses were contributed by the federal government and the remainder by individual states (Rowland, 1994). However, with the passage of welfare reform in 1996, Medicaid funding has been reduced, with the result that many poor people receive less medical care than they did before the legislation was passed (Gwatkin, 2000). (The Social Policy section of this chapter presents more analysis of this situation in the United States and throughout the world.)

Inequalities of Gender. Women are also less likely to get adequate health care in the United States. A major survey of health-care inequalities, conducted in 2002 by the Kaiser Family Foundation, found that about one woman in four skipped or delayed needed health care in the course of a year, while more than one in five could not afford to fill at least one prescription during that time. Sixteen percent of men skipped or delayed care, and 13 percent did not fill a prescription. The report's authors noted that these disparities actually add to the nation's health-care costs because eventually women who cannot afford routine medical care will become more ill, and their medical costs will be higher because they were not able to get adequate care earlier.

Like the poor and minorities who suffer from unequal access to health-care services, women who delayed or skipped care often did so because they lacked insurance: One-fifth of those surveyed reported being uninsured. Among low-income women, one-third had no health insurance. Nor did having a job guarantee access to health benefits: Nearly 60 percent of women without health insurance worked full time or part time (Allen, 2002).

The High Cost of Health Care

Unequal access to health care is related to its cost, which in recent decades has been very high. In fact, because of the rapid rates of increase in the cost of medical care in recent years, the American health-care system is often said to be in crisis. Problems like containing hospital expenses and the costs of new diagnostic technologies, the cost of prescription drugs, the effects of malpractice lawsuits, and problems with managed care and other medical insurance systems are all specific aspects of the general crisis in health-care economics in the United States. Other nations have some of the same problems and some different ones, depending on how they fund their health-care systems, but this analysis focuses primarily on conditions in the United States.

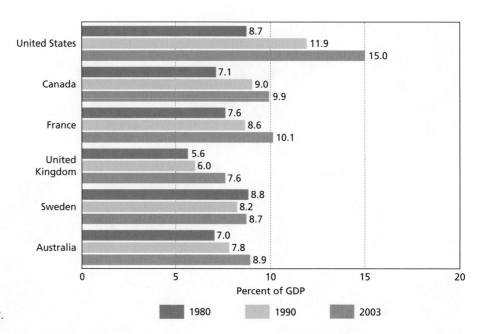

Figure 2–2 Spending on Health Care, Selected Countries

Source: Data from *Statistical Abstract,* 2007.

Expenditures on health care in the United States amounted to $5,804 per capita in 2002, a more than fivefold increase over the 1980 level of $1,002 per capita (*Statistical Abstract,* 2007). It is true that all the highly developed nations have had high levels of health-care spending, as can be seen in Figure 2–2. Nevertheless, the United States has seen the highest increases in these expenditures, despite a slowing in the rate of inflation in medical costs in the past several years.

Declining personal incomes due to global wage competition; dwindling government resources at the state and federal levels; the steady arrival of new drugs, new procedures, and advanced technologies; and the difficulty of persuading people to change risky behaviors mean that Americans are likely to spend a higher proportion of their incomes on health care in coming years. The nation's health-care expenses will rise faster than they did at the end of the 1990s. Many of the salient facts and trends in health-care costs can be gleaned from a careful look at Figure 2–3. Here we see that the largest expenditures are for hospital care and physicians' clinical services. But the costs of these medical services have actually decreased as a proportion of total health-care costs, while the costs of prescription drugs and other personal health-care services (nonprescription drugs, homeopathic remedies, diet plans, etc.) are increasing.

Hospitals. Until the mid-1980s, hospital costs rose at a dramatic pace, primarily because hospitals had little incentive to keep costs down. Both patients and physicians were often discouraged from using hospitals on an outpatient basis, and hospitals offered few self-care facilities for patients who could look after themselves. This situation was aggravated by health insurance programs like Blue Cross, which enabled hospitals to raise their fees almost at will. Expensive medical technologies are another important factor in the increase in hospital costs, as is the aging of the population, which increases the demand for hospital services.

In recent years the rate of increase in hospital costs slowed somewhat, largely as a result of improvements in the efficiency of hospital administration. Among the techniques that have been used to reduce the level of hospital costs are preadmission testing in outpatient departments and physicians' offices and a reduction in the average length of hospital stays. In addition, many procedures that were formerly performed on an inpatient basis have been moved to outpatient and office settings. Other factors in the reduction of the overall level of hospital care are the increased use of second opinions and an increase in care by nonhospital providers such as nursing homes and home health agencies (Atkins, 1999; White, 2007).

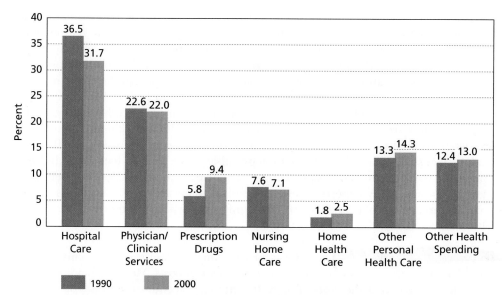

Figure 2–3 Distribution of National Health Expenditures, by Type of Service: 1990 and 2000. *Although remaining the largest contributors to spending on health services overall, the proportion of national health expenditures devoted to physician and clinical services and hospital care declined from 1990 to 2000. In the same period, the share spent on prescription drugs increased by over half to 9.4% of U.S. health spending.*

Source: Centers for Medicaid and Medicare Services (CMS), Office of the Actuary, National Health Statistics Group.

Unfortunately, these various measures to control costs have not been fully successful. And as more patients are treated outside of hospitals or stay in hospitals for shorter periods, the costs of home care of the ill are rising rapidly. Another problem is that severe measures to reduce hospital costs have a disproportionate impact on the poor and the elderly, who are more likely to suffer from chronic illnesses that may require hospitalization. These and similar situations illustrate the tendency of cost-control efforts in one area to result in higher costs elsewhere, and they provide an argument for comprehensive reform of the nation's health-care system.

Physicians. During much of the twentieth century, a shortage of physicians, together with an increasing demand for medical services, helped doctors command high fees. The supply of doctors has grown significantly since 1950, but this growth has not necessarily led to improved access to medical care or to lower costs. A look at the distribution of physicians will indicate why. People living in cities and suburbs can afford high-cost, specialized medical care. These places also tend to be more attractive than rural locales to physicians. As a result, physicians who engage in private practice tend to be clustered in metropolitan areas, producing shortages elsewhere. Even in densely settled urban areas, poor sections may have too few practicing physicians. However, it should be noted that rural areas have small populations that cannot support major institutions like teaching hospitals, where many physicians practice and conduct research.

Another cause of the increase in the cost of physicians' services is specialization. At the turn of the twentieth century, the majority of the nation's doctors were general practitioners; by 2000, less than 8 percent were. One reason for the high degree of specialization is the rapid increase in medical knowledge, which means that physicians can become competent only in limited areas. Another reason is that high-quality medical care often requires the availability of specialists. The fact remains, however, that specialists command more income than doctors who engage in primary care. A specialist's income may be up to one and one-half times that of a general practitioner. Specialization also increases costs in another way; patients must consult several physicians for a variety of ailments instead of one physician for all of them. Visiting several different physicians multiplies the cost of treatment many times.

A major factor in the high cost of physicians' services is the cost of malpractice insurance. Malpractice litigation has become more frequent for several reasons. Ineffective insurance programs play a significant role. If more people were adequately covered, they would be less likely to go to court to recover their health-care costs. The increasing sophistication of medical technology also plays a part in the rise of malpractice litigation. Although recent advances enable doctors to perform treatments that once would have seemed miraculous, the treatments can be more hazardous for the patients if they are performed incorrectly or without sufficient skill and care. Public expectations about the powers of modern medicine also increase the likelihood of malpractice suits. When the new technology fails, people tend to feel angry and frustrated and to blame the most available representatives of medical science—their physicians. Although many experts believe the cost of malpractice suits accounts for less than 2 percent of total health-care costs, this proportion is huge in dollar terms (Birenbaum, 1995).

Explain how medical technologies can be a mixed blessing for societies with advanced medical care systems.

Medical Technologies. Steadily improving medical technologies, many of which can prolong life, are another reason for high medical costs. Medical sociologists and economists argue that the costs of these technologies account for a disproportionate share of total medical costs in the United States. Because the rate of hospital use, measured in hospital days per person, has remained fairly constant since the 1960s, it is clear that patients are receiving more expensive tests and medical procedures than ever before (White, 2007). The list of advanced medical technologies that did not exist a few decades ago is impressive. It includes invasive cardiology (e.g., open heart surgery and angioplasty), renal dialysis, noninvasive imaging (e.g., sonograms, CAT scans, and MRI imaging), organ transplantation, intraocular lens implants, motorized wheelchairs, and biotechnologies that are yielding new but costly drugs like AZT. Although some of these technologies may reduce the costs of medical care, most studies indicate that they have caused total health-care spending to rise (Freudenheim, 1999).

Prescription Drugs. The cost of prescription drugs is a major factor in the high cost of health care. The cost of prescription drugs now accounts for about 45 percent of the annual increase in U.S. health-care costs, making it the single most controversial aspect of the health-care crisis and the one receiving the most attention in Congress and other social-policy arenas. Most of the increase is due to increases in the use of existing drugs, but about one-third is attributable to the development and marketing of new drugs (Hogan, Ginsburg, & Gabel, 2000).

Throughout the industrialized world, advances in pharmaceutical research and technologies are bringing new and more effective drugs to market each year. These remedies often result in major savings for employers and individuals when measured in terms of lower rates of absence from work. But their costs threaten to accelerate the rate of increase in overall medical expenses. Total spending for prescription drugs increased over the past decade, due especially to the demand for new drugs to combat depression, allergies, arthritis, hypertension, and elevated cholesterol.

Demographic and Cultural Factors. Another set of explanations for the high cost of health care in the United States can be traced to demographic and cultural factors. Demographic factors refer to aspects of population growth and change, while cultural factors refer to specific ways of life, beliefs, and norms of behavior that may contribute to health and illness.

Among the primary demographic factors influencing the cost of health care is the aging of the U.S. population, a phenomenon that is mirrored in many parts of the world but is particularly salient in Western urban industrial nations. The baby boom cohort, the generation of Americans born in the 15-year period after World War II, includes a disproportionately large number of dependent and working poor people. As shown in Figure 2–4, as this extremely large segment of the population passes through the life span, it exerts a strong influence on national social issues. Members of

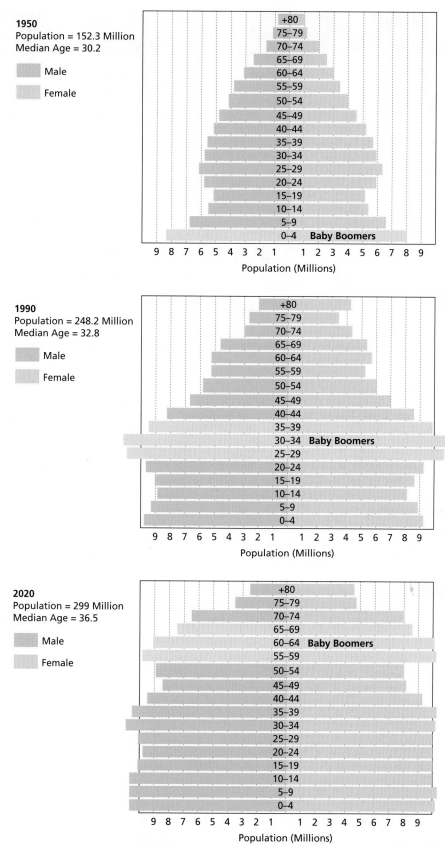

Figure 2–4 Impact of the Baby Boom on the U.S. Population, 1950–2020

Source: Data from the Census Bureau and the United Nations.

TABLE 2–2	Percentage of the Adult Population Considered to be Obese

Obesity rates are defined as the percentage of the population with a Body Mass Index (BMI) over 30 kg/m^2. The BMI is a single number that evaluates an individual's weight status in relation to height (weight/height^2, with weight in kilograms and height in meters). For Australia, the United Kingdom, and the United States, figures are based on health examinations rather than self-reported information. Obesity estimates derived from health examinations are generally higher and more reliable than those coming from self-reports because they preclude any misreporting of people's height and weight. However, health examinations are only conducted regularly in a few countries.

Country	2003	Country	2003	Country	2003
United States	30.6	France	9.4	Luxembourg	18.4
Australia	21.7	Germany	12.9	Mexico	24.2
Austria	9.1	Greece	21.9	New Zealand	20.9
Belgium	11.7	Hungary	18.8	Norway	8.3
Canada	14.3	Ireland	13.0	Spain	13.1
Czech Republic	14.8	Italy	8.5	Sweden	9.7
Denmark	9.5	Japan	3.2	Switzerland	7.7
Finland	12.8	Korea	3.2	United Kingdom	23.0

Source: Statistical Abstract, 2007.

this cohort are living longer than previous generations and are likely to require costly medical services as they encounter the chronic illnesses of old age. Now entering their retirement years, they are becoming more concerned about health care and income security. The resulting pressure on the nation's health-care system, according to some analysts, threatens to bankrupt the Social Security and Medicare systems unless changes are made in the taxation system that funds these entitlement programs.

Cultural factors that raise the cost of health care in the United States include aspects of lifestyle such as heavy use of tobacco and alcohol, unhealthy diet, high stress, sedentary activities like driving and watching television, and at the opposite extreme, activities that increase the likelihood of broken bones and orthopedic surgery.

Obesity. In the past three decades, **obesity** has become much more prevalent among Americans than it was during the mid-twentieth century. Today about 60 percent of Americans are overweight and 26 percent (about 54 million people) are obese. Another 6 million are "super-obese," meaning that they weight at least 100 pounds more than they should.

Table 2–2 shows that the United States leads other advanced industrial nations in rates of obesity, although the condition also affects large proportions of the populations of the United Kingdom, Australia, New Zealand, and Mexico.

Major health and social impacts of obesity include the following:

- Obesity increases the risk of illness from about thirty serious medical conditions.
- Obesity is associated with increases in deaths from all causes.
- Earlier onset of obesity-related diseases, such as type 2 diabetes, is being reported in obese children and adolescents.
- Obese individuals are at higher risk for impaired mobility.
- Overweight or obese individuals experience social stigmatization and discrimination in employment and academic situations.

Among the chief causes of obesity among Americans are an increasingly sedentary lifestyle (especially as people grow older), lack of exercise, and consumption of unhealthly, high-caloric, and fatty foods. Consumption of fast foods at an early age makes American children develop cravings for high-sugar, high-fat diets, which predispose them to obesity later in life.

The Centers for Disease Control and Prevention (CDC) estimates that about 280,000 Americans die each year as a direct consequence of obesity, although the immediate causes of death are quite varied; heart disease, diabetes, and stroke are especially prevalent consequences of obesity. Second only to smoking as a cause of illness and death, obesity, like smoking, is directly related to trends in individual behavior—and, many critics would add, to the influence of corporations that market unhealthy foods to eager consumers.

Smoking. Smoking remains the leading high-risk behavior associated with poor health, untimely death, and extremely high health-care costs. In consequence, many health experts consider preventing tobacco use, especially among young people, to be among the nation's most important health challenges. According to the Department of Health and Human Services' Substance Abuse and Mental Health Administration (SAMHSA), more than 57 million individuals currently smoke, putting themselves at risk for serious health consequences such as cancer, heart disease, and high blood pressure. In addition, data from the CDC indicate that more than 430,000 deaths per year in the United States are attributable to tobacco use, making tobacco the leading preventable cause of death and disease in the nation.

Adolescents and young teenagers are at particularly high risk for smoking. Every day, 3,000 young people become regular tobacco users, and one-third of them will eventually die from smoking-related diseases. The U.S. Centers for Disease Control (2004) estimates that smoking-related deaths worldwide will reach 10 million per year by 2030, with 70 percent of deaths in developing countries. The negative effects of smoking and high consumption of fast foods and unhealthy diets tend to be worst among the poorer segments of the population and among the young, many of whom are also from low-income families.

Risky Behaviors and Costly Procedures. Costly injuries due to skiing, rock climbing, mountain biking, skateboarding, and roller skating are associated with higher-income adolescents and young adults. Sports injuries are only one among many examples of how features of American culture drive up the cost of medical care and health insurance. More than those of other highly developed societies, American culture emphasizes seeking the most up-to-date medical treatments, even when those treatments have not always proven helpful. Bone marrow transplants to fight advanced cancers, hormone replacement therapy for women after menopause, and the indiscriminate use of MRI or CAT scans are all examples of questionable procedures or practices that increase costs for all health-care consumers. At the same time, Americans have shown great reluctance to support any health-care system that would limit their ability to seek whatever medical treatment they desire, and this drives up the cost of insurance and means that people who are less able to pay medical bills will postpone important preventive treatments (Toner & Stolberg, 2002).

Unequal Access. Unequal access to medical services is another important cause of the rising cost of health care. As the number of poor people without medical insurance (many of whom are immigrants) increases, so does the cost of treating illnesses that could have been avoided with better preventive care (e.g., tuberculosis, asthma, AIDS, and hypertension). Also, poor people are more likely to suffer from the effects of inadequate diet, lack of exercise, and exposure to harmful and addictive drugs (especially tobacco and alcohol) than more affluent Americans. On the world scene, the United States stands out among the advanced nations as the one that does the least to ensure adequate health coverage for the neediest segments of its population. The causes and consequences of this situation are discussed in later sections of the chapter.

TABLE 2–3	Potential Cost Savings from Early Preventive Medicine or Social Services

Early or Late Intervention: Pay Now or Pay Later

$600	Prenatal care for a pregnant woman for 9 months
$2,500	Medical care for a premature baby for 1 day
$842	A small child's nutritious diet for 1 year
$4,000	Special education for a child with a mild learning disability for 1 year
$8	A measles shot
$5,000	Hospitalization for a child with measles
$5,000	Drug treatment for an addicted mother for 9 months
$30,000	Medical care for a drug-exposed baby for 20 days
$135	School-based sex education per pupil for 1 year
$50,000	Public assistance for a teenage parent's child for 20 years
$2,000	Six weeks of support services so parents and children can stay together
$10,000	Foster care for a child for 18 months

Source: Children's Defense Fund, 2004.

Inadequate Protection

We often hear it said that an ounce of prevention is worth a pound of cure. It is certainly true that the heavy burden on the American health-care system would be alleviated if greater emphasis were placed on the prevention of illness. (This will become especially clear in the discussion of AIDS later in the chapter.) Table 2–3 presents some comparisons between the cost of early preventive medicine (or related social services for young children) and the much higher costs society incurs when it does not invest in prevention. In an ideal society, all citizens would have comprehensive health insurance that would encourage preventive measures as well as the treatment of disease and injury. But if prevention is not possible, at least there should be some form of protection. Given that both as individuals and as a society we seem unable to prevent a wide variety of illnesses and chronically disabling conditions, there is clearly a need for some means of protecting citizens from the potentially devastating economic impact of major health-care expenditures.

For much of the nation's history, individuals paid for their own health care, or if they had insurance, they paid for the insurance themselves. As a result, the poor and the near-poor often received medical care only in the most extreme emergencies. Along with the New Deal legislation of the 1930s—which included the establishment of Social Security, the extension of pension benefits for employed Americans, and other social-welfare legislation—the United States began to establish a system of health insurance whose costs were shared by employers, individuals, and government.

There are now three categories of health insurance: commercial insurance companies that sell both individual and group policies (e.g., Blue Cross and Blue Shield); independent prepaid groups, or **health maintenance organizations (HMOs);** and public insurance. Public insurance includes two programs designed to help the medically needy—Medicare and Medicaid—which were enacted by Congress in 1965. Medicare is paid for by Social Security taxes. It is designed to cover some of the medical expenses of people aged 65 and over. Medicaid, an assistance program financed from tax revenues, is designed to pay for the medical costs of people of any age who cannot afford even basic health care. Administered by the states with funds from the federal budget and from the states themselves, Medicaid now insures one in seven Americans and pays for 40 percent of births and 50 percent of nursing home costs (Toner & Stolberg, 2002). At this writing, almost every state in the nation is facing dramatic increases in

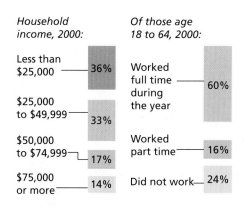

Figure 2–5 Household Income and Employment Status of the Uninsured

Source: "Decade After Health Care Crisis, Soaring Costs Brings New Strains," Robin Toner & Cheryl Gay Stolberg, New York Times, August 11, 2002. © 2002 by The New York Times. Reprinted by permission of The New York Times Graphics.

the demand for Medicaid services, especially for elderly people who need nursing home care and children whose parents lack health insurance. At the same time, most states are experiencing cuts in funding for Medicaid, which is producing a health-care crisis for millions of the most vulnerable Americans.

What are the similarities and differences between Medicare and Medicaid?

The Uninsured. More than 45 million Americans lack health insurance, an increase of about 5 million since 2000. This figure represents about 18 percent of the U.S. population. Much of the increase has occurred in families in which one or both parents are working full time. As we see in Figure 2–5, 60 percent of people age 18 to 64 who are uninsured work full time. The very poor who are out of the labor force qualify for Medicaid, and the elderly are eligible for Medicare. Young people who are subject to frequent periods of unemployment and minority workers who are employed at jobs with no health benefits are especially likely to be uninsured. Children, the most vulnerable segment of the population, have been losing out the most as the proportion of uninsured people in the U.S. population has risen.

Most people in the United States, other than those over 65 and those on Medicaid, receive their health insurance benefits from their employers, although they may also pay into the insurance plan. The lack of insurance among many active workers stems from this fact because, as we see in Figure 2–6, the smaller the firm, the less likely it is to provide health insurance benefits for its employees. And although the share of small firms offering insurance has tended to increase, this trend is sensitive to economic conditions.

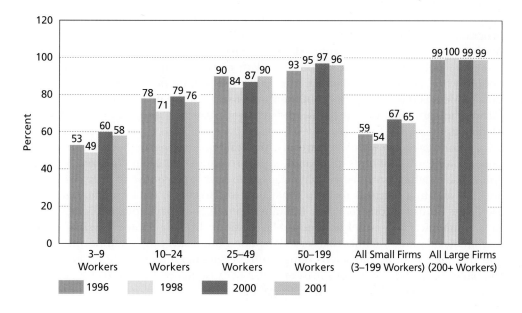

Figure 2–6 Percentage of Firms Offering Health Benefits, by Firm Size: 1996–2001

Source: Employer Health Benefits, 2001 Annual Survey, The Kaiser Family Foundation and Health Research and Educational Trust. Copyright © 2001. Reprinted by permission of Henry J. Kaiser Family Foundation.

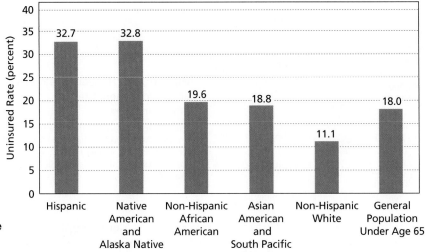

Figure 2–7 Probability of Being Uninsured, by Race and Ethnicity

Source: U.S. Census Bureau, 2004.

Minority status also increases one's probability of being without medical insurance in the United States. Figure 2–7 shows that in the general population under age 65 there is an 18 percent probability of being uninsured, but among African Americans, Native Americans, Hispanics, and Asians the probability is far higher, in most cases two times or more than for white Americans. Most of these disparities can be traced to the fact that if one is not on public insurance, either Medicare or Medicaid, one must either pay privately for insurance or be provided with an insurance plan on the job. Because far higher proportions of minority workers are employed by firms with limited or no health insurance plans, the probability of not having health insurance is higher as well. (See the On Further Analysis box on page 45 for further discussion of the special situation of Hispanics.)

Another group that lacks sufficient health insurance is the elderly population. Many older people believe, incorrectly, that Medicare and other insurance programs will cover the cost of long-term care in nursing homes. As a result, elderly people whose families are unable to care for them may find their savings exhausted after less than a year in a nursing home (Pear, 1998).

Medicaid and Medicare have been helpful to many Americans, but a number of ills plague these programs. First, there is inequity in the distribution of services. The poorest people continue to receive the fewest services. There are also inequities in geographic distribution. In addition, a number of factors have caused the Medicare program to fall short of its goal of providing full access to health care for the elderly. Among them is the requirement of deductible payments and coinsurance (additional insurance policies that must be purchased to ensure complete medical coverage). People who are financially secure can meet this requirement, and the poor can turn to Medicaid for this portion of their expenses. But the near-poor aged must still forfeit the care they need because they cannot pay for it and are not eligible for Medicaid.

A second problem with Medicare and Medicaid is their cost to the public and their impact on health-care costs in general. Both programs have been criticized for waste and abuse by administrators and physicians, who have no incentive to keep costs down and few auditing controls to keep them ethical. Hospitals, for example, have used Medicare funds to construct new buildings, purchase superfluous equipment, and hire nonmedical personnel such as public-relations directors. Some physicians operate "Medicaid mills"—clinics that serve the poor—often carrying out unnecessary tests and treatments. Many physicians refuse to treat patients under Medicaid because of the paperwork and regulations involved, and because many doctors' offices are inaccessible to the poor, the Medicaid mills are often their only source of health care.

Aside from wanting to help people who are less fortunate, what are some of the reasons that lack of medical insurance among a large proportion of Americans is a problem for all?

On Further Analysis

DISPARITIES IN HISPANIC HEALTH CARE

Why should Hispanics in the United States be almost three times as likely as non-Hispanic whites to lack health insurance? (Refer to Figure 2–7.) The answer to this question requires that we explore the meaning of the term *Hispanic*. Often, social categories that lump together large numbers of quite diverse people can mask important trends. In the case of Hispanics, further analysis of the Hispanic subgroups in the United States reveals great variations in rates and sources of health insurance.

The accompanying chart shows the differences in health insurance coverage among the major Hispanic groups in the United States. Cuban Americans, the majority of whom live in Florida and have been in the United States since the 1960s if not earlier, have by far the highest rates of job-based or other private insurance (65%). Puerto Ricans, like Cuban Americans, have lower rates of noninsurance, but they have the highest rates of public insurance (Medicaid and Medicare) because they are American citizens with long histories of job discrimination and residence in low-income urban ghettos. People of Central American or Mexican descent have the lowest rates of job-based insurance and, in consequence, extremely high rates of noninsurance. At the same time, they are most often found among the ranks of the working poor, in occupations like landscaping, dishwashing, and casual labor. Any improvements in coverage for the working poor would greatly benefit these Hispanic subgroups, but they would also benefit society as a whole, which is already paying higher hospital costs as poor people seek emergency room and hospital care for severe illnesses that in many cases could have been prevented had they been eligible for outpatient clinic visits.

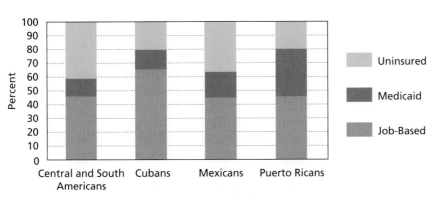

Health Insurance Coverage Among Latino Subgroups

Source: Kaiser Family Foundation, 2000. Copyright © 2000 by UCLA Center for Policy Research and Kaiser Family Foundation. Reprinted by permission of Henry J. Kaiser Family Foundation.

Cost Shifting. Part of the high cost of medical care in the United States is due to the nation's "crazy quilt" system for funding health care. Private insurance companies, managed care medical companies, Medicare, Medicaid, and veterans' health care plans cover health costs to varying degrees for different categories of citizens. But they may also seek to shift the costs of care to other companies and health care agencies whenever possible. The tendency for the costs of treating people with serious illnesses to be transferred from one insurance system to another is called **cost shifting.** The most prevalent form of cost shifting is the practice of many insurance companies of refusing coverage for people with serious chronic illnesses like diabetes, cancer, and AIDS.

Because many doctors and hospitals believe they have a moral obligation to treat sick people even if they do not have insurance, hospitals end up with over $10 billion a year in treatment costs that are not reimbursed by public or private insurance. These costs are passed along to insured patients in the form of higher fees, driving up the premiums charged by insurance companies. This has the effect of shifting the burden to private firms that provide health coverage for their employees (Birenbaum, 1995). This situation, in turn, causes employers to reduce their health insurance costs, often by reducing the number of employees covered under their benefit plans. Since the uninsured tend to use hospital emergency rooms as their main source of primary medical care, the rising number of uninsured people only worsens the problem of cost shifting.

The practice whereby insurance companies attempt to limit hospital stays and otherwise seek to influence the course of a patient's medical care—for example, by reviewing doctors' treatment plans—has created widespread controversy in recent years. Membership in HMOs grew steadily in the past two decades but has been declining in recent years as patients look for greater flexibility in their plans. In HMOs patients pay a fixed premium for services (usually covered by their insurance plans) and must use doctors and hospitals approved by the HMO. Preferred provider organizations (PPOs) are becoming more popular because they allow patients to use any doctor or hospital, but patients are charged less if they use those on an approved list. These plans are a reaction to the more restrictive aspects of the managed-care system in effect during most of the 1990s, but they also move closer to the older and more expensive "fee for service" model (Toner & Stolberg, 2002).

In sum, although insurance plans, both public and private, were originally intended to solve many of the problems and inequities of the American health-care system, in many ways they have compounded existing difficulties.

Women and Health Care

Since the late 1960s some of the strongest criticisms of the health-care system have come from the women's movement. Advocates of improved health care for women argue that in American society women are forced to play subordinate roles in every social institution, including health care. As part of an effort to enhance the power of women, they have campaigned for the legal right to terminate unwanted pregnancies through safe, nonexploitive abortions, as well as for more control over their own medical care, especially in the areas of obstetrics and gynecology. This activism has had some influence on the delivery of health care to women, but the permanence of these gains is far from assured.

One of the first issues around which the women's movement was able to mobilize mass support was abortion. Although the majority of the American public opposed the procedure during the 1960s, increased publicity about birth defects (notably those caused by the use of thalidomide, a tranquilizer, during pregnancy) helped change many people's attitudes. In the late 1960s, as state legislatures began to liberalize restrictions on abortion, a number of women's groups demonstrated and lobbied aggressively not merely for a loosening of restrictions but also for outright repeal of all limitations on access to abortion. In 1973, in *Roe* v. *Wade,* the U.S. Supreme Court affirmed the right of all women to obtain abortions early in pregnancy. Since then, however, opponents of abortion have succeeded in gaining the passage of legislation that restricts federal funding of abortion, a topic to which we return in later chapters.

The controversy over abortion awakened many women to larger problems in the health-care system, and the women's movement has continued its efforts to make medical personnel more sensitive to the physical and psychological needs of women. Feminists point out that in many ways health-care organizations have placed their own interests ahead of the needs and preferences of their clients. In the case of childbirth, in most states infants must be delivered by a licensed doctor. Because the birthing process usually occurs in a hospital with the participation of a number of specialists, mothers lack the supportive presence of one person from the beginning of labor until the birth of the infant. Moreover, until recently the hospital was dominated by high-status male physicians who retained exclusive command of relevant medical knowledge, making it difficult for women to challenge established procedures (Gabay & Wolfe, 1997). Thus, efforts to win acceptance of midwives, who perform deliveries in the home and are present throughout the childbirth process, have been only moderately successful. The work of nurse midwives, for example, is usually limited to hospitals and performed under medical supervision, whereas that of lay midwives, who practice outside of medical control, is not fully legal in all states (Katz Rothman, 1994).

Other critics of the health-care system as it relates to women have called for less intervention in the birth process itself. Anesthesia, induced labor, and surgical

This class for expectant mothers and their mates illustrates how such classes help involve fathers in the preparations for and in the actual birth of their children. In the past, fathers were often deprived of such opportunities to share the unforgettable experience of birthing.

practices such as Caesarian sections and the use of forceps have come under attack. Some of these forms of intervention not only can cause harm to both mother and infant but can also inflate the cost of delivery. As a result of these criticisms, classes in prepared childbirth taught by nurse practitioners have become widespread. Such classes prepare a woman (and often her partner as well) for the experience of childbirth by describing the process in detail and teaching a variety of techniques for reducing or eliminating pain during labor and delivery. These techniques not only make it possible to avoid excessive use of anesthetics but also greatly reduce the woman's fear and anxiety about giving birth. Some hospitals have also granted women a greater say in decisions that affect their deliveries, such as whether a mate or friend may be present in the delivery room.

Women's groups have also criticized the nature of gynecological care in the United States. It is argued that the simple fact of being female has been "medicalized"; that is, certain conditions, such as pregnancy and menstruation, have been defined in terms of health and illness (Katz Rothman, 1994). This has permitted "experts," especially gynecologists and psychiatrists (see Chapter 3), to achieve professional dominance over women, with results that not only are economically beneficial to physicians but also contribute to women's relative lack of power in society (Riessman, 1983).

Although many politically active women concern themselves with issues of reproductive care and abortion, medical researchers and health administrators point out that women and their needs are vastly underrepresented in medical research. Eighty percent of health-care workers are women, yet women remain largely absent from the leadership ranks of medicine. The National Institutes of Health (NIH), the most important source of funds for medical research, spend less than 20 percent of their research budget on women's health issues, even though breast cancer alone claims the lives of about 40,000 women a year. Moreover, until recently most of the studies of heart disease and smoking used only male subjects, and the possible unique needs of women were unresearched (Ness & Kuller, 1999). In 1990, in response to the latter criticism, the NIH created an Office of Research on Women's Health. The office provides funds for studies designed to fill gaps in scientific knowledge that result from the exclusion of women from past experiments. In addition, proposals for studies that use only male subjects must be justified on scientific grounds.

The Disabled and Handicapped

Another important population from the standpoint of health-care needs is people who are disabled or handicapped, usually as a result of automobile and industrial accidents. Automobile accidents are a major cause of paralysis and other permanent disabilities, in addition to other serious injuries that often require hospitalization and costly surgery. Until recently, the disabled and handicapped were literally forgotten people. They were excluded from work, school, and society both by active discrimination and by barriers imposed by a world designed for the able-bodied. Steps, curbs, and narrow doorways and aisles—impassable obstacles to wheelchairs, for example— are only a few of the aspects of everyday life that still impede the physically disabled. Although the situation has improved since the 1960s as a result of the political organization of the disabled themselves, many problems remain.

The disabled suffer from extremely high unemployment rates. Of the 22 million people with a work disability, fewer than one-quarter are employed (*Statistical Abstract*, 2007). In addition, many handicapped people are underemployed—assigned to low-level, low-paying jobs—because employers are afraid to offer them challenges. In many instances Social Security regulations contribute to the problem by limiting the amount of money a handicapped person can earn and still receive benefits. For all these reasons, the majority of the handicapped are poor.

Numerous studies have shown that when disabled people are hired, they usually dispel all the negative myths that surround them. An overwhelming majority prove to be dedicated, capable workers; they have only a slightly higher-than-average absentee rate, and their turnover rate is well below average. The disabled are neither slower nor less productive than other workers and have excellent safety records.

Almost 32 million Americans have deformities or orthopedic impairments; another 33 million have visual or hearing impairments (*Statistical Abstract*, 2007). In addition, advances in medical science have made it possible for many people to survive serious accidents, usually with handicaps. Technology is also making it possible for many disabled people, who would have been bedridden or housebound in the past, to be mobile and to acquire new skills. Improved health care and prevention of disease have

Today disabled people refuse to be denied active and productive roles in society.

meant that more people than ever before are living to an advanced age and are incurring the disabilities that often occur in old age.

The disabled and handicapped have emerged as a recognized minority group. Like women and blacks, they are demanding an end to the discrimination that keeps them out of jobs and out of the mainstream of life. They oppose efforts to place them in special programs or schools, except during the necessary phases of rehabilitation or therapy. Special programs, they claim, are the ghettos of the handicapped. As we will see in the Social Policy section, in recent decades some far-reaching legislation has been enacted in an attempt to address the problems of the disabled and handicapped.

Ethical Issues

As medical technology has improved and life-prolonging procedures have become more available and dependable, a number of complex ethical issues have arisen. Some of the new medical technologies, such as heart and kidney transplants, are extremely costly and cannot be provided to all patients who might benefit from them. Thus, the question arises of how to choose the patients who will undergo these procedures (Callahan, 1994).

The availability of life-prolonging equipment and procedures has also given rise to new questions about the meaning of life and death. State legislatures across the country have been debating the question of whether death occurs when the heart stops beating or when the brain stops functioning. Courts have been required to decide whether patients should have the right to die by ordering life-prolonging treatments to be terminated.

In recent years a related issue, assisted suicide, has come to the fore. Michigan doctor Jack Kevorkian became the personification of the right-to-die issue when he helped a 54-year-old woman with Alzheimer's disease kill herself, using an intravenous device that allowed the patient to receive a lethal drug by pressing a button. The doctor was arrested and charged with first-degree murder; later the charges were dropped, but the doctor was ordered to refrain from using the suicide device in the future. Kevorkian continued to defy the authorities in Michigan and eventually was sentenced to a term in prison. Although many doctors and health authorities condemn the practice, Kevorkian's sensational methods brought the right-to-die issue to national attention.

The controversy over the removal of life support for Terri Schiavo called attention to the problem of death with dignity in a situation in which a patient is on life support but has left no clear "advance directives." To her parents and the lay public, it seemed that Schiavo was responding to voices and other stimuli. But the neurologists who examined her believed that she had no awareness or other higher brain functions, and that with life support she might live in a vegetative state for an indefinite length of time. Although individuals who are in a persistent vegetative state may appear somewhat normal, they do not speak and are unable to respond to commands. (For more on this subject, go to **www.ninds.nih.gov/disorders/coma/coma.htm**.)

Schiavo's family was divided on whether to remove life support, with her husband asserting that she had told him she would never want to live in such a hopeless condition. Right-to-life groups, along with political leaders, including President Bush, Florida Governor Jeb Bush, then House Majority Leader Tom DeLay, and many others, supported the right-to-life advocates and soon made Schiavo a national symbol of their desire to create a "culture of life" rather than of death. Every court, including the U.S. Supreme Court, ruled in favor of Shiavo's husband's assertion of his wife's right to die with dignity. Life support was removed, but demonstrations continued to be held outside her hospital until she finally expired.

Every opinion poll conducted about how Americans actually felt about the case showed that strong majorities believed that the courts had acted wisely and that government should not interfere in what most people consider highly personal and extremely emotional issues.

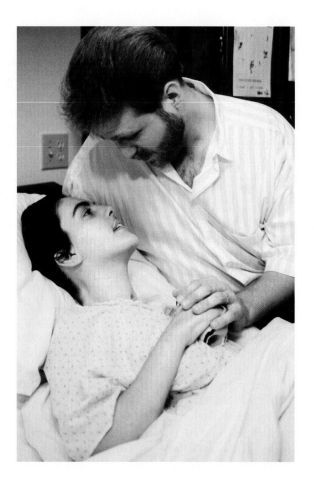

To win support for their demand that she be maintained on life support indefinitely, groups opposed to removal of Terri Schiavo's feeding tube often used photos and television clips that showed her seemingly alert, with her eyes wide open. But an autopsy conducted after her death showed that her brain had atrophied to less than half its normal size during her many years of illness and she would have had no chance of ever regaining consciousness.

End-of-Life and Advanced Directives. Although religious beliefs explained many of the differences of opinion in the case, even a slim majority of evangelical Protestants supported the decision: Forty-six percent favored removal; 44 percent were opposed. Sixty-three percent of Roman Catholics favored removal; 26 percent were opposed. Seventy-seven percent of nonevangelical Protestants favored removal; 18 percent opposed (**www.religioustolerance.org/schiavo7.htm**).

As the populations of the urban industrial nations continue to age, and given the appearance of ever-more sophisticated methods for prolonging life, the number of ethical, legal, and technical questions about life's end grows as well. Imagine that your elderly parent has had a stroke. Doctors express little hope that consciousness can be restored or that life-support systems could be removed without causing death. This is not a rare situation. Unless your family and the terminally ill parent have prepared advanced directives for dealing with the situation, much agony and prolonged suffering can ensue for everyone concerned. Advanced directives have two parts: a living will, which tells doctors and hospitals how the patient wants to be cared for should he or she become terminally ill, and a health-care proxy, which designates an advocate, usually a close family member, who can make sure that those wishes are honored (Aitken, 1999). Daniel Callahan, one of the nation's leading experts on medical ethics, comments further on these points in the Unintended Consequences box on page 51.

Privacy and Patients' Rights. Another major medical-ethical issue in the United States concerns patients' right to privacy and control over their medical records. Insurance companies wish to share patients' medical records, and there are good medical reasons, as well as economic ones, for doing so. If hospitals, doctors, and insurance companies could draw on a single national database of patient records, the nation's medical system would benefit from faster processing and reduced waste. But

Problems of Health and Health Care

Unintended Consequences

LIFE-SAVING TECHNOLOGIES

All medical policies and technologies have both intended and unintended consequences. The new life-saving technologies also create situations in which people who wish to die can do so by refusing treatment. Policies and laws designed to protect people's rights can also become a means of protecting their right to die.

Medical researcher Daniel Callahan (2003) has long been one of the nation's strongest advocates of patients' rights and the use of advanced directives. He notes, however, that after ten years of efforts to educate patients and their families about their rights to care in the face of death, over 40 percent of terminally ill patients do not have advanced directives. Even when such directives exist, doctors and other hospital personnel are often unwilling to implement them if it means not trying heroic measures to sustain life. "The culture of medicine," Callahan has written, "in league with that of American hospitals and the health care system, all push in the direction of aggressive treatment, of frequent deafness to patient wishes, and toward a curious unwillingness to take prognosis information as seriously as it should be" (1995, p. 533; see also 1997).

For Callahan and other medical ethicists, the problems of advanced life-saving technologies are hardly limited to the dying patients. He is one of a growing number of health-care experts who believe new policies will have to be established to determine who has access to many life-saving medical procedures. In his view, priority should be given to preventive medicine and to the needs of groups that are particularly at risk—for example, prenatal care for the poor—rather than to high-cost efforts to save the lives of individuals whose chances of surviving and leading a comfortable life are minimal. Every person should have the right to humane care, not cure, he believes; expensive medical resources should not be devoted to marginal cases such as 18-ounce babies or quadriplegic teenage victims of automobile accidents.

Callahan and other researchers and policymakers have yet to agree on an equitable system for rationing expensive medical treatments. However, this failure does not deny the importance of the issue so much as it points to the immense political and ethical difficulties involved.

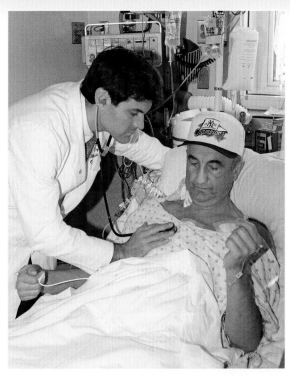

This man is recovering from an open-heart operation to clear blocked arteries. This procedure, which depends heavily on advanced medical technologies, is becoming almost routine in American medicine, but it also helps account for the rapid increase in health-care costs.

patients' advocacy groups fear that systematic sharing of medical records would also allow insurance companies to deny coverage to people with serious medical problems like AIDS and many other illnesses. In 2002 the Bush administration ruled that patients did not need to give prior approval for their records to be shared, opening the way to both the positive and negative consequences of the flow of private medical information. Because the administration did not take any measures that would help fund the creation of a state-of-the-art medical database, critics argued that the ruling was primarily a gift to the major medical insurance corporations. This issue promises to remain an extremely controversial aspect of health-care policy in coming years, and we will return to it again in the Social Policy section of the chapter.

AIDS—A MODERN PLAGUE

The social problems related to health care became especially acute in the mid-1980s with the spread of a previously unknown disease: *acquired immune deficiency syndrome (AIDS)*. This disease is caused by the *human immunodeficiency virus (HIV)*, which attacks the body's

As medical researchers strive to find a cure for AIDS, educators and policymakers use posters like this one to make people more aware of the need to engage in "safer" forms of sexual behavior.

immune system. An unusual feature of HIV is the long period of latency—up to ten years—between the time of infection and the appearance of the disease. During this period there may be no visible symptoms. Once it has been rendered ineffective by the virus, however, the immune system is unable to combat other diseases that routinely infect humans, such as pneumonia, cancer, and tuberculosis, and death is almost inevitable.

It is not certain what proportion of people infected with HIV will actually develop AIDS-related illnesses, but the number who do so remains high. In 1996 AIDS researchers discovered that treatment with a combination of anti-AIDS drugs, all costly, is effective in preventing the onset of AIDS symptoms and, in some cases, in eliminating the presence of HIV altogether. But these treatments are available mainly in the more affluent nations and to the more affluent patients; they are not widely available in Africa and other regions where the spread of HIV continues at epidemic rates and is associated with heterosexual transmission through unprotected sex.

AIDS is a "pandemic," or global epidemic. In the United States deaths from AIDS have decreased dramatically since 1996, due primarily to expensive drug treatments, which are available mainly in more affluent nations. Elsewhere in the world, especially in impoverished African and Asian countries, the rate of infection is soaring. The World Health Organization (WHO) estimates that almost 40 million people are infected with HIV; almost 85 percent of them are in the developing nations of Asia and sub-Saharan Africa. In Zimbabwe, for example, 25 percent of the adult population is thought to be HIV positive, largely through heterosexual transmission. Infection rates are rising rapidly in the economically and politically chaotic nations of the former Soviet Union. India, with an estimated 5.1 million cases, has the world's highest number of cases, although given India's huge population, the rate of infection is relatively low (UNAIDS, 2004). (See Figure 2–8.)

Why is HIV/AIDS considered a "pandemic," and where is it spreading most rapidly?

Prospects for coping with the AIDS epidemic in poor nations are particularly gloomy because of the high cost of advanced treatments. In the United States the cost

North America
1,000,000

Western Europe
610,000

Eastern Europe
& Central Asia
1,400,000

East Asia
1,100,000

Caribbean
440,000

North Africa
& Middle East
540,000

South &
South-East Asia
7,100,000

Latin America
1,700,000

Sub-Saharan
Africa
25,400,000

Oceania
35,000

Number of people living with HIV/AIDS	Total	39.5 million
	Adults	37.2 million
	Women	17.7 million
	Children <15 years	2.3 million
People newly infected with HIV	**Total**	**4.3 million**
	Adults	3.8 million
	Children <15 years	640,000
AIDS deaths	**Total**	**2.9 million**
	Adults	2.6 million
	Children <15 years	380,000

Figure 2–8 Global Estimates of HIV/AIDS Epidemic, 2006

Source: UNAIDS, 2007. Courtesy of UNAIDS.

of the multidrug therapy that has proven effective in suppressing the deadly AIDS symptoms can average $750 a month. This is a fortune for people in poor nations like South Africa, where about 8 percent of the population is HIV positive and the annual per capita income is $6,000. But some encouraging changes are occurring. It appears that a short, four-week course of even one anti-AIDS drug, AZT, during late pregnancy and delivery can halve the rate of HIV transmission from mothers to their babies. There is also evidence from some third-world nations that rates of condom use are rising as AIDS education finally begins to take effect. In the urban parts of Senegal and in Uganda, studies show that there has been an enormous increase in safe sex practices. Unfortunately, these vital changes are slow to occur, and there has not been nearly enough investment in programs to change the behaviors that lead to infection. (This subject is discussed further in the Social Policy section.)

In the United States, at least 524,000 people have died of AIDS since 1981 (U.S. Centers for Disease Control, 2005). In 2004, however, the number of AIDS deaths in the United States fell below 18,000. (The record high of about 43,000 was reached in 1995.) These changes are due primarily to the spread of new treatments and to lower rates of infection as a result of intensive education and safe sex campaigns begun years ago. But AIDS experts now fear that complacency and a return to unsafe sexual practices could once again increase the HIV infection rate. The U.S. Centers for Disease Control (2005) estimates that the number of AIDS cases in the United States increased by almost 1,000 between 2001 and 2003. It is clear that in the United States, as elsewhere, the epidemic is not over.

The HIV virus is transmitted through the exchange of body fluids, that is, directly from an infected person's blood, semen, or vaginal secretions into another person's bloodstream. Transmission can occur through sexual activity that leads to torn membranes; through blood transfusions, sharing of hypodermic needles, and other means;

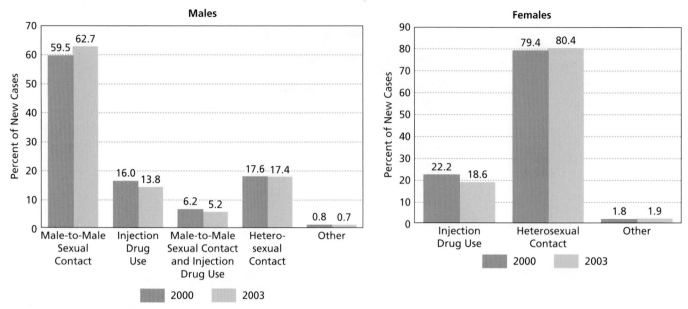

Figure 2–9 Routes of AIDS Transmission Among Males and Females, United States

Source: U.S. Centers for Disease Control, 2005.

or from an infected mother to her unborn or newborn infant. The disease is not transmitted by mere contact with skin—by a handshake or a hug, for example—or through the air as a result of a sneeze or cough. It is not transmitted by sharing meals, bathrooms, or beds with infected individuals or by casual contact in the home, school, or workplace. The primary means of transmission are sexual intercourse, especially anal intercourse, and sharing of needles by drug users.

AIDS is sometimes erroneously referred to as a "gay disease" because in the United States it first appeared in male homosexuals between the ages of 20 and 49, and the majority of AIDS deaths have occurred among this population. But as indicated in Figure 2–9, AIDS is by no means limited to homosexuals. At present about 63 percent of new AIDS cases in the United States are among men who have had sex with other men; about 30 percent of new cases (a figure that seems to be accelerating) are found in women. In Canada the trends are similar: Twenty-seven percent of new cases are now occurring among women, compared to 8.5 percent in 1995. In all the wealthier nations, poor women who are members of minority groups are at especially high risk (UNAIDS, 2004). While the majority of women who contract the HIV virus are infected through the use of contaminated needles associated with intravenous drug use, other drugs—particularly crack cocaine—are also associated with high-risk behavior among women in the United States and other nations where these drugs are available. The realization that non-IV drugs like crack are implicated in the AIDS epidemic (because women and men in crack houses engage in sex with many partners, thereby greatly increasing their risk of infection) emerged in part from the pioneering research of sociologist Claire Sterk (1988, 2000), who spent hundreds of hours interviewing street women about their drug and sexual behavior.

AIDS and Global Poverty

On a more global basis, a major underlying factor in the spread of AIDS among women is dire poverty. Delegates at the World AIDS Conference in Barcelona in 2002 warned that contrary to what many people may think, the global AIDS epidemic is in its early stages and promises to have worsening effects on prospects for economic and social development. In southern Africa, for example, life expectancies have actually been decreasing

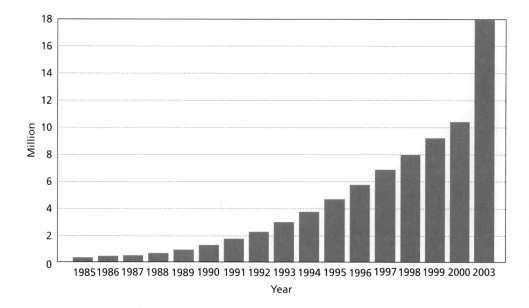

Figure 2–10 Number of Children (ages 0–14) Who Lost Their Mother or Both Parents to HIV/AIDS

Source: UNAIDS/UNICEF/USAID, 2002, 2005. Courtesy of UNAIDS, USAID, and UNICEF.

due to the enormous number of relatively young and productive people who are dying of AIDS-related diseases. Rates of infection are increasing most rapidly in the world's poorest regions, especially in Africa, India, and China. In contrast to the more affluent regions of the world, transmission in these poorest regions is through heterosexual sex and thus infects increasing numbers of women and their babies, as Figure 2–10 shows.

In southern Africa and other regions of that impoverished continent, high rates of HIV transmission are often found among the most mobile populations: miners who travel to distant copper or gold fields, long-distance truck drivers, migratory agricultural workers. Away from home for long periods, these migrants, who are primarily males, frequent local prostitutes, who are typically the daughters of destitute families and, with increasing frequency, orphans of the AIDS epidemic themselves. In her pioneering work on AIDS in the mining regions of southern Africa, biologist Helen Epstein reports that local researchers found that 80 percent of local prostitutes and 30 percent of male miners were HIV positive. But even more shocking was her finding that in the township about fifteen miles from the mines, 60 percent of the women between the ages of 20 and 30 were HIV positive. Epstein and other researchers found that these women were not prostitutes and were not promiscuous, but had long-term relationships with miners who often failed to use condoms with them precisely because they were not prostitutes. Invariably, the young women were from extremely poor households and were utterly lacking in alternatives to the relationships they had with the miners, which helped them survive (Epstein, 2002).

Similar situations abound throughout the world wherever women are driven to high-risk sexual behavior due to the effects of extreme poverty, often made far worse by civil war, corruption, and the faulty economic policies of national and world leaders (Stiglitz, 2002).

AIDS Orphans

Researchers at the World AIDS Conference warned that there are now 15 million orphans of the AIDS epidemic, over 80 percent of whom live in sub-Saharan Africa in nations largely lacking institutions of health and social welfare adequate to cope with this growing emergency. Figure 2–10 shows the alarming acceleration in the number of children who have lost their mother or both parents to the disease since 1985 (UNAIDS, 2004).

These children are the hardest hit when their parents fall ill and waste away. Adolescents in AIDS-stricken families are typically forced to drop out of school to care for their dying parents and then for their orphaned siblings. The surviving children are most often left homeless, shunned, and ostracized by the stigma that still attaches to AIDS in Africa and in many other societies throughout the world. Some orphaned children try to manage on their own in child-headed households, while others are driven to beg or find other means to survive in the streets. Orphaned girls frequently become targets of abuse by older men seeking uninfected sexual partners.

For AIDS victims and their families, the impact of the disease is devastating. Not only must they deal with fear and grief, but they must also cope with shame. Because AIDS is associated with homosexuality and drug abuse, relatives and close friends of the patients feel stigmatized. They may become angry at the patient and blame themselves for failing to rescue him or her from a dangerous lifestyle (Ayala, 1996). "Having AIDS is a little bit like being treated as if you're a leper," says a therapist who works with AIDS patients and family members (quoted in Walker, 1987).

Although certain drugs, such as AZT, may slow the onset of AIDS symptoms, to date there is no cure for AIDS. The only defense against it is prevention. At present, therefore, behavioral changes are the only means of stopping the spread of the virus. Indeed, AIDS is different from most other diseases in that individuals can choose, at least in theory, to avoid infection. The battle against the AIDS epidemic is thus a social as well as a biological one. While scientists conduct research in an effort to find a cure, educators, social scientists, and policymakers are attempting to influence the behavior of large numbers of people. But efforts to control behavior—especially sexual behavior—raise a variety of moral and ethical issues: Should people be required to undergo testing for the presence of the HIV virus? Should they be required to reveal the names of individuals with whom they have had sexual contacts? Should drug addicts be given clean needles? Should condoms be distributed in public schools? Just how controversial this subject is will become clear in discussions of AIDS-related issues at several points in this book.

Thus, AIDS is having a major impact not only on individuals and their loved ones but also on the health-care system itself. The HIV virus can be detected almost immediately, and in most cases months or years go by before severe symptoms appear. Therefore, there is ample time for medical intervention. But treatment for AIDS is complex and prolonged. Because it destroys the body's ability to fight disease, the presence of AIDS is signaled by the onset of many different illnesses, ranging from pneumonia to various forms of cancer. In the terminal stages, the patient often suffers from acute illnesses like meningitis. Thus, treatment for the illnesses associated with AIDS is complex and usually requires long periods of hospitalization and intensive care. The health-care system, already overburdened, is severely strained by the need to provide expensive care for hundreds of thousands of AIDS patients. Health insurance costs are also increasing as more AIDS cases develop.

Clearly, AIDS is a great deal more than a serious illness. It can, in fact, be viewed as three epidemics rolled into one: the spread of the HIV virus; the epidemic of the disease AIDS; and the social, political, psychological, and ethical reactions to the disease and those who suffer from it (Bozette, 1998). AIDS has had a profound effect on American society—on its ways of living and dying and on its debates over health care, sex education, drug abuse, and social justice. It has had an especially dramatic effect on sexual behavior. There has been a resurgence of traditional sexual mores and values not just among the groups most at risk, but throughout the population (Laumann et al., 1994).

What are the major differences between the ways in which AIDS is spread in the developing regions of the world and the ways in which it is spread in developed regions?

EXPLANATIONS OF HEALTH-CARE PROBLEMS

Why do we have such difficulty improving the quality of health-care services and providing more equal access to them? The explanations offered by medical sociologists depend to a large extent on the perspective from which they view the problem. Conflict theorists, for example, tend to view the problem as a feature of capitalism: The poor get less medical care because they get less of everything in American society. Those who approach this question from a functionalist perspective have sought the answers in medicine's development into a complex and costly social institution. And from an interactionist perspective, many of the problems of health care in the United States and other highly developed nations can be traced to cultural factors, including the way people are taught to interact with one another. In this section we briefly discuss each of these approaches to the explanation of health-care problems.

Class and Class Conflict

Sociologists often point out that social class, measured by the income and wealth a household has at its disposal, goes a long way toward explaining the types of illnesses experienced by members of that household and the kinds of health care they receive. We have already suggested that lack of access to good medical care causes higher rates of illness and death among the poor. Until the early twentieth century, the ill health of the poor was caused largely by infectious diseases. Today medical science is able to control and cure such diseases much more effectively, with the result that by themselves they no longer account for tremendous differences in health between the poor and the nonpoor. The chief obstacles to good health in developed nations are lack of access to good medical care, inadequate knowledge about health, failure to take preventive medical action, and delay in seeking treatment, all of which are especially prevalent among the poor (Cockerham, 2006).

In fact, as control of chronic diseases like cancer becomes more important, the differences between the health of the poor and that of the nonpoor are likely to increase; that is, the poor will still have higher rates of illness and death than the nonpoor because of their relative lack of access to high-quality medical care.

In a classic analysis of the relationship between social class and ill health, Lee Rainwater (1974) suggested that lack of access to medical care is not the only factor that affects the health of the poor: Just being poor promotes poor health. The poor, for example, cannot afford to eat properly, so they are likely to be weak. They often live in the most polluted areas and hence are susceptible to respiratory diseases. Because they cannot afford proper housing, they are exposed to disease-carrying refuse and rodents. Perhaps most important, their lives are filled with stress due to constant worry about getting enough money to pay for necessities. Such long-term stress can cause both physical and mental illness. It also makes it difficult to react to minor signs of ill health (Birenbaum, 1995). A cough is likely to be dismissed if one does not have enough to eat; only a much worse cough will prompt a visit to a clinic, and by then it may be too late. The poor also seem to feel middle-aged earlier than the nonpoor. As a result, they are likely to accept illness and disability as somehow natural, even in their thirties.

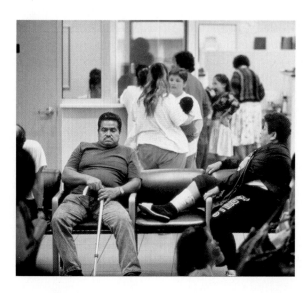

Crowding in hospital emergency rooms reflects the tendency of people who lack medical insurance to seek primary care at an emergency room in lieu of visiting a private physician.

Social scientists who see class conflict as a basic cause of social-class differences in health and unequal access to medical care are skeptical of the increasing privatization of the American health-care system. They point out that as public hospitals are replaced by hospitals run for profit, there is a tendency to avoid treatment of less profitable patients (Tuckett, 2003).

Studies have shown that as more hospitals are managed by for-profit or not-for-profit corporations, as opposed to the public sector, they are indeed less likely to provide services like drug counseling, suicide prevention, and AIDS treatment (Himmelstein et al., 1999). Both public and private hospitals share the duty to accept all patients who require emergency care, but private hospitals can decide to eliminate their emergency facilities altogether, and the requirement for emergency care does not extend to nonemergencies.

Social scientists who view health-care problems from a conflict perspective often explain the outcomes of conflicts over medical policy in terms of conflict between classes. For example, in a study of the social, political, and psychological impact of AIDS in America, Dennis Altman (1987) showed that as long as AIDS was perceived as a disease of homosexuals and intravenous drug users, members of the middle and upper classes did not put pressure on the government to invest heavily in its treatment and cure. Altman and others have pointed out that because AIDS strikes disproportionately at less advantaged citizens and members of minority groups, it is often thought of as "their" disease.

Institutions and Health Care

Functionalist explanations of health-care problems focus on features of health-care institutions themselves. Sociologists with this institutional orientation point out that every society is faced with the problem of distributing health-care services among its members. The United States uses a marketplace approach, which views health care as a commodity subject to the demands and spending power of consumers. Canada, by contrast, views health care as an entitlement of citizenship and extends full coverage to all its legal residents.

Since health-care costs are lower in Canada and many medical professionals feel the quality of care in that nation is at least equal to the quality of care in the United States, there are many advocates for a comparable "universal and single-payer" insurance system in the United States. A recent survey of family practice doctors found, for example, that 65 percent favored a single-payer health insurance plan like those that exist in other advanced nations, notably Canada and the United Kingdom (*Family Practice Management*, 2004). Opponents of the Canadian system point out, however, that it deprives the well-off of the higher-quality health care they can afford. The broad sociological issue here is how to improve health-care institutions in order to provide the best possible care for the greatest number of people. Most medical sociologists do not agree that health care should be treated as a commodity available in higher amounts and quality to those most able to afford it. But this does not mean that they believe the Canadian model could be imported to the United States without a great deal of compromise.

There are a number of functionalist arguments for why a service that has come to be viewed as a basic human right should not be treated as a commodity:

- **Information**—A consumer is not in a position to shop for medical treatment in the same way that one shops for other products or services, because the need for such treatment cannot be evaluated by the consumer.

- **Product uncertainty**—The consumer does not have sufficient knowledge to judge the effectiveness of sophisticated treatments.

- **Norms of treatment**—Medical care is performed under the control of a physician. A patient does not direct his or her own treatment.

- **Lack of price competition**—Prices for doctors' services are not advertised and are not subject to true competition.

- **Restricted entry**—There are numerous barriers to entry to medical school. Many qualified applicants are turned down because of a limited number of places.

- **Professional dominance**—Many health-care services restricted to physicians could be performed by trained technicians. This restriction has created a monopoly.

- **Misallocated supply**—An abundance of specialists encourages the use of expensive and sophisticated treatments when simpler ones would be just as effective (Dlugacz, 2006).

Health and Social Interaction

The relatively poor health of Americans is due in part to features of our lifestyle, including sedentary occupations, nonnutritious diets, lack of proper exercise, environmental pollution, and cigarette smoking (Cockerham, 2006; Gochman, 1997). But if activities like smoking are detrimental to health, why do people engage in them? Interactionist explanations of social problems related to health care often draw on studies of patterns of sociability (i.e., interaction among people in groups) and the ways in which people are socialized in different societies and communities. Features of a society's lifestyle, such as smoking, drinking, and diet, are deeply ingrained in the way people interact with one another. Very often we eat, drink, or smoke as much to be sociable as to sustain ourselves. Advertising reinforces these patterns by associating consumption with sociability, as you can see by completing the following phrases: "It's _____ Time"; "Welcome to _____ Country."

Excessive eating, leading to obesity, and high rates of alcohol consumption are among the health problems related to patterns of sociability in an affluent society. But as noted earlier, the most pervasive and serious problems are created by smoking. Each year smoking causes serious illnesses among an estimated 8.6 million Americans, approximately 440,000 deaths, and $157 billion in health-related economic costs. National surveys indicate that 23 percent of Americans are regular smokers, although as Figure 2–11 indicates, there are important regional differences. Rates of smoking

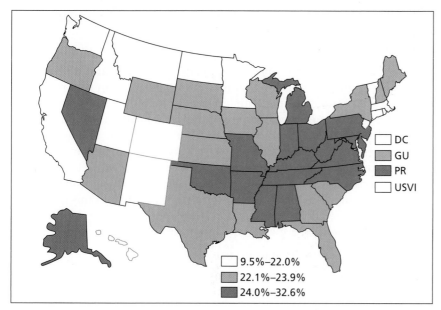

Figure 2-11 Prevalence* of Current Cigarette Smoking among Adults Age 18 or Over, by State or Area

Source: U.S. Centers for Disease Control, 2004.

□	DC
▨	GU
▤	PR
□	USVI

□ 9.5%–22.0%
▨ 22.1%–23.9%
▨ 24.0%–32.6%

*The percentage of all adults in each state/area who reported having smoked ≥ 100 cigarettes during their lifetimes and who currently smoke every day or some days.

Note: DC = District of Columbia
GU = Guam
PR = Puerto Rico
USVI = U.S. Virgin Islands

are highest in Alaska and West Virginia and lowest in Utah, Connecticut, New Jersey, and California.

In addition, women often expose unborn infants to the negative effects of smoking, especially low birthweight. More than 1,100 deaths a day and a greater number of serious illnesses are directly attributable to cigarette smoking, and recent research has shown that passive smoking (breathing air that contains cigarette smoke) is a serious environmental hazard. Since 2002 there have been significant cuts in funds available to the states to help pay for antismoking campaigns and education, and in consequence few states are meeting the minimum funding requirements set for by the U.S. Centers for Disease Control (2004).

Interactionist perspectives on issues like smoking and health typically focus on the way communications (e.g., advertising images and messages) seek to connect the use of tobacco with particular lifestyles. They may also take a more explicitly critical look at the way tobacco companies directly or indirectly influence those communications. For example, a study by Kenneth E. Warner at the University of Michigan found that "the higher the percentage of cigarette advertising revenues, the lower the likelihood that a magazine will publish an article on the dangers of smoking" (quoted in Carmody, 1992, p. D22).

It is helpful to think of the major sociological perspectives as conceptual tools to be used in analyzing a complex social problem like the prevention and treatment of physical illnesses. No single perspective explains all the important issues, but together they go a long way toward a full explanation. The functionalist view is most helpful in pointing out how social institutions like hospitals should function, why they do not function effectively, and how they could be improved. The conflict perspective allows for more insight into the influence of inequalities of wealth, education, and power on access to and quality of medical care. The interactionist perspective points to the way differences in people's perception of social conditions such as the AIDS epidemic influence their behavior toward others.

Social Policy

The American health-care system is once again in crisis. At this writing, a number of major proposals are under discussion that may eventually result in true reform of the system. We noted earlier that the United States is the only advanced industrial nation in the world that does not have a system of universal health coverage. But it is extremely unlikely that the next administration and Congress will be willing or politically able to pass legislation to create a Canadian-style single-payer system in which the federal government uses tax funds to pay for medical care. Instead, new legislation designed to provide something approximating universal health coverage will continue to build on and seek to improve the existing system. We will return to this issue after describing previous efforts to address problems of health and health care.

As we have seen, the salient facts include the following:

- Too many households lack medical insurance.

- The costs of medical goods and services are mounting (especially for prescription drugs and advanced medical procedures).

- Medical malpractice insurance costs are forcing hospitals and doctors to curtail services in some instances.

- The costs of insurance for those who are covered are rising (Fineman, 2002).

In comparison with other advanced industrial nations, the United States is doing a relatively poor job of providing health care for its population, especially its poor and its minority populations. More affluent individuals and families tend to get excellent medical care in the most up-to-date care facilities, and they largely account for the 20 percent who are satisfied with their care. Recent surveys show, however, that the majority of Americans are increasingly anxious about the future of their insurance benefits and their ability to pay for their medical costs as they grow older (Creighton, 2002; Kaiser Family Foundation, 2005).

All the major industrial nations are having difficulty coping with the demands on their health-care systems brought on by aging populations with more chronic illnesses. None of them has found easy solutions or avoided the need for compromises and less-than-perfect solutions. But in the United States—as compared to Canada, France, Germany, England, and the Scandinavian nations—there is an even greater lag in arriving at reforms of health-care institutions that address the major problems (Mechanic, 2005).

In Canada and some of the social democracies of Western Europe, the problems arising from aging populations, lack of coverage for the poor, the challenge of controlling health-care costs, and a host of other issues are addressed through what is known as a single-payer system. In 1946 Canada introduced national legislation to extend health care to all, regardless of age, occupation, preexisting conditions, or income. Today all citizens and legal residents of Canada are covered by the Canadian Medicare system; doctors who provide direct, fee-for-service medical care to private patients cannot participate in the national system. Each of Canada's provinces has its own system of health-care providers, but to receive federal funding the system must provide comprehensive services for anyone in the province. In this way everyone is entitled to the same quality of services. Relatively few Canadians complain about the system or about lack of access to doctors. In the United States, in contrast, 14 percent of survey respondents say that they have not visited a doctor because of inability to pay (Cockerham, 2006).

There are some drawbacks to the Canadian system. It is less well equipped with advanced medical technologies. Moreover, hospitals and doctors are allocated a fixed amount for their services, which keeps costs in check but also results in longer hospital stays and a higher rate of hospital admissions than in the United States. But because there are no insurance forms or billing procedures, there are far fewer clerks and other nonmedical service workers employed in the system (Cockerham, 2006). Administrative costs are thus far lower than they are in the United States (less than 1 percent of all medical expenses compared to over 6 percent in the United States). In recent years, however, the rising costs of medical care have placed strains on the Canadian system and have contributed to already high federal and provincial tax rates, something that frightens American lawmakers who might otherwise be attracted to the more equitable Canadian system.

Managed Care

In place of a comprehensive and universal health-care system, the United States has been moving toward a system termed **managed care.** The term *managed care* refers to a wide range of health plans and practices that depart from the traditional model of private health insurance provided by one's employer. In the traditional model, insured patients chose their physician; physicians treated patients with absolute clinical autonomy; insurers generally paid physicians whatever they billed on a fee-for-service basis; and employers paid premiums for their workers to private insurers, regardless of the cost. Managed care has altered all these arrangements by setting limits on individual medical visits or treatments—that is, by managing care.

The rise of managed care has tended to limit patients' ability to freely choose their doctors, because patients in most plans, and especially HMOs, receive full coverage for services only if they choose a physician within the plan's network. In some plans, patients are required to go to a primary-care physician to obtain a referral to a specialist. Physicians' clinical decisions are now subject to external review by insurance plans, with the ironic result that U.S. physicians experience more intrusion into their clinical work than do physicians anywhere else in the industrialized world—even though the American Medical Association has long opposed national health insurance as a threat to doctors' clinical autonomy.

Insurance Reform

Both physicians and patients have come to believe that managed care is leading to a reduction in the quality of health care. Empirical data on this subject are inconclusive, but in such situations feelings are often more important than facts. In the past few years efforts have been made to enact patients' bills of rights and other laws that regulate managed-care plans. Almost all of the states now have patients' rights legislation, and Congress is debating federal legislation that would permit patients to sue HMOs, guarantee access to specialists, and establish procedures for appealing health plan decisions that deny coverage or medical care.

Medicare, the predominant insurance program for people over 65, and Medicaid, which is intended for the nonworking poor and disabled, are federal- and state-funded insurance outside the employer-based system. Although Medicare costs continued to increase steadily during the late 1980s and early 1990s, by 1999 there was some evidence that government attempts to regulate the Medicare program, combined with low rates of inflation, had at last succeeded in reducing the annual rate of increase in Medicare spending from 10 percent to a mere 1 percent between 1998 and 1999. In the past three years, however, rapidly rising prescription drug costs, together with a slow recovery from recession, have again caused Medicare costs to rise and state and federal health-care budgets to become dangerously strained. This aspect of the overall health-care crisis has given rise to new legislative efforts to pass a federal prescription drug bill that would increase the proportion of drug costs paid for by public funds. In 2002 Congress failed to pass such a bill after weeks of efforts to compromise and intense lobbying by patients advocacy groups on one side and private insurance companies on the other (Carey & Naresh, 2002; Draper, Hurley, & Short, 2004).

In 2003, at the urging of the Bush administration, Congress passed legislation to extend coverage of some prescription drugs for people over age 65 who receive medical benefits through the Medicare system. Before this legislation passed, the average senior citizen was spending $2,322 on prescription drugs each year. The new law offers more than 40 million beneficiaries these options: (1) They may keep any private prescription drug coverage they currently have; (2) they may enroll in a new, freestanding prescription drug plan that has yet to be created; or (3) they may, if they have an extremely low income and no personal wealth, obtain drug coverage by enrolling in a Medicare managed-care plan. Medicare subsidizes the cost of coverage for about 14 million low-income beneficiaries. Other beneficiaries face significant gaps in coverage and, as a result, are still liable for up to $3,600 in annual expenses.

In the 2006 congressional elections, Democrats promised to revise the prescription drug law to allow Medicare to negotiate with drug producers to secure the lowest possible prices, something that the version currently in effect prohibited. Since large health management agencies like the Public Health Service and the Veterans Administration do conduct such negotiations and do secure lower prescription drug prices, this seemed to be a logical next step toward cost saving under the new drug plan. At this writing, however, intense lobbying by the insurance industry and the drug companies, which do not want to engage in direct negotiations with a powerful government agency, has thwarted efforts to pass this legislation in Congress.

Working, but without Health Care

The current crisis in the U.S. medical care system is significantly worsened by a large-scale retreat from employer-provided health insurance. The understanding that employees and their families would receive health insurance coverage from their employer in the private or public sector, long a cornerstone of the U.S. system, is coming unraveled. The proportion of Americans with insurance provided by their employers has declined to 61.3 percent, from 63.6 percent in 2000. In 2006 the number of people with employer-sponsored coverage fell by 1.3 million, to 175.3 million, even as the total population grew by 3.9 million. Increasingly, small companies, and companies that compete with companies in other nations that pay their workers much less in wages and benefits, are claiming that they have no choice but to cut employee benefits, especially costly medical insurance. Large corporations like Ford Motor Company note that producing automobiles in Canada saves about $5,000 per new vehicle because in Canada workers' health care costs are paid through the national health care system, and the same is true in the European nations whose autos compete with those produced in the United States.

The Disabled and Handicapped

The first significant measure that affected the disabled and handicapped was the Rehabilitation Act of 1973, which prohibited government agencies and contractors from discriminating against the handicapped and mandated affirmative-action plans for hiring and promotion. A related act, the Education for All Handicapped Children Act of 1975, required that handicapped children be provided with a "free appropriate public education" in the least restrictive environment appropriate to their needs—often an ordinary classroom in a public school. This policy is sometimes called *mainstreaming*. Critics of this act point out that it costs twice as much to educate a handicapped child in the public school system as it does to educate a nonhandicapped child; supporters emphasize the substantial reduction in Medicaid and disability costs that it can achieve.

The most far-reaching legislation affecting people with physical and mental disabilities is the Americans with Disabilities Act (ADA), which was passed in 1990. This act bars discrimination against the disabled in employment, transportation, public accommodations, and telecommunications. It requires employers that receive federal funds to provide equal opportunity for employment and for participation in programs and services to otherwise qualified people with disabilities. Employers must make reasonable accommodations to the disabilities of those individuals—that is, they must make facilities physically accessible; restructure job duties and modify work schedules; purchase or modify equipment; and provide readers, interpreters, or other support services. In addition, public accommodations and transportation facilities must be accessible to people in wheelchairs, and telephone companies must provide relay services that allow hearing- or voice-impaired people to place and receive calls.

At the turn of the present century there were signs that judges were in a mood to curtail somewhat the rights of disabled persons under the ADA. The Supreme Court ruled in 1998 that persons with medically treatable disabilities (as opposed to permanent ones) are not eligible to sue their employers under the act. And as we will see in the next chapter, many states are seeking to curtail the rights of people with mental disabilities (Falk, 1999).

Social Policy and AIDS

The discovery of new treatments for people with HIV, based on intensive drug therapies and costly medications, raises many difficult policy issues. As more low-wage workers, immigrants, and indigent persons are moved off Medicare or have their Medicare support reduced as a result of welfare reform, it becomes less likely that they will receive the new treatments. Even more affluent HIV and AIDS patients may not receive the new treatments if their insurance plans are inadequate or delayed.

Elsewhere in the world, changes in the pattern of HIV transmission mean that more babies will be born with AIDS in coming years, and more costly treatment will be required for AIDS patients in nations that can hardly afford to treat existing cases. Most world health authorities acknowledge that in the absence of a vaccination against AIDS, the only realistic policy to prevent the further spread of the disease is educational programs, especially those directed at young women and adolescents.

Because the incidence of AIDS is increasing most rapidly among very poor people, particularly members of minority groups, many AIDS activists fear the disease will become a neglected issue (Ayala, 1996). But the spread of AIDS among the poor in the more affluent nations means that the policies needed to prevent or slow its spread throughout the world are similar in both rich and poor nations. Again the key is more effective education about the risks of unprotected sex, needle sharing among drug users, and promiscuous sex. Increasingly, these messages will need to be directed at women everywhere. Thus, WHO recommends the following measures:

- *Prevent HIV infection in women* by protecting the human rights of women and girls, increasing education opportunities for girls and young women, increasing women's access to economic activities, and other measures.

- *Reduce the impact of HIV/AIDS on women* by including women living with HIV/AIDS in the development of HIV/AIDS policy and prevention and care programs; encouraging voluntary, confidential testing; and supporting programs that work with families of women living with the disease.

- *Care for women with HIV/AIDS* by providing appropriate health and welfare services, ensuring that women have access to contraceptive measures, increasing access to child care and other support services, and similar policies (WHO, 2001).

Effective educational programs are often hampered by ideological and religious differences within a population. In the United States, for example, to avoid arousing the anger of conservative groups, the government has been careful not to issue AIDS brochures and materials that seem to promote sexual activity. The AIDS Commission has pointed out that this restriction actually serves to prolong the epidemic. Many groups at risk of contracting AIDS need very straightforward verbal and pictorial descriptions of the kinds of behavior they must avoid. They need plain language and blunt warnings. But pictures of people shooting drugs and engaging in sexual contact are not likely to gain the approval of local panels. The commission strongly urges policies that would reduce the power of local panels and permit the creation of more effective communications to target populations.

Numerous other policy issues are related to the AIDS epidemic. One area of controversy is how to prevent AIDS among intravenous drug users and their sex partners. Proposals include increasing the availability of treatment for drug users, providing for safer injection, and initiating more prevention programs (Des Jarlais, 1987). Programs in which addicts exchange old needles for new, sterile needles have been extremely controversial. They have been initiated in some American cities on a demonstration basis but have not yet received adequate support to increase their scope, as they have in Holland and some other European nations.

Despite the grim statistics, there are signs that the AIDS epidemic can be controlled at a reasonable cost. In Thailand, where AIDS is concentrated among drug users and sex workers, a national AIDS prevention program has had a major impact. An extensive public information program and a program to promote consistent condom use by sex workers have produced dramatic changes in the behavior of the most affected population groups. Within a few years, the number of men visiting prostitutes decreased, condom use for commercial sex rose from 14 percent to over 90 percent, and the number of patients with sexually transmitted diseases decreased by 90 percent (Deame, 2005).

Among major funders of efforts to eradicate AIDS, the United States' leadership is considered essential. Bush administration policies favor funding for faith-based organizations in many developing nations, which has the benefit of avoiding dependence on the corruption-plagued governments of many extremely poor nations in Africa and elsewhere. But at the same time, the United States favors programs that teach abstinence from sex as the primary means of preventing the spread of this sexually transmitted disease. It does not favor the distribution of condoms, nor does it fund needle-sharing programs for drug users, even though they have been shown to be effective in reducing AIDS transmission among intravenous drug addicts, a major cause of the disease in the United States, Russia, and much of Eastern Europe. Conservative administrations in the United States, Africa, and Asia tend not to condone funding for sex education and reproductive health programs (including programs about safe sex) when they are directed at groups such as prostitutes, drug users, or others whose behavior is considered immoral. In the global battle against AIDS, however, these groups are those most in need of education and assistance in practicing safe sex, not only because they are deserving of care, but also because they are instrumental in the spread of the disease into the general population.

Future Prospects

As the 2008 presidential election approaches, health-care reform is once again a major campaign issue. No one can say with any certainty whether a new president and a new Congress (one that is likely to have a larger Democratic majority than the present Congress) will be able to pass new, more comprehensive health-care bills. But the electorate is clearly demanding progress in this area, as shown in most national polls, and a number of states—including California, often a trendsetter—are moving toward legislation that would provide coverage for a much larger proportion of Americans without medical insurance. Such legislation would require companies that do not provide health care plans to contribute to a national health-care fund, which would then provide insurance along the lines of Medicare. Congress would also be asked to increase federal spending for health-care coverage for children who currently lack it. Much of the cost of the new coverage would be covered by increases in taxes for Americans earning over $200,000 a year, the same group that has enjoyed large cuts in taxes during the Bush administration. There would also be cost savings as a result of efforts to streamline the federal system and the creation of a national health insurance agency to administer new plans paid for by contributions from employers. The last provision is highly controversial because it would move the United States closer to a single-payer system like those of Canada and the European nations.

Depending on who wins the 2008 presidential election and how the congressional elections unfold, there will be either continued piecemeal efforts to reform the system, as we see in various state-level proposals, or a larger and more ambitious federal effort to move toward universal health care coverage. It is certain, however, that any efforts to widen the role of government in health care will generate fierce political debates, as they did in 1992 after the election of President Clinton. It remains to be seen whether the American electorate will send a determined enough message to its political leadership to overcome the opposition of insurance companies, drug companies, and private health maintenance organizations.

GOING BEYOND LEFT AND RIGHT

At this writing, almost every major health initiative, either in the United States or globally, is fraught with issues that originate in deep ideological divisions and moral dilemmas. Among these issues are end-of-life measures, research on stem cells taken from unused human embryos (that is, ones not used in fertility clinics), funding for women's reproductive health, funding for safe sex practices to reduce the spread of sexually transmitted diseases like AIDS, and reform of the health-care system itself. These issues are all subjects of intense debates between Christian conservatives, who are opposed to any form of intervention in ending life and to any system that seems to resemble "socialized medicine," and liberal advocates of health policies that feature individual choice and a role for government in providing more equal access to high-quality health care. The U.S. population is deeply divided on these issues, although as we have seen in the case of Terri Schiavo, there is a large majority that believes individuals must be free to make their own final choices without governmental intervention. Over the next few years, it is likely that this belief, along with the shared perception that the nation must move beyond the current stalemate over policies such as whether to permit stem cell research, will break through the present ideological impasse.

Any attempt to reform the health-care system generates intense political debate and lobbying efforts in Congress and in state legislatures. Current proposals, however, have been crafted so as to minimize such opposition and the accompanying ideological debate. The popular reform measure that would require employers who do not provide health coverage to pay into a fund for working, but uninsured, families is an example. Although opponents of the proposal claim that it will force small companies to let some workers go, other companies that currently pay health benefits can counter with the argument that it is only fair for all employers to pay some share of the cost of providing health care for the nation's citizens. In other words, proposals that promise to increase health-care coverage but do not stimulate unified opposition (e.g., by all employers) have a much better chance of success than do those that tend to deepen existing political and ideological divides.

Summary

- Health care is considered a social problem when members of a society have unequal access to health-care institutions and the quality of the care provided is low relative to its cost.

- Health care is distributed very unequally in the United States. The use and availability of medical care are directly related to socioeconomic class and race. People in the lower classes tend to have higher rates of untreated illnesses and disabilities and higher mortality rates for most diseases than do people in the middle and upper classes.

- Unequal access to health care is related to the cost of obtaining it. Health-care costs increased fourfold between 1980 and 1999. The cost of prescription drugs is a major factor in the high cost of health care in the United States.

- Cultural factors that raise the cost of health care in the United States include aspects of lifestyle such as heavy use of tobacco and alcohol, unhealthful diet, and lack of exercise. Obesity is a major health problem in the United States and other affluent nations.

- Many Americans lack adequate health insurance. Public insurance programs (Medicaid and Medicare) have helped the poor and the elderly obtain greater access to health care, but there remain large numbers of people who are not covered by health insurance, either public or private. Minority status increases one's probability of being without medical insurance.

- The controversy over legalized abortion has revealed many problems in the treatment of women by the medical establishment and has led to efforts to make medical personnel more sensitive to women's physical and psychological needs. These include efforts to win acceptance of midwives, to decrease medical intervention in the birth process, and to increase research on women's health issues.

- The disabled and handicapped encounter special problems related to their condition. They suffer high unemployment rates, and the majority are poor.

- Improved medical technologies and life-prolonging procedures have given rise to ethical issues such as how to determine when death occurs and whether individuals have a right to die.

- The social problems related to health care have become especially acute as a result of the AIDS epidemic. The disease is especially prevalent among homosexuals and intravenous drug users, but the rate of infection is accelerating among the heterosexual population. There is no cure for it, and at present behavioral changes are the only defense against the spread of the virus.

- Conflict theorists believe social class goes a long way toward explaining the types of illnesses experienced by members of a household and the kinds of health care they receive.

- Functionalist explanations of health-care problems focus on features of health-care institutions themselves.

- The interactionist perspective on health-care problems points to the role of lifestyle features such as poor diet; lack of exercise; and smoking, including passive smoking, or breathing air that contains cigarette smoke.

- In the past two decades the nation has turned increasingly toward a managed-care system. However, many patients and physicians believe managed care is resulting in lower-quality care.

- Policy measures that affect the disabled and handicapped include the Education for All Handicapped Children Act of 1975, which requires that handicapped children be provided with free public education in the least restrictive environment appropriate to their needs, and the Americans with Disabilities Act of 1990, which bars discrimination against the disabled in employment, public accommodations, and other areas.

- Policy issues related to the AIDS epidemic include how to give costly treatment to those who cannot afford it and how to educate the general public, especially women, about ways to avoid infection.

Key Terms

obesity, p. 40
health maintenance organization (HMO), p. 42

cost shifting, p. 45
managed care, p. 61

Social Problems Online

An enormous range of material about AIDS is available to students and professors on the Internet. For example, there are homepages for organizations of AIDS activists in the United States and throughout the world. But for basic information about the disease, its spread, its control, and the latest research developments, a good place to start is the homepage of a major public agency like the CDC in Atlanta.

The CDC has a homepage at **www.cdc.gov** with numerous links to specific AIDS/HIV Web sites. Each Web page has links to the other CDC sites (e.g., the CDC's mission, addresses of regional centers, information for travelers, and news bulletins about infectious diseases), as well as links to non-CDC Web pages and e-mail addresses. Each CDC Web page has a search tool that allows the user to find related resources such as additional Web pages, online articles and reports, press releases, and graphics.

After connecting to the CDC homepage, one of the first places the user might want to browse is the National Center for HIV, STD, and TB Prevention (NCHSTP) page. Click on the center's highlighted name or enter its address—**www.cdc.gov/nchstp/od/nchstp.html**. The NCHSTP page contains links to fact sheets and brochures about AIDS/HIV and other sexually transmitted diseases. There are links to U.S. and worldwide statistics on AIDS/HIV. Another interesting site with a more international focus is WHO's site, which can be reached at **www.who.int/en/**.

The Gay Men's Health Crisis has a Web page at **www.gmhc.org** that stresses education and activism. In addition to providing basic information about AIDS/HIV, it contains useful discussions about HIV testing and living with AIDS/HIV.

Research Navigator

Follow the instructions on pages 26–27 of this text to access the features of Research Navigator. Once at the Web site, enter your Login Name and Password. Then, to use the Content Select database, use keywords such as "managed care," "AIDS," and "obesity," and the search engine will supply relevant and recent scholarly and popular press publications. Use the *New York Times* search-by-subject archive to find recent news articles related to problems of health and health care and the Link Library to find relevant Web sites organized by the key terms associated with this chapter.

On the Navigator, go to the EBSCO host and type in "The Future of Fitness." Whose research is reported on in this article, and what is the condition being studied? What are three factors discussed in the article that help explain why the condition has become so much more prevalent recently? How does social stigma contribute to the severity of the condition among young people? Do you think governments ought to be doing something about this condition, and if so, what policies would you recommend?

3

PROBLEMS OF MENTAL ILLNESS
and Treatment

Dominant Trends

- An increasing proportion of Americans are receiving treatment for mental disorders, a proportion that has grown from about one-fifth in the 1990s to about one-third at present.

- The World Health Organization reports that, worldwide, one in four patients visiting a health service has at least one mental, neurological, or behavioral disorder, but most of these disorders are neither diagnosed nor treated.

- Most middle- and low-income countries devote less than 1 percent of their health expenditures to mental health. Consequently, mental health policies, legislation, community care facilities, and treatments for people with mental illness are not given the priority they deserve.

- The parity movement in mental-health care advocates legislation that would end practices whereby insurance companies discriminate against people with mental illnesses and chemical dependencies.

- Research studies estimate that about one in six returning servicepeople will be in need of mental-health services as a result of their experiences serving in Iraq.

Approximately one out of every four Americans suffers some form of mental disorder in a given year. These disorders range from mild depression and anxiety to severely debilitating psychoses like schizophrenia and manic depression (Barry, 2002). An estimated 3.5 million Americans suffer from severe mental illnesses, especially schizophrenia and manic-depressive illness. At least 40 percent of these individuals are not being treated for their illness, and many of them are found among the homeless on the streets of the nation's cities (Kessler et al., 2005).

The wars in Iraq and Afghanistan are again bringing issues of mental health to national attention. According to Karen H. Seal and associates at the Veterans Administration Medical Center, approximately 25 percent of men and woman returning from military duty in those conflicts have a diagnosed mental health problem, and half of those individuals have more than one such problem. The most frequent diagnosis is post-traumatic stress disorder; other diagnoses include anxiety disorder, depression, substance use disorder, and other behavioral or psychological problems. Those who are most at risk for serious mental health problems are the youngest soldiers and those with the greatest exposure to combat (Seal, 2007).

Around the world, mental illness is a "profoundly underestimated" social problem. Approximately 80 percent of the world's 450 million mentally disabled people live in developing nations (U.S. Surgeon General, 2005). While basic physical health has improved worldwide, mental health has remained stagnant or deteriorated. Ironically, increases in the incidence of clinical depression, schizophrenia, dementia, and other forms of chronic illness have been a side effect of improved physical health in many parts of the world. More people are living to the ages at which the risk of severe mental illness increases (Brundtland, 2001; WHO, 2005).

The mental problems of the aging U.S. population are also a growing concern for researchers and policymakers as well as for millions of elderly people and their families. Depression is extremely common in the elderly, usually worsened by isolation and chronic pain. Alzheimer's disease, a degenerative brain disorder that destroys memory, has been increasing in prevalence. Recent progress in research and development of treatments for depression and possible treatments for Alzheimer's is encouraging, but the problems brought on by mental illnesses among the elderly are likely to increase as the elderly population grows, a subject to which we return in Chapter 9.

MENTAL ILLNESS AS A SOCIAL PROBLEM

The terms **mental disorder** and **mental illness** are often used interchangeably, and that is how they are used here. However, in formal social-scientific writing, mental illness is usually reserved for mental disorders that require hospitalization or for which close medical supervision would normally be recommended. Most people who seek help from mental-health institutions are unlikely ever to be hospitalized (Cockerham, 2006).

Until the mid-twentieth century, a large proportion of people who were classified as mentally ill and admitted to mental hospitals were actually suffering from physical ailments like epilepsy and brain tumors (Barry, 2002). Today researchers are learning about the biological origins of many mental illnesses, including schizophrenia, autism, and alcoholism (Sapolsky, 2004). As we discover the biological bases of some mental illnesses, we also gain information about the social conditions—such as physical abuse, neglect, and severe stress—that may bring on the mental breakdowns that cause people to cease functioning "normally."

The specific relationships between biological factors and certain types of mental illness are considered in detail in psychology and genetics courses. For our purposes here, it is enough to be aware that mental illness, whatever its causes, is a source of serious social problems not only because of the number of people affected but also in terms of the extent to which social institutions are strained by efforts to care for them.

The mental disorders that cause severe social problems are the most extreme forms of mental illness. Of these, the most sensational are those that threaten the social order—sociopaths who become serial killers (e.g., Jeffrey Dahmer) or severely mentally ill individuals with hostile and suicidal tendencies who are not receiving mental health treatment. The gunman who killed 32 people at Virginia Tech University in 2007, Seung-Hui Cho, did not receive the mental health treatment ordered by a judge who declared him an imminent threat to himself and others. Neither the court nor community mental health officials followed up on the judge's order. In consequence, students at the university were not protected when Cho went on a suicidal rampage (Schulte & Jenkins, 2007). The number of individuals with such disorders may be small, but they constitute an especially serious social problem because they are so violent and irrational.

Table 3–1 indicates that among the ten leading causes of role impairment—that is, people reporting that they cannot work or perform their normal daily activities because of illness—are three mental illnesses: generalized anxiety disorder, panic, and major depression. Each of these ranks ahead of major physical illnesses such as high

TABLE 3–1	Ten Leading Causes of Role Impairment Days	
Rank	**Condition**	**Mean Monthly Impairment Days**
1	Cancer	10.9
2	Heart disease	6.6
3	Ulcer	5.8
4	Generalized anxiety disorder	5.5
5	Panic	5.1
6	Major depression	4.3
7	Arthritis	4.0
8	High blood pressure	3.9
9	Diabetes	3.6
10	Asthma	3.0

Source: Reprinted with permission from the *Diagnostic and Statistical Manual of Mental Disorders,* Fourth Edition, Text Revision, (Copyright 2000). American Psychiatric Association.

blood pressure, arthritis, and diabetes (Kessler et al., 2005). Role impairment, especially inability to meet one's work obligations, costs the United States billions of dollars in lost productivity each year.

Less threatening to public safety and perceptions of security, but far more widespread as a social problem, are severely ill individuals (often diagnosed as psychotic) who cannot care for themselves without specialized attention. This includes people who are classified as mentally ill and chemically addicted, who are also especially likely to be indigent and homeless (Cockerham, 2006).

For the mentally ill themselves, their problem is a terrible affliction. They experience such symptoms as unimaginable fear, uncontrollable hallucinations, panic, crushing sadness, wild elation, and roller-coaster mood swings. For society as a whole, their illness presents a range of social problems: stress in family life, heavy demands on health-care institutions, moral and ethical problems (e.g., whether to permit the plea of insanity in criminal cases), the cost of treatment to society, and so on. All of these can be aggravated by the social stigma attached to mental illness. It can be said that the mentally ill suffer twice: They suffer from the illness itself, and they also suffer rejection, as if their illness were their own fault. This is not nearly as true for physical illness, and this factor alone marks off mental illness for special consideration in the study of social problems.

In the United States panic attacks and phobias are the most common form of mental problem. Phobias include severe fears such as fear of going outside, fear of heights, or fear of being in an enclosed space. Phobias and panic attacks affect an estimated 20 million Americans in any given year. Another 18 million suffer from depression, including manic depression, major depression, and minor depression. Alcoholism, classified as a mental illness, has been diagnosed in approximately 14 million people. To complicate matters, about 6 million Americans have a substance abuse disorder along with one or more severe or relatively severe mental disorders like schizophrenia. These individuals are often referred to as mentally ill chemical abusers (MICA) and are a particularly problematic population in major urban centers (Kessler et al., 2005; National Institute of Mental Health, 2007).

A distressing aspect of the general problem of mental illness is the social impact of **deinstitutionalization,** or discharging patients from mental hospitals directly into the community. Some of these patients are not able to function as normal members of society, and the consequences can be painful both for them and for those who come into contact with them. Others may suffer from less severe problems caused by rejection

Before the development of modern medicine, and extending into the present in some regions of the world, mental illness was believed to be the result of demonic possession of a person's mind; the remedy, known as exorcism, was (and still is) performed by religious authorities, as shown in this woodcut from medieval Europe.

and stigma. As we will see later in the chapter, it has been difficult to develop (or consistently fund) effective means of treating such individuals outside mental hospitals.

Policymakers at every level of society look to sociologists and other social scientists for basic research on the causes of mental illness and on the effects of major policy initiatives like deinstitutionalization or community treatment, as well as for recommendations on how to deal with trends in mental illness. Thus, in addition to sponsoring research on medical approaches to treatment and rehabilitation, the National Institute of Mental Health (NIMH) funds studies of the social epidemiology of mental illness—by which we mean not simply its distribution in the population but also its impact on families, communities, and welfare institutions, as well as the associated problems of homelessness and social dependency.

Perspectives on Mental Illness

In studying social problems related to mental illness, the basic sociological perspectives can help clarify the relevant issues and explain some aspects of the origins of mental disorders. The interactionist perspective focuses on the social construction of mental illness, that is, on how our definitions of "normal" and "deviant" behavior in social situations lead to definitions of mental disorders. To a large extent, the definition of mental illness is the province of psychologists and psychiatrists. Their diagnoses result in labels like "schizophrenic" or "depressed." Research by sociologists who have studied the interactions among people who are thought of as mentally ill suggests that such a label may cause one to define oneself as ill and to behave in ways that confirm the self-definition (White, 1998).

Conflict theorists tend to focus on how mental illness may be associated with deprivation and inequality, including unequal access to appropriate care. The emergence of a two-class system of mental-health care in the United States is a central concern of this sociological perspective. Typically, more affluent patients with less severe mental illnesses receive higher-quality private care, whereas severely ill patients, often reduced to poverty by their illnesses, are shunted into budget-starved public institutions (U.S. Congress, 2001).

From a functionalist perspective, mental illnesses constitute a social problem because they challenge our ability to provide effective treatment. This is especially true in societies marked by rapid social change, in which people do not have long-standing attachments to others in their immediate social surroundings or are often separated from their families, or in which systems of treatment have been changing rapidly and it is not clear how people with mental disorders should be helped (Cockerham, 2006).

Suicide and Mental Illness

In October 1999, on the stressful anniversary of the shootings and suicides at Columbine High School, the mother of a student who had been paralyzed in the shootings walked into a pawn shop that sold handguns. As she was examining a pistol, she took bullets from her purse, inserted them into the gun, and shot herself. This grisly and public suicide is an example of a much larger social problem. Many social scientists believe suicide has reached epidemic proportions in the United States and other nations. The sensational suicide of Carla June Hochhalter is a reminder of the complexity of suicide and its links to mental illness. Just that week, her daughter had shown some important progress in her recovery. But for severely depressed individuals like this mother of a shooting victim, small signs of hope can produce unexpected and irrational reactions. Suicide is the most extreme of such behaviors.

Every 17 minutes someone commits suicide in the United States. Suicide ranks third among causes of death for young people, and it is the second highest cause of death among college students. The rate of suicide, especially among teenagers and young adults, has been increasing steadily since 1950. Men and women report suicidal thoughts with equal frequency, but young men are over three times more likely to kill themselves than are women. The likelihood of a male teenager or young adult committing suicide has increased by over 200 percent since midcentury (King, 1999). In the United States this year, suicide will claim more young men than will AIDS, heart disease, and all other major illnesses. Around the world, WHO estimates that suicide is responsible for almost 2 percent of all deaths. This puts suicide well ahead of war and homicide (WHO, 2005).

The continuing suicide bombings associated with Al Qaeda terrorism and insurgency in Iraq call attention to the large number of people susceptible to the notion that their lives can gain meaning from suicidal acts of murder. Political suicide may draw upon individuals with mental illnesses, but it is a form of suicide best considered separately, as we do in Chapter 16. Many people might believe that anyone who commits suicide or murder is insane, but the causes of suicide are far more complex. Kay Redfield Jamison, an expert on the subject, notes that half of all people with bipolar disease (manic depression) will make a suicide attempt, as will about one in five people with major depression. People who have suffered neurological damage before birth, often because of alcohol or cocaine use by the mother, may experience severe mood disorders that can lead to suicide. And there is mounting evidence that genetic factors are responsible for some mental illnesses as well as for impulsiveness, aggression, and violence, which increase the risk of suicide. Unfortunately, our knowledge of the possible biological antecedents of suicide is still developing while the toll of suicide mounts. Although drugs like lithium and antidepressants are somewhat effective in decreasing rates of suicide among risk-prone individuals with histories of mental disorders, there are as yet no therapies to correct genetic damage at the neurological level (Jamison, 2000).

Research by Kay Redfield Jamison (2000) and others calls attention to the social aspects of suicide's causes and treatment. Depression, for example, can be brought on by chronic anxieties over money and loss of work, as can marital discord. It often engenders further depression or abusive behavior and substance abuse, which can accelerate a downward spiral toward suicide. Among the elderly, loss of mental capabilities (dementia) is associated with depression and suicidal tendencies. But not all suicide is irrational and related to mental illness. People commit suicide to avoid severe embarrassment, to escape debt, to express strong political protest, and to avoid

These volunteers are working at a suicide prevention hotline. Once they have received training in how to talk to callers, they can be quite effective in helping them find appropriate professional assistance.

severe suffering due to physical illness. These reasons suggest that suicide can be the result of rational choices, even though the act itself requires an extremely strong emotional state if it is to succeed. In the young, however, suicide is almost always the result of depression or other forms of mental illness.

The shootings and suicides at Virginia Tech and Columbine and the hidden epidemic of suicides by teenagers and young adults inevitably raise questions about intervention and prevention. It is extremely difficult, however, to predict who will commit suicide among the far larger population of individuals who cope with suicidal thoughts. It is also true that suicide can produce localized suicide epidemics among peers. Strategies for peer counseling and suicide awareness, therefore, are extremely important. Jamison (2000) and other researchers tend to be highly critical of federal health-care policies that have decreased insurance coverage for the treatment of mental illness and deny adequate coverage and therapies to the mentally ill, a subject to which we return in the Social Policy section of the chapter.

THE SOCIAL CONSTRUCTION OF MENTAL ILLNESS

Defining Mental Illness

When social scientists say that mental illness is socially constructed, they are highlighting aspects of those illnesses that help define how both the mentally ill and "normal" people behave. The usefulness of this approach becomes clear if we consider some alternative views of mental illness. In this section we look briefly at three different explanations of mental illness: (1) the medical model, which asserts that mental illness is a disease with physiological causes; (2) the deviance approach, which asserts that mental illness results from the way people considered mentally ill are treated; and (3) the controversial argument that mental illness is not a disease but a method governments use to define certain people as being in need of isolation and "treatment."

The Medical Model. The most familiar school of thought holds that a mental disorder should be viewed as a disease with biological causes. That is, a mental disorder is primarily a disturbance of the normal personality that is analogous to the physiological disturbance caused by physical disease. It can be remedied primarily by treating the patient. Once this has been done, the patient will be able to function adequately.

Research in the biological sciences, especially genetics, has uncovered strong evidence to support biological explanations of mental illnesses like schizophrenia, manic depression, childhood autism, senility, and even alcoholism (to which we will return in Chapter 4). In addition to disorders that are classified as mental illnesses, many of which have been found to have somatic causes, there are a host of mental disabilities that usually appear at birth, such as Down syndrome, cerebral palsy, and brain damage caused by birth trauma; such disorders present unusual and difficult challenges to those afflicted by them.

Research on the medical model of mental disorders arose in reaction to the older notion that mentally disturbed people are mad or "possessed" and should be locked up, beaten, or killed. It made possible serious investigation of the causes and cures of mental disorders and was responsible for the development of virtually all the systems of mental-health care and therapeutic treatment in existence today—systems that are still largely in the hands of medically oriented personnel. It has helped reduce the stigma and shame of mental disorder because, after all, "illness can happen to anyone."

Nevertheless, the concept of mental disorder as a disease has certain disadvantages. Because it concentrates on individuals and their immediate environment (often their childhood environment), it tends to disregard the wider social environment as a possible source of the problem. In addition, especially for hospitalized patients, the medical model can lead to impractical criteria of recovery—people may have gained considerable insight into their inner tensions but are still unable to function adequately when they return to the outer tensions of home, job, or society. It is also true that many mental illnesses, which may or may not be caused by an individual's physiology, may be brought on, alleviated, or worsened by conditions in that person's social environment.

Mental Illness as Deviance. Neither social nor biological scientists know precisely what kinds of interactions among the multitude of physical and social conditions that affect human beings may cause mental illness in some cases or lead to remission or recovery in others. We do know, however, that the way a mentally ill person is treated once the illness has been diagnosed can have a lasting impact on that person's behavior and on his or her chances of leading a happy and productive life.

The concept of mental disorder as a disease holds that something about a person is abnormal and that the fundamental problem lies in his or her emotional makeup, which was twisted, repressed, or otherwise wrongly developed as a result of genetic or chemical factors or events early in life. Although this theory seems to explain some mental disorders, many observers believe other factors need to be taken into account, especially the constant pressure exerted by modern society. Out of this has developed the view that mental disorder represents a departure from certain expectations of society—that it is a form of social deviance.

In this connection the idea of **residual deviance** is useful. According to Thomas Scheff (1963), who formulated the concept, most social conventions are recognized as such, and violation of those conventions carries fairly clear labels: People who steal wallets are thieves, people who act haughtily toward the poor are snobs, and so on. But there is a large residual area of social convention that is so completely taken for granted that it is assumed to be part of human nature. To use Scheff's example, it seems natural for people holding a conversation to face each other rather than to look away. Violation of this norm seems contrary to human nature.

Scheff (1963) suggests that residual deviance occurs in most people at one time or another and usually passes without treatment. What causes it to become a mental disorder in some cases is that *society decides to label it as such*. When this happens, the role of "mentally ill person" is offered to the deviant individual. Because such people are often confused and frightened by their own behavior—as well as by other people's reactions to their behavior—during a time of stress, they are likely to be particularly impressionable and may accept the role offered to them. Once this happens, it becomes difficult for them to change their behavior and return to their "normal" role.

If this is so, mental disorder may actually be caused by some of the attempts to cure it. By treating a patient in a separate institution, the mental-health profession certifies that the individual is indeed a patient and that he or she is mentally ill (Berrios, 1995). The point of this concept of mental disorder as deviance is thus that the disorder may be a function not only of certain individuals' inability to comply with societal expectations but also of the label attached to those who deviate (Barry, 2002; Cockerham, 2006).

Problems in Living. A third approach to understanding mental disorder has been offered by Thomas Szasz, a psychiatrist who has generated considerable controversy by contending that mental illness is a myth. Although this is not a widely accepted view, it does call attention to the relationship between diagnosis and repression. Szasz does not claim that the social and psychological disturbances referred to as mental illness do not exist; rather, he argues that it is dangerously misleading to call them illnesses. Instead, he believes, they should be regarded as manifestations of unresolved problems in living.

The significance of Szasz's basic argument is that it concerns justice and individual freedom. As he sees it, a diagnosis of mental disorder involves a value judgment based on the behavioral norms held by psychiatrists. Referring to certain behaviors as illnesses allows doctors to use medicine to correct what are essentially social, ethical, or legal deviations. Not only is this logically absurd, Szasz contends, but it is also dangerous.

Szasz (2003) believes that individual liberty can be unwittingly sacrificed through too great a concern for the "cure" of "mental illness." This issue has come to the fore in connection with the forcible removal of homeless individuals from city streets. The presence of these people, who are often shabby and dirty and may behave in bizarre ways, offends "normal" citizens. As we will see later in the chapter, the interpretation of this lifestyle as a sign of mental illness has been used to justify the involuntary placement of the homeless in shelters or hospitals, where they are out of sight. We will also see that sensational crimes by mentally ill people, such as incidents of sudden violence in which schizophrenic individuals push unsuspecting pedestrians off train platforms, along with public concern about links between mental illness and violent crimes in schools, have produced renewed efforts to enforce mandatory institutionalization (Phillips, 1998).

When sociologists speak of the social construction of mental illness, they incorporate all these approaches into their explanations. They recognize that there is often a biological basis for mental illness. In fact, medical and genetic discoveries are making possible more effective treatments. But social-scientific research also finds that mental illness is often aggravated by the fact that mentally ill people are treated as social deviants. Sociologists therefore also study instances in which the label of mental illness is a convenient way of ridding society of people who are troublesome. (The nations of the former Soviet Union were notorious for this technique, but it has been used in societies all over the world at one time or another.) Most important, sociologists recognize that the classification of mental illnesses and decisions about how they should be treated are determined by how we think about the causes, consequences, and possibilities of treating mental disorders. Even the diagnosis of mental illness requires the emergence of a common set of perceptions among mental-health professionals, a point that becomes clear if we look in more detail at the problems of diagnosis.

Classification of Mental Disorders

Clinicians and researchers need a common language to discuss mental disorders. It is impossible to plan a consistent program of treatment for a patient without an accurate diagnosis, and it is impossible to evaluate the effectiveness of various forms of treatment without clearly defined diagnostic terms.

In 1973, in an effort to deal with these problems, the American Psychiatric Association (APA) embarked on a controversial and ambitious revision of its manual of mental disorders. The new manual, released in 1980 and referred to as the *Diagnostic and Statistical Manual of Mental Disorders,* third edition, or simply as *DSM-III,* represented the work of hundreds of scientists and professionals in the field of mental-health care. A revised edition, *DSM-IV,* was published in 1994, and the most recent revision, *DSM-IV-TR,* appeared in 2000. Widely regarded as a major advance in the scientific description and classification of mental disorders, *DSM-III* had a significant impact on treatment. Among other things, it made an important contribution to the separation of mental disorders from behaviors (such as homosexuality) that deviate from societal norms but are not necessarily a result of mental illness.

Although, as we will see shortly, labeling theorists continue to believe that the diagnostic categories of psychiatrists reflect the biases of the people who create them, *DSM-III* and *DSM-IV* resolved some of the more controversial issues in the classification of mental disorders. In general, however, the manual continues to represent the illness model. To a large extent it seeks to attribute mental dysfunctions to physiological, biochemical, genetic, or profound internal psychological causes. The major categories of the illness model, as presented in *DSM-IV,* are shown in Table 3–2.

A number of familiar terms are not used in *DSM-IV.* Chief among them is *neurosis,* the older term for a wide range of disorders in which the individual suffers from severe anxiety but continues to attempt to function in the everyday world, usually through a variety of subterfuges or defense mechanisms, such as denial of problems or

TABLE 3–2	Categories of Psychological Disorders Listed in the *Diagnostic and Statistical Manual of Mental Disorders*, 4th ed.

DISORDERS EVIDENT IN INFANCY, CHILDHOOD, OR ADOLESCENCE
These disorders that begin prior to adulthood include mental retardation, attention-deficit hyperactivity, anorexia nervosa, bulimia nervosa, stuttering, sleepwalking, and bedwetting.

ORGANIC MENTAL DISORDERS
Psychological or behavioral abnormalities associated with temporary or permanent dysfunction of the brain resulting from aging, disease, or dugs; include delirium and dementia.

PSYCHOACTIVE SUBSTANCE USE DISORDER
Disorders resulting from excessive and persistent use of mind-altering substances like alcohol, barbiturates, cocaine, or amphetamines.

SCHIZOPHRENIA
Characterized by symptoms such as delusions or hallucinations and deterioration from a previous level of functioning, with symptoms existing for more than six months. Examples include catatonic schizophrenia and paranoid schizophrenia.

DELUSIONAL DISORDERS
The key feature is the presence of a delusion (e.g., belief that one is being persecuted). It is often difficult to clearly differentiate delusional disorders from paranoid schizophrenia.

MOOD DISORDERS
These disorders, also known as affective disorders, involve extremes in emotion; they include major depression and bipolar (manic-depressive) disorder.

ANXIETY DISORDERS
The key symptom, anxiety, is manifest in phobias, generalized anxiety disorder, panic attacks, or obsessive-compulsive disorder.

SOMATOFORM DISORDERS
The presentation of physical symptoms such as paralysis without medical explanation. Examples include somatization disorder, hypochondriasis, and conversion disorder.

DISSOCIATIVE DISORDERS
Involves a splitting or disassociation of normal consciousness; includes psychogenic amnesia, psychogenic fugue, and multiple personality.

PSYCHOSEXUAL DISORDERS
Disorders characterized by sexual arousal by unusual objects or situations (fetishism) or by sexual dysfunctions such as inhibition of sexual desire.

PERSONALITY DISORDERS
Chronic, inflexible, and maladaptive personality patterns that are generally resistant to treatment, such as the antisocial personality disorder.

DISORDERS OF IMPULSE CONTROL
These include kleptomania, pyromania, and pathological gambling.

Source: Reprinted with permission from the *Diagnostic and Statistical Manual of Mental Disorders,* Fourth Edition, Text Revision, (Copyright 2000). American Psychiatric Association.

projection of one's own problems onto another person (e.g., perceiving others as hostile or angry rather than acknowledging these traits in oneself). The new classification system replaces this term with more specific ones like *affective disorder, anxiety disorder, somatoform disorder,* and *psychosexual disorder.* In everyday usage, however, the term *neurosis* continues to appear with some frequency.

Diagnosis or Label?

Just as some physical illnesses may be culturally defined, so may certain mental disorders. The medical model assumes that patients present symptoms that can be classified into diagnosable categories of mental illness. But there is a growing belief that at least some psychiatric diagnoses are pigeonholes into which certain behaviors are placed arbitrarily. According to labeling theorists, the diagnosis of schizophrenia has been especially subject to misuse. Although there is little agreement about its origins, causes, and symptoms, it is the most commonly used diagnosis for severe mental illness. To labeling theorists, this suggests that diagnoses of mental illnesses tend to reflect cultural values, not scientific analysis. People are not "schizophrenic" in the sense that they manifest definite symptoms; instead, their behavior violates society's norms and expectations. For example, a person who sees visions might be considered perfectly normal, even admirable, in many cultures, although in the United States he or she would probably be regarded as disturbed.

The problem with labeling people as mentally ill is threefold: It makes us perceive certain behaviors as "sick," something to be eliminated rather than understood; it gives public agencies the right to incarcerate people against their will simply for not conforming; and it causes those people to define themselves as rule breakers and undesirables and allows them to fulfill that image. Many studies have demonstrated the influence of societal factors on the diagnosis of mental illness as well as the vagueness of such diagnoses. Rosenhan (1973), in a classic study that will be described more fully later in the chapter, found that psychologists and psychiatrists on the staffs of several mental hospitals were unable to determine accurately which of the people they interviewed were mentally healthy and which were mentally ill. Greenley (1972) found that the attitudes of the families of patients in a mental hospital were a critical factor in how the patients' illnesses were defined. If the family insisted that the patient be released, the psychiatrist in charge would generally agree. Upon being discharged, the patient would be defined, both in the doctor's conversations and in official records, as being well enough to leave. When there was no pressure for a patient to be released, the patient generally was defined as being too sick to leave the hospital.

Despite the undeniable influence of labeling on the diagnosis and treatment of mental illness, recent large-scale research has shown that interviewers with basic training in the diagnosis of mental illness can spot people with serious mental disorders like schizophrenia and severe depression quite accurately. Such research is vital to our knowledge of the extent of mental illness in a population (Horowitz & Scheid, 1999; Kessler et al., 2005).

Mental Illness Among Combatants in Afghanistan and Iraq. Even when research findings are available and widely publicized, there is no guarantee, especially with mental illnesses, that effective action will follow. A case in point is the gap that existed until quite recently between what is known about the incidence of mental illness among soldiers who have witnessed violent death on battlefields and the provision of adequate mental-health services for them. Once called shell shock or combat fatigue, what is now known as post-traumatic stress disorder, or PTSD, was frequently confused with cowardice or weakness and was a severe problem in past wars. Now mental-health researchers understand that an individual may develop PTSD after witnessing or experiencing any traumatic event. The treatment of soldiers with PTSD may improve as a result of a recent, highly publicized study of the mental-health needs of soldiers returning from Iraq and Afghanistan, conducted a few months after their return. It found that one in eight American GIs serving in those countries reported symptoms of PTSD. The symptoms of this disorder may be quite severe and can include flashbacks, nightmares, feelings of detachment, irritability, trouble concentrating, and sleeplessness. According to Charles W. Hoge of the Walter Reed Army Institute of Research, studies of past wars' effects on mental health were conducted years later, making it difficult to compare the latest results with those from the Vietnam or Persian Gulf wars (Hoge, Messer, & Castro, 2004). The research also showed that fewer than half of returned soldiers with symptoms of PTSD seek help, mostly out of fear of being stigmatized or hurting their careers. As a consequence of these findings, the U.S. Department of Defense began administering mental-health questionnaires to all soldiers after they have returned home. Although this is clearly a major step forward, at this writing funds for treatment of veterans with mental-health problems related to their service in Iraq or Afghanistan remain inadequate (Albernaz, 2005). In 2007 a special report to the U.S. military by the American Psychological Association revealed that the military's mental-health system is overwhelmed and understaffed, with almost 40 percent of mental-health positions in military hospitals and bases unfilled (Borenstein, 2007).

Situations like this one remind us that the members of a society, especially mental-health professionals and political leaders, are continually negotiating the definitions and thus the possible treatments of mental disorders. We will see in the next section that a large number of factors—including whether people are rich or poor; live in a central city, a suburb, or a rural area; are black, white, or Hispanic, male or female—can affect how, and even if, their illnesses are diagnosed and treated.

INEQUALITY, CONFLICT, AND MENTAL ILLNESS

Sociologists and experts on mental-health care have continually refined their research concepts and tools in order to trace the relationships between mental illness and inequalities of social class, race, ethnicity, and gender. Sociologists are interested in the relationship between social factors like poverty and the incidence of mental disorders. Is mental disorder associated with social class and with conflicts over the distribution of social rewards? Does it occur more frequently in urban centers than in rural areas or suburbs? In what population groups is it most prevalent? Would changes in social conditions prevent or alleviate certain mental disorders?

Incidence versus Prevalence of Mental Disorders

Epidemiologists—social scientists who study the course of diseases in human populations—make a distinction between the incidence of a disease or disorder and its prevalence in a given population. Incidence and prevalence are important concepts in studying how mental illness is related to social variables such as inequality, race, gender, and age. The *prevalence* of mental illness usually refers to the estimated population of people suffering from one or more mental illnesses at any given time. The term *incidence* refers to the annual diagnosis rate, or the number of new cases of mental illness diagnosed each year. The rate of incidence of childhood autism, for example, is between 1 in 500 and 1 in 1,000 children, depending on the diagnostic criteria used. Autism affects five times as many boys as girls, and although it is difficult to know exactly how many Americans suffer from the disease at any given time, autism advocacy groups agree that autism currently affects at least 400,000 people in the United States (autisminfo.com, 2007).

The study of incidence and prevalence of mental disorders is complicated by the difficulty of ascertaining the prevalence of mental disorders. We can count the number of patients in mental hospitals and, somewhat less accurately, those receiving treatment in clinics and other outpatient facilities. It is far more difficult to obtain reliable statistics on the number being treated in private practice. Moreover, any number of people who would qualify as emotionally disturbed are not under treatment at all and therefore do not appear in most estimates of the incidence of mental disorders. Consequently, any statistics on treated mental disorders must be viewed as only a very rough estimate of the total number of people suffering from these problems.

Despite these difficulties, sociologists have reached several tentative conclusions about the relationship between mental disorders and patterns of inequality in a society. It should be noted that research on the impact of inequality is often conducted from a conflict perspective. Conflict theorists call attention to the ways in which inequalities of wealth and power produce inequalities in access to effective treatment for mental disorders. Underlying these inequalities is class conflict. The poor demand more services and better care from public institutions, while those who are better off believe the poor bring their troubles on themselves and do not deserve expensive care facilities and treatment programs. Conflict theorists also emphasize that poverty itself is a social problem that can produce severe stress in those who experience it. Life in poverty is associated with higher exposure to crime and violence, which adds to the stress of everyday life. In some individuals such extreme stress can precipitate mental illness (Kozol, 1988; Snow, 1993).

Social Class and Mental Disorder

Long before sociologists began to make systematic studies of social conditions and mental disorders, the connection between the two had been recognized. It was only in the 1930s, however, that serious sociological study of this relationship began, and although the research results are not in perfect agreement, they offer some useful information.

One pioneering study (Faris & Dunham, 1938) investigated the residential patterns of 35,000 hospitalized mental patients in Chicago. The highest rates of mental disorder were found near the center of the city, where the population was poor, of very mixed ethnic and racial background, and highly mobile. Although this number included many cases of organic psychosis due to syphilis and alcoholism in the skid row districts, it also included a significantly high rate of schizophrenia throughout the area. Conversely, the lowest rates of mental disorder were found in stable, higher-status residential areas.

We now know that the early research was somewhat misleading in suggesting that psychoses are more likely to occur among people who are poor and live in run-down areas. It has been shown that people with schizophrenia and drug-induced organic disorders tend to inhabit the poorer areas of cities, partly because they usually have limited incomes and also because they feel more comfortable where there are people like themselves.

Another classic study, the Midtown Manhattan Study, went beyond treatment to include a random sample of 1,660 adult residents of midtown Manhattan (Srole et al., 1978). The researchers found that almost 23 percent were significantly impaired in mental functioning, including many people who were not under treatment. One of the factors investigated was socioeconomic status, not only that of the subjects but also that of their parents. Among subjects considered seriously impaired in mental functioning, the percentage with lower-class parents was twice the percentage of those with upper-class parents. This finding suggests that socioeconomic status has a strong influence on the mental health of children.

It should be kept in mind that studies like these tend to come up with widely divergent estimates of the proportion of mentally ill individuals in various populations. Some of these differences are due to the use of different data-collection techniques and different definitions of mental illness. The studies are consistent, however, in reporting that only a minority of the cases observed have ever received treatment (Barker, Manderscheid, & Gendershot, 1992; Horowitz & Scheid, 1999; Regier et al., 1993).

All the studies just described agree that psychosis in general and schizophrenia in particular are much more common at the lowest socioeconomic level than at higher levels. They do not indicate, however, whether most schizophrenic individuals were originally in the lowest class or whether they drifted down to it as the disorder worsened. In other words, they fail to make clear whether low socioeconomic status is primarily a *cause* or an *effect* of serious mental disorder. Other research has attempted to address this question.

Can we say that poverty causes mental illness?

The Drift Hypothesis.

Some researchers reject a poverty or social-stress hypothesis as an explanation of the preponderance of mental illness in the lower classes. Instead, they propose the **social-selection,** or **drift, hypothesis,** which holds that social class is not a cause but a consequence of mental disorder. In this view, mentally disordered people tend to be found in the lower classes because their illness has prevented them from functioning at a higher class level and they have "drifted" downward to a lower class. This interpretation is partially supported by a study of a population of over 16,000 individuals in southern Appalachia (Harkey, Miles, & Rushing, 1976), which found that the primary effect of psychological disorder is to retard upward mobility (although it does not necessarily contribute to downward mobility). A study of Dutch schizophrenics also supported the social-selection theory (Fox, 1989).

Studies like these, though not conclusive, provide evidence that low social class does not cause mental illness. Instead, a low social-class position is associated with mental disorders, most likely as a result of a process in which the mentally ill drift downward in society. A review of existing studies on this subject, together with an analysis of new data from repeated interviews with a large sample of Americans, lends further support to the drift hypothesis. Sociologists and mental-health experts on the study team found that a wide variety of mental illnesses impair individuals' ability to develop their skills and advance in the world of work and thus prevent them from

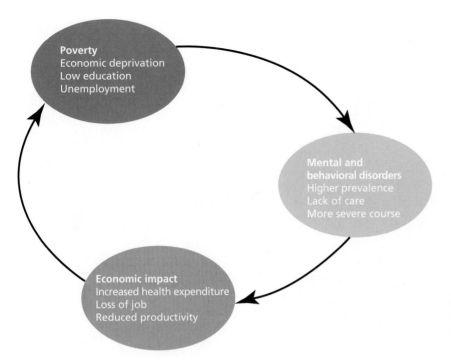

Figure 3–1 The Vicious Cycle of Poverty and Mental Disorders

Source: World Health Organization, 2001.

attaining social mobility. In short, it is more often the case that mental disorders produce low socioeconomic status than that low socioeconomic status produces mental disorder (Miech et al., 1999; National Institute of Mental Health, 2007). The interconnectedness of social factors associated with mental illnesses can be represented as a "vicious cycle of poverty and mental disorders," as shown in Figure 3–1.

What is the drift hypothesis, and how does it help explain the relationship between mental illness and poverty?

Mental Disorder and Urban Life

Whatever the precise relationship between mental illness and social class, there is no doubt that people who live in lower-class communities or neighborhoods, especially in central cities, experience high levels of stress. This aspect of their social environment can bring on bouts of mental illness. The presence of high rates of mental illness in urban settings leads many people to assume that there is a connection between city life and mental disorder. However, because there has been little research in this area, no conclusive test of this assumption is available. Investigation is made more difficult by the fact that mental disorder is more likely to be diagnosed and treated where facilities are readily accessible—which usually means in and around cities. Studies of treated mental disorder, therefore, are of limited usefulness in making urban–rural comparisons.

A feature of urban life that has received particular attention in studies of the causes of mental illness is crowding in the home. Research on this subject has generated considerable controversy. A survey of Chicago residents (Gove, Hughes, & Galle, 1979) measured both objective crowding (number of persons per room) and subjective crowding (excessive social demands and lack of privacy). The results indicated that household crowding has a number of adverse consequences, including poor mental health. However, this conclusion has been challenged by critics who contend that complaints of lack of privacy and excessive demands by others may themselves be signs of mental disorder (Booth, Johnson, & Edwards, 1980).

Research on crowding and child development offers substantial evidence that children growing up in crowded apartments, neighborhoods, and child-care facilities can suffer a variety of disorders that may put them at risk for more severe mental disorders later in life. In a study of 10- to 12-year-old children of working-class parents living in India (Evans et al., 1998), the researchers found that chronic residential crowding is

Most cities have run-down areas where people from other neighborhoods and outlying areas congregate. Often suffering from the consequences of multiple problems (poverty, homelessness, mental illness, alcoholism), these individuals feel less deviant in these areas than in more "respectable" parts of the city.

associated with difficulties in behavioral adjustment at school, poor academic achievement, and impaired parent–child relationships. Recent research on crowding in U.S. prisons also shows a high correlation between crowded conditions and the onset of symptoms of mental illness. Increasingly, people with mental illnesses who commit misdemeanors are being sent to prison, where crowding and other adverse conditions worsen their symptoms. And as prison populations in the United States have reached historic highs, it is no surprise to researchers that mental-health problems among the incarcerated are exploding (Freudenberg, 2001).

Other Factors

A variety of other factors have been investigated in an attempt to discover their relationship to mental disorder. Among these are race and sex.

Race. Race does not appear to be a significant variable by itself. Instead, racial differences in mental health can be explained in terms of social class. Poor people, of whom a large proportion are black or Hispanic, are much more likely to be seen as needing hospitalization than are members of the middle and upper classes, more of whom are white. The latter are more likely to be seen as needing outpatient psychotherapy. The poor are also much more likely to deal with public agencies, including mental-health centers, and to live in deteriorated urban environments (Gaw, 1993; Miech et al., 1999).

Sex. Women and children are much more likely than adult men to be diagnosed with severe depression, but again it appears that poverty and the stress it causes are more important than biological differences between the sexes. Women and children account for about 75 percent of people living below the official poverty line in the United States, so unless researchers look at the incidence of mental illness among men and women at each major income level, they will be confounding gender with socioeconomic inequality (National Institute of Mental Health, 2005). When this is done, it appears that women are more likely to experience depression, anxiety, and phobias, whereas men are more likely to suffer from autism and schizophrenia. In a classic study of this important subject, Phyllis Chesler (1972, 2005) suggested that the nature and incidence of mental disorder among women are a reflection of women's secondary status and restricted roles. Women are expected to conform to rigidly defined standards of behavior—to be passive, dependent, and emotional, for example, in accordance with traditional feminine roles. Because mental-health professionals are predominantly male, women who behave in nontraditional ways are more likely to be defined as mentally ill.

Chesler (1972) cites a study in which mental-health clinicians were asked to identify healthy male traits and healthy female traits. The researchers found that the standards of mental health for men and women differed according to traditional sex-role stereotypes. Thus, healthy women were considered to be unaggressive, submissive, excitable, and vain. Other studies cited by Chesler confirm that such attitudes do indeed serve as a basis for the decisions of mental-health professionals. For example, the major difference between female ex-mental patients who were rehospitalized and those who were not was that the former had refused to perform their domestic "duties"—cleaning, cooking, and the like. Females were also more likely to be called schizophrenics when they behaved in ways considered acceptable for men.

The question of whether men and women have different rates of psychosis has not been fully resolved. Men are thought to be more susceptible than women to schizophrenia; however, in a review of existing research, Dohrenwend and Dohrenwend (1975) found that half of the studies they investigated reported schizophrenia to be more prevalent among men, whereas the other half found it to occur more frequently among women. On the other hand, a study based on the criteria listed in *DSM* found significantly more men than women among schizophrenic patients (Lewine, Burbach, & Meltzer, 1984).

Although the evidence on schizophrenia, the most serious mental illness, is contradictory, there is widespread agreement among researchers that women tend to have significantly higher rates of depression than men and that men exhibit significantly higher rates of personality disorders. Women who are single parents and in the labor force have the highest rates of depression (Cockerham, 2006; Jamison, 2000; Mirowsky, 1985).

Age. In contrast to most severe and disabling physical diseases, mental illness begins early in life. The most recent incidence research in the United States and worldwide

Loss of a job or failure to pay the rent may leave families struggling to survive on city streets.

shows that 50 percent of all lifetime cases begin by age 14. Three-quarters have begun by age 24 (Kessler et al., 2005; WHO, 2005). Mental disorders therefore can be thought of as the chronic diseases of the young. Anxiety disorders, such as panic attacks, often begin in late childhood, eating and mood disorders in late adolescence, and substance abuse disorders in the early twenties. Young people with mental disorders suffer disability when they are in the prime of life, when they would normally be most productive, whereas extremely disabling physical illnesses like heart disease and cancer tend to strike adults in the later years of their working lives. The risk of mental disorders declines as people mature out of the high-risk age range. Prevalence increases from the youngest group (age 18–29) to the next-oldest age group (age 30–44) and then declines, sometimes substantially, in the oldest group (age 60+). Although it is true that seniors have increasing rates of depression after age 70, this is often due to loss of loved ones and to physical conditions such as progressive dementia (National Institute of Mental Health, 2005).

How is the incidence of mental illness related to age, and especially to adolescence?

INSTITUTIONAL PROBLEMS OF TREATMENT AND CARE

The treatment of mental disorders has undergone enormous changes in the past century and remains one of the most controversial aspects of mental health in all societies. In this section, we review the major approaches to the treatment of mental illness as well as changes in mental-health institutions. We will see that although there has been a great deal of progress in treating mental illness, many problems remain, especially in creating and maintaining effective institutions for the treatment and care of the mentally ill (Horowitz & Scheid, 1999; Kessler et al., 2005).

Methods of Treatment

The two major approaches to the treatment of mental disorders are psychotherapy (sometimes called insight therapy) and medical treatment in the form of **psychotropic drugs** or electroconvulsive therapy. Although these approaches are sometimes used simultaneously, they involve different groups of mental-health professionals, who often have difficulty coordinating the diagnosis and treatment of their patients. The problem of coordination is discussed more fully in the Social Policy section of the chapter. In this section, we briefly review the most important methods of treatment.

Nonmedical Forms of Treatment. Patients who undergo psychotherapy are helped to understand the underlying reasons for their problems so that they can try to work out solutions. The process involves some form of interaction between the patient and the therapist or among patients in groups. Among the major forms of psychotherapy are psychoanalysis, client-centered therapy, and various types of therapy and support groups.

Developed by Sigmund Freud in the late nineteenth century, psychoanalysis seeks to uncover unconscious motives, memories, and fears that prevent the patient from functioning normally. Patients may use various methods of exploration and discovery, including dreams and free association. Client-centered therapy was developed by Carl Rogers in the 1940s. This approach emphasizes current problems rather than unconscious motives and past experiences. The patient sets the course of the therapy, while the therapist provides support. In therapy and support groups, people attempt to solve their problems through interaction with one another. Therapy groups are led by professionals; support groups are organized by people who have experienced the same problems as the other participants, for example, Alcoholics Anonymous, Overeaters Anonymous, and Gamblers Anonymous. Another important type of group therapy is family therapy, in which family members work with the help of a trained professional to overcome their difficulties.

Still another nonmedical approach, hypnosis, can help patients recall deeply repressed but significant memories that may be blocking their progress toward understanding and dealing with their problems. Hypnosis is often used successfully in the treatment of milder mental disorders but has not had a major impact on the treatment of psychoses.

Medical Approaches to Treatment. Medical treatments, particularly chemotherapy and shock treatment, are applied to the most severe mental illnesses, such as schizophrenia and manic depression. Control over these treatments is in the hands of medical or clinical psychiatrists, whereas insight therapies are practiced by other professionals, including licensed psychologists, clinically trained social workers, and lay therapists. None of the latter is authorized to prescribe drugs, shock treatment, or hospitalization.

Before the late 1930s severe psychosis was treated in a variety of ways: by confining the patient in a straitjacket; by administering sedatives; by wrapping the patient in moist, cool sheets; or by immersing the patient in a continuous flow tub for hours at a time (Sheehan, 1982). Then a more drastic treatment was introduced: electroconvulsive therapy, in which an electric shock produces a convulsion and brief unconsciousness. This frightening and dangerous treatment has produced dramatic results with deeply depressed patients and some schizophrenics. However, the effects tend to be temporary, and it is not clear how much brain damage the treatment causes. Moreover, it often results in long-term memory loss.

In the 1940s and early 1950s shock treatment was used extensively, sometimes in coercive and excessive ways (Squire, 1987). The procedure was modified in the mid-1950s and made somewhat safer, but in the 1960s and 1970s it fell into disfavor as drug therapies became increasingly popular. Recently, interest in this form of treatment has revived, partly because drug therapies have turned out to be less effective than anticipated (Regier, 1991).

The other important medical approach to treatment, chemotherapy, involves treating patients with a variety of drugs, ranging from mild tranquilizers to antidepressants and antipsychotic agents. The development of the antipsychotic drugs has made it possible to control the most incapacitating aspects of schizophrenia and paranoia. This, in turn, often permits the patient to return to the community, with occasional periods of hospitalization when stress or other problems cause more severe symptoms of the disorder to recur. But these powerful drugs cause side effects when they are administered over long periods (Cockerham, 2006). Of all the recent innovations in drug therapy, the administration of antidepressants, especially Prozac, has had the greatest impact and has relieved severe and debilitating symptoms in millions of people (Jamison, 2000).

Chemotherapy is also used in the treatment of anxiety. This usually involves the use of mild tranquilizers such as Valium and Xanax. It is generally believed that chemotherapy should be used in conjunction with some other form of therapy, because drugs alone can rarely bring about significant long-term changes in behavior.

Changes in Mental-Health Treatment and Care

Lack of treatment is one of the most persistent social problems associated with mental illnesses. The most recent national-level research finds that the prevalence of mental disorders in the United States did not change significantly from 1990 to 2003 (29.4 percent between 1990 and 1992 and 30.5 percent between 2001 and 2003), but the rate of treatment increased. Among patients with any mental disorder, 20.3 percent received treatment between 1990 and 1992, and 32.9 percent received treatment between 2001 and 2003. But this important improvement should not mask the far greater problem of lack of treatment among the large majority with mental disorders. Moreover, about half of those who receive treatment for emotional problems did not actually have disorders that met the diagnostic criteria for a mental disorder. The most important improvements were among people seeking help for emotional issues from their family doctors or from counselors and therapists; there were no significant increases in treatment among those with severe mental illnesses such as bipolar disorder or schizophrenia. The study concluded that

> Despite an increase in the rate of treatment, most patients with a mental disorder did not receive treatment. Lack of treatment is especially problematic for the young who are afflicted with mental illness. Young people typically experience long delays—sometimes decades—between first onset of symptoms and when they seek and receive treatment. The recent data also reveals that an untreated mental disorder can lead to a more severe, more difficult to treat illness, and to the development of co-occurring mental illnesses. (Kessler et al., 2005)

To effectively address the needs of people with mental disorders, a variety of institutions and approaches, all working together, are required. Schools, hospitals, families, community centers, and law enforcement agencies need to become more aware of mental-health problems and how to deal with them. In affluent nations, including the United States, part of the reason why so many cases of mental disorder go untreated has to do with lack of coordination and failure to overcome problems of stigma, discrimination, and lack of support in the person's social environment. But as we will see shortly, changes in mental-health systems and problems of funding mental-health institutions are also a major problem. Figure 3–2 provides a useful overview of the range of needs and institutions that must be addressed to effectively cope with mental disorders (WHO, 2001).

A good example of the difficulty of filling the needs outlined in Figure 3–2 is the case of children who experienced the 9/11 terrorist attacks. Recent research indicates that while large numbers of children continue to suffer from one or more symptoms of PTSD, the vast majority are untreated, largely due to lack of understanding of the symptoms, problems of coordination between institutions (families, schools, mental-health agencies), and lack of adequate funding for special programs to deal with the situation. (See the On Further Analysis box on page 88.)

Figure 3–2 Needs of People with Mental Disorders

Source: World Health Organization, 2001.

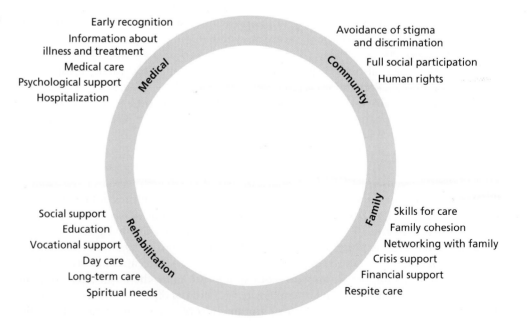

Treatment Institutions

The forms of treatment described earlier are carried out in a variety of settings. Psychotherapy and other nonmedical forms of treatment generally occur in nonhospital settings such as psychologists' offices. Medical treatments, in contrast, often require hospitalization. In addition, some patients are so seriously ill that they cannot be cared for outside a hospital or asylum. In this section we discuss issues related to the care of the mentally ill in hospitals and other institutions.

Mental Hospitals. In the late nineteenth and early twentieth centuries, mental-health care meant, in practice, mental hospitals. During this period, the ties among members of extended families were being weakened as a result of increased mobility. The smaller nuclear family was less well equipped to care for its disabled members and began to look to the state for assistance (Curtis, 1986). Institutions like mental hospitals were developed to meet this need. In such institutions the insane were to be sheltered from a hostile world, kept from harming themselves or others, and given help and treatment. Hospitals were built in secluded spots and surrounded by high walls and locked gates. Within the walls, all the patient's needs were to be met. But the purpose of the hospital was not merely to protect patients from society and, if possible, to cure them; it was also to protect society from the patients. The old stereotype of the "raving lunatic" persisted, and gradually security came to be considered more important than therapy.

For the sake of economy and efficiency, the present system of enormous hospitals developed, each housing several thousand patients and staffed largely by aides whose main job is to keep things quiet on as low a budget as a state legislature can decently supply. Staffing these hospitals is a perennial problem. Salaries are usually low; working conditions are often unattractive or discouraging; and professionally trained personnel are almost irresistibly tempted by private hospitals, clinics, or private practice, where the rewards, both monetary and in terms of visible therapeutic achievement, are much greater. Consequently, public institutions must depend heavily on partially trained personnel, particularly attendants or nursing aides. These attendants, though not fully qualified, have the most contact with the patients, and typically they control most aspects of the patients' daily life, including access to doctors.

There is evidence that hospitalization may not always be the best solution to mental illness, even in good hospitals. Long-term studies have shown that patients who do not improve enough to be discharged within a short period are likely to remain hospitalized for a very long time, if not indefinitely. This effect is due in part to the inadequacies of the hospital. It also seems to be a consequence of hospitalization itself, a position taken by Erving Goffman (1961). Goffman developed the concept of the total institution, which may be defined as "a place of residence and work where a large number of like-situated individuals, cut off from the wider society for an appreciable period of time, together lead an enclosed, formally administered round of life" (p. xiii).

Goffman (1961) regarded the mental hospital as a prime example of a total institution. His field research and work in mental hospitals convinced him that because inmates are constantly subject to its control, the hospital profoundly shapes their sense of self. In general, mental hospitals downgrade patients' desire for self-esteem and emphasize their failures and inadequacies. Uniform clothing and furniture, a regimented routine, and the custodial atmosphere of the hospital make patients docile and unassertive. Because the psychiatric approach requires cooperation, staff members often encourage patients to view themselves as sick and in need of help. Any act of self-assertion or rebellion will probably be interpreted as further evidence of illness, and patients will be expected to take that view of themselves. Release from the hospital is often contingent on the patient's accepting, or appearing to accept, the official interpretation of his or her hospital and prehospital life. Goffman

On Further Analysis

9/11 AND SCHOOLCHILDREN

Many of the people who watched in horror as the World Trade Towers became a flaming death scene experienced symptoms of PTSD—sleeplessness, attention problems, depression, recurring nightmares, and more—for days after the event. This was true even of people who saw the events on television (Foner, 2007). But children in New York City were especially prone to suffer one or more symptoms of PTSD long after the event. Here are segments of the testimony of psychiatrist Christina W. Hoven, who directed a study for the New York Department of Education of children's lingering psychological difficulties as a consequence of their experiences on 9/11:

To better appreciate the complexity and challenges faced by the New York City Board of Education, as they struggled to address this situation, I want to identify a few issues that contributed to our conceptualizing the study the way we did, that is, to view the aftermath as a probable citywide phenomenon, not just a Ground Zero event:

1. There are approximately 1.2 million children enrolled in the New York City public schools.
2. Approximately 750,000 of them take public transportation every day, including subways, buses, and boats, passing through tunnels and going over bridges on their way to school.
3. Whereas only 35,000 people reside in the area surrounding Ground Zero, more than twenty times that number commute there to work each day. Similarly, the schools near Ground Zero, especially the specialized middle and high schools, are attended primarily by students living outside that area, coming every day from each of the boroughs of NYC.

Briefly summarizing our findings, we observed throughout the City a higher than expected prevalence of a broad range of mental-health problems or psychiatric disorders among NYC public schoolchildren. It is estimated that as many as 75,000 (10.5%) New York City public schoolchildren in grades

4 to 12 have multiple symptoms consistent with post-traumatic stress disorder (PTSD); and that 190,000 (26.5%) have at least one of the seven assessed mental-health problems (excluding alcohol abuse).

NYC public school students were exposed to the effects of the attack in different ways. Almost all the students in Ground Zero, and two-thirds of children in the remainder of the City, experienced some type of personal physical exposure to the attack, such as being near the cloud of smoke and dust, having fled to safety, having had difficulty getting home that day, and/or continuing to smell smoke after 9/11.

Having a family member exposed to the attack—that is, having a family member killed, injured, or in the World Trade Center at the time of the attack but who escaped unhurt—was more frequent among students in schools outside of Ground Zero than among students in schools near Ground Zero.

We know that previous exposure to trauma elevates an individual's response to any new trauma. We found that nearly two-thirds (64%) of New York City public schoolchildren had been exposed to one or more traumatic events *prior* to 9/11, including seeing someone killed or seriously injured, [or] seeing the violent/ accidental death of a close friend or family member. Again, a disproportionate number of the children with previous exposure go to schools outside of the Ground Zero area.

Exposure to the media was also very high; almost two-thirds (62%) of the surveyed population spent a lot of their time learning about the attack from television . . . . Rates of the other psychiatric disorders [estimated for the city's 1.2 million children from random sample surveys] were as follows:

• 8 percent with major depressive disorder (MDD);

• 10 percent with generalized anxiety disorder (GAD);
• 12 percent with separation anxiety disorder (SAD);
• 9 percent with panic attacks;
• 11 percent with conduct disorder;
• 5 percent with alcohol abuse (grades 9–12 only).

All of these reported mental-health problems were determined to be associated with impairment; that is, they were so severe as to indicate a need for immediate further assessment and appropriate intervention. Yet, at least two-thirds of children with probable PTSD following the 9/11 attacks have not sought any mental-health services from school counselors or from mental-health professionals outside of school. (Hoven, 2002)

As part of the effort to help children cope with their fears and understand their feelings, the Messages Project collected notes and drawings sent to New York City schoolchildren from other children throughout the world. This one is from a group of Oregon elementary school children.

(With permission of the New York City Department of Education.)

concluded that in most cases there is a high probability that hospitalization will do more harm than good.

Goffman's (1961) research has received heavy criticism, particularly for not having conducted enough empirical research on enough hospitals to determine whether all mental hospitals could be called total institutions. Moreover, although Goffman's view has had a great influence on the way people think about mental hospitals (and jails), he is accused of having himself been influenced by the literary power of his ideas and images rather than by the force of empirical data (McEwen, 1988; Scull, 1988).

The classic study by Rosenhan (1973) mentioned earlier illustrates the conditions prevailing in many mental hospitals. This research project involved eight normal people, or pseudopatients, who were admitted to a mental hospital and diagnosed as schizophrenics. Their only symptom was a fabricated one: They said that they had heard voices on one occasion. Although the pseudopatients spent some time in the institution and were recognized as normal by their fellow inmates, the staff continued to think of them as schizophrenic. Some were released with the diagnosis of "schizophrenia in remission," and none was ever thought to be cured. In a follow-up study, a hospital that had heard of these findings was informed that over a period of three months some pseudopatients would attempt to gain admission to the hospital, and staff members were asked to judge which applicants were faking illness. Over the three-month period at least 41 patients were judged to be pseudopatients. In fact, none of those patients was faking.

The results of this study were widely cited as supporting the labeling theory in that the diagnosis of illness—or health—was applied regardless of the actual condition of the patient. But here we are interested in what the pseudopatients observed while in the hospital. As much as possible, staff members were separated from patients by a glass enclosure; psychiatrists, in particular, almost never appeared on the wards. When pseudopatients approached staff members with questions, the most common response was to ignore the questions or mumble something—avoiding eye contact with the patient—and quickly move on. Patients were sometimes punished excessively for misbehavior, and in one case a patient was beaten. In sum, the atmosphere was one of powerlessness and depersonalization.

Community Psychology. The increased use of chemotherapy in the treatment of mental disorders caused a revolution in mental-health care. It began in the hospitals in the 1950s. As a result of the introduction of psychotropic drugs,

> Thousands of patients who had been assaultive became docile. Many who had spent their days screaming subsided into talking to themselves. The decor of the wards could be improved: Chairs replaced wooden benches, curtains were hung on the windows. Razors and matches, once properly regarded as lethal, were given to patients who now were capable of shaving themselves and lighting their own cigarettes without injuring themselves or others or burning the hospital down. (Sheehan, 1982, p. 10)

But the revolution went far beyond hospital care. New "wonder drugs" like Thorazine made it possible to release hundreds of thousands of hospitalized patients (Cockerham, 2006; Sperry, 1995), who were supposed to receive outpatient treatment in their own communities.

Outpatient treatment for mental disorders is far from new, but until the 1960s it was confined largely to less severe disorders and to the upper and middle classes. With the passage of the Community Mental Health Centers Construction Act in 1963, the idea of easily accessible, locally controlled facilities that could care for people in their own communities—community psychology—was established.

The community psychology movement arose from two basic sources: (1) awareness that social conditions and institutions must be taken into account in dealing with individual mental-health problems; and (2) the idea that psychologists or psychiatrists should be able to contribute to the understanding and solution of social problems. The guidelines laid down for the centers provided for a wide range of mental-health care in the community and for coordination with, and consultative assistance to, other community agencies. Other nations, particularly Belgium and France, had had great success in developing residential treatment facilities for mentally ill individuals who were able to live among the general population.

The Community Mental Health Centers Construction Act set up a sophisticated support system to aid newly released patients, many of whom need considerable help in relearning the skills of everyday life and social interaction. The cornerstone of this system is the halfway house, a small, privately run residential community, usually located in an urban area, in which ex-patients are helped to make the transition from the hospital to normal life. They may receive therapy from a psychiatrist; they may be trained for a job and helped to obtain or keep one; and they are able to practice fitting into a community in which behavior is not subject to hospital regulations.

Under optimal conditions, halfway houses are capable of providing high-quality care; however, a variety of obstacles have prevented them from meeting the needs of many discharged mental patients. Operating almost in a vacuum—with no working relationship with the state mental hospitals from which they receive patients—many halfway houses soon found themselves with far more patients than they had staff or facilities to handle. This problem was exacerbated as hospitals rushed to reduce their patient loads long before community support systems were in place. In addition, halfway houses and other community mental-health centers face the enormous problem of lack of funds. The insurance coverage of mentally ill patients tends to favor hospital care, and the coverage for mental problems is inferior to that available for physical illnesses. As a result, halfway houses, nursing homes, and other community mental-health facilities have found it difficult to meet the growing demand for services (Hazlett et al., 2004).

Cost Shifting and the Two-Class Mental-Health System.   For over a century the public mental-health system, including state and local services, has subsidized the private mental-health system through the technique of cost shifting (see Chapter 2). As it provides mental-health services to people who cannot pay for them, including the uninsured, the public system has always tended to "absorb the private system's bad risks, difficult patients, and high-cost cases. Because the public system historically has been underfunded and has provided charity care, it has been perceived as inferior to the private care system" (Goldman, Frank, & McGuire, 1994, p. 74). And as severe mental illnesses like schizophrenia often reduce their victims to poverty, the public system has always been further burdened with the stigma of treating these individuals.

The resulting two-class system of care has persisted despite the change from a system dominated by large state mental hospitals to one of community mental-health care. The failure of community mental health is ironic, because never before in the history of mental illness has it been possible to do so much to alleviate the suffering of the mentally ill through drug therapy and social services (National Advisory Mental Health Council, 1993). At present, however, the number of untreated indigent mentally ill persons, many of whom are also chemically addicted, remains extremely large and is a significant social problem in many parts of the nation. To understand more about the origins of this problem, we turn to a discussion of released mental patients and the problem of homelessness.

Deinstitutionalization and Homelessness

We noted in the preceding section that beginning in the mid-1950s large numbers of mental patients were deinstitutionalized, or released from mental hospitals. The

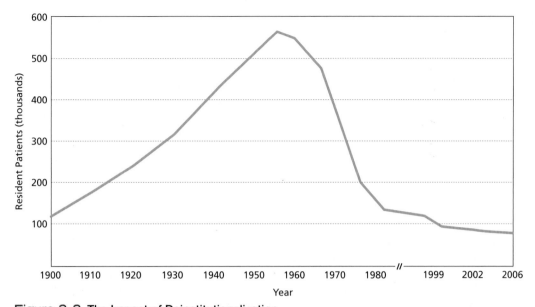

Figure 3–3 The Impact of Deinstitutionalization

Source: From "The Homelessness Problem" by E. I. Bassuk; © 1984 by Scientific American, Inc.; all rights reserved; also *Statistical Abstract,* 2006.

prominent medical sociologist David Mechanic (1990) has noted that in the United States, "We have emptied out mental institutions, reducing the number of public mental hospital beds from a peak of 559,000 in 1955 to 110,000 today, but have not developed effective systems of community care" (p. 9). As Figure 3–3 shows, deinstitutionalization reversed a trend that had extended throughout the early twentieth century, in which the population of state mental hospitals increased fourfold. During that time, mental hospitals were subjected to intense criticism, but the solutions proposed involved increasing the funding of hospitals, not the wholesale release of their inmates.

The trend toward deinstitutionalization is generally attributed to the introduction of psychotropic drugs, which greatly reduce the disruptive behavior of patients and make it possible to treat them outside of the hospital. However, some experts on mental-health care believe other factors besides the drug revolution played a role in deinstitutionalization. One was the expansion of federal health and welfare programs, which resulted in "the emergence of a new philosophy regarding what was possible and desirable in the provision of mental-health care for the seriously mentally ill" (Gronfein, 1985, p. 450). In other words, although the advent of psychotropic drugs certainly played an important role in deinstitutionalization, they were not the cause of large-scale discharges. It would be more accurate to say that the use of psychotropic drugs reinforced a trend that began at about the same time in response to a combination of factors, including not only expanded federal welfare programs but also the fiscal crises developing in many states, as well as growing demands for protection of the rights of the mentally ill (Wilton & Wolch, 1996).

Throughout the 1960s and 1970s it was hoped that reductions in the hospital population would be accompanied by equivalent reductions in the incidence of mental disorders. This hope proved vain. Far from decreasing, the incidence of mental disorders increased. At the same time, the funding of community mental-health care was cut back. Of the 2,000 community mental-health centers planned in 1963, fewer than 1,000 have been established. As a result, hospital emergency rooms are often crowded with psychiatric patients. In addition, large numbers of former patients are homeless (*Harvard Mental Health Newsletter,* 2005).

The presence of deinstitutionalized mental patients among the homeless is due partly to their tendency to congregate in central-city neighborhoods, which are unable to provide the services they need. It has also been caused, in part, by the passage of laws designed to protect the rights of the mentally ill. Because only patients who are demonstrably dangerous may be involuntarily committed to mental hospitals, most mentally ill patients receive only brief, episodic care (Bassuk, 1984). Chronically disturbed people who are not dangerous to themselves or others are released into the community. Some find housing in single-room occupancy (SRO) hotels or cheap rooming houses, but these forms of housing are far less available today than they were in the 1950s and 1960s because landlords have either abandoned them or converted them into condominiums. As a result, mentally ill people often end up on the streets (Jencks, 1995).

Homeless mentally ill individuals are highly visible, contributing to the widespread impression that a large proportion of homeless people have mental disorders. It has been estimated that between 30 percent and 60 percent of the homeless are seriously mentally ill. Social-scientific research has found, however, that the majority of the homeless are individuals who have been caught in a cycle of low-paying, dead-end jobs that fail to provide the means to get off the streets (Snow, 1993). In one study, 164 homeless people in Austin, Texas, were tracked over a 20-month period. Approximately 10 percent were found to have psychiatric problems of varying degrees of severity. Even among this group, more than 50 percent registered for job referrals at the Texas Employment Commission at least once. The researchers concluded that the erroneous notion that the homeless are predominantly mentally ill is explained by four interconnected factors: undue emphasis on the causal role of deinstitutionalization, the medicalization of homelessness (i.e., viewing it as an illness instead of a social condition), the high visibility of the homeless mentally ill, and the difficulty of assessing the mental status of the homeless (Bassuk, Browne, & Bruckner, 1996; Jencks, 1994).

The fourth factor was emphasized by a New York State judge in a case involving a homeless woman who had been involuntarily hospitalized under a program to remove seriously disturbed people from New York City streets. The judge ordered the woman released on the ground that the city had failed to prove that she was mentally ill. (The ruling was subsequently reversed by a court of appeals.) "The issue for most homeless people," he said, "is not whether they are mentally ill, but housing" (quoted in Barbanel, 1987). The crisis in housing for low-income individuals and families will be discussed further in Chapters 6, 10, and 13.

Even though the proportion of mentally ill individuals among the homeless may have been exaggerated, there is no doubt that a frequent outcome of untreated mental disorder is rejection and homelessness. Homelessness usually is the final stage in a long series of crises and missed opportunities, the end result of a gradual process of disengagement from supportive relationships and institutions. The situation is especially severe for the mentally ill. They are isolated. Family members and friends have become tired and discouraged or are unable to help. Social workers are overburdened and cannot give them the attention they need, and the mentally ill themselves cannot communicate their needs adequately. In addition, the mentally ill encounter hostility from other residents of the urban communities in which they try to exist (Dickey et al., 1997).

As a result of experiences like these, the homeless, especially those who are mentally disturbed, tend to be extremely afraid of strangers. This is one explanation why they often reject offers of shelter and efforts to help them. The fear experienced by some homeless people is so great that it can be overcome only with effort and patience. However, much of the assistance offered to these individuals is perfunctory and uncaring, serving only to further isolate them from society. (See the Current Controversies box on page 93.)

It should be pointed out that mental illness can be a consequence of homelessness as well as a factor that leads to social isolation (*Harvard Mental Health Newsletter*,

Current Controversies

FAILURES IN DEALING WITH CASES OF DANGEROUS MENTAL ILLNESS

The mass murder at Virginia Technical University in Blacksburg, Virginia, in April 2007 raised once again the question of how society can protect itself against psychotic killers. When Seung-Hui Cho, an undergraduate student with a history of rather serious mental illness, killed thirty-two students and teachers in a campus rampage, the tragedy also raised questions about how a person with such a history was able to easily buy firearms without any of the required background checks. The lesson from this and similar cases is that far more attention needs to be given to enforcement of existing laws dealing with the monitoring of possibly dangerous mental patients.

As university authorities and reporters gathered the gory facts after the Blacksburg killings, it appeared that the killer had been examined at the university's mental health facility and had been singled out as a potential danger to himself and others. His roommates had urged him to get help, and female students whom he had stalked warned others about him. Although the troubled student did visit mental health facilities, his case "is a classic example of some of the flaws in the outpatient treatment system." (Schulte & Jenkins, 2007, p. A1).

Cho, an English major at Virginia Tech, had written strange essays filled with violence and threats that frightened his teachers and classmates. He referred to himself as Question Mark, never made eye contact, and rarely spoke. When two undergraduate women complained that Cho had sent them instant messages and left cryptic lines from "Romeo and Juliet" on their dry-erase boards, he finally came to the attention of police. The women decided not to press charges and the police met with Cho and warned him to leave the women alone. The same night, Cho e-mailed a roommate saying that he might as well kill himself. The roommate contacted the police, who brought Cho to the New River Valley Community Services Board, the government mental health agency that serves Blacksburg. There mental health professionals examined Cho and found him to be "mentally ill and in need of hospitalization," according to court papers. That was enough to have him temporarily detained at Carilion St. Albans Behavioral Health Clinic in Christiansburg,

a few miles from campus, until a special justice could review his case in a commitment hearing.

The next day, the special judge decided that Cho was an imminent danger to himself as a result of mental illness and ordered him into involuntary outpatient treatment. Although details of the case are still being investigated, it appears that there was no effective follow-up after Cho was released. Court officials claim that they have no authority or resources to follow up such cases. Virginia Tech mental health officials claimed that they are never informed when a person is referred to their facilities by the court. According to these officials, the court's orders for mandatory treatment are directed at the individual, not the agency. In fact, Virginia law does specify that the local mental health agency "shall monitor the person's compliance" and if the person does not appear for treatment he or she can be remanded to the judge and possibly committed to a mental hospital. But these procedures and regulations were not routinely followed due to confusion about responsibilities and lack of resources to monitor such individuals.

At this writing, it appears that although Virginia's mental-health care statutes contained adequate legal language for dealing with possibly

dangerous individuals, no attention was paid to enforcement of these regulations, and this is a common situation throughout the United States. The same negligence applies to the enforcement of firearms laws that bar people with severe mental-health problems from purchasing weapons.

Virginia is one of only eight states requiring that people be an "imminent" danger to themselves or others before they can even be brought before a judge. Under these high standards, only the most dangerous cases are considered and involuntary hospitalization is usually required, although this was not true in Cho's case. After events like the Virginia Tech massacre there are always recriminations and fingers pointed at officials who did not act on time. But when gun legislation is not enforced, and when resources are not put into the monitoring of possibly dangerous mental patients, it often takes tragedies like the Virginia Tech massacre to bring about changes in policies and the commitment of adequate resources to protection of the public in the future. Will this occur as a result of the Virginia Tech shootings? It is up to informed citizens like readers of this text to keep the pressure on legislatures to make sure that appropriate changes in policy and practice are made.

Students and faculty mourning on the Virginia Tech campus.

2005). People who lose their homes suffer severe stress. They experience hunger, lack of sleep, and physical illnesses ranging from asthma to tuberculosis. In addition, they are "disorganized, depressed, disordered . . . immobilized by pain and traumatized by fear" (Kozol, 1988). To the uninformed observer, such individuals resemble the former mental patients who have also ended up on the streets, and their disordered appearance helps perpetuate the belief that all homeless people are crazy.

Social Policy

T he political battles surrounding mental-health care in the United States focus largely on the issue of *parity,* or eliminating the discrimination against mental illness that is inherent in existing health insurance plans—which helps produce the two-class system of mental-health care. Parity is highly desirable, but insurance company executives fear that it could increase the costs of insurance paid by employers. Large corporations typically impose a $50,000 life-time limit on mental-health care, whereas the limit for physical-health care may range from $750,000 to $1 million. Thus, health insurance experts fear that an unintended consequence of parity legislation would be to actually reduce the number of people covered by any form of mental-health insurance (Pear, 1998). In 1990 mental-health care accounted for 9 percent of all health-care costs, but by 2000, due to the lack of parity in health-care payments, the proportion had dropped to 3 percent. Managed care cut the costs of mental-health services and care by 54 percent while cutting other medical costs by 8 percent. The Surgeon General's *Report on Mental Health* opposed this trend. It ranked mental illness second only to heart disease as a cause of disability, and it reported that only one-third of the 20 percent of Americans who need psychiatric treatment in any given year received it (cited in Houghton & Houghton, 2002).

What is meant by "parity" in mental-health policy?

Without adequate coverage for mental-health care, people who suffer from severe mental illnesses are often forced into poverty. Once on the streets, they may be treated in public institutions, but in an era of shrinking budgets this, too, becomes problematic. State and municipal governments are often unwilling or unable to assume the burden of caring for the mentally ill. Some provide shelters for the homeless, but these cannot hope to replace the mental hospital or the halfway house. Shelters offer minimal medical, psychological, and social services. Generally understaffed, they are open only at night and cannot provide the supervision and support needed by disturbed individuals.

Some *re*institutionalization has occurred as a result of the public outcry over the plight of the homeless mentally ill. This is especially true of patients under constant medication, who need careful monitoring because their tolerance of and need for psychotropic drugs are constantly changing. If they receive adequate treatment outside as well as inside the hospital, this revolving-door system is reasonably effective. However, such situations are rare.

An important problem in caring for the mentally ill is the lack of coordination of treatment. Because of the division of mental-health care between insight therapists and medical practitioners, there is a widespread tendency to see psychotherapy and medical treatment as mutually exclusive. Yet a patient who is on medication needs to have enough insight to be able to take the medicine in the prescribed dosage at the correct intervals. It follows that there must be a high level of coordination of treatment between social workers and others in the patient's social world, on one hand,

and the clinical personnel who prescribe medication and decide whether patients should be hospitalized, on the other.

Problems of treatment and supervision of nonhospitalized patients stem in part from certain characteristics of the organization of mental-health institutions. According to one expert (Meyer, 1985), the mental-health-care system lacks integration or structure. The various types of organizations that provide mental-health services differ greatly in the types of cases they handle, the way they are staffed and funded, the way they relate to other mental-health organizations, and many other respects. In addition, they are constantly changing, and they are continually under attack for failures both real and imagined. There is a need for what Meyer terms "institutional coordination" such as that which exists in education. Educational institutions also differ greatly, but they are held together by shared definitions of the nature of education, the requirements for teaching, the meaning of degrees and credit, and so on. Similar agreements are needed in the field of mental-health care—for example, agreements on the definition of treatable problems, appropriate professionals, funding responsibilities, and the like. (See the On Further Analysis box on page 96.)

Future Prospects

In the absence of a comprehensive approach to health care, including mental-health care, it is likely that there will be further deterioration in the treatment conditions for people with severe mental illnesses. This population currently depends heavily on the social safety net of public mental-health services (Thompson, 2007). However, decreasing insurance coverage will probably force more severely ill patients into an already heavily burdened public system. People with moderate mental illnesses like chronic depression, who need extensive rehabilitation or long-term care, are even less likely to receive the care they need because of inadequacies in coverage and the fact that (as they usually are not indigent) they are ineligible for care in public institutions.

As the number of untreated and poorly treated mental patients increases, many experts anticipate that their problems will become so visible on the streets and in residential neighborhoods that an alarmed public will again realize the need for a balanced public and private approach to comprehensive coverage for mental-health care. This may be an overly hopeful scenario, however. The costs of such an approach would be extremely high and would require a far more generous spirit than now exists among American voters.

One promising approach to the problems of the severely mentally ill is being promoted by the National Alliance for the Mentally Ill. This program began in Wisconsin in the early 1970s and has been developed in a number of mental-health centers since then. It calls for a program of assertive community treatment (PACT) for people with severe and persistent mental illnesses like schizophrenia, bipolar disorder, and other psychoses. PACT uses a multidisciplinary team that provides comprehensive, client-centered care on a round-the-clock basis. Seventy-five percent of this care is provided in community settings, including homes, workplaces, restaurants, laundromats, and grocery stores. Models of assertive community-based care are also being developed in Great Britain and Australia. They are achieving considerable success because mental-health workers are reaching out to the mentally ill where they are and when they are in need, rather than waiting for them to appear in clinics or to be incarcerated.

GOING BEYOND LEFT AND RIGHT

Whose responsibility are the mentally ill? This question does not give rise to as many moral or ideological debates as some other social problems, but there are controversies nonetheless. In this chapter, for example, we have described the failure of the

On Further Analysis

ATTENTION DEFICITS, EATING DISORDERS, AND SOCIAL POLICY

Two eating disorders, anorexia nervosa (AN) and bulimia nervosa, affect twice as many girls and young women as boys and men. In contrast, attention deficit hyperactivity disorder (ADHD) is almost twice as common among boys and young men as it is in girls and young women. Together, however, they constitute two of the most common and problematic mental health problems among children and adolescents in the United States. These disorders present quite different challenges to mental-health professionals and policymakers because untreated ADHD is associated with poverty status and AN is more often found in wealthier families.

Children with ADHD have difficulty staying focused on a task, cannot sit still, often act without thinking, and rarely finish tasks. If untreated, the disorder can have long-term effects on the child's ability to make friends or do well at school or work. Over time, children with ADHD may develop depression, poor self-esteem, and other emotional problems. Research sponsored by the National Institute of Mental Health (NIMH) (2001) reports that

ADHD affects an estimated 4.1 percent of youths ages 9 to 17 in a six-month period.

About two to three times more boys than girls have ADHD.

Children with untreated ADHD have higher than normal rates of injury.

ADHD often co-occurs with other problems, such as depressive and anxiety disorders, conduct disorder, drug abuse, or antisocial behavior.

Symptoms of ADHD usually become evident in the preschool or early elementary-school years. The disorder frequently persists into adolescence and occasionally into adulthood.

Treatments for ADHD are quite controversial because they tend to combine the use of stimulants such as Ritalin or amphetamines with behavioral therapy. These can help children control their activity level and impulsiveness, pay attention, and focus on tasks. But many parents and parents' groups oppose the medications because of possible side effects and the fear that they will lead to addiction. Although it supports the drug therapies, the NIMH also warns that "Parents need to carefully evaluate treatment choices when their child receives a diagnosis of ADHD. . . . When they pursue treatment for their children, families face high out-of-pocket expenses because treatment for ADHD and other mental illnesses is often not covered by insurance policies. In schools, treatment plans are often poorly integrated. In addition, there are few special education funds directed specifically for ADHD. All these factors lead to children who do not receive proper and adequate treatment." Parents are advised to seek schools with "team based approaches that involve parents, teachers, school psychologists, other mental health specialists, and physicians" (NIMH, 2001). Unfortunately, in low-income communities, many of which are predominantly populated by ethnic and racial minorities, these services are inadequately funded or nonexistent. At the same time, cuts in mental-health treatment for low-income families through Medicare and related programs are being made at both the state and federal levels of government.

Eating disorders affect 2 to 4 percent of children and adolescents in the United States each year, with girls at least twice as likely as boys to suffer from these disorders. They are marked by serious disturbances in eating behavior, such as extreme and unhealthy reduction of food intake or severe overeating followed by self-induced vomiting, accompanied by intense feelings of distress or extreme concern about body shape or weight. Unlike obesity, which is more common among lower-income families whose diets are high in carbohydrates and sugars, eating disorders tend to occur in children from families with more economic and social advantages and higher levels of education who have ample access to healthier foods and diets (Rich & Evans, 2005).

But eating is a highly complex set of behaviors that is influenced, according to NIMH researchers, "by many factors, including appetite, food availability, family, peer, and cultural practices, and attempts at voluntary control. Dieting to a body weight leaner than needed for health is highly promoted by current fashion trends, sales campaigns for special foods, and in some activities and professions" (NIMH, 2001). Many girls and young women who develop eating disorders believe that if their bodies do not conform to the ideal shapes they see in magazines and television, they must reduce their food intake. But when dieting becomes a compulsion not to eat, or to binge and then vomit, the behavior often becomes something that the individual cannot control, even though she frequently denies that there is any problem. At this stage, NIMH (2001) authorities note, "Eating disorders are not due to a failure of will or behavior; rather, they are real, treatable medical illnesses in which certain maladaptive patterns of eating take on a life of their own." If left untreated, severe eating disorders can lead to serious physical ailments such as kidney failure and heart disease.

Both eating disorders and ADHD are being diagnosed with increasing frequency in the U.S. population, indicating a pressing need for new policy initiatives at all levels of government. Mental-health authorities tend to agree that increased public education efforts are needed to educate children and their parents, as well as the general public, about these conditions and what must be done to treat them when they occur (Cumella, 2005).

community mental-health-care movement. There has been no ideological debate over the need to end the warehousing of mentally ill people in isolated state hospitals, especially when new drug therapies have made it possible for them to live more normal lives. But where are they to live? In whose communities? Do we all share the responsibility for their care, or must the communities where the mentally ill are most numerous bear a greater share of the burden?

On the right, there is a tendency to insist on the responsibility of families to care for their mentally ill members. On the left, one hears demands for public funding of mental-health clinics. What are your views on the issue? Does the sociological analysis presented in this chapter help you go beyond the opposing viewpoints?

Family responsibility and adequate funding of public programs need not be incompatible policies. At some point the laws, which are based on social custom, insist that an adult person is no longer the sole responsibility of his or her family. However, lack of adequate funding for public mental-health programs remains a serious obstacle to providing care for such individuals. And the tragic rampage at Virginia Technical University calls attention to the failure to enforce existing laws about selling guns to mentally ill individuals or to adequately monitor their activities and follow up on their treatment. Unfortunately, the likelihood of constructive action to address these problems is diminished by conservative opposition to restrictions on sales of firearms and liberal concerns about the restriction of civil rights. Still, lawmakers who wish to avoid ideological battles can remind the public of the consequences of inaction and invoke tragedies like the Virginia Tech massacre to make their case for effective measures to protect public safety.

Summary

- The mental disorders that cause severe social problems are the most extreme forms of mental illness, in which individuals become violent and irrational. Less threatening, but more widespread as a social problem, are severely ill individuals who are unable to care for themselves without specialized attention.

- There are three different explanations of mental illness: (a) the medical model, which simply asserts that mental illness is a disease with physiological causes; (b) the deviance approach, which asserts that mental illness results from how people considered mentally ill are treated; and (c) the argument that mental illness is not a disease but a way of defining certain people as being in need of isolation and "treatment."

- The American Psychiatric Association's *DSM* has gone a long way toward standardizing the diagnosis of mental illness. However, many researchers believe psychiatric diagnoses are arbitrary and merely amount to labels, describing behavior that is contrary to accepted social and psychological norms.

- Poverty is associated with high exposure to crime and violence, which creates stresses that can precipitate mental illness. In addition, lower-class social status is associated with a greater likelihood of being selected or labeled as mentally ill.

- According to the social-selection, or drift, hypothesis, low-class status is not a cause but a consequence of mental disorder. Mentally disordered people tend to be found in the lower classes because their illness has prevented them from functioning at a higher-class level.

- Research on the correlation between mental illness and such factors as urban life and crowding in the home has not produced conclusive results. Race also does not appear to be a significant variable by itself, but there are differences in the types of mental illnesses suffered by men and women.

- The two major approaches to the treatment of mental disorders are psychotherapy and medical treatment. The major forms of psychotherapy are psychoanalysis, client-centered therapy, and therapy and support groups. Medical treatments such as chemotherapy and shock treatment are applied to the most severe mental illnesses.

- Increasingly, psychiatrists are competing for patients with therapists who rely on insight methods. The services of the latter cost less and therefore are favored by insurance companies and many patients.

- Medical treatments often require hospitalization. Until the mid-twentieth century, this usually meant care in mental hospitals or asylums. However, long-term studies have shown that patients who do not improve enough to be discharged within a short period are likely to remain in the hospital indefinitely.

- The community psychology movement arose in the 1950s, partly as a result of the increased use of chemotherapy in the treatment of mental disorders. Many patients were released from mental hospitals to be cared for in community mental-health centers or halfway houses. The large-scale deinstitutionalization of

mental patients led to a variety of problems, including the tendency of such patients to end up among the homeless.

- Legislative efforts are under way to reduce some of the disparities in insurance coverage between mental and physical illness, a goal referred to as *parity*. Treatment of patients both within and outside mental-health institutions is difficult to achieve, however, because of the lack of coordination of medical and nonmedical treatment.

Key Terms

mental disorder, p. 70
mental illness, p. 70
deinstitutionalization, p. 71

residual deviance, p. 75
social-selection (drift) hypothesis, p. 80
psychotropic drugs, p. 84

total institution, p. 87
community psychology, p. 89
halfway house, p. 90

Social Problems Online

The World Wide Web and associated Internet resources contain a great deal of information about mental health. A user has many choices in investigating the relationship between mental health and homelessness. A good first site to visit is the NIMH's homepage at **www.nimh.nih.gov**. This site contains links to NIMH publications on conditions that affect many homeless people, such as schizophrenia. The National Alliance for the Mentally Ill, which advocates medical treatment of mental illness, has a homepage at **www.nami.org** that features links to publications and book reviews, many of which explore the interconnections between mental health and homelessness. It also presents updates on pending legislation, grassroots advocacy, and recent medical research.

A good Web site with a full range of links to resources on psychiatry, including discussion groups that touch on social problems such as homelessness, is Cyber-Psych at **www.cyberpsych.org**.

Most of the Web resources that are directly concerned with homelessness address the connections between poverty and lack of shelter, but several offer information on mental illness as well. The National Coalition for the Homeless has an interesting homepage at **www.nationalhomeless.org**; it emphasizes advocacy by the homeless and formerly homeless to "create the systemic and attitudinal changes necessary to end homelessness." It provides facts about homelessness and attempts to dispel some of the myths about mental illness and homelessness.

Research Navigator

Follow the instructions on pages 26–27 of this text to access the features of Research Navigator™. Once at the Web site, enter your Login Name and Password. Then, to use the **Content Select** database, use keywords such as "incidence," "depression," and "drift hypothesis," and the search engine will supply relevant and recent scholarly and popular press publications. Use the *New York Times* **search-by-subject archive** to find recent news articles related to problems of mental illness and treatment and the Link Library to find relevant Web sites organized by the key terms associated with this chapter.

Go to Research Navigator and find the article "The Borders of Healing," by Marianne Szegedy-Maszak. In what ways does the article reveal the similarities among victims of major disasters? Does the article suggest that the same kinds of treatments for people traumatized by disasters are effective across cultures? Explain your answer.

ALCOHOL
and other Drugs

Dominant Trends

- Daily smoking among teens has leveled off after years of steady decline. Exploratory smoking among eighth-graders declined from about 50 percent to 25 percent in the past ten years, but the rate of decline has slowed, and more high-school students are trying smoking, a signal that greater efforts must be made to prevent teenage smoking.

- A greater number of teenagers (52 percent) are finishing high school without ever trying illicit drugs, including marijuana, but among the minority who do try and use drugs, there are alarming increases in the use of prescription drugs and amphetamines.

- Adult drinking is a growing problem throughout the world, although far less so in Muslim regions, where drinking is often prohibited.

- Alcohol-related automobile accidents and fatalities have been declining in the United States, largely as a result of public campaigns against drunken driving, together with increased police surveillance.

- The "War on Drugs" continues to fail in its efforts to prevent large-scale importation of drugs into the United States, while it succeeds in maintaining historically high rates of incarceration for nonviolent drug-related offenses.

Ours is a drug-using society. We use drugs to ease pain, increase alertness, relax tension, lose weight, gain strength, fight depression, and prevent pregnancy. Americans of all ages and at all socioeconomic levels consume vast quantities of chemical substances every year. Most of these drugs are socially acceptable, and most people use them for socially acceptable purposes. Alcohol is a drug, as are caffeine and nicotine; these are commonly and widely used as aids to sociability and ordinary activity. But some drugs and some users of drugs are socially defined as unacceptable, and it is these drugs and users that constitute the drug problem.

The uses and abuses of alcohol and other drugs are discussed together in this chapter for a number of reasons. Through its personal and social effects, alcohol abuse is at least as harmful as the abuse of less socially accepted drugs. Moreover, many drugs, including alcohol, offer satisfactions that make them attractive to many people, but they can be habit forming, sometimes with destructive consequences to users as well as to nonusers; thus there are controversies over the causes, consequences, and moral implications of their use. Efforts to control drug use—particularly the "War on Drugs" that has been a cornerstone of American social policy against substance abuse for over twenty years—are increasingly controversial among political leaders and social scientists.

We will see that strategies of interdiction and control are often associated with other social problems, such as violence, racism, and crime. Drastic measures to prevent drug cultivation and importation can also have negative effects on democratic institutions, both in the United States and abroad, with little evidence of success in diminishing drug supplies. Moreover, despite the nation's huge investments in antinarcotics policies, experts on addiction continually find that alcohol abuse is far more prevalent and damaging to individuals and society than any other form of substance abuse.

Abuse of alcohol and other drugs is a growing problem throughout the world. One in four deaths of men aged 15 to 29 in Europe is due to alcohol, and addiction to opiates and cocaine is a growing problem in China, Latin America, Russia, and other nations of the former Soviet Union. Civil strife in drug-producing nations like Colombia and Afghanistan has multiple causes, but the importance of world drug markets as a cause of violence in these and other nations is undeniable. Although this chapter focuses primarily on drug problems in the United States, much of what is learned in this nation has a bearing on drug issues in other nations as well (WHO, 2005).

THE NATURE OF THE PROBLEM

From a pharmacological viewpoint, a *drug* is any substance, other than food, that chemically alters the structure or function of a living organism. So inclusive a definition, however, encompasses everything from vitamins and hormones to laxatives, snake and mosquito venom, antiperspirants, insecticides, and air pollutants. Obviously, this definition is too broad to be of practical value. Definitions that depend on context are more useful. In a medical context, for example, a drug may be any substance prescribed by a physician or manufactured expressly to relieve pain or to treat and prevent disease. In a sociological context, the term **drug** denotes any habit-forming substance that directly affects the brain or nervous system. More precisely, it refers to any chemical substance that affects physiological functions, mood, perception, or consciousness; has the potential for misuse; and may be harmful to the user or to society. In addition to the illicit drugs that attract so much attention, many pharmaceutical drugs are abused as narcotics (Henderson, 2005).

Although the last definition is more satisfactory for our purposes than the original, much broader one, it omits the social bias that has traditionally determined what substances are labeled drugs. When the members of a society have used a habit-forming substance for centuries, that substance may not be classified as a drug in that society even if it has been proven to be harmful. Alcohol and tobacco (nicotine) are examples of such substances, although there is a growing movement to classify nicotine as a drug (Day, 2002).

Drug Abuse

We can define **drug abuse** as the use of unacceptable drugs and/or the excessive or inappropriate use of acceptable drugs in ways that can lead to physical, psychological, or social harm. (See the discussion of drug dependence later in this section.) With this definition, there can be little question that the abuse of both legal and illegal drugs is a social problem.

Like so many other social problems, drug use has both objective and subjective dimensions. The objective aspect is the degree to which a given substance causes physiological, psychological, or social problems for the individual or the social group—the family, the community, or the entire society. The subjective aspect is how people perceive the consequences of drug use and how their perceptions result in social action concerning drug use (norms, policies, laws, programs, etc.). Of course, these subjective perceptions may be based on objective evidence, but very often they are based on past practices and combinations of scientific and folk wisdom about a given substance. Aspirin, for example, is one of the most widely used drugs in the United States. From an objective standpoint, we know that aspirin is often taken in excessive dosages for every real or imagined physical or mental discomfort. Aspirin can cause ulcers, gastrointestinal bleeding, and other ailments. But most Americans believe—this is the subjective aspect—that aspirin is a harmless drug that is dangerous only when taken in massive doses. Thus, aspirin use is part of our overall drug problem in objective terms, but not in subjective terms. For many Americans, the same failure to allow objective facts to shape subjective perceptions is true in the case of alcohol, as we will see later in the chapter.

Other drugs are part of the social problem of drug use because they are perceived as problems even if the way they are used by certain people is not problematic in objective terms. Marijuana is an example. Objectively, there is little evidence that marijuana users damage themselves psychologically or physiologically, although researchers believe marijuana may decrease the user's motivation to concentrate and learn complex material. Yet the subjective view of many Americans, especially those in policy-making positions, is that marijuana is a dangerous drug. This subjective viewpoint is incorporated into laws against marijuana use, and these laws, in turn, foster the illegal traffic in marijuana (MacCoun & Reuter, 2002).

The discrepancy between the subjective viewpoint and objective reality comes to prominence quite often in American political affairs. In 1992, Bill Clinton's admission that he had tried marijuana as a student but had not inhaled became the subject of innumerable jokes during the presidential election campaign. The question of whether George W. Bush had used cocaine as a young man while "sowing his wild oats" was a persistent issue during the 2000 presidential primaries. In the meantime, thousands of Americans are in prison for possession of marijuana. Facing a backlash from an important segment of voters, only the bravest or most secure legislators would seriously consider supporting a bill to legalize or decriminalize the substance (Souder & Zimmer, 1998). Most recently, however, legalization votes in Canada and efforts to make marijuana available for medical use in the United States have stimulated new and far more open debates about marijuana policies, as we will see in the Social Policy section of the chapter.

Other examples of this type of discrepancy could be added. The point is that drugs such as marijuana are treated as social problems within our society's dominant system of norms and institutions. Other drugs, such as alcohol and nicotine, are much less sharply defined as problems even though in objective terms their harmful consequences have been fully documented. In the past fifty years, as the harmful effects of smoking tobacco and heavy consumption of alcohol have been documented and have become a target of policies aimed at prevention and control, these behaviors have also begun to be defined as social problems. Nevertheless, these substances remain legal and continue to be sanctioned in many social settings.

Abuse, Addiction, and Dependence

The difficulty of separating the subjective and objective dimensions of drug use causes a great many problems of definition for experts in the field. The term *drug abuse* is widely used to refer to the objectively harmful consumption of drugs that are subjectively approved of, such as alcohol and tranquilizers. The term also refers to the use—in any amount—of drugs that are subjectively disapproved of, such as cocaine

Drug problems are by no means limited to the United States or other modern nations. In prerevolutionary China, for example, opium addiction seriously weakened the society by depriving it of thousands of productive workers.

TABLE 4–1	Lifetime Prevalence Rates of Use of Different Drugs among High-School Seniors, 2006

Substance	Percentage Ever Using Drugs	Percent Change, 2005–2006
Alcohol	72.7%	−2.4%
Cigarettes	47.1	−2.9
Marijuana	42.3	−2.5
MDMA	6.5	+1.1
Inhalants	11.1	−0.2
Cocaine	8.5	+0.5
Hallucinagens	8.3	−0.5
Tranquilizers	10.3	+0.4
Heroin	1.4	−0.1
Steroids	2.7	+0.1
Amphetamines	12.4	−0.6

Source: Data from National Institute on Drug Abuse (NIDA), 2007.

and marijuana, even if the objective facts about their effects in certain dosages do not indicate that they are harmful. Of course, almost all strongly addicting drugs, such as heroin, are harmful both to the user and to society at any level of use. But many other drugs whose use is considered abusive do not appear to be harmful when they are used sparingly or in small doses. Despite this ambiguity, the National Institute on Drug Abuse continues to support the use of the term, and we will use it in this chapter—except that we define drug abuse as *the use of a drug to an extent that causes harm to the user.*

Like the term *drug,* the term *addiction* is used rather loosely to refer to any habitual or frequent use of a drug, with or without dependence. In fact, addiction is a complex phenomenon that involves the drug user's physical and psychological condition, the type of drug, and the amount and frequency of use. Similarly, precise degrees of dependence are difficult to define because of the physiological and psychological complexity of drug use. Nevertheless, a limited consensus has developed among some experts, and certain definitions are considered acceptable. Physical dependence occurs when the body has adjusted to the presence of a drug and will suffer pain, discomfort, or illness—the symptoms of withdrawal—if its use is discontinued. The word **addiction** is used to describe physical dependence; **psychological dependence** occurs when a user needs a drug for the feeling of well-being that it produces. The word **habituation** is sometimes used to mean psychological dependence.

In the diagnosis and treatment of alcoholism, the terms *dependence* and *abuse* are carefully defined in *DSM-IV.* These definitions are used to determine third-party payments for treatment and to legally determine the presence of alcohol problems. Criteria for alcohol dependence focus on cravings, withdrawal symptoms, and other behavioral measures of feelings associated with alcohol consumption. The criteria for abuse include drinking despite recurrent social, interpersonal, and legal problems resulting from alcohol use. In addition, *DSM-IV* highlights the fact that symptoms of certain disorders, such as anxiety or depression, may be related to the use of alcohol or other drugs.

It is important to note that not all drug use is considered abuse in the sense that it impairs health. A person who is suffering from an illness that requires treatment with morphine, for example, might be addicted but would not be considered an abuser.

However, there can be no doubt that some drugs are not only physically addicting, but also dangerous to society because they compel their users to seek ever larger quantities to maintain a high. These highly addictive drugs can be a major social problem in that thousands of otherwise productive people may disappear from the labor market or become involved in an underground drug economy. The classic example is the city of Shanghai before the Chinese Communist revolution of 1949. It has been estimated that almost 500,000 residents of Shanghai were addicted to opium and had to spend hours in smoking dens each day. Earlier in the twentieth century, thousands of Americans were addicted to a form of opium known as *laudanum,* which they used for headaches and menstrual cramps. In North America today, cocaine is a popular drug that is used in moderation by some people. But its more powerful, smokeable form, known as *crack,* creates an intense desire for more of the drug and can be extremely addicting.

However one defines abuse and addiction, mere knowledge of patterns of use in the general population at a given moment and over time is an essential starting point. This is where social-scientific data play an important role. Monitoring of drug use by people who are arrested, large-scale surveys of alcohol and drug use, and national surveys of the incidence of mental illness—including drug- and alcohol-related disorders—are designed and carried out by professional social scientists. At their most basic level, these surveys establish the prevalence of alcohol, tobacco, and illicit drug use in the general population, as shown in Table 4–1. As noted in Chapter 3, **prevalence** refers to the estimated population of people suffering from a given condition at any given time. Table 4–1 shows the proportion of the population (high-school seniors in this case) that has ever used the substance, regardless of frequency.

Drug prevalence data are especially helpful in comparing the popularity of specific drugs in a population or a segment of a population, such as teenagers. Questions that ask about the use of illicit drugs in the past month, as reported in Figure 4–1, are especially helpful in tracking trends in drug consumption over time. The figure shows a significant decrease in illicit drug use by teenagers and young adults between 1979 and 1992 and a slight increase since then. Figure 4–2 on page 106 shows the increase in smoking among teenagers since 1988.

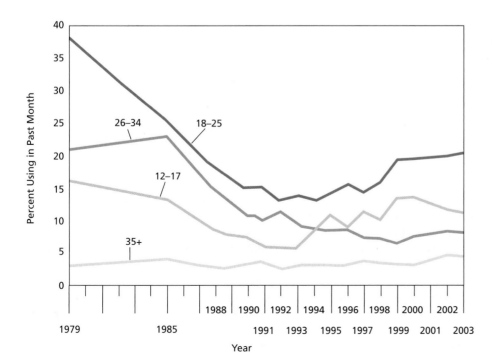

Figure 4–1 Illicit Drug Use, by Age: 1979–2003

Source: National Household Survey on Drug Use and Health, 2005.

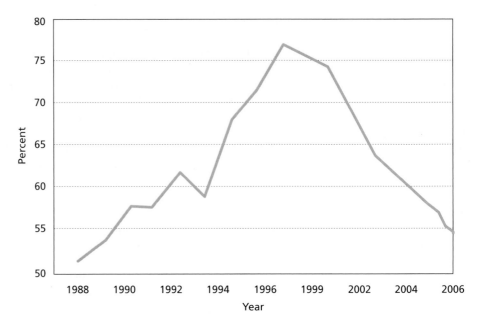

Figure 4-2 Percentage of Teenagers Who Have Tried Smoking

Source: Data from U.S. Centers for Disease Control and Prevention.

ALCOHOL USE AND ABUSE

On average, American adults consume about 22 gallons of beer, 2 gallons of wine, and 1.5 gallons of distilled spirits a year (*Statistical Abstract,* 2006). Despite these high rates of consumption, the problems associated with alcohol abuse—especially chronic inebriation, vagrancy, and drunken driving—arouse less interest and concern than the abuse, or even the use, of other drugs. In contrast to other drugs, alcohol is thoroughly integrated into Western culture. It may also be better adapted to our complex lifestyle because, in addition to relieving tension and reducing sexual and aggressive inhibitions, alcohol seems to facilitate interpersonal relations, at least superficially, whereas other drug experiences, even in groups, are often highly private.

In our society, people have mixed feelings about alcohol. On one hand, alcohol creates warmth and high spirits and promotes interpersonal harmony and agreement ("Let's drink to that"). It has long been used in informal rituals (Christmas eggnog) and formal rites (wine as the blood of Christ) and has been important in the economies of many nations. The growing and harvesting of grapes, grain, and other crops used to produce alcoholic beverages, as well as the brewing, fermenting, distilling, and sale of alcoholic beverages, provide employment, trade, and tax revenues. On the other hand, the problems created by the abuse of alcohol are staggering. They include public drunkenness and disorderly behavior, traffic and industrial accidents, poor social functioning, broken marriages, child abuse, and aggravation of existing conditions such as poverty, mental and physical illness, and crime.

The perception of alcohol as a social problem varies with changes in American culture and increased knowledge about the effects of alcohol use. According to some sociologists, in the early decades of the twentieth century alcohol was a symbol that masked the larger social conflict between the working class, with its large immigrant component, and the upper class, which sought to control the workers and increase their productivity (Gusfield, 1975; Szasz, 1992). In recent years the American public has become more aware of the dangers associated with drinking—for example, the damage it can cause to an unborn fetus and the high correlation between highway accidents and driving while intoxicated. Alcohol is implicated in about 40 percent of all fatal highway accidents in the United States and approximately one-third of all homicides, drownings, and boating deaths. These problems have led to crusades against excessive drinking rather than against alcohol itself. In the 1990s both the

Highway Safety Council and the Council for Accident Prevention reported significant declines in traffic deaths due to drinking and in home accidents associated with alcohol consumption. These decreases seem to indicate that crusades against excessive drinking are having an impact, and their success will surely reinforce efforts to educate the public about its risks.

Problem Drinkers and Alcoholics

According to the National Institute on Alcohol Abuse and Alcoholism (2004), in 1992, 7.41 percent of adults in the United States met the criteria for alcohol abuse or dependence. By 2002, this percentage had risen to 8.46 percent. The National Council on Alcoholism and Drug Dependence estimates that about 76 million Americans have been affected by an alcoholic family member (Small, 2002). Alcohol addicts, or **alcoholics,** have an uncontrollable need for intoxication, and if this need is frustrated, they will develop acute withdrawal symptoms like those of narcotics addicts—uncontrollable trembling, nausea, rapid heartbeat, and heavy perspiration. Some alcohol addicts have physiological symptoms after abstaining for only one day; in fact, alcohol withdrawal is even more likely than narcotics withdrawal to be fatal. Alcoholism may develop after ten or more years of problem drinking; however, many alcoholics go directly from total abstinence to chronic alcoholism. Such cases are believed to involve a complex set of physiological, psychological, and social factors.

Who Drinks?

Obviously, people are not alike in their drinking habits. Several factors seem to be related to whether, how much, and in what ways an individual uses alcohol. Among these are biological and socioeconomic factors, gender, age, religion, and cultural influences.

Biological Factors. Alcoholism appears to be due in part to biological factors (Bowes, 2005). So far, researchers who study the genetic factors linked to alcoholism are able to explain about half the risk for alcoholism faced by any given individual: "Recent genetic studies have demonstrated that close relatives of an alcoholic are four times more likely to become alcoholics themselves. Furthermore, this risk holds true even for children who were adopted away from their biological families at birth and raised in a nonalcoholic adoptive family, with no knowledge of their biological family's difficulties with alcohol" (Carson-DeWitt, 1999, p. 79). These findings are further supported by neurological studies showing that brain function is often different in alcohol abusers and their children. Studies of alcoholism and biogenetic factors also indicate that some ethnic groups, particularly Native Americans, have lower tolerances for alcohol than other groups do, putting them at greater risk for alcoholism, and that some Asian populations have highly negative physiological reactions to alcohol, which tend to diminish their risk of becoming alcoholics (Schuckit & Jefferson, 1999).

Socioeconomic Factors. Drinking appears to be most frequent among younger men at higher socioeconomic levels and least frequent among older women at lower levels. Members of the higher socioeconomic classes drink to excess less often; heavier drinking is found at lower socioeconomic levels and among young people (Kandel, 1991). When drinking is analyzed by occupation, however, a different pattern emerges: Business and professional men are most likely to be heavy drinkers, whereas farmers are least likely to drink heavily. Among women, service workers drink most heavily.

Gender. Recent decades have seen a dramatic increase in alcoholism among adult women. There are several possible explanations, but research has focused on the differences between female and male alcoholics. For both sexes, social factors—the presence of alcoholism in the family, childhood unhappiness, and trauma—are important influences. But for women, increasing rates of alcoholism seem related to their entry into the labor force in large numbers. One study found that married working women are more likely to become alcoholics than are homemakers or single working women. Yet the statistics on female alcoholism may be misleading. As women have become more visible in society, their drinking patterns have become more visible. Perhaps researchers are only now learning to identify the female alcoholic, and many women may still be hiding their drinking problems at home. Moreover, even if there has been an increase in alcoholism among women, it remains true that women have far fewer drinking problems than men do.

Binge drinking—consumption of large amounts of alcohol over an extended period— is a particularly dangerous behavior pattern because it often leads to violence, auto accidents, and other major problems. Bingeing is at least three times more common among male drinkers and among heavy drinkers regardless of gender. But binge drinking by pregnant women is a particular problem because of the resulting danger to fetal health.

Age. Heavy drinking among men is most common at ages 21 to 30; among women, it occurs at ages 31 to 50. In general, older people are less likely than younger people to drink, even if they were drinkers in their youth. (Drinking among young people is discussed more fully in the next section.) Drinking among the elderly is a hidden social problem, however, especially because statistics on alcohol use suggest that drinking diminishes with age. As a larger portion of the population is elderly, the absolute number of problem drinkers in this population segment increases even if the proportion of heavy drinkers (five or more drinks per day) is lower than in other age groups.

Religion. Regular churchgoers drink less than nonchurchgoers. However, within the former group, Episcopalians drink most heavily, and conservative and fundamentalist Protestants drink most lightly. More Catholics than members of other religions are heavy drinkers, whereas fewer Jews are heavy drinkers. One study linked the low rate of problem drinking among Jews with informal processes of social control, such as the association of alcohol abuse with non-Jews and a set of techniques for avoiding excess drinking under social pressure (Brown et al., 2001).

Cultural Influences. Among some groups, alcoholic beverages are normally drunk in moderate amounts at meals. Members of other groups drink after meals or on other occasions, sometimes to the point of drunkenness. It is the latter custom that seems to promote alcoholism, as is illustrated by a comparison of American Jews and Italian Americans, who customarily drink with meals and in the home, and Irish Americans, who are more likely to drink outside the home and/or not at meals. Most Jewish and Italian adults use alcohol and report having done so since childhood, but their rate of alcoholism is quite low; among the Irish, childhood drinking is less likely and alcoholism rates are much higher. One study (Vaillant, 1983) found that Irish Americans are seven times as likely as those of Mediterranean descent (e.g., Italians and Greeks) to be alcoholics.

The correlation between familial drinking patterns and alcoholism has been found to hold true for other groups as well. In ethnic groups in which drinking habits are established by cultural custom, alcohol abuse is rare. But in groups with ambivalent attitudes toward alcohol, including American Protestants and Native Americans, alcoholism rates are high; in particular, drinkers from groups in which alcohol is seldom used are most likely to encounter problems (Ford & Kadushin, 2002). In general, when children grow up with routine, comfortable exposure to alcohol within the family, they are very unlikely to become excessive drinkers when they become adults. Indeed, "the power of the group to inspire moderation of consumption is perhaps the most consistent finding in the study of addictive behavior" (Peele, 1987, p. 189; Small, 2002).

In the past two decades there has been a marked decline in drinking, especially of hard liquor, in many segments of the American public. This is especially true among upwardly mobile members of the middle class. The consumption of distilled spirits declined dramatically during the 1980s, and the consumption of beer also fell. Despite these significant declines, however, rates of alcohol consumption in the United States remain extremely high, and newer products like wine coolers and especially promoted malt liquors threaten to diminish the downward trend in alcohol consumption.

Marketers of alcoholic beverages have attempted to address the problems associated with alcohol consumption through advertising that promotes "moderate" or "responsible" drinking. However, one study identified a number of problems with such ads (Dejong, Atkin, & Wallack, 1992). Slogans like "Know when to say when" and "Drink safely" tend to ignore or gloss over the fact that no level of alcohol consumption is completely risk free; moreover, they do not place sufficient emphasis on the need for some people—drivers, pregnant or nursing women, and people using other drugs—to abstain totally. The ads themselves often undermine the message they are trying to convey; for example, they reinforce the idea that beer consumption is a reward for hard work, a form of escape, a means of promoting romance, and a way of obtaining comradeship, acceptance, and social identity (Kilbourne, 1991; Postman et al., 1987). They also seem to imply that abstinence is not socially acceptable.

Drinking Among Young People

Drinking by teenagers and young adults is among the most serious aspects of alcohol use as a social problem, especially because so many lives are needlessly ended by alcohol-related deaths and patterns of adult alcohol use are established during the teenage and young-adult years. In 2003 about half of all twelfth-graders and 20 percent of ninth-graders reported that they had drunk alcohol in the past month. Alcohol is by far the most frequently used illicit drug among teenagers (who are below the legal consumption age of 21)—rates of use are far higher than those for nicotine or marijuana (see Figure 4–1; U.S. Centers for Disease Control, 2004).

Teenagers who are defined as problem drinkers include those who have had confrontations with teachers or the police because of their drinking. Of these, only a relatively small percentage can be defined as chronically alcoholic. Alcoholic teenagers differ from other adolescent drinkers in that they drink more often and consume greater quantities, often with the intention of getting drunk; they are also more likely to drink alone, to display aggressive or destructive behavior, and to have severe emotional problems.

It is estimated that about 3 million people between the ages of 14 and 17 have problems related to the use of alcohol. Teenage drinking is directly related to social problems such as highway accidents, which claim thousands of lives each year.

The popularity of alcohol among young people is attributed to many factors, including the difficulty, expense, and danger of obtaining other drugs; low legal drinking ages; and the manufacture and advertisement of products that are especially appealing to the young, such as sweet wines and alcoholic beverages that resemble milk shakes. Alarmed at the increase in traffic fatalities caused by young drunk drivers, many states have passed laws that raise the minimum age for the purchase of alcoholic beverages.

Drinking among young people can also be construed as a rebellion against the adult world—an attempt to assert independence and imitate adult behavior. Some authorities believe strict regulations on drinking only make it more appealing. Moreover, prohibition of drinking by the young is extremely difficult in a society in which alcohol is widely used and relatively easy to procure.

Many young people turn to alcohol for the same reasons that their parents do: to have a good time, to escape from the stress of everyday life, and to conform to social norms. A recent study compared teenage males who abstain with those who drink in varying amounts; it found that those whose fathers are nondrinkers are most likely to abstain, but that abstainers tend to have fewer close friends. Moreover, abstainers tend to become somewhat isolated from their peers, the large majority of whom consume alcohol at social gatherings (Leifman, Kuhlhorn, & Allebeck, 1995).

Binge Drinking. Binge drinking among high-school and college students is a particularly serious group behavior and one that has been studied intensely by the Harvard School of Public Health College Alcohol Surveys (CAS). In this study, "binge" drinking among college students was defined, for male students, as the consumption of five or more drinks in a single drinking session and, for female students, as four or more drinks (Wechsler et al., 1998, 2000). The survey included more than 14,000 randomly selected respondents on U.S. college and university campuses. Most notably, the researchers discovered that in 1999, 44 percent reported at least one episode of heavy drinking in the year prior to the survey. This was the same percentage found in the first round of the survey, conducted in 1993, indicating that despite major efforts on some campuses and in the media to convince students that drinking in excess can be extremely dangerous, the behavior has not diminished (Hanson, 2007).

Violence at soccer games in Europe and Great Britain is directly related to binge drinking by youthful spectators. In the United States, similar problems of binge drinking at football games often leads authorities to ban alcoholic beverages at stadiums.

Worldwide, binge drinking is a serious problem among teenagers and young adults, especially in the more industrialized and urban regions of the world. In the United Kingdom and Ireland, about one-third of 15-year-olds admitted to bingeing three or more times in the past month, compared to about 20 percent in the United States. In those nations, also, binge drinking is associated with particular forms of public violence, especially at sports events. Soccer hooliganism, often involving older teenagers and young adults, is a serious problem associated with binge drinking (Lyall, 2004). In the former Soviet Union, public binge drinking is quite common and is often seen in the streets of major cities. But partially due to the cost of buying alcoholic drinks, about 18 percent of teenagers said that they had binged three or more times in the past 30 days (Plant, 2003).

Alcohol-Related Social Problems

Excessive use of alcohol contributes to many different social problems: murder, family violence and divorce, suicide, ruined health, fetal death, and many more. The United States spends approximately $130 billion annually on problems related to alcoholism (Carson-DeWitt, 1999). In this section, we briefly describe a few of these problems.

Health. On average, alcoholics can expect to live 10 to 12 fewer years than nonalcoholics. There are several reasons for this shortened life span. First, alcohol contains a high number of calories and no vital nutrients. Thus, alcoholics generally have a reduced appetite for nutritious food and inevitably suffer from vitamin deficiencies; as a result, their resistance to infectious diseases is lowered. Second, over a long period, large amounts of alcohol destroy liver cells, which are replaced by scar tissue; this condition, called cirrhosis of the liver, is the cause of more than 27,000 deaths each year in the United States (*Statistical Abstract,* 2005). Heavy drinking also contributes to heart ailments, and there is some evidence that alcohol contributes to the incidence of cancer. Finally, alcohol is implicated in thousands of suicides every year.

Drinking and Driving. Tests of the amount of alcohol in the blood of drivers involved in accidents have found a significant connection between alcohol and vehicular accidents. Drinking by drivers, pedestrians, or a passenger is involved in about 40 percent of traffic fatalities, accounting for about 17,000 deaths. In fact, however, as we see in Figure 4–3, there has been a steady decline in the rate of drunk-driving fatalities as measured by the number of traffic fatalities per billion miles driven by U.S.

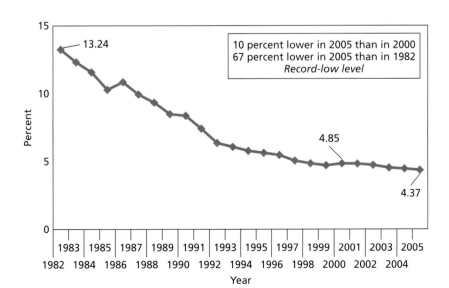

Figure 4–3 Total Drunk-Driving Fatalities, per Billion Vehicle Miles Traveled

Source: U.S. Department of Transportation, National Highway Traffic Safety Administration; Federal Highway Administration Annual Highway Statistics.

Note: Drunk-driving fatalities represent the total number of people (occupants and nonoccupants) killed in motor vehicle traffic crashes in which at least one driver had a blood alcohol content of 0.08 or higher.

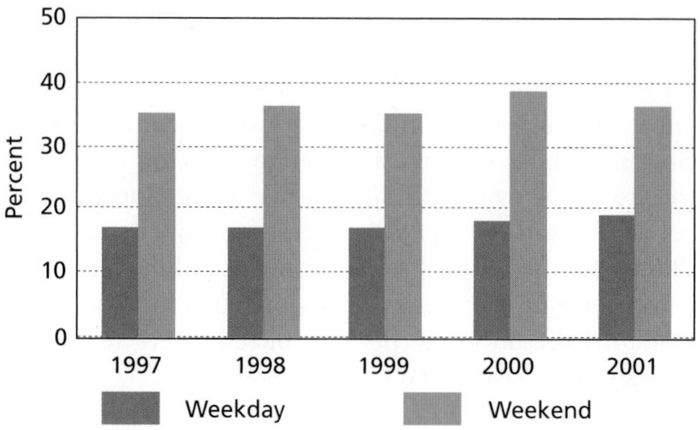

Figure 4–4 Alcohol Involvement among Drivers Involved in Fatal Crashes, by Day of the Week: 1997–2001

Source: National Center for Statistics and Analysis, 2002.

motorists. These declines can be attributed to social policies and enforcement. As states have adopted more uniform laws about driving under the influence of alcohol, and as more funding has been devoted to enforcement of these laws, we have seen welcome declines in alcohol-related driving fatalities. State police and other authorities credit much of this success to the activities of Mothers Against Drunk Driving (MADD) and other voluntary organizations. But 17,000 annual road deaths due to drunk driving is still a large number. Figure 4–4 shows that weekend drinking remains a major factor and that the percent of weekend drunk-driving fatalities has remained relatively constant.

Alcohol and Arrest Rates. In 2004 more than 1,160,000 arrests, or about 12 percent of all nonserious crimes, involved drunkenness or an offense related to violations of the liquor laws (*UCR*, 2005). These criminal acts were minor, such as breaches of the peace, disorderly conduct, and vagrancy. In arrests for major crimes, drunkenness generally does not appear in the charges, although alcohol often contributes to criminal acts. In many homicide cases, alcohol is found in the victim, the offender, or both; each year thousands of homicides are linked to alcohol use. A significant percentage of male sex offenders are chronic alcoholics or were drinking at the time of the offense. The rates for drinking in relation to skilled property crimes, such as forgery, appear to be somewhat lower than the rates for violent and sex-related crimes.

The reasons for the high correlation of drinking with arrests for serious crimes are not fully understood. It has been pointed out that alcohol, by removing some inhibitions, may cause people to behave in unaccustomed ways. Also, as with other drugs, the need to obtain the substance may lead to theft or other property crimes and sometimes to violent crimes like armed robbery. Since chronic alcoholics may be unable to hold steady jobs, their financial difficulties are compounded, perhaps increasing the temptation to commit crimes. Also, the values and self-image of chronic heavy drinkers tend to change as their condition worsens. They are more likely to associate with delinquents or criminals, which may lead them to commit criminal acts themselves.

In addition to its link with serious crimes, alcoholism creates another problem; it places a major strain on the law enforcement system, which must process large numbers of petty offenders. Arrests, trials, and incarcerations of offenders cost taxpayers billions of dollars each year. And many of these arrests involve a small segment of the community—the neighborhood drunk or derelict who may be repeatedly arrested and imprisoned briefly during the course of a year.

Effects on the Family. If the only victims of alcoholism were the alcoholics themselves, the social effects would be serious enough; but other people, especially the families of alcoholics, also suffer. The emotional effect, which is part of any family crisis, is heightened when the crisis itself is socially defined as shameful. The effects of "acts of God," such as fires, illnesses, and accidents, on a family elicit sympathy, but those of alcoholism produce negative reactions. The children of an alcoholic parent frequently develop severe physical and emotional illnesses, and marriage to an alcoholic frequently ends in divorce or desertion. Finally, because alcoholics are often unable to hold jobs, the outcome may be poverty for their families.

Families of alcoholics often cease to function well because of a pattern known as **codependency.** The spouse of the problem drinker, and often the children as well, frequently participate in a pattern of interactions designed to excuse the problematic behavior. Without thinking about it, they may aid the drinker in his or her behavior through various forms of denial. They may even help supply the drinks in an effort to reduce conflict or ease pain. As a result of these activities, they may themselves become dependent on alcohol, despite its negative effects on the family. In many instances the children, too, become problem drinkers later in life.

Alcoholism and Homelessness. Contrary to popular belief, only about 5 percent of all alcoholics and problem drinkers are homeless vagrants; most have jobs and families. Several theories have been advanced to explain the differences between the alcoholics who end up homeless and those who do not. Homeless alcoholics often want to separate themselves from their past, as well as to drink. Lack of social affiliation, a feeling that usually exists for a long time before the person finally becomes a derelict, is another likely cause. Homeless alcoholics have a strong need to escape from the realities of social life—an escape provided by chronic drinking (Rossi, 1989a).

Additional evidence suggests that in some cases alcoholism itself helps produce homelessness. Studies of homelessness in London and in major American cities agree that about half of the urban homeless suffer from alcohol addiction, but this research does not answer the question of the extent to which poverty and homelessness are the result of alcoholism (and addiction to other drugs) or vice versa. In both studies, about 20 percent of the sample said that they were heavy drinkers or alcoholics before their bouts of homelessness began (Fountain et al., 2003; Glasser & Zywiak, 2003). Many homeless men and women are alcoholics who formerly lived in SRO hotels; when the hotels were closed by urban redevelopment, they were cast out onto the streets (Kasinitz, 1989). Life on the streets for alcoholic men and women is extremely stressful and accounts for rates of heart disease that are three times higher than rates for normal populations at equivalent ages (Ober, Carlson, & Anderson, 1997). In the less developed regions of the world, there is also growing evidence that alcoholism is associated with a range of other social problems, including homelessness and the emergence of public drunkenness in urban centers (Beckman, 1995).

Treatment of Alcoholism

Rehabilitation. Alcoholism is increasingly viewed as an illness with a variety of psychological and physiological components; therefore, it is possible to rehabilitate, but not completely cure, many alcoholics (Brick, 2004). A variety of nonpunitive attempts have been made to assist alcoholics in overcoming their addiction or habituation and to help alcoholism-prone individuals handle disturbing emotions and anxieties. The Comprehensive Alcohol Abuse and Alcoholism Prevention, Treatment, and Rehabilitation Act of 1970 created the National Institute on Alcohol Abuse and Alcoholism (to coordinate federal government activities) and the National Advisory Council on Alcohol Abuse and Alcoholism (to recommend national policies). The act also provided grants to states for the development of comprehensive programs for alcoholism, grants and contracts for specific prevention and treatment projects, and incentives for private hospitals that admit patients with alcohol-related problems.

Traditionally, hospitals offered little beyond the "drying out" and release of alcoholic patients; they might treat a specific medical problem caused by alcohol, but not alcoholism itself. The American Hospital Association now advocates hospital alcoholism programs and is attempting to utilize the resources of general hospitals in community treatment programs.

Alcoholics Anonymous. The most impressive successes in coping with alcoholism have been achieved by Alcoholics Anonymous (AA). The effectiveness of this group in helping individual alcoholics is based on what amounts to a conversion. Alcoholics are led to this experience through fellowship with others like themselves, some of whom have already mastered their problem while others are in the process of doing so.

The organization insists that drinkers face up to their shortcomings and the realities of life and, when possible, make amends to people they have hurt in the past. The movement also concentrates on building up alcoholics' self-esteem and reassuring them of their basic worth as human beings. Since its founding in 1935, the group has evolved a technique in which recovered alcoholics support and comfort drinkers who are undergoing rehabilitation. This support is also available during crises, when a relapse seems likely, and on a year-round basis through meetings that the alcoholic may attend as often as necessary.

Alcoholics Anonymous has created special groups to deal with teenage and young adult drinkers. It has also established programs to aid nonalcoholic spouses and the children of alcoholics. Alateen, for example, is for young people whose lives have been affected by someone else's drinking. The alcoholic need not be a member of AA for relatives to participate in these offshoot programs, which developed out of the recognition that an entire family is psychologically involved in the alcohol-related problems of any of its members.

It appears that AA is the most successful large-scale program for dealing with alcoholism; it estimates its membership at over 2 million. According to the AA credo, it is essential for addicts to acknowledge their lack of control over alcohol use and to abstain from all alcoholic beverages for the rest of their lives. This approach sees alcoholism as an allergy in which even one drink can produce an intolerable craving for more. Although precise figures are not available, it seems that more than half the individuals who join AA with a strong motivation to cure themselves are rehabilitated (Brick, 2004). The voluntary nature of the program probably contributes to its success; however, it is unlikely that this approach, with its insistence on total abstinence, could be applied successfully to all alcoholics. This is especially true of alcoholics who reject the spiritual tenets of AA, which teach the recovering alcoholic to seek help from a "higher power," whatever that may mean to the individual. Alcoholics who are unwilling to accept these tenets can often find programs that are related to the twelve steps of the AA program but eliminate the spiritual aspects.

Antabuse. Antabuse, a prescription drug, sensitizes the patient in such a way that consuming even a small quantity of alcohol causes strong and uncomfortable physical symptoms. Drinkers become intensely flushed, their pulse quickens, and they feel nauseated.

Before beginning treatment with Antabuse, the alcoholic is **detoxified** (kept off alcohol until none shows in blood samples). Then the drug is administered to the patient along with doses of alcohol for several consecutive days. The patient continues to take the drug for several more days, and at the close of the period another dose of alcohol is administered. The trial doses of alcohol condition the patient to recognize the relationship between drinking and the unpleasant symptoms. (Similar treatment programs depend on different nausea-producing drugs or electric shock to condition the patient against alcohol; this process is known as **aversion therapy** or **behavior conditioning.**)

Antabuse (or Disulfiram) has gained only limited acceptance in the treatment of alcoholics. Critics claim that its effect is too narrow and that this approach neglects the personality problems of the drinker. They also maintain that the drug does not work for people who are suspicious of treatment or have psychotic tendencies.

Other Programs. A problem drinker or alcoholic who receives help while remaining in his or her family and on the job usually responds better than one who is institutionalized. Community care programs treat these problem drinkers, as well as their families, in an effort to improve their self-image and enhance their sense of security within the family.

Employee assistance programs, a relatively new development, have demonstrated considerable effectiveness in treating problem drinkers in the workplace. Their success depends on their availability on a scheduled basis and during crises, on the maintenance of absolute confidentiality, and on the development of rapport between the counselor and the patient as they explore underlying psychological problems such as loneliness, alienation, and poor self-image. Also important is the patient's desire to remain in the community and to continue working.

The Johnson Intervention. The Johnson intervention, a technique for intervening in the lives of alcoholics or drug abusers, is one of many "tough love" strategies that have emerged in recent years. In this approach, members of a person's social network confront the individual about the damage his or her drinking (or drug use) has caused and the action they will take if treatment is refused. In a study of its effectiveness, researchers found that those who had been subjected to the Johnson intervention were more likely to enter treatment than members of any of the other four groups studied. Moreover, people subjected to this intense pressure from family and friends were more likely to complete treatment than members of other groups who entered treatment (Ford & Kadushin, 2002; O'Farrell, Allwright, & Bedford, 2004).

ILLEGAL DRUG USE AND ABUSE

Commonly Abused Drugs

The major categories of illegal drugs are constantly changing as culture and customs change. In eighteenth-century England, the use of tobacco was forbidden; anyone found guilty of consuming it could be punished by such extreme measures as amputation or splitting of the nose. In the United States, cocaine was introduced to the public early in the twentieth century as an additive to a new commercial soft drink, Coca-Cola. Today the use of illegal drugs embraces an extremely diverse set of behaviors, ranging from recreational use of marijuana to heroin addiction. The most commonly used drugs today, in addition to alcohol, are marijuana, cocaine, the opiates (including heroin and morphine), hallucinogens, amphetamines, and barbiturates. Marijuana use was so widespread in the 1980s that the U.S. Department of Agriculture estimated that the plant ranked among the top five cash crops in some states. The use of cocaine has increased dramatically in recent years, and heroin continues to find a ready market in the United States. The spread of the smokable form of cocaine known as crack is the latest in the series of drug epidemics that have swept North America since World War II. As the crack epidemic wanes, there are indications that heroin use is increasing. Heroin is especially popular among former cocaine addicts. In addition, some young people are again experimenting with psychedelic drugs like LSD and XTC. In short, trends in drug use change quite rapidly, but the most serious social problems associated with illegal drug use have always stemmed from drugs that cause severe psychological and physiological addictions, especially the opiates, cocaine, and amphetamines (Fields, 1999).

Marijuana. Like alcohol, marijuana is a social drug, one that is often used in social gatherings because it is thought to ease or enhance interaction. This accounts for its popularity among the young, who in the 1960s considered it the hallmark of rebellion, as well as among many members of the middle and upper classes. Because the use of marijuana is widespread and there is little evidence that it has detrimental long-term effects or leads to the use of stronger drugs, the federal government has shifted its enforcement efforts to the more clearly addicting drugs. At the same time, the eradication of marijuana crops in the western United States and the interdiction of bulk shipments from the Caribbean and Mexico have reduced supplies, and some dealers have turned to trafficking in more dangerous but less bulky drug products like crack cocaine.

Cocaine. Cocaine, which produces a sense of greater strength and endurance and a feeling of increased intellectual power, can cause paranoid psychoses when taken in large quantities over time. Until the 1980s, because of its high street price, cocaine was viewed as an upper-class indulgence, a pastime of celebrities like actor John Belushi (who died from an overdose). Over the past two decades, cocaine use has become more prevalent in the middle and working classes.

Crack is a form of cocaine that can be smoked rather than ingested through the nasal passages. Commercial cocaine is "cooked" with ether or bicarbonate of soda to form a "rock" of crack. When it is smoked, crack produces an instant and extremely powerful rush that tends to last only about 15 minutes and to cause a strong desire for another rush. This form of cocaine is therefore highly addicting.

Crack is more expensive than cocaine in its powder form, and its use is often associated with an expensive lifestyle. Perhaps for this reason, some athletes, movie stars, and politicians who previously used cocaine have become addicted to crack, with disastrous consequences in some cases. The crack epidemic peaked in the early to mid-1990s, but prevalence data show that almost 4 percent of teenagers in the United States have tried crack. Clearly, therefore, the market for the drug still exists, with all the risks associated with it (Parrott et al., 2004). Violence linked with the distribution and sale of crack continues. In addition, the birth of sickly, low-weight babies with cocaine addictions formed before birth is a serious problem in communities where the effects of the crack epidemic are still being felt.

Heroin. Most heroin users experience a sudden, intense feeling of pleasure; others may feel greater self-esteem and composure. But because heroin slows brain functions, after the initial euphoria the addict becomes lethargic. The acknowledged relationship between crime and heroin addiction results not from the influence of the drug, but from the suffering caused by the lack of it: Withdrawal symptoms are avoided at all costs. Because addicts are seldom employable and a single day's supply of heroin may cost more than $100, most of an addict's day is usually devoted to crime, especially property crimes.

The typical lower-class heroin addict is under 30, lives in an urban area, has serious health problems, and has a greatly reduced life expectancy. The addict frequently suffers from malnutrition, as well as from hepatitis, AIDS, and other infections caused by intravenous injection of the drug. In communities where heroin addicts are numerous and visible, there is often conflict over the advisability of providing free needles so that addicts will not be forced to share illegally purchased hypodermics and risk the mixing of blood that may contain the HIV virus.

Recent evidence from drug markets throughout the world indicates that heroin is again becoming the drug of choice among international dealers, replacing cocaine as the preferred narcotic in many markets. Heroin is appearing in many variations; snortable and smokeable forms compete with the older injectable doses. As we will see shortly, drugs like ecstasy and amphetamines are used by specific drug subcultures, but heroin is the most sought-after drug in world markets, and its impact is likely to remain the most serious (after those of alcohol) throughout the world (Brzezinski, 2002).

Hallucinogens. Hallucinogens, such as lysergic acid diethylamide (LSD), distort the user's perceptions. Despite frequent warnings about "bad trips," studies indicate that long-term adverse reactions to LSD occur primarily when the user has preexisting mental problems. There are no data to indicate that the drug can cause either physical or emotional dependence (Brick, 2004).

Amphetamines. Amphetamines—called "uppers" because of their stimulating effect—are legal when prescribed by a physician, and many people become addicted to them through medical use. In some cases an overdose of one of these drugs can cause coma, with possible brain damage or even death. Amphetamine psychosis is likely to occur when amphetamines are used in high doses over a long period, and abrupt withdrawal may cause suicidal depression in a heavy user.

In young children, some amphetamine-type drugs actually decrease activity and may improve attention span. These drugs are often prescribed for hyperactive children and children diagnosed with attention deficit disorder. Ritalin, the drug most often prescribed in these cases, is the subject of a growing controversy among specialists in child development and education. International medical experts have criticized American physicians for prescribing pills to improve children's behavior without first attempting behavioral therapies. Parents often report that the medication has enormously positive effects on their children's performance in school and their social adjustment with peers. Still, the growing use of these drug therapies is alarming to some experts, who note that Americans took more than 350 million doses of Ritalin in 2000, an increase of 50 percent since 1994 (Murray, 1998; Park, 2001).

Ecstasy, Methamphetamine, and Other "Designer Drugs." So-called *designer drugs*, which are related to the amphetamines, are produced in illegal chemical laboratories, often using readily available over-the-counter pharmaceuticals. The most common of these drugs are MDNA (methylenedioxymethamphetamine), or ecstasy, which is often used in dance clubs that participants call "raves," and methamphematine, or "crystal meth." The latter is a speed drug, or "upper," which is sought after for its effects of reducing sleepiness and producing greater energy. After about two years of steady use, it creates a physiological addiction that is quite difficult to shake. Ecstasy, on the other hand, produces a feeling of empathy or love for others, along with a rush of energy and endurance. As a party drug, ecstasy is quite popular, but early findings show that in high doses it can produce serious illness and even death. There is, nonetheless, a thriving illicit traffic in the drug. Recent data show that teenagers are beginning to increase their wariness and disapproval of the drug, but at the same time, the availability of MDNA has been spreading more widely throughout the United States, Canada, England, and Australia (Johnston et al., 2002; Kalant, 2001).

Of all the contemporary designer drugs, none is causing more concern among law enforcement officials and medical professionals than methamphetamine. At present this drug, which is often manufactured in makeshift "laboratories" in people's homes and garages, is making headlines and appears to be gaining in popularity among teenagers and young adults, especially in rural areas and small towns throughout the nation. Because the drug can be produced using some over-the-counter cold remedies, in many states and communities there are heated debates about whether these medicines should be dispensed only with a doctor's prescription. Some experts on drug use fear that these debates will give rise to a widespread panic about methamphetamines similar to the panic that resulted in the disparities in sentencing for possession of powdered cocaine and its "crack" form, discussed in the On Further Analysis box on page 118. Whether or not these fears are justified, the illegal manufacture of this dangerous drug is clearly a major problem in some communities (Olive, 2004).

Abuse of Prescription Drugs. Abuse of prescription drugs is becoming an ever more serious form of drug use and addiction. The sensational revelations in 2004 that talk show host Rush Limbaugh had become addicted to Oxycontin, a powerful member of the opiate family of prescription drugs, called public attention once again to the availability and danger of a wide array of potentially addictive prescription medicines. Opium-derived pain medicines such as Oxycontin and Vicodin, benzodiazepine tranquilizers such as Valium and Xanax, sedatives and sleeping pills

On Further Analysis

IS THE U.S. WAR ON DRUGS A FAILURE?

While the war on terrorism dominates headlines, the U.S. federal and state governments spend about $30 billion annually on the War on Drugs, first proclaimed by President Nixon in 1972. The administration of George W. Bush has pledged its continued and strong support for the antidrug war and continues to oppose measures that would soften any aspects of the nation's antidrug policies. It opposes relaxation of mandatory sentencing for drug cases as well as legislation to allow medical uses of marijuana, and it pursues vigorous law enforcement policies to crack down on drug markets and drug producers in Asian and Latin American regions where addictive drugs are produced. These are policies that might be considered normal for a conservative administration, but in fact there is a good deal of controversy about the War on Drugs among conservatives themselves. Those who base their conservatism on religious beliefs tend to support the War on Drugs, but those with more secular and philosophical views are increasingly opposed to many aspects of the drug war. As early as 1996, the *National Review*, one of the nation's oldest and most respected conservative journals, made the following statement:

> We urge the stiffest feasible sentences against anyone convicted of selling a drug to a minor. But that said, it is our judgment that the war on drugs has failed, that it is diverting intelligent energy away from how to deal with the problem of addiction, that it is wasting our resources, and that it is encouraging civil, judicial, and penal procedures associated with police states. We all agree on movement toward legalization, even though we may differ on just how far. (*National Review*, 1996)

Conflicts over the success or failure of the War on Drugs can be confusing. How do social scientists use social theory and empirical fact to make judgments about the War on Drugs? Here are a few important questions that will help you draw your own conclusions:

1. Are drugs harder to obtain because of the War on Drugs? If law enforcement at all levels is effective in reducing drug supplies, we should see increases in the prices of drugs on the

Spectacular drug seizures like this one, which netted kilos of cocaine and hundreds of thousands of dollars in illegally transported cash, garner favorable publicity for the U.S. War on Drugs, which otherwise has not had nearly enough victories to significantly increase the prices of street drugs.

street. Where enforcement is especially effective, we should hear about shortages of illegal drugs and decreases in the purity of drugs as dealers "cut" them with additives. In fact, the opposite is true. Data from the 2005 Monitoring the Future database show that American teenagers report easy availability of drugs. The federal government's studies of the prices and purity of illegal drugs find that there have been no significant increases in prices that would indicate decreases in supply (U.S. Drug Enforcement Agency, 2002).

2. Are the high numbers of arrests for drug use and drug dealing, and the costs of prison terms in dollars and in human suffering, justified by decreases in street drug activity? In 2006 the FBI reported that over 45 percent of the approximately 1.6 million arrests for drug abuse violations in the previous year were for marijuana use, about 700,000. Of those, the vast majority were for marijuana possession alone. While this represents a slight decrease from the previous year, it is extremely small. With by far the largest prison population of any major democratic nation, the United States is spending billions of dollars on incarceration with no discernable effect on drug use or supply.

3. Is the War on Drugs changing attitudes about drug use and abuse? This is one area in which we can conclude that the War on Drugs has had modest but important success. Monitoring the Future and other studies do show that over time there has been a significant increase in the number of children and teenagers who disapprove of the use of marijuana and other illegal drugs. Success in public education supports what leaders of nations that supply the United States with cocaine, opiates, and marijuana have been urging for decades. By reducing the U.S. demand for illegal drugs—and public education seems to be one effective strategy for doing so—the United States would also be taking steps to reduce the profitability of importing drugs across its borders and avoid embarrassing itself by supporting drug suppliers in Afghanistan, Colombia, and other nations where many of our political allies are also involved in growing and producing dangerous street narcotics.

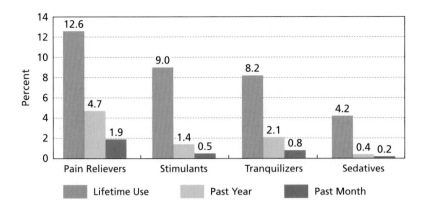

Figure 4–5 Percentages of the Population Age 12 and Older Reporting Nonmedical Use of Prescription-Type Psychotherapeutic Drugs, by Type of Drug
Source: NIDA, 2004.

such as Ambian and the barbiturates, and prescription amphetamines, often dispensed as diet pills, are among the most frequently abused of the widely available but heavily controlled prescription drugs. Figure 4–5 shows that pain relievers, which, because they are derived from opium, are among the most addictive prescription drugs, are also the most commonly abused. Most adults over age 40 who abuse or become addicted to prescription drugs first used the drug under a physician's supervision, as was the case for Rush Limbaugh. But young adults and adolescents tend to obtain the drugs through friends and street dealers. The National Institute on Drug Abuse reports that since the early 1990s abuse of prescription-type drugs has "escalated substantially" across the nation, especially among people between the ages of 12 and 25 (NIDA, 2004). The agency also warns that use of multiple drugs, known as *polydrug use*, is extremely common among abusers of prescription drugs. The mixing of drugs for nonmedical, recreational use has risks that are dangerously underestimated by users.

What do you consider to be the most dangerous drug available today? On what criteria do you base your answer?

Patterns of Drug Abuse

Who Uses Drugs?   The opportunity to use drugs is among the most important factors in illicit drug use. The National Institute on Drug Abuse (NIDA, 1980) reports that acquaintance with a user precedes the first experience with drugs. Although most people who use drugs are likely to pass up the first opportunity to do so, they take advantage of subsequent opportunities. Among professionals, doctors are most likely to use drugs and to become addicted to them because they have the most knowledge about these substances, as well as access to them. For the general public, opportunity and lifetime experience with drugs (more than one or two "experiments") are strongly related to age. Older teenagers and young adults are more likely to use drugs than are older adults, and the younger a person is at the time of the first opportunity, the more likely he or she is to eventually try the drug (Ray, 1996).

The study of drug use in the United States is a social-scientific undertaking of great magnitude. The data come from two major sources. The first source includes reports from public and private agencies that deal with arrest, hospitalization, treatment, or legal matters. These reports offer important evidence about trends in drug use among individuals arrested for crimes or admitted to hospital emergency rooms. But they do not tell us very much about the distribution of drug use in the general population. This information is obtained from large-scale national surveys, the second source.

In an annual survey, Monitoring the Future, conducted by the Institute of Survey Research at the University of Michigan, more than 16,000 high-school seniors are given a self-administered questionnaire (to encourage honesty) about their substance use. Conducted annually since 1975, this survey is an essential barometer of drug use among young Americans. Like all other surveys, however, it has its limitations; in particular, it does not sample young people who have dropped out of school, an important population in the study of drug use. Another important survey is the National Household Survey on Drug Abuse, which is sponsored by the National Institute on Drug Abuse. Other surveys that collect information on various aspects of substance use and abuse are quite common, but these two allow us to track patterns of use from year to year.

Data from the national surveys indicate that drug use among young Americans, and among Americans overall, peaked in the late 1970s, declined until the early 1990s, and began rising again after 1993—although by no means to the levels of the late 1970s. All surveys show that alcohol use among teenagers and young adults occurs at twice the rates of any other substance included in national prevalence studies. Analyses of the prevalence research and opinions about use also indicate that there is a pattern of "intergenerational forgetting" that helps explain these trends. As Lloyd D. Johnston, one of the key researchers in the University of Michigan drug studies, has pointed out, "Each new generation needs to learn the same lessons about drugs if they're going to be protected from them. Unless we do an effective job of educating the newer generations, they're going to be more susceptible to using drugs and have their own epidemic" (quoted in Wren, 1996, p. A11).

Johnston and other drug researchers note that there is an inverse, or negative, relationship between teenagers' disapproval of drugs and their use of drugs like marijuana. This relationship is shown in Figure 4–6, which traces the percentage of teenagers who admit to having used marijuana in the last year and the percentage who disapprove of drug use. Clearly, there is an inverse relationship between the two variables: The more teenagers disapprove of drugs, the less they tend to use or experiment with them.

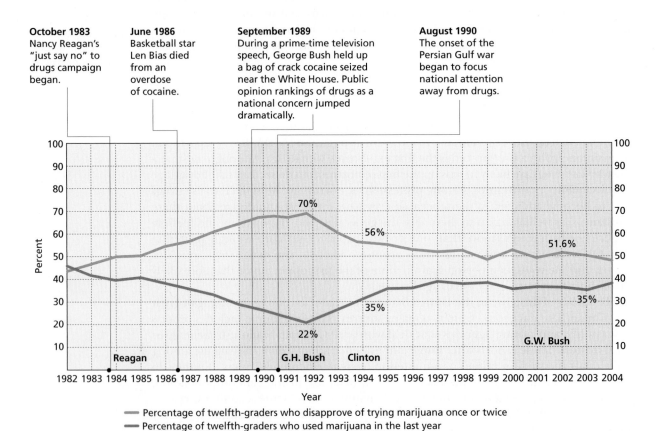

Figure 4–6 Attitudes about Drugs. *This chart shows the percentage of twelfth-graders who used marijuana in the last year, the percentage of twelfth-graders who say that marijuana use is socially unacceptable, and significant events involving drug use.*

Source: Monitoring the Future Study, University of Michigan Institute for Social Research. Copyright © 2005. Reprinted by permission.

The changing curve of disapproval appears to be sensitive both to the campaigns of national leaders and to such events as the arrest of famous athletes who experiment with drugs. In 1999, the Partnership for a Drug Free America, one of the leading public education groups in the movement against drug use, reported a significant increase in the proportion of school-age children who said that drug use is "uncool." On a more pessimistic note, the proportion of students who report that they can easily obtain illicit drugs has not declined appreciably over the past decade.

Marijuana use is an inadequate indicator of teenagers' predisposition to use or experiment with drugs and alcohol more generally. As marijuana use has increased somewhat in recent years, use of cocaine by the same age groups has continued to decline. Also, separate campaigns against tobacco and alcohol may contribute to the belief that of all the possibilities, marijuana is the least dangerous. Frequent use of marijuana can have very negative consequences, especially for young people, because it has been shown to severely diminish the ability to concentrate in school; it can also have deleterious effects on the respiratory system similar to those of tobacco (Brook et al., 1999; Parrott et al., 2004).

Surveys of drug use over time also provide information about its distribution by gender, socioeconomic status, and racial or ethnic background. Table 4–2, for example, clearly shows that there is more drug experimentation and use by men than by women (except among people with higher incomes, for whom levels of use by men and women are more similar). We can see in the table that people with lower incomes have a higher prevalence of illicit drug use in general, as well as a higher prevalence of marijuana and cocaine use. Other studies, however, have found opposite trends. A large-scale survey by Denise Kandel and her associates (Kandel, 1991) showed that affluent teenage students are substantially more likely to experiment with and use illicit drugs than those from modest and poor backgrounds. These differences in findings point to the difficulty of judging trends in illicit drug use from a particular survey, especially where students are concerned, because student surveys miss many people who are out of school and possibly in the labor force (Kandel, 2006).

Surveys of various racial and ethnic groups show that the prevalence of drug use is higher among whites than among blacks, with Hispanics falling somewhere between the two. The figures on annual use and use in the past month reveal that more white than black teenagers are probably frequent users, but this situation is reversed among older age groups. Among adults aged 26 to 34, for example, frequent cocaine users are a far smaller proportion of the population than individuals who have ever used the drug. And among black males in this age group, 5.0 percent had used cocaine in the past month, whereas 1.4 percent of white males had done so. These proportions correspond to the experience of people in black communities, for whom the presence of crack

TABLE 4–2 | **Prevalence Rates of Use of Selected Drugs among Full-time Employed Men and Women Ages 18 to 40 in the General Population, by Sex and Personal Income**

Annual Personal Income	Past Month Use of Any Illicit Drug		Past Month Use of Marijuana		Past Month Use of Cocaine	
	Male	Female	Male	Female	Male	Female
Less than $12,000	24.8%	8.4%	22.8%	7.7%	13.9%	5.8%
$12,000 to $19,999	19.6	9.3	18.9	7.4	10.0	7.3
$20,000 to 29,999	15.2	4.3	12.0	3.6	12.5	4.7
$30,000 or over	8.6	10.8	8.1	5.6	9.4	7.8

Source: National Institute on Drug Abuse, 1999.

cocaine addicts is perceived as a far more serious problem than it is in white or Hispanic communities. Because there are so many more whites, however, these proportions indicate that the number of frequent cocaine users is far higher among whites than among blacks or Hispanics (NIDA, 2003).

How Does Drug Use Spread? Most sociologists and social psychologists agree that drug use is a learned behavior that spreads through groups of peers who influence one another. In the pioneering study described in Chapter 1, Howard S. Becker (1963) traced the career of a marijuana user, showing that users must learn how to smoke the drug and identify their reaction to it as pleasurable. If they are unable to make this identification, they stop using the drug. They also gradually learn that the social controls that work against marijuana use—limited supplies, the need to maintain secrecy, and the definition of drug use as immoral—either do not apply to the peer group or can be circumvented.

The popular view that marijuana is a stepping-stone or gateway to stronger drugs is not supported by research. Becker (1963) found marijuana users to be "noncompulsive and casual" (p. 44), and the National Institute on Drug Abuse (1980) found that in 1979, 30 percent of high-school seniors who were using marijuana tried other illicit drugs. Findings from Europe—especially Amsterdam, where marijuana and hashish are legal—confirm the U.S. research, which shows that a minority of marijuana users experiment with more dangerous drugs (Donohew et al., 1999; Kandel, 2006). A 2002 study by the Rand Corporation found that "Marijuana use precedes hard drug use simply because opportunities to use marijuana come earlier in life than opportunities to use hard drugs" (quoted in Satel, 2005, p. f6). Because U.S. drug policy continues to view marijuana as a "gateway drug" and staunchly opposes legalization of the substance for medical uses, we will return to this subject in the Social Policy section of the chapter.

In explaining the spread of heroin use, Hunt and Chambers (1976) developed a disease model of "initiators" and "susceptible communities," and suggested ways to identify and contain the "contagious" individuals. Hunt and Forsland (1980) found

The U.S. government continues to strenuously oppose legalization of marijuana use for medical purposes, against the wishes of several state legislatures, including California's.

that addicts who moved to a Wyoming community from other locations were "not part of a coherent pattern of growing use (as are native users)" (p. 213) and that discontinuity eventually developed between local users and the newcomers because the latter were "not related to the original friendship groups" (p. 214).

Other research has provided additional evidence that "the most important direct influence on drug use is that of the peer cluster: 'gangs,' best friends, or couples" (Oetting & Beauvais, 1987, p. 133). However, other factors set the stage for involvement in drug-using peer groups. These include the individual's socioeconomic status and neighborhood environment, and the influences of family, religion, and school. For example, drug use is more likely when the family is not intact, when the young person has problems in school, or when the family is forced to live in a neighborhood where young people have ready access to drugs and are exposed to deviant role models (Oetting & Beauvais, 1987). Research on the use of addictive drugs, especially crack cocaine, among women indicates that personal traumas such as severe abuse or the loss of an infant can lead to relapse in drug use or to initial use (El-Bassel, Gilbert, & Schilling, 1996).

If the individual's social milieu contributes significantly to drug use, what effect might a change in milieu have? American soldiers who were addicted to heroin in Vietnam were generally able to kick the habit rather easily when they returned home (Robins, 1973). This shows that people are able to abstain from an extremely addicting drug when their social milieu supports nonuse. It is also an example of the phenomenon that drug researchers term "maturing out," that is, the tendency of drug users to decrease their use of drugs of all kinds, including alcohol, beginning in their late twenties (Neff & Dassori, 1998).

Like most other human behavior, drug use follows trends and fads. What are the recent trends or fads in illegal drug use that are notable in the United States?

Drug Use, Crime, and Violence

The nature of drug-related crimes varies with the drug involved. According to the classic and still definitive study by the National Commission on Marijuana and Drug Abuse (1973), "The only crimes which can be directly attributed to marijuana-using behavior are those resulting from the use, possession, or transfer of an illegal substance." Neither marijuana nor low to moderate use of barbiturates is likely to promote violence, "although high dose use of [barbiturates] has been known to cause irritability and unpredictably violent behavior in some individuals" (p. 159). Amphetamine users, in contrast, seem disproportionately involved in violent crimes such as robberies and assaults, and it is possible that these crimes are "directly attributable to acute reactions to the drug" (p. 160).

Heroin and crack are the drugs most frequently associated with various kinds of criminal behavior. Heroin and crack addicts can rarely support their habit without resorting to crime. In addition, they often already have a criminal history (Inciardi, 1999; Williams, 1992). Studies show that the crimes committed to support a drug habit tend to be money-seeking crimes like shoplifting, burglary, and prostitution. Although these crimes may provide 40 to 50 percent of the addict's income for drug purchases, one study estimated that almost half the annual consumption of heroin in New York City is financed by selling the drug itself, along with the equipment needed to inject it (Inciardi, 1999). All these crimes, considered nonviolent in themselves, nevertheless are often accompanied by violence: "Muggings and armed robberies will be committed regularly by some addicts and occasionally by many; even in burglary, violence may result if the addict is surprised by the victim while ransacking the latter's home or store" (Wilson, 1977, p. 156). The relationship between heroin addiction and crime is supported by evidence that "when the drug users are active in a therapeutic program and presumably not using heroin, criminal activity decreases" (p. 156).

The crack epidemic was also associated with criminal activity. Because crack is produced from large volumes of commercial cocaine, it is expensive; like heroin, it often involves users in the sale of the drug itself or in criminal activities designed to raise money to buy it. In addition, there is evidence that in some communities crack use has led to increases in female prostitution and other crimes (Bourgois, 1995; Inciardi, 1999).

A great deal of evidence indicates that crack and cocaine dealers contributed to the sudden rise in the number of violent deaths and shootings of innocent bystanders in large U.S. cities in the late 1980s and early 1990s (Bourgois, 1995; Williams, 1989). As the crack business became more competitive, with more dealers seeking to serve a steady or somewhat decreasing number of customers, there was increasing violence in communities where retail drug markets thrive. Despite declining murder rates, due in part to an easing of the crack epidemic, we can expect to see continuing use of heavy weaponry in those communities, because assault rifles and automatic rifles are readily available to drug dealers and distributors as well as those who attempt to rob them. (Gun control is discussed in Chapter 5.)

Over 80 percent of all prison inmates have a history of substance abuse, and about 68 percent of those arrested for crimes are drug or alcohol abusers (Bureau of Justice Statistics, 2002). This close association between crime and substance abuse does not prove that drug use actually causes crime. Other factors, such as early abuse, socialization into a criminal peer group, and the lure of seemingly easy gain, frequently help explain how an individual becomes involved in criminal activities (Weiner et al., 2005). But drug and alcohol abuse is clearly a contributing or facilitating influence in the majority of cases. Crimes committed by heroin or crack addicts, however, can often be directly attributed to the individual's efforts to obtain money to purchase illicit drugs (Lyman, 1996). Despite this situation, few probationers and prison inmates are enrolled in substance treatment programs (Blanchard, 1999).

It is evident that there are new patterns of organized crime in the illicit drug trade. New organizations not associated with older crime "families" have sprung up in American cities. They frequently resort to extreme violence in controlling local drug dealing. Since 1990 there have been numerous murders and other violent incidents among Dominican, Vietnamese, Chinese, Colombian, and Russian participants in the organized branches of the cocaine trade, as well as violent killings among native-born Americans of every description.

Drug Use and AIDS

We saw in Chapter 2 that a major means by which AIDS spreads among heterosexual populations is the sharing of needles and syringes by intravenous drug users. In large cities like New York and Moscow, AIDS is a leading cause of death among intravenous drug addicts (Kerr et al., 2005).

Public health officials were slow to realize the extent of AIDS transmission among intravenous drug users. Hence, they were also slow to initiate educational and other programs that might hinder the spread of the disease in this population. Educational programs that focus on sexual practices are inappropriate for this group; drug treatment programs and efforts to prevent addiction in poor communities are needed (WHO, 2005).

Efforts to reach addicts face a number of obstacles. Because their activity is illegal, addicts are reluctant to come forward to be tested for AIDS. Public health workers lack credibility in the eyes of addicts, and attempts to employ ex-addicts in outreach programs encounter resistance from law enforcement personnel. Proposals to give addicts sterile needles on an experimental basis have also been thwarted in many areas. However, needle exchange programs have been tried successfully in New York City and San Francisco, and New York legalized the programs in 1992. Research by Don Des Jarlais and his coworkers in New York showed that as a result of needle exchange programs, especially for heroin users, use of unclean and possibly HIV-infected needles declined from 51 percent to 7 percent. In San Francisco, researchers found that by 1994 almost 64 percent of intravenous drug users had used a needle exchange program within the last year (Paone, Des Jarlais, & Caloir, 1995).

In 2002, WHO sponsored a study of HIV prevalence in 103 cities throughout the world. In 36 cities with needle exchange programs, HIV infections declined by 19 percent annually, but in 67 cities without such programs infection rates increased by

8 percent each year (Campbell, 2005). Remarkable results like these provide strong support for needle exchange and other "harm reduction" programs that seek to reduce the ravages of drug addiction. However, their impact is limited by public opposition to programs that seem to condone drug use.

Outreach programs also face public opposition because it is often believed that narcotics addicts "deserve what they get." But perhaps the greatest obstacle is the attitude of the addicts themselves: "Ninety of 100 guys won't come in [for testing]," said one former addict. "They're either too high or else they're trying to score their fix. They don't want to know if they're sick" (quoted in Freedman, 1987, p. B7).

What is the actual connection between drug use and AIDS? Give an example of how a "harm reduction" strategy can help break that connection. Why do such strategies face political opposition?

Treatment of Drug Abuse

Efforts to rehabilitate narcotics addicts have been impeded by the notion that "once an addict, always an addict." Until recently, statistical evidence supported this belief, and the prospects for returning addicts to normal living were bleak. However, drug use spreads through the peer group and may be reversed with a change in social milieu. And drug use does not necessarily follow a predictable course from experimentation to addiction; instead, it encompasses a wide range of behaviors that may include experimentation, occasional use, regular use, and heavy use (Lipton, 1996; Lyman, 1996). These behaviors stem from the interaction of many complex factors, and efforts to rehabilitate addicts have not always addressed all of them. For example, until very recently it was thought that crack was so highly addicting that existing treatment programs and methods could not be effective. However, researchers at the Addiction Research Center in Baltimore have found that crack is less addicting than nicotine, but more addicting than alcohol. Nine out of ten people who experiment with cigarette smoking become addicted to nicotine; for crack, the figure is one out of six; and for alcohol, it is one in ten.

Crack addiction responds to the same treatment that other drugs require, but because it is especially appealing to people who are depressed and do not have strong social support from family and nonaddict friends, it is important to try to remove the crack addict from the social milieu in which the drug is used. This is the basic strategy of therapeutic communities.

This public service poster, originally the winner of a school contest, turns a familiar cigarette ad into a powerful warning.

Therapeutic Communities. Therapeutic communities are a way to attack the high relapse rate of addicts who are detoxified and returned to the larger society. They enable individuals to reenter social life gradually and at their own pace. This reduces the shock of moving from a protective institutional environment to the much greater freedom of the outside world.

One of the most highly developed therapeutic community programs is operated by Phoenix House. In the Phoenix program, addicts who have completed their treatment are transferred to a Re-Entry House for gradual reintegration into everyday life. Educational facilities are part of the program and include training in vocational skills and preparation for entry into other educational programs.

The Phoenix House approach rests on two key precepts: Addicts must assume responsibility for their own actions, and treatment should address psychological as well as physical difficulties. Phoenix House relies on ex-addicts, who are often more effective in breaking through the barriers of isolation and hostility. In addition, ex-addicts provide living proof that addiction can be overcome. In operation since 1968, the Phoenix House program has helped many addicts recover permanently.

Methadone Maintenance. Methadone, a synthetic narcotic, has been tested extensively and is now used regularly in treatment programs for heroin addicts. In prescribed amounts, it satisfies the addict's physical craving, preventing the agonizing symptoms of withdrawal. Although it does not produce a high, methadone is addicting and therefore offers not a cure, but a maintenance treatment for addicts who do not respond to other types of therapy.

Many people, including addicts themselves, believe methadone keeps addicts dependent on drugs and hence is useful only for a short time while the addict is weaned from heroin. Methadone treatment is sometimes regarded as a form of social control imposed by the dominant culture. (The substance is legally available only through approved programs, which require addicts to report to the treatment center for their daily dosage.) These ambivalent attitudes toward methadone treatment do not seem to deter potential clients. According to one survey, one of the major reasons cited by addicts for not entering treatment earlier was the absence of treatment facilities in their neighborhood (Lipton, 1996).

Narcotic Antagonists. Narcotics users who are weaned from their physical addiction often have a psychological craving for drugs as soon as they return to their normal environment. The need to overcome this problem led scientists to develop **narcotic antagonists,** substances that negate the effects produced by the opiates. By counteracting the positive sensations produced by heroin, narcotic antagonists help motivated addicts overcome their psychological conditioning to the drug.

Social Policy

Social policies that address drug and alcohol abuse take two main forms. One consists of control strategies—that is, attempts to help individuals or groups control their own behavior—coupled with efforts to build local institutions (e.g., residential treatment centers) that provide helping services. The other is law enforcement, meaning attempts to tighten the enforcement of existing laws or to enact new laws designed to deal with the problem more effectively. As control strategies were discussed earlier, this section focuses on law enforcement.

The simplest approach to a problem like drug abuse is to crack down on the sale or use of the drug. This was the rationale for Prohibition, in which the manufacture, sale, or transportation of alcoholic beverages was banned in 1919 by an amendment to the U.S. Constitution. Although Prohibition was repealed in 1933, the attitudes that gave rise to this approach are still in evidence. Chronic drinkers are still thrown in jail to dry out; people are still arrested for possession of a single marijuana cigarette; drug addicts still receive heavy jail sentences. In many places treatment is limited to incarceration.

Repeated arrests of chronic alcoholics merely perpetuate a revolving-door cycle. Offenders are arrested, processed, released, and then arrested again, sometimes only hours after their previous release. Each such arrest, which involves police, court, and correctional time, is expensive and may actually contribute to the labeling process in which an excessive drinker becomes an alcoholic and behaves accordingly.

In the 1980s there was considerable pressure for legislation to reduce the number of automobile accidents caused by drunken driving. In 1984 a Gallup poll found that 79 percent of Americans favored a national law that would raise the legal drinking age to 21 in all states, because statistics indicated that a large percentage of drunken drivers were under 21. Shortly thereafter, President Reagan signed legislation that would deny some federal highway funds to states in which the drinking age was below 21. Now all states require a person to be 21 or older to purchase liquor and beer (other than 3.2 beer in some states).

In addition to attempting to prevent teenagers from driving while drunk, some states have instituted programs in which motorists are stopped for sobriety checks during holiday weekends. Others require first offenders to participate in education programs that stress that alcohol and driving do not mix. Critics of these efforts point out that most drunk drivers are not social drinkers who have overindulged, but chronic alcoholics or problem drinkers. They claim that education programs will not change the behavior of these people; the alcohol addiction itself must be treated. On the other hand, groups like MADD call for strict legal sanctions against people who drink and drive.

Both educational programs and law enforcement efforts seem to have had some effect: The 16,189 alcohol-related traffic fatalities in 1997 represent a 32 percent reduction from the 23,641 reported in 1987 (National Center for Injury Prevention and Control, 2002). Authorities attribute this encouraging change to a number of policies, including direct campaigns against drunk driving, federal pressure on states to raise the drinking age, and the tendency of states to lower the amount of blood alcohol in definitions of drunkenness. But they also point out that much remains to be accomplished.

Many observers believe that the drug problem can be eased by revising drug laws so that they deal with issues more realistically and consistently. The most insistent demands for reform have focused on marijuana. It is considered illogical to classify marijuana with the far more dangerous hard drugs, and even people who do not favor legalization of marijuana may support reductions in the penalties for its possession and sale.

The legalization of marijuana for medical uses has created a major rift between several states and the federal government, which continues to pursue its War on Drugs and regards any movement away from strict enforcement of antidrug laws as an infringement of its authority. California, Nevada, Oregon, Washington, Colorado, and Maine have laws permitting medical uses of the substance, and in 2002 the small city of Santa Cruz made headlines because its mayor and city council defied federal authorities by distributing marijuana publicly after a raid by federal agents on growers of medical marijuana outraged local residents. In 2005 the Supreme Court, in a 6–3 ruling, decided that doctors can be barred from prescribing marijuana for patients suffering from pain caused by cancer or other serious illnesses. The ruling gave clear precedence to federal antidrug legislation over "medical marijuana" laws passed by the states. At the same time, medical use of marijuana has been legalized in Canada, and interest in similar legislation is growing in states throughout the United States.

In another 6–3 vote, the Supreme Court ruled that the Bush administration can bar the cultivation of marijuana for personal use because such use has broader social and financial implications.

With regard to hard drugs, some experts advocate revision of the law and, in some cases, legalization. One argument for the legalization of heroin is that it would drive down the price of the drug so that addicts would no longer be compelled to engage in crime to support their habit; the British system is cited in support of this position. The British view drug addiction as a disease that requires treatment, and they regulate the distribution of narcotics through physicians and government-run clinics. This system does not give addicts unlimited access to narcotics, but it eases the problem of supply. Those who oppose this approach fear that it might tempt people to experiment with drugs. Moreover, the British system is flawed because many addicts do not wish to register their addiction and prefer to find sources in the illegal drug markets (MacGregor, 1990).

What can be said about legalization is that each year more social scientists and law enforcement officials are taking its possibility seriously (Goode, 1999). It should be noted, however, that opposition to legalization is very strong in minority communities, where it is often seen as a form of surrender that is likely to trap even more poor minority people in addiction (Rangel, 1998).

On the other hand, there is a growing outcry in minority communities, and among many parent groups and civil rights advocates, over the continuing erosion of civil liberties in the face of the War on Drugs. Random drug searches in schools, drug testing as a requirement for all school activities, and mass arrests in some communities are giving rise to increased concern that the fight against drug use leads to abuses of government power. The ACLU, the NAACP, and many allies in the civil rights community, to cite one example, are bringing a lawsuit against the authorities of Tulia, Texas, where a biased and seemingly racially motivated drug bust resulted in the arrest of about 15 percent of the community's African Americans on charges of cocaine possession and sale. A jury made up only of whites upheld the arrests and sentenced some of the defendants, most of whom had never been arrested before, to sentences of twenty or more years in prison. At the time, the prosecutor was wanted on criminal charges in a Texas county where he had previously served as prosecutor, yet this information never appeared in court (Yardley, 2000).

The problem of enforcement at the national level is complicated by issues of foreign policy. Through economic and military aid, the United States supports the governments of countries that are major suppliers of illegal drugs, particularly Colombia, Peru, and Bolivia. It has been suggested that the United States should suspend foreign aid to governments that do not cooperate with efforts to stop the flow of drugs into the U.S. market. Other suggestions include imposing trade sanctions on those countries or reducing military assistance. The arrest in 1996 of Mexico's top drug enforcement official on charges of drug trafficking, and the subsequent problems of U.S.–Mexican relations, illustrate the influence of narcotics control efforts on foreign policy. (See the Social Problems: A Global View box on page 129.)

An issue that has generated a great deal of controversy is the testing of public employees for drug use. Appeals court rulings have reversed lower court decisions that such testing violates the Fourth Amendment to the Constitution, which protects citizens against "unreasonable searches and seizures." Many private firms are imposing drug (including alcohol) testing on employees in sensitive positions. This trend has become especially prominent since the *Exxon Valdez* oil spill in 1989.

The Bush administration pledged to renew the more aggressive aspects of the War on Drugs, especially by providing military assistance to drug-exporting nations like Bolivia and Colombia. Since the events of 9/11, the War on Drugs has taken a back seat to the war on terrorism, but the administration has continued to pursue policies such as crop spraying in Latin America and to seek stiffer penalties for drug use and sale within the United States. The U.S. federal government spent over $19.2 billion dollars—or about $609 per second—on the War on Drugs in 2002 (Office of National Drug Control Policy, 2002).

What measures do social scientists use to judge the effectiveness of the U.S. War on Drugs?

Future Prospects

Despite evidence that most aspects of the War on Drugs are not effective, and even have unintended negative consequences, there are almost no prospects for a full-scale

Social Problems: A Global View

DRUG CONTROL IN A BORDERLESS WORLD

The economies and political institutions of Mexico, Colombia, Peru, Bolivia, Barbados, and many other nations of the Caribbean and Latin America have been shaken by the rise of international markets for narcotic substances like cocaine. But the problem is not limited to the Western Hemisphere. In Europe and the nations of the former Soviet Union, the easy flow of drugs across relatively porous national frontiers is an ever-increasing problem of public health and national politics (Inciardi, 1999; Stares, 1996).

The relaxation of borders in Europe is a result of efforts to create a common market and improve the flow of goods and services among the European nations. A necessary step in this direction is to reduce border inspections, which has the unintended consequence of making the movement of illegal substances from one nation to another far easier. Marijuana grown in the Netherlands can be transported easily into France or Germany, which have more stringent laws about drug sales. And hard drugs like heroin and cocaine can pass more easily from Italy or Spain into southern France and then into the lucrative markets of central and eastern Europe and Russia.

In the Western Hemisphere it has proven to be extremely difficult to police national borders for drug shipments. As international trade among Canada, Mexico, and the United States has been encouraged as a result of the North American Free Trade Agreement (NAFTA), drug trafficking among these nations has been unintentionally facilitated. Recent scandals in Mexico, for example, reveal that there has been long-standing collusion between some of that nation's highest political officials and international drug dealers. Diminishing public funds for policing the international flow of narcotics also makes it more difficult to stem the flow of drugs across national boundaries.

---

evaluation and review of this long-standing and largely failed social policy. The political stakes, as most elected officials see it, are too high for them to appear to voters to be "soft on drugs."

GOING BEYOND LEFT AND RIGHT

Is there really a difference between the views of those on the left (liberals and others) and those on the right (conservatives of most descriptions) about drug and alcohol use and abuse? In fact, there are many differences, although there are no monolithic views on either side of the political spectrum. Too many people have had direct experiences with drug and alcohol problems for this to be a partisan issue. Nevertheless, there are some clear differences among major segments of the population. Think about these issues and choose among the following beliefs:

A. You believe that all kinds of mind-altering substances, from alcohol to most illegal drugs, are immoral and must be strongly prohibited. _____

B. You believe that what people want to drink or ingest is their own business, and the state should have no role in saying what they may buy or use. _____

C. You believe that mind-altering drugs like marijuana and LSD and the opiates and amphetamines are dangerous and need to be controlled, but you approve of moderate social drinking. _____

D. You believe that many drugs that are now illegal are no more or less dangerous than alcohol and should not be prohibited. _____

Do you agree with any of these strong but commonly held opinions? No doubt you do. *A* is likely to be a religious conservative, for example, a Southern Baptist or a follower of Islam. *B* could well be a libertarian who mainly desires less government and regulation; *B* could also be a conservative, but more tolerant of different behaviors than *A*. *C* could be on the right or the left. The majority of Americans, spanning all political divisions, drink in moderation (or hope and pretend they do) but feel that society needs to control access to other illegal substances. *D,* who argues against the criminalization of marijuana and other mind-altering drugs, is likely to be on the political left. But some conservatives also support this position.

To go beyond all these differences and divisions, one needs to go back to the facts about alcoholism and drug addiction. One needs to consider the ravages of alcohol in families and entire peoples, such as Native Americans. One needs to see the associations between alcohol and drug abuse and poverty and discrimination. These considerations lead to the idea that society as a whole, through its governmental institutions or its civic and community institutions, has a responsibility to devise policies to deal with the problems of alcohol and drug abuse.

Many conservatives believe that prisons should not "pamper" inmates and that offering them education, rehabilitative treatment, and counseling should not be substituted for "hard time" spent on prison chores and work programs. Many more liberal observers plead for more rehabilitation and drug counseling, and in the past have favored "softer" prison terms. Yet when one considers the costs to society of repeat offenders with drug and alcohol problems, it is clear that whatever our political beliefs, we all stand to benefit from prison drug and alcohol treatment programs.

Summary

- In sociological contexts, the term *drug* refers to any chemical substance that affects body functions, mood, perception, or consciousness; has a potential for misuse; and may be harmful to the user or to society. *Drug abuse* is any use of unacceptable drugs and excessive or inappropriate use of acceptable drugs so that physical or psychological harm can result.

- The issue of drug use has objective and subjective dimensions. The objective aspect is the degree to which a given substance causes physiological, psychological, or social problems for the individual or the social group. The subjective aspect involves people's perceptions of the consequences of drug use and how those perceptions result in social action.

- The word *addiction* is used to describe physical dependence on a drug, in which the body has adjusted to its presence. The word *habituation* is sometimes used to mean psychological dependence, in which the user needs the drug for the feeling of well-being that it produces.

- Alcohol use is widely accepted in Western culture, even though its abuse creates many complex problems. There are many problem drinkers and alcoholics (alcohol addicts) in the United States. It is possible that the tendency to become an alcoholic is an inherited trait.

- Drinking is heaviest at higher socioeconomic levels, among men, among nonchurchgoers, and in cultures whose members do not normally drink alcoholic beverages with meals. Alcohol is the drug that is most widely used by young people. Older people are less likely than younger people to drink, but as the proportion of elderly people in the population increases, so does the number of problem drinkers and alcoholics among them.

- Social problems related to excessive alcohol use include health problems, automobile accidents, criminal conduct, family disorganization, and homelessness.

- Attempts to help alcoholics overcome their addiction take a variety of forms, including group therapy (e.g., Alcoholics Anonymous), Antabuse programs, community care and employee assistance programs, and direct intervention (the Johnson intervention technique).

- The most commonly abused drugs are marijuana, cocaine and its derivative crack, the opiates, the hallucinogens, the amphetamines, "designer drugs," and some prescription drugs. Of these, by far the most widely used is marijuana.

- Drug use is largely a matter of opportunity. The younger one is at the time of the first opportunity to try a drug, the more likely one is to eventually try it.

- It is generally agreed that drug use is a learned social behavior. Users must learn how to use the drug and to identify their reactions to it as pleasant. The most important direct influence on drug use is that of the peer group. People can stop using drugs relatively easily if their social milieu does not encourage drug use.

- The drugs that are most frequently associated with crime and violence are heroin and crack; many addicts cannot hold jobs and must resort to crime to support their habit. Use of crack is also associated with criminal activity and with high rates of murder and violence in large cities.

- The primary means by which AIDS is transmitted among heterosexual populations is the sharing of needles and syringes by intravenous drug users. Efforts to prevent the spread of the virus in this way face a number of obstacles, including legal barriers and public opposition.

- Approaches to the rehabilitation of addicts include therapeutic communities, where individuals prepare to reenter the larger society at their own pace; methadone maintenance, in which a synthetic narcotic is used to wean addicts from heroin; and the use of narcotic antag-

onists, substances that prevent the euphoria produced by opiates.

- Increased emphasis on law enforcement has not solved the problems associated with abuse of alcohol and other drugs. Many people advocate reform of the law, especially for marijuana use. Some also call for legalization of hard drugs, but this remains a highly controversial issue.

Key Terms

drug, p. 102
drug abuse, p. 102
addiction, p. 104
psychological dependence, p. 104

habituation, p. 104
prevalence, p. 105
alcoholics, p. 107
codependency, p. 113

detoxified, p. 114
aversion therapy, p. 114
behavior conditioning, p. 114
narcotic antagonists, p. 126

Social Problems Online

The Internet is a valuable resource for exploring the social and medical problems associated with youthful alcohol consumption. The National Council on Alcoholism and Drug Dependence (NCADD) offers a concise but well-documented overview, *Youth and Alcohol*, which can be accessed at **www.ncadd.org/facts/youthalc.html**. This site stresses the negative health and safety consequences of drinking by young people and highlights some of the usage patterns and attitudes of the young toward alcohol.

The American Society of Addiction Medicine has a medical model of alcoholism, which can be found at **www.ncadd.org/facts/defalc.html**. The address of AA, the world's largest organization concerned with alcoholism, is **www.alcoholics-anonymous.org**. Reflecting its international breadth, AA presents a self-test on alcoholism, information for professionals, and a fact file in English, French, and Spanish.

WHO has an annotated list of its publications on European policy approaches to alcoholism control; these can be found at **www.whoint.en**.

The industry trade group DISCUS, the Distilled Spirits Council of the United States, has a policy of strong opposition to underage drinking. Its Web site is **www.discus.org**.

Research Navigator

Follow the instructions on pages 26–27 of this text to access the features of Research Navigator. Once at the Web site, enter your Login Name and Password. Then, to use the Content Select database, use keywords such as "alcoholism," "medical marijuana," and "methamphetamines," and the search engine will supply relevant and recent scholarly and popular press publications. Use the *New York Times* search-by-subject archive to find recent news articles related to problems of alcohol and drug abuse and the Link Library to find relevant Web sites organized by the key terms associated with this chapter.

Use Research Navigator to find articles about AA. What are some of the key features of AA that these articles describe? What are the "twelve steps" in the AA program? What evidence do any of the articles present to show that AA can be an effective intervention for alcoholics? Is the AA approach limited to alcoholism? Are there twelve-step programs that address the needs of the family members of addicted people?

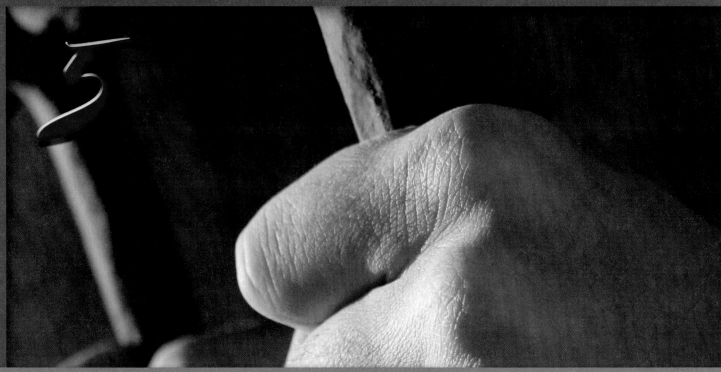

5

CRIME
and Violence

Dominant Trends

- Rates of violent crimes, especially murder and rape, are increasing nationally after years of decline. Only in the Northeast are crime rates still decreasing.

- With almost 1.5 million people in its prisons, a disproportionate number of whom are members of racial or ethnic minorities, the United States continues to lead the world in rates of imprisonment. No other nation jails as high a proportion of its citizens.

- The fourfold increase in the rate of incarceration in the United States since 1980 is due largely to the War on Drugs. Almost one-quarter of all inmates in federal and state prisons are there because of drug-related offenses, most of them nonviolent. Without changes in punishment policies, this trend will continue.

- Today crime increasingly occurs in a global context. The U.S. Department of Justice estimates that international criminal activities coming to its attention have increased by at least 50 percent since 2000.

- Scientific techniques, such as DNA analysis of crime scene evidence and studies of problems administering lethal injections, will continue to shape crime policies and practices.

Americans consistently rank crime among the most serious social problems in the United States. Depending on their concerns about such issues as health care or the state of the economy, they may rank these as more serious problems at a given moment. But for many decades crime has been ranked at or very near the top of the list of major social problems. During the past few years some crime rates have decreased. The public's perception of crime as a serious social problem has similarly abated, although it remains high on any survey list. At the same time, as we will see in this chapter, governments at all levels continue to invest heavily in crime control. As a result, the prison population in the United States has reached record proportions.

It is important to realize that at least some crime has existed in almost all societies. As the French sociologist Émile Durkheim (1895–1950) pointed out, wherever there are people and laws, there are crime and criminals:

> Crime is present . . . in all societies of all types. There is no society that is not confronted with the problem of criminality. Its form changes; the acts thus characterized are not the same everywhere; but, everywhere and always, there have been men who have behaved in such a way as to draw upon themselves penal

repression . . . . What is normal, simply, is the existence of criminality. (p. 65)

According to the *Uniform Crime Reports (UCR)* of the Federal Bureau of Investigation (FBI), between 2005 and 2006 there was a 1.3 percent increase in serious crimes, especially murder and robbery with a deadly weapon (*UCR*, 2007). Although it is too soon to know exactly, this finding may mark the end of the rather steady downward trend in crime that occurred during the economic boom years of the 1990s. Between 1997 and 1998, for example, there was a 6 percent drop in serious crimes, and the 1998 rate was 14 percent below the rate for 1994 and 20 percent below the rate for 1989 (*UCR*, 2002). The smaller reductions and recent increases in crime rates in the past few years reflect a more difficult economic situation, especially for poor and younger Americans, whereas the dramatic declines during the 1990s seem to have been associated with good economic times.

In this chapter we examine these and other trends in crime and violence more fully. We will see that there is a good deal of argument among experts about whether these trends are likely to continue. Another problem is that these statistics are based on reports provided by local police departments, which often contain errors of various kinds.

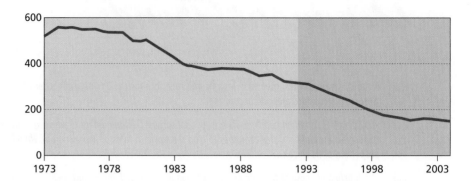

Figure 5–1 Property Crime Rates. *Adjusted victimization rate per 1,000 households*

Source: Bureau of Justice Statistics, 2006.

One reason for the disagreement is that it is extremely difficult to measure actual rates of crime. An annual survey of American households by the U.S. Department of Justice asks respondents detailed questions about their experiences with crime. This survey, known as the National Crime Victimization Survey of the Bureau of Justice Statistics, reveals that the actual rates of violent personal and property crime are several times higher than the official rates presented in the *UCR*, which are based on crimes reported to the police. Many victims do not report crimes because they believe nothing can be done or that the crime was unimportant. Sample surveys of Americans indicate that crimes reported to the police account for about one-third of actual offenses and about 50 percent of violent crimes (Bureau of Justice Statistics, 2006; Reid, 1991).

What are the two main methods for measuring the incidence of crime in the United States?

Even with a large proportion of unreported crimes, statistics showed a rapid increase in crime in the early 1970s. The crime rate continued to increase in the late 1970s, but in the early 1980s it leveled off. Beginning in 1985 there was a steady increase in the absolute number of serious crimes and in the rate of crime per 100,000 inhabitants, which controls for any increase in population size that alone might result in more crime. These trends continued until the early 1990s, when, as just mentioned, the rate of serious crime began to decrease.

In 2005, U.S. residents age 12 or older experienced approximately 23 million crimes, according to findings from the National Crime Victimization Survey. Of these, 77 percent (18.0 million) were property crimes, 22 percent (5.2 million) were crimes of violence, and 1 percent (227,000 were personal thefts (Bureau of Justice Statistics, 2006). Property crimes include theft (including automobile theft) and larceny (including fraud, embezzlement, and other white-collar crimes); violent crimes include murder, forcible rape, robbery, and aggravated assault. (See Figures 5–1, 5–2, 5–3, 5–4, and 5–5 and 5–6 on page 136.)

Figure 5–2 Four Measures of Serious Violent Crime. *Offenses in millions*

Source: Bureau of Justice Statistics, 2006.

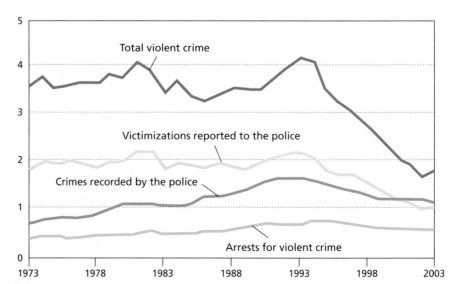

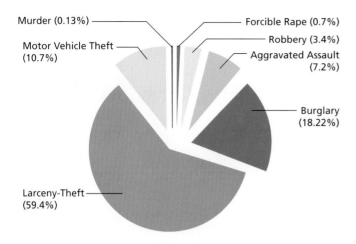

Figure 5–3 Crime Index Offenses, 2005 (Percent Distribution)*

*Percentages do not add up due to rounding.

Source: Federal Bureau of Investigation, *Uniform Crime Reports,* 2006.

Sociologists believe that the recent declines in crime rates were a result of the rapid increase in the number of prison inmates, the waning of the crack epidemic in the largest metropolitan centers, and increases in police forces throughout the nation (Krauss, 1996). Recent increases in violent crime may be a warning sign of a general upturn in crime, especially if the economy continues to produce wide disparities in well-being between rich and poor Americans. It is noteworthy that even the lower rates attained in recent years were higher than those in European nations.

The extent of the nation's crime problem is measured by the **crime index,** developed in the 1930s by the Committee on Uniform Crime Records of the International Association of Chiefs of Police. The crime index collects data on the most serious and most frequently occurring crimes—those that are most likely to come to the attention of the police. These include murder and nonnegligent manslaughter, forcible rape, robbery, aggravated assault, burglary, larceny-theft, motor vehicle theft, and arson. The statistics reported throughout this chapter are taken from the crime index.

Official statistics, of course, do not tell the whole story. It has never been easy, for example, to assess accurately the extent of organized and occupational (white-collar)

What are index crimes? Describe the two main subdivisions of the crime index.

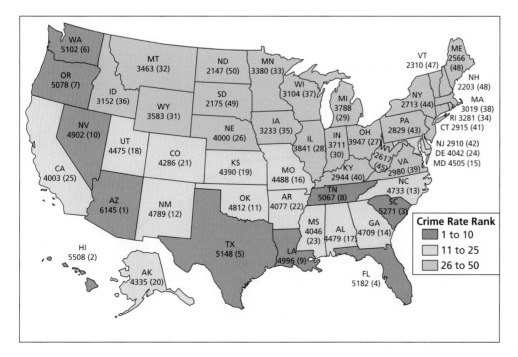

Figure 5–4 Index Crime Rate* and (Rank) per 100,000 Population, 2005

*Total index crime rates derived by adding reported violent and property crime rates.

Source: Federal Bureau of Investigation, *Uniform Crime Reports,* 2006.

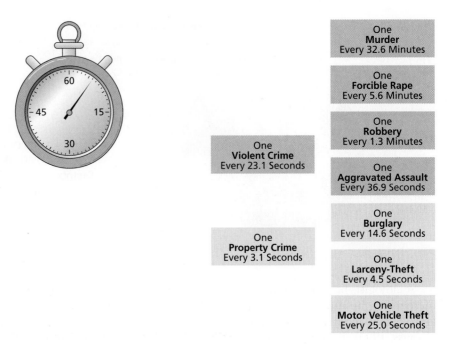

Figure 5–5 The Crime Clock.
The Crime Clock should be viewed with care. The most aggregate representation of UCR data, it conveys the annual reported crime experience by showing a relative frequency of occurrence of Part I offenses. It should not be taken to imply a regularity in the commission of crime. The Crime Clock represents the annual ratio of crime to fixed time intervals.

Source: Federal Bureau of Investigation, *Uniform Crime Reports*, 2006.

crime. Exposures of scandals in government and business show that these types of crimes are far more widespread and pervasive than is generally realized. Not only is the rate of crime itself extremely high, but fear of crime, especially in large cities, significantly affects the lives of many people. Large numbers of Americans feel unsafe in their homes, neighborhoods, or workplaces. Many have stopped going to places they used to go to at night, and fear of violent crime is widespread.

Sociologists who study the effects of media coverage of crime report that attitudes about safety in one's neighborhood and about going out at night in the city in which one resides vary directly with the rate of index crimes in that city; however, reports of crimes in other cities make people feel safe in comparison. The reports that are most closely correlated with fear of crime are those describing sensational murders in one's own city, that is, murders reported on the front pages of newspapers and on television.

Figure 5–6 Violent Crime.
Percent change from 2004.

Source: Federal Bureau of Investigation, *Uniform Crime Reports*, 2006.

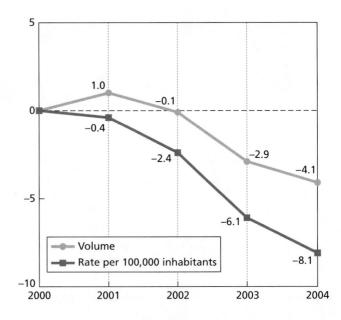

Less sensational murders, even in one's own city, do not have a measurable impact (Liska & Baccaglini, 1990; Schmalleger, 2000). Of course, the crimes that are most likely to generate fear are those that directly affect one's family and friends, even if they are relatively minor.

THE NATURE OF CRIME

There is no single, universally agreed-upon definition of crime. In the words of one of the world's foremost historians of crime, the late Sir Leon Radzinowicz, crime

> is something that threatens serious harm to the community, or something generally believed to do so, or something committed with evil intent, or something forbidden in the interests of the most powerful sections of society. But there are crimes that elude each of these definitions and there are forms of behavior under each of them that escape the label of crime. The argument that crime is anything forbidden, or punishable, under the criminal law is open to the objection that it is circular. But at least it is clear cut, it refers not to what ought to be but to what is, and it is an essential starting point. (Radzinowicz & King, 1977, p. 17)

According to this argument, a **crime** is any act or omission of an act for which the state can apply sanctions. This is the most frequently used definition of crime and the one we will use in this chapter. However, it should be kept in mind that definitions of crime are subject to changing values and public sentiments; moreover, as we will see shortly, factors like police discretion play a major role in the interpretation of particular behaviors as crimes.

The **criminal law** in any society prohibits certain acts and prescribes the punishments to be meted out to violators. Confusion frequently arises because although the criminal law prescribes certain rules for living in society, not all violations of social rules are violations of criminal laws. A swimmer's failure to come to the aid of a drowning stranger, for example, would not constitute a criminal act, although it might be considered morally wrong not to have done whatever possible to save the victim, short of risking one's own life.

Many acts that are regarded as immoral are ignored in criminal law but are considered civil offenses. Under **civil law**—laws that deal with noncriminal acts in which one individual injures another—the state arbitrates between the aggrieved party and the offender. For example, civil law is involved when a person whose car was destroyed in an accident sues the driver responsible for the accident to recover the cost of the car. The driver at fault is not considered a criminal unless he or she can be shown to have broken a criminal law, for instance, to have been driving while intoxicated. Further confusion results from changes in social attitudes, which usually precede changes in criminal law. In some states, for example, old laws that are still on the books continue to define as criminal some acts that are no longer considered wrong by society, such as certain forms of sexual behavior between consenting adults.

Police Discretion

In addition to problems of definition, such as ambiguity about whether loitering is a crime, certain other factors contribute to the difficulty of knowing what crimes are committed in a particular society. A significant factor is the role of police discretion. In practice, the definition of criminality changes according to what the police believe criminal behavior to be. Given the thousands of laws on the books, police officers have considerable discretion about which laws to ignore, which laws to enforce, and how strongly to enforce them. This discretionary power, in turn, gives them many opportunities to exercise their own concept of lawful behavior in decisions about what complaints merit attention, whom they should arrest, and who should be released (deLint, 2000).

Social Problems: A Global View

GLOBALIZATION AND CRIME TRENDS

Globalization refers to the increasing ease of movement of people, goods, services, and information across national borders and throughout the world. Globalization of the world economy is associated with the movement of manufacturing to low-wage areas of the world and the development of multinational corporations that do business in more than one nation (Stiglitz, 2002). But the same processes of globalization are also associated with new forms of crime, such as identity theft and money laundering using cybertechniques and the Internet, or new increases in old forms of crime like sex and drug trafficking and enslavement. Globalization has also encouraged the development of new organized crime groups and facilitated the recent wave of international terrorism (see Chapter 16; National Institute of Justice, 2005).

Trafficking in Humans

In legal terms, *trafficking* refers to "the recruitment, harboring, transportation, provision, or obtaining of a person for labor or services, through the use of force, fraud, or coercion for the purpose of subjection to involuntary servitude, peonage, debt bondage, or slavery" (National Institute of Justice, 2005). United Nations officials estimate that as many as 900,000 people are sold around the world annually. In the United States, human trafficking has become an important and highly profitable criminal market in the past ten years. An estimated 50,000 women and children are trafficked from foreign countries into the United States each year, most for employment that is not available in their own nations, and many for prostitution (Stein, 2003).

The main pipelines for human trafficking stretch from Asia, across Europe, through Central America and the Caribbean, to the United States, often involving multiple border crossings and many payments to corrupt border officials. The largest numbers of people trafficked to the United States come from the less developed regions of the world. The most popular transit route for Chinese, South Americans, and South Asians is through Central America and Mexico. Panama is a major transit point for migrants coming from Colombia, Ecuador, Peru, Cuba, India, and China. South Africa has also become an important transit point into the United States, and traffickers are increasingly utilizing the U.S.–Canadian border as a corridor into the United States.

Traffickers in humans often use a form of enslavement known as *debt bondage* to ensure that their victims cannot easily escape from involuntary servitude. People who are smuggled into wealthy nations by professional criminals typically owe their smugglers many thousands of dollars in addition to the funds they and their friends or families have already advanced to the criminals. The remaining debt can take years to repay, and along with threats about the physical consequences of failure to make payments, it serves to hold people in this form of slavery. Of course, this quite common form of debt bondage is applied to trafficked people in many kinds of work, not only in the sex trades.

Transnational Organized Crime

The majority of trafficking is conducted by global crime organizations. According to the National Institute of Justice (2005), "Transnational organized crime is organized criminal activity across one or more national borders. This type of criminal activity includes trafficking in humans, drugs, weapons, body parts, and endangered species; money laundering; and cybercrime." The breakup of the Soviet empire led to the widespread development of organized crime groups in the former Soviet nations. Some of these groups participated in the purchase of legitimate businesses, especially in oil and other energy resources, along with honest businesspeople, but invariably graft, corruption, and the collusion of political leaders were involved as well; as a result, in Russia and other former Soviet nations it is often difficult to separate organized crime groups from legitimate businesses.

In an important study of police discretion, Michael K. Brown (1988) compared police activities in two Los Angeles Police Department (LAPD) districts and three suburban towns in the Los Angeles metropolitan region. On the basis of interviews with patrol officers and their supervisors, he concluded that "a police bureaucracy has a significant impact on the behavior of patrolmen. . . . Patrolmen in the two divisions of the LAPD are formalistic and more willing to make an arrest in a variety of incidents than patrolmen in small departments, who are consistently more lenient and less willing to invoke the force of the law in the same circumstances" (p. 275). When asked whether they would normally arrest disorderly juveniles on their beat, for example, 28 percent of veteran police officers with five years or more experience in the smaller departments said that they would not arrest the offenders, whereas 65 percent of the LAPD veteran officers said that they would arrest disorderly juveniles.

Police discretion has become a controversial issue in Los Angeles and other major cities. In Los Angeles, where there are more street gangs than in any other U.S. city, the police have developed a policy of issuing what are known as "gang injunctions."

Revolutionary improvements in transportation (commercial air travel) and communication (the Internet) have decreased physical barriers around the world and made it easier for criminals to operate in other countries. For example, leads supplied by the FBI and eBay, Inc., helped Romanian police round up eleven members of a gang that set up fake eBay accounts and auctioned off cell phones, laptops, and cameras that they never intended to deliver (Grow & Bush, 2005).

Money laundering—the movement of vast sums of money from drug deals or other illegal activities—is another major form of global crime. A recent example is the U.S. government's indictment in 2004 of four individuals and two companies in connection with the laundering of more than $7 billion (some estimates range up to $10 billion) from a Russian organized crime syndicate through the Bank of New York. Another organized crime group with branches in Russia and elsewhere in the world was recently convicted of smuggling shiploads of the drug ecstasy from Amsterdam to Los Angeles by way of France, Korea, and Mexico, usually via Federal Express. The crime organization monitored the drug shipments on the Internet using FedEx's package tracking system (Ragavan, 2001).

The key to combating new forms of global crime entails far greater cooperation among the law enforcement agencies of the world's nations.

These women, some of them teenagers, are among the many who have been trafficked by criminals who illegally transport young women and men across international borders for purposes of prostitution.

The rise of global terrorism is encouraging such cooperation. As we will see in Chapter 16, the United States groups the world's nations into three categories or tiers based on the extent to which they are cooperating in combating global crime. The third tier, those with no or minimal forms of interagency cooperation, includes Burma, Cuba, Liberia, North Korea, and Sudan. In 2005 the president, acting on the recommendation of cabinet members, decided to impose sanctions on Burma, Cuba, and North Korea. Liberia and Sudan are also subject to sanctions.

These local policy orders target specific gangs and their members. They order people wearing gang colors off the street, and they ban driving or congregating with other known gang members. This is a response to demands for action to prevent gang crimes. But the wide use of gang injunctions has drawn the criticism of citizens who are concerned about the curtailment of personal liberties and civil rights. The Supreme Court has so far refused to rule on the use of gang injunctions, but the controversy further demonstrates how police discretion can account for important differences in the enforcement of laws from one community to another (Lipsky, 1980; Shoop, 1998). (See the Social Problems: A Global View box above.)

In a classic study of two groups of adolescents in the same high school, William Chambliss (1973) examined how the biases of the local police affected their treatment of middle- and lower-class delinquents. A group of middle-class boys (the Saints) had been truant almost every day of the two-year period during which they were studied. They drove recklessly, drank excessively, and openly cheated on exams. Yet only twice were members of the Saints stopped by police officers; even then, nothing appeared on their school records. The members of the other group (the Roughnecks) all came from lower-class families. Unlike the Saints, who had cars and could "sow their wild oats" in parts of town where they were not known, the Roughnecks were confined to an area where they could be easily recognized; they therefore developed a reputation for being delinquent.

The demeanor of the two groups of boys differed markedly when they were apprehended by the police. The Saints, who were apologetic, penitent, and generally respectful of middle-class values, were treated as harmless pranksters. The Roughnecks, who were openly hostile and disdainful toward the police, were labeled deviant. These results demonstrate that factors such as low income, unemployment, or minority status are not the only ones that have a bearing on the commission of juvenile crimes. Although these factors did account for a higher rate of detection and punishment, the rates of actual misbehavior in Chambliss's study were virtually the same for both groups. Differences in the official records of the two groups reflect the discretionary power of the police. Chambliss's experience with the empirical facts of police discretion and unequal application of state power has made him one of the nation's foremost critical criminologists (Chambliss, 2000).

Problems of Accuracy

Another factor that contributes to the problem of determining the level of crime in a society is that police statistics depend on police reports, which in turn depend on the level and quality of police personnel in a given area. Because police are assigned to lower-income communities in greater numbers, there is a tendency for police records to show higher crime rates for those communities and lower rates for more affluent areas.

If official data on crime are less than fully accurate on a local level, it is possible that similar problems undermine the accuracy of national crime statistics. The standard index of criminal activity in the United States, the *UCR*, supplies racial and economic profiles of people arrested for such crimes as murder, rape, assault, and robbery. Recent data support the long-held assumption that minority group members are more likely than nonminority individuals to be involved in crimes. Yet it must be remembered that *UCR* statistics cite only individuals who are apprehended. If, like the Saints in the Chambliss (1973) study, adult offenders in middle- and upper-class groups are rarely caught or punished, *UCR*-based data become inaccurate. Because it does not profile those who successfully evade apprehension and prosecution, the *UCR* fails to reveal the entire range of criminal activity in the United States.

Acting on this hypothesis, researchers have attempted to devise more reliable ways of tracking criminal activity. Self-report studies, which ask respondents to report their own criminal involvement through an anonymous questionnaire, have provided alternative data. Whereas minority groups have higher crime rates when judged by official data (such as juvenile or criminal court records or the *UCR* index), self-reporting techniques indicate that whites and nonwhites have similar rates of criminal activity. Thus, on one hand, the idea that race is a factor in criminality is called into question when different standards of measurement are used. On the other hand, some criminologists argue that although self-report studies question the distribution of crime in the population, they do not show significant differences in levels of crime from those shown in the *UCR* (Maltz, 1999).

Another attempt to supplement *UCR* data has led to the development of **victimization reports.** These surveys, conducted by the Census Bureau, collect information from a representative sample of crime victims. Comparisons of *UCR* and victimization indexes reveal discrepancies in the data, and depending on which standard is used, different conclusions can be drawn about the correlation between crime and socioeconomic status (Reid, 1993). The *UCR* data reflect only crimes that are reported, yet many victims—through fear, ignorance, or alienation—do not file reports. Victimization surveys indicate that this is particularly true in low-income, high-crime areas. Certain crimes—especially sex-related crimes such as rape and child molestation—are underreported, and the statistics are distorted as a result.

In sum, it appears that the poor, the undereducated, and minority groups have become the victims of selective law enforcement, stereotyping, and misleading statistics. The rich and powerful, in contrast, have been insulated from these problems; they are so seldom sent to prison that when one of them is finally jailed for fraud, embezzlement, or tax evasion, it makes headlines. Some sociologists, noting the difficulty of obtaining accurate information on the incidence of these crimes, have contended that the upper classes may actually have a higher rate of crime than the lower classes (Pepinsky & Quinney, 1991; Reckless, 1973). The discovery of criminal dealings by high officials of Enron and other U.S. corporations in recent years reinforces this hypothesis. It will be helpful to keep these contrasts in mind as we discuss the various types of crimes, including corporate crime.

TYPES OF CRIMES AND CRIMINALS

In this section we review nine major types of crimes and criminals (Siegel, 1999). Six of them have been classified by sociologists according to how large a part criminal activity plays in people's lives; that is, whether or not people see themselves as criminals and the extent to which they commit themselves to a life of crime. To these we add a seventh category, juvenile delinquency, and an eighth, corporate crimes. Two forms of illegal activity—occupational and organized crime—receive more extensive treatment here because their social costs probably exceed those of all the others combined. Hate crimes, a ninth category, are not accorded official status in all states, but the increase in such crimes is an important exception to the recent decline in U.S. crime rates and a subject of much current debate.

Violent Personal Crimes

Violent personal crimes include assault, robbery, and various types of homicide—acts in which physical injury is inflicted or threatened. Although robbery occurs most often between strangers, murders are very often a result of violent disputes between friends or relatives. About 45 out of every 100 murder victims are related to or

Although we think of ourselves as a peace-loving people, we continually resort to violence in defense of what we consider our vital interests. The American Civil War was among the bloodiest in world history.

acquainted with their assailants, and murders initiated by arguments (as opposed to premeditated murders) accounted for over 25 percent of all murders. Murders and aggravated assaults, therefore, are usually considered unpremeditated acts. The offenders are portrayed in the media as normally law-abiding individuals who are not likely to engage in other criminal activities. Some murders may be contract murders, which are committed by hired killers and often linked to organized crime. When weapons are involved, guns account for about 70 percent of murders (*UCR*, 2006).

Despite signs of progress, the level of deadly violence remains higher in the United States than in any other urban industrial nation. Although rates of interpersonal violence may be higher in a few poorer nations, no major industrialized nation has homicide rates as high as those in the United States. For black men in the United States, the chances of living beyond age 40 are worse than in the poorest nations of the world, mainly because of the toll taken by violence. The widespread availability of guns and the contribution of drugs to violence are important factors in this situation, but those who study the problem also point to the pervasiveness of violence in our culture. Increasingly frequent incidents of aggressive driving, often referred to as "road rage," increases in fights at sports events and school outings, rising rates of family violence, and outbreaks of deadly violence in workplaces have drawn attention to the underlying levels of interpersonal violence that result in spectacular and grisly headlines (Elvin, 1999).

Much violent action throughout the world is not recognized as such. This is particularly true of violence associated with the rise or expansion of a political party or social movement; most groups try to forget, justify, or disguise their use of violence for these purposes. Whereas extralegal violent acts like murder, rape, or gang wars elicit public condemnation, other forms of violence are accepted or even praised—for example, those that occur in war. Similarly, in troubled times and in frontier areas, vigilante activities are often approved by the local community as the only available means of maintaining order. In general, violence by or on behalf of the state is less likely to be condemned than violent personal crimes.

Criminal Homicide. Criminal homicide takes two forms: **Murder** is defined as the unlawful killing of a human being with malice aforethought; **manslaughter** is unlawful homicide without malice aforethought. In practice, it is often difficult to distinguish between them. Someone may attack another person without intending to kill, but the attack may result in death. Depending on the circumstances, one case might be judged to be murder and another to be manslaughter. Often the deciding factor is the extent to which the victim is believed to have provoked the assailant.

Paradoxically, most murderers do not have a criminal record. Of course, there are those who use actual or threatened violence as tools in a criminal career, but these are exceptions. As a rule, professional criminals try to keep violence—especially killing—to a "necessary" minimum because of the "heat" it would bring from the law. Most murderers do not see themselves as real criminals, and until the murder occurs, neither does society. Murderers do not conform to any criminal stereotype, and murder is not usually part of a criminal career.

Murder does, however, follow certain social and geographic patterns. Reported murders occur most often in large cities. The murder rate for large metropolitan areas is about 6 per 100,000 people, compared to about 4 per 100,000 in rural counties and 3.5 per 100,000 in cities outside metropolitan areas (*UCR*, 2006). The incidence of murder is unevenly distributed within cities; as Donald T. Lunde (1975) has pointed out, "Most city neighborhoods are just as safe as the suburbs" (p. 38). There are also regional differences; for example, murder is more likely to occur in the South, even though it is one of the more rural parts of the country. This seems to be a result of the culture of the region, which tends to legitimize personal violence and the use of weapons.

Most murderers are men, who generally are socialized to be more violent than women and to use guns for recreation or for military purposes; guns are the most common murder weapon. Many murderers are young; about 45 percent of those arrested

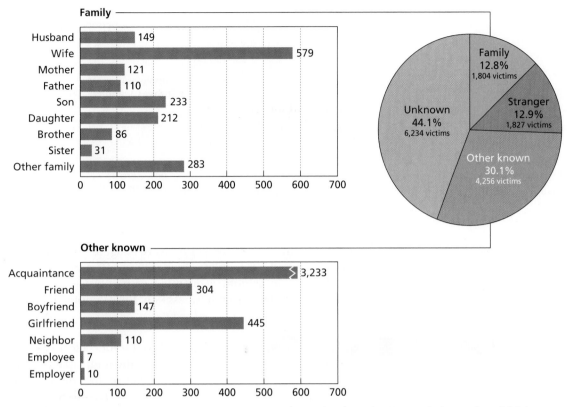

Figure 5–7 **Murder by Relationship**[1]. *Percent Distribution*[2] *Volume by Known Relationship, 2004*

[1]Relationship is that of victim to offender.

[2]Due to rounding, the percentages may not add to 100.0.

Source: Federal Bureau of Investigation, *Uniform Crime Reports*, 2006.

for murder are between the ages of 17 and 34. The victims are young too; about 55 percent are between the ages of 17 and 34 (*UCR*, 2006). More than half of all murder victims are members of minority groups. Most of the time, the killer and the victim are of the same race. In 2004, 85 percent of white murder victims were slain by white offenders, and about 90 percent of black victims were slain by black offenders (*UCR*, 2006).

More significant than the demographic characteristics of murderers and their victims is the relationship between them. Several studies have indicated that this relationship is generally close; often the murderer is a member of the victim's family or an intimate friend. A high proportion of murderers are relatives of their victim, often the spouse. These relationships between murderers and their victims are clearly shown in Figure 5–7. Note the disproportionate number of wives and girlfriends among victims, a stark indicator of the high rates of violence against women in American society.

Most murders occur during a quarrel between two people who know each other well. Both the murderer and the victim may have been drinking, perhaps together, before the event. Even though many homicides occur during the commission of other crimes, these killings, too, are usually unpremeditated—a thief surprised by a security officer, a bank robber confronted by an armed guard, and so on. In addition, some homicides involve police officers, many of whom are killed in the line of duty.

Police officers who are killed in the line of duty are usually attempting to make an arrest, but as Figure 5–8 on page 144 shows, many of their routine duties, such as traffic stops or answering disturbance calls, can also turn deadly for them.

The mentally ill commit murder at the same rate as the general population, but serial killers are almost always psychotic—either paranoid or sexual sadists (Nocera, 1999). These murderers may hear voices commanding them to kill, think they are

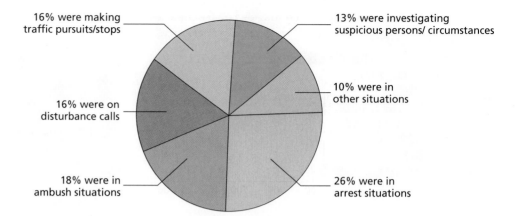

16% were making traffic pursuits/stops

13% were investigating suspicious persons/ circumstances

16% were on disturbance calls

10% were in other situations

18% were in ambush situations

26% were in arrest situations

Figure 5–8 Situations in Which Police Officers Were Killed in the Line of Duty, 2004

Source: Federal Bureau of Investigation, *Uniform Crime Reports*, 2006.

superhuman or chosen for a special mission, or kill to avert imagined persecution. Sadists may torture before killing and/or mutilate their victims afterwards. Unlike most murderers, psychotic killers are seldom acquainted with their victims, who are often representatives of a type or class—rich businessmen, for example, or young middle-class women.

Mass Murderers and Serial Killers. He was a Boy Scout leader, a leader of his church, a father and husband, and a steady worker at his job in the municipal government, but his secret identity was that of a social monster, known by his own designation as the BTK Killer (for bind, torture, and kill). In the summer of 2005 Dennis Rader was sentenced to death after confessing to ten horrible slayings of women between 1974 and 1991. He had first stalked the women and then tortured them, all the while eluding capture and taunting the Wichita, Kansas, police with anonymous notes (Susman, 2005).

Although the people of Wichita were immensely relieved that the murderer who had terrorized their community for so long was finally locked up, the Rader case is another reminder of our society's vulnerability to terroristic acts, whether they are motivated by political ideologies or by psychotic individuals like Rader. There is some

Apprehended in 2005 after years of brutal serial killings in and around Wichita, Kansas, Dennis Rader, the infamous BTK killer, turned out to be hiding the murderous side of his personality while posing as a family man and dedicated leader of his church congregation.

evidence that mass murders (in which four or more people are killed by the same person in a short time) are becoming more frequent. Although the number fluctuates from year to year, some of the worst cases have occurred since 1980.

On July 18, 1984, James Oliver Huberty, a recently fired security guard, opened fire in a McDonald's restaurant, killing 21 people and injuring 20 others. Before the 1995 Oklahoma City bombing, this was the worst massacre by a single person in a single day in U.S. history. In 1989, Theodore ("Ted") Bundy, an articulate and rather charming drifter, was executed for the murder of numerous children and teenagers throughout the United States. These two cases, one a psychotic who murdered in a fit of rage, the other a cool but also psychotic individual who organized a series of killings (and therefore is known as a serial killer), illustrate quite well the types of people who commit mass murders. Generally, a mass murderer like Huberty—or Cho Seung-Hui, the Virginia Tech student who shot thirty-two students and instructors in 2007—kills in a fit of spontaneous rage. In contrast, a serial killer is highly organized and seeks to perfect a murder technique that will prevent detection and apprehension. Most serial killers have deep emotional problems concerning sexuality and describe the act of violence itself as thrilling and compelling (Pakhomou, 2004).

Workplaces like post offices, banks, factories, and even universities are increasingly frequent scenes of mass murders or outbreaks of lethal violence, apparently because of a buildup of rage in a person who fits the profile of a potential mass murderer. Unfortunately, it is extremely difficult to know beforehand whether a person fits that profile. There is a need, therefore, for greater vigilance and more open lines of communication in the workplace (Nigro & Waugh, 1996; Wilgoren et al., 2005).

Occasional Property Crimes

Occasional property crimes include vandalism, check forgery, shoplifting, and some kinds of automobile theft. These crimes are usually unsophisticated, and the offenders lack the skills of the professional criminal. Because occasional offenders commit their crimes at irregular intervals, they are not likely to associate with habitual lawbreakers. Nonprofessional shoplifters, for example, view themselves as respectable law-abiders who steal articles from stores only for their own use. They excuse their behavior on the grounds that what they steal has relatively little value and the "victim" is usually a large, impersonal organization that can easily replace the stolen article (Schmalleger, 2000; Siegel, 1999).

Neither nonprofessional shoplifters nor nonprofessional check forgers are likely to have a criminal record. Like vandals and car thieves, they usually work alone and are not part of a criminal subculture; they do not seek to earn a living from crime.

Occupational (White-Collar) Crimes

The phenomenon of occupational crime was defined and popularized by sociologist Edwin H. Sutherland, first in a 1940 article and then in his 1961 book *White Collar Crime*. Sutherland analyzed the behavior of people who break the law as part of their normal business activity: corporate directors who use their inside knowledge to sell large blocks of stock at tremendous profits; accountants who juggle books to conceal the hundreds of dollars of company funds that they have pocketed; firms that make false statements about their profits to avoid paying taxes. Such acts tend to be ignored by society. They rarely come to the criminal courts, and even then they are rarely judged as severely as other kinds of criminal activities. Since Sutherland first described it, the category of occupational crime has also come to include such acts as false advertising, violations of labor laws, price-fixing, antitrust violations, and black-market activities.

The occupational offender is far removed from the popular stereotype of a criminal. Few people imagine that a lawyer or stockbroker is likely to engage in illegal activities. Because of their respectable appearance, it is difficult to think of these offenders as criminals. In fact, occupational offenders often consider themselves respectable citizens and do everything possible to avoid being labeled as lawbreakers—even by themselves.

Sutherland's theory of **differential association** asserts that occupational criminality, like other forms of systematic criminal behavior, is learned through frequent direct or indirect association with people who are already engaging in such behavior. (We discuss this theory later in the chapter.) Thus, people who become occupational criminals may do so simply by going into businesses or occupations in which their colleagues regard certain kinds of crime as the standard way of conducting business.

A good example of occupational crime is the insider trading that frequently occurs in the securities industry. Some stockbrokers and major shareholders may be privy to inside information about an impending corporate merger or a change in the financial condition of a company that will affect the price of its stock. Brokers who possess such information are prohibited from either profiting from it themselves or selling it to others who may be able to profit from it. Nevertheless, in the 1980s the senior partners of several large brokerage houses were convicted of using inside information to make hundreds of illegal stock transactions worth many millions of dollars (Auletta, 1987).

Embezzlement. Embezzlement, or theft from one's employer, is usually committed by otherwise law-abiding people during the course of their employment. Embezzlement occurs at all levels of business, from a clerk who is stealing petty cash to a vice-president who is stealing large investment sums. Most cases are not detected, and companies are often unwilling to prosecute for fear of bad publicity. In the United States, more than 13,000 people a year are arrested for embezzlement (*UCR*, 2006).

Donald Cressey's (1953) book *Other People's Money* is a classic study of embezzlers. On the basis of interviews with convicted embezzlers, Cressey concluded that three basic conditions are necessary before people will turn to embezzlement. First, they must have a financial problem that they do not want other people to know about. Second, they must have an opportunity to steal. Third, they must be able to find a formula to rationalize their criminal act—such as "I'm just borrowing it to tide me over."

Fraud. Fraud, or obtaining money or property under false pretenses, can occur at any level of business and in any type of business relationship. A citizen defrauds the government by evading the payment of income taxes; workers defraud their employers by using company property or services for their personal benefit; an industry defrauds the public when its members agree to keep prices artificially high. The cost of fraud may run from a few cents to millions of dollars, and the methods may be as crude as the butcher's thumb on the scale or as sophisticated as the coordinated efforts of dozens of lawyers, executives, and government officials. More than 200,000 people are arrested for fraud each year in the United States (*UCR*, 2006).

Within this category, the incidence of crimes committed through computer technology has increased dramatically. Computer crimes are quite diverse, ranging from data diddling, or changing the data stored in a computer system, to superzapping, or making unauthorized use of specialized programs to gain access to data stored in a computer system. In 1999, the first conviction for creation of a computer virus (the Melissa virus) was handed down. No doubt many more will follow. And along with the boom in electronic commerce has come a rash of online fraud. The rising volume of online sales is resulting in a surge of revenue lost to fraud, estimated at $2.8 billion in 2005 (CyberSource Corp., 2006).

Corporate Crimes

Corporate crimes include, but are not limited to, environmental crimes, illegal credit card manipulations, insider trading in financial institutions, intimidation of competitors and employees, illegal labor practices, defrauding of pension plans, falsification of company records, bribery of public officials, and computer crimes. Because it is so often undetected or unpunished, there are no reliable estimates of the cost of corporate crime to the public (Salinger, 2004; Sherrill, 1997).

Disclosures of corporate crime in the tobacco and food industries have commanded large headlines and been the subject of movies like *The Insider*. But measured in terms of loss of public and private funds, the single worst example of corporate crime in American history occurred toward the end of the 1980s (Sherrill, 1997). It is known as the savings and loan scandal, and in the early 1990s it was estimated that it would cost taxpayers up to $500 billion, not to mention the large amounts of unprotected savings lost by individuals. In fact, the seizure and sale of properties involved in the scandal eventually reduced the overall financial damage (Foust, 1993). However, to assess the impact of this crime one needs to realize that this single major loss to taxpayers was over twenty times greater than the total value of property reported stolen each year in other kinds of crimes.

The spectacle of high-level corporate officials testifying before Congress or paraded before law enforcement officials and television cameras during the "corporate crime wave" of 2002 brought the subject of corporate crimes to the attention of a world audience. Authorities charged executives of Enron, Tyco, Arthur Andersen, WorldCom, and many other firms, some of them among the largest and most powerful companies in the United States, with fraud and other criminal activities. Millions of Americans lost funds invested in the securities (stocks and bonds) of these companies after key executives sold their shares at high prices and reaped millions of dollars in personal gains, knowing that very shortly the shares' value would drop sharply. Not only was this "insider trading" illegal, but the values of the stocks themselves had in many cases been illegally inflated, and accountants and company executives often colluded to hide the way they were "cooking the books"—that is, reporting false profit statements in order to keep the value of the firm's securities high (Colvin, 2002).

Companies involved in corporate crime after the bursting of the high-technology investment "bubble" after 2000 were often shielded from careful scrutiny by their close relationships with public officials. The Enron Corporation, which has been charged not only with stock manipulation and accounting fraud, but also with illegally causing the rise of electricity prices in California in 2001, had extremely close ties to

Enron's former CEO, Kenneth Lay, shown here, and other company officers bilked investors in the energy trading company of millions of dollars. They sold their own Enron shares at a profit while lying to their employees and to investors about the company's imminent bankruptcy. Eventually Enron's possessions were sold at auction for a pittance and Enron became a symbol of one of the worst corporate crime waves in U.S. history.

numerous members of the Bush administration, including Vice-President Cheney and President Bush himself. Although it does not appear that either political leader colluded with Enron in its illegal dealings, their ties to Enron executives helped create an aura of great power and respectability around the corporation that helped mask its criminal activities from the public (Dunham & Salczak, 2002).

In the aftermath of the corporate scandals of recent years, Congress has passed new legislation (discussed in the Social Policy section of the chapter) and prosecutors have aggressively pursued criminal investigations of many corporations accused of falsifying their accounts, including Health South, Adelphia, Tyco, and AIG, one of the nation's largest insurance companies. But the acquittal of former Health South CEO Richard Scrushy shows how difficult it can be to convict executives of corporate crimes. These cases are extremely complex and difficult for juries to comprehend. The wealthy defendants can afford the best defense attorneys, in contrast to poor criminals, who must rely on overworked and poorly paid public defenders. Moreover, the plea that the executive on trial was merely accepting the reports of subordinates, which Scrushy used effectively in his defense, has proven to be persuasive for some juries (Salinger, 2005). Nevertheless, since 2002 prosecutors have charged 1,300 executives and won convictions or obtained guilty please from 693 of them (Iwata, 2005).

What is corporate crime, and how has it affected the United States in recent years?

Public-Order Crimes

In terms of sheer numbers, public-order offenders constitute the largest category of criminals; their activities far exceed reported crimes of any other type. Public-order offenses include prostitution, gambling, use of illegal substances, drunkenness, vagrancy, disorderly conduct, and traffic violations. These are often called *victimless crimes* because they cause no harm to anyone but the offenders themselves. Society considers them crimes because they violate the order or customs of the community, but some of them, such as gambling and prostitution, are granted a certain amount of tolerance.

Public-order offenders rarely consider themselves criminals or view their actions as crimes. The behavior and activities of prostitutes and drug users, however, tend to isolate and segregate them from other members of society, and these individuals may find themselves drawn into criminal roles.

Prostitution is a particularly relevant example of public-order crime because of the way young women (and young men or adolescents) are exploited by older adults in the sex trade, both in the United States and, increasingly, in third world nations with thriving "sex tourism" industries (Wonders & Michalowski, 2001). Prostitution is illegal everywhere in the United States except in some counties of Nevada. Although there is little pressure on other states to follow Nevada's example, many arguments have been offered in support of legalization. It is claimed that prostitution will continue to exist regardless of the law and that recognizing this fact would bring many benefits: Legalization would make prostitutes' incomes taxable; it could eliminate or reduce the frequent connection of prostitution with crime and government corruption; and health regulations for prostitutes could be enacted and enforced, reducing the incidence of venereal disease. It has been suggested that legalization of brothels would result in a reduction of streetwalking and public solicitation, which disturb residents of the neighborhoods where they occur.

Many advocates of legalization point to class differences in the enforcement of the laws. Unless they are very indiscreet, call girls and their upper-middle-class customers are seldom targets of police action. It is the lower-class prostitutes, with their lower-class customers, who bear the brunt of antisolicitation laws.

It has also been pointed out that prostitution is usually a victimless crime because the customer participates willingly and generally has few complaints. Because most laws against prostitution and solicitation require specific evidence of an offer to exchange sexual favors for money, a major means of curbing prostitution is entrapment by plainclothes officers posing as customers. This method is objected to as unjust in that it singles out only one partner in the crime; if a prostitute commits a crime, so does the customer. A few states and cities now have laws (rarely enforced effectively) under which a man can be jailed for as much as a year and fined up to $1,000 for offering to pay for sexual services.

Entrapment of participants of either sex is protested by civil libertarians, who argue that it is a violation of the right to privacy. They favor legalization on the ground that sex for a fee is a private matter between consenting adults. Supporters of legalization argue that it is harmful to the social order to have laws on the books that are routinely flouted; because laws against prostitution are not enforced effectively, it would be better not to have them at all.

Still another argument for legalizing prostitution is that prostitutes would no longer be viewed as lawbreakers. This change in status might go a long way toward reducing the tension and stress experienced by most prostitutes. Legally at least, they would no longer have to define themselves negatively; moreover, they would no longer be constantly in fear of arrest, even though by other norms prostitution would still be regarded as a social problem.

Some experts continue to argue against legalization. They believe that society is the ultimate victim of prostitution and that legalization would not necessarily remove the prostitute from exploitation by pimps or organized crime figures. Moreover, it might encourage more young women to enter "the life." They therefore question whether any benefits would accrue from legalization (Williamson & Cluse-Tolar, 2002).

Organized Crime

Organized crime is a term that includes many types of criminal organizations, from large global crime syndicates that originated in Sicily and Italy (the Mafia), and more recently in Russia, to smaller local organizations whose membership may be more transient. Based on research in England, British sociologist Dick Hobb makes this observation:

> Contemporary serious crime groups possess the ability to splinter, dissolve, mutate, self-destruct, or simply decompose. For instance, I found that a group dealing in amphetamines splintered into both legal and illegal enterprise when a key member was arrested for a crime totally unconnected with their business. They were not bonded by some mysterious brotherhood of villainy, their collaboration was temporary and sealed with money. (1997, p. 57)

The groups that we usually think of as representing organized crime tend to be large and diversified regional or national units. They may organize initially to carry on a particular crime, such as drug trafficking, extortion, prostitution, or gambling. Later they may seek to control this activity in a given city or neighborhood, destroying or absorbing the competition. Eventually, they may expand into other types of crime, protecting their members from arrest through intimidation or bribery of public officials (Salinger, 2004).

Unlike other types of crime, organized crime is a system in which illegal activities are carried out as part of a rational plan devised by a large, often global organization that is attempting to maximize its overall profit. To operate most efficiently, organized crime relies on the division of labor in the performance of numerous diverse roles. Within a typical organized crime syndicate in a large metropolitan area, there will be groups in the stolen car and parts business, others in gambling, and still others in labor rackets. In each of these and other businesses there will be specific occupations like enforcer, driver, accountant, lawyer, and so on. Another major feature of organized crime is that the crime syndicate supplies goods and services that a large segment of the public wants but cannot obtain legally. Without the public's desire for gambling or drugs, for example, organized crime's basic means of existence would collapse.

In recent years the American FBI has investigated large and well-organized crime syndicates on the Mexican border that deal in international drug smuggling, as well as

In Sicily, where the Mafia maintains a powerful grip over community leaders, social activists use photos of Mafia killings to stimulate local and international protest.

a growing number of Russian crime syndicates that have been caught moving large amounts of illegally gained money through U.S. and European banks (Shaw, 1999). These large, globally organized crime organizations derive huge profits from supplying illegal goods and services to the public. Their major source of profit is illegal gambling in the form of lotteries, numbers games, off-track betting, illegal casinos, and dice games. Much illegal gambling is controlled by organized crime syndicates that operate through elaborate hierarchies. Money is transferred up the hierarchy from the small operator, who takes the customer's bet, through several other levels until it finally reaches the syndicate's headquarters. This complex system protects the leaders, whose identities remain concealed from those below them. The centralized organization of gambling also increases efficiency, enlarges markets, and provides a systematic way of paying graft to public officials.

Closely related to gambling and a major source of revenue for organized crime is *loan sharking*, or lending money at interest rates above the legal limit. These rates can be as high as 150 percent a week, and rates of more than 20 percent are common. Profits from gambling operations provide organized crime syndicates with large amounts of cash to lend, and they can ensure repayment by threatening violence. Most of the loans are made to gamblers who need to repay debts, to drug users, and to small businesses unable to obtain credit from legitimate sources.

Drug trafficking is organized crime's third major source of revenue. Its direct dealings in narcotics tend to be limited to imports from abroad and wholesale distribution. Lower-level operations are considered too risky and unprofitable and are left to others.

Organized Crime and Corruption. Organized crime could not flourish without bribery. By corrupting officials of public and private agencies, the syndicate tries to ensure that laws that would hamper its operations are not passed, or at least not enforced.

Corruption occurs at all levels of government, from police officers to high elected and appointed officials. It is especially effective with individuals in more powerful positions because they can prevent lower-level personnel from enforcing laws against organized crime activities. If the cooperation of the police chief can be obtained, for example, a police officer who tries to arrest gamblers may be shifted to another assignment or denied a raise or promotion. Other officers will quickly learn from this example.

Conventional and Professional Crimes

Conventional offenders tend to be young adults who commit robbery, larceny, burglary, and gang theft as a way of life. They usually begin their criminal career in adolescence as members of juvenile gangs, joining other truants from school to vandalize property and fight in the streets. As juvenile offenders, they are not organized or skillful enough to avoid arrest and conviction, and by young adulthood they have compiled a police record and may have spent time in prison.

Conventional offenders could be described as semiprofessional, since their techniques are not as sophisticated as those of organized and professional criminals, and they move into a criminal life only by degrees. For this reason, their self-concept as criminals develops gradually. By the time they have built up a criminal record, they have usually identified fairly strongly with criminality. The criminal record itself is society's way of defining these offenders as criminals. Once they have been so defined, it is almost impossible for them to reenter the mainstream of society.

Because only a small percentage of conventional crimes results in arrest, most offenders in this category are convinced that crime does pay. Moreover, the life of a successful criminal has a certain excitement, and many criminals are seduced into a life of crime by the excitement they experience in the criminal act itself (Siegel, 1999). Not only the sudden windfall of money but also the thrill of getting away with an illegal act and the release of tension after it has been committed can become part of the reward system (Katz, 1988). Because offenders associate mostly with other criminals, they develop a shared outlook that scorns the benefits of law-abiding behavior.

Young criminals who escape arrest often develop into lifelong professional criminals. Professional criminals are the ones we read about in detective novels or see on television: the expert safecracker with sensitive fingers; the disarming con artist; the customer in a jewelry store who switches diamonds so quickly that the clerk does not notice; the counterfeiters who work under bright lights in the basement of a respectable shop. This class of criminals also includes the less glamorous pickpockets, full-time shoplifters and check forgers, truck hijackers, sellers of stolen goods, and blackmailers.

Professional criminals are dedicated to a life of crime; they live by it and pride themselves on their accomplishments. These criminals are seldom caught, and even if they are, they can usually manage to have the charges dropped or a sentence reduced. Meyer Lansky, a particularly successful thief who was a top figure in a national crime syndicate, spent only 3 months and 16 days in jail out of a criminal career that spanned over 50 years (Plate, 1975). These are the cleverest of all criminals, with the most sophisticated working methods.

Professional criminals tend to come from higher social strata than most people who are arrested for criminal activities. They frequently begin as employees in offices, hotels, and restaurants, with criminal life as a sideline. Eventually their criminal careers develop to the point at which they can make a living almost entirely from criminal activities. This phase usually starts at the same age at which conventional criminals are likely to give up crime. As criminologist E. M. Lemert put it, "Unemployment occasioned by old age does not seem to be a problem of con men; age ripens their skills, insights, and wit, and it also increases the confidence they inspire in their victims" (quoted in Quinney, 1979, p. 245). Most professional criminals enjoy long, uninterrupted careers because experience improves their skill at avoiding arrest. They often justify their activities by claiming that they are simply capitalizing on the fact that all people are dishonest and would probably be full-time criminals themselves if they had the ability and opportunity. Many are employed in operations carried on by organized crime syndicates (Salinger, 2004).

Cybercrime. A rapidly growing area of professional crime involves the use of computers and the Internet to defraud unsuspecting victims. The term *cybercrime* includes many types of crime, from money laundering by terrorist and organized crime groups to identity theft, in which victims' credit card or bank account numbers are stolen by computer "scammers" and used to pay for goods and services. According to one report,

> These new scammers are average students, bored stay-at-homes, and low-end criminals who have discovered how easy it is to pick the locks on the Web. Their specialty is phishing, creating fake sites that sucker people into giving up account numbers and other sensitive information online. (The spelling alludes to the phone "phreaks" of decades past, who pilfered long-distance phone service.) They get technical help from any of 50 or more gangs of professional criminals, operating mostly in Russia and Eastern Europe, where legions of unemployed programmers have found steady work as freelance hackers.
>
> The scams are incredibly effective. In the 12 months through April 2004, 57 million Americans said they received what they believed was a phished e-mail, reports the consultancy Gartner. Of those, 1.8 million people took the bait, and 980,000 claimed they were scammed as a result. (Goldman, 2004, p.1)

Identity Theft. The vast increase in the use of credit cards, in person or via the Internet, has resulted in an explosion in the crime of identity theft, which occurs when official identity cards and account numbers are copied or stolen and used for illegal purchases or other activities. Identity thieves use your personal information to impersonate you and either open new accounts with your background information or take existing accounts and spend as much money as they can in as short a time as possible before moving on to someone else's name and identifying information. Recent surveys have found that within the last twelve months, 9.3 million Americans were victims of identity theft, for a total cost of $52.6 billion.

Contrary to popular belief, most thieves still obtain personal information through traditional rather than electronic means. In cases in which the means of theft are known, 68.2 percent of the information was obtained off-line and only 11.6 percent online. Conventional methods—lost or stolen wallets, misappropriation by family and friends, and theft of paper mail—are among the most common ways in which thieves gain access to personal information.

Juvenile Delinquency

Historically, children have been presumed to lack the criminal intent to commit willful crimes; hence, juvenile law is designed primarily to protect and redirect young offenders rather than to punish them. There is a separate family court system for dealing with juvenile offenders, and their sentencing is limited. Within those limits, however, judges have wide discretion in dealing with youthful offenders and can choose the approach that they feel will be most effective.

In recent years there has been increasing dissatisfaction with the workings of juvenile law (Jacobs, 1990). Some critics contend that law enforcement authorities have too much latitude in interpreting juvenile behavior and that standards differ too much from one community to another (Bennett, DiIulio, & Walters, 1996; Traub, 1996). The epidemic of violent youth crime—especially the violence that broke out in some U.S. schools in the late 1990s and the extremely violent gang warfare that coincided with the crack epidemic—created a public perception that young people were becoming especially prone to violence and crime. In fact, however, the long-term aging of the American and European populations and the waning of the crack epidemic have tended to help reduce youth crime and violence (*The Economist*, 2002).

As noted in the preceding chapter, many young people become involved in drug commerce at the retail level, especially because as juveniles they often run somewhat less risk of incarceration than people over 18 years of age. Involvement in petty sales and other aspects of drug commerce puts juveniles at risk of addiction and, increasingly, of violent death. As the demand for cocaine and crack abates while law enforcement pressure continues, there is an escalation of violence, often involving automatic

Arrests in the War on Drugs often lead to felony convictions for youthful offenders. As a consequence of efforts to lengthen prison terms for people with multiple felony convictions, these early episodes could greatly increase the risk of eventual life imprisonment.

weapons, among drug dealers and their associates. Thus, in some large American cities the homicide rate among juvenile males has reached record levels.

Teenagers arrested on minor sales or possession charges often begin a career in and out of detention centers and jails, where they are initiated into the world of professional crime (Sullivan, 1989). Young women who become involved in the drug world and associated illegal hustling often trade sexual services for drugs and thus are recruited into the culture of prostitution. Although prostitution may not be considered a serious crime, it places young women at serious risk of violent death or injury and of sterility or death from sexually transmitted diseases.

Status offenses, such as running away and vagrancy, are a very common reason for arrests of juveniles. In 2005, about 90,000 juvenile runaways were arrested in the United States, of whom 59 percent were females (*UCR,* 2006). This is one of the few types of arrest in which the usual gender distribution is reversed. The reason so many girls are runaways is that they are far more likely than boys to be abused, both sexually and otherwise, in their homes.

Hate Crimes

It is perhaps appropriate to follow juvenile crimes with a discussion of hate crimes. Many of the most sensational recent crimes that were motivated by deep hatred for people of other groups have been committed by teenagers and young adults. The killings at Columbine High School in Colorado and those of James Byrd, Jr., in Texas and Matthew Shepard in Wyoming are hate crimes that most readers will remember vividly. Even when they do not result in murder and mayhem, these criminal acts reveal hatreds and violent propensities that go far beyond what we usually categorize as juvenile crime. Hatred of gays or people of other races and religions is widespread in all societies, but the propensity to express it through violent acts tends to be a phenomenon of youth and young adulthood. Yet the emotions that motivate the deeds are taken from the adults who socialize young people. Throughout the world—in Kosovo, Rwanda, Northern Ireland, Israel, Pakistan, Russia, the United States, and elsewhere—adult hatreds spawn violence, which is often carried out by the young.

In an exhaustive study of hate crimes, the FBI concluded that 61 percent of such incidents were based on race, 13 percent on sexual orientation, and another 10 percent on ethnicity or national origin. Intimidation, the single most frequently reported hate crime offense, accounts for 41 percent of the total; damage, destruction, or vandalism of property for 23 percent; simple assault for 18 percent; and aggravated assault

TABLE 5–1	Hate Crimes Committed in 2005	
Bias Motivation	**Incidents**	**Offenses**
Total	7,163	8,380
Single-Bias Incidents	7,160	8,373
Race:	3,919	4,691
Anti-White	828	935
Anti-Black	2,630	3,200
Anti-Native American/Alaskan Native	79	95
Anti-Asian/Pacific Islander	199	231
Anti-Multiple Races, Group	183	230
Religion:	1,227	1,314
Anti-Jewish	848	900
Anti-Catholic	58	61
Anti-Protestant	57	58
Anti-Islamic	128	146
Anti-Other Religion	93	102
Anti-Multiple Religions, Group	39	42
Anti-Atheism/Agnosticism/etc.	4	5
Sexual Orientation:	1,017	1,171
Anti-Male Homosexual	621	713
Anti-Female Homosexual	155	180
Anti-Homosexual	195	228
Anti-Heterosexual	21	23
Anti-Bisexual	25	27
Ethnicity/National Origin:	944	1,144
Anti-Hispanic	522	660
Anti-Other Ethnicity/National Origin	422	484
Disability:	53	53
Anti-Physical	21	21
Anti-Mental	32	32
Multiple-Bias Incidents[1]	3	7

[1]A *multiple-bias incident* occurs when two or more offense types are committed in a single incident.

Source: Federal Bureau of Investigation, *Uniform Crime Reports*, 2006.

for 13 percent (Gondles, 1999). Table 5–1 shows that the most common hate crimes are those involving racial hatred, but crimes against people of other religions and against people who are gay or merely appear to be gay are major categories of hate crime as well.

The 1994 Crime Act defines a hate crime as "a crime in which the defendant intentionally selects a victim, or in the case of a property crime, the property that is the object of the crime, because of the actual or perceived race, color, national origin, ethnicity, gender, disability, or sexual orientation of any person." Thirty-seven states have statutes addressing hate crime, and others have pending legislation in this area. But the major controversy surrounding the issue of hate crimes is whether the federal government needs a stronger law that sets greater penalties for crimes motivated by hatred against specific social groups.

GANGS, GUNS, AND VIOLENT DEATH

Why is the homicide rate in the United States as much as 20 times those found in other industrialized nations? There is no one answer, but important explanations may be found in an analysis of changing patterns of juvenile violence, the increased firepower available to violent people, and the inability of American society to agree on appropriate controls on lethal weapons. Figure 5–9 shows that gun-related crimes rose dramatically during the crack epidemic of the 1980s and early 1990s and were declining rapidly at the turn of the century, only to stabilize in the current period. In 2005 about 68 percent of all murders, 42 percent of all robberies, and 21 percent of all aggravated assaults reported to the police were committed with a firearm. According to data from the National Center for Health Statistics, in 2001 about 39 percent of deaths resulting from firearms injuries were homicides, 57 percent were suicides, 3 percent were unintentional, and 1 percent were of undetermined intent.

Franklin E. Zimring (1985), one of the nation's foremost experts on guns and gun control, states that the "proportion of all households reporting handgun ownership has increased substantially over a twenty-year period" (p. 138). On the basis of survey research, Zimring and associates estimate that between one-fourth and one-third of all American households have one or more handguns (Zimring & Hawkins, 1997). This represents an enormous increase since the late 1950s, when the proportion was probably well below one in ten households. Studies of the relationship between handgun possession and homicide find that when people arm themselves out of fear and a desire for protection, there is also an increased risk of fatalities from accidents involving guns, as well as homicides caused by mistaken recourse to fatal force—as in the tragic case of a Japanese exchange student in New Orleans who was killed when he approached the wrong house in search of a party to which he had been invited (Reiss & Roth, 1993).

Gangs and Violence

In many sensational headlines, one reads of brutal violence by juvenile gangs in large cities. In Los Angeles, the Crips and Bloods are said to be especially violent gangs engaged in the distribution of crack cocaine. In Chicago and elsewhere, violence is attributed to the activities of armed gangs of various kinds. Residents of public housing projects routinely must negotiate with gang leaders to ensure the safety of their buildings and grounds and prevent gang members from killing children (Vankatesh, 2000). In the depressed manufacturing city of Paterson, New Jersey, rumors of a pending violent act by local gangs caused parents to keep their children home from school (Hanley, 2002).

In the 1980s and early 1990s there was an upsurge of gang activity and gang-related violence in smaller cities and suburban areas, most often associated with drug dealing. More recently, skinheads and other groups of teenagers and young adults have

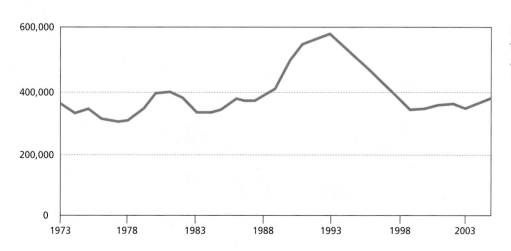

Figure 5–9 Crimes Committed with Firearms, 1973–2005

Source: Federal Bureau of Investigation, *Uniform Crime Reports,* 2006.

committed hate crimes, often involving violent attacks on homosexuals, Jews, and Asian immigrants (Males, 1998). Today much lethal gang violence is still associated with the sale and use of crack cocaine or other illicit drugs, especially in some smaller cities and towns and in specific inner-city communities.

The rate of weapons-related homicide has decreased recently, largely because of a decline in gang-related shootings. Figure 5–10 shows that weapons offenses vary greatly by region of the country; the highest rates are found in the South and Southwest and in urban areas in the Northeast. Figure 5–11 shows that the rate of death due to firearms is from three to six times the rate in Western nations with comparable levels of industrial and urban development. Although gun possession and deaths due to firearms are problems that extend well beyond the phenomenon of youth gangs, early involvement in crime, gangs, and weapons possession among teenagers, of whom the large majority come from poverty-stricken and socially isolated neighborhoods, is a strong signal that creative programs to combat poverty and neglect are urgently needed in communities throughout the nation.

Gangs range from the peer groups that hang out on street corners to the well-organized, hierarchical gangs of crime syndicates. The latter often include contract killers, professional murderers who kill for money. But killings related to organized crime account for only a small percentage of all murders. Do deaths caused by other types of gangs account for the remainder? This does not seem to be the case.

Juvenile and young-adult gangs often begin as street corner cliques and become incorporated into a larger gang confederation. These organizations are often located in poor, segregated communities, where much of their activity is dedicated to the defense of local territory, or turf (Vankatesh, 2000). But experts on the sociology of gangs are quick to point out that there are many types of juvenile gang structures and many different types of gang activity, not all of which are violent or criminal.

In a thorough study of gang confederations in Milwaukee, John M. Hagedorn (1988; Hagedorn, Torres, & Giglio, 1998) found that while gangs in large cities like Los Angeles, Chicago, and New York have been present more or less continuously for generations, in smaller cities and suburban areas gangs may be a new phenomenon. And simply because a community does not have recognizable gangs does not mean that gangs may not form in the near future. Much depends on relations between teenagers and the police, on the drug trade and its control, and on how young people perceive the need (or lack of it) to defend their turf from other teenagers. Thus, in Milwaukee, although there is some fighting, especially as young men strive to gain prestige within the gangs, there is relatively little gang warfare or homicide attributable to gang warfare. In Chicago, in contrast, there seems to be far more gang-related homicide, especially among Hispanic gangs.

A large majority of the gang members Hagedorn (1988) interviewed admitted owning at least one handgun. He concludes that the problem of violence and homicide is

Figure 5–10 Weapons Offense Rates, by State

Source: Federal Bureau of Investigation, *Uniform Crime Reports,* 2006.

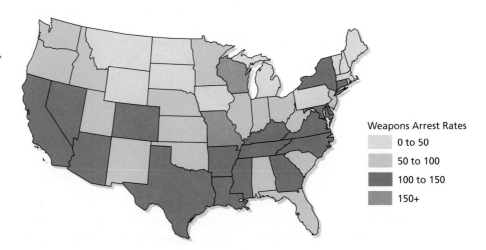

Weapons Arrest Rates
- 0 to 50
- 50 to 100
- 100 to 150
- 150+

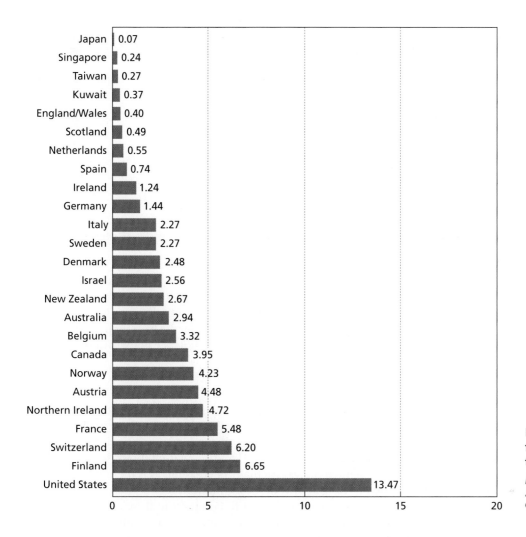

Figure 5–11 Death Rates from Firearms, Selected Countries. *Average Annual Deaths per 100,000 Population*

Source: Data from World Health Organization, 2001.

related more to the increasing availability of guns and the involvement of some gangs in the illegal drug industry than to inherent features of the gangs themselves; this conclusion is shared by most students of gang behavior. Martin Sanchez-Jankowski (1991), one of the nation's foremost authorities on violent gangs, notes that contrary to what some members of the public—and some sociologists—think, gang members typically do not like violence and the risks to personal safety that it entails. But most gang members believe that "if you do not attack, you will be attacked." This worldview implies that much gang violence is premeditated with the goal of taking the opponent by surprise. In addition, Sanchez-Jankowski notes, "the injuries incurred as a result of organizational violence [in the gang] become the social cement that creates group bonds in a deviant individualist setting." Overall, he concludes, gang violence "is understood to be the instrument used to achieve objectives that are not achievable in other ways" (p. 177).

Another study of gang activity and involvement in drug dealing supports Hagedorn's conclusions and reinforces the idea that high rates of lethal violence are attributable more to the widespread use of guns than to the presence of gangs themselves. Terry Williams (1989) spent three years following the activities of a mobile drug "crew" in New York. This small and highly entrepreneurial gang was in the retail crack business. Its success depended on discipline—on ensuring that members did not become too high to function in their jobs or so careless that they became victims of violent robberies. Williams, like Hagedorn, documents the widespread and routine possession of handguns, but he also notes the increasing availability of more powerful automatic weapons and submachine guns.

As noted earlier, rates of gun violence, homicide, and aggravated assault reached their peaks in the early 1990s. It is likely that the waning of the crack epidemic is part of

TABLE 5–2	Number and Membership of Youth Gangs	
	Youth Gang Membership	Number of Gangs
1996	846,500	31,000
1997	816,000	30,500
1998	780,200	28,700
1999	840,500	26,000
2000	772,500	24,500
2002	731,500	21,500

Source: National Youth Gang Center, 2004.

the reason for the recent declines in those rates. But the United States had extremely high homicide rates even before the advent of crack; drugs alone, therefore, do not provide a sufficient explanation. The availability of easily concealed handguns, together with the traditions of interpersonal violence that date from the frontier period of American history, probably accounts for much of the deadly violence in the United States.

Recent Trends

Is the United States in the midst of a rise in violent youth gang activity? Government officials in the U.S. Bureau of Justice and other political leaders, including First Lady Laura Bush, have gone on record saying that the problem is worsening. However, survey research sponsored in large part by the Justice Department itself shows that the number of gang members in the United States is actually decreasing, as is the public's perception of problems related to gang activity in local communities. As Table 5–2 shows, the number and total membership of gangs has declined significantly since 1996. The data in Table 5–3 indicate that from rural counties to inner-city communities, reports of gang activity declined between 1996 and 2004. Nevertheless, it remains true, especially in major cities like Chicago and Los Angeles, that street gangs, made up largely of teenagers and young adults, account for about half of all homicides. And almost 80 percent of survey respondents in major cities report problems with local gangs.

Shortly after Laura Bush spoke out against gang violence, the FBI announced a new anti-gang initiative in which it would seek the reclassification of gangs as "criminal organizations and enterprises" in order to be allowed to prosecute gang members

TABLE 5–3	Law Enforcement Agency Reports of Gang Problems, 1996–2004		
	Average Percentage of Respondents Reporting Gang Problems		
Area Type	1996–1998	1999–2001	2002–2004
Rural Counties	24.3	13.5	12.3
Smaller cities (population 2,500 to 49,999)	36.5	25.9	28.4
Suburban counties	56.0	40.8	40.0
Larger cities (population 50,000 or more)	85.6	77.6	79.8

Note: To account for regular year-to-year fluctuations, 3-year averages are shown.

Source: U.S. Department of Justice, Office of Justice Programs, 2006.

under federal racketeering statutes, which carry tougher sentences. But with more people in prison in the United States than in any other nation, sociologists are concerned that further increases in the prison population only serve to increase gang activity, which often relies on prisons for recruitment and training. Indeed, James Short, an expert on gangs at Washington State University, believes that "excessive incarceration" could provide a pool of available recruits for years to come ("Going Global," 2005).

CONDITIONS AND CAUSES OF CRIME AND VIOLENCE

In this section we consider several explanations for crime, beginning with nonsociological ones and continuing with various sociological approaches based on the theoretical perspectives described in Chapter 1.

Biological Explanations of Crime

A medieval law stated that "if two persons fell under suspicion of crime, the uglier or more deformed was to be regarded as more probably guilty" (Ellis, 1914; quoted in Wilson & Herrnstein, 1985, p. 71). This law and others like it illustrate the age-old and deep-seated belief that criminality can be explained in terms of certain physical characteristics of the criminal. An example of this point of view is the theory of crime advanced by an Italian physician, Cesare Lombroso, in the late nineteenth century.

Lombroso was convinced that there is a "criminal man" (or woman), a type of human being who is physically distinct from ordinary human beings. In the course of his examinations of convicts both before and after their deaths, he developed the concept of *criminal atavism*—the notion that criminality is associated with physical characteristics that resemble those of primitive humans and lower primates: a sloping forehead, long arms, a primitive brain, and the like. Lombroso believed, in short, that there was such a thing as a "born criminal." Although this explanation was wrong, it served to initiate scientific inquiry into the causes of crime.

In the twentieth century, Lombroso's theory and other biologically based explanations of crime have been discredited and supplanted by sociological theories. However, some theorists (e.g., Wilson & Herrnstein, 1985) defend the identification of biological characteristics that appear to be predisposing factors in criminal behavior rather than full explanations of it. They believe certain inherited traits, such as an extra Y chromosome or a particularly athletic physique, may be correlated with a greater than average tendency to engage in criminal behavior.

Research on the possibility of a link between criminality and an extra Y chromosome has consistently found that no such relationship can be demonstrated. Although new efforts to establish genetic or other biological origins of criminality are also likely to fail, most sociologists agree with Troy Duster, who argues that such studies can help, because if they properly account for social variables such as racism and class inequality, they will counteract the notion of a biological basis for crime in the lower classes or among some racial groups (cited in Horgan, 1993; Ossorio & Duster, 2005).

Biology, Violence, and Criminality

Is violence simply part of human nature? Because it is such a common occurrence, some social scientists have argued that human aggressive tendencies are inherent or instinctual. According to this view, only social organization keeps violent tendencies under control. Other experts argue that aggression is natural, but violence is not. In an exhaustive review of research on the causes of interpersonal violence, a panel of experts convened by the National Academy of Sciences concluded that there is no solid evidence to support neurological or biological explanations of violent behavior. The panel did note, however, that findings from studies of animals and humans point

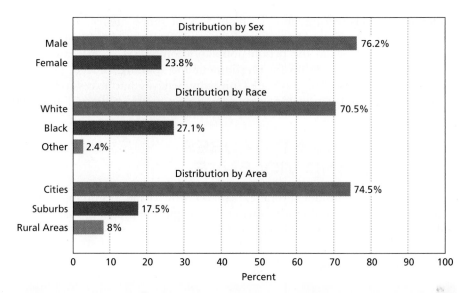

Figure 5–12 Total Arrests, by Sex, Race, and Area: 2004

Source: Data from Federal Bureau of Investigation, *Uniform Crime Reports,* 2006.

to several features of the nervous system as possible sources of such explanations and recommended continued research (Reiss & Roth, 1993). Given the weight of evidence in favor of social and psychological explanations of violent behavior, this recommendation drew considerable criticism from social scientists (Kornblum, 1993).

In her response to the report, Dorothy Nelkin (1995), a well-known evaluator of scientific panels, argued that "biology is not destiny" and "it is not necessary to explain through biology why a child exposed to poverty and racism might become violent." The real source of violence, she believes, can be found in the growing inequality in the United States and other societies (Duster, 2003). This is an important sociological viewpoint, to which we will return in later chapters.

Gender and Crime

Since nations began collecting systematic statistics on crime, analysts have realized that men are far more likely than women to commit crimes. Indeed, gender is one of the most obvious correlates of criminality. Although there are significant variations from one society to another, numerous studies of crime in different countries demonstrate that the gender gap is universal. Males are two to five times as likely to be arrested as females (Steffensmeier & Allan, 1996). As women have gained greater social equality with men in industrialized countries, however, the ratio of male to female arrests has decreased, although men still lead in most categories of crime. (See Figure 5–12.)

The different arrest rates for men and women seem to be a result of different patterns of socialization. In our society men have traditionally been raised to be more aggressive than women, and they have therefore been more likely to commit certain crimes. Women have generally been regarded more protectively by the police and the courts; therefore, they have been less likely to be arrested and, if arrested, less likely to be punished severely, especially if they are wives or mothers. Despite the persistent differences in arrest rates of women and men, with men more than eight times more likely to appear in official crime statistics, rates of crime by women increased rapidly in the second half of the twentieth century. As more women are socialized under conditions of deprivation and abuse, we can expect that larger numbers will be recruited into street hustling, prostitution, and shoplifting, which in turn will account for increasing numbers of arrests (Friedman, 1993; Miller, 1986). Indeed, today women make up about 12 percent of the total prison population in the United States, compared to only 7.7 percent in 1997 (*Statistical Abstract,* 2006).

Age and Crime

Criminologists have found age to be more strongly correlated with criminal behavior than any other factor (McKeown, Jackson, & Valois, 1998). The age of the offender is closely related not only to crime rates, but also to the types of crimes committed. Data from several nations, including England, Wales, and France, provide evidence that the correlation between age and crime holds across geographic boundaries (Gottfredson & Hirschi, 1995; Hirschi & Gottfredson, 1983).

Teenagers and young adults accounted for 44.3 percent of arrests in the United States in 2005, and 29.1 percent of all arrests were of people under the age of 21. A solid majority of arrests for property crimes—54.0 percent—were of people under 25 (*UCR*, 2006). Although young people may be arrested more than older offenders because the young are less experienced, it is clear that many teenagers and young adults, especially those who become involved in gang activities, are enticed by opportunities to commit various kinds of thefts. Automobile and bicycle thefts and vandalism are among the major juvenile crimes, although they are by no means limited to the young.

Violent Youth Crime. Figure 5–13 shows the rate of arrests for violent crimes per 100,000 boys and girls ages 10 to 17. The graph clearly shows that violent youth crime peaked in 1994 and then began to decline quite sharply. This positive shift is not due to any one factor, but part of the explanation simply has to do with the longer-term trend toward an older population and a relative decline in the size of the youth cohorts. The 2000 census revealed that the U.S. population is aging quite rapidly. In 1980 the median age of Americans was about 30, and by 2000 it was over 35. The median age measures the age at which half the population is over that age and half under it. As the median age creeps upward, fewer people are in the younger age cohorts and more are in the elderly ones. We will see in Chapter 9 that these changes are of extreme importance in any society, and that the aging of the U.S. population carries with it many vital policy issues. But if we look for a moment at the declining proportional size of the youthful population, the census figures reveal that between 1980 and 2000 the number of people between 18 and 24 fell by about 6 million. This change led many criminologists and sociologists to support the hypothesis that as the youthful population declined, there would be a decline in crimes committed by youth—a decline that could be measured in a number of ways, including the number of young people arrested and the number incarcerated.

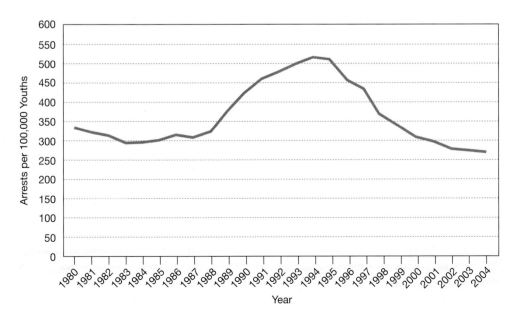

Figure 5–13 Arrests of Youths, 1980–2004

Source: Office of Juvenile Justice, 2006.

It appears that the combined effects of increased arrests and imprisonment for drug possession and sales, greater use of mandatory sentencing for drug and other felony arrests, longer prison sentences, and increased capacities of state prisons throughout much of the nation have all contributed to rising prison populations, despite demographic changes that would otherwise contribute to decreases in crime and incarceration (Marvell & Moody, 1997). From 1980 to 2001 the number of people arrested on drug charges increased from about 581,000 to more than 1.5 million. The prison population (all levels) of those convicted and sentenced on drug charges went from 40,000 to 453,000 in the same period. Fifty-eight percent of those sentenced to prison under federal mandatory sentencing guidelines were not engaged in criminal violence, and four out of five were either black or Hispanic. These facts help explain why, as we see in Figure 5–13, the rate of arrests of young people can decrease while the number of those incarcerated can continue to rise (Barlow & Kauzlarich, 2002; King & Maurer, 2002; Wacquant, 2001).

Another explanation for declining arrests of young people is that in many cities and towns the crack epidemic has waned, and with it the tendency for youth gangs to resort to violence—although, as noted earlier, youth violence and gangs continue to plague many communities. Experience in gangs and socialization into the adult world of crime (either by older gang members or by professional criminals) often carries young people into lives of crime, but most young people who have engaged in juvenile delinquency do not become career criminals. Moreover, young adults who have been involved in crime often seek more constructive and less risky alternatives as they grow older.

How are age and crime correlated?

It is fortunate for society that some criminals give up crime in their late twenties or early thirties, for reasons that are not clear to criminologists (Gottfredson & Hirschi, 1995). Perhaps they marry and find their family life more rewarding than crime. For these individuals, family responsibilities seem to be a more powerful inhibitor of criminal behavior than rehabilitation or coercion. This "maturing out" is a subject of great interest to sociologists. In a study of the criminal careers of juvenile males in three urban communities of whites, African Americans, and Latinos, respectively, Mercer Sullivan (1989) found that as the boys grew older there was an increasingly marked convergence in their tendency to reduce their criminal activity in favor of increased income from legitimate sources. Sullivan attributes this change to their greater maturity, their recognition that sanctions were becoming more severe, and their perception that their opportunities to hold real jobs were better than they had been when they were younger.

Sociological Explanations of Crime

Demographic factors do not offer a complete explanation of crime. They do not, for example, explain why some juveniles and young adults drift into long-term criminal careers or why some young people never commit crimes. Nor do they tell us why some individuals, such as white-collar criminals, begin breaking laws during adulthood and middle age (Barlow & Kauzlarich, 2002). Thus, in addition to demographic analyses of crime, sociologists have proposed a number of theoretical approaches to explain why some people become criminals and others do not.

The first theoretical approach discussed here has evolved from conflict theory; it claims that most crime is either a form of rebellion by members of lower social classes or a form of illegal exploitation by the rich and powerful. A second approach, derived from the functionalist perspective, holds that crime stems from the uncertainty about norms of proper conduct that accompanies rapid social change and social disorganization. A third major explanation applies the interactionist perspective to the study of how people drift toward criminal subcultures and become socialized for criminal careers.

Conflict Approaches to the Study of Crime. Conflict theorists identify inequalities of wealth, status, and power as the underlying conditions that produce criminal behavior. Groups in society that are more disadvantaged than other groups, such as the poor and racial minorities who experience discrimination, are thought to be likely to rebel against their situation. Criminality, in this view, is one way in which disadvantaged individuals act out their rebellion against society (Quinney, 1979).

Inequality and Crime. As noted earlier in the chapter, official statistics show a high incidence of crime among members of the lower socioeconomic classes. Those statistics have fueled a sociological debate over the relationship between social class and criminality. For much of the twentieth century many sociologists believed people in lower socioeconomic classes were more likely than those in higher classes to commit crimes. Criminologists Charles R. Tittle, Wayne J. Villemez, and Douglas A. Smith (1978) analyzed existing studies of crime and class status to determine whether the inverse relationship between class status and the commission of crime always held. When they examined data from arrest records, they found evidence to support the prevailing view. But when they reviewed data from self-report studies, they found no link between class and crime. On the basis of these results, the investigators concluded that "it is time to shift away from class-based theories to those emphasizing more generic processes" (p. 654).

Cross-cultural research on crime suggests that rapid increases in inequality, rather than long-standing patterns of poverty and wealth (e.g., as in India), tend to produce increases in crime (Bunnell, 1995). For example, in the nations of the former Soviet Union there have been rapid increases in poverty and in the number of wealthy individuals, many of whom have made their fortunes in connection with organized crime or other criminal activity. This rapid social change, in which it is no longer clear what the rules of behavior are or whether laws will be enforced, tends to produce lawlessness, corruption, and crime.

In the past two decades, as the total U.S. prison population has grown to record levels, the conflict perspective on crime has gained new adherents. Joseph Califano (1998), former secretary of Health and Human Services, is an example. Califano is highly critical of theories of crime that suggest only punishment can deter people from committing crimes. He sees the failure of U.S. drug policy and the failure to provide adequate rehabilitation as major causes of the boom in prison populations—which, he believes, only increases the chances that people in prison will become criminal recidivists later in their lives. In other words, in Califano's view it is conflicts in American society over how to deal with drug and alcohol abuse that result in some types of crime and, more important, in the dramatic increases in the prison population. More critical theorists, however, still view major differences in income in a society as the most important contributor to crime (Wacquant, 2003).

Race and Crime. Every study of crime based on official data shows that blacks are overrepresented among those who are arrested, convicted, and imprisoned for street crimes. According to official statistics, blacks are arrested at higher rates than whites on charges of murder, rape, robbery, and other index crimes.

In any society one can find differences in crime rates among various racial and ethnic groups. Chinese and Japanese Americans have lower crime rates than other Americans; Hungarian immigrants to Sweden have higher crime rates than native Swedes; Scandinavian immigrants to the United States get into less trouble with the police than do Americans of Anglo-Saxon descent (Reckless, 1973). In the case of black Americans, however, the differences are pronounced; for example, "If blacks were arrested for robbery at the same rate as are whites, there would be half as many robbers arrested in the United States" (Wilson & Herrnstein, 1985, pp. 461–462).

It is possible that the overrepresentation of blacks in official crime statistics is due to greater surveillance of black communities by the police and to the greater likelihood that blacks who commit crimes will be arrested and imprisoned. One expert has calculated that about 80 percent of the disproportion in the rates of imprisonment can be attributed to the disproportion in arrest rates (Blumstein, 1982). However, victimization surveys show that police and court bias cannot be the sole cause. Blacks are far more likely than whites to be victims of crime, and it is unlikely that these higher victimization rates are caused by whites who enter black neighborhoods to commit crimes (Wilson & Herrnstein, 1985).

A more plausible explanation is the disproportionately high percentage of blacks in the lower classes, which, as we saw earlier, are associated with higher crime rates. But economic disadvantage alone cannot fully account for the racial disparity in crime rates. The higher arrest rates for blacks persist even when socioeconomic status is taken into consideration. Moreover, offenders who commit numerous crimes begin to exhibit delinquent behavior early in life, before their outlook has been affected by such factors as failure to find a good job (Adler, Mueller, & Laufer, 1995).

Research by William Julius Wilson (1996a) points to the growing isolation of some black communities from sources of jobs and income. This trend is especially marked in and around cities that have lost large numbers of manufacturing jobs, which once provided a relatively decent livelihood for African American and other minority workers. In communities where legal employment is in short supply, people often turn to illegal activities.

Racial Profiling. Are black Americans more likely to commit crimes, or are their higher arrest rates a function of discriminatory police profiling? The National Household Survey of Substance and Drug Abuse finds that roughly the same proportion of blacks and whites—12 percent to 13 percent—say that they use illegal substances. Yet 37 percent of those arrested for drug-related crimes such as trafficking or possession are black (Duster, 2004; Russell, 1999).

In many minority communities, feelings against racial profiling are profound and bitter. The phrase "driving while black" sums up much of the attitude; it seems as if merely being an African American driver is a crime. Cole (2000) has gathered large amounts of data to support this perception. His data show that wherever police have broad discretion, they disproportionately stop and search minorities. The following are among the many examples he cites:

- Reviewing police videotapes, the *Orlando Sentinel* found that in 1992 in Volusia County, Florida, on a road where approximately 5 percent of the drivers are identifiably black or Hispanic, 70 percent of those stopped and 80 percent of those searched were black or Hispanic.

- Analyzing some 16 million driving records, the *Houston Chronicle* found that in 1995 blacks who traveled in white enclaves of Houston were twice as likely as whites to be ticketed for traffic offenses.

- In 1998 the American Civil Liberties Union (ACLU) reported that during a nearly three-year period 70 percent of the drivers stopped and searched on Interstate 95 in Maryland were African American, whereas only 17.5 percent of the drivers and speeders on that road were black.

- A 1998 analysis of police records found that in Philadelphia African Americans were subject to both car stops and pedestrian stops at rates that were disproportionate to their representation in the population.

- According to the New Jersey attorney general, 77 percent of the motorists stopped and searched by New Jersey state troopers are black or Hispanic, even though only 13.5 percent of the drivers on New Jersey highways are black or Hispanic.

- A 1999 ACLU analysis of Illinois traffic data found that Hispanics account for less than 8 percent of the state's population but for 27 percent of those stopped and searched by drug-interdiction units.

This evidence suggests that racial profiling is a nationwide problem (Cole, 2000).

The Functionalist View: Anomie Theory. Anomie theory, also known as the goals-and-opportunities approach, is favored by many scholars who seek explanations of crime. Robert K. Merton (1968) argues that a society has both approved goals and approved ways of attaining them. When some members of the society accept the goals (e.g., home ownership) but do not have access to the approved means of attaining them (e.g., earned income), their adherence to the approved norms is likely to be weakened, and they may try to attain the goals by other, socially unacceptable means (e.g., fraud). In other words, criminal behavior occurs when socially approved means are not available for the realization of highly desired goals.

Anomie, the feeling of being adrift that arises from the disparity between goals and means, may vary with nationality, ethnic background, bias, religion, and other social characteristics. Some societies emphasize strict adherence to behavioral norms—the case in Japan, for example—and for them the degree of anomie may be fairly low. Others place relatively more emphasis on the attainment of goals and less on their being attained in socially approved ways. Merton (1968) maintains that the United States is such a society. Identifying anomie as a basic characteristic of American society, he lists several kinds of common adaptations. One of these, innovation, consists of rejecting approved practices while retaining the desired goals. This seems to characterize the behavior of certain lower-class gang members, who have adopted socially approved goals but abandoned socially approved methods of attaining them.

This rejection of approved practices occurs widely in groups with the greatest disjuncture among goals, norms, and opportunities. In this country it is most often found among those who have the greatest difficulty in obtaining a good education or training for high-paying jobs, particularly members of disadvantaged minority groups. Higher crime rates among such groups are not automatic, but they can be expected when the goals that people internalize are dictated to them by a society that at the same time erects barriers to the attainment of those goals by approved means. If more attainable goals were set for people in lower socioeconomic classes, presumably there would be less disjuncture between goals and means and hence less anomie. For example, if low-cost rental housing were more widely available as a goal, more poor people could see how even low-wage jobs would improve their lives. When only luxury homes are available (and shown as models on television), the poor sense the futility of conventional jobs or other approved means.

Since the initial formulation of the anomie approach, research seems to have provided at least some support for its basic premise, although there are types of crimes that it fails to explain adequately, such as assault for purposes other than monetary gain. This omission is related to the question most frequently raised about Merton's theory: Are financial success and material possessions only middle-class goals? Do members of the lower classes have different values and aspirations? Many sociologists believe people in the lower classes tend to hold two sets of beliefs simultaneously. That is, they share the norms and values of the larger society but are forced to develop standards and expectations of their own so that they can deal realistically with their particular circumstances. For example, people in the lower classes share with the affluent the view that crime is bad, but they lack conventional means to attain such goals as secure jobs. They may consider illegal "hustles" as an alternative means to some goals, especially when these crimes seem justified by the behavior of others outside their communities whom they observe buying drugs or sex or other illicit goods and services. It is not surprising, therefore, that studies have supported Merton's view that anomie, rather than poverty itself, is a major cause of crime and delinquency (Conklin, 2007).

Interactionist Approaches: Differential Association and Delinquent Subcultures. Interactionist explanations of criminal behavior focus on the processes by which individuals actually internalize the norms that encourage criminality. This internalization results from the everyday interaction that occurs in social groups. Interactionist theories differ in this respect from anomie theory, which sees criminal behavior as the result of certain aspects of social structure. Two examples of interactionist theories of criminality are Edwin Sutherland's theory of differential association and the subcultural approach to the study of juvenile delinquency.

Differential Association. Introduced by Sutherland in 1939, the approach known as *differential association*, with some later modifications, still seems to explain the widest range of criminal acts. According to this theory, criminal behavior is a result of a learning process that occurs chiefly within small, intimate groups—family, friends, neighborhood peer groups, and the like. The lessons learned include both the techniques for committing crimes and, more important, the motives for criminal behavior. The law is defined not as a set of rules to be followed but as a hindrance to be avoided or overcome.

Briefly stated, the basic principle of differential association is that "a person becomes delinquent because of the excess of definitions favorable to violation of law over definitions unfavorable to violation of law" (Sutherland & Cressey, 1960, p. 28). People internalize the values of the surrounding culture, and when their environment includes frequent contact with criminal elements and relative isolation from noncriminal elements, they are likely to become delinquent or criminal. The boy whose most admired model is another member of his gang or a successful neighborhood pimp will try to emulate that model and will receive encouragement and approval when he does so successfully.

Although a child usually encounters both criminal and noncriminal behavior patterns, these encounters vary in frequency, duration, priority, and intensity. The concepts of frequency and duration are self-explanatory. *Priority* means that attitudes learned early in life, whether lawful or criminal, tend to persist in later life, although this tendency has not been fully demonstrated. *Intensity* refers to the prestige of the model and the strength of the child's emotional ties to that person.

Delinquent Subcultures and Conflicting Values. The legal definition of crime ignores the effect of social values in determining which laws are enforced. Although judges and prosecutors use criminal law to determine the criminality of certain acts, the process of applying the law involves class interest and political power: One group imposes its will on another by enforcing its definition of illegality. For example, authorities are not nearly as anxious to enforce laws against consumer fraud as they are to enforce laws against the use of certain drugs. Consumer fraud is often perpetrated by powerful business interests with strong political influence. The drug user, on the other hand, usually lacks power and public support.

The issue of class interests is especially relevant to the study of delinquent subcultures. Albert K. Cohen (1971), for example, viewed the formation of delinquent gangs as an effort to alleviate the difficulties gang members encounter at the bottom of the status ladder. Gang members typically come from working-class homes and find themselves measured, as Cohen put it, with a "middle-class measuring rod" by those who control access to the larger society, including teachers, businesspeople, the police, and public officials. Untrained in such "middle-class virtues" as ambition, ability to defer gratification, self-discipline, and academic skills, and therefore poorly prepared to compete in a middle-class world, they form a subculture whose standards they can meet. This delinquent subculture, which Cohen described as nonutilitarian, malicious, and negativistic, "takes its norms from the larger culture, but turns them upside down. The delinquents consider something right, by the standards of their subculture, precisely because it is wrong by the norms of the larger culture" (p. 28).

Other sociologists do not believe that the formation of delinquent subcultures is a frustrated reaction to exclusion by the dominant culture. Instead, they see delinquency as a product of lower-class culture. A study of street gangs by Walter Miller (1958), for example, identified six "focal concerns" of lower-class culture that often lead to the violation of middle-class social and legal norms:

1. *Trouble.* Trouble is important to the individual's status in the community, whether it is seen as something to be kept out of or as something to be gotten into. Usually there is less worry about legal or moral questions than about difficulties that result from the involvement of police, welfare investigators, and other agents of the larger society.

2. *Toughness.* Toughness comprises an emphasis on masculinity, physical strength, and the ability to "take it," coupled with a rejection of art, literature, and anything

else that is considered feminine. This is partly a reaction to female-dominated households and the lack of male role models both at home and in school.

3. *Smartness.* In the street sense of the term, *smartness* denotes the ability to outwit, dupe, or "con" someone. A successful pimp, for example, would be considered smarter than a bank clerk.

4. *Excitement.* To relieve the crushing boredom of ghetto life, residents of lower-class communities often seek out situations of danger or excitement, such as gambling or high-speed joyrides in stolen automobiles.

5. *Fate.* Fate is a major concern because lower-class citizens frequently feel that important events in life are beyond their control. They often resort to semimagical resources such as "readers and advisers" as a way to change their luck.

6. *Autonomy.* Members of this group are likely to express strong resentment toward any external controls or exercise of coercive authority over their behavior. At the same time, however, they frequently seem to seek out restrictive environments, perhaps even engineering their own committal to mental hospitals or prisons.

Research by Gerald Suttles (1970) and Elijah Anderson (1992, 1999) on the street corner culture of delinquents and other groups provides evidence of continuity in these values. Anderson, for example, writes that lower-class life has an internal coherence that is seldom appreciated by the casual observer. Both show that teenagers and young adults in lower-class street corner groups make careful distinctions based on trust and confidence. They may be labeled street people by the larger society, but among themselves they continually rank each other according to notions of respect and trust derived from their life on the street.

Compare and contrast biological and social explanations of crime.

CONTROLLING CRIME

Efforts by the police, courts, and other agencies to control crime need to be understood as part of society's much larger system of social control (Conklin, 2007). In its broadest sociological sense, **social control** is the capacity of a social group, which could be an entire society, to regulate itself according to a set of "higher moral principles beyond those of self-interest" (Janowitz, 1978, p. 3). The Ten Commandments are a good example of what is meant by such values as they are translated into norms of everyday life. All of a society's ways of teaching the young to conform to its values and norms (i.e., *socialization*), together with the ways in which people in a society reward one another for desired behaviors, contribute to social control. But every society also includes members who deviate from its norms, even strongly held norms like the prohibition against murder or thievery. Viewed in terms of the problems created by such deviance, social control can be defined somewhat more narrowly as "all the processes by which people define and respond to deviant behavior" (Black, 1984, p. xi).

Techniques of social control range from informal processes such as gossip, ridicule, advice, and shunning to the formal processes embodied in the actions of the police, courts, corrections officers, and others who work in the criminal-justice system and in related systems like the mental-health and juvenile-justice systems. These formal systems of social control, established by government, are so important and complex and subject to so much study and debate that in this chapter we focus on them more than on the informal processes. Nevertheless, it is important to recognize that without the great array of informal controls that exist in every community and society, none of the formal systems would be of much use. If the police and the courts and other formal institutions of social control are at all effective, it is because most people are law-abiding and these institutions need deal only with a relatively small minority (which may still be a very large number in absolute terms).

Most formal systems of social control rely on coercion rather than on reward. Surely this is true of courts and prisons. But it is not true by definition. In a prison or other correctional facility, a person can be rewarded for behavior that is defined as positive and as having favorable consequences for the individual and for society. The fact that coercion and punishment often far outweigh persuasion and reward reflects the different goals society has incorporated into its institutions of criminal law, that is, police, prosecution, and corrections (Garland, 2005). As we examine how these formal institutions of social control operate (and sometimes fail to operate), we need to remember that formal efforts to control crime can be classified under four headings: retribution-deterrence, rehabilitation, prevention, and reforms in the criminal-justice system. The last category includes efforts to improve society's ability to deal with all kinds of crime; it is discussed in the Social Policy section of the chapter.

Retribution-Deterrence

Retribution and deterrence—"paying back" the guilty for their misdeeds and discouraging them and others from committing similar acts in the future—have historically been the primary focus of efforts to control crime. Only relatively recently has rehabilitation of offenders—attempts to give them the ability and motivation to live in a law-abiding and socially approved manner—gained wide acceptance. The correctional system, however, is still largely punitive. Although retribution no longer follows the "eye for an eye, tooth for a tooth" formula (in which slanderers had their tongues cut out, thieves had their hands amputated, and rapists were castrated), the retributive orientation can be seen in public demands for longer sentences for such crimes as murder.

The punishments meted out to murderers, forgers, and other offenders are meant to serve several purposes. Besides the often-cited goals of preventing crime and rehabilitating offenders, punishment serves to sustain the morale of those who conform to society's rules. In other words, law-abiding members of society demand that offenders be punished partly to reinforce their own ambivalent feelings about conformity. They believe that if they must make sacrifices to obey the law, someone who does not make such sacrifices should not be allowed to "get away with it." Even those who view criminals as sick rather than evil, and who call for the "treatment" of offenders to correct an organic or psychological disorder, are essentially demanding retribution (Barlow & Kauzlarich, 2002).

In recent years, the public's desire for more retribution has resulted in pressure in many states to restore capital punishment and to restore more punitive, as opposed to rehabilitative, forms of correction. In 1995, for example, Alabama reinstituted the penal practices of chain gangs and rock breaking, practices that were far more common in southern prisons a century ago than they are today.

Some criminologists, such as James Q. Wilson (1977, 1993), have suggested that society needs the firm moral authority derived from stigmatizing and punishing crime. Although Wilson grants that prisoners must "pay their debts" without being deprived of their civil rights after release from prison and without suffering the continued indignities of parole supervision and unemployment, he stresses the moral value of stigmatizing crime and those who commit it: "To destigmatize crime would be to lift from it the weight of moral judgment and to make crime simply a particular occupation or avocation which society has chosen to reward less (or perhaps more) than other pursuits. If there is no stigma attached to an activity, then society has no business making it a crime" (1977, p. 230).

Laws that establish penalties for crimes are enacted by the states and by the federal government. But concern for the rights of citizens faced with the power of the state to enforce laws and inflict punishment is a prominent feature of the U.S. Constitution. The Fourth Amendment guarantees protection against "unreasonable searches and seizures"; the Fifth Amendment guarantees that citizens shall not be compelled to testify against themselves or be tried more than once for the same crime (double jeopardy) or be deprived of due process of law; the Sixth Amendment guarantees the right to a public trial by an impartial jury, the right to subpoena and confront witnesses, and the right to legal counsel; the Eighth Amendment prohibits "cruel and unusual punishment" and "excessive" bail or fines.

The trend toward "hard time" incarceration for both teenage and adult offenders is growing throughout the United States. It has yet to be determined whether these measures actually reduce recidivism.

It is important to note these points because they are at the heart of conflicts about how fairly laws are enforced and how impartially justice is meted out. In the controversy over capital punishment, for example, opponents argue that it has become a form of cruel and unusual punishment. Others argue that because those who are condemned are often unable to afford adequate counsel, they have been deprived of their rights under the Sixth Amendment. Whatever one believes about such controversies, it is clear that the Constitution establishes the basis for protection of individual rights but also leaves much discretion to citizens and lawmakers to establish the ground rules for how justice is to be carried out.

The role of the sociologist in these debates is to help establish a scientific basis for decision making. Empirical data collected by social scientists and government statisticians can be used to compare homicide rates in states that have the death penalty and states that do not. When this is done, as in Figure 5–14 on page 170, the results provide dramatic support for the contention that the death penalty does not deter murderers. As a form of retribution, it allows victims' family members to feel that justice has been done, but the data show that murder rates in states like Texas and Louisiana, where the death penalty is legal and executions routine, remain higher than average despite capital punishment.

Many social scientists also cite the negative effects of the severe anti-drug-dealing and anti-gun-possession laws put into effect in New York during the 1970s. In the years since these laws were passed, there have been significant increases in rates of drug dealing and arrests on drug and gun possession charges, despite much higher penalties for these offenses (Califano, 1998). Critics of such findings point out that very often criminals ask themselves before committing a crime, "Will I be punished if I am caught, and how severe will the punishment be?"

Research on the deterrent effects of punishment for crimes other than murder is made extremely difficult by the fact that very few perpetrators of these crimes are actually caught and sentenced. For many decades, researchers have been able to show that whatever the punishment, a high likelihood of arrest is the greatest deterrent to crime. However, the arrest rate for property crimes is only about 18 percent, and for all index felonies it is only 20 percent (*UCR*, 2006). These rates are based on crimes reported to the police. Because far more crimes are committed than are known to the police, the actual rates are even lower.

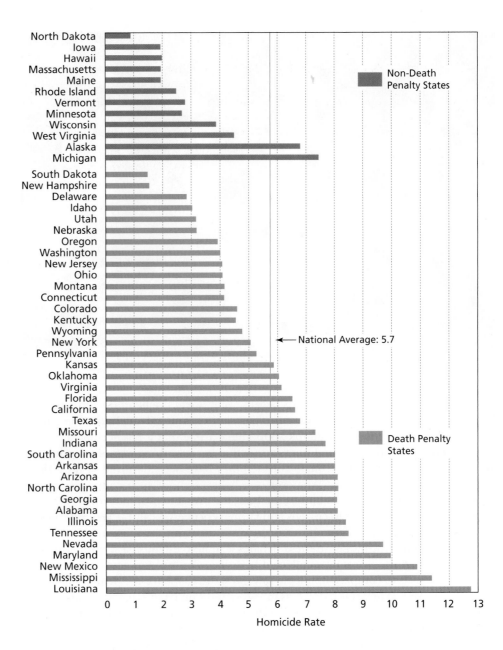

Figure 5–14 Homicide Rates in Death Penalty and Non-Death-Penalty States

Source: Data from *Uniform Crime Reports,* 2004.

Rehabilitation

The idea of rehabilitating offenders, which has developed only during the past century and a half, rests on the concept of crime as a social aberration and the offender as a social misfit whose aberrant behavior can be modified to conform to society's norms—in other words, "cured." As yet there are no clear guidelines concerning the form of rehabilitation that will be most effective with a particular kind of offender. Rehabilitation usually includes varying amounts of counseling, educational and training programs, and work experience. In the past, the programs that have had the most success have been those that prepare criminals to enter the world of legitimate work and help them actually secure and hold jobs after incarceration. However, such ambitious programs are unlikely to be implemented on a large scale.

By the 1990s both the ideal and the practice of rehabilitation in prisons and among paroled offenders had reached a low point in what has historically been a cyclical process. Efforts to institute rehabilitation programs often follow efforts to increase the severity of sentencing. When it is shown that longer sentences and harsher punishment do not prevent crime or repeated offenses, society tends to shift toward efforts to rehabilitate criminals (Conklin, 2007; Friedman, 1993).

Studies of **recidivism**—the probability that a former inmate will break the law after release and be arrested again—have found no conclusive evidence that various approaches to rehabilitation, such as prison counseling programs or outright discharge, are more effective in reducing recidivism rates than more punitive alternatives. All that can be said is that some of the rehabilitation experiments undertaken to date—in particular, those that include extensive job training and job placement—have been more successful than others.

In an in-depth study of the juvenile-justice system and rehabilitation, sociologist Mark Jacobs (1990) found that professionals in the system—court officials, parole officers, psychologists, correctional administrators, and others—often believe they must "screw the system" to make it rehabilitate rather than do further harm to juvenile offenders and young "persons in need of supervision." (The latter is a court-designated category of juveniles who are judged by their parents and others to be highly at risk of falling into a criminal subculture; courts can order these children to be placed in foster homes or residential care facilities even if they have committed no crimes.)

Jacobs's (1990) study showed that rehabilitation is hampered by a maze of organizations and regulations. Juveniles are shuttled from one jurisdiction or program to another and are often the victims of inadequately funded training programs and haphazard supervision by overburdened caseworkers. Given the extreme splintering of the system—family courts, juvenile courts, schools, parents, parole officers, correctional officers, psychologists, and many more—the young offender is often deprived of the rehabilitation to which he or she is entitled. And no coherent set of laws holds anyone in the system accountable for the youth's rehabilitation; that is, no single institution, group, or person can be said to be at fault. In such a no-fault society, Jacobs argues, rehabilitation will remain a distant ideal.

The nature of the prison system itself is a major hindrance to rehabilitative efforts. Prisons remove offenders from virtually all contact with society and its norms, then subject them to almost continual contact with people who have committed crimes ranging from murder and petty larceny to homosexual rape and fraud (Garland, 2005). Often inmates are abused by their guards. A notorious case, probably indicative of more widespread patterns of abuse, was revealed in a 1992 court ruling against 119 former officials and guards at a Georgia prison for women; inmates were able to prove that they had been subjected to sexual abuse and rape over a period of several years (Applebome, 1992).

Within prison walls, offenders are punished by being deprived of liberty, autonomy, heterosexual contacts, goods and services, and the security normally obtained from participation in ordinary social institutions. At the same time, prisoners create a social order of their own. Adherence to the norms of prison life, which may be necessary for both mental and physical well-being, further separates inmates' goals and motivations from those of the larger society and makes it more difficult for them to benefit from whatever rehabilitative measures are available.

The most common type of rehabilitation program consists of work training. However, prison work is generally menial and unsatisfying, involving such jobs as kitchen helper or janitor. The difficulty of rehabilitating offenders in prison has led to various attempts to reform them outside prison walls. This approach seems to have several benefits. Treating offenders without exposing them to all the deficiencies of the prison system not only reduces the antisocial effects of prolonged exposure to a criminal society but also reduces the cost of custodial facilities and personnel. This makes treatment resources more available to those who seem to have the best prospects for rehabilitation. Perhaps the oldest and most widely used system of this kind is the *work release* program, in which prisoners are allowed to leave the institution for part of the day or week to work at an outside job. Although this type of program was first authorized in Wisconsin in 1913, it has become widely used only since the mid-1950s. Today many states and the federal government have authorized various kinds of work release programs.

The idea of releasing convicted felons into society, even for limited periods, has met with considerable opposition, but in general such programs seem to work well. Besides removing convicts from the criminal society in the prison, work release programs reimburse the state for some of the costs of supporting them and allow the prisoners to support their dependents, thereby helping them stay off the welfare rolls. In addition, a work release program is a practical step toward reintegrating offenders into society because many of those who successfully complete the program retain their jobs after release. In fact, in a classic study Martinson (1972) found that the most effective single factor in rehabilitating offenders is a program of training for work following release; work during the prison term itself; and above all, job placement and training during probation.

At present there are two competing tendencies in corrections in the United States with regard to work and occupational training. On one hand, state prison systems are seeking to put prisoners to work, usually at unskilled jobs, on contracts with private businesses that will reduce soaring prison costs. On the other hand, there has been a decrease in the number of job training programs that prepare inmates for productive work after incarceration (Califano, 1998; Gondles, 1999).

The controversy over youthful offenders raises further questions about what kinds of corrections are most appropriate for this segment of the criminal population. So far it does not appear that more punitive programs, or "boot camps," are more effective than others. In addition, it is extremely costly to keep teenagers in prison or detention; the costs range from $20,000 to $90,000 per year, depending on the state and the particular form of incarceration (Belluck, 1996). Many states, therefore, are experimenting with programs in which youthful offenders can attend school or job training while in prison or in lieu of prison (Barlow & Kauzlarich, 2002).

Programs like these are controversial because violent offenders are expected to do "hard time." In consequence, a few states (New Jersey, Texas, Florida, and California) have created residential training schools for juvenile offenders. This is an old concept that is being modified with new techniques for supervision, mentoring, and training (Snyder & Sickmund, 2006). Although such programs may not work for the most violent or hardened young criminals, many penologists believe that when young inmates can be released to their communities with new skills and education, more positive options are open to them and they are less likely to drift back into a criminal lifestyle (Sadd & Grinc, 1996). But many young offenders return to extremely troubled families and peer groups. The more contact they have with professionals who can help them find alternatives to a violent home or neighborhood group, the better their chances—and society's—of avoiding crime and violence (Belluck, 1996; Gardner, 2005).

Large centers like this one in Prattville, Alabama, and "boot camp" detention centers that specialize in harsh treatment, have been prone to abuses such that juvenile detention authorities throughout the United States are examining their juvenile detention policies.

Prevention

The idea of preventing crime and delinquency before they occur is an attractive one, but like rehabilitation, it is difficult to implement. Aside from the deterrent effect of punishment, crime prevention is customarily defined in three different ways: (1) the sum total of all influences and activities that contribute to the development of a non-deviant personality; (2) attempts to deal with conditions in a person's environment that are believed to lead to crime and delinquency; and (3) specific services or programs designed to prevent further crime and delinquency.

Programs based on the first definition include measures designed to improve the social environment, such as improved housing and job opportunities for ghetto dwellers. Although one of their goals may be the reduction of crime and delinquency in the target area, this is rarely their primary goal. Moreover, studies of youths involved in antipoverty programs have not demonstrated a positive correlation between such participation and reduced delinquency rates. The most positive results are found in evaluations of Job Corps and other education, job training, and social-skills programs in which young people at risk are given a chance to leave their neighborhood peer groups.

The second definition includes efforts based on Sutherland's theory of differential association (Sutherland & Cressey, 1960), such as efforts to reduce children's exposure to the antisocial and/or illegal activities of people around them, to improve their family life, and to create a viable and conforming social order in the community itself. Several projects of this sort have been attempted; some, like the Chicago Area Project (discussed shortly), have had notable success.

Most crime prevention programs attempt to work within the third definition—prevention of further delinquency and crime. They include well-established approaches such as parole, probation, and training schools, as well as more experimental programs. It is difficult to compare these approaches with those attempted under the other two definitions because they deal with quite different sets of circumstances.

An early prevention program, the Chicago Area Project, was established in the mid-1930s in the Chicago slums, where immigrant families were no longer able to control their children because of a weakening social order. The project sought to develop youth welfare programs that would be viable after the project leaders had left. It was assumed that local youths would have more success than outside workers in establishing recreation programs (including summer camping), community improvement campaigns, and programs devoted to teaching and assisting delinquent youths and even some adults who were returning to the community after release from prison. The project not only demonstrated the feasibility of using untrained local youths to establish welfare programs but also indicated a possible decrease in the delinquency rate (Kobrin, 1959). This model has been used successfully in many communities to diminish gang violence.

It is difficult to prove the effectiveness of preventive measures. Although they seem to fail at least as often as they succeed, the difficulty may lie more in the specific kinds of services offered than in the concept of prevention itself. When delinquency prevention seems to fail, there are often signs that there were some beneficial effects, even if they were not of the desired magnitude. It should be kept in mind that most of the programs described here are experimental and have not been attempted on a large scale. Delinquency prevention needs further research and more government funding (Hagedorn, 1988; Williams & Kornblum, 1994).

According to Charles Silberman (1980), one of the major problems with programs designed to control juvenile delinquency is that they place too much emphasis on methods of policing, more efficient courts, and improved correctional programs, and too little emphasis on community programs that give families the support they need to deal with delinquency:

> If a community development program is to have any chance of success, those in charge must understand that the controls that lead to reduced crime cannot be imposed from the outside; they must emerge from changes in the community

itself and in the people who compose it. Hence the emphasis must be on enabling poor people to take charge of their own lives—on helping them gain a sense of competence and worth, a sense of being somebody who matters. (p. 430)

I n their efforts to reduce crime, governments at all levels experience more frustration than success. In a few short periods, such as the present period of relative and sustained affluence in the United States, crime rates have fallen, or at least the rates of some crimes have, but such lulls have been temporary. As crime historian Lawrence M. Friedman (1993) points out, crime is far too complicated and diverse and too firmly embedded in American culture to be controlled and eliminated. Whenever one kind of crime is reduced, criminals invent others. And social change is constantly at work on the criminal-justice system, producing a recurrent pattern of criminalizing, decriminalizing, and recriminalizing certain behaviors.

The fact that important decreases in some categories of violent crimes were announced in recent years also calmed public fear of crime somewhat. For the first time in recent memory, in fact, the public rated educational quality above crime and drugs as the foremost issue facing the nation in coming years. Crime and terrorism remain major concerns of Americans, especially the elderly and residents of central cities, but according to the National Opinion Research Center (NORC), citizens are beginning to question such policies as mandatory sentencing, the "three-strikes" policy, and some aspects of the War on Drugs, which have resulted in large increases in the prison population (Conklin, 2007).

Mandatory Sentencing

In 2005 the U.S. Supreme Court, in a surprising 5–4 decision, struck down the federal mandatory sentencing law, which had been in effect for 21 years and had required

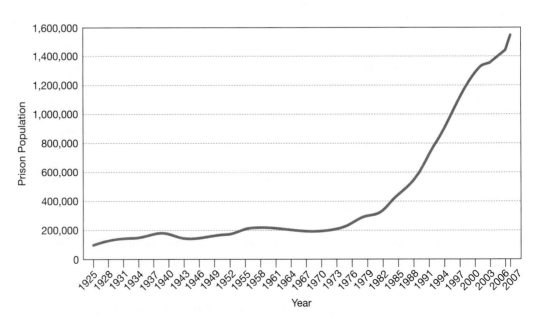

Figure 5–15 State and Federal Prisoners, 1925–2007

Source: Reprinted by permission of The Sentencing Project, 2007.

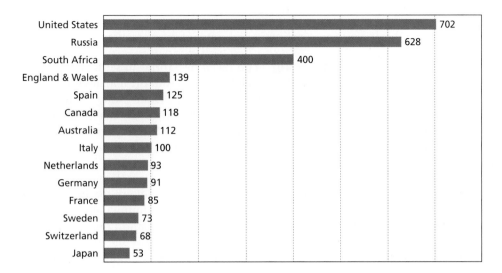

Figure 5–16 Incarceration Rates* for Selected Nations

*Number of people in prison per 100,000 population.

Source: Copyright © 2005 by International Centre for Prison Studies. Reprinted by permission of King's College London.

judges to impose specific sentences in criminal cases. Advocates of mandatory sentencing, like advocates of California's "three-strikes" policy (now in effect in about half the states), claimed that these measures remove career criminals from society. But the majority of the Supreme Court justices found that mandatory sentencing violated the constitutional guarantees of due process and the right of trial by jury. The Court's ruling turned the mandatory sentences for specific crimes into guidelines. Although many advocates of mandatory sentencing were infuriated by the decision, at this writing there does not appear to be enough support in Congress to challenge the ruling through new mandatory-sentencing legislation (Green, 2005).

Arrest and Incarceration

In 2005 about 10 million violent and major property crimes were committed in the United States. Of these, only about 20 percent were cleared by arrests, and even fewer ended in convictions, making crime an attractive pursuit for many people (*UCR*, 2006). Even the relatively small number of people apprehended presents an almost insurmountable burden for existing correctional systems. Court calendars and prison cells are so overloaded that there is continual pressure to find ways to reduce sentences or to create new forms of corrections. One of the most controversial yet widespread strategies is **plea bargaining,** in which the offender agrees to plead guilty to a lesser charge and free the courts from the need to conduct a jury trial. By this means most of those who are convicted of serious crimes receive shortened sentences. Plea bargaining has been criticized for allowing dangerous criminals to receive mild sentences. It has been estimated, however, that if the plea-bargaining process were reduced to even 80 percent of serious crimes, the number of trials would double and put an enormous strain on the court system (Reid, 1993).

The Prison Paradox. As crime rates have decreased over the past few years, rates of imprisonment of Americans have increased, as shown in Figure 5–15. The U.S. rate of incarceration, 702 inmates per 100,000 population, now ranks the United States well ahead of Russia as the nation most likely to use imprisonment, with rates six to eight times higher than other urban industrial democracies (see Figure 5–16). What explains this paradox of declining crime and rising numbers in U.S. prisons? Among the explanations are mandatory sentences at the state and federal levels. These sentencing rules maintain larger numbers in prison for longer periods, thus increasing prison populations, and ensure that while fewer crimes may be committed, those who are arrested are more likely to face lengthy prison terms. As states rushed to build new prisons—often located in areas with high unemployment rates—work in the prisons becomes a major

How does the United States compare to other major democracies in terms of its rate of incarceration?

feature of the regional economy, so that decreases in prison populations are threatening and result in lobbying efforts to maintain high rates of incarceration.

Racial Disparities in Sentencing. The racial disparities in sentencing in the United States are dramatic. One out of every eight African American males is incarcerated on a given day, and state laws that bar former felons from voting result in the "felony disenfranchisement" of over 1 million African American men, a situation that can be of decisive importance in states like Florida, in which Republican state officials vigorously apply felony rules to eliminate voters who might otherwise vote against their party's candidates.

Alternatives to Incarceration. The costs of imprisonment are soaring, causing many states to question mandatory sentencing and seek community alternatives to incarceration. Alabama, which until recently ranked with Texas and Louisiana among states with the highest rates of imprisonment, faced a budget crisis due in large part to the costs of running its prisons. In 2004, the Alabama Sentencing Commission found that the state pays $26 a day to house an individual in prison but only $11 a day to divert a prisoner into intermediate sanctions. Another recent report on Alabama's corrections system found that the state pays $9,000 per person per year for incarceration versus $2,000 for community corrections programs. In consequence, Alabama is now a national leader in developing prison diversion programs and new forms of community corrections (Carter Goble Associates, 2005).

More than 100,000 juveniles are incarcerated on any given day, even though they make up a smaller proportion of the total population than they did in the 1970s. Adult prison populations have also reached extremely high levels. However, of the 6 million people in custody in all U.S. correctional systems, only about 20 percent are in prisons. The majority are under community supervision through probation or parole. (**Probation** is supervision of offenders who have not been sentenced to jail or prison; **parole** is supervision of people who have been released from prison.) And although both probation and parole were originally intended for nonviolent offenders, they are increasingly being used for those who have committed felonies because of the costs of incarceration and the problems of overcrowded prisons.

Recidivism rates are quite high among felons who are placed on probation. Research indicates that from one-half to two-thirds are rearrested, a situation that indicates the continuing need to develop a greater array of sentencing options and rehabilitation strategies while ensuring public safety (Garland, 2005). Faced with these problems, many states have been seeking alternatives to conventional incarceration and parole. Community corrections, in which the offender provides a service to social-welfare agencies or neighborhood associations, is one approach. Another is house arrest and monitoring by electronic devices.

Occupational and Corporate Crimes

A variety of legal reforms have been proposed to curb occupational and corporate crimes. One approach would be to increase the penalties for such crimes. In 2002, in the aftermath of the Enron scandal and other corporate fraud cases, Congress passed the Sarbanes-Oxley Act, which makes it mandatory for the directors of public corporations (those whose shares are traded on the stock exchanges) to sign off on annual audits and accept responsibility if accounting fraud is revealed. The law provides stiff new penalties for corporate fraud.

Obviously, stronger enforcement must accompany legal reform if it is to be meaningful, and this means more money and personnel for enforcement agencies. To detect more income tax cheating, for example, the IRS must hire more auditors. To detect more white-collar crime, the FBI must devote more resources to investigations in this area. Similarly, once a case against occupational offenders has been won in court, the judge must be willing to invoke the full penalty allowed under the law.

These two approaches—legal reform (particularly tougher penalties) and stronger enforcement—would probably deter much occupational crime. More than most other types of crimes, occupational crimes involve calculation, planning, and the weighing of gains against costs. Increasing the costs of crime as well as the risk of detection might lead occupational criminals to conclude that honesty is more profitable.

Organized Crime

It is particularly hard to fight organized crime, for several reasons. A major one is the difficulty of obtaining proof of syndicate activities that will be accepted in court. Witnesses rarely come forward; either they fear retaliation or they themselves are too deeply implicated. Since the top levels of the syndicate's hierarchy are so well insulated from those below them, witnesses are rarely able to testify against them. Documentary evidence is equally rare, since the transactions of organized crime are seldom written down. Finally, corruption hinders effective prosecution of organized crime.

Despite these obstacles, in recent decades the FBI has made immense progress in its battle against organized crime; today numerous reputed syndicate leaders are under indictment or in jail. Experts credit this breakthrough to a number of factors, of which the most prominent is that the FBI now devotes about one-quarter of its personnel to combating organized crime. Other important factors are using undercover agents in long-term investigations, pooling the resources of agencies that formerly competed with one another, and giving the FBI jurisdiction in narcotics cases. Especially significant has been the use of sophisticated surveillance techniques and computer technology. The witness protection program, in which witnesses are offered new identities, support, and protection in moving away from their organized-crime contacts, has also proven successful in a number of instances. An example is the successful arrest and conviction of mob boss John Gotti and his son, both major organized-crime figures who were notorious for flouting the law.

Public-Order and Juvenile-Justice Reforms

Many criminologists and legal authorities agree that there are too many laws that make certain behaviors (such as truancy) illegal only for children, as well as too many laws that address nonviolent victimless crimes like adultery, homosexuality, prostitution, and drunkenness. Offenders in both categories account for 40 percent of the caseload in both juvenile and adult courts. In addition, abuse at home often causes juveniles to become runaways. When they are apprehended for this offense, they spend even more time in juvenile detention. The large number of arrests of juvenile runaways has led experts such as Edwin M. Schur (1973) to advocate a thorough reform of the concept of juvenile justice that would tolerate a broader range of behaviors and define as crimes only specific antisocial acts. Similarly, many citizens advocate lessening of penalties for possession of drugs like marijuana. The conservative mood of the nation makes such reforms unlikely, however.

By the early 1990s rates of juvenile crimes and the number of juveniles in criminal detention had risen dramatically. These trends, combined with the impact of some highly sensational juvenile crimes, have tended to blur the distinction between juvenile and adult offenders. In 1996, for example, a 12-year-old boy became the youngest inmate of a high-security prison. He and his 13-year-old accomplice had been convicted of dropping a small child from a 14-story building in Chicago. The sentencing itself, carried out under a new Illinois law, was an example of the trend toward judging serious juvenile crimes on the same basis as adult crimes.

Fears of an increase in juvenile crimes are supported by statistical evidence, and victims of these crimes are calling for tougher penalties (Snyder & Sickmund, 2006). But the trend toward greater punitiveness has its critics, who believe sending young offenders to prison will simply produce more super-predators (Males, 1996).

In addition to proposals directed at law enforcement agencies, some small-scale community-based approaches have been attempted. An example is the House of Umoja in Philadelphia. This program, which combines surrogate family relationships with job opportunities and placement counseling for youths, has virtually eliminated street violence in a ghetto neighborhood. A similar program in Ponce, Puerto Rico, provides a wide range of services to an entire community; one of its achievements has been to cut the delinquency rate in half despite a rapidly growing teenage population (Kornblum & Boggs, 1984). Maryland, New York, and other states are also experimenting with programs that provide intensive home surveillance and counseling for delinquents from high-crime and poor neighborhoods.

Despite these and other measures, many experts agree that the problem remains far from a solution. None of the approaches taken so far has been shown to be successful. As a result, public policy toward serious juvenile crime is in a state of considerable confusion, and opinions on what can be done vary widely. At present, many states are diverting juveniles charged with felonies to adult courts, where they face adult prison sentences. Currently about 200,000 minors each year are so diverted, the vast majority of them facing convictions on drug and property crime offences (Bilchik, 2003).

The Department of Justice holds that the problem of juvenile crime is caused by the breakdown of family and community controls and that until these are strengthened, there is little that federal funds can accomplish. However, members of the Congressional Select Committee on Children argue that the rate of poverty among children has increased to almost 20 percent at the same time that there have been immense cuts in child welfare services (32 percent), juvenile delinquency prevention programs (55 percent), and drug and mental-health treatment programs (30 percent). Most law enforcement officials believe that without more resources to address joblessness, lack of education, and lack of housing and recreational facilities, and to provide drug treatment on demand, there will be little overall improvement in the juvenile crime situation (Snyder & Sickmund, 2006; Travis & Petersilia, 2001).

Gun Control

In recent decades there has been increasing demand for stricter federal supervision of the purchase and sale of firearms, particularly the cheap handguns that are readily available in many areas. However, opponents of gun control legislation, represented primarily by the National Rifle Association (NRA), constitute one of the most powerful interest groups in the nation. The NRA draws much of its strength from areas of the nation where hunting is popular and where there is a strong feeling that people need to protect themselves and their families. Members of the NRA claim that gun control measures would violate the "right to bear arms" that is contained in the Second Amendment to the United States Constitution. This is a strong position and one that most political leaders are unwilling to challenge directly.

In 2005 the Bush administration and Republican leaders in the House of Representatives, especially Majority Whip Tom DeLay, refused to seek renewal of the ban on assault weapons passed in 1994 as part of a broad legislative effort to institute some forms of gun control (Sontag, 2005). The administration was also well aware that the public's conservative mood favored a strong stance in favor of the individual's right to self-defense. These attitudes are visible in recent opinion polls, like the one shown in Table 5–4, which show that although a slim majority of Americans still support strict gun control measures, that support has been steadily eroding from its high point in 1993.

Opponents of gun control claim that the decision to commit murder has nothing to do with possession of a gun; a killer can stab, strangle, poison, or batter a victim to death. Gun control, therefore, would make little difference. Although this argument sounds logical, it ignores the lethal potential of guns, which are about five times more likely to kill than knives, the next most commonly used murder weapon. And since most murders are spontaneous results of passion rather than carefully planned acts, it

TABLE 5–4	Responses to Gallup Poll on Gun Control

In general, do you feel that the laws covering the sale of firearms should be made more strict, less strict, or kept as they are now?

Date	More Strict	Less Strict	Kept as Now	No Opinion
2004	54%	11%	34%	1%
1999	68	6	25	1
1993	72	5	22	1
1988	64	6	27	3
1986	60	8	30	2
1981	65	3	30	2
1980	59	3	30	2
1975	69	3	24	4

Source: The Gallup Poll. All rights reserved. Reprinted with permission.

follows that the easy availability of guns is likely to increase the death rate in criminal assaults. In most cases murders are a result of three factors: impulse, the lethal capacity of the weapon, and the availability of the weapon. Strict gun control would eliminate or at least reduce the latter two factors.

A significant majority of the American public has long favored tighter controls over firearms that stop short of a complete ban on handguns. This support for gun control correlates most closely with the nation's murder rate. Throughout the 1980s and 1990s the murder rate varied between about 8 and 10 per 100,000. Table 5–4 demonstrates that high poll numbers favoring gun control in the early part of the period correlate to a high murder rate (associated with the crack cocaine epidemic, among other factors). The lower figures in the mid-1980s correlate with a lower murder rate. When the murder rate increased in the early 1990s, support for gun control moved upward again. But even as political leaders and the majority of the public joined the outcry against widespread availability of heavy firepower, the NRA experienced its largest jump in membership ever. And in fact, public opinion on the basic issues of gun control was altered, but not dramatically (Birnbaum, 1999).

In 1993, in response to what had come to be perceived as a national epidemic of gunshot injuries and deaths, as well as the earlier shooting of President Reagan and his press secretary Matthew Brady, Congress finally passed the Brady Act and other legislation to limit the access of felons to handguns and assault weapons. In 1996 Congress attempted to repeal the ban on assault weapons, but the repeal was vetoed by President Clinton. During the Bush administration, as noted earlier, support for gun control, and even the ban on assault weapons, declined as the National Rifle Association and its allies continued to hold sway over a majority of Republican elected officials. The shootings at Virginia Polytechnic Institute in Blacksburg in 2007 led to renewed calls for better enforcement of existing laws requiring background checks for gun buyers. But even this devastating mass murder has not resulted in a strong push for gun control among Democrats, who, like the Republicans, tend to fear the influence of gun advocates (Milite, 2007).

Not all antigun, antiviolence policy is made at the federal level. Many states and municipalities have recognized that the alarming increase in the number of youths aged 10 to 17 who are arrested for violent crimes demands more creative approaches than simply trying them in adult courts and locking them up with adult prisoners. In the wake of the rash of killings in 1999, California passed both a ban on assault weapons and a "gun a month" law that limits handgun purchases to one every 30 days.

While the political debate has continued, there have been quite successful efforts to decrease the number of available guns in high-risk communities—that is, places where there have been recent histories of high murder rates and deaths of bystanders. Since 1991 Congress and the Justice Department have cooperated in instituting experimental programs to decrease the number of guns carried in "high-risk places at high-risk times" (Sherman, Shaw, & Rogan, 1995). Perhaps the most important of these is the Kansas City Gun Experiment, part of the Justice Department's Weed and Seed program in which local authorities were given wide latitude in planning strategies to reduce gun violence. The Kansas City experiment attempted to show a relationship between seizures of guns and reduced crimes committed with guns. A target police beat, covering a neighborhood where homicides were 20 times above the national average, was selected. The beat was patrolled by officers with special training in detecting people who were carrying weapons. On another beat, similar in demographic and crime characteristics, the police continued to use their traditional methods. After 29 weeks of operations, statistics showed that gun crimes had dropped significantly on the beat with the special patrols. Drive-by shootings also decreased, as did homicides of all kinds. In patrolling the beat, the police concentrated on likely gun carriers in special hot spots, where crimes had often been committed in the past. Since the focus was on crimes committed with guns, it is not surprising that there was little difference between the two beats in other violent crimes or in property crimes.

From a policy standpoint, the most important conclusion of the experiment is that "the police can increase the number of guns seized in high crime areas at relatively modest cost" (Sherman, Shaw, & Rogan, 1995, p. 9). Specially trained patrols seize about three times as many guns over a similar period as do traditional police patrols. Similar programs of community policing and gun interdiction (funded by private foundations as well as by the federal government) are likely to become a major area of antiviolence policy in high-crime communities throughout the nation.

An important issue related to gun control is the extent to which women who are heads of households will choose to arm themselves with handguns for protection. Because the number of female-headed households is rising rapidly, any increase in the propensity of women to arm themselves could raise the overall level of handgun ownership to 50 million in the next decade. But research shows that women are still far more reluctant than men to purchase handguns; female-headed households are half as likely to have handguns as male-headed households (Zimring, 1985). This suggests that the outcome of the political battle over handguns may eventually depend on how both sides manage to appeal to female voters.

Future Prospects

As the nation has turned its attention to the consequences of terrorism and the war in Iraq, the fear of crime has decreased, as has the widespread support that once existed for more severe sentencing and the treatment of juveniles as adults (Barrette, 2007). Does this mean that there will be changes in the harsh mandatory sentencing measures that many states have passed since the early 1980s? Does the public's concern about the erosion of civil liberties due to the policies of the Bush administration in its so-called war on terror mean that there will be more efforts to bring about prison reform and rehabilitation? At this writing, it is not at all clear if this will be the case. In California, for example, efforts to steer public opinion away from policies that favor large-scale incarceration and severe punishment meet with strong opposition from well-organized lobbying groups, such as the state's union of prison guards, that benefit economically from the existence of prison populations in their midst. This is also true to varying degrees in other large states, such as Illinois, New York, and Texas. Also, as we have seen in this chapter, as the gap between the rich and the poor continues to widen, it is likely that there will be slow but steady increases in some forms of violent and property crime. These increases are likely to continue to motivate those who take a hard line about imprisonment. Eventually, once issues of terrorism and international warfare are eased in the public mind, it is likely that there will be another round of prison reform and revisions of what most judges and many criminal lawyers see as overly harsh sentencing guidelines that have resulted in the politically embarrassing levels of imprisonment in the United States.

GOING BEYOND LEFT AND RIGHT

There are many differences among people on the liberal left and the conservative right concerning crime and its control. Liberals believe that crime is caused by social-structural factors, such as poverty, and recommend rehabilitative strategies for offenders. Conservatives stress personal responsibility and the rights of crime victims. Are there no areas of common ground? Yes, there are. Sociology offers some important ones, especially if one thinks globally.

Indeed, on the global level the differences between left and right diminish, at least when confronted by the threat of organized criminal attacks on the rule of law. If a society like Russia or Italy or even, in some specific cases, the United States cannot protect its citizens against criminal victimization and organized crime, it can no longer claim to be the legitimate representative of its people, nor can it guarantee order within its borders or contribute to world peace. These are fundamental issues of human existence. When President Bush speaks out forcefully against widespread corruption in many of the world's nations, he stresses a theme that unites people with divergent political views (although some may wish that he spoke more forcefully about corporate and political corruption in the United States). Without the rule of law, the distinctions between left and right are absurd. A sociological analysis of global crime shows us that policies to address the threat of criminal victimization are vital to economic and social well-being at all levels of society.

A good example of the move toward international cooperation in enforcing the rule of law is the global movement among world leaders to combat illegal trafficking in human beings, either for sexual markets or as what is essentially a form of slave labor. President Bush and many other world leaders have taken forceful steps against the international trafficking of women and children, for example, a subject to which we will return in later chapters.

Summary

- The criminal law prohibits certain acts and prescribes punishments to be meted out to offenders. In practice, the definition of criminality changes according to what law enforcement authorities perceive as criminal behavior.

- Researchers have attempted to find more reliable ways of tracking criminal activity. Self-report studies and victimization surveys provide useful data; both are used to supplement the FBI's *Uniform Crime Reports*.

- Violent personal crimes include assault, robbery, and the various forms of homicide. Robbery usually occurs between strangers, murder between friends or relatives.

- Occasional property crimes include vandalism, check forgery, shoplifting, and so on. Offenders are usually unsophisticated and unlikely to have a criminal record.

- Occupational, or white-collar, crimes are committed by people who break the law as part of their normal business activity. They include such acts as embezzlement, fraud (including computer crimes), and insider trading in the securities industry. Occupational offenders have a respectable appearance and often consider themselves respectable citizens.

- Corporate crimes include a variety of illegal practices of private corporations, including environmental crimes, insider trading, illegal labor practices, defrauding of pension plans, and the like. Such crimes are extremely difficult to control.

- Public-order offenses include prostitution, drunkenness, vagrancy, and the like. They are often called victimless crimes because they cause harm only to the offender.

- Organized crime is a system in which illegal activities are carried out as part of a rational plan devised by a large organization for profit. The profits come largely from supplying illegal goods and services to the public.

- Conventional criminals commit robbery, burglary, and other crimes as a way of life, usually beginning their criminal careers as members of juvenile gangs and developing into professional criminals, who are dedicated to a life of crime and are seldom caught. They include safecrackers, check forgers, and blackmailers. An increasingly common form of conventional crime is cybercrime, especially identity theft.

- Teenagers and young adults account for almost half of all arrests in the United States. The majority of arrests for property crimes are of people under 25 years of age. In addition, many young people become involved in drug commerce at the retail level. Status offenses like running away and vagrancy are another common reason for arrests of juveniles, especially young women.

- Hate crimes are crimes in which the defendant intentionally selects a victim based on the actual or perceived race, color, national origin, ethnicity, gender, disability, or sexual orientation of that person. They are often carried out by young people, acting on emotions taken from the adults who socialize them.

- The much higher rate of homicide in the United States than in other urban industrial nations is sometimes attributed to violence by juvenile gang members, but the available evidence indicates that it is not the presence of gangs per se but the ready availability of guns that accounts for the prevalence of lethal violence in American cities.

- Various explanations of the causes and prevalence of crime have been suggested. They include biological explanations; demographic factors (including gender and age); and sociological explanations based on conflict theory, functionalism, and interactionism.

- Conflict approaches to the study of crime see inequalities of wealth, status, and power as the underlying conditions that produce criminal behavior. These inequalities are thought to explain the overrepresentation of blacks in official crime statistics. A related problem is racial profiling, in which blacks are more likely than people of other races to be subjected to searches, arrests, and other actions by law enforcement authorities.

- The functionalist explanation of crime is based on anomie theory, in which crime is considered to be the result of a disparity between approved goals and the means of achieving them.

- Interactionist explanations include differential association, in which criminal behavior is said to be learned from family and peers, and theories about the origin and character of delinquent subcultures.

- Efforts to control crime take four forms: retribution-deterrence, rehabilitation, prevention, and reform of the criminal-justice system. Retribution-deterrence focuses on punishing the criminal and attempting to deter others from committing similar crimes. The idea of rehabilitating offenders rests on the concept of cure; the most successful form of rehabilitation is work release. Programs to prevent crime and delinquency include parole, probation, training schools, and more experimental programs.

- Proposals for reform of the criminal- and juvenile-justice systems include imposing harsher and more specific penalties for conventional crimes, increasing the penalties for occupational and corporate crimes and improving law enforcement in this area, repealing laws dealing with status and public-order offenses, and passing more stringent gun control legislation. Recently there has been increased emphasis on punishment and incapacitation as opposed to rehabilitation. However, higher rates of imprisonment have resulted in severe overcrowding of the prison system, leading to proposals like community corrections and house arrest.

Key Terms

crime index, p. 135
crime, p. 137
criminal law, p. 137
civil law, p. 137
victimization reports, p. 140
murder, p. 142

manslaughter, p. 142
differential association, p. 146
embezzlement, p. 146
fraud, p. 146
organized crime, p. 149
status offenses, p. 153

anomie, p. 165
social control, p. 167
recidivism, p. 171
plea bargaining, p. 175
probation, p. 176
parole, p. 176

Social Problems Online

The Internet offers a plethora of resources on crime and the criminal-justice system. Starting with the FBI at **www.fbi.gov/**, one can locate several sources of information about current and historical investigations. Clicking on Most Wanted Fugitives brings up the Internet's version of the "wanted" poster. On the FBI's homepage are links to monographs about the agency's most famous cases, hotlines on current unsolved crimes, congressional testimony, and downloadable files that contain statistics from the *Uniform Crime Reports.*

The U.S. Department of Justice, at **www.usdoj.gov/**, has a regularly updated homepage with links to various agencies and projects. The Violence Against Women Office has a Web site at **www.usdoj.gov/vawo/** with information on the National Domestic Violence Hotline, copies of federal legislation and regulations, and ongoing research reports and studies. The Bureau of Justice Statistics, at **www.ojp.usdoj .gov/bjs/welcome.html**, provides statistics, most in downloadable format, about crimes and their victims, drugs and crime, and the criminal-justice system. It also has links to other sources of data on crime.

The Federal Bureau of Prisons site can be accessed at **www.bop.gov/**. It provides statistics on the federal prison population (inmates and staff) broken down by age, ethnicity, race, sentences, types of offenses, and other variables. The bureau's Program Statements can be accessed. Research documents pertaining to the prison system are available, and most can be downloaded.

Research Navigator

Follow the instructions on pages 26–27 of this text to access the features of Research Navigator. Once at the Web site, enter your Login Name and Password. Then, to use the Content Select database, use keywords such as "index crimes," "hate crime," and "racial profiling," and the search engine will supply relevant and recent scholarly and popular press publications. Use the *New York Times* search-by-subject archive to find recent news articles related to problems of crime and violence and the Link Library to find relevant Web sites organized by the key terms associated with this chapter.

Go to Research Navigator and choose "Sociology" in the subject box. Then, after pressing the letter "c," choose "crime" as the subject. Go the Web site of the Bureau of Justice Statistics. Find the interactive heading on jails. From 1995 to 2004, what was the increase in the number of inmates per 100,000 population? What is another term for this type of number? What are some explanations for the fact that while crime rates are decreasing, rates of incarceration are still increasing in the United States?

6

POVERTY AMID *Affluence*

Chapter Outline

Dominant Trends

- Income and wealth disparities have reached extremes not seen since the Great Depression of the 1930s. In 2005, the top 10 percent of Americans collected 48.5 percent of all reported income.

- More of the nation's poor are working full time. The working poor rate—the ratio of the working poor to all individuals in the labor force at least 27 weeks—rose from 4.7 percent in 2000 to 5.6 percent in 2004. For the most part, these are working heads of families whose incomes do not afford them adequate shelter or health care.

- As the proportion of households living in poverty increases, so does the number of impoverished children, which is now over 20 percent of all U.S. children.

- Poverty continues to strike minority households at far greater rates than is true for nonminorities. About 26 percent of Native Americans, 25 percent of African Americans, and 23 percent of Latinos have incomes below the official poverty level, compared with about 10 percent of the white population.

- Increases in poverty are accompanied by increases in homelessness. About 1.35 million children—nearly 2 percent of the nation's total—are homeless.

In the United States and throughout the world, the gap between rich and poor is widening. Worldwide, the gap between rich and poor is also a cause of growing concern. Of the 6.4 billion people on the planet, about 1.2 billion are so poor that they must subsist on the equivalent of a dollar a day or less. Although the poor in the United States do not routinely face starvation or the possibility of economic catastrophes like famine, the decline of their health and the growing precariousness of their access to the means of existence result in a wide array of social problems.

We will see in this chapter that there are wide ideological differences among the various policies proposed for dealing with poverty. There are also many different explanations for the persistence of poverty amid growing affluence. But despite the differences in ideology, most observers of inequality in the United States would agree with a statement by Senator Edward M. Kennedy: "As a society we must answer an increasingly urgent question. What can we do to close the widening gap in income and skills that leaves too many Americans unable to participate fully in the American Dream?" (quoted in Stevenson, 2000, p. 3).

Unfortunately, in the wake of globalization and the impact of terrorism on the U.S. economy, rates of poverty in the United States have been increasing steadily since the turn of the century. From 2001 to 2004, poverty rates increased each year; between 2003 and 2004, the number of people living below the official poverty threshold rose by 1.1 million. Between 2004 and 2005, the latest year for which figures are available, the overall poverty rate remained unchanged, with an estimated 37 million people living in poverty according to the most conservative official statistics. Poverty rates for African Americans and Latinos remained unchanged, but those for non-Hispanic whites rose. Only Asian Americans experienced modest decreases in poverty rates (U.S. Census Bureau, 2006). By almost any standard measure, the United States ranks as one of the wealthiest nations in the world. GDP—the total market value of all final goods and services produced within the United States in one year—is almost $9 trillion. If we divide the GDP by the total population to derive the per capita GDP, a crude but commonly used measure of the comparative wealth of nations, we find that the United States ranks well above most other countries, with a GDP of over $35,000 per person. Other advanced industrial nations, such as France, Germany, Denmark, and the United Kingdom, fall below this figure by $10,000 or more (*Statistical Abstract*, 2006).

In the United States, wealth is concentrated in the hands of a relatively small number of people, while many other Americans can barely make ends meet or are living in poverty. American households have a median income of $46,326; about 43 percent enjoy incomes above $50,000 (U.S. Census Bureau, 2006). Indeed, we will see in this chapter that the gap between the rich and the poor has widened in the past decade, that the level of living of most Americans has been declining, that the concentration of wealth in the hands of a few fortunate people has been increasing, and that policymakers are engaged in an intense debate over how to address the problem of persistent poverty. In the first section of the chapter we briefly examine the consequences of the inequality that characterizes American society. Later we explore some theories that attempt to explain the presence of poverty in one of the world's most affluent nations, as well as social policies aimed at reducing or eliminating poverty.

Although this chapter focuses on poverty in the United States, it is important to note that a growing gap between the haves and the have-nots exists throughout the world. One-fifth of the world's people live in the richest nations (including the United States), and their average incomes are 15 times higher than those of the one-fifth who live in the poorest nations. In the world today there are about 160 billionaires and about 2 million millionaires, but there are approximately 100 million homeless people. Americans spend about $5 billion per year on diets to lower their caloric intake, while 400 million people around the world are undernourished to the point of physical deterioration (United Nations Development Programme, 2005). These growing disparities between rich and poor throughout the world have direct effects on the situation of the poor in the United States because many jobs are "exported" to countries where extremely poor people will accept work at almost any wage. The increase in world poverty also contributes to environmental degradation and political instability and violence, which drain resources that might be used to meet a nation's domestic needs.

The experience of poverty is based on conditions in one's own society. People feel poor or rich with reference to others around them, not with reference to very poor or very rich people elsewhere in the world. The experience of living in the United States as a teenager in a family for which every penny counts—and there is rarely enough money for new clothes or a family car or trips outside of town—can be as difficult to bear as life in poverty anywhere. That the poor in the United States are relatively better off than the poor in Bangladesh is of little comfort.

In many less-developed countries, poverty is increasing as unemployment and population growth outstrip economic development.

THE HAVES AND THE HAVE-NOTS

Although equality of opportunity is a central value of American society, equality of outcome is not (Cox & Alm, 2000). Most Americans believe everyone should have the same opportunity to achieve material well-being (equality of opportunity). They do not object to inequality in the actual situation of different groups in society (equality of outcome). Thus, the middle-class standard of living is the norm that is portrayed over and over again in media representations of American lifestyles. But this image ignores both the handful of extremely rich Americans and the tens of millions who share only minimally in the nation's affluence. To observe inequality and understand its impact, we need only compare a few aspects of the lives led by the affluent and the poor in our society.

The affluent live longer and better and can afford the best medical care in the world, the finest education, and the most elegant possessions. In addition, by discreetly influencing politicians, police officers, and other public officials to promote or defend their interests, they can obtain social preference and shape government policies. This capacity to purchase both possessions and influence gives the extremely wealthy a potential power that is grossly out of proportion to their numbers.

For the poor, the situation is reversed. Although America's poor people seldom die of starvation and generally have more than the hopelessly poor of the third world, they lead lives of serious deprivation compared not only to the wealthy but to the middle class as well. This relative deprivation profoundly affects the style and quality of their lives. It extends beyond mere distribution of income and includes inequality in education, health care, police protection, job opportunities, legal justice, housing, and many other areas. The poor are more frequently subject to mental illness than other Americans. They require more medical treatment and have longer and more serious illnesses. Their children are more likely to die than those of the more affluent, and their life expectancy is below the national average. They are more likely to become criminals or juvenile delinquents, and they contribute more than their share of teenage pregnancy, alcoholism, and violence to American society.

The Rich

Economist Paul Samuelson has provided a vivid metaphor for the disparity in the distribution of income in the United States: "If we made an income pyramid out of a child's blocks, with each layer portraying $1,000 of income, the peak would be far higher than the Eiffel Tower, but almost all of us would be within a yard of the ground" (quoted in Blumberg, 1980, p. 34). Whatever measure or standard is used, the implications are the same: The rich own more, earn more, and use more—much, much more—and they have been doing so for a long time.

Net worth, a frequently used measure of wealth, refers to the value of savings and checking accounts, real estate, automobiles, stocks and bonds, and other assets minus debts. Surveys by the Federal Reserve Board suggest that 1 percent of all households hold over one-third of all personal wealth. The distribution of income is even more unequal: The wealthiest 20 percent of households receive almost 50 percent of all income, while the poorest 20 percent receive less than 5 percent (*Statistical Abstract*, 2006).

The United States has a long history of attempting to redistribute wealth through taxation and other policies. These policies have been instituted for three reasons: (1) The wealthy get more out of the economic system and can afford to pay more taxes; (2) they have a greater investment in the economic system and should pay more to maintain it; (3) redistributing some income from the rich to the poor is fair and just in a democratic society. Ideas such as these led to the establishment in the 1930s of President Franklin D. Roosevelt's New Deal, which, together with the Great Society legislation proposed by President Lyndon B. Johnson in the 1960s, created most of this country's welfare institutions and programs.

The United States is now considered a **welfare state,** meaning that a significant portion of the GDP is taken by the state to provide certain minimum levels of social welfare for the poor, the aged, the disabled, and others who would not be able to survive under conditions of market competition. In a welfare state, governments at all levels attempt to smooth out the effects of recessions and economic booms through such devices as graduated income taxes, public-sector employment, economic incentives for private firms, unemployment insurance, and the transfer of some wealth from the rich to the poor.

In general, the competition for resources—not only income and wealth but also what they can buy (health care, comfortable housing, expensive education, etc.)—heavily favors the rich. For example, people in upper income brackets have many legal ways to avoid taxes. If they purchase real estate, they can obtain substantial tax reductions for mortgage interest payments at the same time that the property is increasing in value. In addition, the wealthy can make tax-free investments that are not available to those who are less well-off. The income from municipal bonds—which are commonly sold in denominations of $5,000—does not have to be reported on tax returns.

Several other aspects of the welfare state's programs have turned out to be what is sometimes called **wealthfare,** or subsidies for the rich. For example, government import–export policies are designed to protect certain industries, such as textiles or steel, and the jobs of their employees. However, when the government limits imports of a certain product, competition is stifled and consumers must pay the prices demanded by domestic manufacturers. When the government agrees to rescue failing corporations, as it has done with railroads, banks, and aerospace companies, the owners of substantial portions of the corporations' capital are most likely to benefit. It can be argued that the poor are relative losers in these situations, since less government money is available for social programs. Similarly, when government revenues are raised through such means as sales taxes on gasoline, those with less money effectively bear a greater share of the burden because the proportion of tax they pay is higher relative to their smaller incomes than it is for the rich. Corporations are heavy users of the nation's resources but pay a declining share of taxes to help pay for roads, education, improvements in air quality, and the like. Figure 6–1 shows this decline, expressed as a percentage of the nation's gross domestic product from 1942 to 2003.

Figure 6–1 Corporate Income Taxes as a Percentage of Gross Domestic Product, 1942–2003

Source: Congressional Budget Office, 2003.

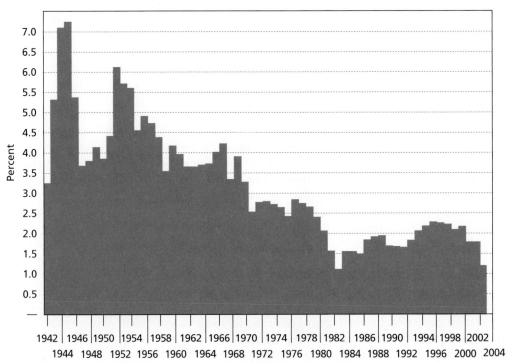

TABLE 6–1	Average Income Received by Each Fifth of Households, 1977, 2000, and 2005		

| Household Groups | Average After-Tax Income (Estimated) | | |
	1977	2000	2005
One-fifth with lowest income	$10,000	$10,188	$19,178
Next lowest one-fifth	22,100	25,331	36,000
Middle one-fifth	32,400	42,252	57,660
Next highest one-fifth	42,600	65,690	91,705
One-fifth with highest income	74,000	139,950	166,000

Source: U.S. Census Bureau, 2006.

Are the Rich a Social Problem? By the turn of the century, the 400 richest Americans had amassed a total net worth of $1 trillion more than the GDP of China (Galewitz, 1999). At the same time, increasing numbers of low-wage workers had seen the value of their earnings diminish even in a period of low inflation. The gains of the rich and the losses of the nonrich are clearly shown in Table 6–1. Note the extraordinary growth in income of the top one-fifth of American households. Average household income for this 20 percent was $166,000, while the average for the 20 percent of American households in the lowest income group was less than $20,000.

We return to this issue in the discussion of corporate power in Chapter 12. Here it is sufficient to point out that although there is no consensus in American society that the rich themselves are a social problem, there is evidence of concern that the ethic of individual success and enrichment may hamper efforts to develop new policies to address the problems of poverty (Reich, 1998).

The Poor

Although the rich are able to take advantage of various ways of improving their situation, the poor face an entirely different set of circumstances. They are part of a society that has the means to greatly alleviate poverty but instead has adopted policies that actually increase the percentage of the poor. In the pointed words of an unusual pastoral letter issued by a committee of Roman Catholic bishops in 1984, "The level of inequality in income and wealth in our society . . . today must be judged morally unacceptable" (quoted in Briggs, 1984). Today the situation of the poor, especially those working in the lower ranks of the labor force, has become still worse. There are several reasons for this, including technological changes that eliminate certain kinds of jobs, globalization (which exports jobs to lower-wage regions of the world), the reluctance of the middle and upper classes to share their wealth with less fortunate members of society, and the general attitude of Americans toward poverty.

Many people believe the poor are largely to blame for their own poverty. The argument is as follows: "The poor as a class consists of the unemployed, who are responsible for their condition because they will not work. If they could be persuaded to work for a living or were forced to take jobs, poverty could be eliminated. What we have now is a group of freeloaders who are getting by on welfare." The inaccuracy of this argument is evident when one examines the data on poverty and work.

Of the 37 million people classified as living below the official poverty line in 2004, 13.0 million (17.8 percent) were children under the age of 18; another 3.5 million (9.8 percent) were over 65 years old (*Statistical Abstract*, 2006). Millions more were

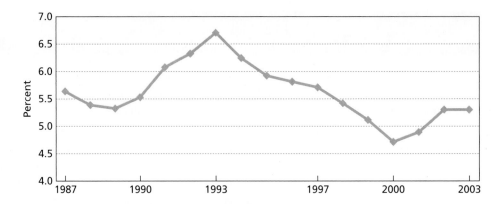

Figure 6–2 Poverty Rates of Persons in the Labor Force for 27 Weeks or More, 1987–2003

Source: Bureau of Labor Statistics, 2005.

female heads of households with children younger than 18 and no husband present, or were ill, disabled, or going to school; of the remainder, the majority worked either full or part time in the previous year, but their wages were not sufficient to elevate them above the poverty threshold.

Members of minority groups are especially likely to be included among the poor. The median income of minority families is about 67 percent of that of white families (U.S. Census Bureau, 2006), and unemployment rates for black and Hispanic workers average about double the rate for white workers.

The Working Poor. We see them working all around us, in restaurant kitchens, on landscaping crews, installing roofs in the hot sun, taking care of our loved ones. The **working poor** are often from immigrant backgrounds, but this is by no means always true. According to the U.S. Department of Labor (2005), "the working poor are individuals who spent at least 27 weeks in the labor force (working or looking for work), but whose incomes fell below the official poverty level. Of all persons in the labor force for at least 27 weeks, about 7.4 million people, or almost 4 percent of the nation's labor force of about 140 million workers, were working at wages so low that they remained below the official poverty threshold in 2003." Of these working poor individuals, more women than men were poor (3.9 million and 3.5 million, respectively).

Who are the working poor? Why is it so difficult for poor people who are working full time to raise themselves out of poverty?

Charting the poverty rates of working people in the United States from the 1980s to the present, as shown in Figure 6–2, reveals the extremely strong impact of recessions and economic good times on these workers at the bottom of the wage scale. During the recession of the early 1990s, there was a spike in the proportion of workers who were working at below-poverty wages. Throughout the economic good times of the 1990s, these rates declined steadily. They began to increase dramatically after 2000, due in part to economic deregulation and failures in the enforcement of labor standards.

The Severely Poor. In addition to those who are working but cannot escape from poverty because of low wages, an increasing proportion of people in the United States are working part time at extremely low-paying jobs, or are out of the labor force and receiving minimal benefits. Sociologists often consider severely poor people or households to be those living at 50 percent of the poverty threshold. In recent years, according to the U.S. Census Bureau, the percentage of the population considered severely poor has reached a 32-year high. Between 2000 and 2005 the percentage living at half of the poverty threshold increased by 26 percent. This descent into severe or "abject" poverty can be found throughout the nation, from the largest cities to the smallest rural communities. According to a study of severe poverty by Amy Glasmeier (2005),

> The abjectly poor in America are individuals living on $5,250 a year. For a family of three, two adults and a child, the level of income is $6,922; for a family of four, $10,222. This level of poverty in comparative terms is only slightly above the poverty line originally set in the 1960s and affords a person little more than food and shelter.

The $5,250 for an abjectly poor individual means a bare bones budget of $ 437/month. Of that total, no more than $50 is available per week for food, or $7.14 day—about two big Macs and a drink, or 1200–1600 calories a day and 120 grams of fat. The residual income supports a housing expenditure in the same range of $200/month, which in most places in the country yields a bed in a group home, leaving about $37 for incidentals.

Even more sobering is the fact that the number of severely poor is growing rapidly. In 1975 the severely poor were 30 percent of the population in poverty. Today a dismaying 43 percent of persons in poverty are severely poor by national standards. But more embarrassing than the share of the poverty population truly poor is the increase in the number of persons descending into severe poverty. While the rate of new entrants moving into poverty is somewhat stable, those who are becoming truly poor are increasing at a rate 56 percent higher than the growth rate of new entrants into poverty.

POVERTY AND SOCIAL CLASS

In every society people are grouped according to their access to the things that are considered valuable. These groupings of people are variously called classes, status groups, or strata, depending on the classification scheme used. Whatever the name, the phenomenon being described is **social stratification**—a pattern in which individuals and groups are assigned to different positions in the social order, positions that enjoy varying amounts of access to desirable goods and services.

The stratification of individuals and groups according to their access to various occupations, incomes, and skills is called **class stratification.** A social class is a large number of people who have roughly the same degree of economic well-being; people enter or leave a given class as their economic fortunes change. Marxian social theory emphasizes this form of stratification. For Marx and his followers, the basic classes of society are determined by ownership or nonownership of the means of production of goods and services. The owners are called capitalists, and those who must sell their labor to the capitalists are the workers.

Marx referred to members of capitalist societies who are poor and not in the labor force as the **lumpenproletariat.** This class is made up of people at the margins of society who either have dropped out of the capitalist system of employment or have never been part of it at all. Marx thought of the lumpenproletariat as comprising the criminal underworld, street people, the homeless, and all the other categories that make up the dregs of humanity. He believed capitalism would always impoverish the working class because the owners of capital would seek to exploit the workers to the fullest extent possible, and as a result the lumpenproletariat would expand and become ever more dangerous to the stability of capitalist societies.

The German sociologist and historian Max Weber was critical of the Marxian perspective. Weber accepted most of the Marxian analysis of economic classes, but he did not believe capitalism would inevitably cause the expansion of the lumpenproletariat. Moreover, he pointed out that other valued things besides wealth are distributed unequally in modern societies. For example, status (or prestige) and power are both highly valued, and their distribution throughout society does not always coincide with the distribution of wealth. People who have made their money recently, for example, are often accorded little prestige by capitalists who made their money much earlier.

In their studies of the American system of social stratification, social scientists have developed a synthesis of the Marxian and Weberian approaches. They have devised designations like upper class, upper-middle class, middle class, working class, and poor, which combine the Marxian concept of economic class with the Weberian concept of status.

Sociologists have pointed out that the ways in which we distinguish among these class levels have both *objective dimensions,* which can be measured by quantifiable variables such as income or membership in certain clubs, and *subjective dimensions,*

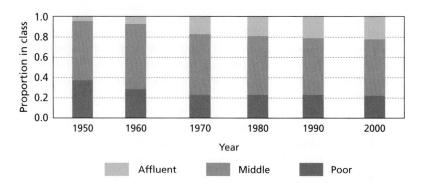

Figure 6–3 Distribution of U.S. Families by Income Class, 1950–2000

Source: Massey & Fischer, 2003.

which are the ways in which we evaluate ourselves and others (and the way we feel about people in the various objective classes). Objectively, we base our estimations of social-class position more or less on the Marxian model. Major employers and powerful political leaders are assigned to the upper class. Managers of large firms and relatively wealthy people with successful businesses and professional practices are in the upper-middle class. People who are employed as middle-level managers and lower-paid professionals (e.g., technicians) are in the middle class. People who work in factories or depend on hourly wages are assigned to the working class. People who lack steady work or drift back and forth between legitimate employment and other ways of obtaining income are the poor.

Research on the distribution of the wealth and income in the United States shows clearly that the gap between the affluent and the poor is widening as more people become affluent, more become poor, and fewer are found in the middle levels of the class hierarchy. Research by Douglas Massey and his associates shows that after 1950, due to a booming economy and to the effects of social legislation such as minimum wages, unemployment insurance, and above all, Social Security to help lift the elderly out of poverty, the proportion or the poor or lower classes decreased and the middle class grew dramatically (Massey & Fischer, 2003). These trends are illustrated in Figure 6–3, but what the graph does not show is the even more rapid increase in the poor as a social class in recent years. As noted elsewhere, for the first five years of the new century the number of families below the poverty line in the United States (the "poor" category in the graph) has been growing steadily (Leonhardt, 2005).

The subjective dimension of social class becomes evident when people are asked to identify the class to which they belong. For example, the proportion of people who classify themselves as poor is considerably lower than the proportion who are so classified by the Census Bureau. Part of the reason for this is that many poor people have low-paying jobs and hesitate to identify themselves as poor even when they are; they place themselves in the working class. Moreover, as Mary R. Jackman and Robert W. Jackman (1983) have pointed out, respondents who do identify themselves as poor might not do so if the same category were labeled "lower class" (Gilbert, 1993).

All the categories mentioned earlier are used to discuss the American stratification system, but they are extremely difficult to define scientifically. The designations "middle class" and "working class" are especially problematic. In the 1950s and 1960s, when the GDP doubled each decade, it appeared that the distinctions between the working and middle classes were becoming blurred and meaningless. For a period of about 20 years, it seemed that the United States and Canada were experiencing a convergence in social classes as more and more people shared in the benefits of expanding wealth. Workers—defined in the Marxian sense—were adopting lifestyles that seemed to make them indistinguishable from the middle class of salaried employees and professionals. In that period only the extremes of social stratification were easy to identify: the wealthy at the top and the poor at the bottom. Otherwise, the incomes of most Americans were giving them access to what sociologist David Riesman called the "standard package" of goods and services available in a wealthy society (Riesman, Glazer, & Denney, 1950). That package included a home, a car, and such consumer goods as TV sets, air conditioners, and washing machines (Blumberg, 1980).

The development of welfare state institutions in the United States from the 1930s to the end of the 1960s supported the notion that the classes were converging toward a generalized level of affluence. The growing strength of labor unions allowed workers to bargain for higher wages and better benefits than ever before. The growth of mass educational institutions made education available to more people and provided training for new jobs and professions. Social-welfare programs like Social Security, workfare, food stamps, Medicare and Medicaid, affirmative-action programs, youth programs, unemployment insurance, and many other kinds of government support seemed to offer the hope that the degree of inequality in American society would be reduced still further. However, events of recent decades have reversed the trend toward greater affluence for all, and the gap between the poor and the affluent has increased. We will return to this subject in later sections of the chapter.

THE NATURE OF POVERTY

Poverty is a deceptively simple term to define. Certainly the poor have less money than other people. In addition, the money they do have buys them less. The poor must often purchase necessities as soon as they have cash (e.g., when a welfare check arrives). They cannot shop around for sales or bargains, and they are often victimized by shopkeepers who raise their prices the day welfare checks are delivered. When they buy on credit, the poor must accept higher interest rates because they take longer to pay and are considered poor credit risks. Inflationary price increases affect the poor first, and more severely. The cost of essential consumer goods, ranging from rice and sugar to toilet tissue and soap, may rise suddenly (e.g., when energy costs increase as a result of a crisis in the Middle East), but the wages of the lowest paid people and government income assistance payments rise slowly if at all.

For most people, poverty simply means not having enough money to buy things that are considered necessary and desirable. Various formal definitions of poverty have been offered. John Kenneth Galbraith (1958) stressed the sense of degradation felt by the poor and concluded that "people are poverty stricken when their income, even if adequate for survival, falls markedly behind that of the community" (p. 245). Poverty may mean a condition of near starvation, bare subsistence (the minimum necessary to maintain life), or any standard of living measurably beneath the national average. To deal more effectively with poverty as a social problem, a generally agreed-upon, scientifically based, and more specific definition is needed.

The Poverty Line

Official U.S. government definitions of poverty are based on the calculation of a minimum family "market basket." The U.S. Department of Agriculture regularly prepares estimates of the cost of achieving a minimum level of nutrition, based on average food prices. It is assumed that an average low-income family of four must spend one-third of its total income on food; thus, by multiplying the family food budget by four, the government arrives at a poverty income that can be adjusted for the number of people in the household and for changes in the cost of food. The official, food-based poverty line can also be adjusted to account for the tendency of rural people to supplement their incomes with subsistence agriculture and gardens. The official measure is also corrected each year or even more often for changes in the cost of living as measured by the consumer price index (CPI). In 2005 this inflation-corrected, official poverty line for a family of four was $19,350. By this measure, more than 37 million people, or 12.7 percent of the U.S. population, were below the poverty line (U.S. Census Bureau, 2005).

Census reports issued in the spring of 2005 revealed that the nation had experienced the largest increase in its poverty population since the late 1970s. Then, a few months later, Hurricane Katrina brought the problems of poverty and race to national attention in far more vivid ways.

This official poverty measure was developed in 1965 by Mollie Orshansky, an economist at the Social Security Administration, who reasoned that the only acceptable measure of the adequacy of a person's level of living is food consumption. But although this definition was accepted as the official means of establishing a poverty line, there has been continuing controversy and debate over definitions of poverty and their implications for social policy.

During the Reagan administration, conservative social scientists and policymakers were critical of the way poverty is measured. In particular, they argued that if benefits provided to the poor, such as food stamps, Medicaid, and housing, are included in the calculation of income, the extent of poverty is much less than is generally believed. Others have argued that the CPI overestimates the impact of rising prices on the poor. These differences in measurement could affect whether millions of Americans are classified above or below the official poverty line.

But those who believe the existing poverty measures actually underestimate the size of the poor population also have strong arguments on their side. First, there is the argument that taxes, alimony, out-of-pocket health-care expenses, and many work-related expenses should be excluded from the income figures used to determine poverty status because this money cannot be used to purchase food and other necessities of life. Second, the official poverty definition does not take into account regional differences in the cost of living and therefore neglects hundreds of thousands of poor people in high-cost cities like Washington, D.C., while overestimating the number of poor people in rural areas, where the cost of living is lower. Finally, many researchers and advocates for the poor note that the poverty threshold is extremely low and that people living well above that level are still quite poor.

When the poverty formula was first developed, such conveniences as telephones and indoor plumbing were not part of Americans' expectations of a minimally adequate level of living. And at that time far fewer children lived with one parent and far fewer women were employed. Child care, a significant expense for most working families (and essential if a single parent is to work), was not the major and necessary expense it is today. With these factors in mind, poverty scholar Patricia Ruggles (1990) suggests that the official estimate of the poverty line based on food prices should be recalculated at regular intervals on the basis of changing definitions of minimal consumption.

The idea that poverty is relative rather than absolute is nothing new. In 1956 Victor Fuchs proposed that any family may be classified as poor if its income is less than half of the median family income. By this definition, about 20 percent of the population would be considered poor. Contrary to the Orshansky formula or any arbitrary income standard, the use of such a relative standard implies that poverty will exist as long as income distribution remains unequal. And in fact, the proportion of poor people in America has tended to remain stable when measured by the Fuchs formula.

Who Are the Poor?

Since the passage in 1935 of the Social Security Act, which established federal old-age pensions (Social Security), unemployment insurance, and Aid to Families with Dependent Children (now Temporary Assistance to Needy Families, or TANF), the nation has made great strides in its effort to combat poverty. Although it remains true that far too many citizens live in poverty, it is not true, as some argue, that programs to combat poverty have had negative effects or no effect at all (Murray, 1984). Figure 6–4 shows clearly that over the same period poverty among people under the age of 18 has been increasing. Figure 6–5 on page 196 shows that other nations, such as Ireland, the United Kingdom, France, and Israel, also have large numbers of poor children, but these nations dramatically reduce their rates of child poverty through government assistance. As William O'Hare (1996), a noted expert on the demographics of poverty, points out, "These findings suggest that the public sector in other developed countries does more than the United States to lift poor children out of poverty" (p. 37). The primary reason for child poverty is birth into a single-parent family or the breakup of a two-parent family. It is worthwhile, therefore, to look more closely at the link between poverty and single-parent families.

Poverty and Single-Parent Families. Of all children under the age of 18 in the United States, 17.8 percent are living in poverty. The situation is especially severe for children in single-parent families headed by women. In 2004, 30.5 percent of female-headed families were below the poverty threshold, and in such families the average income was about 60 percent less than the median income of all families (U.S. Census Bureau, 2005).

As we have seen, severe poverty is far too often experienced by children and mothers. Much of the increase in severe poverty seems to be due to a decrease in subsidies for low-income children and their mothers. In 1995, for instance, some 88 percent of poor children received food stamps. By 2000, the figure had dropped to 70 percent. Families

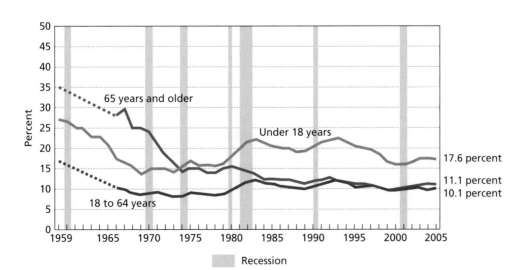

Figure 6–4 Poverty Rates, by Age: 1959–2005

Note: The data points are placed at the midpoints of the respective years. Data for people 18 to 64 and 65 and older are not available from 1960 to 1965.

Source: U.S. Census Bureau, 2007.

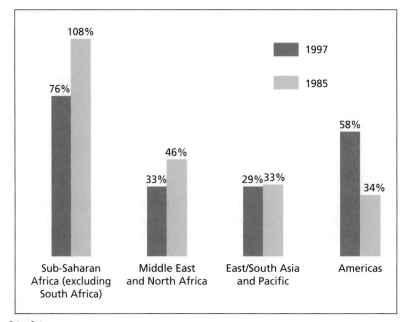

Russian Federation 26.6%
United States 26.3%
United Kingdom 21.3%, Italy 21.2%

Australia 17.1%, Canada 16.0%
Ireland 14.8%, Israel 14.7%
Poland 14.2%, Spain 13.1%
Germany 11.6%, Hungary 11.5%

France 9.8%, Netherlands 8.4%
Luxembourg, Switzerland 6.3%
Belgium 6.1%, Denmark 5.9%
Austria 5.6%, Norway 4.5%
Sweden 3.7%, Finland 3.4%
Slovakia 2.2%, Czech Republic 1.8%

Figure 6–5 Child Poverty in Industrialized Countries. *Percentages of children who are likely to be living in a poor family (defined by a household disposable income less than half the country's overall median income).*

Source: Bradbury & Jäntti, 1999; *Statistical Abstract,* 2006.

How are race, gender, and poverty related in the United States?

that are technically eligible for assistance seem not to receive it once they leave the welfare rolls, often because women are intimidated about requesting aid or because it is being withheld by states and municipalities. The declines in food aid to poor children highlight the stark differences between the United States and most other affluent nations in the efforts made at the national level to combat child poverty.

Child Poverty and the Frayed U.S. Safety Net. The United States leads the affluent nations in the proportion of its children it allows to live in poverty. As shown in Figure 6–5, only the Russian Federation ranks higher than the United States on this negative measure of children's well-being, but that nation is no longer considered affluent or a superpower. Most other affluent industrial nations have far more effective and generous *social safety nets,* welfare systems that assist significant proportions of children and their families in their efforts to escape poverty. Research by sociologists Lee Rainwater and T. M. Smeeding has found that in the United States, social-welfare policies lift only 17 percent of children out of poverty, but in Canada 60 percent and in France 70 percent of children escape poverty due to government assistance (Rainwater and Smeeding, 2003).

Most industrial nations, including Canada and France, do a far better job helping parents in low-income families obtain child care services that will allow them to work steadily while their children are adequately cared for. In the United States, in contrast, child care is often a major obstacle for single mothers who want to work and could be successfully employed. Parents in the labor force must find ways to cope with the unpredictable time demands of children. Most single parents have access to some form of daily child care, often local day-care centers or reliance on friends and especially on grandmothers. Indeed, recent studies show that one in ten grandparents is either taking full responsibility for rearing a grandchild or providing regular day care. And fully four in ten who are not providing these major services say that they see their grandchildren every week (Lewin, 2000). But what happens when the child is ill, or when it snows, or when children are having difficulties in day care or in school? Then it becomes necessary for the working parent to have other resources to draw on.

Paternal involvement and child-support enforcement are other major areas of concern for poor mothers struggling to work and raise children simultaneously. The 1996 welfare act includes tough language about paternity and child-support enforcement, but so far there appear to have been only sporadic increases of enforcement at the state level. Too often men are unable to pay court-ordered child support payments, and there is little provision in the act to allow fathers to replace cash payments with services like child care or transportation. Negative incentives abound but are fitfully enforced, while positive incentives and programs to increase the employability and income of fathers of low-income children are underfunded (Wolk & Schmahl, 1999).

Poverty and Minority Groups. It should be noted that although whites are by far the largest group among poor families, blacks and other racial minorities are overrepresented. For example, about 26 percent of Native Americans, 25 percent of African Americans, and 23 percent of Latinos have incomes below the official poverty level, compared with about 10 percent of the white population. The median income of white families is approximately $50,000, whereas that of black families is about $30,000 and that of Hispanic families is about $35,000 (U.S. Census Bureau, 2006).

Several factors are thought to be responsible for the lower earning power of blacks and other minority workers. Among the most important are low wages, discrimination, and educational deficits. The proportion of people of African American or Latino background working at low-wage and minimum-wage jobs is higher than the proportion of whites in such jobs. After the Republicans lost control of Congress in 2006, the Democrats made good on their promise to raise the minimum wage. Eighty-two Republicans joined 233 Democrats in the House to pass the legislation, which also passed the Senate and was signed into law by President Bush. The law raises the minimum wage from $5.15 per hour to $7.25 per hour in three increments over a period of two years and two months. While this is good news for wage workers, even at the higher minimum wage a family of three supported by a minimum-wage worker would have an annual income that falls below the poverty threshold, though not quite as far as before the new legislation was passed.

The discrimination experienced by blacks, Chicanos, Puerto Ricans, Native Americans, and other minority groups in housing, education, and health care exacerbates the effects of low income. In fact, discrimination often accounts for their inability to find higher-paying employment. Members of these groups are often forced to pay higher rents and to live in dilapidated or deteriorating dwellings, and the quality of predominantly minority schools is often inferior to that of predominantly white schools. In these and other areas, the disparity between blacks and whites in both opportunity and treatment is evident. (These problems are discussed more fully in Chapter 7.)

Although the educational gap between minorities and whites is narrowing, members of minority groups who have less education experience greater difficulty finding jobs that will lift them out of poverty than do whites with the same levels of education. Figure 6–6 on page 198 shows this clearly. Poverty rates for blacks and Hispanics with a high-school education or less are significantly higher than those for whites with comparable education.

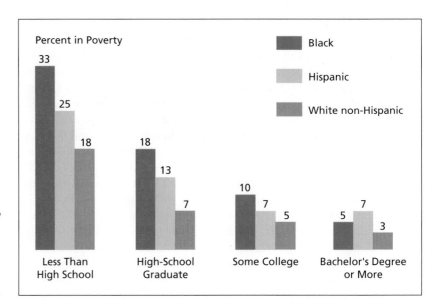

Figure 6–6 Poverty Rates, by Education and Race or Ethnicity

Source: Lichter & Crowley, 2002. Copyright © 2002. Reprinted by permission of The Population Reference Bureau.

Poverty and Geography. The 2000 Census revealed that poverty rates continue to vary widely among the states, but the gaps are narrowing somewhat. Table 6–2 lists the states by the percentage of their population below the official poverty threshold. Many of the states with the highest poverty rates are still found in the South and West, but states like California and New York, with large metropolitan populations including many poor households, also rank above the national average.

In fact, although the general distribution of poverty revealed by these numbers has persisted for decades, there have been some important improvements. In the 1990 census, New Hampshire had a 6 percent poverty rate, but Mississippi, then the leader, had a 25 percent rate. There has been some convergence toward the U.S. mean of 12.6 percent, and the gaps between states with high and low poverty rates is narrowing somewhat.

Note in the table that states with larger rural areas, like Arizona, New Mexico, and those of the Deep South, have high poverty rates, often because rural areas tend to have weaker educational institutions and far less diverse labor markets. Impoverished American Indian reservations and the migrant labor camps of Mexican agricultural workers are also pockets of poverty hidden from mainstream America. The growing isolation of poor people, whether in rural or urban areas, makes it ever harder to convince more comfortable Americans that the consequences of growing up poor are shared by all citizens in the form of higher health-care costs, higher crime rates, and a growing level of cynicism about the possibility of achieving the American dream for all.

Rural Poverty. Although urban poverty is probably more familiar to most people, about one-fifth of poor people live in rural areas and another third in suburban areas. Rural poverty is not as visible as urban poverty. Separated from the mainstream of urban life, the rural poor are largely hidden on farms, on Indian reservations, in open country, and in small towns and villages. Unemployment rates in rural areas are far above the national average. Largely because of the technological revolution in agriculture and other occupations, poorly educated, unskilled workers have been left with no means of support.

The majority of the rural poor are white, but a high percentage of southern blacks, Native Americans, and Mexican Americans are poor as well. Census figures consistently indicate that people living in rural areas have lower incomes, higher poverty rates, higher unemployment, and lower educational attainment than those living in metropolitan areas (U.S. Census Bureau, 2006). Certain areas that have historically been poor, such as many counties in Appalachia, much of the Mississippi Delta, and the arid

TABLE 6–2	U.S. States Ranked by Poverty Rate

State	Percent of Population Below Poverty	State	Percent of Population Below Poverty
District of Columbia	21.3	South Dakota	11.8
Mississippi	20.1	Missouri	11.6
Louisiana	18.3	Illinois	11.5
New Mexico	17.9	Colorado	11.4
Alabama	16.7	Iowa	11.3
Texas	16.2	North Dakota	11.2
Oklahoma	15.6	Pennsylvania	11.2
West Virginia	15.4	Florida	11.1
Arizona	15.2	Nevada	10.6
South Carolina	15.0	Wyoming	10.6
Tennessee	14.9	Washington	10.2
Kentucky	14.8	Wisconsin	10.2
New York	14.5	Massachusetts	10.1
Georgia	14.4	Alaska	10.0
Arkansas	13.8	Idaho	9.9
Montana	13.8	Maryland	9.7
California	13.2	Nebraska	9.5
North Carolina	13.1	Connecticut	9.3
UNITED STATES	12.6	Delaware	9.2
Indiana	12.6	Virginia	9.2
Maine	12.6	Utah	9.2
Kansas	12.5	Hawaii	8.6
Ohio	12.3	Minnesota	8.1
Rhode Island	12.1	Vermont	7.6
Oregon	12.0	New Jersey	6.8
Michigan	12.0	New Hampshire	5.6

Source: U.S. Census Bureau, 2006.

regions of the Southwest outside of the cities and irrigated farming areas, as well as many other rural areas, have experienced steady declines for at least twenty years. Those declines are accompanied by increases in the correlates of poverty: infant mortality, family dissolution, out-migration of the younger and better-educated population, and malnutrition (Harrington, 1987).

Among the rural poor are migrant workers who, following the harvest, live in tar-paper shacks with few possessions. The rural poor also include Native Americans on reservations, who often lead lives of destitution and regimentation, with decisions made for them by faraway bureaucrats. Other poor populations in rural areas are out-of-work coal miners, as well as farmers and farmworkers who cannot compete with automated production techniques.

Attempting to escape poverty, many of the rural poor migrate to urban areas, where they discover that the problems of the countryside are magnified. In the cities, lack of money is aggravated by higher living costs, overcrowded and inadequate housing, poor nutrition, insufficient medical care, unsanitary health conditions, and other

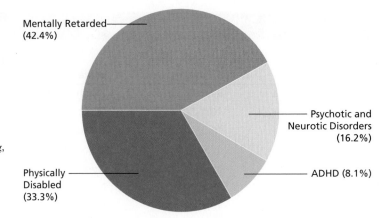

**Figure 6–7 Children
with Disabilities Receiving SSI**

Source: Meyers, Lukemeyer, & Smeeding,
Focus (Newsletter of the Institute for
Research on Poverty, University of
Wisconsin—Madison), 19, no. 1,
Summer–Fall, 1997, p. 51; U.S. Census
Bureau, 2006.

serious problems. The desired jobs are unobtainable because the demand for unskilled labor has declined drastically. In addition, as businesses move to the suburbs, transportation to work becomes unavailable or too expensive. As a result, rural immigrants frequently end up on the urban welfare rolls.

The Dependent Poor. Americans have an ambivalent attitude toward poverty. We recognize that the poor are not always responsible for their situation, yet those who must turn to public assistance (sometimes referred to as the dependent poor) are often pictured as lazy, shiftless, or dishonest. Their private lives are scrutinized, and the constant presence of social workers and welfare investigators in their homes denies them the basic right of privacy.

A significant proportion of the dependent poor are people who have struggled with disabilities from childhood. Many people who have not studied poverty closely fail to understand the outstanding importance of this fact. Approximately 1 million poor children in the United States receive Supplemental Security Income (SSI) because they have disabilities. As Figure 6–7 shows, the largest proportion are mentally retarded. Slightly over 8 percent have ADHD, a disability that often severely impedes the educational attainment of children from poor families. Although childhood disabilities are not unique to poor families, children in low-income households are more likely to be chronically ill or disabled because of the environmental risks of low-income neighborhoods as well as deficiencies in nutrition and health care. Moreover, not only does childhood disability correlate highly with later adult dependence, but it can also create extreme hardship for single parents already burdened by the basic effects of poverty (Meyers, Lukemeyer, & Smeeding, 1997).

Although many poor parents face the difficulties of dealing with children's disabilities, all poor people who depend to some degree on public assistance are victims of myths and misconceptions like those listed in the On Further Analysis box on page 201.

As noted earlier, a significant proportion of the poor are in two-parent families in which at least three-fourths of the family's income is derived from work. This large group is known as the *working poor.* These families are poor primarily because the breadwinners have limited skills, making it difficult for them to compete in the job market, and as a result their incomes from work are not sufficient to lift them above the poverty level.

Note that in a family with two wage earners who have jobs that pay slightly more than the minimum wage—say, $6 an hour—the workers' combined annual income would be about $25,000 a year (assuming that each works 50 weeks a year). After taxes, this income would be reduced, although a family with children would qualify for the Earned Income Tax Credit, which would more than offset deductions for Social Security and payroll taxes, except it would not be paid until after the end of the tax year. In any case, this family would barely be making enough to be above the poverty level of about $19,000 a year for a family of four.

On Further Analysis

MYTHS ABOUT POVERTY IN THE UNITED STATES

As if they did not have enough to cope with, poor people are often stigmatized as lazy, dishonest, and unable to help themselves. In fact, as we have seen, the poor are an extremely diverse population, and the vast majority are among the hardest working people in the nation. Here are seven common myths that a sociologically informed citizen should be able to debunk:

Myth 1: The vast majority of the poor are blacks or Hispanics.   Poverty rates are higher among blacks and Hispanics than among other racial/ethnic groups, but they do not make up the majority of the poor. Non-Hispanic whites are the most numerous racial/ethnic group in the poverty population.

Myth 2: People are poor because they do not want to work.   Half of the poor are not of working age: About 40 percent are under age 18; another 10 percent are age 65 and older. Many poor people have jobs but earn below-poverty wages. Many poor individuals cannot work because of a serious disability or because they must care for family members.

Myth 3: Poor families are trapped in a cycle of poverty that few escape.   The poverty population is dynamic—people move in and out of poverty every year. Less than 15 percent of the poor remain in poverty for five or more consecutive years.

Myth 4: Welfare programs for the poor are straining the federal budget.   Social-assistance programs for low-income families and individuals accounted for less than 12 percent of federal expenditures in 2005. A much larger share of the budget goes to other types of social assistance, such as Social Security, which mainly go to middle-class Americans.

Myth 5: The majority of the poor live in inner-city neighborhoods.   Less than half of

One of the most persistent myths about poverty is that poor people do not want to work. Yet every time there is a natural disaster and people are thrown out of work, and every time an employer advertises a few job openings, hundreds of hopeful applicants line up for hours just to submit an application.

the poor live in central-city areas, and less than one-quarter live in high-poverty inner-city areas. Over one-third of the poor live in the suburbs, and more than one-fifth live outside metropolitan areas.

Myth 6: The poor live off government welfare.   Under the new rules for public assistance, which require welfare recipients to work after two years of public assistance, welfare itself accounts for a diminishing proportion of the income of poor adults. Well over half of the income received by poor adults comes from wages or other work-related activity. Perhaps the most pernicious myth about the poor is that they do not share the work ethic of the middle class—that they are lazy or shiftless and would much rather be on welfare than work. Many

studies have shown that the poor strongly share the work ethic and regret being on welfare (Jencks & Swingle, 2000). The research indicates that there are no differences between the poor and the nonpoor in life goals and willingness to work; the differences are that the poor lack confidence in their ability to succeed, and hence they accept welfare or low-wage work as a necessity.

Myth 7: Most of the poor are single mothers and their children.   Female-headed families represent just 38 percent of the poor. About 34 percent of the poor live in married-couple families, 22 percent live alone or with nonrelatives, and the remainder live in male-headed families with no wife present. (Rainwater & Smeeding, 2003)

Event Poverty

Very often such families are prone to what is known as *event poverty*. In the event of illness, loss of one of the jobs, marital discord, or pregnancy, for example, the family could easily lose half its income and then plunge well below the official poverty level (Ellwood, 1996; McKernan & Ratcliffe, 2002). When a plant or other place of employment closes abruptly, hundreds of workers may be thrown out of work to join, even for a brief period, the ranks of the poor. Or a family may become impoverished because of high medical bills (we return to this subject shortly) or, as we have seen so dramatically in 2005, because they have lost everything in a storm or other natural disaster.

Why were so many more people below the poverty line than people in the middle and upper classes killed by Hurricane Katrina and the resulting flood?

Hurricane Katrina—Poverty, Race, and Class. People throughout the world were horrified by the images coming from the destroyed city of New Orleans and many towns and villages on the Mississippi Gulf Coast in the aftermath of Hurricane Katrina. President Bush stated that there had never been a more serious disaster in the nation's history, but it took many days and weeks for the extent of the tragedy to be fully understood. In addition to the thousands of dead, hundreds of thousands of people lost their homes and all their possessions, as well as their jobs and their incomes. People with the means to flee the city and region were those most likely to have sought shelter elsewhere, out of harm's way, but they often lost most of their possessions. People who lacked automobiles, or who were too old or infirm, were caught in the storm, and many perished. For those who survived inside the city of New Orleans, the experience of being neglected while authorities tried to organize relief efforts engendered further suffering and bitter reactions of anger and hostility. In the atmosphere of normlessness (anomie), a small number of people began looting and sniping at police and hapless civilians. The poor and those now thrown into poverty by the storm were most likely to be victimized by the lawlessness. Every aspect of the tragedy was heightened by the fact that those experiencing the worst suffering and willful neglect were poor African American residents of the central city, some of whom had been herded into the Superdome or other "shelters" without adequate preparation to accommodate their needs. Many died, and many more were traumatized by the experience.

When all the facts are known, Katrina will no doubt have added many tens of thousands to the ranks of the poor in the United States. The storm revealed once again the deep divides between people with the material means to escape and survive and those, especially the poor and minorities, who are most vulnerable and who suffer the greatest losses in such disasters.

This family, attempting to flee to safety and shelter after Hurricane Katrina, was among the thousands of African American, Latino, and white families made homeless by the storm. Because they often lacked the means to escape, poor African Americans were disproportionately affected by the disaster.

Immigration and Poverty. Immigration is a different kind of life event that may be associated with poverty or efforts to escape from it. In many of the world's wealthier nations, an increasing proportion of the poor are immigrants. This is certainly true in the United States. Almost 25 percent of the increase in poverty since the early 1970s has occurred among recent immigrants and their children. Although the majority of Hispanics are neither impoverished nor immigrants, poor people from Mexico, Central America, and the Caribbean are among the largest immigrant groups today. Many live in the poorest city neighborhoods and rural counties. Most of the adults work full time, often in the lowest paying and most undesirable jobs. Most lack health insurance, and many fear that changes in welfare laws will make it impossible for them to send their children to school or to receive the same benefits as others who pay taxes.

The issue of whether poor and unskilled immigrants drive down the wages of the working poor and represent a burden to taxpayers generates a great deal of controversy. It is often used by politicians who wish to capitalize on the resentment some Americans already feel toward immigrants. In 1994, for example, California voters passed Proposition 187, which asserted that the state's welfare benefits were a "magnet" for immigrants from Mexico and made illegal immigrants ineligible for state aid, including public education (Rodriguez, 1999). Although it was quickly declared unconstitutional by the California supreme court, the idea of denying access to food stamps and other forms of public assistance remained popular and was incorporated as a highly controversial policy of the 1996 welfare reform act.

In 1997 a panel of experts convened by the prestigious National Academy of Sciences released a comprehensive study that examined the impact of immigration on the U.S. economy as a whole and on low-wage workers in particular. The study found that "the vast majority of Americans are enjoying a healthier economy as a result of the increased supply of labor and lower prices that result from immigration" (quoted in Pear, 1997, p. 1). The analysis also showed, however, that competition from low-wage immigrant workers "lowered the wages of high-school dropouts by about 5 percent, which accounts for about 44 percent of the total decline in wages of high-school dropouts from 1980 to 1994" (p. 24).

Recent census data confirm the fact that first-generation immigrants and their families experience far higher rates of poverty than do non-immigrants, largely because they are most heavily represented among the nation's low-wage workers. (See Figure 6–8.) Note that compared with white, non-Hispanic households, immigrant households are almost twice as likely to fall below the official poverty threshold.

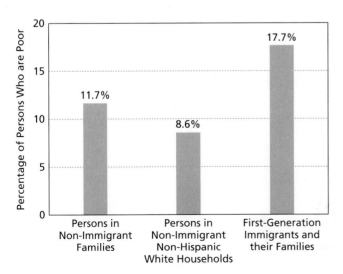

Figure 6–8 Poverty among First-Generation Immigrants and Non-Immigrants (Poverty Rates)
Source: U.S. Census Bureau, 2005.

CONCOMITANTS OF POVERTY

"Poverty," said George Bernard Shaw, "does not produce unhappiness; it produces degradation." Most Americans take for granted a decent standard of living—especially good health care, decent education and housing, and fair treatment under the law. In this section we examine the impact of poverty in each of these areas.

Health Care

The number of uninsured Americans rose by 1.3 million between 2004 and 2005 and has increased by almost 7 million since 2000 (National Coalition on Health Care, 2007). Low-wage workers increasingly find that employers do not offer health insurance, and the rising costs of medical care and insurance make it impossible for many to afford their own private insurance plans. For people in this situation, the leading cause of poverty is catastrophic illness and the resulting medical bills.

By almost every standard, the poor are less healthy than the rest of the population. For example, the mortality rates for poor infants are far higher than those for infants in more affluent families, and poor women are much more likely to die in childbirth. Poor women are also far more likely to give birth to their children in a municipal hospital. Inadequately housed, fed, and clothed, the poor can expect to be ill more often and to receive less adequate treatment. The health problems of the poor are not limited to physical ailments. Rates of diagnosed psychosis are higher among the poor, and they are more likely to be institutionalized and to receive shock treatment or chemotherapy in lieu of psychotherapy. As shown in Figure 6–9, the less income people have, the more likely they are to report that their health is "fair or poor." Of all the population groups in the United States, the poor are the least likely to have health insurance.

In their analysis of the impact of welfare reform on poor households, Christopher Jencks and Joseph Swingle (2000) found that "health insurance coverage has fallen for almost all groups, including single mothers, since the early 1990s." Health insurance coverage for single-parent families fluctuated between 81 percent and 82 percent from 1987 to 1993. By 1998 it averaged only 79 percent. "The reason for declining coverage is clear," the authors note. "When a single mother goes on welfare, she is automatically enrolled in Medicaid. In 1993, when the welfare rolls peaked, 40 percent of all single mothers said they had Medicaid. As the rolls fell, Medicaid coverage fell too." As a result, by the end of the 1990s only about 33 percent of single mothers had Medicaid coverage. As single mothers took "workfare jobs" or found jobs themselves in

Figure 6–9 Americans Reporting "Fair" or "Poor" Health, by Annual Family Income

Source: Lichter & Crowley, 2002. Copyright © 2002. Reprinted by permission of The Population Reference Bureau.

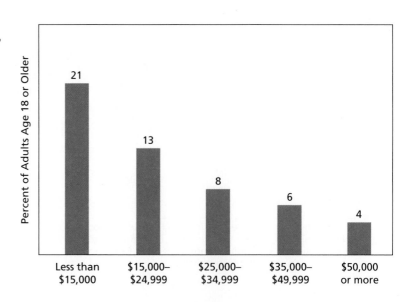

the labor force, private coverage increased somewhat. But that increase has not been sufficient to offset the decline in Medicaid.

Since the inception of Medicare and Medicaid in 1965, the poor have had greater access to various medical resources. But there are problems with almost all insurance programs: Coverage is often inadequate, it begins only after a specified deductible expense has been reached, and many people do not know exactly what is covered. Recent reductions in funding for Medicaid are resulting in more curtailments of medical benefits for the poor. Throughout the nation, the drive to reduce Medicare costs and close public hospitals is reducing access to health care and hospitals, especially for immigrants.

Along with the large increase in poverty in the early years of the new century came even more rapid increases in the number of Americans without health insurance. This was particularly significant for the nation's children, 29 percent of whom lacked health insurance in 2005 and thus were least likely to receive the preventive medical care that children in other affluent nations receive. In the wake of Hurricane Katrina, the situation became even worse. When the full extent of the disaster became evident, the Congressional Black Caucus held a press conference to highlight the urgent need for further government assistance. Representative Elijah Cummings (D-MD) pointed out that many of the people now devastated by the hurricane were "already living in poverty and destitution even before the hurricane came." He urged the government to do more. "We cannot allow it to be said by history that the difference between those who lived and those who died in this great storm was nothing more than poverty, age, or skin color."

Education

In every respect, poor children get less education than those born into more affluent families. They receive fewer years of schooling, have less chance of graduating from high school, and are much less likely to go to college. They are apt to be taught in overcrowded classrooms, often by inexperienced teachers, and to receive little if any individual attention. Moreover, most teachers come from a middle-class background and have little training in working with disadvantaged children. They bring to the job the expectation that poor children will read, speak, and behave poorly and perform poorly on tests, and that their parents and home life do not encourage academic achievement. It is not surprising that these expectations become self-fulfilling prophecies.

In recent decades considerable research has been devoted to the question of how effective preschool programs are in counteracting the effects of poverty. A review of that research concluded that children who attended preschool programs had higher intelligence scores at the age of 6, were less likely to be assigned to special-education classes, were less likely to be held back, and were less likely to drop out or be classified as delinquents (Duncan, Brooks-Gunn, & Marx, 1998).

The low educational attainment of poor children tends to perpetuate poverty. In general, the less educated have lower incomes, less secure jobs, and more difficulty in improving their economic condition. Children of parents with less than a high-school education generally do not do as well in school as children whose parents have completed high school. Thus, the cycle in which poverty and education are linked is passed from one generation to the next.

Housing and Homelessness

The poor are likely to live in housing that is overcrowded, infested with vermin, in need of major repairs, lacking basic plumbing facilities, and inadequately heated. More than half of such housing is in rural areas. Poor people who live in cities are unable to move around and use the city's resources but are often forced to move from one bad situation to another because of fire, crime, and other misfortunes. They are isolated and segregated both economically and racially.

Racial segregation increases when middle- and upper-income families leave the city. Cities also lose businesses when more prosperous citizens leave, and consequently their tax revenues decline. This leaves poor residents with fewer jobs and less adequate police protection and other services. Suburban zoning requirements, such as minimum lot sizes, are designed to attract newcomers who add more in taxes than they require in services. Suburban restrictions on multiple-dwelling structures have the same purpose: to prevent low-income housing from being erected and to keep out low-income and minority families.

People who live in their cars while they work at jobs that do not pay enough for them to afford local housing are homeless. So are people sleeping over the warm air of exhaust grates in the alleys of urban office buildings. Women seeking safety from abusive spouses by sleeping with their children in a local women's shelter may have a home, but during the time they are in the shelter, they too are homeless. A recent analysis of national census and survey data found that about 1.35 million children—nearly 2 percent of the nation's total—are homeless (Bernstein, 2000). As these examples suggest, it is extremely difficult to actually count the homeless or even to adequately describe all the forms homelessness can take (Burt, 1994). In an effort to fill in some of the knowledge gaps, the U.S. Department of Housing and Urban Development conducted a survey in shelters, soup kitchens, and other programs; some of the results are shown in Figure 6–10.

One notable finding of the survey is the disproportionate number of African American men among the homeless. Note also the relatively high proportion of veterans compared to the entire population. Insufficient income and lack of a job, both aspects of the homeless person's poverty status, rather than lack of available housing, appear to be the major obstacles to finding a home. Not shown in the charts is that the same survey found that the majority of the homeless had worked for pay in the past month, another indication that the combination of low wages and lack of affordable housing prevents many people from securing more permanent shelter. As housing prices move beyond the reach of the homeless and as their ability to move up the income ladder weakens, the demand for affordable housing will only increase.

Rehabilitation of existing structures has been advocated as one solution to the housing problem, one in which the poor need not be uprooted from familiar surroundings. But the cost of rehabilitating antiquated structures in deteriorating neighborhoods is too high, and the potential return on the investment too low, to appeal to private builders. Because poor families cannot afford rentals or purchase prices that would be profitable to owners and builders, it is extremely difficult to induce private industry to provide low-income housing. Each year, therefore, the lack of housing for the poor becomes more serious, a subject to which we return in Chapter 13.

Justice

As noted in Chapter 5, poor people are more likely than members of the middle and upper classes to be arrested, indicted, convicted, and imprisoned, and they are apt to be given longer sentences for the same offenses. Conversely, they are less likely to receive probation, parole, or suspended sentences. Also, adolescents who are poor are more apt to be labeled juvenile delinquents. Affluent children who commit crimes are likely to be sent to a psychiatrist and left in their parents' custody; poor children who commit crimes are likely to be sent to a correctional institution.

Because of the position of poor people in society, the crimes that they are most likely to commit (property theft and assault) tend to be the ones most disapproved of by those who make the laws—the middle and upper classes. These crimes also tend to be the most visible and widely publicized ones. Members of the middle and upper-middle classes tend to commit white-collar crimes—embezzlement, price-fixing, tax evasion, bribery, and so on. Although these crimes involve much more money than street crimes or property theft and may even pose a greater threat to social institutions, they tend not to be regarded as

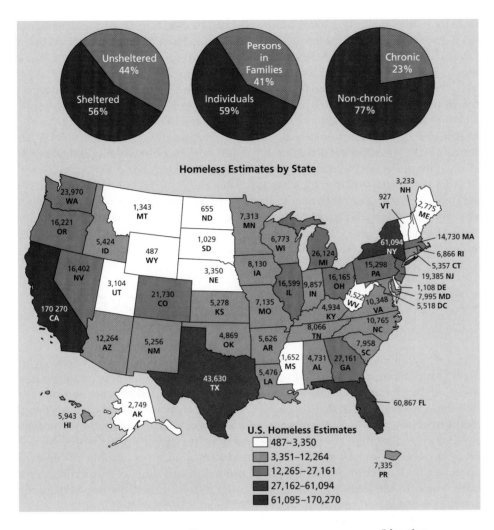

Homeless Estimates by State

U.S. Homeless Estimates
- 487–3,350
- 3,351–12,264
- 12,265–27,161
- 27,162–61,094
- 61,095–170,270

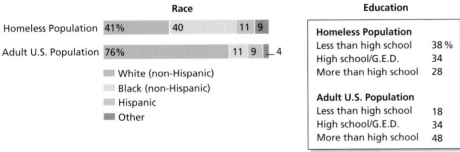

Race

Homeless Population 41% 40 11 9

Adult U.S. Population 76% 11 9 4

White (non-Hispanic)
Black (non-Hispanic)
Hispanic
Other

Education

Homeless Population
Less than high school	38 %
High school/G.E.D.	34
More than high school	28

Adult U.S. Population
Less than high school	18
High school/G.E.D.	34
More than high school	48

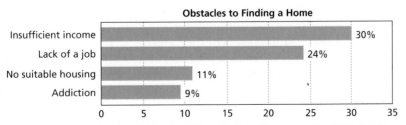

Obstacles to Finding a Home

Insufficient income 30%
Lack of a job 24%
No suitable housing 11%
Addiction 9%

0 5 10 15 20 25 30 35

Figure 6–10 Characteristics of the Homeless Population, Compared to U.S. Adult Population

Source: Adapted from Slobin, 1999. Copyright © 1999 by The New York Times Company. Reprinted by permission; National Coalition to End Homelessness, 2007.

serious by the criminal-justice system. Moreover, white-collar crimes are rarely publicized. Even if they are arrested, prosperous citizens are more likely to be able to afford bail, to know their rights, to be competently defended, and to receive brief sentences. But an indigent defendant who is unable to post bail may be kept in jail for months.

Under the law, every accused person has the right to be represented by counsel, and some cities, counties, and states provide public defenders. But many large cities and a majority of the states lack public-defender services, and in federal courts there are neither paid defenders nor funds to compensate court-appointed counsel, who serve on a voluntary basis. When public defenders and court-appointed lawyers are provided, they may not have the financial resources or time required for extended investigations.

Inadequate defense is one of the reasons that the poor are more likely to be convicted and, if they are, to receive more severe sentences than those who are better off. And poor individuals who have been arrested and convicted are likely to be sentenced to overcrowded jails, where few inmates can be truly rehabilitated. Upon release, they bear a stigma that makes it difficult to find or hold a job.

EXPLANATIONS OF PERSISTENT POVERTY

Structural Explanations

Structural explanations of poverty incorporate elements of both the functionalist and the conflict perspectives described in Chapter 1. They attribute poverty to the functioning of the dominant institutions of society, such as markets and corporations. When these major social structures change, conflicts arise as large numbers of people attempt to adjust to new conditions and new forms of social organization. For example, in a society dominated by agrarian production and agricultural markets, the poor tend to be people who lack land or whose land is unsuitable for farming. Or they may be people who have been forced off their land and have come to towns and cities to look for work. In industrial societies, the poor tend to be those who have been unable to acquire the skills or knowledge that would enable them to find and keep jobs in factories or other businesses.

During various periods of American history, some groups migrated to the cities in an attempt to escape from an impoverished rural life. Others migrated when they were forced off the land by the mechanization of farming, by the consolidation of farms into larger units, and by the pressure of competition with large agribusinesses. All these changes in the social structure of farming created a class of poor people who were forced to sell their labor for whatever wages they could obtain. Since the Civil War, entire population groups, including U.S.-born blacks and Appalachian whites with neither land nor marketable skills, have been forced into the cities, where they compete with newly arrived immigrants and other groups for menial, low-paying jobs.

The Marxian structural explanation would add to the causes of poverty just mentioned the case of the impoverished industrial worker. Increasingly, according to the Marxian view, the poor are industrial workers displaced from their jobs through the efforts of capitalists to find ever-cheaper sources of labor, to automate their production systems and thereby eliminate the need for workers, or to move their factories out of the country altogether. This trend, which is characteristic of all unregulated capitalist societies, creates a "reserve army of unemployed," which, in its desperate search for income of any kind, drives down wages for all workers.

Contemporary social scientists may not agree with Marx's theory, but they tend to agree that changes in macro social patterns of growth have a lot to do with increasing poverty. Nobel-Prize-winning economist James Tobin (1994), for example, points out that in the early twentieth century, when U.S. society was undergoing rapid industrialization and urbanization, the "rising economic tide" reduced poverty by increasing employment and providing the revenue needed to invest in education, housing, jobs, and greater income security for the elderly. Now, with slow economic growth, there are

Abandonment of inner-city housing in the 1970s and 1980s helped create the low-income housing crisis of the 1990s.

fewer "good jobs" to lift people out of poverty and less money to invest in the programs needed to help poor families achieve upward mobility.

Closely related to structural explanations like the one offered by Tobin are those that emphasize the dual market for labor. In studies of the migrations of blacks and other groups to the cities, sociologists have found that there is a dual labor market in which favored groups are given access to the better jobs—those that offer secure employment and good benefits. Other groups, usually minority groups and migrants, are shunted into another segment of the labor market in which the jobs pay extremely poorly and offer no security or benefits (Lister, 2004; Wilson, 1996a).

Still another structural explanation of poverty maintains that the state, through its efforts to eliminate poverty, actually causes it. This explanation has both radical and conservative proponents. The radicals argue that whereas low wages and unemployment cause a great deal of poverty, the state's welfare and relief programs actually perpetuate it. They claim that the state uses programs like unemployment insurance to prevent rebellions by the poor that might otherwise challenge the existing capitalist order; yet it does not use its power to ensure that all citizens can work for a decent wage (Piven, 2004; Piven & Cloward, 1972). Arguing in a somewhat similar vein but from a conservative point of view, George Gilder (1993) claims that poverty in America is generally caused by well-meaning but misguided liberal welfare policies, which rob unemployed workers of the initiative to develop new, marketable skills and rob society of capital that should be invested in new businesses to produce new wealth and new jobs. The high proportion of the poor who work or are actively seeking work constitutes a strong argument against this claim.

These structural theories discuss the causes of poverty and the origins of the lower class in terms of the structure of the society in which the poverty occurs. Other theories, to which we now turn, attempt to explain the perpetuation of poverty. They examine why certain individuals, families, and groups tend to remain poor even in good economic times and in spite of what appear to be ample opportunities for education and personal advancement.

What do sociologists mean by "structural" forces in society that are associated with greater numbers of low-income and poor people in the labor force? What aspects of globalization engender these structural forces?

Cultural Explanations

Cultural explanations of poverty are based on the interactionist perspective in sociology. In this view, through the ways in which they are brought up and socialized and through their interactions in everyday life, people become adapted to certain ways of life, including poverty. These ways of life persist because they become part of a group's culture.

Proponents of the cultural approach argue that a "culture of poverty" arises among people who experience extended periods of economic deprivation. Under these conditions, new norms, values, and aspirations emerge and eventually become independent of the situations that produced them, so that eliminating the problem does not eliminate the behaviors that have been developed to deal with it. The result is a self-sustaining system of values and behaviors that is handed down from one generation to the next (Entman & Rojecki, 2000; Lewis, 1968; Murray, 1984).

The idea that there is a culture of poverty that arises among chronically poor individuals and families is highly controversial. William J. Wilson (1996a), a noted expert on inner-city poverty, rejects the concept, claiming that it is a global label that does not fit in many instances. But he recognizes that long spells of poverty may have long-term consequences for children and grandchildren: "As the disappearance of work has become a characteristic feature of the inner-city ghetto, so too has the disappearance of the traditional married-couple family" (p. 31). He attributes this decline in family norms to the despair felt by the poor, especially impoverished men. This despair also leads to higher rates of suicide, homicide, incarceration, and addiction, which in turn decrease the pool of eligible men in poor communities.

A culture-of-poverty explanation for the decline in two-parent families in the inner city and among poor people elsewhere would argue that children in poor families are socialized to believe that it is permissible to father babies and not take responsibility for them or that it is acceptable to spend long periods on welfare. Wilson's (1996a) research finds little evidence that such norms are widespread. Instead, poor people in inner-city ghettos and elsewhere share the same values and express the same aspirations as more affluent Americans, but their confidence in attaining them is greatly diminished by their negative life experiences. They may develop certain styles of language and expression that look like a separate culture to outsiders, but this, according to Wilson, hardly qualifies as a culture of poverty.

Sociologist Herbert J. Gans (1995) is also critical of the culture-of-poverty thesis. Gans stresses the heterogeneity of the poor, noting that some are in families that have been poor for generations, while others are poor only periodically; some have become so used to coping with deprivation that they have trouble adapting to new opportunities; and some are beset by physical and emotional illnesses. He is critical of the idea that culture is holistic, that no element of it can be changed unless the entire culture is altered. Instead, he argues that behavior results from a combination of cultural and situational influences.

Gans (1995) maintains that the ultimate solution to the problem of poverty lies in the discovery of the specific factors that constrain poor people in reacting to new opportunities when these conflict with their present cultural values. He and Wilson (1996a) believe we must examine the kinds of changes needed in our economic system, social order, and power structure and in the norms and aspirations of the affluent majority that permit a poor class to exist. These are all themes that emerge again in considerations of social policy and poverty.

Social Policy

As is evident throughout this chapter, the extent of poverty in the world's most affluent society is a matter of continuing controversy. So is the question of what can be done about it. This question is intimately bound up with attitudes toward the poor themselves: Are the poor to blame for their own poverty? Do they avoid work? Would providing more jobs for the poor do any good? One's views on these issues have a lot to do with one's opinions about government intervention on behalf of the poor.

Reform of "Welfare as We Know It"

In 1996 Congress passed the Personal Responsibility and Work Opportunity Reconciliation Act, more widely known as "welfare reform." This legislation is largely targeted toward the parents of children in households whose incomes fall below the poverty line. Female single parents who were formerly entitled to monthly payments or assistance through the AFDC program are now required to obtain jobs or enroll in work training programs to qualify for supplemental assistance through their state governments. These state payments are subsidized by federal government grants. We will describe some of the changes brought about by welfare reform shortly. Few policy changes have received more attention or generated more confusion or ideological controversy.

Advocates of welfare reform, including both Republicans and Democrats, point to dramatic decreases in the number of people, especially female single parents, receiving various types of "welfare" payments under the TANF program. They may also cite abundant examples of people who have succeeded in finding real employment. These individuals often gain greater self-esteem and pride from their jobs than they ever experienced in the far more passive but frustrating life lived from one AFDC check to another. But have these far-reaching changes actually improved the lives of female single parents? The answers are not fully known, but much of the data suggests that a great deal of caution should accompany the generally enthusiastic welcome that welfare reform has received so far.

Boosted by a booming economy, welfare officials have found it far less difficult than anticipated to find jobs for clients. Caseloads have dropped by over 50 percent in many states. At the same time, the earnings and employment of poor people have increased. Figure 6–11 shows clearly that income from public welfare has decreased from about 50 percent to less than 20 percent of the budgets of poor female-headed families, to be replaced by income from earnings, as required by the welfare reform law. But as noted earlier, in too many cases the earned income is insufficient to adequately support families or lift them above the official poverty threshold (Lichter & Crowley, 2002).

As noted earlier, the 1996 welfare reform bill ended the 60-year-old program known as AFDC, originally part of the landmark Social Security Act of 1935 (DeParle, 2004). Under the new legislation, parents whose household incomes fall below a given

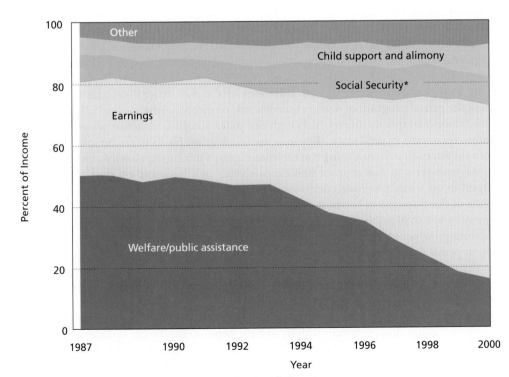

Figure 6–11 Income Sources for Poor Female-Headed Families with Children, 1987–2000

Source: Lichter & Crowley, 2002. Copyright © 2002. Reprinted by permission of The Population Reference Bureau.

*Includes SSI (Social Security Insurance) for disabled workers.

TABLE 6–3	Key Provisions of the 1996 Personal Responsibility and Work Opportunity Reconciliation Act (PRWORA)

- Establishes TANF. TANF replaces former entitlement programs (such as Aid to Families with Dependent Children) with federal block grants; devolves responsibility for welfare programs from federal to state government; and uses time limits and work requirements to emphasize the move from welfare to work.

- Tightens eligibility standards for SSI child disability benefits.

- Requires states to enforce strong child support programs for collecting child support payments from absent fathers.

- Restricts eligibility for welfare and other public benefits for recent immigrants. PRWORA denies illegal aliens most benefits, except emergency medical services. It also allows states to provide federal cash assistance to legal aliens already in the country and to use state funds for cash assistance to aliens not eligible for federal funds.

- Provides resources for foster care data systems and a federal child welfare custody study.

- Establishes a block grant to allow states to provide child care for working parents.

- Alters eligibility criteria and benefits for child nutrition programs.

- Tightens national standards for food stamps and other benefits. It reduces benefit levels and denies most benefits to childless able-bodied adults unless the person is working or in training.

- Limits eligibility for TANF receipt. It sets a five-year time limit for TANF and bars people convicted of drug-related crimes from TANF for life.

Source: Adapted from Whitener, Weber, & Duncan, 2001.

level (depending on the size of the household) are no longer entitled to federal funds administered through state and county welfare agencies. Instead, the states receive block grants, large sums of money earmarked for specific purposes, to be used for assistance to the poor. Thus, instead of AFDC payments, people now receive checks from Temporary Assistance to Needy Families (TANF). (See Table 6–3.)

As in the past, the cash amounts vary widely from one state to another, with Mississippi and Alabama on the low end and California and New York on the high end. The critical difference, however, is that federal requirements now specify that after two years of welfare payments under the new system, an able-bodied recipient must enroll in a training program or find work. The federal law also places a five-year limit on all payments to individual households in an attempt to prevent "chronic" welfare dependency. As long as the states conform to the broad mandates of the new federal program, they may shape the actual program of work requirements, monthly payments, and other policies to suit their own specific needs. Although the states are under intense pressure to shift welfare recipients to paid work, they may use block grant funds to create jobs or to supplement wages that do not bring the recipient up to a minimum monthly income.

We have seen in this chapter that despite years of a booming economy, which has helped many former welfare clients find decent jobs, the picture for the poorest segments of the population began to improve but has worsened again as a result of recession and the loss of public funding. Does this mean that the welfare reforms are actually harming poor people, especially poor children? How social scientists answer this question depends to a great extent on their ideological positions on the left–right spectrum. On the right, social scientists often claim that welfare reform is working extremely well. It has reduced welfare rolls by almost half in many states. Most important from the conservative perspective, it is claimed that the reforms discourage welfare dependency by increasing work opportunities and reducing family breakdown. Supporters of the new system also claim that work rather than welfare dependency builds independence and self-esteem. They note that there is a 20 percent exception in the laws that allows the states to waive the rules for the neediest clients, so that flexibility and the possibility of humane treatment are built into the law (Besharov & Germanis, 1999).

Liberal critics of welfare reform argue that the new system is increasing the number of homeless people and people who lack health insurance, and that it is, in effect, a form of government enforcement of underpaid work. "At first glance," writes Frances Fox Piven (1999), "the campaign to reform welfare seemed to be entirely about questions of the personal morality of the women who subsist on the dole. The problem was, the argument went, that a too generous welfare system was leading women to spurn wage work for lives of idleness and for what Senator Orrin Hatch called 'the deep, dark pit of welfare dependency.'" Piven argues that the reforms drew on popular stereotypes and prejudices toward "black and Latina minorities who were widely understood to be the main beneficiaries of welfare, and also tapped the energy and excitement evoked by talk of women and sex and sin." She believes that the real motivation behind welfare reform was to enforce low-wage work. She and other critics of both the old and the new welfare systems believe that education and job creation are vital to getting people off the dole. To them, the ironies of the new system are clear:

> A good many Americans are frustrated by low and declining wages and overwork. They are anxious that their family life is eroding now that neither parent has time to do the cooking and caretaking that sustains families. They have been encouraged to vent their frustrations on welfare. In the process, they are supporting a reconfiguration of policy that will worsen the terms of their own work and wear away at their own families while gripping them ever more tightly in the cultural vise that compels low wage work no matter the terms. (p. 32)

Piven (1999), Gans (1995), and many other welfare critics on the left side of the political spectrum argue that with all its faults, AFDC was a relatively small federal program. It never cost more than about 1 percent of the federal budget, and fewer than 5 million people were on the rolls. They maintain that beginning in the early 1980s the welfare poor were targeted as examples of the failure of liberal antipoverty policies. To afford tax cuts and budget reductions before the economic boom of the late 1990s, it was necessary to cut programs for the most vulnerable and politically powerless segments of the population. The poor are foremost among these groups. So are immigrants, whose benefits are also scheduled for cuts under the new policies being formulated in many states. The idea that some people could subsist on payments that transferred funds from the more well-to-do to the poor, and that in some cases they could live that way for years without any work requirement, became an easy target for those who wished to decrease federal spending. On this last point, conservative social scientists would certainly agree. From their perspective, the liberals who were critical of the old AFDC program failed to make adequate reforms when they had control of Congress.

So what is the truth about welfare reform? The answer is that there is no single truth. Instead of a national program and set of policies dealing with cash assistance, the United States now has fifty-one different systems for the states and the District of Columbia. This makes the task of analyzing which mix of financial incentives, work supports, and work obligations is most effective extremely difficult (Kaplan, 2002). Different state policies are still being evaluated. Positive claims based only on reduction of the welfare rolls should never be taken as the full measure of the program's success. Neither should claims based on the experience of the poorest of the poor. Far more careful evaluation of the actual conditions experienced by parents and children in the new welfare systems are required. In the meantime, it is important for social scientists to conduct politically neutral analyses of the empirical facts. The results of one such analysis are presented in the Unintended Consequences box on page 214.

The United States also attempts to provide a safety net of social-insurance programs for all taxpayers and their dependents, not only those who are already quite poor. Some social-insurance programs are intended to compensate for loss of income, regardless of income level or need. Through unemployment insurance, for example, cash benefits are paid for short periods to insured workers who are involuntarily unemployed. Unemployment insurance was created by the same act of Congress that established the

Unintended Consequences

EFFECTS OF WELFARE REFORM

Christopher Jencks and colleagues at Harvard's Kennedy School of Public Policy are continually reviewing new studies of the welfare reform policies. Here are some of their observations:

More single mothers are working. That is the good news. The bad news is that a large minority of the women who leave the welfare rolls do not find or keep jobs. Follow-up studies show that most mothers who leave the welfare rolls find jobs, but a large minority do not. Moreover, some of those who find jobs soon lose them and do not appear on the welfare rolls. Between 1987 and 1996, about 10 percent of all single mothers fell into this category. By 1998 the proportion had climbed to 12 percent.

Incomes are rising at the top but not at the bottom. Most social-scientific and journalistic accounts of welfare reform in different states or cities provide abundant evidence of successful transitions to work, often after many years of welfare dependence. Kathryn Edin and Laura Lein's (1997) empirical work on poor women's incomes demonstrates that even the more successful job holders experience economic hardship and must often resort to the help of family and friends.

Doubling up? Liberal critics of welfare reform often speculate that when single mothers cannot make ends meet, they will increasingly move in with relatives. So far, the doubling-up hypothesis is not confirmed.

The proportion of single mothers living with relatives has not increased.

Less health insurance coverage. As we saw earlier in the chapter, there have been significant increases in the proportion of poor people, especially single mothers, who are not covered by health insurance. Once people leave welfare to begin working, they may not be eligible for Medicaid even though their employer does not offer health insurance.

More marriage? Conservatives hoped that welfare reform would encourage morality, especially through encouragement of marriage and discouragement of single motherhood. The results suggest otherwise. Wisconsin, for example, began welfare reform efforts early. It has reduced its welfare rolls more than any other large state, yet the proportion of Wisconsin children born to single mothers has not fallen. In fact, "the proportion climbed from 27.1 percent in 1994 to 28.5 percent in 1998—an increase of 1.4 points—at a time when the increase for the nation as a whole was only 0.2 points."

Aside from these economic and moral considerations, two facts stand out: "First, almost all mothers who are working tell interviewers that they prefer work to welfare. Second, many working mothers report problems finding satisfactory child care." Reports provide a great deal of anecdotal evidence that young children are being left alone, sometimes for long periods. "These reports suggest that welfare reform could end up helping parents but hurting their children. Because we have no reliable system for monitoring children's well-being, we will probably never know how welfare reform affected them" (Jencks & Swingle, 2000, p. 49).

Jencks and others who are evaluating the impact of welfare reform are especially cautious about the fact that so far the policies have been implemented in a favorable economic climate. No one knows what might happen if unemployment rates began to rise and an economic contraction was under way. In addition, Jencks issues this warning:

Some single mothers can't manage both employment and parenthood simultaneously. Even those who have the energy and skill to juggle work and parenthood often earn so little that they cannot make ends meet without additional help. If such help is not available, the long-term impact of welfare reform on both single mothers and their children could well turn out to be like the long-term impact of deinstitutionalization on the mentally ill: good for some but terrible for others. This is a worst-case scenario. But it is a possibility we should bear in mind as states keep cutting their welfare rolls. (Jencks & Swingle, 2000, p. 51)

Social Security system; however, the responsibility for administering unemployment insurance was delegated to the states, which were given broad latitude in setting eligibility standards and levels of benefits. As a result, the amount and duration of unemployment benefits vary greatly from one state to another. In Massachusetts, a worker who is unemployed after paying into the system beyond the minimum period is eligible for more than $200 a week for 15 weeks. In South Carolina, a worker who has paid into the system is eligible for only $150 per week for 9 weeks (Edelhoch, 1999).

Other forms of social insurance include workers' compensation programs, which provide wage replacements to insured workers who suffer occupational injuries, and veterans' compensation plans, which issue benefits to disabled veterans to make up for their loss of earning potential. Social Security payments to the elderly also fall into this category. Cash income-support programs are provided for unemployable people, those who are not covered by any form of social insurance, and those with special needs. Veterans' pensions fall into this category.

Income-in-kind programs provide goods and services, such as food, housing, and medical care, to the poor. These programs include public housing and urban renewal, health plans like Medicare and Medicaid (see Chapter 2), and food supplements like the commodity distribution program (which distributes surplus farm products to poor households) and food stamps (which in effect provide discounts on food purchases).

Welfare Policies and Growing Inequality

We have seen throughout this chapter that the United States faces serious social problems due to the widening gap between the haves and have-nots. Figure 6–12 shows that the share of income earned by most Americans has been declining since the mid-1970s, with a brief exception during the 1990s, so that today 90 percent of the population takes in only slightly more than 50 percent of the nation's annual income whereas the top 1 percent enjoys over 20 percent of all income. Between 2001 and 2005, due in large part to extremely generous tax cuts, corporate compensation policies, and gains in the financial markets, the top 1 percent of the population averaged over $5 million a year, and the top 0.01, the richest segment, now earns over $25 million a year. During the same period, due to welfare reform, increasing declines in health-care coverage for low-income workers, and decreasing employer payments into pension plans, Americans who are not rich have seen continual erosion of their social safety net.

In his thorough review of antipoverty policies in the United States and other nations, William J. Wilson (1987) notes that the countries that rely least on public assistance (e.g., Sweden and West Germany) instead emphasize such policies as family and housing allowances, child care services, and various types of work incentives. Thus, the cornerstone of their antipoverty policies is employment policies that make it easier for adults to manage their work and family lives without undue strain on themselves and their children (Kamerman & Kahn, cited in Wilson, 1987).

How should the United States address the dependency issue? One answer frequently given by social scientists and policymakers is that a serious effort should be made to increase the income of low-wage workers so that the working poor, by far the largest category of poor households, will not be forced to live in poverty. Another, similar approach would be to provide incentives for people on welfare to work if they are able to do so.

Figure 6–13 on page 216 shows some of the relationships that Wilson refers to. The Northern European nations devote large percentages of their annual GDP to major aspects of social welfare: pensions, health care, education, cash transfers (such as unemployment insurance), and housing. The English-speaking nations rank lower in terms of the generosity of their welfare programs, with the United States lagging behind most of them. Historical differences among these nations help explain these differences. Many of the European nations have stronger labor unions, as well as stronger traditions of state intervention in the economy. The English-speaking nations, on the other hand, have have stronger beliefs in limited government and personal responsibility for one's own well-being. Despite these differences, there is a rising tide of public opinon and

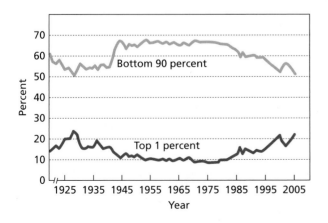

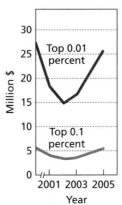

Figure 6–12 Share of Individual Income Earned by Bottom 90 Percent, Top 1 Percent, and Top 0.01 Percent of U.S. Population, 1925–2005

Source: Johnston, 2007. (Data: Thomas Piketty, Paris School of Economics and Emmanuel Saez, University of California, Berkeley, from I.R.S. data).

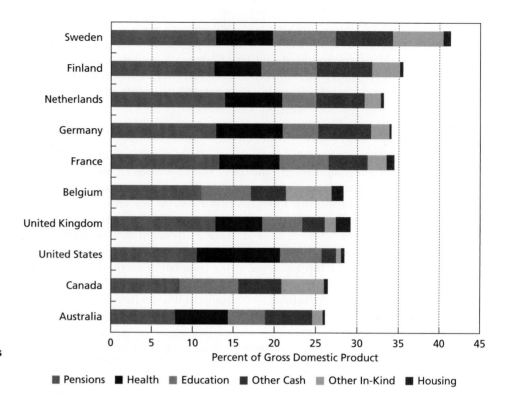

Figure 6–13 Size and Composition of Social Welfare Expenditures, Selected Nations

Source: Garfinkel, Rainwater & Smeeding, 2005.

Legend: ■ Pensions ■ Health ■ Education ■ Other Cash ■ Other In-Kind ■ Housing

concern among political policymakers that the United States needs to do a better job of addressing the problems of the impoverished and social welfare more generally.

As noted earlier in the chapter, a person who works full time all year at the minimum wage cannot earn enough to keep even a two-person family above the poverty line. To support a family of four, a worker must earn 60 percent more than the minimum wage (Ellwood, 1987). There are a variety of possible approaches to this problem. One recommended approach is income supplements, which could include wage subsidies, medical protection, and expansion of the earned income tax credit (EITC). The EITC was instituted in 1975 as a means of reducing the total tax bill of low-income taxpayers with dependent children. Originally, the credit was 10 percent of earned income up to $4,000, with a smaller credit for amounts between $4,000 and $8,000, but in the 1980s it was extended to somewhat higher incomes. If the credit exceeds the amount of tax due, an eligible individual can receive a payment from the Internal Revenue Service. In some respects, therefore, the EITC can be viewed as a negative income tax (Romich & Weisner, 2004).

Numerous proposals have been made to modify or extend the EITC. In one approach, a household could designate a principal earner whose wages would be subsidized if they were below a specified level; this would increase the reward for working. Another suggestion is to expand the EITC and allow it to vary by family size; this would help protect larger families and encourage low-income workers with families to return to work. A third approach is to convert the current tax deduction for children into a refundable tax credit.

Future Prospects

One of the most difficult problems in attempting to improve the condition of the poor is what to do about people living in highly concentrated or segregated poor neighborhoods. We saw earlier that the ghetto poor of central cities are a minority of all poor households, but they are highly visible and therefore are the focus of a great deal of attention, much of it negative and mean-spirited (Gans, 1995; Wilson 1996a). As long as large numbers of people live in inner-city neighborhoods where there has been a drastic loss of jobs and opportunity, it will be difficult for workfare or any other training and work approaches to make much of a difference. And decreases in welfare payments, Medicare services, and disability payments are likely to increase the economic and social stress in these impoverished areas of urban America.

A policy innovation that holds promise is a set of experimental programs designed to move people from areas of concentrated poverty to communities where they will have more opportunity. These programs were motivated in large part by an important court decision about what is known as the Gautreaux project in Chicago. The city of Chicago and the state of Illinois were ordered to assist residents of public housing in an extremely poor neighborhood to move to better neighborhoods outside the inner city. Evaluations of how the families who moved fared in the job market and in schools were generally favorable (Rosenbaum et al., 1996). In consequence, the Department of Housing and Urban Development has developed a program known as Moving to Opportunity. Although the program is still in the evaluation stage, families that are selected to move to new housing in neighborhoods with better job and educational opportunities are showing statistically significant gains in important social indicators, especially family income. Unfortunately, the experimental results also show that many of the people who were helped to move to better neighborhoods were unable to improve their economic condition over the full five years of the experiment, primarily because the weak economic recovery of recent years meant that they often moved to areas where jobs were unavailable.

Recent research shows some promising results and some important disappointments that reveal how complex the problems are. Among teenagers whose families participated in the Moving to Opportunity experiments, girls did much better than boys as measured by educational achievement, staying out of trouble (and jail), and rate of non-sports-related personal injuries. In fact, boys whose families moved to higher-income neighborhoods actually showed negative changes as measured by these variables (Clampet-Lundquist et al., 2006; Ludwig & Kling, 2006; Turney et al., 2006).

In the aftermath of Hurricane Katrina and the increase in destructive weather-related events throughout the nation, the United States faced an unprecedented regional crisis in its supply of low-income housing. But that was only one aspect of the disaster. As noted earlier, the storm revealed to a shocked nation and world many of the dire consequences of traumatic loss, especially for people already living in poverty. Days after the storm, Congress began appropriating emergency funds for the evacuation, relocation, and rebuilding of shattered communities, but at this writing it is by no means clear what the longer-term consequences of the disaster may be for antipoverty policies in the United States.

GOING BEYOND LEFT AND RIGHT

Referring to earlier antipoverty policies, President Ronald Reagan said, "We fought a war on poverty, and poverty won." People on the left often claim that unlike the War on Drugs or the war on terrorism, the war on poverty was abandoned too soon. This point was driven home, to the embarrassment of many Americans, in the aftermath of Hurricane Katrina. Twenty-eight percent of New Orleans residents lived below the poverty threshold, and this population was by far the least likely to have cars or other means of transportation to safety. Although they may differ on the best approaches to dealing with poverty, most Americans can agree that the sight of poor children and their parents living on the streets, either because of a natural disaster or because of homelessness caused by other forces, is unacceptable.

As vulnerable people on the margins of an enormously affluent society, the poor are often made to suffer before wiser policies are formulated to meet their needs. But opportunities for adequate child care, decent education, and job training do not negate the widely shared desire that we end welfare dependency by asking people who are able to do so to work for their incomes. We can begin to go beyond the left–right impasse by achieving a better balance between work requirements and opportunities to meet those requirements and by doing far more to address the housing and health care needs of poor children and families.

In 2007 the Supreme Court affirmed the right of employers of home-health-care workers not to pay overtime, even though these low-income workers are routinely asked to work longer than standard hours. Since this policy affects millions of women and men who work at or slightly above the minimum wage, and who care for our loved ones, their plight is not an issue of left or right, and at this writing Congress is preparing to address the issue of their right to earn a living wage.

Summary

- Although the United States ranks among the wealthiest nations in the world, many Americans are living in poverty. In the past two decades, the gap between the rich and the poor has widened.

- The United States has a long history of attempting to redistribute wealth through taxation and other policies. In so doing, however, it has actually provided more opportunities for the rich to get richer than for the poor to escape from poverty.

- About 37 million people live below the official poverty line. They include children, elderly people, single mothers, ill or disabled individuals, and students, as well as people who work either full or part time at poverty-level wages.

- The stratification of individuals and groups according to occupation, income, and skills is called class stratification. The Marxian view of stratification holds that classes are determined by economic measures. This view has been supplemented by those of Weber and his followers, who pointed out that other valued things besides wealth, such as status and power, are distributed unequally in modern societies. American society can be divided into five main classes: the upper class, the upper-middle class, the middle class, the working class, and the poor.

- Poverty can be defined in a variety of ways. It can mean a condition of near starvation, bare subsistence, or any standard of living that is measurably below the national average. Official definitions of the poverty line are based on the consumer price index. Alternative measures have been proposed that take into account changing definitions of minimal consumption.

- A large proportion of the poor are children, many of them in single-parent families. Blacks and other racial minorities are overrepresented among the poor. Poor people living in rural areas include migrant workers, Native Americans on reservations, and farmers. Many of the poor are working at low-paying jobs.

- Concomitants of poverty include poor health and unequal access to health services, inadequate education, substandard housing and homelessness, and discrimination in the criminal-justice system.

- Structural explanations of poverty attribute it to dominant social institutions such as the dual market for labor. The cultural explanation holds that extended economic deprivation creates a culture of poverty with its own norms and values. The situational approach interprets the behavior of the poor as an adaptation to their environment.

- The 1996 welfare reform bill replaced AFDC with a system of block grants to the states to be used for assistance to the poor. After two years of welfare payments under the new system, able-bodied recipients must enroll in a training program or find work. Evaluations of the new system find that more single mothers are working, but a large minority of the women who leave the welfare rolls do not find or keep jobs. They also find that the incomes of the poorest of the poor are not rising, and that increasing numbers of poor people lack health insurance.

- Proposals for alleviating the problems of people who work at low-wage jobs include modifying or extending the earned income tax credit (a means of reducing the total tax bill of low-income taxpayers with dependent children), enabling single mothers to work part time while receiving welfare payments, and reforming the child-support system so that fathers are held accountable for the support of their children.

Key Terms

welfare state, p. 187
wealthfare, p. 188

working poor, p. 190
social stratification, p. 191

class stratification, p. 191
lumpenproletariat, p. 191

Social Problems Online

There are several Web sites on the Internet with data and analyses of poverty in the United States as well as debates about welfare policies. To get a numerical account of poverty and wealth in America, start at the U.S. Census Bureau's homepage at **www.census.gov/**. Click on Subject A–Z and then on "P" to find Poverty in the menu. Information concerning poverty areas, historical poverty tables (1959–2004), poverty thresholds by family size and number of children, and the like can be found there. For related areas, check Income and Wealth.

The Census Bureau also offers links with organizations such as the Institute for Research on Poverty, which is located at **www.ssc.wisc.edu/irp**. It is a university-based center (University of Wisconsin, Madison) whose mission is to research "the causes and consequences of poverty and social inequality in the United States." Clicking on the Publications section of the institute's homepage brings up a menu of choices, such as Discussion Papers, Special Reports, and so forth.

The University of California Berkeley Data Archives & Technical Assistance Center, at **http://ucdata.berkeley.edu:7101/**, provides data sets on a variety of subjects related to welfare and poverty. For summaries of welfare reform and its impact on adolescents, health care, immigration, and the like, browse the Economic Success Clearinghouse at **www.financeproject.org/irc/win.asp**.

The Urban Institute, **www.urban.org/**, is a policy research organization that investigates social and economic problems. The Cato Institute, at **www.cato.org**, is a think tank that emphasizes market-based rather than government-driven policies. For research papers and data related to welfare and poverty, visit the Brookings Institution at **www.brook.edu/**.

Research Navigator

Follow the instructions on pages 26–27 of this text to access the features of Research Navigator. Once at the Web site, enter your Login Name and Password. Then, to use the Content Select database, use keywords such as "poverty threshold," "working poor," and "class identification," and the search engine will supply relevant and recent scholarly and popular press publications. Use the *New York Times* search-by-subject archive to find recent news articles related to poverty and the Link Library to find relevant Web sites organized by the key terms associated with this chapter.

Go to Research Navigator and choose Sociology; under Topics, choose Poverty. Then choose the U.S. census and click on the table dealing with Families by Number of Working Family Members and Family Structure, Below 100 Percent of Poverty. What does the category of 100 percent of poverty represent? (Hint: 125 percent of poverty refers to households below the poverty line up to those making 125 percent more than the poverty threshold for their family size.) What percentage of married-couple families are in this category? What percentages of male-headed and female-headed single-parent families? What percentage of families with one working member are in poverty? What percentage of single-parent families in which the "female householder" (usually the mother) is working are in poverty?

RACISM, PREJUDICE, and Discrimination

Dominant Trends

- *Parity in educational attainment between whites and African Americans is a dominant trend, but the achievement gap for Latinos and Native Americans remains a considerable problem.*

- *Racial and ethnic segregation in local communities continues to present obstacles to school desegregation. Almost 70 percent of black and 75 percent of Latino children attend predominantly minority schools.*

- *The widening income gap in the United States and Europe affects people of color disproportionately because they are more heavily concentrated in lower-wage jobs. The gap in wealth between the haves and the have-nots is becoming an even more serious obstacle to racial and ethnic equality.*

- *Disparities in rates of imprisonment continue without much improvement. Although they account for 12.5 percent of the population, for example, blacks make up 44 percent of the prison population, with severe consequences for the entire society.*

Why did Hurricane Katrina take such a heavy toll on minorities, the poor, and women and children? Many thousands of people from all social classes and from all racial and ethnic groups lost their property, but why were African Americans, Latinos (especially Mexicans), women, and children most likely to be among the dead? It is not difficult to answer these questions: In the United States the poor are disproportionately women and children of color. This is especially true in large cities like New Orleans, where, when the order was given to evacuate the city, people without the means to leave were trapped. But why were the inequalities in New Orleans so extreme? Answers to this question require more understanding of the history and sociology of American racism, prejudice, and discrimination.

The United States prides itself on its ethnic and racial diversity and on the progress it has made since the Civil War toward greater tolerance and racial harmony. At the same time, when one looks at the conditions of life in inner-city ghettos or on Indian reservations and at the continuing struggle against racial and ethnic hatreds, it becomes clear that the gains have been modest. In the early twentieth century the United States was still characterized by deep racial and ethnic divisions. Its educational and economic institutions were marked by sharp patterns of racial and ethnic exclusion, its communities rigidly segregated along racial lines. Indeed, when he surveyed the situation of prejudice and discrimination in the 1930s and 1940s, the eminent Swedish social scientist Gunnar Myrdal called the situation of "poor and suppressed" minorities in the land of freedom and opportunity "the American dilemma." Although much has changed since that time, racial and ethnic prejudice is still a significant problem in many areas of American life. And we will see in this chapter that many aspects of inequality in our society are the results of past patterns of racial and ethnic discrimination (Rees, 2007; Wilson, 1996a).

Shortly before the storm ravaged the Mississippi Gulf Coast and destroyed scores of communities and cities, the U.S. Census Bureau had confirmed that its latest surveys showed that poverty and lack of health insurance had increased quite markedly, just as the share of income enjoyed by the richest 20 percent of the population also increased. Poverty rates continue to be more than twice as high for minorities as for non-Hispanic whites. Among African Americans, 24.4 percent of households are below the poverty threshold, compared to 10.5 percent of non-Hispanic white households. For Hispanics of any race, the poverty rate is 22.1 percent of households, and for Asian Americans it is 10.6, reflecting the more predominantly middle-class composition of Asian households in the United States (U.S. Census Bureau, 2006).

As we have seen in earlier chapters, a frequent consequence of poverty is lack of health insurance. In the United States, the number of uninsured individuals grows by an average of 800,000 each year. But the burden of this inequality is hardly shared equally among the different racial groups. In 2005, 11 percent of non-Hispanic white households lacked health insurance, as did 20 percent of African American, 29 percent of Latinos, 19 percent of Asian Americans, and 24 percent of American Indians and Alaskan Natives (U.S. Census Bureau, 2005). Increasingly, adult members of minority groups who report low income are working full time for employers who do not pay for health insurance, but their wages are too low to allow them to afford health care insurance for themselves and their children.

The most vulnerable households in America are those headed by women with children under the age of 18. Here the poverty rates do not differ significantly between whites and minority groups, with almost half of these households found below the poverty level. But as we saw in the case of New Orleans, black single-parent families are heavily concentrated in inner-city neighborhoods, so that when disaster struck, African American and other women of color and their children were most likely to be unable to leave the city for economic reasons and were disproportionately affected by the disaster and its aftermath.

All these conditions and trends that contribute to the inequalities and disadvantages faced by minority groups have their origins in the history of American racism, prejudice, and discrimination—especially in the legacies of conquest of Native Americans and the history of slavery, reconstruction, and the continuing struggle for minority civil rights (Agoustinos and Reynolds, 2001).

THE CONTINUING STRUGGLE FOR MINORITY CIVIL RIGHTS

Although the constitutional bases for racial equality were established in the 1860s and 1870s with the ratification of the Thirteenth, Fourteenth, and Fifteenth Amendments, it was not until the mid-twentieth century that the rights guaranteed by these amendments began to be exercised effectively. Starting with Supreme Court decisions that affected specific, small areas of life, black Americans began to work their way toward equality. A major legal breakthrough came in 1954 with the historic decision in *Brown* v. *Board of Education of Topeka* that "separate educational facilities are inherently unequal." The Supreme Court later applied this "separate cannot be equal" doctrine to a wide range of public facilities.

The Civil Rights Act of 1964 was another important step. Unlike the civil rights acts passed in 1957 and 1960, the 1964 act provided a means for fighting discrimination in employment and public accommodations and for denying federal funds to local government units that permitted discrimination. There followed the comprehensive Voting Rights Act of 1965 and a federal prohibition against housing discrimination in the Civil Rights Act of 1968. Subsequent affirmative-action orders by President Lyndon B. Johnson aided the enforcement of these new laws; in addition, the Johnson administration set up new programs, such as Head Start, to counter the effects of discrimination.

But the discrepancy between legal equality and actual inequality remained. The impatience of some American blacks developed into anger, and in August 1964 a riot erupted in Watts, a black section of Los Angeles. By the time the wave of violent protest set off by the Watts riot subsided, it had struck almost every major urban center in the country. In 1967, following especially destructive riots in Newark and Detroit, President Johnson appointed the National Advisory Commission on Civil Disorders (1968) to investigate the origins of the disturbances and to recommend ways to prevent or control them in the future. Its findings suggested that there had been very little change since Myrdal's study. Describing the basic causes of the disorders, the commission stated,

> The first is surely the continuing exclusion of great numbers of Negroes from the benefits of economic progress through discrimination in employment and education, and their enforced segregated housing and schools. The corrosive and degrading effects of this condition and the attitudes that underlie it are the source of the deepest bitterness and at the center of the problem of racial disorder. (p. 203)

The commission concluded that "our nation is moving toward two societies, one black, one white—separate and unequal" (p. 1).

Although the situations of other minority groups—Native Americans, Chicanos (Mexican Americans), Hispanic Americans (especially Puerto Ricans and Cubans), Asian Americans, and some white ethnic groups—have received less intensive study, they are similar to that of black Americans. One form of discrimination to which these other groups are particularly vulnerable is harassment at the voting booth, largely because of some individuals' inadequate command of English. The 1975 extension of the Voting Rights Act attempted to alleviate this problem by requiring cities with sizable "language minority" populations to provide bilingual ballots in elections; it also permanently banned the use of literacy tests as a prerequisite for voting.

In recent years there has been a major influx of immigrants from Asian countries, especially Korea, Vietnam, Cambodia, India, and Pakistan. Their experience has shown that small groups with education, business experience, and some funds, coupled with cultural values that stress family cohesion and extremely hard work, have less difficulty in adapting to their new environment (Kim, 1983). On the other hand, large populations that gather in concentrated settlements, as Vietnamese immigrants have done in Texas and California, have been targets of racial hostility. Thus, it appears that the larger a group and the more segregated it is, the more hostility it encounters (Portes, 1995; Sears, Sidanius, & Bobo, 2000).

In the same vein, Stanley Lieberson (1990) argues that when an immigrant group is small, it is relatively easy for it to develop an occupational niche or specialty, as the Greeks and the Chinese have done in the restaurant industry. He cites a study showing that 14.8 percent of Greek immigrants were working in the restaurant industry and 9.4 percent of Swedish immigrants were carpenters. But when an immigrant population grows, it becomes far more difficult for it to retain control of an occupational niche and expand it enough to accommodate newcomers. Later arrivals, therefore, are more dependent than earlier immigrants on the general labor market.

The terrorist attacks on the United States in 2001 showed quite vividly how national and world events can quickly change the fortunes of particular minority groups. According to the U.S. Commission on Civil Rights (2001),

> For those of Middle Eastern descent or appearance, September 11 ushered in fear of reprisal and concern for personal safety. Some Muslims, Arab Americans, and Southeast Asians have paid a high price for sharing a similar appearance or cultural and religious background of the accused terrorists. In the months after the attacks, reports of harassment and assaults against these groups soared; as did complaints of workplace bias and allegations of racial profiling by law enforcement and airline personnel.

The situation of immigrant groups highlights the problems of minority status in the United States. But before we can discuss these problems in detail, we must gain a clearer understanding of the meaning of the term *minority* as it is commonly used today.

This scene in an ethnic neighborhood highlights the growing ethnic and racial diversity of the American population.

THE SOCIAL CONSTRUCTION OF MINORITIES

One often hears the claim that due to immigration and differences in the birthrates of various groups within the population, the United States is rapidly becoming a "nation of minorities." This claim refers especially to the increasing numbers of Latinos, Asians, and other groups, but it does not address the more important sociological aspects of the term *minority*. From the standpoint of social problems, the most significant minorities are those that do not receive the same treatment as other groups in society. But how and why does such a situation come about? Before we can begin to answer these questions, it is important to define three terms that are central to the discussion: *racial minorities, ethnic minorities,* and *assimilation.*

Racial minorities are groups of people who share certain inherited characteristics, such as eye folds or brown skin. Most experts believe that the biologically determined racial groups into which humanity is divided—caucasoid, mongoloid, and negroid— are strictly social categories and that the actual hereditary differences among them are meaningless (Gould, 1981; Thernstrom & Thernstrom, 2002). This is known as the "social constructionist" explanation for the existence of racial minorities. Race is a socially constructed concept in that people take what are actually rather trivial biological distinctions and "construct" ideas about more general differences among groups. Historically, when it is convenient for those in power to do so, they have used socially constructed ideas about racial superiority and inferiority to justify slavery or other extreme forms of racial dominance (Ore, 2006).

Ethnic minorities are made up of people who share cultural features, such as language, religion, national origin, dietary practices, and a common history, and who regard themselves as a distinct group. When members of either a racial or an ethnic minority take on the characteristics of the mainstream culture by adapting their own unique cultural patterns to those of the majority, as well as by intermarrying, **assimilation** occurs.

Can you explain the difference between race and ethnicity by applying these terms to American citizens who are descended from African slaves? (Hint: Discuss both their race and their ethnicity.)

It should be noted that the term *minority* as used here does not refer to a group's numerical strength in the population. This is true even though in most cases minority groups lack both numerical superiority and other means of counteracting unequal treatment.

All minority groups have their own particular characteristics, but the following are sociologically significant (Feagin, 1996; Simpson & Yinger, 1985):

1. Minorities are subordinate segments of a complex society.

2. Minorities tend to have special physical or cultural traits that are seen as undesirable by the dominant segments of the society.

3. Minorities develop a group consciousness or "we feeling."

4. Membership in a minority is transmitted by a rule of descent—one is born into it—which can impose the minority status on future generations even if by then its special physical or cultural traits have disappeared.

5. Members of a minority, whether by choice or by necessity, tend to practice **endogamy**—that is, to marry within the group.

There is no clear line between totally dominant and totally minority groups; rather, any given group can be placed at some point along a continuum of "minorityness." Various immigrant groups in the United States have moved along this continuum, edging progressively closer to equality and shedding some or all of their distinctive minority characteristics. It should be emphasized, however, that the physical distinctiveness of racial minorities has made the attainment of assimilation and equality much more difficult for them than for other immigrant groups, which are defined largely by cultural traits. Thus, racial minorities have tended to remain minorities much longer than nonracial minorities.

The characteristics just listed apply somewhat less accurately to nonracial and nonethnic minority groups. The aged, for example, constitute a minority group in terms of both absolute numbers and the treatment they receive, yet they are not born into it. Membership in the homosexual minority is not transmitted from one generation to another. Nevertheless, these groups share the major characteristics of minorities: subordinate status, special traits, and increasingly, group self-awareness.

Subordinate status is the principal characteristic of a minority group. In almost any society the desire for some goods, whether tangible or intangible, exceeds the supply, and groups within the society are likely to compete for them and for the power to control them. The groups that gain the most power dominate the other groups, controlling their access to the desired goods and often to other goods—social, economic, political, and personal—as well. The dominant group need not be the most numerous; it must merely be able to prevent other groups from effectively challenging its power (Plous, 2003).

Once established, however, the dominant–subordinate relationship is not fixed for all time. Either through the efforts of the subordinate group itself or as a result of changing legal or economic conditions, power relationships can be altered. We can see in our own society that women are not as subordinate as they were only a generation ago. Similarly, in southern counties where blacks considerably outnumber whites, extensive voter registration has enabled the formerly subordinate blacks to become politically significant. On a broader scale, most of the former colonial areas of Africa and Asia are independent nations, and some countries that formerly lacked influence, such as Japan and China, are now world powers.

Despite these examples of long-term change, it is usually very difficult for members of a subordinate group to attain a share of power and influence. The dominant group naturally wants to protect its privileged position. Among the weapons it uses to do so are prejudice and discrimination.

DEFINING RACISM, PREJUDICE, AND DISCRIMINATION

Racism is behavior, in word or deed, that is motivated by the belief that human races have distinctive characteristics that determine abilities and cultures. Racists believe in this erroneous concept of race; they also believe that their own race is superior and

White supremacists like those shown here are open and explicit about their hatred for racial minorities and about their desire to live in a "racially pure" society—which is, given the history of racial mixing over generations, a biological impossibility.

therefore ought to dominate or rule other races. Racism may be an attribute of an individual, or it may be incorporated into the institutions (social structures and laws) of an entire society. Nazi Germany, South Africa under apartheid, and the United States before the civil rights era of the mid-twentieth century are examples of societies and nations that incorporated racist beliefs in their social institutions. Societies that have attempted to eliminate racism from their institutions continue to struggle with the legacies of their racist histories. These legacies often appear in the form of prejudices, discrimination, and incidents of overt racism—such as the killing of a black man, James Byrd, Jr., by white supremacists who chained him to the back of a truck and dragged him along the ground until he died. Although the townspeople of Jasper, Texas, where the incident occurred, were shocked by the ghastly killing, the murder revealed the continuing presence of extreme racism in the United States.

Discrimination is "the differential treatment of individuals considered to belong to a particular social group" (Williams, 1947, p. 39). To treat a member of a subordinate group as inferior is to discriminate against that person. Members of the dominant group tend to use one standard of behavior among themselves and a different standard for any member of a subordinate group.

Discrimination is overt behavior, although it may sometimes be difficult to observe—as in tacit agreements among real estate agents to steer members of minority groups to particular blocks or neighborhoods. To justify the behavior to themselves, people tend to rationalize it on the ground that those whom they discriminate against are less worthy of respect or fair treatment than people like themselves (a perspective to which we return later in the chapter). Moreover, people tend to be *ethnocentric*—to see their own behavioral patterns and belief structures as desirable and natural and those of others as less so. These two tendencies usually result in **prejudice**—an emotional, rigid attitude—against members of the subordinate group (Simpson & Yinger, 1985).

But while prejudices are attitudes, not all attitudes are prejudices. Both share the element of *pre*judgment—the tendency to decide in advance how to think about a situation or event. Unlike other attitudes, however, prejudice involves an emotional investment that strongly resists change. Prejudiced people tend to be so committed to their prejudgments about a particular category of people that even in the face of rational evidence that the prejudgment is wrong, they will maintain their prejudice, even defend it strongly, and denounce the evidence.

TABLE 7–1	A Typology of Prejudice and Discrimination

	Discrimination (the Behavior)	
Prejudice (the Attitude)	Yes	No
Yes	Outright bigotry	Latent bigotry
No	Institutional discrimination	Integration (both psychological and institutional)

Source: Adapted with the permission of The Free Press, a Division of Simon & Schuster Adult Publishing Group, from *Social Theory and Social Structure* by Robert K. Merton. Copyright © 1949, 1957 by The Free Press. Copyright © renewed 1977, 1985 by Robert K. Merton. All rights reserved.

It is important to note that prejudice need not always involve antipathy. One can be prejudiced in favor of a person or group, with a similar degree of disregard for objective evidence. Prejudice is based on attitude; it is a tendency to think about people in a categorical, predetermined way. Discrimination, on the other hand, involves behavior. It is overt unequal treatment of people on the basis of their membership in a particular group. Prejudice and discrimination are closely related, and both are often present in a given situation.

Robert Merton (1949) outlined four possible relationships between prejudice and discrimination: unprejudiced and nondiscriminatory (integration), unprejudiced and discriminatory (institutional discrimination), prejudiced and nondiscriminatory (latent bigotry), and prejudiced and discriminatory (outright bigotry). (See Table 7–1.) Although it is possible to be both completely free of prejudice and completely nondiscriminatory—or, on the other hand, to be a complete bigot—most people fall somewhere between these two extremes. It is possible to be prejudiced against a particular group but not to discriminate against it; it is also possible to discriminate against a particular group but not to be prejudiced against it.

For example, the builders of a new, expensive cooperative apartment house may not be personally prejudiced against Jews, but they may refuse to sell apartments to Jewish families—that is, they may discriminate against Jews—out of fear that the presence of Jewish families would make it more difficult to sell the remaining apartments. This is a clear case of institutional discrimination (the lower-left cell in Table 7–1). Or the reverse may occur: In a corporation that holds a government contract, and hence is subject to federal equal employment opportunity regulations, the personnel director may be very prejudiced personally against both blacks and women but may hire a black woman as a management trainee—that is, not discriminate against her—to comply with the law. This is an example of latent bigotry (the upper-right cell).

Suppose the builders were confronted with a different situation: a black family attempting to buy one of their apartments. They might very well discriminate out of both personal prejudice and concern for profits—a case of outright bigotry (the upper-left cell). On the other hand, there can be situations in which legal controls prevent latent bigotry from affecting such behaviors as the sale of a house to a black family but cannot prevent social isolation of the family after the sale. These examples illustrate the difficulty of keeping personal prejudices from leading, sooner or later, to some form of discrimination, particularly if a significant number of people share the same prejudice (Ore, 2006).

How do racial discrimination and prejudice continue to produce inequalities in the United States? Include issues of income, wealth, and educational attainment in your answer.

ORIGINS OF PREJUDICE AND DISCRIMINATION

We have said that prejudice and discrimination are weapons used by a dominant group to maintain its dominance. It would be a mistake, however, to see them as always, or even usually, consciously used weapons. Unless the subordinate group mounts a serious challenge to the dominant group, prejudice and discrimination are likely to seem part of the natural order of things. Their origins are numerous and complex, and to explain them it is necessary to consider both the felt needs of individuals and the structural organization of society. Do patterns of prejudice and discrimination result from the aggregation of individual attitudes and behaviors, or are these attributes of individuals shaped by the society of which they are members? In fact, neither argument excludes the other; both are possible. To blame prejudice and discrimination wholly on warped personalities or wholly on oppressive social structures is to oversimplify (Plous, 2003).

Prejudice and Bigotry in the Individual

Frustration-Aggression. At one time or another most human beings feel frustrated. They want something, but because of events or other people they cannot get it. This can lead to anger and to aggression, which may be expressed in any of several ways. The most obvious way is to strike at the source of the frustration, but often this is impossible; frustrated individuals do not know the source, or are subjectively unable to recognize it, or are in a position in which they cannot risk such an action. Whatever the reason, the results are the same: They are unable to vent their anger on the real source of their frustration.

Instead, the aggression is often directed at a safer and more convenient target, usually one that somewhat resembles the real source of the frustration. In other words, the aggression is displaced onto a **scapegoat.** When this displacement is not limited to a particular person but is extended to include all similar people, it may produce a more or less permanent prejudice.

For example, suppose a middle-aged man who has been working for twenty years at the same job is told by his young supervisor that his job will soon be eliminated as a result of automation. The man is understandably angry and frightened. But if he were to vent his aggression on the supervisor, he would almost certainly be fired. That evening, as he is telling his woes to friends at the local bar, a young man comes in for a beer. The middle-aged man accuses the youth, and "all you lazy kids," of being a good-for-nothing and ruining the country, and only the intervention of the bartender prevents him from assaulting the young man.

It is fairly clear that this man has displaced his aggression toward his young supervisor onto all young people. Rather than dealing with the supervisor and the whole range of factors that led to the elimination of his job, he blames the problems of the country on young people; that is, he uses them as a scapegoat.

Projection. Another source of prejudice and discrimination is **projection.** Many people have personal traits that they consider undesirable. They wish to rid themselves of those traits, but they cannot always do it directly—either because they find the effort too difficult or because they are unable to admit to themselves that they possess those traits. They may relieve their tension by attributing the unwanted traits to others, often members of another group. This makes it possible for them to reject and condemn the traits without rejecting and condemning themselves. Since the emotional pressures underlying projection can be very intense, it is difficult to counter them with rational arguments.

An often-cited example of projection is white attitudes toward black sexuality. Historically, many whites saw blacks as extremely promiscuous and uninhibited in their sexual relations, and there was much concern about protecting white women from sexual attacks by black men. Actually, white men enjoyed virtually unlimited sexual access to black women, particularly slaves. White society, however, regarded overt sexuality as unacceptable, and it is likely that white men felt some guilt about their sexual desires and adventures. To alleviate their guilt, they projected their own lust and sexuality onto black men—a much easier course than admitting the discrepancy between their own values and behavior.

Professor John Satter and other sit-ins at a lunch counter in Jackson, Mississippi, were sprayed with mustard, ketchup, and sugar by a crowd of white teenagers. Civil disobedience and peaceful protests such as sit-ins made an enormous contribution to changing patterns of segregation in the United States in the 1950s and 1960s.

Prejudice and Bigotry in Social Structures

The emotional needs of insecure individuals do not explain why certain groups become objects of prejudice and discrimination. To understand this, we need to look at some larger social processes.

As noted earlier, in many societies the demand for more than the available supply of certain goods gives rise to a competitive struggle, which usually results in the dominance of one group and the subordination of others. Even if the initial competition is for economic goods, the contest is ultimately a struggle for power and, hence, a political process. Once established, political dominance is likely to be reinforced by economic exploitation. Slavery and serfdom are the most obvious forms of exploitation, but "free" workers may also be exploited. Migrant farmworkers, illegal aliens, and unorganized clerical and service workers are examples of the latter.

Economic exploitation is one form of discrimination practiced by the dominant group against a subordinate group. Historically, the subordinate group has consisted of unskilled workers. In the case of African Americans, for example, unskilled jobs were plentiful and available (at low wages) before the 1940s. With the development of protective labor legislation (e.g., minimum wage, antidiscrimination, and workers' compensation laws), employers could no longer use the subordinate group as a source of cheap labor. African Americans were systematically denied jobs as white-dominated unions maintained control over skilled jobs and employers sought cheaper unskilled labor by transferring basic manufacturing operations abroad (Sears, Sidanius, & Bobo, 2000).

Discrimination can take many other forms. Some of these are practical: Members of the subordinate group may be legally prevented from owning property or voting, or may be terrorized into submission, as often happened to strikers early in the labor movement. Some forms of discrimination are symbolic, as when African Americans were refused service in restaurants before the civil rights movement. All are aimed, consciously or unconsciously, at keeping the subordinate people "in their place."

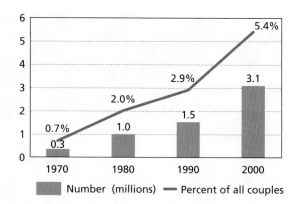

Figure 7-1 U.S. Interracial Couples, in Millions and as Percent of All Married Couples: 1970 to 2000

Source: Population Reference Bureau, 2005.

Cultural Factors: Norms and Stereotypes

Social Norms. A **social norm** is a commonly accepted standard that specifies the kind of behavior appropriate in a given situation. It is relevant to our discussion because, although it does not tell us why prejudice and discrimination begin, it helps explain how and why they are perpetuated.

Social norms are learned in a process that begins almost at birth. Small children soon learn what kind of behavior elicits the approval of their parents and what kind is likely to elicit a rebuke. The same process continues as they encounter other significant adults. Gradually children internalize the values and norms of their society. They receive approval from parents and other adults, and later from their peers, when they behave in socially acceptable ways; they experience disapproval when they do not.

A good example of a social norm that pertains to minority–majority relations is **homogamy,** the requirement that one must marry a person similar to oneself in religion, social class, and race or ethnicity. This has been a particularly strong norm in the United States for race. Before the civil rights movement of the 1960s, many states had laws that prohibited racial intermarriage. Racially mixed couples often encountered severe hostility, and many felt compelled to move to places like Greenwich Village in New York City or Hyde Park in Chicago, where there were similar couples and they could feel less "deviant."

Recent research shows, however, that the norm of homogamy is far weaker today than it was even 30 years ago. (See Figure 7–1.) Today interracial couples account for over 5 percent of all married couples, and the number of such marriages has doubled since the early 1980s (Population Reference Bureau, 2005). Although the Gallup Poll does not ask Americans about the racial makeup of their own marriages, poll responses show that Americans are significantly more accepting of interracial marriage than in the past. In 1960, only 20 percent of Americans approved of marriage between "whites and nonwhites." By 1983, 43 percent said they approved of marriage between blacks and whites, and in the most recent survey, 73 percent of Americans expressed approval of black–white marriages (Gallup, 2004).

Stereotyping. Still another source of prejudice and discrimination is **stereotyping,** or attributing a fixed and usually unfavorable or inaccurate conception to a category of people. Whereas social norms are concerned primarily with behavior and only indirectly with attitudes, stereotyping is basically a matter of attitude.

Usually a stereotype contains (or once contained) some truth, but it is exaggerated, distorted, or somehow taken out of context. Stereotyping has much to do with the way humans normally think. We tend to perceive and understand things in categories, and we apply the same mental process to people. We build up mental pictures of various groups, pictures made from overgeneralized impressions and selected bits of information, and we use them to define all members of a group regardless of their individual differences. Thus, we come to assume that all Native Americans are drunks, all African Americans are lazy, all residents of Appalachia or the Ozarks are hillbillies, all Puerto

The body language and clothing style of many inner-city young people, known as the "cool pose," often leads to labeling these teenagers as members of a "dangerous underclass."

Ricans are short, all Italians are gangsters, all Jews are shrewd, all English people are reserved, all Swedes are blond, all Frenchmen are amorous, all old people are senile, and so forth. None of these generalizations will stand up to even perfunctory analysis, yet many people habitually use them in thinking about minority groups. For example, social scientists in the United States believe young black males are victimized by stereotypes that portray them as violent and swaggering. In studies of the "cool pose" of inner-city black men, Robert Majors finds that this essentially defensive posture is often misinterpreted as a threatening pose, even by black middle-class individuals, and can lead to discrimination and prejudice (cited in Goleman, 1992).

It should be noted that stereotyping is not confined to any particular group, nor is it unique to the United States. Throughout the world it follows well-established patterns based on in-group/out-group distinctions and hostilities (Paul, 1998).

The three approaches just described—psychological, social-structural, and cultural—should not be viewed as mutually exclusive. As Milton Yinger (1987) has pointed out, human problems like racial disharmony are best viewed from all three of these perspectives, not just one.

INSTITUTIONAL DISCRIMINATION

If discrimination is a socially learned behavior of members of dominant groups, designed to support and justify their continued dominance, it is reasonable to expect that it will be built into the structure of society. To members of a society who are socialized to believe that members of certain groups "just are" to be treated as inferiors, it would be perfectly natural to formulate public policies and build public institutions that discriminate against them.

To some extent, this is exactly what has happened in the United States. If many blacks, Chicanos, Native Americans, Puerto Ricans, women, and members of other minority groups do not have equal protection of the law in their dealings with public institutions, it is not necessarily because of the conscious prejudices of public officials. Such **institutional discrimination** is an unconscious result of the structure and functioning of the public institutions and policies themselves.

For example, people living near reservations often believe Native Americans are lazy and incompetent, unable to exercise initiative or do anything to improve their often deplorable condition. What such people fail to realize is the degree to which this apparent incompetence is a result of the way Native Americans are governed. Their ability to handle their own affairs has been hampered by an administrative structure that denies them opportunities to learn new ways of doing things while simultaneously rendering old tribal ways ineffective. As Gary D. Sandefur and Marta Tienda (1988) have written,

> Native Americans collectively have been victims of discrimination and persecution throughout the history of the development of the United States. The contemporary expression of subjugation and discrimination has changed considerably from the blatant destruction experienced a century ago... Despite substantial increases in educational attainment over the past few decades, many Native Americans remain unprepared to compete in a highly technical and bureaucratized world of work. Consequently, there persist income and employment differentials relative to comparably schooled whites.... To the extent that job possibilities on reservations remain limited while large shares of Native Americans reside on them, the prospects for economic parity with whites probably will not be realized. (pp. 8–9)

It should be noted that Native Americans are by no means a homogeneous group. They have been lumped into a single category ("Indians"), but in fact they constitute a variety of peoples with vastly different cultures. Despite the poverty and hardship they have experienced on segregated reservations and the racism they often experience outside them, many of these groups have succeeded in preserving their traditional identities while adapting to the ways of the larger society.

Racial Profiling. Racial profiling refers to the practice by law enforcement personnel, security agents, or any person in a position of authority of disproportionately selecting people of color for investigations or other forms of discrimination, which often include invasions of privacy. To a large degree, racial profiling is a form of institutional discrimination because representatives of social institutions, such as the police or intelligence organizations, unfairly single out certain groups, distinguished

Many young Americans experience racial integration for the first time in their lives when they join the armed services.

On Further Analysis

"DRIVING WHILE BLACK"

African Americans assert that they are unfairly singled out for traffic stops and other investigations, which, if initiated because of their race, are violations of their civil rights. In the 1990s such racial profiling became a major racial controversy along the I-95 corridor between New Jersey and Maryland, as many African American drivers complained that they were being unfairly stopped and their cars searched for drugs. The authorities in New Jersey and Maryland, as well as in other states, pleaded that they were merely stopping drivers whose behavior (e.g., speeding) warranted such action. Some of these incidents led to altercations and the arrests of drivers, as well as a few incidents of violence on both sides. But the authorities denied that they were actually practicing racial profiling. Finally, a sound research project by John Lamberth of Temple University provided the data and

analysis that prevailed in the courts and forced the authorities in New Jersey and Maryland to change their practices. Here is what the research showed in the Maryland case, which is similar to that of New Jersey (see accompanying table).

Lamberth commented as follows:

These results are consistent with the work I did in the case of *State of New Jersey* v. *Pedro Soto et al.,* in which we conducted both a rolling survey and a stationary survey to determine motorist and violator populations on the southernmost segment of the New Jersey Turnpike (which ends 19 miles from the northern terminus of I-95 in Maryland). There, 98 percent of the drivers were violating traffic laws and 15 percent of the violators were black. While I would not expect I-95 in northern Maryland and the southern portion of the

New Jersey Turnpike to have identical numbers of minority motorists and violators, the similar percentages discerned in the surveys support and confirm their reliability.

When he looked at the statistics for stopping and searching, however, here is what he found: "Between January 1995 and September 1996, the Maryland State Police reported searching 823 motorists on I-95, north of Baltimore. Of these, 600, or 72.9 percent, were black. Six hundred and sixty-one, or 80.3 percent, were black, Hispanic, or other racial minorities." In other words, even though the data on driving violations show that almost everyone could be stopped in violation of the law—because almost everyone exceeds the speed limit—the police were stopping minority drivers at a rate that was 316 percent greater than for whites (Lamberth, 2000).

Drivers and Traffic Law Violators by Race from I-95 Corridor Survey

	White	Black	Other	Unknown	All Minority
Number of Drivers Observed	4,341	973	241	186	1,214
Number of Violators Observed	4,000	938	232	184	1,170
Percent of Drivers (by race)	75.6%	16.9%	4.3%	3.2%	21.1%
Percent of Violators (by race)	74.7%	17.5%	4.4%	3.4%	21.8%

by racial characteristics, in seeking to enforce rules or laws. From the authorities' viewpoint, this behavior may be justified by the belief that their suspicions correspond to realistic probabilities of wrongdoing by members of those groups. Thus, after 9/11, Arab Americans, Indian American Sikhs wearing turbans—in fact, anyone with swarthy skin and a beard—have been far more likely than lighter-skinned individuals to be searched at airports. Many Muslim immigrants and Americans, and Arab Americans of any religion, have accepted this behavior as the inevitable consequence of heightened security after the terrorist attacks. But others cannot help feeling that their status in the United States is diminished and threatened.

Racial profiling has also been a major subject of controversy among African Americans and other people of color who are disproportionately stopped while driving and searched for possible drug possession, according to the theory among law enforcement personnel that such people are more likely than others to be involved in drug use and drug dealing. Conservative social scientists, such as Heather MacDonald (2001), argue that racial profiling is justified because the facts show that African Americans and Latinos are indeed disproportionately likely to drive fast and also to be carrying drugs than whites. But as we see in the On Further Analysis box on page 233, the best research on this issue to date has convinced judges in many courts that indeed racial profiling violates the civil rights of innocent people and must be curtailed.

Since it would be difficult to discuss all categories of institutional discrimination against all minority groups, we focus on four major categories: education, housing, employment and income, and social justice. But the patterns we describe apply to other categories as well, such as health care and consumer issues.

Education

A question that generates a great deal of emotion in the United States is whether black, Puerto Rican, Chicano, and Native American children should attend the same schools as white children. This question underlies such issues as busing to achieve racial balance, high-quality education for all, and public tax support for private schools.

Americans take public school systems very seriously. Undoubtedly, one reason is that in this country education has generally been seen as the road to social and economic advancement. It is almost an article of faith that American children should get more education than their parents and achieve higher social and economic status. (This subject is discussed in detail in Chapter 11.)

Since the 1940 census, which was the first to ask about educational attainment, the average number of years of school completed by all Americans has increased steadily. (See Figure 7–2.) Despite these gains, members of minority groups still have less chance of finishing high school or attending college than do whites. In 2004 about 15 percent of whites age 25 and over had not completed high school; the comparable figures for blacks and Hispanics were 20 percent and 43 percent, respectively (*Statistical Abstract*, 2006). Thus, although Figure 7–2 indicates a significant gain in educational parity since World War II, large differences remain. The greatest difference is in the attainment of a college diploma plus graduate training. In 2004 among Americans age 25 and over, only about 17 percent of blacks and 11 percent of Hispanics had completed four years of college or more, compared to about 27 percent of whites (*Statistical Abstract*, 2006).

In an important recent study of how minority achievement in education and in the labor force is related to parents' wealth, Dalton Conley (1999) found that one's parents' own level of education and their net worth (not only income, but the total of all owned assets, or wealth) are the two best predictors of the quality of higher education their children will receive. Since African American students tend to come from far less

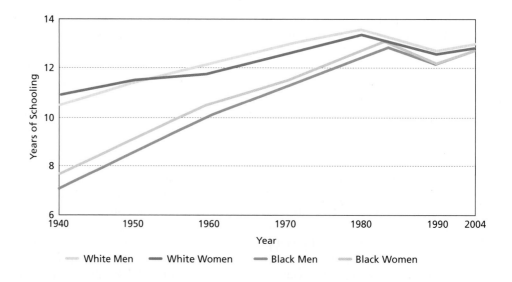

Figure 7–2 Average Years of Schooling Completed by Persons Age 25–29, by Race and Sex: 1940 to 2004

Source: Data from Farley, Bianchi, & Colasanto, 1979; and *Statistical Abstract*, various years.

| TABLE 7–2 | Mean Earnings, by Highest Degree Earned |

Characteristic	Total Persons	Not a High School Graduate	High School Graduate Only	Some College, No Degree	Level of Highest Degree				
					Associate's	Bachelor's	Master's	Professional	Doctorate
All persons	$36,308	$18,826	$27,280	$29,725	$34,177	$51,194	$60,445	$112,845	$89,734
White	37,376	19,264	28,145	30,570	34,876	52,459	60,787	115,523	92,125
Black	28,179	16,516	22,823	26,711	30,391	42,285	51,974	96,368	69,780
Hispanic	25,824	18,981	24,163	26,459	31,710	40,949	58,814	81,186	—*

*Base figure too small to meet statistical standards for reliability of a derived figure.

Source: *Statistical Abstract,* 2005.

wealthy homes than white students do, their ability to go to the prestigious universities and colleges that produce the most entrants into the professions and the world of finance and business is far more limited. This means that although as we have seen, blacks and other minorities are reaching parity in educational attainment with whites, and in some states African Americans are exceeding whites in their rates of high-school graduation, their inability to pay the costs of an elite higher education presents a major barrier to their full equality in a labor market that demands increasingly sophisticated skills and in which success often hinges on personal contacts established in college.

We have long assumed that higher education leads to higher income. There is no doubt that among people working at this time, the more highly educated usually receive substantially higher salaries than those with little education. Evidence also suggests that even better than a sheepskin is a white skin, for minority group members at all levels of education earn less than their nonminority counterparts. (See Table 7–2.) As educational requirements for the labor force increase, it becomes ever more urgent for members of minority groups to enter colleges and universities (Evangelauf, 1992). Despite recent gains, minority enrollment rates are lower than they would be under conditions of equality.

Unequal Access to High-Quality Schooling. Throughout the United States, school administrations are under pressure to raise standards and increase performance, especially in underachieving schools, which are often found in communities with high proportions of low-income black and Hispanic households. The causes of this situation and policies to address it are among the most hotly contested issues in American public life at this time. We deal in more detail with educational issues in Chapter 11. Relevant here is the issue of minority segregation and poor schools, along with the retreat from policies to achieve school desegregation (Patterson, 2001).

In its *Brown* v. *Board of Education* decision the Supreme Court mandated integration "with all deliberate speed" but was vague on actual remedies to be used. The decision effectively wiped out **de jure segregation**—segregation required by law—and by finding that "separate but equal" schooling was inherently unequal, it set in motion decades of sporadic efforts to achieve more racially balanced classrooms. To do so, states and municipalities had to address **de facto segregation,** segregation resulting from housing patterns, economic inequalities, gerrymandered school districts, and the departure of middle-class families from communities with increasing rates of minority households and poor or mediocre schools (Orfield, 2001).

Throughout much of the last thirty years, busing of students, primarily minority students, to schools outside their neighborhoods has been the primary remedy for desegregation. Today, however, busing is largely considered to have been a failure. At the same time, no alternative strategies are being implemented to achieve school desegregation. Demands for higher standards and higher achievement are not generally matched with increases in funding for schools in lower-income minority neighborhoods. Public schools in the United States are typically funded from local property taxes, so wealthier communities can afford to pay higher salaries to teachers and hire more experienced teachers than can financially strapped inner-city schools. States often attempt to correct this imbalance with supplemental funding, but the results are extremely mixed.

A study by the Harvard Project on School Desegregation found that resegregation of the races is increasing. This is true despite the growing diversity of minority enrollments as a result of recent immigration (discussed in Chapter 14). Resegregation is occurring most rapidly in the South, but the races are increasingly separate in schools in other regions as well. The study also found that over the past three decades the following changes have occurred (Cutler, Glaeser, & Vigdor, 1999; Orfield, 2001):

- Enrollment of Hispanic students has increased 218 percent, and nearly 75 percent of Latino schoolchildren attend predominantly minority schools.

- Enrollment of black students has risen 22 percent, and 69 percent of African American children attend schools where at least half the students are from minority groups.

- Enrollment of white students has declined by 16 percent, and the vast majority of white students attend schools that are 80 percent or more white. This finding holds even for white students who live in generally nonwhite areas (often because of white enrollment in private schools). At the same time, black and Hispanic students generally remain in black- and Hispanic-majority schools even when they live in the suburbs.

- Schools with mostly black and Hispanic students are eleven times more likely to be in areas with concentrated poverty than are schools with predominantly white students.

- Poverty compounds the problems of segregation and is linked to lower classroom performance and achievement. The research shows that schools with many poor children lack advanced courses and well-qualified teachers. Such schools are more likely than others to have children who drop out, suffer from untreated health problems, and do not attend college.

- The research reveals that black students are most likely to go to majority-black schools in the following states, in order of severity: Michigan, Illinois, New York, New Jersey, and Maryland. The top states for Hispanic student concentration are, in order, New York, Texas, New Jersey, California, and Illinois.

Housing

School desegregation is an extremely difficult issue to address when such a high proportion of minority and nonminority people live in segregated neighborhoods to begin with. Housing segregation—the separation of minority groups into different regions, cities, neighborhoods, blocks, and even buildings—has diminished somewhat in recent years as a result of immigration into formerly segregated neighborhoods, but as we will see in this section, it remains a serious obstacle to the achievement of racial and ethnic harmony (Lewis Mumford Center for Comparative and Regional Statistics, 2005; Meyer, 2000).

In an important series of studies of residential segregation and poverty in the United States, sociologists Douglas Massey and colleagues found that although some decrease in housing segregation has occurred in urban regions, the largest cities,

TABLE 7–3	Trends in Black-White Segregation in 30 Metropolitan Areas with Largest Black Populations, 1970–2000			

Metropolitan Area	1970	1980	1990	2000
Northern areas		(Percentages)		
Boston	81.2%	77.6%	68.2%	65.7%
Buffalo	87.0	79.4	81.8	76.7
Chicago	91.9	87.8	85.8	80.8
Cincinnati	76.8	72.3	75.8	74.8
Cleveland	90.8	87.5	85.1	77.3
Columbus	81.8	71.4	67.3	63.1
Detroit	88.4	86.7	87.6	84.7
Indianapolis	81.7	76.2	74.3	70.7
Kansas City	87.4	78.9	72.6	69.1
Los Angeles–Long Beach	91.0	81.1	73.1	67.5
Milwaukee	90.5	83.9	82.8	82.2
New York	81.0	82.0	82.2	81.8
Newark	81.4	81.6	82.5	80.4
Philadelphia	79.5	78.8	77.2	72.3
Pittsburg	75.0	72.7	71.0	67.3
St. Louis	84.7	81.3	77.0	74.3
Average	84.5	80.1	77.8	76.6
Southern areas				
Atlanta	82.1%	78.5%	67.8%	65.6%
Baltimore	81.9	74.7	71.4	67.9
Birmingham	37.8	40.8	71.7	72.9
Dallas–Ft. Worth	86.9	77.1	63.1	59.4
Houston	78.1	69.5	66.8	67.5
Memphis	75.9	71.6	69.3	68.7
Miami	85.1	77.8	71.8	73.6
New Orleans	73.1	68.3	68.8	69.3
Norfolk–Virginia Beach	75.7	63.1	50.3	46.2
Tampa–St. Petersburg	79.9	72.6	69.7	64.5
Washington, D.C.	81.1	70.1	66.1	63.1
Average	75.3	68.3	66.5	65.3

Source: Reprinted by permission of the publisher from *American Apartheid: Segregation and the Making of the Underclass* by Douglas S. Massey and Nancy A. Denton, p. 222, Cambridge, MA: Harvard University Press. Copyright © 1993 by the President and Fellows of Harvard College; Logan, 2004.

including Chicago, Cleveland, Detroit, New York, and St. Louis, have failed to significantly reduce housing segregation (Fischer & Massey, 2004). The figures in Table 7–3 are percentages based on a calculation of how many of each city's African American residents would have to move out of their segregated neighborhoods to achieve an even distribution of their numbers throughout the city's neighborhoods. Poverty, unemployment, homicide, AIDS, and many other problems of urban centers are heightened by the segregation of racially distinct and poor households in blighted urban communities. This study confirms what many others have shown: Failure to enforce federal laws against housing discrimination continues to produce rates of black segregation that are far higher than those experienced by any other group in U.S. history.

A practice that contributes to high rates of segregation is **racial steering,** in which real estate brokers refuse to show houses outside of specific areas to minority buyers. Before the landmark judicial decisions of the 1950s, racial steering was enforced through *restrictive covenants*—agreements among homeowners not to sell their property to people designated as undesirable. Although restrictive covenants are now illegal, racial and ethnic steering still occurs unofficially in many all-white neighborhoods. Because it operates below the surface, with no written agreements, racial steering is difficult to detect or prevent (Farley, 1996; Herbert, 1999).

Massey and others who study racial and ethnic segregation assert that more *audit research* is needed to show lawmakers that racial steering and other forms of discrimination exist and that laws against them must be enforced far more rigorously. In audit research, a black or minority couple is sent to real estate agents and shown (or not shown) certain types of housing. Then a white couple is sent to the same agents and the results are compared; this process is repeated many times with different agents to determine whether a systematic pattern of discrimination exists (Massey & Denton, 1993).

The housing problems of another minority group, Native Americans, provide further examples of how segregation and faulty application of social policies worsen an already difficult situation. Until the early 1960s Native Americans were excluded from plans for public housing. They lived on reservations, where some had adequate housing, especially on the more well-to-do reservations, but many more lived in tar-paper shacks, drafty log houses, ragged tents, abandoned automobile bodies, and hillside caves. When public housing did become available on the reservations, failure to build adequate housing with federal funds, often due to corruption, resulted in poor and extremely depressing housing conditions in the new buildings (Nagel, 1996).

The problem of inadequate housing on Indian reservations is related to the federal government's long-standing policy of taking Native American children away from their homes to be educated in boarding schools. This had the effect of weakening the family. Depressed by the destruction of their families and convinced of their powerlessness, some Native American tribes have difficulty developing the patterns of leadership needed to argue their case effectively with the government or to develop their own communities (Sandefur, 1996; Sandefur & Tienda, 1988).

Employment and Income

The idea of work as a way to improve one's social status is deeply ingrained in American culture. Although it is no longer as pervasive as it once was, the work ethic still holds that if you really want a job, you can find one, and that if you work hard, you will make money. The corollary to this is the notion that if you are wealthy, you deserve your wealth because you worked for it, and if you are poor, it is because you are lazy. Thus, one hears the argument that if only blacks, Puerto Ricans, and Native Americans would make an effort to find jobs and stick to them, they could improve their lot in life. This view ignores the fact that discrimination is no less prevalent in employment than it is in education and housing.

In some ways discrimination in employment is a direct result of discrimination in education. We have already noted the relationship between income and education. Since today the chances of finding even an entry-level job without a high-school diploma are slim, lack of education means that many minority group members will spend their lives underemployed or unemployed (Wilson, 1987). This, in turn, means a low income, resulting in inferior housing, with the likelihood of a poor education for the next generation, and so on—a cycle of discrimination that is built into the system.

Is there any escape from this situation? What about jobs that do not require much formal education, jobs that one learns mostly through apprenticeship and are represented by many labor unions?

Historically, labor unions have been in the forefront of battles for civil rights, but union locals often resisted minority demands for membership. William Gould (1968) pointed out a basic conflict between the rhetoric of union leadership and established union policies and practices. Unions, like other institutions, are resistant to internal changes or economic sacrifices to accommodate the demands of minority workers. There are only so many jobs to go around, and those who have them want to keep them. This has meant that union-sponsored job training programs are generally closed to minority workers. Progress in opening apprenticeship and training programs has been slow. Although in 1983 blacks accounted for 26 percent of union members, by 2000 this figure had fallen below 24 percent. This negative trend has been reversed in recent years with renewed effort by organized labor to bring in new members, increasing numbers of whom are members of racial minority groups.

The employment problem among minority groups is particularly devastating for young black and Hispanic men. In the absence of legitimate means of getting ahead, many turn to various forms of illicit activity. In addition, without hope for a steady income, they often find it economically impossible to form stable families. And this situation shows few signs of improving; the employment gap between young white men and black and Hispanic youths increased in the 1990s despite the narrowing of the educational gap.

Research has shown that focusing on income differences can be deceptive. Although it is true that in the past thirty years there has been a trend toward income parity among African Americans, some Latino populations, and whites, the same is not true for assets, such as first and second homes and other costly material possessions or capital-generating investments. In their influential research on asset inequality, Melvin Oliver and Thomas Shapiro (1995) found that about a third of Americans own almost no assets other than a car. More recent research by the Pew Foundation shows that the asset gap between whites and people of color is widening. Although there is a growing black middle class whose members do own property and have bank accounts and pension funds, it is far outnumbered by those who own almost nothing and have no assets to fall back on during hard times. Asset inequality has a profound impact on intergenerational inequality. People with property and investments can will their estates to their children so that they have some material advantages as they establish homes of their own. This is not possible for those with no assets, whatever their ethnic or racial background.

Table 7–4 highlights the profound gap between the wealth (homes, autos, and savings) of blacks and Hispanics and that of white households in the United States. In 2002, the median net worth of white households was over $88,000, but for blacks it was just under $6,000 and for Hispanics it was about $8,000, or just under 9 percent of the net worth of white families (Kochhar, 2004). In their earlier research on the wealth gap, Paul Oliver and Thomas Shapiro found that well over 50 percent of Hispanic and black families were living from paycheck to paycheck, with no other financial assets at all (Oliver & Shapiro, 1995). Sudden loss of a job or a rental apartment, as occurred to thousands of people in the Gulf coast region after Hurricane Katrina, clearly reveals the human consequences of this condition.

Research on impoverished ghetto neighborhoods by William J. Wilson (1996a) emphasizes that the economic and social distance between the small middle class and the poor is widening. Blue-collar manufacturing work once helped create a relatively secure black and Latino middle class. As manufacturing has disappeared from many metropolitan areas, finding a decent job is often a matter of good basic education and interpersonal skills. Inadequate schools and the growing isolation of poor African Americans in segregated inner-city neighborhoods make it difficult for young people to learn the vocabulary and mannerisms of the dominant white middle class. In consequence, many

TABLE 7-4	Median Net Worth of Households, by Race and Ethnicity: 1996–2002 (2003 dollars)

	Median Net Worth ($)						Percent Change
	1996	1997	1998	1999	2001	2002	1996 to 2002
Hispanic	6,961	7,801	7,167	10,495	6,213	7,932	14.0
Non-Hispanic Black	7,135	7,013	7,873	8,774	5,905	5,988	−16.1
Non-Hispanic White	75,482	77,368	79,905	86,370	86,286	88,651	17.4
All Households	53,160	54,547	54,663	59,762	58,957	59,706	12.3

Net Worth Relative to Net Worth of Non-Hispanic Whites (%)						
	1996	1997	1998	1999	2001	2002
Hispanic	9.2	10.1	9.0	12.2	7.2	8.9
Non-Hispanic Black	9.5	9.1	9.9	10.2	6.8	6.8

Source: The Wealth of Hispanic Households: 1996 to 2002, R. Kochhar, Pew Hispanic Center, 2004; http://pewhispanic.org/files/reports/34.pdf

employers have had negative experiences with African Americans, especially young men, and tend to be wary of employing them.

Wilson (1996b) also notes that some employers are simply racist and discriminate because of their own prejudices. But employers often come to feel that poor African American males from ghetto neighborhoods lack a work ethic or basic educational skills. Employers' perceptions vary from one type of work to another, but often they share the notion that black males' lives are complicated by other social problems and that they do not understand what employers require in a new worker. Wilson and others who have studied this problem call for social policies that provide more opportunities for young men and women from segregated communities to find jobs at which they can succeed and opportunities to get more training for work (Reich, 1992; Wilson, 1996a). (We return to these subjects in the Social Policy section of the chapter.)

Why were the effects of Hurricane Katrina so much more severe among minority women and children than among whites?

Justice

Philosopher and social theorist Cornel West (1994) recounts an all-too-familiar tale of the daily injustices faced by African Americans and other nonwhites. While driving to a college lecture, he remembers, "I was stopped on fake charges of trafficking cocaine. When I told the police officer I was a professor of religion, he replied, 'Yeh, and I'm the Flying Nun. Let's go, nigger!'" (p. xv). Such degrading experiences with the police and other street-level authorities enrage members of minority groups, who know that those who are poor and powerless may receive far worse treatment in the justice system.

The American system of justice is based on two premises that are relevant to this issue: (1) Justice is blind—racial, ethnic, economic, or social considerations are irrelevant in the eyes of the law—and (2) any accused person is considered innocent until proven guilty in a court of law. But do these assumptions apply equally to everyone?

As noted in Chapter 5, minority groups are overrepresented in official arrest records, and it seems probable that in general they are more likely to be arrested and charged with a crime, whether or not they are guilty. The higher arrest rates among minorities are due partly to the higher arrest rates among the poor in general (who, as noted earlier, include a disproportionate number of minority group members), but there is considerable evidence that discrimination plays a role in who is arrested. In 2005 the federal Bureau of Justice Statistics released a report that showed the effects of racial profiling by police agencies in the United States. (Racial profiling is discussed in the On Further Analysis box on page 233.) This practice often leads to highly discriminatory actions. Thus, the federal report found that blacks and Hispanics were roughly three times more likely than whites to "experience police threat or use of force" during interactions with the police. In addition, they were almost three times more likely to be arrested and three times more likely to have their person or their vehicle searched (ACLU, 2005).

Following arrest, the obstacle of the bail system must be overcome. It is here that the American criminal-justice system may be most discriminatory. To begin with, bail involves money: Those who have it can usually arrange to be released after arrest and await their trial in freedom, subject only to the limitations of the bail agreement. Those who do not have money are punished, in effect, because of the long delay between arrest and trial in many jurisdictions (particularly in big cities). They are compelled to wait in jail—often for months, sometimes for more than a year—until their case comes up. This borders on punishment before conviction and certainly runs counter to the precept of presumed innocence (Feagin, 1996). Even those who can pay bail can rarely afford costly legal counsel, and those who are detained have little opportunity to prepare a defense. This inequality in the administration of justice extends to the sentencing process. Although blacks account for only about 12.5 percent of the population, they make up about 44 percent of the prison population (*Statistical Abstract*, 2005); whites are much more likely to be released on their own recognizance or given suspended sentences.

Imprisonment and Employment Discrimination. All black males who seek employment are subject to racial discrimination. Black men who have served prison terms for nonviolent crimes face far greater discrimination in the job market than do white ex-offenders. These difficult truths are revealed in an "audit survey" conducted by sociologist Devah Pager (2003). She sent prospective applicants to answer employment ads. Figure 7–3 shows that even among the applicants without a criminal record, the effect of race was very large: Thirty-four percent of the white applicants were called back for an interview, while only 14 percent of the black applicants—whose

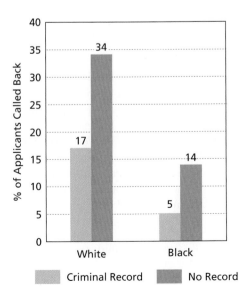

Figure 7–3 Effect of a Criminal Record in the Milwaukee Audit Sample

Source: Pager, 2003.

resumes listed the same qualifications as those of the whites—were called back. Fourteen percent of whites with criminal records were called back, compared to only 5 percent of similar black applicants. Note that the research shows that a white applicant with a prison record was more likely to be called for a job interview than a black applicant without a prison record. Since one in five black males in the United States has a prison record of some kind, often the result of inadequate legal representation, the stigma that follows them into the job market is an extremely important problem that can lead to negative consequences such as recidivism.

Racial inequalities in Capital Punishment. In capital crimes, the probability that minority offenders would be more likely to receive the death penalty—because of the effects of prejudice and inability to afford good legal counsel—prevented the Supreme Court from reinstituting capital punishment for many decades. In 1977, however, the Court reversed its position and the death penalty was reinstated. Since then, the issue of racial bias in the application of the death penalty has also reappeared in many states.

David C. Baldus, the nation's leading expert on the subject and the author of numerous studies that have influenced the courts, notes, "Some people are being sentenced to death based on race, and I find that morally and legally objectionable" (quoted in Eckholm, 1995, p. B1). In fact, studies by Baldus and others show that the race of the defendant is not significant in explaining whether the death penalty is applied in murder trials. What is highly significant is the race of the victim. About half of the people murdered in the United States each year are black, but since 1977, 85 percent of those sentenced to death have killed a white person.

In the important case of *McCleskey* v. *Kemp* (1987), it was argued that the death sentence of a black defendant convicted of killing a white police officer should be revoked because there was evidence of systematic discrimination in similar cases. In a 5–4 decision, the Supreme Court denied the appeal. More recently, in 1994 Congress rejected a requirement that federal sentencing guidelines for the death penalty must be based on quantitative studies of racial patterns in sentencing in capital cases and that these findings must be given important courtroom standing. But for Baldus and others who study patterns of racial preference in sentencing, the issue is not to increase the number of executions for murderers of black people but to end racial biases of all kinds in the administration of justice (Eckholm, 1995).

Political Discrimination

Members of minority groups are systematically courted by politicians for their votes, but at the same time patterns of political discrimination can be found throughout the United States. Frequently, when politicians in power fear that members of a particular minority group will vote as a more unified bloc, they try to make it more difficult for them to register and vote. Although we may take it for granted that all citizens have the right to vote and to express their opinions freely, it was not until Congress passed the Voting Rights Act of 1965 that many extremely discriminatory practices, such as poll taxes and tests prior to registration, were banned throughout the United States. The Voting Rights Act began to bring the United States into conformity with the Universal Declaration of Human Rights, which it had signed in 1946. This declaration is extremely important because it clearly establishes standards and practices that preserve individual and group rights, including the rights to participate in the political process. According to the Universal Declaration's section on the Right to Participate in Government,

1. Every citizen shall enjoy the following rights and opportunities:
   a. to take part in the conduct of public affairs, directly or through freely chosen representatives;

b. to vote and to be elected in genuine periodic elections, which shall be by universal and equal suffrage and by secret ballot that guarantees the free expression of the will of the voters; and

c. to have access, under general conditions of equality, to the public service of his country.

2. The law may regulate the exercise of the rights and opportunities referred to in the preceding paragraph only on the basis of age, nationality, residence, language, education, civil and mental capacity, or sentencing by a competent court in criminal proceedings.

On Native American reservations, in segregated ethnic communities, and in racial ghettos, rates of political participation tend to be significantly lower than in nonminority communities. These differences are often the result of historical patterns of domination and discrimination that prevented members of particular groups in specific places from voting. To overcome these patterns, special efforts to register and mobilize these formerly disenfranchised voters are required. But registration drives frequently encounter opposing tactics by incumbents who wish to retain their power and fear the influence of new voters. Two current forms of political discrimination are felony disenfranchisement and anti-voter-fraud campaigns.

Felony disenfranchisement. In many states, people convicted of a felony may lose the right to vote (also known as the *franchise*), often permanently. This is known as *felony disenfranchisement*. With the world's highest rates of imprisonment, the United States is also the world's leader in felony disenfranchisement, a dubious distinction that has an enormous impact on the political fate of minority groups. Consider the following statistics:

- An estimated 3.9 million Americans, or one in fifty adults, have currently or permanently lost the ability to vote because of a felony conviction.

- 1.4 million persons disenfranchised for a felony conviction are ex-offenders who have completed their criminal sentence. Another 1.4 million of the disenfranchised are on probation or parole.

- 1.4 million African American men, or 13 percent of the black adult male population, are disenfranchised, reflecting a rate of disenfranchisement that is seven times the national average. More than one-third (36 percent) of the total disenfranchised population are black men.

- Ten states disenfranchise more than one in five adult black men; in seven of these states, one in four black men is permanently disenfranchised.

- Given current rates of incarceration, three in ten of the next generation of black men will be disenfranchised at some point in their lives. In states with the most restrictive voting laws, 40 percent of African American men are likely to be permanently disenfranchised (Manza & Uggen, 2006).

In the 2000 presidential election, had former felons who had completed their sentences been allowed to vote, experts agree that since a significant proportion are African Americans and others who tend to vote Democratic, there is no question but that Grorge W. Bush would have lost Florida's Electoral College vote and, hence, the election. In Florida, along with a few other southern states, lifetime felony disenfranchisement dates back to the era of the Civil War and was used to systematically bar nonwhites from voting. In the aftermath of close elections in Florida and elsewhere since 2000, many states, including Florida, are revising these discriminatory laws, as we will see in the Social Policy section of the chapter (Manza & Uggen, 2006).

Anti-Voter Fraud Campaigns. Civil rights groups note that recent state and federal efforts to investigate voter fraud and institute new systems of voter identification can be seen as attempts to block higher minority voter turnouts. Some members of the Bush administration claim that voter fraud is widespread, especially in minority-dominated voting districts, which tend to be in large cities where voters most often vote Democratic. In 2007 the Justice Department was rocked by scandal when it was revealed that the administration appeared to have fired several federal prosecutors for political reasons; especially likely to be fired were prosecutors who were reluctant to aggressively pursue groups that were registering minority voters, even when there were no findings to support a claim of actual or potential voter fraud. Attorney General Albert Gonzales appears to have been involved in the firings, but at this writing the controversy is unresolved. One consequence, however, is that anti-voter fraud campaigns that target minority voters are far less likely to be a problem in the 2008 elections because of the attention that has been directed at them.

SOME CONSEQUENCES OF PREJUDICE AND DISCRIMINATION

The harmful effects of prejudice and discrimination are not limited to minority groups. As the Supreme Court noted in its decision in *Brown* v. *Board of Education of Topeka,* the lives of members of the dominant group are also stunted by the artificial barriers and warped perceptions that such social divisions create. Here, however, we will consider the effects on the subordinate group, since they are usually more serious.

What happens to people who must live with institutionalized discrimination and the prejudice that accompanies it? There are, of course, effects on the individual personalities of minority group members. And both individuals and groups develop protective reactions against prejudice and discrimination.

First, consider the effects of discrimination on individual personalities. In his groundbreaking work *Children of Crisis,* Robert Coles (1968) documented some of the effects on the first black children to attend desegregated schools in the South. These children were subjected to blatant discrimination and bitter prejudice, including mob action against them and their parents. Coles observed the children for several months, focusing on how they depicted themselves and their world in drawings. His account of the drawings of one black girl, Ruby, is fascinating. For months Ruby would never use brown or black except to indicate the ground. However, she distinguished between white and black people:

> She drew white people larger and more lifelike. Negroes were smaller, their bodies less intact. A white girl we both knew to be her own size appeared several times taller. While Ruby's own face lacked an eye in one drawing, an ear in another, the white girl never lacked any features. Moreover, Ruby drew the white girl's hands and legs carefully, always making sure that they had the proper number of fingers and toes. Not so with her own limbs, or those of any other Negro children she chose (or was asked) to picture. A thumb or forefinger might be missing, or a whole set of toes. The arms were shorter, even absent or truncated. (p. 47)

At the same time, Jimmy, a white classmate, always depicted blacks as somehow related to animals or extremely dirty and dangerous. After about two years of contact with Ruby and other black children in his school in New Orleans, Jimmy grew less fearful of blacks, and the change was reflected in his drawings. Coles concluded that children were conditioned to fear and distrust members of the other race, but that with continuing friendly contact, these prejudices were broken down and the children eventually helped change their parents' attitudes as well. To this day Ruby Bridges, now a grown woman with children of her own, and Dr. Coles are friends who share a strong bond, having struggled together for social justice. Coles recently wrote a children's book about Ruby's experiences (Judson, 1995).

The most common reaction against inequality during the past few decades has been public protest. Following the success of the Montgomery bus boycott of 1955 and 1956 (when blacks stopped riding buses until discriminatory seating rules were eliminated), a broad social movement for desegregation emerged. Initially led by Martin Luther King, Jr., the movement was directed against laws that enforced or created a statutory inequality—that is, an obstruction maintained for the purpose of denying minority groups the rights and privileges enjoyed by other Americans. In the 1960s, however, as progress slowed and resistance increased, minority protests sometimes took more violent forms. Anger, frustration, and rage provoked urban riots across the country. Often the catalyst was the arrest of a black by white police officers, who served as visible symbols of the attitudes of the white majority. At no time, however, did a majority of blacks approve of the violent protests (National Advisory Commission on Civil Disorders, 1968).

By the mid-1970s the frequency of riots had diminished considerably. The recession during this period caused both whites and blacks to suffer from high unemployment rates and inflation, and expectations of progress were reduced. Moreover, the end of the Vietnam War and the draft caused a general decline in protest movements. There may also have been a sense that riots had reached the limits of their effectiveness and that more deliberate, better organized efforts were necessary. In addition, it is possible, as Frances Piven and Richard Cloward (1997) have theorized, that welfare rolls were increased in response to the riots and that this had the effect of mollifying blacks.

A different kind of racism is often experienced by young upper-class blacks. This type of prejudice is considerably more subtle and more difficult to confront than open bigotry. It may take the form of excessive highway stops by police or patronizing comments (e.g., "Blacks are not good swimmers because their bodies are less buoyant than those of whites") or simple lack of awareness (e.g., "I never think of you as black"). Blacks are still prevented from renting apartments or buying homes in certain neighborhoods, and racist incidents in schools and restaurants are common. In the words of one young black woman, "The old racism seems . . . ever ready to resurface with a vengeance" (Russell, 1987, p. 2).

Research by sociologist Joe R. Feagin (1991; Feagin & McKinney, 2003) in major metropolitan areas also documents the persistence of discrimination and prejudice against middle-class blacks in public places. Feagin's black respondents mentioned case after case of avoidance by whites; of rejection or extremely poor service in public establishments; of verbal epithets, public harassment, and other threats. Feagin also found, however, that black citizens are increasingly asserting their rights even in embarrassing social situations and demanding redress and apologies from business owners.

The consequences of prejudice can also be seen in the events following the collapse of communism, the easing of the cold war, and the rise of anti-Western terrorism. In many areas these stunning changes also rekindled nationalist passions. The conflicts among different nationality groups in the former Soviet Union, Bosnia, and the Middle East remind us again of the fierce power of ethnic and racial sentiments and their ability to violently disrupt political and economic institutions. In the United States, growing tensions among different groups have also caused outbreaks of violence. Even before the series of arson fires in black churches in 1996, the FBI had reported that crimes motivated by racism and bias against minority groups (including homosexuals and religious groups) were becoming more frequent. And sociologist Jack McDevitt found in analyzing 452 cases of crimes motivated by prejudice that the majority (57 percent) involved "turf defense"; that is, they occurred when people walking, driving, or working in a neighborhood were attacked for being different from those living there (cited in Goleman, 1990; see also Meyer, 2000).

What are the current trends in school desegregation in the United States? Why is this an important issue in addressing racial prejudice and inequalities?

Social Policy

A half-century after the civil rights movement of the 1950s and 1960s, it is fair to say that race remains the single most important issue in American politics. Although it is not often discussed in these terms, the outcomes of elections for national offices like senator and president often are determined in states where race remains a major political issue. After the American Civil War, the North tended to vote Republican, the party of Lincoln and emancipation, as did most African Americans. The South was a bastion of Democratic voting and was referred to as the "solid South." In the 1930s, a majority of voters in the northern states shifted to the Democratic party, but these voters tended to be far more liberal than southern Democrats, who were known as "Dixiecrats."

The passage of the Civil Rights Act of 1964 changed this pattern dramatically. White voters in the South, especially those with more conservative opinions who favored traditional forms of racial segregation, began to support Republican candidates who were opposed to the policies of the more liberal Democrats. Many southern political leaders actually switched their party affiliation from Democrat to Republican. In much of the South and Southwest, this is the current racially divided political reality, although there are many exceptions in particular voting districts.

In response to the demands of blacks and other minority groups for a more equal share in the benefits of the American way of life, various programs have been instituted to alleviate the effects of prejudice and discrimination. For the most part, these programs are favored by more liberal voters and opposed by more conservative ones, which helps explain why such initiatives tend to wax and wane in different presidential administrations. In this section we examine some of the approaches and goals of these programs and evaluate their effectiveness.

Job Training

A persistent political demand, especially by conservatives, is the need to reduce taxes and shrink the size and responsibilities of government. These demands make it increasingly difficult for governments to take the initiative in creating employment and training programs. At the same time, major U.S. corporations have been "downsizing," or eliminating as many jobs as possible, to increase their profitability. This tends to create situations in which more qualified workers compete with less well-trained or experienced ones for a limited number of jobs. Members of minority groups, especially blacks and Puerto Ricans, Mexicans in some states, and Native Americans—all groups that have experienced discrimination in the past—suffer the most severe consequences of these changes.

Recent setbacks cannot erase the programs' positive contributions. Besides those who received job training and secured higher-paying jobs, many people improved their skills in other ways. Some entered counseling programs and went to school, and hence were able to keep their jobs; others qualified for high-school equivalency diplomas, thereby improving their chances of finding employment.

Affirmative Action

The most controversial policy designed to redress past institutional discrimination is **affirmative action.** This term refers to policies based on a body of federal law originating in the 1964 Civil Rights Act that bans discrimination on the basis of race, religion, sex, or national origin in such areas as employment, education, and housing. Affirmative-action programs require institutions that have engaged in discriminatory practices to increase opportunities for women and members of minority groups (Kahlenberg, 1996). The policy is controversial because, with the goal of correcting past patterns of discrimination, institutions such as universities and businesses must make special efforts to recruit minority applicants, and those efforts may in effect represent discrimination against white applicants. Affirmative-action policies are also controversial because they often appear to divide both majority and minority groups into those who support the policy and those who believe it represents a form of "reverse discrimination." This is true not only in the United States, but also in South Africa, Europe, and other regions of the world (Alexander & Jacobsen, 1999).

In an effort to enable members of minority groups to receive the same educational opportunities as whites, beginning in 1965 the federal government required schools to establish goals for minority enrollment and in some cases to set quotas that specify the number of minority students to be admitted each year. These policies met with considerable opposition. Charging that affirmative action is reverse discrimination, critics focused on the Supreme Court case of Alan Bakke, a white student who was refused admission to the medical school of the University of California at Davis even though his grades were higher than those of many black students who were admitted under an affirmative-action program.

The fight against the medical school's program was led by Jewish organizations, which viewed quota systems as a threat to the advancement of Jews in American society. Emphasis on educational achievement had caused the relatively small Jewish population to be overrepresented at institutions of higher education, even though they had been subject to quotas in the past. Many Jews feared that quotas would again limit their access to colleges and universities to roughly the same small proportion as their numbers in the general population.

Those who support affirmative action cite a major difference between discriminatory quotas and policies designed to extend the opportunities available to victims of past discrimination. Describing affirmative action as a societal commitment to bringing blacks and other minority groups to a position of equality in the professions, they adamantly deny charges of reverse discrimination. The few whites who lose the opportunity to attend professional schools because of affirmative-action programs are, they argue, victims not of racism but of an effort to eradicate racism from the college and university environment (Kahlenberg, 1996).

The Supreme Court's decision in the *Bakke* case straddled these opposing points of view. The medical school's system was struck down, but the Court did not extend its ruling to all preferential admission systems. Affirmative action in college and professional school admissions remained in effect and continued to generate a great deal of rancorous conflict and political agitation, especially from conservative opponents of the policy. In 1996 California voters passed a statewide referendum, known as Proposition 209, that ended affirmative-action programs in public college admissions and in government hiring and contracts. A similar referendum passed in Washington State, and even earlier Texas had begun to dismantle affirmative-action programs in colleges and universities. On the other hand, a referendum against affirmative action was soundly defeated in Houston in 1998, and other states have failed to pass similar legislation, a sign that Americans remain extremely divided over what to do to redress past patterns of racial and gender discrimination (Staples, 1999).

Three years after Proposition 209 was passed in California, data on college admissions revealed a precipitous drop in enrollments of Latino and black students in the more prestigious colleges in the University of California system and even lower minority enrollments in professional schools. In 1999, therefore, the state's Civil Liberties Union brought suit against the state on behalf of minority high-school students. The suit was filed on behalf of four black and Hispanic students at Inglewood High School in Los Angeles, which offers only three advanced-placement courses. Inglewood's student population is 97 percent black. Beverly Hills High, which is 91 percent white, offers fourteen advanced-placement courses. Surprisingly, University of California Regent Ward Connerly, a conservative African American who championed

Student Breakdown (2001–2002)

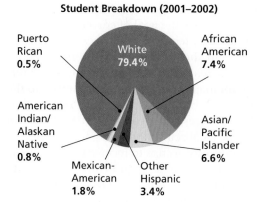

Minority Enrollment

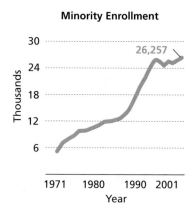

Figure 7–4 Fighting for a Piece of the Pie. *Although the number of minority students in U.S. law schools is growing, whites still make up the bulk of the student body.*

Source: American Bar Association, 2002.

Proposition 209 and other initiatives like it throughout the nation, joined the supporters of the suit. Although he opposes any form of affirmative-action quota system or preferential selection, he and others are appalled by the drastic results of Proposition 209 and realize that other measures, such as more effective high-school preparation and better outreach to gifted minority students, are still needed (Alexander & Jacobsen, 1999).

Figure 7–4 shows that although minority enrollment in law schools is increasing, African Americans continue to be underrepresented in those schools. Most experts believe that without some effort to recruit qualified minority candidates, this pattern will continue.

Although it is too soon to know the fate of affirmative-action policies, it seems likely that preferential selection systems of any kind will continue to come under attack, at least in public institutions like universities and agencies of government. The same is not entirely true of private businesses. Major corporations like Texaco and Verizon have affirmative-action recruitment policies for women and minorities and will maintain those policies because they fear negative publicity and wish to please all segments of the vast markets they serve. This may not be true of all corporations, but it has been a pattern for many of the large corporations that operate in global markets.

Although affirmative-action policies remain under attack, efforts to redress past patterns of discrimination will no doubt continue. In 1997, for example, southern African American farmers were successful in suing the government for past discrimination in farm loans, which deprived hundreds of independent minority farmers of the opportunity to make a living from the land. Under the agreement reached between the United States and the black plaintiffs, each farmer is entitled to receive $50,000 tax free and to have his or her federal loan debts erased. The debts average $100,000. Farmers with the most damaging claims can seek more compensation through arbitration, the courts, or the Department of Agriculture's administrative process (Cannon, 1999).

Analyses of employment data show that even at exactly the same levels of education and training and even with the same college grade point averages, white male college graduates earn 10 to 15 percent more per hour than comparable female, black male, or Asian male graduates (Sears, Sidanius, & Bobo, 2000). As social scientists continue to document persistent patterns of discrimination in opportunities and in the treatment of minorities, efforts to correct these inequities will persist.

Education for Equality

In an influential study entitled *American Apartheid,* Massey and Denton (1993) demonstrated that native-born blacks are (and have always been) far more segregated than any other racial or ethnic group in the United States. Persistent patterns of housing discrimination, documented in careful studies by the federal government during the 1980s, show that real estate agents, banks, local governments, and even the federal government have engaged in a variety of discriminatory housing practices or have failed to enforce legislation designed to guarantee freedom of choice in housing decisions. The extremely high rates of racial segregation in U.S. communities are reflected in increasing segregation in public schools (Plous, 2003).

A study released in 2002 by researchers at the Harvard School of Education confirms what many observers feared: The lack of vigorous enforcement of antidiscrimination legislation and the increasing segregation of blacks and some Hispanic groups in U.S. cities have resulted in a reversal of the twenty-year trend toward decreasing school segregation (Frankenberg & Lee, 2002). Table 7–5 lists the most rapidly resegregating school districts in the United States. Many of them are located in fast-growing metropolitan regions of the South and Southeast. Table 7–6 on page 250 demonstrates that the same trend (though it is original segregation rather than resegregation) is preventing Latino and white students in many metropolitan regions from gaining experience in interacting with one another in the public schools. These dramatic findings, however, are unlikely to stimulate renewed efforts to develop policies to promote desegregation. As few groups wish to resort to busing, it is unlikely that there will be renewed attempts to bus children to achieve racial integration.

TABLE 7–5 | Most Rapidly Resegregating Districts, Black Exposure to Whites: 1986–2000

Districts	Change
Clayton Co., GA	−45.0
Alief, TX	−42.4
Gwinnett Co., GA	−41.7
Cobb Co., GA	−40.5
Irving, TX	−39.0
Arlington, TX	−34.3
Minneapolis, MN	−33.2
Aldine, TX	−33.2
Klein, TX	−31.8
Fremont, CA	−31.0
Anaheim, CA	−30.9
Richardson, TX	−30.8
Mesquite, TX	−29.4
Adams-Arapahoe, CO	−28.7
Prince William Co., VA	−28.6
Mt. Diablo, CA	−27.9
Baltimore Co., MD	−26.8
Garden Grove, CA	−26.2
Pasadena, TX	−26.1
Clark Co., NV	−24.7

Source: Frankenberg & Lee, 2002.

TABLE 7–6	Most Rapidly Segregating Districts, Latino Exposure to Whites: 1986–2000

Districts	Change
Clayton Co., GA	−58.7
Gwinnett Co., GA	−48.3
Cobb Co., GA	−45.7
Alief, TX	−43.6
Adams-Arapahoe, CO	−40.9
Arlington, TX	−40.2
DeKalb Co., GA	−39.9
Irving, TX	−39.9
Birmingham, AL	−39.5
Anaheim, CA	−33.1
Richardson, TX	−33.0
Minneapolis, MN	−32.2
Prince William Co., VA	−31.4
Mesquite, TX	−31.0
Orange, CA	−30.8
Mt. Diablo, CA	−30.7
Fremont, CA	−30.7
Pasadena, TX	−30.5
Klein, TX	−29.3
Aldine, TX	−29.2

Note: This table shows segregation—as opposed to the resegregation in Table 7–5—because Latino students have never experienced significant integration with white students and have instead become steadily more segregated since the late 1960s.

Source: Frankenberg & Lee, 2002.

Recognition of the problems of segregated and unequal schooling is also likely to spur efforts to increase funding for preschool programs that address the needs of children in communities where segregation and discrimination have produced persistently high rates of school failure. **Head Start** is a blanket term that refers to federally funded preschool programs aimed at preparing disadvantaged children for school. They are quite popular among parents, administrators, and education activists (Klein, 2007).

At its inception in the 1960s and during its early years, Head Start was a showcase program. Early studies found improvements of 8 to 10 points in the IQs of 480 children in a Head Start program conducted in Baltimore in the summer of 1965 (Levitan, 1968). These immediate, measurable gains in cognitive achievement heralded an enormous expansion of Head Start operations and a push for year-long programs throughout the country. From small beginnings, Head Start grew until it cost several hundred million dollars a year, served approximately 400,000 children, and was widely supported.

The initial goals of Head Start and its early popularity obscured some basic flaws. First, although the concept of early intervention was popular among researchers on child development, and their research did in fact suggest that there is real potential for intellectual improvement through early-childhood training, there remain few unchallenged guidelines for exactly what is to be taught, how, when, and by whom.

Project Head Start, a preschool enrichment program for disadvantaged children, was begun in the 1960s. Evaluations of the achievements of children from Head Start programs indicated that such programs have lasting beneficial effects that more than justify their expense.

Second, it is argued that Head Start does too little, too late, to be effective. According to this view, the most important period in a child's emotional, social, and intellectual development is the first three years of life, when the child begins to acquire language and learns to manipulate his or her surroundings. Parents, not teachers, therefore, are the most important educators, and for intervention to be effective, it must begin during infancy in the child's own home. (These issues are discussed further in Chapter 11.)

Future Prospects

The desolate blocks of un-rebuilt black New Orleans are a vivid reminder of the racial disadvantage Hurricane Katrina exposed, and the costly war in Iraq, whose burdens are disproportionately borne by minority groups, has added to the growing inequality in American society. These factors combine to create social forces that strongly influence African Americans, Latinos, and Native Americans. As the 2006 election demonstrated, they are angry and motivated to vote. This means that the nation is likely to see the passage of social policies that will begin to address the problems of people who are not wealthy and white. But what form will these policies take?

In employment, education, health care, and criminal justice—all institutions in which minorities have a high stake—it is highly significant that for the first time in American history powerful members of these groups are leaders of major committees in Congress. Representative Charles Rangel, for example, is chair of the House Ways and Means Committee, which has a key role in determining what social policies actually receive government funding. Passage of new legislation such as increases in the minimum wage, health-care reform, immigration laws, and funding for education, student scholarships and loans, and local community development can make enormous differences in the lives not just of minority groups, but of all Americans who live on modest incomes.

In response to attacks on affirmative action, school desegregation, and many other policies designed to integrate American society, and perhaps as a consequence of continuing immigration into the nation's large cities, minority groups are increasingly developing a form of "identity politics." (See the Current Controversies box on page 252.)

Current Controversies

IMMIGRATION

Should legal immigration to the United States be curtailed? Are immigrants a threat to the social mobility of African Americans and other minority groups that experienced racism and discrimination earlier in U.S. history? Should immigrants qualify for the same social benefits as citizens? These and many related questions are high on the political and policy agenda in the United States. Welfare reform policies single out illegal immigrants, and in some cases legal immigrants, for restrictions of benefits. Congress is now debating a new round of restrictions on the flow of legal immigrants into the United States.

Immigration is also a burning issue in many other nations, especially in Western Europe, where anti-immigration sentiment is on the rise and is inspiring the hopes of nativist political parties, just as it is in the United States. Nativism is the idea that only native-born persons deserve the full benefits of citizenship and that foreigners are a danger to the stability of the society. Nativism is an old issue in nations with histories of immigration. But why is it undergoing such a resurgence now? Many of the answers to these questions depend on some knowledge of the current immigration situation in the United States and other countries.

The U.S. Immigration Act of 1986 increased the quotas of immigrants significantly and at the same time attempted to decrease the flow of illegal immigration from Mexico and other nations (Portes & Rumbaut, 1990). Legal immigration increased from a level of about 60,000 per year to more than 900,000 (counting refugees, who are included under another law). Some of the major supporters of the increased quotas were employers represented by the U.S. Chambers of Commerce and the National Association of Manufacturers. The employers were frank in their argument that the nation needed the energies and motivation of workers who were willing to produce well at low wages. But in the ensuing decade it proved difficult to decrease the flow of illegal immigrants. At the same time, legal immigrants made their presence felt quite dramatically in certain areas of the country, particularly in the Northeast, Florida, California, and Texas.

Social scientists who study U.S. immigration argue that the combined flow of legal and illegal immigrants is not enough, in a nation with a low overall birthrate, to significantly disrupt the economy, and in fact it can be a spur to economic growth (Waldinger, 2001). Although this may be true, increasing numbers of citizens in California and other immigrant-receiving areas feel otherwise, and this perception of economic and social competition from immigrants has clearly stimulated the rise of nativist feelings.

At this writing it is not clear if immigration policies will become more restrictive in the United States. Congress will again consider immigration reform and will no doubt again debate measures designed to decrease immigration, both legal and illegal. But an unusual coalition is emerging, made up of representatives of high-technology industries, civil rights groups, immigrant and ethnic associations, and some conservative research organizations, all of which argue in favor of continued high levels of immigration (Jacoby, 2002). So although it is not clear how restrictive the new immigration policies will become, it is apparent that immigration is changing the nature of minority affairs in the United States. There are so many new groups representing different ethnic and racial backgrounds in the nation's largest cities that simple distinctions like "black and white" are less and less relevant, and the building of new coalitions among older and newer minorities is a major political trend.

This trend emphasizes the need for a minority group to recognize its own culture within the larger society and to work to develop strong schools, strong neighborhoods, and new forms of employment. Critics of identity politics fear that it will further divide the United States into competing ethnic and racial groups (Gitlin, 1996). But others, like Cornel West (1994), argue that "without some redistribution of wealth and power, downward mobility [especially of minority group members] will continue to drive people into desperate channels" (p. 116).

GOING BEYOND LEFT AND RIGHT

Conservatives tend to dislike affirmative action because it often discriminates against individuals who themselves are not responsible for past patterns of racism and discrimination. Liberals want to redress old patterns of racial and ethnic inequality and argue that when other considerations are equal, race or descent may be valid criteria for allocating scarce resources like scholarships.

Where do you stand on these difficult issues? Most likely you are among the majority who would like to see less racism and discrimination and more equality, but are also opposed to "reverse discrimination." So what solutions do sociologists propose?

William J. Wilson and many others argue for race-blind social policies that will not create reverse discrimination but will address past patterns of racism and the inequalities they engendered. Such policies would create jobs where there is high unemployment and increase educational and training opportunities wherever people need them, thus dealing with the needs of people on a class basis rather than in terms of their race or ethnic status. Many conservatives have doubts about any government-sponsored program to deal with inequality, but they are more willing to entertain such race-blind policies than those directed at particular groups.

An example of race-blind social policy in the interests of increasing diversity and equality of opportunity is the practice recently instituted by Harvard and other private universities of awarding full scholarships to students who have been accepted by the university but whose families earn less than $50,000 per year. Since more nonwhite than white students fall into this category, this strategy is showing some success.

Summary

- The United States has a long history of inequality. Although much progress has been made toward legal equality as a result of the civil rights movement, inequality remains a significant problem in American society.

- Racial minorities are made up (or "constructed") of people who share certain inherited characteristics. Ethnic minorities are made up of people who may share certain cultural features and who regard themselves as a unified group. The principal characteristic of any minority group is subordinate status in society.

- Racism is behavior motivated by the belief that human races have distinctive characteristics that determine abilities and cultures. Discrimination is the differential treatment of individuals on the basis of their perceived membership in a particular social group. It is overt behavior. People rationalize it on the ground that those against whom they discriminate are less worthy of respect or fair treatment than people like themselves. This reasoning results in prejudice against the subordinate group.

- Prejudice and discrimination have several sources. Among these are individual psychological factors, including frustration-aggression (which involves displacing anger onto a scapegoat) and projection (in which people attribute their own undesirable traits to others). Other factors include social structure (especially economic competition and exploitation) and the norms and stereotypes of a particular culture.

- Institutional discrimination is discrimination that is built into the structure and form of society itself. One form of institutional discrimination is racial profiling, the practice by people in positions of authority of disproportionately selecting people of color for investigations or other forms of discrimination.

- Institutional discrimination is especially evident in the educational system. Here the most prominent issue is achievement in school. Desegregation through busing is largely considered to have been a failure, but no alternative strategies have been suggested.

- Another area in which institutional discrimination is evident is housing. Housing segregation is widespread, resulting in a clear division between whites in the suburbs and blacks and other minority groups in the cities. Among the causes of housing segregation is racial steering by real estate agents.

- Discrimination is also prevalent in employment, often as a direct result of discrimination in education. Those who lack education are often underemployed or unemployed, which results in low incomes and the likelihood of a poor education for the next generation. Even when their educational levels are similar, however, blacks and members of other minority groups are often paid less than whites.

- Members of minority groups are more likely than whites to be arrested and charged with a crime. Following arrest, they face discrimination under the bail system, in which those who lack the money to post bail must wait in jail for their cases to come to trial. Political discrimination against minorities may take the form of felony disenfranchisement and anti-voter fraud campaigns.

- Prejudice and discrimination have a number of harmful consequences. Among the most destructive is lack of self-esteem among those who are discriminated against. Other reactions are separatism and protest, sometimes leading to riots. There are many indications that racism and racial stereotypes persist, including violence directed against blacks, as well as more subtle forms of racism like patronizing remarks.

- The gains made by minority groups since the 1960s faced major challenges in the 1990s and continue to do so. Affirmative action and equal employment opportunity have come under attack. Efforts to increase educational equality through preschool programs have been more successful, and advocates of Head Start are seeking to convince legislators to expand the program.

Key Terms

Social Problems Online

Yale University's Web site on American Ethnic Studies, **www.library.yale.edu/rsc/ ethnic/internet.html**, is an excellent place to start browsing the Web for its rich resources on ethnic and racial issues. It has links to many of the other sites mentioned here. One interesting site is the Historical Society of Pennsylvania at **www.hsp.org**. Its Balch Institute for Ethnic Studies is concerned with the reduction and prevention of intergroup tensions and violence.

Several Web resources are concerned with discrimination in American society. One of them is the National Fair Housing Advocate, **www.fairhousing.com**/, which keeps track of legal cases that involve housing discrimination throughout the nation. It links organizations that call for fair-housing practices, and it provides updated information on federal guidelines, job openings, articles, news, and so forth. Another important resource is the National Association for the Advancement of Colored People (NAACP), the nation's largest civil-rights organization; it has a Web site at **www.naacp.org**/.

Research Navigator

Follow the instructions on pages 26–27 of this text to access the features of Research Navigator. Once at the Web site, enter your Login Name and Password. Then, to use the Content Select database, use keywords such as "endogamy," "racial steering," and "affirmative action," and the search engine will supply relevant and recent scholarly and popular press publications. Use the *New York Times* search-by-subject archive to find recent news articles related to problems of racism, prejudice, and discrimination, and the Link Library to find relevant Web sites organized by the key terms associated with this chapter.

Use Research Navigator to access the Internet. Search for the Lewis Mumford Center for Comparative Urban and Regional Statistics. Find their linked Web site on residential segregation and choose your own metropolitan region. What are the trends in black–white segregation from the 1980s to the present? What are the trends in white–Hispanic segregation? Can you explain what a segregation index is? What, for example, is the meaning of a black–white segregation index of 65? What are some of the consequences of housing segregation for other aspects of social life, such as education?

8

GENDER
and Sexuality

Chapter Outline

Dominant Trends

- With 52 percent of the world's total population, but more than 60 percent of the world's impoverished population, women continue to press for political and economic rights. These demands often conflict with traditional cultural values and will continue to generate much conflict and efforts to repress women's desire for access to education, health care, and political influence.

- In the United States, median earnings of working women are still 20 percent lower than those of men working at the same jobs. Women's organizations will therefore continue to push for equal pay for equal work.

- Worldwide, violence against women remains a severe problem, and in the United States about 115,000 women are raped each year, evidence that the problem of violence is by no means limited to developing areas of the world.

- Women and their political allies will continue to press for better family and work policies, since women are three times as likely as men to experience interruptions in their work histories due to child rearing.

- While same-sex marriage is opposed by about 50 percent of the U.S. population and is banned by the constitutions of eighteen states, there is growing acceptance of its legitimacy. Massachusetts, New Jersey, New York, and other states are moving toward legalization of same-sex marriages.

Over the past several decades, women have made many notable gains. They are increasingly entering occupations that were traditionally dominated by men—about 32 percent of mathematical and computer scientists are women, for example, as are 35 percent of lawyers and judges. Moreover, the gap between the earnings of men and women is narrowing. In 2004 the median earnings of women who worked full time were about 76 percent of those of men, compared to 68 percent in 1985 (*Statistical Abstract,* 2005). The remaining gap can be explained largely by differences in education and work experiences. A significant obstacle to income equality is that women are three times as likely as men to have had interruptions in their work history because of childbearing, child care, illness, disability, and unemployment.

From a global perspective, women face an array of daunting social problems. These include dire poverty, severe lack of rights in many cultures and nations, AIDS, forced marriage, rape and other violence, enslavement in sex industries, and societal failure to recognize and develop their full human potential. At the same time, there are many positive indicators of the improving status of women throughout the world. Rates of literacy are increasing; more women are gaining political rights in

more nations; and there is an increasingly active global array of women's organizations working to achieve the rights and empowerment goals set forth at the historic Beijing Conference in 1995. In many impoverished regions, it is the efforts of women to form economic cooperatives, develop women's reproductive health clinics, and carry forward the fight for women's political rights that provide the greatest impetus to positive social change and economic development. But in these and many other regions, the extent to which women remain subordinate to men, a subordination that is often reinforced by religious norms, remains a severe obstacle to further development (Ashford, 2001).

Despite the gains of recent decades, sex discrimination and stereotyping continue to limit the opportunities of women. Globally, women are beset by hunger and violence far more than are men. In the United States, women are still shunted into the "girl's ghetto": housekeeping; retail trades; insurance; real estate; and service positions such as secretary, receptionist, telephone operator, and clerk. About 60 percent of working women in the United States are employed in these kinds of jobs (Fenstermaker & West, 2002). There are thirteen women senators and sixty-two women representatives in the U.S. Congress. In both chambers the numbers doubled during the 1990s, but few women think the present

TABLE 8–1	Median Weekly Earnings, by Employment Characteristics: 2007

Occupation	Women	Men
All workers	$615	$759
Management, professional, and related	816	1,162
Service	795	516
Sales and office	532	715
Farming, fishing, and forestry	—	340
Construction and extraction	588	662
Production	423	630
Transportation and material moving	436	584

Source: Bureau of Labor Statistics, 2007.

proportions are sufficient, especially as women make up more than 50 percent of the population. Even when women are in the same professions or occupations as men, their salaries are lower; subtle and persistent discrimination in employment and salaries is still widespread. (Table 8–1 shows the wage gap for selected occupations.)

In the 1970s and early 1980s efforts to combat these inequalities centered on ratification of the Equal Rights Amendment to the U.S. Constitution. However, by the June 30, 1982, deadline for ratification, only 35 of the required 38 states had ratified the amendment. The amendment was reintroduced in Congress in 1983, but in the House of Representatives it fell six votes short of the two-thirds majority needed to send it to the states for ratification. Thus, women do not yet have legal assurance of equal rights in American society.

TRADITIONAL SEX ROLES

In Chapter 7 we suggested that prejudice—a predisposition to regard a certain group in a certain way—often becomes the justification for discriminatory behavior. That is, if we believe a certain group is "inferior" or "different," we can easily defend less-than-equal treatment of its members. We also suggested that the norms of society are an important source of prejudice and discrimination. If an entire society is prejudiced against a certain group and discriminates against it, such actions will be accepted as natural and right by most members of that society.

Until fairly recently, it was widely accepted that the only desirable roles for a woman were wife, mother, and homemaker, and that her entire life should revolve around them. The roles themselves emphasized that a woman should be nurturing and skilled in the emotional aspects of personal relationships. A man, on the other hand, was expected to be a leader and provider, a highly rational person who would not let emotions get in the way of action. These expectations often caused men to deny their emotions and thus made them less able to enjoy many aspects of life in their families and communities (Andersen & Collins, 2007).

Betty Friedan (1963) was one of the first contemporary feminists to identify and criticize the traditional view of female roles, which she labeled "the feminine mystique":

The feminine mystique says that the highest value and the only commitment for women is the fulfillment of their own femininity. It says that the great mistake of Western culture, through most of its history, has been the undervaluation of this femininity. It says this femininity is so mysterious and intuitive and close to the creation and origin of life that man-made science may never be able to understand it. But however special and different, it is in no way inferior to the nature of man; it may even in certain respects be superior. The mistake, says the mystique, the root of women's troubles in the past, is that women envied men, women tried to be like men, instead of accepting their own nature, which can find fulfillment only in sexual passivity, male domination, and nurturing maternal love. . . . The new mystique makes the housewife-mothers, who never had a chance to be anything else, the model for all women . . . a pattern by which all women must now live or deny their femininity. (p. 43)

So pervasive was this view, and so thoroughly was it internalized by both men and women, that Friedan called women's dissatisfaction with their traditional roles "the problem that has no name."

Today many people think of the traditional roles of women and men as somewhat outdated. At the time that Friedan (1963) wrote her book, the traditional roles formed the basis for social behavior. Women were considered too delicate to do "men's work" and therefore were legally denied many career and job opportunities. Men were supposed to be dominant and unemotional, to "act like a man." For women, chastity and fidelity were considered major virtues; for men, promiscuity was considered natural. Women and men were thought to be different and hence were treated differently by social institutions—including the government and the legal system. The entire range of social norms and values reflected different standards of behavior for men and women, which few people questioned.

This double standard is not unique to our society. In many Latin American and Muslim countries, the status of women is far more subordinate than in our own. Few women in those societies have the freedom that men have or are able to pursue careers outside the home. And although women in eastern European countries have greater equality with men, disparities exist there as well. For example, most of the physicians in Russia are women, but female physicians receive lower pay than male physicians.

This traditional hierarchy is extremely resistant to change. Women and men are shaped by the culture in which they are raised, so that most adults are thoroughly indoctrinated or socialized for the roles their culture has prescribed for them. Change is

In traditional Muslim societies, women are not permitted to show their face or other parts of their body outside the home. Although many women accept this norm and feel that it protects them, others believe that it conflicts with their desire for greater equality.

suspect because it threatens their identity. Thus, many women oppose attempts to give them equal status with men. It was a women's organization—Stop-ERA, led by Phyllis Schlafly—that led the battle to prevent ratification of the Equal Rights Amendment.

It seems clear that there is considerable variation in the types of behavior that are considered appropriate for men and for women, and that to a large extent these behaviors reflect the values of a particular society more than any innate or "natural" qualities. Whereas it was once supposed that behavioral differences between men and women are innate, today we know that these differences are largely learned through socialization. And although it was once believed that there are universal standards of masculine and feminine behavior, in fact the standards in other societies are very different from our own (Scott, 1999; Susser & Patterson, 2001).

GENDER IDENTITY AND SEXUAL ORIENTATION

In their research on gender and sexuality, social scientists find that, contrary to what most people believe, there is not a clear "binary" male–female distinction between the sexes—either in the way people who are biologically male or female actually think of themselves (gender identity) or in how they prefer to behave sexually (sexuality). A great deal of confusion and suffering occurs because of mistaken ideas about gender and sexuality, and about how we think men and women should behave, as we will see in this section.

Gender versus Sexual Identity

Our **gender identity,** a sense of maleness or femaleness, is typically formed by age 3. According to the gender-role norms of each society, which prescribe how males and females should behave, the child is expected to exhibit maleness or femaleness as they are defined in that society's culture (Bussey & Bandura, 1999; DeLamater & Friedrich, 2002). An extremely important aspect of one's overall self-concept, gender identity may emerge in late adolescence as a stable, self-confident sense of manhood or womanhood, or alternatively, the individual may feel conflict about his or her gender identity and about how to play the roles typically assigned to one's gender—as when a girl is discouraged from playing competitive sports.

Sexual identity, a sense of one's attractiveness to others and a sense of comfort with one's body and one's feelings of sexual arousal, also emerges in the course of childhood and adolescence. It includes *sexual orientation,* that is, whether one is attracted to members of the opposite sex (heterosexual) or to members of the same sex (homosexual), and *sexuality,* or how one actually behaves sexually.

Human sexual development is never complete; it is a continuous process that begins at conception and ends at death. The principal forces that shape one's sexual identity are biological maturation and aging; the progression through the socially defined stages of childhood, adolescence, adulthood, and later life; and the qualities of one's social relationships during each of these stages. These social and biological forces combine in ways unique to each individual to influence the person's sexual identity, attitudes, and behavior. For this reason, there is wide variation in sexual attitudes, behaviors, and lifestyles. Despite claims to the contrary by people with narrow ideas about sexuality, social scientists find that this diversity contributes to the vitality of society (DeLamater & Friedrich, 2002).

Transgendered and *intersexual* individuals, for example, are a diverse group that includes people who feel a strong identification with the other gender; people who cross-dress occasionally or regularly; and people who actually change their bodies—under medical supervision and through the use of hormones and surgery—to look, feel, and act more like members of the other sex. People whose genes, genitals, or reproductive organs are not clearly male or female are intersexual. Although their numbers are relatively small, transgendered and intersexual people often find themselves being mistreated or stigmatized for violating, willingly or unwillingly, their society's "binary" (i.e., male–female) definition of gender and "normal" sexuality. As a legal expert on the subject notes, "The law, by clinging to a binary system that blindly ignores the existence of intersexuals and the importance of self-identity, reinforces the perception that intersexuality is unacceptable" (Greenberg, 1998, p. 265). To learn more about intersexuality, visit the Intersex Society of North America Web site, **www.isna.org/**

Homosexuality

Among the many variations in sexual identity, homosexuality is the most controversial in U.S. society and the one that sheds the most light on the nature of sexuality and gender identity. We turn therefore to a more detailed discussion of this form of sexual orientation.

The brutal murder of college student Matthew Shepard, who was kidnapped, beaten, and left to die on a fence along a Wyoming highway, along with many other incidents of violence and harassment against gay people in the United States and elsewhere, indicate why homosexuality is a social problem. Although millions of gays find immense satisfaction and fulfillment in their lives, controversies raised by antigay groups, discrimination against gays and lesbians, battles over the rights of same-sex partners, and struggles by gay people to win acceptance of same-sex marriages often force them into painful confrontations with some "straight" people. In one sense, gays and lesbians share the difficulties of any minority group, but the conflicts centering on sexuality and gender in the United States often compound the problems, as we will see in this section (Fulton et al., 1999; Rosario, 2002).

Homosexuality is a sexual preference for members of one's own sex. Some people are exclusively homosexual; others may engage in same-sex behavior only under special circumstances, such as imprisonment; still others have both homosexual and heterosexual experiences. Both males and females may be homosexual; male homosexuals are usually referred to as gays and female homosexuals as lesbians.

It is difficult to determine the number of gay and lesbian individuals in the United States. An often-cited estimate based on the original research of Alfred Kinsey (Kinsey, Pomeroy, & Martin, 1948), which included 17,000 interviews, places the proportion of gay or lesbian Americans at 10 percent. Kinsey found that 37 percent of the male population had had physical contact to the point of orgasm with other men at some time between adolescence and old age. The extent to which respondents had engaged in same-sex behavior varied, with 10 percent of the sample reporting that they had been more or less exclusively homosexual for at least three years.

Recent surveys of sexual behavior in the United States and other Western societies have found lower percentages, varying between 1 percent and 4 percent, of men who indicated that they had had same-sex relations in the year prior to the survey (Laumann et al., 1994; Schmidt, 1997). Gay-rights activists and survey research experts agree that although the Kinsey figures may be high estimates, the fluctuations in recent survey data suggest that sensitive questions about sexual behavior are subject to rather high levels of error because respondents may not feel comfortable about answering truthfully (Rosario, 2002).

In the most recent survey of Americans' sexual attitudes and behaviors, the National Center for Health Statistics sponsored a survey of more than 12,000 males and females between the ages of 15 and 44. To protect their privacy and encourage full disclosure, respondents were allowed to type their answers on a laptop computer without the interviewer knowing them. Figures 8–1 and 8–2 on page 262 show that same-sex experiences are more common among women, especially teenagers and college-age women, than among men. These findings confirm what many social scientists have observed: Women are more likely then men to be able to experience same-sex attraction without necessarily defining themselves as gay or lesbian over their entire lifetimes (Lewin, 2005).

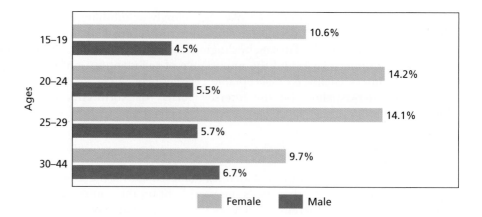

Figure 8–1 Sexual Experiences with Member of the Same Sex during Lifetime

Source: Lewin, 2005.

In our society, homosexuality has alternately been regarded either as a sin or as the effect of some physical or mental disturbance; until the rise of the gay-rights movement in recent decades, it was considered too shameful and indecent to be spoken of openly. Although society has become more tolerant of open discussions of sexual orientation, many prejudices still prevail. Surveys consistently show increasing public tolerance of homosexuality, but almost half of all Americans believe gays and lesbians should be barred from certain jobs for which they may be qualified, particularly jobs involving young people (NORC, 1999). Elsewhere in the world, a similar picture of increasing acceptance and persistent problems also prevails. In Europe, there is growing acceptance of same-sex behavior, and gay people are far less closeted about their sexual identity than they were a generation ago. But in the Islamic world, although homosexuality is not uncommon, it is severely persecuted; in fundamentalist nations like Iran, it can result in harsh and even deadly sanctions. In India, gay communities are emerging in major cities, and in parts of Africa homosexuality is becoming more accepted. Throughout much of Africa, however, it remains a taboo subject and leads to clandestine, closeted behavior (Epprecht, 2004).

Social-Scientific Perspectives on Sexual Orientation. In the early decades of the twentieth century, social scientists generally viewed homosexuality as a form of social pathology brought on by the disorganization of families and communities that were experiencing the effects of rapid urbanization and industrialization. Sociologists tended to regard homosexuality, along with prostitution, as an individual

Figure 8–2 Number of Partners in Last 12 Months

Source: Lewin, 2005.

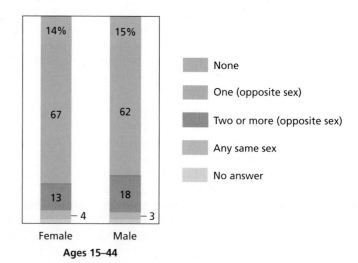

response to the disorganization of family life. Psychologists attempted to treat it as an illness with physiological causes.

Sigmund Freud and other founders of the psychoanalytic movement realized that many homosexuals are well-adjusted, productive adults. Freud also believed homosexuality is a stage that all people pass through on the way to developing heterosexual desires. Homosexuals, in his view, have been "arrested" and have failed to develop further. The Freudian perspective on homosexuality did not become a dominant viewpoint, however. The majority of American social scientists continued to view homosexuality as an illness that should be cured through some kind of therapy.

Kinsey's study of the sexual behavior of American males (Kinsey, Pomeroy, & Martin, 1948) marked a turning point in the understanding of same-sex behavior from both a scientific and a popular point of view. This work was extraordinary because it was based on interviews with thousands of ordinary Americans rather than with people who had requested psychiatric treatment. It revealed a wide gap between sexual norms and actual behavior and questioned the idea that there is a clear dichotomy between heterosexual and same-sex attraction. Kinsey and subsequent sex researchers began to believe that sexual feelings toward same-sex friends are not abnormal or deviant and that hostility toward gays and lesbians is often a response to the severe conflict that people feel, but deny feeling, about this attraction and society's condemnation of it.

Despite the torrent of criticism that greeted Kinsey's studies when they first appeared, other social scientists soon published findings that supported his conclusion that gays and lesbians cannot be distinguished from nonhomosexuals in psychological terms. The most famous of these studies were conducted by psychologist Evelyn Hooker during the 1950s. Hooker showed that it is not possible to distinguish homosexuals from nonhomosexuals with any of the standard projective tests available in clinical psychology. She went on to show that alleged homosexual obsessions (with anonymous sex, for example), where they exist, are caused not by homosexuality itself, but by stigmatization and rejection. If gays and lesbians are a deviant group in society, she reasoned, they are so not because of any inherent feature of same-sex attraction but because of their rejection by the larger society (Hooker, 1966).

Thomas Szasz (1994)—who, as we have seen, was one of the founders of labeling theory—carried this perspective a step further. He argued that psychiatrists and others who labeled homosexuality an illness were merely taking the place of the church in identifying gays and lesbians and punishing them for their deviant sexual behavior. As noted earlier, all the professional scientific associations that deal with human sexuality support the official position of the American Psychological Association as set forth in its arguments before the Supreme Court in the 2003 Texas sodomy case (discussed further in the Social Policy section of the chapter):

> Decades of research and clinical experience have led all mainstream mental health organizations in this country to the conclusion that homosexuality is a normal form of human sexuality. Homosexuality—defined as a pattern of erotic, affectional, and romantic attraction principally to members of one's own sex—has consistently been found in a substantial portion of the American adult population. (Ogden, 2003, p. 1)

Who Becomes Gay or Lesbian? To date, there is no convincing evidence that same-sex attraction is biologically determined. Biologists tend to agree that evidence from studies of twins reared apart and from other research seems to indicate that there is a strong genetic component in sexuality, but this does not mean that there are direct links between specific sexual behaviors and genetic transmission (Pillard & Bailey, 1998). A large proportion of gays and lesbians find the origins of their sexual preference in their earliest experiences as children, and hence they tend to accept the hypothesis that same-sex attraction has a strong genetic component (Robertson, 2005). Opponents of homosexuality, especially among conservative Christian groups, tend to reject biological explanations because they view homosexuality as a "lifestyle preference" that is voluntary and could be changed through therapy or religious conversion (Fulton, Gorsuch, & Maynard, 1999; Jones, 1999).

Sociologists, psychiatrists, and anthropologists, like gays and lesbians themselves, are increasingly inclined to view same-sex attraction as a biologically based trait in some individuals, but they often argue that environmental factors can play a role in shaping actual sexual behavior. While human beings may or may not have a basic need for sex, social scientists often find that sexual expression is shaped by experience (Seidman, Fischer, & Meeks, 2006). However, psychiatrists and psychologists have not succeeded in identifying any early experiences that result in homosexuality. Certain situations do seem to be frequent in the case histories of homosexuals: The family often includes a dominant or seductive mother and a weak, detached, or overly critical father—factors that discourage the male child from identifying with male role models. Yet it is not clear why homosexuality develops only in some children who are reared under these conditions; many researchers, in fact, question whether homosexuality is caused by a pathological family situation at all.

One study of the process by which an individual becomes a homosexual (Troiden, 1987) emphasized the importance of labeling. The process of gaining a homosexual identity was divided into four stages: (1) sensitization, (2) dissociation and signification,* (3) coming out, and (4) commitment. In this model, the gay identity is subject to modification at each stage, and the later stages do not inevitably follow the earlier ones. The third stage, coming out, marks the point at which the individual defines himself or herself as homosexual and becomes involved in the homosexual subculture. The specific means through which this occurs may vary, as can be seen in Table 8–2.

Lesbianism. It is even harder to estimate the number of lesbians in the United States than it is to estimate the number of gays, especially as social norms make it easier to conceal female same-sex attraction. A single woman who does not date men is usually assumed to be uninterested in or afraid of sex rather than being suspected of lesbianism. Also, it is considered more acceptable for women to share an apartment or to kiss or touch in public than it is for men (Gallagher & Hammer, 1998). Finally, laws against homosexuality are usually concerned primarily with the activities of males.

Although as individuals lesbians are as diverse as gays, there are some general differences between the ways in which males and females manage same-sex behavior.

TABLE 8–2	How Do Gay Men Define the Term "Coming Out"?[a]		
		Responses	
		Percent	Number
To admit to oneself a homosexual preference, or decide that one is, essentially, homosexual		31	77
To admit to oneself a homosexual preference *and* to begin to practice homosexual activity		27	41
To start actively seeking out other males as sexual partners		9	13
First homosexual experience as a young adult (i.e., after middle teens)		8	12
A homosexual experience that triggers self-designation as homosexual		1	2
Other		3	5
		99	150

[a]Informants were asked to define what the term *coming out* meant to them—that is, how they would use the term.

Source: Richard Troiden, "Becoming Homosexual," *Psychiatry: Journal for the Study of Interpersonal Processes* (November 1987), 42: 362–373.

*These terms refer to the mental processes by which sexual feelings and/or activity are distinguished from sexual identity.

Many of these differences appear to arise from differences in socialization. Gays and lesbians, as much as heterosexuals, are affected by society's expectations about the kinds of behavior that are appropriate for members of each sex. Well before a girl begins to experience same-sex tendencies, she is absorbing society's assumptions about how females should act—for example, that they should be less aggressive than males and that sex is permissible only as part of a lasting emotional relationship. Moreover, sexual experiences usually begin later for females than for males. A boy is likely to have a sexual experience to the point of orgasm—usually through masturbation—relatively early in adolescence, whereas for a girl the corresponding experience is likely to occur in late adolescence or early adulthood. It is therefore likely that a girl will learn to think in terms of emotional attachment and permanent love relationships before she develops any strong sexual commitment; when that commitment appears, whether heterosexual or homosexual, it does so in the context of love. Thus, for most of the lesbians studied by Gagnon and Simon (1973), the first actual sexual experience came late, during an intense emotional involvement.

These differences in development and socialization underlie many of the subsequent differences in the behavior of gays and lesbians. The lower level of sexual activity among lesbians, for example, parallels the behavior of women in general. Lesbians typically come out at a later age than do gays. When a lesbian does come out, she usually looks for one partner and remains with her as long as the relationship is satisfying. When she lacks a partner, she is less likely than a male to look for one-night stands and hence spends less time in the gay bars and other gathering places that are so important to gays (Robertson, 2005).

As in the case of male homosexuality, a special category of lesbianism is found in prisons. Many women who are in prison have experienced severe abuse by male partners or parents and feel angry and estranged from men. In prison they form friendships that may lead to sexual relations, a pattern that may endure later in life (Miller, 1986).

The Gay Subculture. When we speak of the gay subculture, we are referring to the visible institutions of the gay community. *The Advocate,* "the national gay and lesbian newsmagazine," is an example of such an institution. An undetermined proportion of gays remain in the closet; that is, they do not participate openly in the life of the gay community. It is the declared homosexuals who create the gay subculture and have mobilized to bring about changes in laws and social norms that would create a more tolerant climate for all homosexuals.

The gay subculture may be found in most big cities in the United States, which have large gay populations in neighborhoods such as Greenwich Village and Chelsea in New York City and the Castro district in San Francisco. Gay institutions in these communities, which provide services and serve as meeting places for gays, include certain parks, restrooms, movie theaters, public bathhouses, gyms, and bars. Cities with large gay populations also support businesses—restaurants, boutiques, barbershops, bookstores, travel agencies, repair shops, and so forth—that cater primarily to a gay clientele. Certain doctors, dentists, and lawyers also have largely gay clienteles. The growth of such businesses has fostered a sense of community among gays. In New York and San Francisco, for example, it is possible for gays to live, work, shop, and be entertained in a largely gay milieu. In 1999 Chicago unveiled a commemorative statue for gay rights in the growing gay community on the city's north side, another indication of the political and cultural influence of gay people in major American cities.

A major function of the gay subculture is to give its members a way to understand and accept their sexual orientation. This function is performed not only by gay bars and similar meeting places but also by some gay-rights organizations. These groups work to abolish laws that discriminate against gays and to persuade gays themselves and society in general that there is nothing shameful or harmful about same-sex orientation. Since the advent of the AIDS epidemic, they have also worked to propagate knowledge about safe sex and to lend support to those stricken by the disease (Duggan & Hunter, 2006).

The emergence of gays and lesbians as political actors has added to the legitimacy of same-sex relationships. To cite just one example, Barney Franks, an openly gay member of Congress, has used his power wherever possible to push for equality not only for gays and lesbians, but also for women, minorities, and others who, like himself, have experienced homophobia, racism, and sexism.

SEXISM AND GENDER INEQUALITY

Sexism is the counterpart of racism and ageism, which are discussed in Chapters 7 and 9, respectively. It may be defined as the "entire range of attitudes, beliefs, policies, laws, and behaviors discriminating against women (or against men) on the basis of their gender" (Safilios-Rothschild, 1974, p. 1). In this section we describe several factors that contribute to sexism around the world and in the United States.

Power and Male Hegemony

Sociologists who study gender relations call attention to persisting patterns of male dominance throughout the institutions of modern societies. R. W. Connell (1995), for example, has analyzed how dramatic inequalities in the distribution of power in societies often deprive women of opportunities to realize their full potential. Connell's research shows that wherever possible, males attempt to preserve their hegemony (controlling power) over women. In relations marked by hegemony, domination by one group, class, or gender over another is achieved by a combination of political and ideological means. Although political power or coercion is always important, ideologies can be equally important. In gender relations these ideologies differ from one culture to another. In parts of the Islamic world, male dominance is enforced by religious principles that emphasize female dominance over the home and male dominance over the world outside the home. In parts of the United States, ideologies that portray men as soldiers, athletic heroes, and managerial leaders, and women as homemakers and nurturant spouses, reinforce male dominance.

Connell's (1995) work shows that in much of the industrialized world men still have much greater access than women to cultural prestige, political authority, corporate power, individual wealth, and material comforts. Individual men or small groups may be confused or insecure about these inequalities. Others, such as gay men or men with feminist ideals, may join with women in rejecting male hegemony. But despite all the recent feminist criticism and despite all the documented struggles by women to assert their equality and make gains in the workplace, men continue to be dominant. With some notable exceptions (the occasional woman boss or female political leader), male–female relations are structured so that women are subordinate. This subordination is reinforced by the symbolic equation of masculinity and power.

One of the unfortunate aspects of ideologies that support male dominance is that even people victimized by them tend to believe that they are true. Thus, many women have attitudes that are prejudicial to women, causing them to undervalue the work of other women and to set up psychological barriers to their own achievement. Matina Horner (1970) found that many women were motivated to avoid success, fearing that the more ambitious and successful they became, the less feminine they would be. Research on the influence of stereotypes focuses on how women may become obsessed with their appearance and their efforts to please males or live up to an image of femininity largely created by men. Sharlene Hesse-Biber (1996) attributes the rise of problems like anorexia and compulsive dieting to the commercialization of images of women's bodies and the prevalent notion that one cannot be too thin.

Power held by men creates significant barriers to equality because men still hold most positions of authority in American society. Although this is even more true in many other nations, women in the United States have yet to achieve the same degree of access to positions of power that is enjoyed, for example, by Scandinavian women.

This is one of the infamous photos of prisoner abuse at the American detention center for Iraqi prisoners known as Abu Ghraib. This treatment of a male prisoner by a female guard violated Islamic norms of male–female power relations. To date, only lower-level enlisted military personnel, such as the soldier shown here, have been disciplined for the abuses.

And as is evident in Figure 8–3, when power is measured by the presence of women in legislative bodies, the United States ranks quite low (Ashford, 2001).

In her study of gender and sex roles, sociologist Cynthia Epstein (1993) found that there have been many positive changes in corporations and the professions, but that inadvertent and at times open hostility toward women remains a problem in many organizations. The continuing presence of sexism is revealed by the fact that white males still hold about 95 percent of the top management jobs in major U.S. corporations and less than 3 percent worldwide (Wirth, 2002).

How do power and patriarchy operate in societies to produce inequalities between men and women?

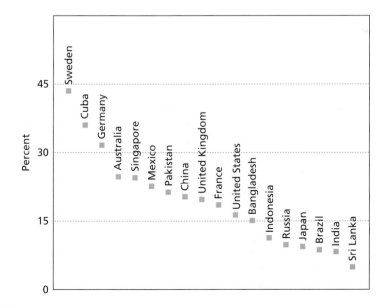

Figure 8–3 Percentage of National Legislative Seats Held by Women, Selected Nations

Source: Inter-Parliamentary Union, 2005, www.ipu.org.

Stereotyping

As we saw in Chapter 7, one source of prejudice and discrimination is stereotyping—attributing a fixed and usually unfavorable and inaccurate conception to a category of people. Stereotypes often make it easier to justify unequal treatment of the stereotyped person or group.

Among the traditional stereotypes about women is the belief that they are naturally passive, domestic, and envious. Friedan (1963) referred to this set of stereotypes as "the feminine mystique." However, Marc Fasteau (1974) has pointed out that there is a "masculine mystique" as well—a set of stereotypes about men that limits their ability to function fully and effectively. The masculine stereotype is that all men are tough, unemotional, and dominant; and however unrealistic and inaccurate this stereotype is, many men (and women) believe it. Many men avoid performing traditionally "female" tasks, such as washing dishes or working as a secretary, for fear that their masculinity will be questioned. And men who might prefer the role of homemaker feel compelled to seek careers in business because they have been socialized to believe that domestic work is not masculine (Rensenbrink, 2001).

Not only does the masculine stereotype limit the freedom of men to engage in any activity or occupation they choose, but it also limits their personal relationships. Many men believe that they cannot discuss their feelings with other men. Instead, they tend to be extremely competitive. They also feel compelled to try to dominate women instead of relating to them as equals (Benokraitis & Feagin, 1986; Gould, 1974; Kimmel, Hearn, & Connell, 2005).

Sexism and Employment

Sexism is perhaps most evident in the employment status of women. Women are concentrated in lower-status jobs at the low end of the pay scale. The vast majority of retail clerks, typists, and secretaries are women, whereas men account for the largest proportions of corporate directors, white-collar administrators, and blue-collar supervisors. It could be claimed that these differences are due to differences in educational attainment. However, this is not the case. For the past several decades men and women have received the same amount of schooling. Although men hold more bachelor's and graduate degrees than women do, more men than women drop out of high school, so the average educational attainment is the same in each group (England, 2000; England, Herbert, & Kilbourne, 1994).

Unequal Pay for Equal Work. The difference between wages paid to male and female occupations is often referred to as the gender wage gap. Table 8–3 indicates that even in occupations in which women are the large majority of workers—such as housecleaners, nurses, or clerical workers—men in these occupations earn more, as measured by average weekly earnings for full-time workers and by the earnings ratio, which divides women's earnings by those of men. The differences are particularly striking in such occupations as physicians or lawyers and judges, which require years of professional education and experience yet still show wide gaps in earnings.

This type of pay inequity, as well as unequal access to certain jobs, has given rise to debates over "comparable worth"—the idea that the pay levels of certain jobs should be adjusted to reflect the intrinsic value of the job; holders of jobs of comparable value would then be paid at comparable rates. This concept is discussed in more detail in the Social Policy section of the chapter.

Wage and job discrimination are illegal under the Equal Pay Act of 1963 and the Civil Rights Act of 1964, yet they continue to exist. About 3,000 charges of sex discrimination are filed with the Equal Employment Opportunity Commission each year. In a major recent sex discrimination settlement, more than 5,000 women who formerly worked for the Rent-A-Center Corporation of Plano, Texas, the nation's largest rent-to-own

TABLE 8–3	The Gender Wage Gap in Selected Occupations with Estimated Earnings of Under $20,000

Occupation	Percent Women	Men's Wages	Women's Wages	Earnings Gap	Earnings Ratio (%)
Waiter/waitress	69	$346	$301	$45	87
Cleaning & building service occupations	40	382	307	75	80
Cashiers	76	313	276	37	88
Food preparation and service	50	325	294	31	90
Maids and housemen	80	348	297	51	85

Occupations with Estimated Earnings Between $20,000 and $34,000

Occupation	Percent Women	Men's Wages	Women's Wages	Earnings Gap	Earnings Ratio (%)
Bus driver	45	$506	$401	$105	79
Sales worker; retail & personal	56	470	301	169	64
Mechanics & repairers	5	649	627	22	97
Construction trades	2	599	475	124	79
Truck drivers	4	573	407	166	71

Occupations with Estimated Earnings Above $34,000

Occupation	Percent Women	Men's Wages	Women's Wages	Earnings Gap	Earnings Ratio (%)
Accountants & auditors	60	$953	$690	$263	72
Securities & financial services sales	33	1,118	641	477	57
Physicians	31	1,553	899	654	58
Teachers, college & univ.	38	1,020	805	215	79
Lawyers & judges	29	1,448	1,054	394	73
Economists	48	1,148	785	363	68

Other Occupations in Which the Majority of Workers Are Women

Occupation	Percent Women	Men's Wages	Women's Wages	Earnings Gap	Earnings Ratio (%)
Registered nurse	91	$890	$782	$108	88
Social worker	71	637	589	48	92
Admin. support, including clerical	77	563	449	114	80
Teachers, except college and universities	74	827	673	154	81

Source: Data from Bureau of Labor Statistics, 2005.

company, were awarded a total of $47 million in damages. Over many years the company had systematically promoted men instead of women, and the women, finding themselves in dead-end jobs, typically left the company and found new jobs with different employers. After a suit was filed with the federal Equal Employment Commission, the company eventually settled with the plaintiffs. Unfortunately, however, hundreds of such claims are pending before the commission, and many others have never been filed because of fear or lack of knowledge on the part of those women who have been discriminated against. But large awards such as this at least serve to remind large employers that such discrimination is illegal.

TABLE 8–4	Earnings of Full-Time Female Managers for Each Dollar Earned by Males		
Sector	1995	2000	Change
Entertainment and recreation	83 cents	62 cents	−21 cents
Communications	86	73	−13
Finance, insurance, and real estate	76	68	−8
Business services and repairs	82	76	−6
Other professional services	88	83	−5
Retail trade	69	65	−4
Professional medical services	90	88	−2
Public administration	80	83	+3
Hospital and medical services	80	85	+5
Education	86	91	+5

Source: "Earnings of Full-Time Female Managers for Each Dollar Earned by Males," from *How to Shrink the Pay Gap* by T. Gutner, *Business Week.* Copyright © 2002 The McGraw-Hill Companies. Reprinted by permission of *Business Week.*

Despite occasional victories like the one just described, there is a significant earnings gap between men and women in the American labor force. This is evident in Table 8–4, which is taken from a federal General Accounting Office study released in 2002. The table shows that between 1995 and 2000, while the economy was booming, women in managerial positions actually lost ground in comparison with men as the male–female pay gap widened in most economic sectors. It is difficult to know exactly why this gap widened, but the most likely hypothesis, advanced by employment experts such as Heidi Hartmann, president of the Institute for Women's Policy Research in Washington, is that during the 1980s the pay gap was narrowing, so political activists paid less attention to it. Moreover, the relative lack of women in top leadership positions in American corporations makes it unlikely that pay equity will be seen as a problem that those in power should deal with. According to Catalyst, a not-for-profit organization dedicated to advancing women in business, women hold only 11 percent of the board seats at Fortune 1000 companies (Shapiro Snyder, 2002).

For Minority Women, an Even Wider Wage Gap. African American and Latino women, the fastest growing demographic segment of the U.S. labor force, face the most severe consequences of unequal pay for equal work. Sixty percent of black working women, for example, are in clerical, sales, or service occupations, which pay lower wages than other sectors of the job market. Women's mean earnings for all occupations are about $500 per week, but for service occupations they are about $300. Figure 8–4 shows that the wage gap for black women is 10 percent wider than the gap for white women, while for Hispanic women it is a full 20 percent wider. Even among educated minority women, the wide gap persists. Among full-time year-round workers, black women with B.A. degrees make only about $1,500 more per year than white men with only a high school education.

Sexual Harassment

Among the most persistent and difficult aspects of sexism is sexual harassment. The tumultuous Senate hearings on the confirmation of Clarence Thomas as a Supreme Court justice focused national attention on the range of behaviors that may be viewed as forms of sexual harassment. The charges leveled against Thomas by Anita Hill, a

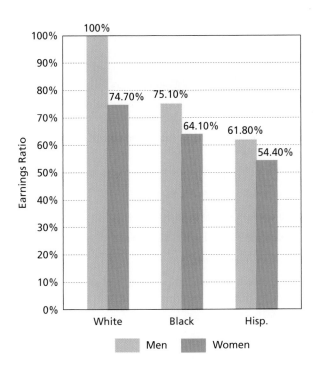

Figure 8–4 The Wage Gap, by Gender and Race/Hispanic Origin

Source: Data from Bureau of Labor Statistics.

former employee, included making lewd and suggestive comments, requesting sexual favors, and similar behaviors that are often labeled "flirtation" when they occur outside the workplace. Partly as a result of the Hill–Thomas controversy and partly as a consequence of women's continual struggle against harassment, people throughout the nation have been drawn into a national debate over its nature and significance.

The controversy has focused on serious forms of harassment, including date rape, as well as on behaviors that are viewed as annoying if not dangerous. In 1993, for example, the students and faculty of Antioch College in Ohio published a set of written rules that require verbal consent at every stage of sexual intimacy. Although the rules have been the subject of much satire and derision, they represent a model for dealing with a highly sensitive and often taboo subject.

Such episodes are bringing people closer to a consensus about the norms of conduct between men and women. An increasing number of Americans are recognizing that one person's joke or offhand comment can create another's hostile environment. In an attempt to provide a less subjective description of **sexual harassment,** the Michigan Task Force on Sexual Harassment developed the following definition:

> [Sexual harassment] includes continual or repeated verbal abuse of a sexual nature, including but not limited to graphic commentaries on the victim's body, sexually suggestive objects or postures in the workplace, sexually degrading words used to describe the victim, or propositions of a sexual nature. Sexual harassment also includes the threat or insinuation that lack of sexual submission will adversely affect the victim's employment, wages, standing, or other conditions that affect the victim's livelihood. (Stover & Gilles, 1987, p. 1)

Although sexual harassment has been a common feature of work and community life for well over a century, the problem came under public scrutiny only recently as a result of court decisions and government attempts to punish offenders. Many thousands of complaints of sexual harassment are filed each year in agencies at all levels of government; of these, less than 10 percent are filed by men (Richmond-Abbott, 1992). The formal complaints represent a small fraction of the incidents of harassment that occur in workplaces, schools, community associations, and public settings (Hippensteele & Pearson, 1999).

What can YOU do to help prevent sexual assault?

- Ask the management of restaurants and business to remove materials depicting women as sexual objects.
- Do not patronize restaurants that exclusively hire women based on physical characteristics.
- Discourage friends from eating at or doing business with such places as well.
- Report catcalling men at workplaces to the management.
- Pay attention to the words you use in reference to women.
- Pull friends and associates aside and correct them in their useage.
- Do not refer to women with dehumanizing words.
- Reflect on your own behavior and work on changing any sexist, controlling, or abusive behaviors of your own.
- Women—You need to respect each other and stick up for other women.
- Men—Ask women how they would like you to help prevent sexual assault.

Taking these kinds of steps demonstrates to others that a sexually charged atmosphere in the wrong context is damaging to men and women alike.

A CHALLENGE: Think of one more way that YOU can help prevent sexual assault, email it so that it can be listed here. Let me know if you want credit for your post or if you want it posted anonymously.

Ads like this one in a school newspaper encourage men and women to be more assertive in combating date rape and other forms of sexual assault.

Source: Reprinted by permission of rivervision.com.

Even rape, the most brutal form of violence against women short of murder, is significantly underreported, often because women fear the stigma of having been raped more than they desire justice. Data from the FBI show that in 2003 just over 93,000 rapes were reported to local police departments; of those incidents, just over 40,000 resulted in arrests. But victimization surveys reveal that an estimated 112,000 women were raped in 2003, and another 76,000 were subjected to unsuccessful rape attempts, for a combined total that is twice the number of reported rapes (Bureau of Justice Statistics, 2005; *UCR*, 2004).

Sexual harassment is also extremely common in schools and other educational institutions. A recent random sample survey of 2,064 public school students in the eighth through eleventh grades found the following:

- Eighty-three percent of girls and 79 percent of boys report having ever experienced harassment.
  - The number of boys reporting experiences with harassment often or occasionally has increased since 1993 (56% vs. 49%), although girls are still somewhat more likely to experience it.
  - For many students, sexual harassment is an ongoing experience: Over 1 in 4 students experience it "often."
  - These numbers do not differ by whether the school is urban, suburban, or rural.
- Seventy-six percent of students have experienced nonphysical harassment, while 58 percent have experienced physical harassment. Nonphysical harassment includes taunting, rumors, graffiti, jokes, or gestures. One-third of all students report experiencing physical harassment "often or occasionally."
- There has been a sea change in awareness of school policies about harassment since 1993. Seven in 10 students (69%) say that their school has a policy on sexual harassment, compared to only 26 percent of students in 1993.
- Nearly all students (96%) say they know what harassment is, and boys' and girls' definitions do not differ substantially.

Despite these positive changes, the majority of students say they fear sexual harassment in any form, and if this survey adequately represents the school population of the United States, they have reason on their side. The report warns that too many parents and teachers still believe sexual teasing, taunts of "faggot" or "slut," are normal aspects of adolescence. But when such behavior is accepted or not sanctioned in some way, it makes it more likely that sexual harassment in the person's adult life will also go unreported and unsanctioned (American Association of University Women, 2001).

Homemaking

In a review of research on changing sex roles and housework, sociologist Janet Z. Giele (1988) observes that women continue to bear the primary responsibility for child care and housework even if they are employed. Men with working wives have begun to take on a greater share of this burden, but inequalities remain. Time budget studies show that when one measures solo time spent with children, fathers average 4.5 hours a week and mothers 19.6 hours; however, men with working wives who themselves support nontraditional sex roles spend significantly more time with their children than do men who lack such ideals. Researchers have also noted that wealth permits working couples to displace housework and child-care responsibilities onto hired domestic helpers, which may ease their burden but also increases inequalities of race and class in their communities.

Elsewhere in the world, especially in Asia, Africa, and many parts of Latin America, homemaking remains a predominant concern of women. Indeed, although they may be involved in producing or selling goods and services, third-world women are also responsible for much of the work that sustains life in rural villages and small towns. In consequence, experts often point to the need for literacy programs and reproductive and public health instruction as vital to the future of women's efforts to become fully empowered citizens of their nations (Mbere, 1996).

We have seen in this chapter that women and men in the same occupations are often paid unequally. How may sexism help explain these differences?

SOURCES OF SEXISM

We have described some of the causes of the subordination of women from a historical viewpoint and indicated some of the major inequities that women face in our society. In this section we discuss in some detail the processes by which American institutions reinforce and perpetuate sexism.

Socialization

In her book *The Second Sex,* the famous French philosopher and sociologist Simone de Beauvoir (1972) described how, as children, women are often socialized for roles in which they are not expected to compete with men in any way. Often, she observed, women are discouraged from studying more challenging subjects like mathematics, science, and philosophy. Instead, they are expected to learn the domestic skills of cooking and running a household, and the emotional skills of soothing children's and men's bruised feelings. These observations signal the immense importance of sex-role socialization in forming our attitudes and behavior as men and women.

Socialization is the process whereby we learn to behave according to the norms of our culture. It includes all the formal and informal teaching that occurs in the home and in the school; among peers; and through agents of socialization like radio, television, the church, and other institutions (Kornblum, 2008). Through socialization people internalize to varying degrees the roles, norms, and values of their culture and subculture, which become their guides to behavior and shape their deepest beliefs.

Most socialization takes place in the course of interaction with other people; how others react to what we do will eventually influence how we behave. We are also socialized through popular culture—largely through television, films, and books. Socialization may be consciously imposed, as in compulsory education, or it may be subtle and unconscious, conveyed in the nuances of language. According to Eleanor Maccoby and Carol

Jacklin (1977), common myths about sex differences, such as "girls are more suggestible than boys" and "boys are more analytical than girls," reinforce sex-role socialization.

In her review of research on gender socialization in families, Marie Richmond-Abbott (1992) notes,

> As infants become toddlers, parental interaction with them continues to be sex-differentiated. In certain studies, both parents emphasized achievement for boys and urged them to control their emotions. Both parents characterized their relationship to their daughters as having more warmth and physical closeness. They believed the daughters were more truthful and showed a reluctance to punish them. They discouraged rough-and-tumble play for girls and doll play for boys. They were more likely to let boys be independent. (p. 69)

Some research emphasizes the importance of peer socialization in schools and neighborhoods. Barrie Thorne (1994), for example, spent many hours watching children and adolescents interacting in school classrooms and play yards. She notes that whereas adolescent girls usually dream of love and intimacy, "the heterosexual marketplace all too often involves exploitation. Active efforts to get and keep a boyfriend lead many young women to lower their ambitions, and the culture of romance perpetuates male privilege" (p. 170).

Education

Education represents a more formal type of socialization. Considering how much time children spend in school, the socialization they receive there inevitably affects how they behave. Several studies have indicated that, by and large, schools reinforce traditional sex-role stereotypes and socialize children into traditional sex roles.

In recent years much emphasis has been placed on ridding the schools of bias against female achievement and increasing gender equality. Greater emphasis on girls' sports and on more equal participation in the school's political activities and newspapers, for example, attests to increased concern for sex-role equality. But some major problems remain. For example, women continue to achieve less well than men in math and science, and far fewer women than men are recruited into the ranks of

In 2006, Nancy Pelosi, a member of Congress from San Francisco, became the first woman to be elected Speaker of the House of Representatives. Pelosi waited until her children were old enough to care for themselves before considering her first run for Congress.

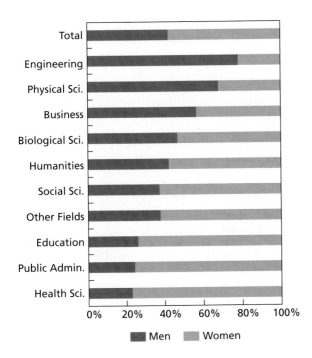

Figure 8–5 Graduate
Enrollment, by Gender: Fall 2005

Source: Council of Graduate Schools, 2006.
"Graduate Enrollement and Degrees:
1986–2005."

engineers and scientists. Figures 8–5 and 8–6 confirm these facts. Note that since 1960 the numbers of women receiving degrees in law and medicine, academic Ph.D.s, and even business have risen dramatically. Engineering degrees have increased at a far slower rate, and women now account for only about 20 percent of engineering degrees in the United States. Although Figure 8–6 shows that the professional gender gap will narrow in coming years, the data still raise questions about why women lag behind men in engineering and related technical fields.

A study by the American Association of University Women (cited in Richmond-Abbott, 1992) found that girls and boys start school with similar levels of skill and

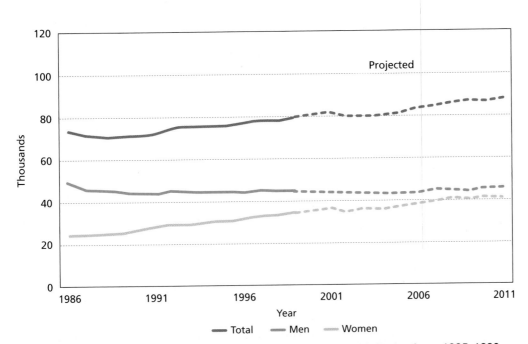

Figure 8–6 First Professional Degrees, by Sex of Recipient, with Projections: 1985–1986
to 2010–2011

Source: National Center for Education. U.S. Dept. of Education.

confidence, but that by the end of high school, girls trail boys in science and math. After reviewing more than 100 articles and reports of research conducted during the past ten years, the authors reached several conclusions:

Teachers pay less attention to girls than to boys.

Girls lag in math and science scores, and even those who do well in these subjects tend not to choose careers in math and science.

Reports of sexual harassment of girls are increasing.

Textbooks still ignore or stereotype women and girls, and omit discussion of pressing problems such as sexual abuse.

Some tests are biased against females and thereby limit their chances of obtaining scholarships.

Black girls are particularly likely to be ignored or rebuffed in schools.

Clearly, continued efforts are needed to address these inequalities of socialization if more women are to be attracted to the sciences.

An especially insidious form of sex segregation occurs during career counseling, which often channels young people into careers on the basis of sex rather than ability. Counselors frequently advocate traditionally female occupations for young women who are qualified and eager to enter so-called "male preserves." A girl who is a good math student may be told to go into teaching; a boy with equal skills may be directed toward engineering. However, more recent research indicates that there have been quite positive changes in adolescent girls' attitudes about what they can achieve and that young women are more aware of opportunities in formerly male-dominated fields like law enforcement and business (Fox, 2005; Richmond-Abbott, 1992).

What are some of the reasons that women are underrepresented in American scientific and engineering institutions?

The Family

Although many women report great satisfaction as mothers and homemakers, this traditional role often gives a woman a subordinate status within the home, limits her freedom, and leaves her feeling unfulfilled (Susser & Patterson, 2001). Some researchers argue that more feminist researchers distort the extent to which women are dissatisfied with their homemaking roles. They believe many women would appreciate the opportunity to devote more time to mothering and homemaking. Although this perception is surely true for a certain proportion of women with children, it does not apply to the growing number of women who are single parents, who must work to survive. And Heidi Hartmann (1994) of the Institute for Women's Policy Research points to the following data from the Bureau of Labor Statistics:

While the number of women who collect any kind of paycheck has nearly doubled, climbing to 57 million over the past 20 years, the number of women working at two or more jobs has quintupled, soaring from less than 650,000 to over 3 million. Similarly, the number of women working in their own businesses has nearly tripled, rising from 1.38 million to over 4 million; more than a third of those holding multiple jobs worked in their own businesses. (p. 16)

As a result of these changes, more and more women are facing the challenge of balancing work and family roles.

Even in many nontraditional marriages in which there is a great degree of equality between husband and wife, the husband often has a more privileged position. One study found that even when both members of a couple are professionals, the woman is often forced into a somewhat subordinate position because it is assumed that the man's career is more important or more likely to be successful than the woman's. As a result, wives in professional pairs are less likely than their husbands to be satisfied with their careers (Crittenden, 1999).

Language and the Media

The language used in the media (and in textbooks) often reinforces traditional sex-role stereotypes through overreliance on male terms and a tendency to use stereotypic phrases in describing men and women. The use of male pronouns in referring to neutral subjects—"The typical doctor enjoys his leisure"—also implies that women are excluded from an active social life.

Whereas sexism in everyday language is subtle and unconscious, in advertising it is often blatant. According to sociologist Barbara Ehrenreich (1992), the importance of sexist themes in advertising and the way in which advertisements capitalize on women's anxieties about their appearance are revealed by the fact that over the past 30 years 1.6 million women have undergone breast enlargement operations, often with dubious medical results.

Typically, far fewer women than men are portrayed in the media as employed, although more than half of all women work outside the home. Few women are shown in executive positions; instead, they play largely decorative roles. Moreover, the vast majority of buying decisions are portrayed as being made by men, particularly decisions involving major purchases like cars. Recent advertising campaigns have sought to attract the growing population of female executives by presenting successful business-women and female scientists to endorse products. But the patterns of sexism in advertising remain strong: Sex appeal and sexual stereotypes are still used to sell many products.

Organized Religion

Women attend church more frequently, pray more often, hold firmer beliefs, and cooperate more in church programs than men do; yet organized religion is dominated by men (Giroux, 2005; Mills, 1972). In their theological doctrines and religious hierarchies, churches and synagogues tend to reinforce women's subordinate role. Explicit instructions to do so can be found in the Bible: "A woman must be a learner, listening quietly and with due submission. I do not permit a woman to be a teacher, nor must

Here is an example of a sexist advertising strategy often used to get men to notice a new car model.

woman domineer over man; she should be quiet. For Adam was created first, and Eve afterwards; and it was not Adam who was deceived; it was woman who, yielding to deception, fell into sin" (Timothy 2:11–15).

Historically, organized religion has reinforced many secular traditions and norms, including the traditional view that men are primary and women secondary, and that a woman's most important role is procreation. In Judaism, women are required to obey fewer religious precepts than are men because less is expected of them. Orthodox Jewish males recite a prayer each morning in which they thank God that they are not women. The Catholic Church still assumes authority over a woman's sexual behavior, forbidding the use of birth control devices because they prevent reproduction.

Most churches bar women from performing the most sacred rituals or attaining the highest administrative posts. The consequences of this practice have been summed up as follows:

> As long as qualified persons are excluded from any ministry by reason of their sex alone, it cannot be said that there is genuine equality of men and women in the church. . . . By this exclusion the church is saying that the sexual differentiation is—for one sex—a crippling defect which no personal qualities of intelligence, character, or leadership can overcome. In fact, by this policy it is effectively teaching that women are not fully human and conditioning people to accept this as unchangeable fact. (Daly, 1970, p. 134)

In recent decades there have been some changes. The movement to allow women to hold leadership positions in churches and synagogues has had some success: In more liberal denominations (e.g., Episcopalians, Presbyterians, and Reformed Jews), women may be ordained as ministers and rabbis. Within the Catholic church there are groups of women devoted to changing the norm against female priests, but they encounter severe resistance from traditionalists in the Catholic hierarchy (Ecklund, 2003).

Government

The federal government has a long history of discrimination against women. A 1919 study by the Women's Bureau (a federal bureau created by Congress) found that women were barred from applying for 60 percent of all civil-service positions, notably those involving scientific or other professional work. Women were placed in a separate employment category, and their salaries were limited. The professionals in the Women's Bureau, for example, were required under an act of Congress to receive half the salaries received by men for doing the same work in other federal agencies.

Although discrimination against women has received less overt support from the government in recent years, patterns of discrimination still exist at all levels of government. In state and local governments, for example, women face a "glass ceiling" that causes them to be underrepresented in high-level jobs and concentrated in lower-level, nonexecutive positions. The 1964 Civil Rights Act, which prohibited discrimination on the basis of sex, specifically excluded federal, state, and local governments from its provisions. Thus, women who work for the government are concentrated in clerical or service-type jobs, whereas most administrative posts are held by men (Nussbaum, 1999).

The Legal System

There are many legal barriers to sexual equality. For example, many state labor laws passed during the late nineteenth and early twentieth centuries set work standards designed to protect all workers; they established the maximum hours people could be required to work, the maximum weights they could be required to lift, and so on. The Supreme Court found, however, that such restrictions were unconstitutional in the case of male workers because they violated constitutional liberties. Women, on the other hand, could still be subject to these restrictions. In its decision in *Lochner* v. *New*

Susan Wood, the director of the FDA's Office of Women's Health, resigned in 2005 in protest over the agency's decision to keep the morning-after pill, called Plan B, off pharmacy shelves for the foreseeable future. The drug, which is essentially a double dose of the common birth control pill, lowers the risk of pregnancy by 89 percent and had won the approval of scientists.

York (1908), which upheld a state law limiting the number of hours women factory workers could work, the Court stated,

> History discloses the fact that woman has always been dependent on man. He has established his control at the outset by superior physical strength, and this control in various forms, with diminishing intensity, has continued to the present. . . . Differentiated by these matters from the other sex, [woman] is properly placed in a class by herself, and legislation designed for her protection may be sustained, even when like legislation is not necessary for men, and could not be sustained.

This decision in effect legalized and perpetuated state laws that differentiated between men and women. As late as 1965, the Equal Employment Opportunity Commission stated that state laws designed to protect women were not discriminatory.

A related issue is sexual harassment on the job. As noted earlier in the chapter, this harassment is widespread and usually intentional. It includes touching and staring at a woman's body, requesting sexual intercourse, and sometimes actual rape. Verbal abuse and derogatory language are common. Although there are legal prohibitions against sexual harassment in the workplace, laws of this type are hard to enforce because it is often difficult to define a particular incident as sexual harassment. Another serious problem with existing laws is that a woman who files a complaint may have to endure years of procedures and hearings before she can win a chance at redress (Kaminer, 1999).

The problem of legal differentiation between men and women exists in other areas as well. Some state educational institutions are permitted to exclude women, either from their student bodies or from their faculties. Many technical high schools admit only boys; many high schools prohibit pregnant or married girls from attending but admit unmarried fathers or married boys.

Credit for low-income women is another area in which past patterns of discrimination have led to strange and unintended social change. The Equal Credit Opportunity Act, passed in 1974, makes it illegal to discriminate against women in many types of credit transactions. As a result, it is now somewhat easier for women to qualify for home loans as single parents or widows. At the same time, the laws have made it possible for credit card companies to flood the market with easy credit, even for very poor Americans, many of whom are single mothers. Between 1983 and 1995 the percentage of all U.S. families holding a credit card rose from 65 percent to over 77 percent, and the average monthly balance in constant dollars rose from $751 to $1,852. In the mid-1990s about 36 percent of poor families had credit cards, with an average monthly balance of $1,380. In essence, in the United States the problem is not lack of credit, but the dangers of too easy access and the temptation to run up unmanageable bills as part of the struggle to make ends meet (Grow & Epstein, 2007).

On a global scale, however, lack of access to credit remains a major challenge for women and social policymakers. A pioneer in this regard is Dr. Muhammad Yunus, winner of the 2006 Nobel Peace Prize and founder of the Grameen (meaning "rural") Bank in Bangladesh. This bank lends small amounts of money to women who wish to start businesses or build new homes. It began when Yunus found himself surrounded by begging women, to whom he loaned $30 rather than giving the money away. He then began working with women to establish a rotating credit fund. Eventually, his activities became the Grameen Bank, which now has more than 1,000 branches in 34,000 villages and makes loans totaling about $369 million a year, with repayment rates higher than those of commercial banks in the United States (Munti, 2007).

Why were so many of the people who suffered the worst effects of Hurricane Katrina women, especially women of color?

SOURCES OF HOMOPHOBIA

Hostility, violence, or discrimination directed at people because they are, or are suspected of being, gay or lesbian, is known as **homophobia** (Fone, 2000). Gregory M. Herek, who has conducted extensive research on homophobia, finds that hostility toward gays is a common aspect of the male gender identity in the United States and elsewhere, and that it begins to be expressed at an early age. Heterosexual masculine identity, with its emphasis on physical violence and power, seems to be enhanced by expressing hostility toward gay people—that is, by expressing or asserting who one is not and thereby affirming who one is (Herek, 2002).

Sociologist Nancy Chodorow (1999) points out that homophobia is often associated with distorted notions of masculinity and can result in "gay bashing" and even murder. But in discussing the term *homophobia* itself, Chodorow says,

> Phobias imply fear and avoidance, but homophobia is really a counterphobia, which, in its extremes, leads to attacks and seekings out, and which is constituted by virulent hatred that I think we can only understand in terms of primitive splitting and projection—more like ethnic hatred of those who are so threateningly like someone that all likeness has to be denied and difference exaggerated.

The Matthew Shepard case, she notes, is a tragic example of extreme homophobia in action. Shepard's attackers had to represent him as someone who was about to attack them sexually. "I do not want to minimize the anti-homosexual prejudice against women or the fear of lesbians and lesbian sex," Chorodow continues, "because to do so, to put all the emphasis on male norms of masculinity, actually risks contributing to a prejudiced and one-sided view of homophobia" (Chodorow, 1999).

In recent years there has been a decrease in homophobia, at least as measured by opinion surveys. The General Social Survey conducted by the National Opinion Research Center, for example, asks a random sample of Americans whether admitted homosexuals should be allowed to speak in schools or universities. Over time, there has been a decrease in the percentage who would bar gays and lesbians from teaching in public schools, but a significant percentage, about 33 percent, would continue to deny them this right because of their sexual orientation. The same survey shows a trend toward greater acceptance of adult same-sex relations, but a majority, albeit a

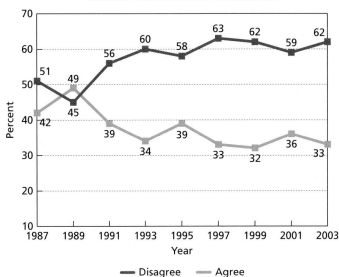

School boards ought to have the right to fire teachers who are known homosexuals

Figure 8–7 Percentage of Americans Who Agree or Disagree That Gays Should Be Barred from Teaching in Public Schools

Source: Times Mirror Center/Pew Research Center.

decreasing one, of Americans still feel that adult same-sex relations are always wrong. (See Figure 8–7.)

Tolerance for alternative sexual lifestyles, including homosexuality, is growing; however, the number of extremely hostile homophobic people remains sizable. Although they may not approve of homosexual relationships, there is also evidence that a growing majority of Americans concede that the homosexual lifestyle must be tolerated. Gallup Poll results indicate that by the turn of the present century, a majority (52 percent) regard homosexuality as an acceptable lifestyle, compared to 44 percent who consider it unacceptable (Herek, 2002).

The positive trend in public opinion regarding homosexuality, like the changes in attitudes toward equal rights for women, is a result of years of political organizing. Gay activists and their allies continue to confront homophobia and develop campaigns to assert the legitimacy of gay and lesbian lifestyles. But these campaigns also result in political backlash and homophobia in the more conservative and antigay communities of the United States. In her study of confrontations between gay activists and liberal supporters, and antigay, conservative activists in a small city in Oregon, sociologist Arlene Stein shows that eventually, after the strident political campaigns and local referendums are over, there will be a growing realization that "people are not going to change so easily and that they need to live together, and from this comes a much-needed effort to at least sit down face-to-face and begin to come to terms with strangers" (Stein, 2001, p. 228).

Explain what is meant by homophobia. Have you ever encountered homophobia? What, in your opinion, can be done to counter homophobia?

Social Policy

The Women's Movement

The women's movement in the United States was officially founded in 1848, when a women's rights convention held in Seneca, New York, was attended by 300 women and men, many of whom, like Elizabeth Cady Stanton and Lucretia Mott, were active in the abolitionist movement. The Seneca convention endorsed a platform that called for the right of women to vote, to control their own property, and to obtain custody of their children after divorce. After women won the right to vote in the 1920s, the women's movement receded from public consciousness until the 1960s, a decade characterized by considerable activism and numerous social movements (Banaszak, 2006).

The resurgence of the movement in the 1960s occurred in a context of widespread social change. In 1963, the year in which Friedan's *The Feminine Mystique* appeared, the President's Commission on the Status of Women published its recommendations for equal opportunity in employment. In 1964 Congress passed the Civil Rights Act, which included a provision (Title VII) that made it illegal to discriminate against women in promotion and hiring. But the Equal Employment Opportunity Commission (EEOC), established to enforce Title VII, was unwilling to serve as a watchdog for women's rights. As a result, in 1966 a pressure group, the National Organization for Women (NOW), was founded. Its stated purpose was "to take action to bring women into full participation in the mainstream of American society *now*, exercising all the privileges and responsibilities thereof in truly equal partnership with men."

Attitudes about gender roles have undergone a major transformation since the resurgence of the women's movement. Although, as we have seen, significant inequalities and double standards continue to exist, they are far less sharply defined than they were in earlier decades. However, in the late 1970s and early 1980s the women's movement encountered increasing opposition, and its momentum slowed. The Equal Rights Amendment failed to obtain ratification by the required number of states. Opposition to more liberal abortion laws was well organized and vocal, and the movement faced severe challenges in several other areas. Nevertheless, reproductive choice remained a dominant theme of the movement, one that could unite women with diverse interests; this was evident in the massive 1988 free-choice rally in Washington, D.C., which drew more than 500,000 marchers. With the election of President Clinton in 1992, the movement gained greater influence in Washington, and women voters played an important part in Clinton's reelection in 1996.

On a global level, what Jessie Bernard (1987) refers to as the "feminist enlightenment" has made significant progress in recent years. Women throughout the world have benefited in many ways, ranging from improved health and education to expanded economic and political opportunities. Much of this progress can be attributed to the role of the United Nations as a platform for women's issues. Throughout the late 1970s and the 1980s, women became increasingly skilled at using the United Nations' information and communication systems effectively. These efforts continue to build momentum throughout the developing world (Susser & Patterson, 2001).

Changes in Child-Rearing Practices

Perhaps the greatest obstacle to equality of the sexes is the "motherhood ethic"—the idea that women are most fulfilled as mothers and that children, particularly young children, require a mother's constant attention if they are to grow up healthy and well adjusted.

It is evident that children need loving, consistent care and attention and the chance to build a relationship with one or two caring adults who are present on a regular basis. However, there is no evidence that those adults must be female. In fact, the absence of male figures can be harmful to a growing and developing child (Bronfenbrenner, 1981). Many social scientists have found that an important prerequisite for full sexual equality is for fathers to share equally in the process of child rearing (and homemaking in general). This does not mean that all fathers or all mothers must do exactly half the work involved in raising children and keeping house. But political activists who organize efforts to reduce gender-based discrimination argue that society should encourage men to contribute as much to family life as women do.

Several steps could be taken to make it easier for men and women to share domestic tasks. For example, parental leaves could enable men or women who want to take some time to raise a child to do so without losing their jobs. Another approach is to upgrade the importance of part-time work by institutionalizing many of the benefits of full-time work, such as unemployment insurance and seniority. This would make it easier for men and women to share the responsibilities of supporting the family and taking care of the home and children.

In 1990 Congress passed a family and medical leave act that would have guaranteed unpaid leave with job security to men and women in firms with fifty or more employees. President George H. W. Bush vetoed this legislation. However, during his first campaign for the presidency, Bill Clinton made family leave one of his key campaign promises. As soon as he was elected, Congress again passed the Family Leave Act, and Clinton signed the legislation. During the administration of George W. Bush, there have been no significant improvements in family leave policy or in the provision of child care to lower-income families, but with the Democratic takeover of Congress in 2006 these issues are again high on the congressional policy agenda.

Changes in the Educational System

To eliminate sexism in education, teachers and school administrators must become more sensitive to their own stereotypes about boys and girls (or men and women) and treat members of both sexes equally—for example, by paying equal attention to male and female students and not assigning tasks according to traditional sex-role stereotypes. One way to counteract the idea that only women take care of children is to attract more male teachers for the lower grades. Another is to eliminate traditional occupational and role stereotypes from the standard curriculum. Thus, in opposing the nomination of John Roberts as Chief Justice of the Supreme Court, Eleanor Smeal, a national spokesperson for women's rights, wrote:

> As the Gulf Coast and New Orleans tragedy reveals, our nation still has a deep race and class divide. We must have a federal judiciary that will not unravel the legal gains and guarantees decades of civil rights and women's rights struggles have produced. We again call on President Bush to choose a moderate woman jurist to fill Sandra Day O'Connor's historic seat. (Smeal, 2005)

During the 1980s, progress toward greater equality in education slowed. In 1984, for example, the Supreme Court ruled in *Grove City College* v. *Bell* that legislation prohibiting sex discrimination in education applied only to programs receiving federal aid, not to entire institutions. This ruling allowed colleges to bar women from certain courses or to deny them equal athletic opportunities with men. The *Grove City* decision was reversed by an act of Congress in March 1988. Schools and other institutions that accept federal funds are required to end discrimination in all of their programs and activities.

As noted in the preceding chapter, laws that challenge or eliminate affirmative action for minorities and women have been passed in California, Florida, Washington State, and elsewhere in the United States since the mid-1990s. At this writing, however, it is by no means clear how far-reaching this retreat from the goals of affirmative action will be. Many educators are especially concerned about the impact on the entry of women into science programs. In recent years there have been some vigorous efforts to recruit women and minorities into such programs, but these efforts are threatened by the retreat from affirmative action (Barinaga, 1996; Steinberg, 1996). During the 2004 presidential election campaign, moderates in both major parties warned that full-scale retreat from affirmative action would be a major blow to the goal of an inclusive society. Thus, affirmative action, like abortion, remains one of the most divisive political issues in the United States.

From a global perspective, women are by far more impoverished than men, and about 500,000 women living in poverty die during childbirth each year. Effective investment in education for women therefore is the single most important way to improve the social and economic conditions not only of women but of children as well. With more education comes the ability to make better health decisions, especially in the vital area of reproductive health. And education is a key to the eventual political empowerment of women (Patanjali, 2005).

Changes in the Legal System

Many laws and statutes discriminate against women. Some states, for example, still require that women be given longer sentences than men for the same crimes, on the assumption that female criminals require more rehabilitation; conversely, many states treat women offenders more leniently than men, on the assumption that women require the state's protection. In Alabama, women were excluded from jury duty until 1966, when a federal court ruled that this practice was unconstitutional. However, the Supreme Court has upheld the right of states to keep women from being automatically selected for jury duty: In many states women must volunteer or they will not be called.

Title VII of the Civil Rights Act of 1964 forbids discrimination on the basis of sex. However, as we have seen, wage and job discrimination against women remains widespread. Complicated rules for filing discrimination complaints, a huge backlog of cases, lack of enthusiasm in enforcing the act, and loopholes in the act itself have all reduced its effectiveness. Despite these obstacles, in 1988 women in California won a major victory against sex discrimination in employment. In a multimillion-dollar settlement, the State Farm Insurance Company agreed to pay damages and back pay to thousands of women who had been refused jobs as insurance sales agents over a thirteen-year period. The women had been told that a college degree was required for sales agents, even though men who lacked a degree were hired.

One area in which some progress has been made toward greater equality is known as **comparable worth.** The concept of "equal pay for comparable work," rather than "equal pay for equal work," has won some support in recent years. This concept holds that the intrinsic value of different jobs can be measured and that jobs found to be of comparable value should receive comparable pay. It is intended to correct the imbalance in earnings caused by the fact that many women hold jobs in relatively low-paying fields. Comparable worth received a major boost in 1983 when a federal judge ordered Washington State to raise the wages of thousands of women employees. Although the decision was appealed, it drew national attention to the fact that jobs held mainly by women are paid at rates that average 20 percent below those for equivalent jobs held mainly by men (Nagypal, 2004).

Critics of the comparable-worth concept claim that there is no such thing as an intrinsic value of any job. A job is "worth" what a person is paid for doing it. Discrimination may or may not be present, but many other factors go into determining the wages of all workers. Moreover, comparable worth could turn out to be very costly; in the Washington State case, which was eventually settled out of court, the state increased the salaries of 35,000 employees, at a total cost of $482 million. By 1990 the average salary for all jobs in Washington State had increased by 20 percent from the 1986 level as salaries were adjusted to ensure comparable worth. The gap in wages between men and women had been reduced from 20 percent to 5 percent (Hartmann, 1995a; Kilborn, 1990). As we have seen in this chapter, however, there remains a substantial gap overall between men's and women's wages in some occupations, and women's wages lag behind men's in all occupations (Gutner, 2002). Federal pay equity legislation, which began to make its way through Congress at the end of the Clinton administration, stalled after the Republican victories in 2000 and 2002, and it is unlikely that there will be renewed action on this issue in the foreseeable future (Kessler-Hams, 2002).

Reproductive Control

Abortion is probably the single most controversial social and political issue in the United States. Reproductive rights are controversial in many other parts of the world as well, although the specific cultural practices and behaviors involved may differ. In France, for example, authorities have approved the use of "morning after" contraceptives on an emergency basis for teenagers in schools, something that would be unheard of in the United States, where more conflicted attitudes about sexuality divide the population. In much of Europe, abortion is an issue, but not one that results in major political movements or violence against doctors, as it has in the United States.

Antiabortion laws were passed in the mid-nineteenth century, when "certain governments and religious groups desired continued population growth to fill growing industries and new farmable territories" (Sanford, McCord, & McGee, 1976, p. 217). Another reason given for the passage of these laws was to protect women against the danger of crude "backstreet" operations. Yet women continued to have abortions, legal or otherwise, and many deaths and injuries resulted. Those who could afford the services of expensive doctors stood a better chance of survival than did poorer women, who had to risk highly unsanitary and often degrading conditions.

In the mid-1950s agitation against the existing laws caused a few states to permit abortions under limited circumstances. Women could apply for abortions, but the decisions were made by doctors and hospitals. As a result of bureaucratic red tape and high costs, patients who could afford private physicians were able to benefit most from the reformed laws, while many poorer women continued to have few alternatives to illegal abortions.

In the 1990s the antiabortion movement suffered some setbacks because of the Clinton administration's strong support for pro-choice policies. In 1994, for example, the Supreme Court ruled that organizers of violent protests against abortion clinics may be prosecuted under federal racketeering laws. Nevertheless, the movement continues to pursue strategies whose effect is to make it more difficult for women to have abortions. Since the Court's landmark ruling in *Roe* v. *Wade* (1973), more than 1,000 bills dealing with abortion have been introduced in Congress, mostly designed by pro-life activists in the interest of curtailing access to abortion and other reproductive services. As a result of these and other activities of antiabortion groups, the "choice" to have an abortion is not always feasible for many women. For instance, 94 percent of nonmetropolitan U.S. counties have no abortion provider, and 86 percent of family planning clinics report regularly experiencing at least one form of harassment by protesters. It is no surprise that abortion remained a central concern of voters in the 2000 and 2002 elections. In 2002, before the election, the House passed a bill that would permit hospitals and clinics to refuse to perform abortions without any penalties such as loss of Medicaid or other public funds. The bill did not pass in the Senate, but with the Republican victories in the 2002 congressional elections, such legislation is likely to receive greater support (Carey & Goldreich, 2002).

In 2007 the Supreme Court ruled that certain forms of late-term abortion could be declared illegal, regardless of the danger to the woman's health if the pregnancy were continued. This decision reversed years of precedent holding that a woman's risk of death or severe health consequences was more important than the life of the fetus. A bitterly divided Court voted 5–4 in this historic case. In her dissenting opinion, Justice Ruth Bader Ginsburg said that the majority's opinion "cannot be understood as anything other than an effort to chip away a right declared again and again by this court, and with increasing comprehension of its centrality to women's lives" (quoted in Mears, 2007).

Related to reproductive control is the availability of sex education and contraception. Clearly, the need for abortion decreases as education and the availability of contraceptive devices increase. Many pregnancies among young women could be prevented by education about birth control. As former Surgeon General Joycelyn Elders pointed out in her 1993 confirmation hearings, sex education in the United States is vague or haphazard. Many poor women have less access than more affluent women to sex education and contraception.

A 1995 study by social scientists at the University of California found that half of the fathers of babies born to women between the ages of 15 and 17 were 20 or older. In other words, young women are often at risk of pregnancy not from peers but from older men, a problem that experts believe calls for stricter enforcement of statutory rape laws and far more attention to practical education about sexuality and birth control in low-income communities, where this problem is most severe (Steinhauer, 1995). However, both in the United States and in the programs it funds elsewhere in the world, the Bush administration has emphasized an "abstinence only" approach to sexuality among unmarried people and has barred sex education and anti-HIV education efforts that teach about condoms and other forms of birth control. These policies have drawn the bitter opposition of women's and gay advocacy groups while winning the approval of many conservative and fundamentalist religions organizations (Meckler, 2002).

Changes in Men's Roles

The issues of women's rights have often eclipsed the need for men to examine and change their own sex roles. Inspired by the successes of women, however, many men are exploring the roles that have also limited them in the past, and they are discovering a new freedom in moving toward sex-role egalitarianism. Although the shift in male attitudes appears mainly among educated men in their twenties and thirties (Kimmel & Messner, 1992), there is reason to believe that sex-role stereotyping among men of all ages is changing. The growing presence of women in the work force is leading to greater egalitarianism as women become breadwinners and men participate more freely in child rearing and housework. Progress in this direction is slow, however; even when they work outside the home, women still do most of the food shopping and cooking (Kimmel, Hearn, & Connell, 2005).

The opening up of fields that have traditionally been "male" or "female" to members of both sexes is likely to remain an important goal of the women's movement and civil-rights organizations throughout the United States. Labor shortages in some parts of the nation are also likely to encourage employers to actively recruit women for non-traditional occupations. Clearly, policy initiatives in the area of comparable worth and efforts to combat gender discrimination will continue to occupy legislators at every level of government, and there will surely be increased concern about how to fund these policies. An unintended consequence of the conflict between desired policies and the ability to make the actual changes is that women continue to shoulder more than their fair share of domestic responsibilities. (See the Unintended Consequences box on page 287.)

Gay Rights

The furor over extending civil rights to gay individuals and couples continues in many regions of the United States. The issue of gay rights took a significant turn when the Supreme Court ruled in *Romer* v. *Evans* that Colorado's constitutional amendment barring legislation that protects gays from discrimination was unconstitutional. But this decision does not represent a real gain for gay men and lesbians; it simply overturns a statute that barred such legislation. Discrimination in housing, jobs, and welfare benefits still exists.

The issues of same-sex marriage, gays in the military, and custody of children in same-sex households remain extremely controversial (Fineman, 1996). In North Carolina, for example, Fred Smith, who is gay, lost custody of his two sons because he was living with a male partner. The Defense of Marriage Act, which bars the federal government from recognizing same-sex unions, was passed by Congress and signed into law by President Clinton in 1996, largely because the majority of Americans continue to feel that same-sex marriages should not be condoned. However, a growing number of corporations, including Disney, Xerox, and IBM, now extend health insurance and other benefits to members of same-sex unions despite vociferous criticism from conservative organizations, and Vermont recently passed legislation granting same-sex couples all benefits given to heterosexual couples.

Unintended Consequences

GREATER EQUALITY INCREASES DOMESTIC BURDENS

"You know how in a new relationship you give and you give," said Marie Benedict, a 35-year-old hotel concierge from La Costa, California, who is in the midst of a divorce. "You try to be superwoman. I worked and I did everything. My husband did nothing."

National survey research shows that the situation is similar for the large majority of working women. Although the burden of trying to be a superwoman was not the main reason Benedict gave for the failure of her marriage, the stress and unfairness she felt certainly contributed to the couple's problems. The women's movement is dedicated to ending the double standard that specifies that women must bear the majority of domestic responsibilities even if they are full-time workers. In the past thirty years the movement has made a great deal of progress toward ending discriminatory policies that prevent women from entering occupations formerly reserved for men,

and it has made much progress in changing how women think of themselves—as people who can pursue a career and compete with men, for example—yet the traditional sex roles of domestic life are proving extremely difficult to change.

Recent polls have consistently found that although more women are in the work force and have less time at home, they are still the primary caregivers and meal planners in their households. Over 90 percent of women report that they do most or all of the cooking and kitchen cleanup. Among married couples, less than 20 percent of men report that they do most of the shopping. These studies show that more men are taking on household responsibilities, but the proportions who do so remain small (Robinson & Godbey, 1996).

The strength of the norm that requires women to take primary responsibility for the home can be seen in the case of Houston Oiler

David Williams. Williams missed an important game to be with his wife for the birth of their first child. "It was the most unbelievable thing that I've ever seen and I wouldn't have missed it for anything in the world," he said. Team officials threatened to discipline Williams for "wimping out," claiming that showing up for the game was equivalent to going to war. Eventually, however, they were forced to back down in the face of widespread public protest.

From the perspective of social policy, the persistence of the double standard is a fascinating unintended consequence of the women's movement and one difficult to resolve through further policies. Greater gender equality in the labor force without concomitant progress toward sharing domestic roles has increased the stress and fatigue felt by women. But since the problem lies at the level of the couple and the family, it does not lend itself to direct policy solutions.

Laws that try to control same-sex behavior have come under attack as violations of constitutional rights and attempts to legislate private morality. Those who support such laws usually argue that they are necessary to protect young boys from seduction. They believe that legalizing same-sex behavior will encourage more people to become gay. Against this view must be set the loss suffered by society when gays are legally or informally prevented from pursuing certain careers because of their sexual preference, together with the cost of the suffering imposed on them and their families by society's rejection.

The AIDS epidemic has raised the stakes in dealing with gay issues because it has revealed the need for open discussion of sexual practices among gays and heterosexuals alike (Rochman, 1999). In the opinion of many social scientists, the only effective way to limit the spread of AIDS is through public education aimed at reducing high-risk sex, that is, through campaigns that promote safe sex practices. This approach runs the risk of creating even more negative attitudes toward gays by publicizing their sexual activities and appearing to condemn them. Some communities and gay organizations have managed to publish guidelines for less risky sex without being either moralistic or judgmental. In contrast, governments at all levels have been unwilling to become involved in education about high-risk sex (Altman, 1987). Although public service announcements about safe sex and condom use are more visible and widespread each year, the United States continues to lag far behind other affluent and highly literate societies in its acceptance of sex education and explicit discussion of AIDS and related problems (Fenstermaker & West, 2002).

At this writing, the reaction to hate crimes like the murder of Matthew Shepard has caused some opponents of gay rights to express far more conciliatory views than in the past. The late Reverend Jerry Falwell, previously an outspoken opponent of gays and their civil liberties, met with gay activists and spoke in favor of stronger protection of gay rights. The fact remains, however, that most Christian fundamentalists continue to regard gays and lesbians as deviant sinners (Giroux, 2005).

Future Prospects

In coming years, the women's movement is likely to focus on single-parent families and, within this group, the special needs of low-income, female-headed families. With almost half of all marriages ending in divorce and about one-fourth of all households headed by single parents or unrelated individuals, it is certain that the politics of child care and aid to children will be at the forefront of feminist concerns (Andersen & Collins, 2004). There will also be greater emphasis on family and work policies, including pressure to extend family leave policies so that both men and women can take time off when a new baby comes. Will that leave be paid, as it is in so many European nations? Such a policy is unlikely to be approved in the United States, since, as with health care, employers rather than the state or federal governments would be expected to pay for it (Banaszak, 2006). Child care and early childhood education, on the other hand, are likely to be subject of significant new initiatives and funding, a reflection of the new, more women-friendly Congress.

Another area in which policy changes are likely is same-sex marriage. In 2007 the Massachusetts Legislature defeated a call for a statewide referendum on the issue. As a result, gay marriage remains legal in that state. Other liberal states, such as New Jersey and New York, where gay civil legal unions are legal, are considering legalizing same-sex-marriage. But in far more states the ban on gay marriages also extends to civil unions, so that gay and lesbian couples still face major obstacles in those states. President George W. Bush has repeatedly called for a constitutional amendment that would proclaim marriage to be a legal union between a man and a woman, and thereby ban same-sex marriages. In the 2006 congressional elections, voters in eleven states passed such bans.

GOING BEYOND LEFT AND RIGHT

It would be difficult to imagine an area of life in which there is more ideological and moral conflict in the United States than sexuality and gender. People on the ideological right believe strongly that it is wrong to have sex outside of marriage or engage in homosexual practices. Among people on the ideological left, there are perhaps more shadings of opinion, but the central attitude is one of tolerance: Sex of any kind between consenting adults is permissible.

As you become more sociologically informed, must you become tolerant of behaviors that you do not condone? If you have liberal views on these issues, can you simply ignore the feelings of those who oppose your views? The answer to both questions is no. As sociologically informed citizens, we can examine our own feelings and beliefs, set limits for ourselves, and seek to convince others through persuasion.

At the same time, we are learning that a society of people with diverse and strong opinions must still achieve social peace. Some compromises will be necessary. Look at our social policies to see how we arrive at compromises we can live with. For example, we are moving toward a society in which homosexual unions are granted more of the rights and benefits of heterosexual unions, but we do not seem ready to view gay marriage as legitimate. Our feelings about this issue will differ, but as sociologically informed people, we will understand why the situation exists.

Similarly, issues like abortion often divide a group into conservatives and liberals. There are no easy ways to resolve conflicts over sexual norms or over "the right to choose" abortion versus "the right to life." But in many areas of gender relations that seem highly conflicted, there is room to establish a common ground of reasoned social policy. Consider the storm over welfare reform, for example. Poor women throughout the nation are facing new work requirements. Often they will also face the problem of obtaining adequate child care. Conservatives have been loath to commit sufficient funds to pay for the new demands that will be placed on the already overburdened system of public day care. Liberals often fixate on government solutions to problems like this even though there may be alternatives in nongovernment institutions. A sociological approach must emphasize the need to look at child-care funding in the context of different communities. What resources are currently available in the public and private sectors? How can private and public funds be used to increase these resources? Thinking along these lines will avoid ideological battles and may produce some improvement in the availability of care for the nation's needy children.

It is notable in this regard that abortion, perhaps the most controversial of all the gender-related issues, may be played down as a central issue on both the left and the right, or at least among Republicans and Democrats. Democratic proponents of privacy and choice, such as Hillary Clinton, are seeking a middle ground, although neither she nor others like her would call for reversal of *Roe* v. *Wade*. On the Republican side, candidates like Rudolph Giuliani are outspoken in their disapproval of abortion on moral grounds yet also wish to protect women's individual rights, so they take a more moderate stand on abortion. Much will depend, however, on the actions of the Supreme Court and, above all, on who is elected President in 2008.

Summary

- Until fairly recently it was widely accepted that the only desirable roles for a woman were wife, mother, and homemaker; men were required to be leaders and providers. Today those roles are viewed as outdated or as representing only some of the roles that may be adopted by people of either sex.

- The types of behavior considered appropriate for men and women reflect the values of a particular society. They are largely learned as a person is socialized into his or her culture.

- Our gender identity, a sense of maleness or femaleness, is typically formed by age 3. Sexual identity, a sense of one's attractiveness to others and a sense of comfort with one's body and one's feelings of sexual arousal, also emerges in the course of childhood and adolescence. It includes sexual orientation—that is, whether one is attracted to members of the opposite sex (heterosexual) or to members of the same sex (homosexual)—and sexuality, or how one actually behaves sexually.

- Sociologists have viewed homosexuality as a product of social disorganization, as an illness with physiological or psychological causes, as a product of societal labeling, and as a set of institutions in conflict with the institutions of straight society.

- It is not known what causes people to become homosexual. An important factor may be the social environment in which a person grows up. Recent research has emphasized the importance of the labeling of the individual as homosexual.

- Homosexuals differ greatly in the ways in which they satisfy their sexual desires and cope with the attendant problems, in their willingness to come out, in their ties to the straight world, and in their marital status.

- Lesbians are less conspicuous than male homosexuals and find it easier to conceal their sexual preference. They are more likely to view their relationships in terms of emotional attachment and tend to come out at a later age than do male homosexuals.

- Gay institutions and businesses are concentrated in areas with a large homosexual population. These give homosexuals a way to understand and accept their sexual orientation.

- Sexism is the range of attitudes, beliefs, policies, laws, and behaviors that discriminate against the members of one sex. One source of sexism is the persistence of male dominance in the institutions of modern societies. Sexism also stems from popular stereotypes about women and men. It is especially evident in employment and contributes to the earnings gap between men and women. It can also take the form of sexual harassment.

- The primary source of sexism is socialization, particularly in the family, where children are treated differently on the basis of their sex. More formal socialization occurs in school, where traditional sex-role stereotypes are reinforced. Later, the role of homemaker often perpetuates a woman's subordinate status, and even in two-earner marriages the husband may have a more privileged position.

- Other sources of sexism are language and the media, which reinforce stereotypes; organized religion, in which women have a subordinate role; and a legal system that assumes that men are wage earners and women are homemakers.

- Hostility, violence, and discrimination directed at people because they are homosexual, or suspected to be homosexual, is known as homophobia.

- The women's movement has striven to eliminate sexism from American society, and there is evidence that it has had an impact on attitudes about gender roles.

- A significant step toward sexual equality would be for fathers to share equally in child rearing and homemaking. This could be encouraged by upgrading part-time work and providing day care for preschool children. Changes are also needed in the educational process so that children of both sexes are treated equally. In 1993 Congress passed the Family Leave Act, which allows employees of either sex to take unpaid leave to care for family members; the legislation was signed by President Clinton. At present an important issue is access to affordable, high-quality child care.

- Many laws and statutes discriminate against women. Job discrimination on the basis of sex is forbidden by law, but for the most part such laws have not been strongly enforced. Some efforts to counteract job discrimination have focused on the concept of comparable worth, or measuring the intrinsic value of jobs and paying the holders of jobs of comparable value at comparable rates.

- Another area in which legislation plays an important role is abortion. Abortion laws have been greatly liberalized since the 1950s, but the issue remains highly controversial.

Key Terms

gender identity, p. 260
sexual identity, p. 260
homosexuality, p. 261

sexism, p. 266
sexual harassment, p. 271
socialization, p. 273

homophobia, p. 280
comparable worth, p. 284

Social Problems Online

In searching for resources about women, a good place to start is the U.S. Census Bureau's site at **www.census.gov**/. It contains a great deal of demographic data that are easy to find. For a statistical profile of the population, which includes data on women, go to the bureau's population profile (**www.census.gov/population/www/pop-profile**). The profile is divided into several short essays with colorful graphs on a number of topics, such as labor force participation and family arrangements, almost all of which compare women and men. Return to the Bureau's homepage and click on the Subjects A to Z box for a list of more than 100 categories. For example, B will take you to Business, which includes an entry for Survey of Business Owners that is linked to a page with data on women-owned enterprises categorized by gross receipts, number of employees, and annual payroll. Other areas that highlight the demographic differences between men and women include Household and Families, Immigration, and Poverty.

The Feminist Internet Gateway (**www.feminist.org/gateway**) has what it calls a "mediated listing of the best on the 'net" that provides links to Web resources, both domestic and international. Among other topics covered are global feminism; women and girls in sports; violence against women; and feminist arts, literature, and entertainment. For users interested in political organizations, there is a link to the National Organization for Women (NOW), at **www.now.org**, which features calls for action; press releases; and the NOW newspaper, as well as a history of the organization. A more conservative political organization is the Eagle Forum (**www.eagleforum.org**/).

Research Navigator

Follow the instructions on pages 26–27 of this text to access the features of Research Navigator. Once at the Web site, enter your Login Name and Password. Then, to use the Content Select database, use keywords such as "gender," "sexism," and "homophobia," and the search engine will supply relevant and recent scholarly and popular press publications. Use the *New York Times* search-by-subject archive to find recent news articles related to problems of gender and sexuality, and the Link Library to find relevant Web sites organized by the key terms associated with this chapter.

Go to this site—**www.cdc.gov/nchs/data/series/sr_23/sr23_024.pdf**. This will bring you to a U.S. government report entitled *Teenagers in the United States: Sexual Activity, Contraceptive Use, and Childbearing, 2002* (Centers for Disease Control, Vital and Health Statistics, Series 23, number 24, December 2004). In the table of contents, go to the section entitled "Strengths and Limitations of the Data." What justifications do the report's authors give for exposing facts about the intimate lives of young Americans? What types of visual aids were used by interviewers to enhance the quality of the data? Which of the report's findings were of interest to you from a sociological viewpoint? Why do you believe these are sociologically significant findings?

9

AN AGING
Society

Chapter Outline

Dominant Trends

- As global health conditions improve and fertility rates continue to fall in most regions of the world, the world's population is aging. This means that the population over age 60 is increasing everywhere, although the rates of growth in elderly populations are not evenly distributed throughout the world.

- Throughout the world, the proportion of people over age 65 will continue to increase, although the largest increases will be in the developing nations. In the developed nations, the proportion of aged people in the population is approaching 20 percent, with Italy, Sweden, Japan, Greece, and Spain now having more people over age 65 than children ages 1 to 14.

- In the United States, the aging of the baby boom cohort will greatly accelerate the rise in the proportion of elderly people in the population, so that by 2013 an estimated 14 percent will be over age 65.

- Increasing proportions of elderly people in the developed nations will mean more pressure on retirement systems, higher health-care costs, more calls to open borders to new and younger immigrants, and more demands for improvements in social safety net policies.

The aging of baby boom cohorts is creating a worldwide surge in the proportion of elderly people in nations throughout the world. People who were born in the 1940s and 1950s, and are now in their early 50s or soon will be, are poised to enter late adulthood. As they begin to feel their age physically and socially, these changes exert major influences on their societies (Riley, 1996). Among these influences are the likelihood of increased conflict between the generations over scarce public resources; increasing immigration to offset the loss of large numbers of retired people from national labor forces; and changing attitudes toward youth, infirmity, and death (Quadagno, 2002). In the United States, as we will see in this chapter, the elderly exert an increasing influence over social policy, in large part because of their special needs and concerns.

As Figure 9–1 on page 294 shows, the phenomenon of an aging population is hardly limited to the United States. In fact, whereas the proportion of Americans over age 65 is expected to reach 18 percent in 2023, in Italy, Japan, and Germany this high percentage will be reached in only a few years. In this context it is important to realize that throughout most of the world's history the proportion of people over 65 never exceeded 2 or 3 percent. Now people over 65 account for 14 percent of the population in the developed nations, and the percentage may be as high as 25 percent thirty years from now. The number of people over 65 in the industrialized nations is projected to increase by about 90 million, while the number of people under 65 will fall by an estimated 40 million (Cole & Durham, 2007).

On a global basis, as shown in Table 9–1 on page 295, the phenomenon of aging differs considerably from one region of the world to another. The populations of Asian nations—including China and India—include far fewer elderly people than those of Europe and North America, but these nations are entering a phase of rapid aging and by 2030 are expected to be aging societies, with proportions of elderly people equal to those found in Western nations today. The nations of sub-Saharan Africa and the Middle East, in contrast, will not face the problems of dealing with rapidly aging populations for many more decades.

The main factors that affect a population's general "youth" or "age" are changes in the fertility rate, the infant mortality rate, and the life expectancy of people at older ages. In social terms, age is one of the major factors in determining groupings and role assignments in a society. How old people are plays a large part in how they feel about themselves and what society expects of them. And the way in which a society thinks about its aged members depends very much on the value its culture attaches to age as opposed to youth. Our culture places a

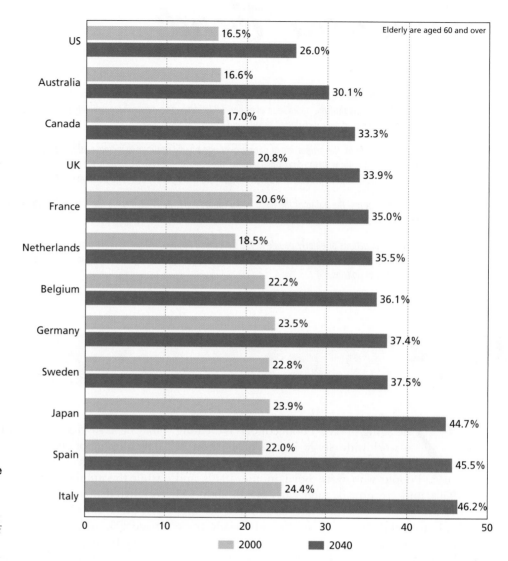

Figure 9–1 Number of Elderly as a Percentage of the Population

Source: Watson & Howe, 2003.

Note: Projections assume constant fertility rates and constant rates of improvement in mortality.

Aging of populations is occurring most rapidly in advanced industrial societies. Does this mean that it is not a problem elsewhere in the world?

high value on youth, and consequently it tends to devalue aging because it is associated with changes in physical appearance that detract from the image of youth. This is a feature of most Western cultures, but it is particularly prevalent in the United States.

AGING AS A SOCIAL PROBLEM

Aging places stress on society as well as on the individual. A major source of structural strain in societies is the long-term failure of social institutions to accommodate the increasing proportion of the population that is elderly. For example, the family has failed to adapt to the presence of older members, and there is considerable strain in the labor force as younger workers find their careers blocked and older ones are forced to leave their jobs before they are ready to do so. The result, according to Matilda White Riley (1987), a pioneering sociologist who helped develop the U.S. Office on Aging, is that "human resources in the oldest—and also the youngest—strata are underutilized, and excess burdens of care are imposed upon strata in the middle years" (p. 10).

The social problems associated with certain age groups, especially the very young and the very old, are aggravated by three factors, which all have an impact on the roles assigned to people of different ages (Binstock & George, 2001): labeling, the concept of work as the basis of personal value, and economic deprivation. These three factors are inextricably linked, and each reinforces the others. Labeling leads to discrimination

TABLE 9–1	Percent of Population in Older Age Groups, by Region: 2000, 2015, and 2030		
Region	Year	65 Years or Older	80 Years or Older
Asia	2000	5.9	0.9
	2015	7.8	1.4
	2030	12.0	2.3
Europe	2000	14.7	3.0
	2015	17.6	4.7
	2030	23.5	6.4
Latin America/Caribbean	2000	5.6	1.0
	2015	7.6	1.5
	2030	11.5	2.5
Middle East/North Africa	2000	4.4	0.6
	2015	5.5	0.9
	2030	8.4	1.4
North America	2000	12.4	3.3
	2015	14.7	3.9
	2030	20.0	5.4
Oceania	2000	10.1	2.3
	2015	12.4	3.1
	2030	16.3	4.4
Sub-Saharan Africa	2000	2.9	0.3
	2015	3.1	0.4
	2030	3.6	0.5

Source: Kinsella & Phillips, 2005. (Data from the Population Reference Bureau)

against older workers, which reduces their responsibility while they are still on the job and forces them to retire. Characterized as weak and incompetent, older people often lose their self-confidence and begin to conform to the stereotype. Retirement often removes people from the mainstream of life and diminishes their status and social contacts, consigning still-vital people to a vaguely defined position on the fringe of society. In a world where one's job is the basis of one's worth and acceptance, retired people are relegated to a position of low esteem. Individuals who once described themselves as accountants, salespeople, or secretaries are suddenly and arbitrarily looked on as noncontributors, a status that reduces both their incomes and their responsibilities.

In the past several decades, the economic status of the aged as a group has improved markedly; the average income of older people is about 90 percent of that of younger adults (Quadagno, 2002). The elderly are not a homogeneous group, however, and the situation of those who live alone is not as comfortable as that of couples. The very old (those over 85) and members of minority groups are less well off than white, "young-old" couples. Moreover, although on the whole the elderly are faring much better than they have in the past, this improvement is due largely to public policies designed to alleviate the problems faced by aging individuals. Such policies do not reach the entire older population. Thus, there are still large numbers of older people who experience economic insecurity because of their vulnerability to major costs, such as medical expenses that are not fully covered by insurance (Binstock & George, 2001). We return to some of these issues later in the chapter.

Much of what we say about the elderly also applies to young people not yet in the labor force. Young people in American society are frequently dependent on others for support and lack the power to assert their needs as citizens. In most states, for example, it is unlawful for people under the age of 21 to purchase alcoholic beverages, yet they can be drafted for military service and may vote in national elections. This is not to argue that young people should drink or that the laws should be changed, but it points to the inconsistency in society's treatment of the young as dependent in some cases and responsible in others.

The problems of different age groups are a vast subject in the social sciences, and it is necessary in this chapter to dwell primarily on those that confront the aged. As our aging society produces an ever larger population of elderly people, the problems of the elderly become increasingly evident and require more attention from both researchers and policymakers.

Perspectives on Aging

Aging as a social problem is often studied from the point of view of one or more of the basic perspectives described in Chapter 1. From the functionalist perspective, for example, aging is a problem because the institutions of modern society are not working well enough to serve the needs of the dependent aged. The extended family, which once allowed elderly people to live out their lives among kin, has been weakened by greater social mobility and a shift to the nuclear family as the basic kinship unit. (See Chapter 10.) The elderly are rendered useless as their functions are replaced by those of other social institutions. As grandparents, for example, older people once played an important part in socializing the young, teaching them the skills, values, and ways of life of their people. Now those functions are performed by schools and colleges, for it is assumed that the elderly cannot understand or master the skills required in today's fast-changing world. Instead, they must be cared for either at home or in institutions like old-age homes, which remove this burden from the productive members of society.

Interactionists take a different view. They see the term *elderly* as a stigmatizing label; it suggests that older people are less valuable because they do not conform to the norms of a youth-oriented culture. Interactionists view the elderly as victims of **ageism**—forms of prejudice and discrimination that are directed at them not only by individuals but also by social institutions. The remedy is to fight ageism in all its forms. (Ageism is discussed more fully later in the chapter.)

Finally, conflict theorists believe that the problems of the elderly stem from their lack of power to shape social institutions to meet the needs of people who are no longer in their productive years and have not accumulated the means to preserve their economic and social independence. In this view, the aged must resist the debilitating effects of labeling and the loss of their roles by banding together in organizations, communities, and voting blocs that will assert their need for meaningful lives and adequate social services. (Table 9–2 summarizes the major sociological perspectives on aging.)

TABLE 9–2	Major Sociological Perspectives on Aging
Perspective	**Why Aging Is a Social Problem**
Functionalist	Social institutions do not adequately serve people as they grow older (e.g., the family is no longer capable of providing adequate care).
Interactionist	The elderly are stigmatized and are victims of ageism because they do not conform to the norms of a culture that emphasizes youthfulness.
Conflict	The problem of the elderly is their relative lack of power; when they organize for political action, they can combat ageism.

THE ELDERLY IN AMERICA TODAY

Research on nomadic societies has found that in some situations, especially in times of scarcity or when they impede the group's mobility, elderly individuals may be badly mistreated and even encouraged to die (Hooyman & Kiyak, 2005). Explorers and anthropologists have also cited instances of mistreatment in some tribal societies. But in many settled agrarian societies, the status of adults actually increases with age. In many African and Asian nations, for example, decisions about land tenure, kinship, and ceremonial affairs are the province of the aged. In the United States and most Western countries, the productive and cultural roles of the aged have been weakened by industrialization and the migration of family members to cities. In this sense, then, the problems of the aged are part of the larger complex of social changes known as **modernization,** which has been described as the transformation of societies to urbanized and industrialized ways of life based on scientific technologies, individualized rather than communal or collective roles, and a cosmopolitan outlook that values efficiency and progress. Thus, many of the problems faced by the aged in America today are social problems that arise from the nature of modern Western society.

Modernization produces far-reaching changes in societies, but clearly the terms *modernization* and *progress* are not equivalent. With modernization come new social problems and, sometimes, new solutions. Modernization is usually associated with increasing length of life, but this is a positive change only when the quality of life is also enhanced. For many people, however, as the life span increases, so does the pain associated with old age.

Technological and scientific advances have reduced the infant mortality rate and eliminated or provided cures for many formerly fatal diseases. Because many of these advances, such as antiseptics and antibiotics, occurred within a short time (often within this century), record numbers of people began living to old age. As the population of elderly people increased, modern societies all over the globe began to deal with poverty and illness among their elderly citizens. Pension plans, Social Security, and medical-care systems had to be developed to address their needs.

From the earliest periods of human prehistory (before written evidence of human civilization appeared) to the present, the average life expectancy has increased by about forty years. In prehistoric times a person could expect to live into his or her early forties; now life expectancy is approaching 80 in some societies. Great surges in life expectancy occurred with the transition from hunting-and-gathering to agrarian societies, with the development of modern techniques of sanitation and water supply, and with the discovery of the causes of diseases and of antibiotics and techniques for preventing many major illnesses. In the past twenty or thirty years, however, there has

Many older people cherish the opportunity to spend time with children and participate in their education.

been a deceleration in the rate of increase in life expectancy (Binstock & George, 2001). There are biological limits to how long humans can live, and although there may be small shifts in life expectancy in the future, we cannot project past advances indefinitely.

We can expect, however, that the number of elderly people who are alive but unwell will increase. As more people live longer, the proportion with major medical problems increases, as does the need for costly medical care. Although most of us wish to live longer lives, the negative side is that we are likely to suffer longer and more as we do so. For society as a whole, this means an increased need to improve the quality of life for the most elderly among the population and to find ways to care for a growing number of frail and ill elderly people (Lee, 2007).

Urbanization, like advances in medical and other technologies, is another major change associated with modernization. The increasing tendency for people to live in cities and for cities and metropolitan regions to dominate the life of modern societies has also affected the lives of the elderly. It has created new jobs for mobile workers who are willing to relocate from rural areas or small towns to large cities or from the older industrial cities of the North and Midwest to the newer urban centers of the Sunbelt. The resulting migration has led to differing concentrations of elderly and younger people in different parts of the nation. Figure 9–2 illustrates quite dramatically how decreases in employment in rural areas and in the older manufacturing cities have created high concentrations of elderly people in counties throughout the Midwest and Plains states.

In counties with high proportions of elderly residents, such as Smith County, Kansas, there is a need for creative entrepreneurs who are willing to help their elderly neighbors remain independent as long as possible. In many rural counties in the Midwest, a variety of services are provided for elderly people, such as minor home repairs, errands, and monitoring of medical needs. These enable older people to live happily on their own and may be harbingers of trends elsewhere in the nation (Heumann, McCall, & Boldy, 2001).

Age Stratification

Matilda White Riley and Joan Waring (1976; Riley, 1996) have described the process of **age stratification.** Age, they point out, operates like race or class in segregating people into different groups or strata. Like the class system, age stratification limits the kinds of roles that the members of each group can hold. Some degree of age stratification seems acceptable and even inevitable. People are attracted to their peers and to those with whom they share common experiences and concerns, and certain activities seem to attract members of particular age groups. However, "Many of these age-related differences in access to the good things in life are violations of societal ideas of equity or harmony. They inhibit communication and understanding between generations. They can create a sense of relative deprivation or inadequacy and feelings of hostility with reference to other age strata" (Riley & Waring, 1976, p. 363).

Age stratification may produce some of the disengagement that is so common among elderly people in the United States. Young people who are denied jobs and opportunities to play rewarding roles often react by engaging in deviant behaviors, including crime. Old people may react by becoming dependent or uninvolved or by manifesting the kinds of behavior that are labeled as "senile."

Age stratification may also lead to age segregation and conflict. From childhood we are segregated into age groups, classes, and clubs; the retirement community, restricted to people of specified ages, continues this process. In the wake of age segregation come suspicion, mistrust, and hostility. The young lack confidence in their elders; the old often fear the young. Isolation of age groups and intergenerational conflicts are common.

It is possible that many conditions that exist today will be reversed in the future. For example, the middle-aged have traditionally enjoyed a better position than the elderly. But that position could be eroded by a combination of factors, including a

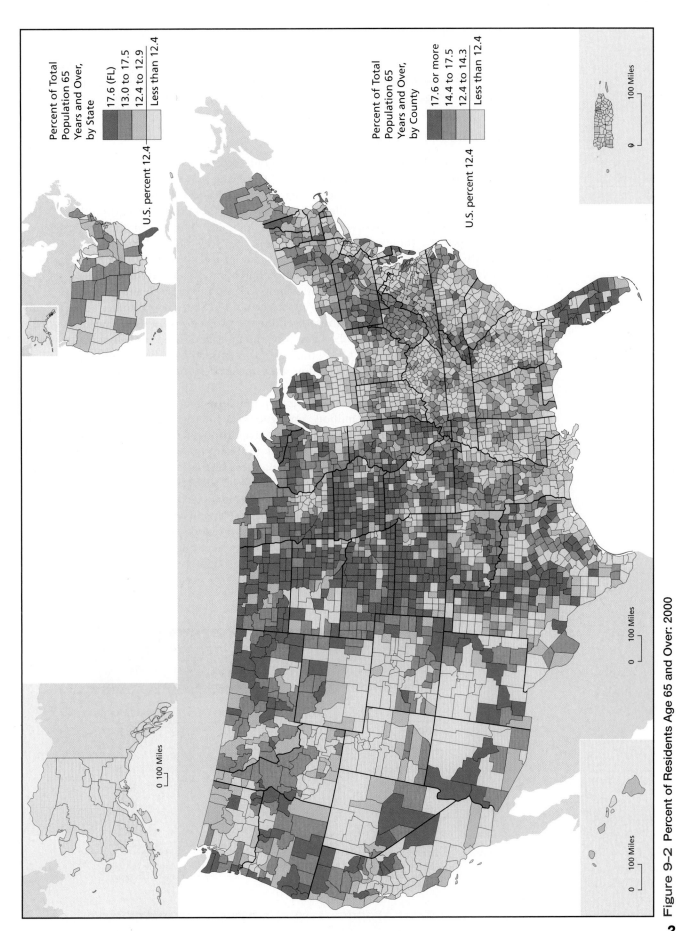

Figure 9-2 Percent of Residents Age 65 and Over: 2000

Source: U.S. Census Bureau, Census 2000 Summary Fig. 1. American Factfinder at *factfinder.census.gov* provides census data and mapping tools.

Percent of Total
Population 65
Years and Over,
by State

17.6 (FL)
13.0 to 17.5
12.4 to 12.9
Less than 12.4

U.S. percent 12.4

Percent of Total
Population 65
Years and Over,
by County

17.6 or more
14.4 to 17.5
12.4 to 14.3
Less than 12.4

U.S. percent 12.4

lower median wage for male heads of households, larger percentages of infants born out of wedlock and children living in female-headed households, and higher educational attainment among individuals currently approaching old age (Riley, 1987). The effect of these trends may counteract the "normal" relationship between the old and the middle-aged and perhaps produce new forms of tension between generations.

Who Are the Elderly?

Anyone over 65 is commonly considered old. Recently, however, social scientists have begun to identify specific groups within the growing population of the elderly (Altman & Shactman, 2002). People between the ages of 65 and 75, who are still inclined to be healthy and active, are called the "young-old." Those over 75, a group that is more likely to require support services, are the "old-old." Those over the age of 85 may be termed the "oldest old." Another group, the "frail elderly," consists of those over 65 who, because of poor health or economic problems, cannot carry out the basic activities of life without help. Assistance may range from full-time nursing care to the delivery of a hot meal each day or help with shopping or cleaning.

Although the oldest elderly people in the United States now number about 4.2 million, or about 12 percent of those over age 65, projections indicate that this figure is likely to increase to almost 22 percent by the middle of the twenty-first century. This will occur because by about 2010 the post–World War II baby boom generation will be entering this age group. Thus, as time goes by, far larger numbers of Americans will be elderly. (See Table 9–3.)

The elderly portion of the American population grows larger in each decade. In 1900 there were about 3 million Americans over the age of 65; in 2000 there were almost 35 million. More important, the proportion of the population over 65 has more than tripled, increasing from about 4 percent in 1900 to 12.4 percent in 2000, and it is continuing to increase. Demographers in the U.S. Census Bureau estimate that in the twenty-first century the elderly will be the fastest growing segment of the population as the huge baby boom generation enters its later years.

Two-thirds of the elderly live in urban areas, many in central cities. For them, as we saw in the aftermath of Hurricane Katrina, the problems of aging are complicated by the problems of the urban environment: crime, decaying neighborhoods, the shortage of affordable housing, and congestion. (See Chapter 13.)

TABLE 9–3	Percent of Total Population 65 and Over, 1950 to 2050 (projected)

Year	Percentage
1950	8.1
1965	9.5
1984	11.8
1995	13.1
2010	13.8
2030	21.2
2050	21.8

Source: Adapted from *Our Aging Society, Paradox and Promise,* edited by Alan Pifer and Lydia Bronte. Reprinted by permission of W.W. Norton & Company. Copyright © 1986 by Carnegie Corporation of New York.

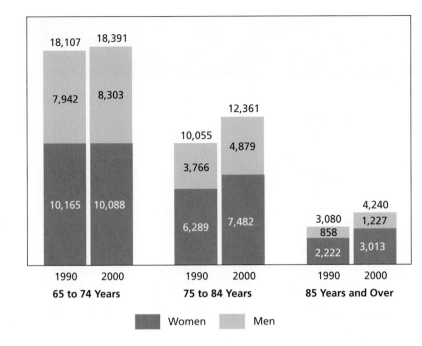

18,107   18,391

7,942   8,303

12,361

10,055

3,766   4,879

10,165   10,088

6,289   7,482

4,240

3,080   1,227

858

2,222   3,013

| 1990 | 2000 | 1990 | 2000 | 1990 | 2000 |

65 to 74 Years   **75 to 84 Years**   **85 Years and Over**

■ Women   ■ Men

Figure 9–3 Population
65 Years and Over, by Age
and Sex: 1990 and 2000
(in thousands)

Source: Data from U.S. Census Bureau.

Although most elderly people live in urban areas, they also represent the highest proportion of the population of small towns. This phenomenon is a result of the patterns of migration that have occurred since World War II, when many people moved from farms to small towns. Many of those people are now elderly. In turn, their children have relocated from small towns to suburbs or cities. Another important pattern of migration is the movement of retired people to the West and South. In some parts of the United States, such as Miami and south Florida and parts of Arizona and southern California, the elderly have become a dominant group and exert considerable political influence. The 2000 census showed rapid increases in the proportion of elderly people, especially those in their advanced years. Thus, we are likely to see even more population growth in the counties that are most attractive to elderly people (Hooyman & Kiyak, 2005).

The Uneven Graying of America. The 2000 census also revealed that although, as expected, the elderly population is continuing to grow rapidly, it is not evenly distributed over the continent. The average proportion of people over 65 in American counties is 12.4 percent, but the boom in retirement communities is producing far higher proportions in some areas.

During the last decade, the most rapid increases in the elderly population were among the oldest of the old, those over 85. Their ranks grew from about 3 million in 1990 to well over 4 million in 2000, for an increase of 38 percent. In contrast, the population aged 65 to 74 increased by less than 2 percent. (See Figure 9–3.)

As people age, they often move to communities where the climate is warmer and there is an infrastructure of services and institutions (elder-care residential developments, hospitals, and nursing care facilities). Table 9–4 on page 302 shows that the proportion of the elderly in certain cities far exceeds the U.S. average of 12.4 percent. Does this mean that such cities are becoming "gray ghettos"? Although there are clearly sections of cities like Clearwater, Florida, and Scottsdale, Arizona, where the elderly are the dominant demographic group, the figures show that in the cities themselves there remains a good deal of age diversity. The census shows that there are only ten counties for which the percentage of people over 65 exceeds 30 percent, and half of these are in Florida.

The census also shows (as we see in Figure 9–2) that in the Midwest and some of the western Plains states the proportion of elderly people is far higher than the national

TABLE 9–4	Ten Places of 100,000 or More Population with the Highest Proportion of Their Population 65 Years and Over: 2000		

| Place | Total Population | Population 65 Years and Over | |
		Number	Percent
Clearwater, FL	108,787	23,357	21.5
Cape Coral, FL	102,286	20,020	19.6
Honolulu, HI	371,657	66,257	17.8
St. Petersburg, FL	248,232	43,173	17.4
Hollywood, FL	139,357	24,159	17.3
Warren, MI	138,247	23,871	17.3
Miami, FL	362,470	61,768	17.0
Livonia, MI	100,545	16,988	16.9
Scottsdale, AZ	202,705	33,884	16.7
Hialeah, FL	226,419	37,679	16.6

Source: U.S. Census Bureau.

average, but these individuals have not migrated to the Sunbelt and are often far less well served by health-care and other elder-care institutions, especially when they can no longer drive relatively long distances for needed services.

Ageism

Many attitudes that are prevalent in modern society contribute to ageism, the devaluation of the aged. One of these is the inordinate value placed on youthful looks, especially for women (Whitbourne, 2005). Older adults do not meet the standards of youthful beauty, and many people may be repelled by the appearance of the aged. Another source of ageism is the belief that the old are useless; since they do not work and cannot reproduce, they serve no purpose. Those who do hold jobs are resented for occupying a position that a young person probably needs. Because it is so deeply rooted in the social and psychological fabric of our culture, ageism is extremely difficult to eliminate. Ageism as a social problem is also confounded with sexism. Feminist social scientists ask, with reason, whether ageism would be the problem it is in U.S. society if men outlived women instead of the reverse (Friedan, 1993).

Ageism prevails in the government. The Administration on Aging, an agency of the Department of Health and Human Services, has low status and limited access to decision makers. When Congress makes budget cuts, programs for the aged are a frequent target. When states and municipalities have to cut their budgets because of recession or regional depression, they often reduce programs for the aged as well as those for the poor. The elderly fare no better in business and industry. Although the Age Discrimination in Employment Act of 1967 prohibits discrimination against workers between the ages of 40 and 65, little is done to enforce it. Critics have pointed out that the law itself exhibits ageism because it does nothing for workers over the age of 65, who probably need even more protection.

Ageism is reflected in the practice of mandatory retirement. This takes a heavy toll on the health, self-respect, social status, and economic security of older people. Retirement isolates the old from the mainstream of American life. The daily social contacts of the working world are gone, and reduced income may bring reduced mobility or prevent participation in social activities. The status of a productive worker is replaced

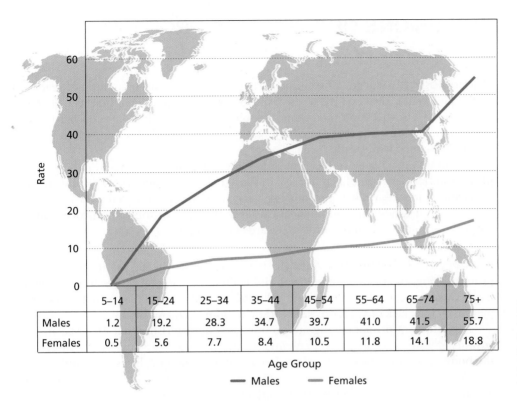

Age Group	5–14	15–24	25–34	35–44	45–54	55–64	65–74	75+
Males	1.2	19.2	28.3	34.7	39.7	41.0	41.5	55.7
Females	0.5	5.6	7.7	8.4	10.5	11.8	14.1	18.8

— Males　— Females

Figure 9–4 Worldwide Distribution of Suicide Rates (per 100,000), by Gender and Age

Source: World Health Organization, 2003. Reprinted by permission of WHO.

by a new status with low prestige and a negative image. Mandatory retirement can thus be considered the most serious and pervasive form of ageism.

The mass media play a part in promoting ageism. Just as women and minority groups must contend with negative images in the media, so must old people. Television, which does so much to shape and maintain attitudes, persists in portraying the elderly as weak in both body and mind, and as a burden on their relatives—or else as unnaturally wise or kindhearted. Newspapers and magazines also contain ageist images. Howard P. Chudacoff (1989) found that only in the past fifty years have newspapers and other communications media begun to stress "age-appropriate behavior." Song lyrics, for example, are often concerned about looking young and not looking old.

The difficulties of the old in modern societies are mirrored by their higher-than-average suicide rate. As Figure 9–4 demonstrates, throughout the developed world the suicide rates of elderly males are far higher than the average number of suicides per 100,000 in the general population. And elderly men are far more likely to kill themselves than are women. The suicide rate for women is similar in all age groups, although it is somewhat higher for elderly women than the average for all women. For men, however, the differences are enormous. Older men are almost five times more likely to commit suicide than are older women.

Although declining health, loss of status, and reduced income play a part in suicides by the elderly, lack of relationships with family, friends, and coworkers seems to exert the most consistent influence (Hooyman & Kiyak, 2005). An analysis of suicides by elderly people in Pinellas County, Florida, over a period of nine years indicated that widowed males were more likely than any other group of old people to commit suicide. Elderly women were more likely to have extended family ties, friends, and club memberships that provided social restraints against suicide. Elderly men who enjoyed these kinds of contact were less likely to commit suicide. This finding mirrors the classic finding by Émile Durkheim (1897/1951), one of sociology's founders, that people of any age who lack social attachments are more likely to commit suicide than are people with active social lives among family and friends.

What is ageism, and what specific forms does it take?

DIMENSIONS OF THE AGING PROCESS

Physiological Aspects of Aging

Chronological Aging. Chronological aging, the simple accumulation of years, is a largely automatic process. We know from our own observations, however, that not everyone ages at the same rate. Some people look and act middle-aged before they leave their twenties, whereas some 50-year-olds radiate the vitality and health that are usually associated with youth.

The dramatic increase in life expectancy and the growing population of older people in America have stimulated interest in the aging process and its causes. The field of study and practice known as **gerontology** has grown. Among other concerns, gerontologists attempt to identify the physical causes and effects of the aging process and to control the factors that diminish the rewards of a long life.

Primary and Secondary Aging. There are two categories in the aging process: **primary aging,** the result of molecular and cellular changes, and **secondary aging,** an accelerated version of normal aging (Whitbourne, 2005) that is caused by environmental factors: lack of exercise, stress, trauma, poor diet, and disease.

The effects of primary aging are seen in the characteristics that we associate with advancing years, such as gray hair, wrinkles, and increased susceptibility to disease. As the body ages, its systems degenerate. The brain, for example, loses thousands of cells daily from birth onward. Some of the body's systems, like the skin, are able to regenerate their cells, although they do so less effectively with each passing year. Others, like the kidneys, lack regenerative powers and eventually wear out. More significant, however, is a general decline in the body's immune defenses, which fight off infections like pneumonia. As a result, elderly people often die of diseases that would not usually be fatal to younger people (Quadagno, 2002).

Aging is a gradual process; not all of the body's systems age at the same rate. The process of decline usually starts relatively early in life. By the mid-twenties the skin begins to lose its elasticity and starts to dry and wrinkle; by 30 the muscles have begun to shrink and decrease in strength. As time passes, the capacity of the lungs is reduced, and less and less air is drawn into the body; circulation slows and the blood supply decreases; bones become brittle and thin; hormonal activity ebbs; and reflexes become slower. Aging is not a disease in itself, but it does increase susceptibility to disease. In old age, therefore, disease becomes chronic rather than episodic.

Some researchers are convinced that each of us carries a personal "timetable" for aging within our cells, a timetable controlled by our genes. Others believe secondary aging factors are also involved. The role of stress is particularly important. One of the most salient age-related changes is the decline in homeostatic capacity—the ability to tolerate stress. This makes older people more susceptible to stress, and it takes them longer to return to normal after being exposed to a stressful situation.

The reduced capacity to cope with stress is a result of primary aging; stress itself is an agent of secondary aging. Together they may be responsible for many of the illnesses that plague the elderly. Older people are confronted by numerous stress-producing situations, including widowhood, the death of friends and family members, and loss of status and productivity. Studies have demonstrated that such illnesses as leukemia, cancer, and heart disease often strike in the wake of stress-producing life changes (Bond, Coleman, & Peace, 2007).

There is evidence that many of the effects of aging are neither inevitable nor irreversible. For example, reduced oxygen intake, diminished lung capacity, and slow circulation—and related mental and physical problems—are results not just of age, but also of the inactivity that may come with it. New developments in drug therapy and exercise are producing some dramatic changes in health and well-being among elderly populations. An annual federal survey of 20,000 people aged 65 and over showed a steady decrease in chronic disabilities in the 1980s and early 1990s. In part this is occurring because of new medications that can diminish depression and chronic pain. Gerontologists are increasingly pursuing a preventive strategy to slow the aging process and ensure that a longer life span is a blessing rather than a painful and expensive curse. The preventive strategy accepts biological aging as a given but assumes that physical and mental decline, disability, and disease can be staved off or delayed through medical advances, diet, and exercise (Binstock & George, 2001).

Psychological Dimensions of Aging

The aging process produces psychological effects as well as physical ones. Social factors also influence the psychological consequences of aging. Self-concept and status are particularly important as aging occurs. One theory views older people as trapped in a shrinking social environment—their world grows smaller and smaller as they leave work, as their friends and relatives die, and as their mobility decreases; at the same time, their social status changes and they become less influential and less important.

New roles always require some adjustment, but for the elderly this adjustment is complicated because their new roles are poorly defined; there are few role models or reference groups on which they can pattern their behavior. Because of the nebulous quality of their new status, older people become dependent on labels and on the opinions of others for their self-definition. In our society the labels applied to the old are consistently negative because they are based on an ethic that equates personal worth with economic productivity (Hooyman & Kiyak, 2005; Riley, Kahn, & Foner, 1994).

This negative labeling is one of the causes of the psychological difficulties experienced by the aged. The old tend to rely on the image imposed on them, even though that image is a negative one. They internalize it, and eventually their self-image and behavior correspond to the weak, incompetent, useless image that has been forced on them. It is widely believed, for example, that intellectual ability declines with age. As a consequence, many people are reluctant to place older individuals in positions of authority or to retrain or reeducate them. Research has shown, however, that this belief is incorrect. Reflexes and responses slow down, but in the absence of organic problems, intellectual capacity remains unchanged until very late in life.

False assumptions about the inevitability of the condition known as senility account for much of this misunderstanding. Contrary to what many people believe, the human brain does not necessarily deteriorate with age. It is not unusual for the brain to function well for over nine decades. At age 86, Artur Rubinstein played the piano better than ever, and George Burns continued cracking jokes at machine-gun speed until he died at the age of 100.

Negative attitudes about the elderly cause many people to consider an older person senile when in fact that person is merely depressed. Depression can cause such symptoms as confusion and loss of certain intellectual abilities. Even elderly people who do become senile do not immediately lose all their capacity for intellectual functioning. Rather, they undergo progressive memory loss. This may be accompanied by gradual decreases in the abilities to calculate, think abstractly, imagine, speak fluently, or orient oneself in time and space. Eventually this deterioration affects the entire personality, but it is a gradual process (Bond, Coleman, & Peace, 2007).

Social and Cultural Dimensions of Aging

The Aged as a Minority Group. Social gerontologists frequently refer to the aged as a minority group, pointing out that the elderly exhibit many characteristics of such groups. (See Chapter 7.) Like members of racial and ethnic minorities, the elderly are victims of prejudice, stereotyping, and discrimination. They are thought to be inflexible, a burden on the young, and incompetent workers. However, some social scientists argue that although the elderly share many of the characteristics of minorities, they are not a true minority group. Unlike traditional minority groups—such as blacks, Native Americans, and Jews—the elderly do not exist as an independent subgroup;

everyone has the potential to become old. Some gerontologists suggest that it would be more accurate to describe the elderly as a "quasi-minority," reflecting their unique position in our society (Quadagno, 2002).

The potential power of this quasi-minority is enormous. Not only are the elderly increasing as a proportion of the population, but they themselves are changing significantly. As can be seen from their turnout at elections, they are a political force to be reckoned with. People over 65 vote at higher rates than does the total voting-age population. Thus, as the population grows older, political leaders will be unable to ignore the power wielded by the elderly at the ballot box. In addition, many people remain active in voluntary associations even into their eighties. They play a much larger role in organizational life than most younger people assume (Riley, 1996).

Myths and Stereotypes about the Elderly. Popular culture characterizes old people as senile, lacking in individuality, tranquil, nonproductive, conservative, and resistant to change. These beliefs persist despite abundant evidence to the contrary. Many of the myths about older workers, for example, were disproved when they were drawn into the labor force during World War II. Other studies have demonstrated that the elderly are no more difficult to train than the young; in addition, they have a lower than average absentee rate and compare favorably with younger workers in accident rates and productivity.

Some of the most pernicious myths about the elderly are directed against older women. In our society women become devalued much sooner than men; therefore, in old age women tend to have a more negative image than men. Among the most common and damaging stereotypes are the following:

1. *Health.* Older women are seen both as hypochondriacs and as having more health problems than older men. A number of investigations, including the noted Duke Longitudinal Study of Aging, have shown that there are neither objective nor subjective differences in physical health between men and women. In fact, elderly women are more likely than younger women to avoid seeking necessary medical care, and elderly men are more likely than younger men to go to a doctor (Bond, Coleman, & Peace, 2007).

2. *Marriage.* In a society in which women have traditionally achieved worth only through marriage, widowhood or remaining single are viewed in a very negative light. Older women in particular are characterized as "mateless." This reflects the fact that females tend to outlive males; moreover, older men who want to remarry after the death of a spouse have a greater chance of finding a partner their own age or younger.

3. *Widowhood.* According to a popular stereotype, a widow continues to base her identity on that of her dead husband. This is generally untrue; older women demonstrate a strong sense of personal identity.

4. *The rocking-chair image.* Older women are characterized as grandmotherly types who confine their interests to knitting and rocking by the fireside. A number of studies have shown that there is little difference between the leisure activities of older men and those of older women or between those of people in their middle and later years (Quadagno, 2002).

One of the most widely accepted stereotypes about the old is that they are sexually inactive because they lack both desire and ability. A number of studies have proved that this view is incorrect (Smolowe, 1996). Research has shown that although sexual interest and activity tend to decline with age, sex continues to play an important role in the lives of older people. However, elderly men enjoy more sexual interest and activity than elderly women. The principal reason for this distinction is that elderly men are more likely to have a readily available, socially sanctioned, and sexually capable partner.

Many age-related changes in sexual behavior have their antecedents in middle age. Women who have been sexually active throughout their adult lives continue to enjoy sexual activity in old age. Those who have had a less than satisfactory sex life tend to use age as an excuse for avoiding sex (Quadagno, 2002).

CONCOMITANTS OF AGING

Victimization of the Elderly

The media often portray the old as victims of fraud and violence. Although this kind of reporting may alert the elderly to potential dangers, it also serves to reinforce their image as weak, incompetent, and easy targets. The elderly themselves do not share this view—only about 6 percent of people aged 65 and older believe they are "very likely" to be victims of violent crimes (NORC, 2002).

Because many elderly people live in high-crime areas, they run a risk of being victimized. When this does happen, they suffer more than members of other age groups. They are likely to sustain more serious injuries during a physical assault and to recover more slowly. Often alone and isolated, old people may lack friends and family members who can provide the emotional support that helps dispel the fear and depression that often follow victimization.

Elderly people are frequent victims of a wide variety of business crimes that prey on their desire for security and comfort. Phony home-repair schemes, medical quackery, mail fraud, and schemes to bilk the elderly of their savings abound in areas where there are high proportions of older people living in private homes or apartments. Law enforcement authorities cannot accurately state the amount of loss caused by such swindles, but it is estimated to total hundreds of millions of dollars annually.

Elder Abuse

In the United States and other aging societies there is growing awareness of mental and physical abuse of elderly people. This is especially true in societies where employment opportunities and upward mobility for the working-age population are decreasing. These conditions are highly correlated with deteriorating care and even abuse of the

The failure to send buses and coordinate the evacuation of thousands of elderly nursing home residents was among the most egregious failures of the federal response to Hurricane Katrina.

elderly. In testimony before Congress, it was estimated that there are at least 1.5 million cases of physical abuse of elderly people in the United States each year, and many experts view this as a conservative estimate because it does not include mental cruelty or severe neglect, which can be as damaging as physical abuse. Although much of the abuse reported to authorities occurs in private households, a significant proportion of reported cases occur in nursing homes and other institutional settings (Heisler, 2007).

Health Care and the Aged

Today individuals either do not encounter the infectious diseases that formerly killed people of all ages or, if they do, they survive them. They live longer, and in their later years, as their health declines, they become more prone to chronic illnesses, which develop over a long period and are often expensive to treat. Thus, the elderly tend to require increasing amounts of costly medical care, which they may be unable to afford. To complicate matters further, physicians have a tendency to lump together elderly people in a single category, even though an 80-year-old person may be "younger" physiologically and in better health than a 65-year-old person with numerous health problems. Because physicians view older patients largely in terms of chronological age, they often do not give them the same level of care that they give to younger patients.

Many people assumed that with the passage of Medicare and Medicaid the problem of health care for the elderly would be eliminated. These programs have alleviated some health-related problems, but they have not been completely successful; thousands of elderly people still lack adequate care. The failure of comprehensive medical-care reform in 1994 created uncertainty about the future of health services for the elderly. The elderly poor are especially vulnerable to projected cuts in services and state requirements that they enroll in managed-care systems to maintain their eligibility (Kinsella & Phillips, 2005). As the number of elderly people in the United States and other industrialized nations continues to increase, the problems of funding adequate health coverage for the elderly, for whom long-term care is often a necessary and costly requirement, remains a major issue, as we will see in the Social Policy section of the chapter.

For those who are covered by Medicare and Medicaid, these programs are extremely important. Thirty-five percent of Medicaid expenditures are for the care of elderly people. Medicare covers most hospital costs but only half of physicians' bills; the charges that are not covered can quickly become an enormous financial burden. Moreover, most nursing-home care is not covered, nor are prescription drugs, dental care, hearing aids, eyeglasses, and many other health services. About two-thirds of the elderly have private health insurance in addition to Medicare, but even they can encounter high medical costs if they become seriously ill (Hooyman & Kiyak, 2005).

Although the problem of medical care for the aged is inextricably linked to the national crisis in health services, some aspects of the problem are unique to the aged. One of these is institutionalization. There are about 1.5 million people in nursing homes—often not because they require constant attention, but because no alternative services are available (*Statistical Abstract,* 2006). Unnecessary institutionalization of the elderly is costly in terms of both public spending for Medicare and Medicaid and the negative psychological effects on the occupants.

Economic Discrimination

Older workers are frequent targets of job discrimination. The most common form of discrimination at work is mandatory retirement, a life-altering experience with social, economic, and emotional effects. The practice of mandatory retirement gives companies a tool for cutting labor costs. In a tight economy a company can simply retire its older employees, who earn higher salaries, and replace them with younger workers, who are usually paid less.

Older workers also encounter job discrimination when seeking new employment. The 1967 Age Discrimination in Employment Act is designed to protect workers between the ages of 40 and 65 and has not succeeded in eliminating discrimination against those over 65. Employers can no longer advertise for applicants "under 30," but a phrase like "one to three years' experience" accomplishes the same goal. When they do obtain interviews, older workers are often rejected as "overqualified," a euphemism for "too old." For these reasons, older unemployed workers remain jobless longer than younger ones.

The Social Security system has been modified so that the retirement age will increase in the next few years. However, the purpose of the change was to reduce financial pressure on the program, not to counteract economic discrimination against the elderly. In fact, it can be argued that public policies toward the aged should be reexamined in light of the improved economic situation of older people today (Kinsella & Phillips, 2005). A key issue in American society is how to devise social policies that extend income and medical benefits to the needy elderly while asking those who are affluent to assume a larger share of their own support. (We return to these issues in the Social Policy section of the chapter.)

Multiple Jeopardy. To be old, black (or Hispanic or Native American), and female in U.S. society is to experience multiple jeopardy—to face more hardships than one would face if one were in just one or two of these categories.

Although the elderly as a group have fared better economically in recent years than they did in the past, this is not true of aged blacks. In a report to the House Committee on Aging, the National Caucus and Center on Black Aged (1987) pointed out that elderly blacks are three times as likely as elderly whites to be poor—in fact, about one-quarter of blacks and one-fifth of Hispanics aged 65 and over live below the poverty line. (See Table 9–5.) Moreover, their health is poorer than that of whites, and they have fewer contacts with social-service workers. Their old age is a bitter culmination of the discrimination they have suffered all their lives. Most are ineligible for Social Security because their jobs were menial ones that were not covered by the program. Their health is poor because of inadequate diet and the effects of stressful work. In addition, a high percentage of black women live alone.

Poverty among the elderly is not much worse in the United States than in the United Kingdom, Germany, or Norway, but compared with advanced nations like Sweden and Canada, the United States has a long way to go. Also, the poverty rate among children is higher in the United States than in any of the other nations. Because poverty among children is associated with a wide range of problems, including poor health, crime, and underachievement in school, it is likely that the effects of childhood poverty will in many cases persist throughout life, making it more difficult to reduce poverty among the elderly (Quadagno, 2002). Figure 9–5 on page 310 indicates that during the 1990s the United States made good progress in reducing poverty among the elderly and among juveniles, but even at its lowest, about 16 percent, the poverty rate for

TABLE 9–5	Poverty, by Race, for Persons Age 65 or Older (in thousands)		
Race	Total Number	Over 65	Percent
White	23,468	2,739	9.1
Black	8,602	680	23.8
Hispanic	8,555	439	21.4
All races	34,570	3,576	10.4

Source: Statistical Abstract, 2005.

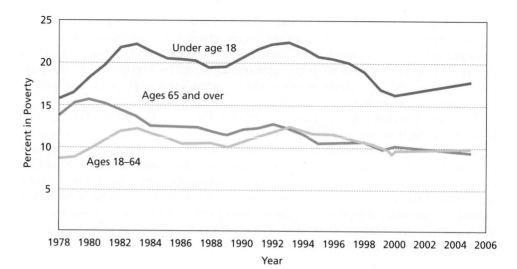

Figure 9–5 Persons Living in Poverty, by Age: 1978–2005

Source: Statistical Abstract, 2006.

youth under age 18 was far higher than, for example, the 5 percent rate in Canada (U.S. Census Bureau, 2006).

Women of all races face disadvantages in old age. As they move away from the ideal of female attractiveness established by a youth-oriented society, they are increasingly devalued. There are more than 20 million elderly women in America (*Statistical Abstract*, 2006), and many of them have financial problems. Because their salaries were lower than those of men, their pensions and Social Security benefits are also lower. The Social Security system gives no credit for homemaking, the principal occupation of most women until recent decades. Older women who want to work suffer the double burdens of age and sex discrimination.

How do aging, minority status, and gender contribute to the problem of multiple jeopardy for some people?

Family Problems

One of the most pervasive myths about the aged is that they are abandoned by their children. In reality, however, the majority of old people who live alone do so voluntarily; they often wish to live near their children but not with them. However, many elderly people do live with one of their children, and those who do not live with their children see them frequently (Binstock & George, 2001).

The institutionalized elderly are not typical. They represent a special population who are, on the average, a decade older than most elderly people; in addition, they suffer severe, chronic physical or mental ailments. Most of them have outlived their spouses and relatives; many have also outlived their children.

Placing an aged relative in an institution is usually a difficult experience. Most families have endured severe personal, social, and economic stress in attempting to avoid doing so; the decision is made reluctantly. The spouse is usually very old, and the adult children are approaching their later years and often are subject to competing demands from ill spouses or their own children (Burbank, 2006).

The problems of caring for the elderly at home are complicated by the fact that as more people live to an extremely old age, the total family unit also ages. People aged 65 may have to provide 24-hour care for parents aged 90 while experiencing economic and health problems of their own. There may be two generations of elderly people in one family, requiring different degrees of care. Moreover, the mobility that is characteristic of Americans may leave parents and their adult children separated by thousands of miles, making home care impossible (Bond, Coleman, & Peace, 2007).

The high divorce rate, the growing number of single-parent families, and the trend toward smaller families also affect the possibilities for home care for the aged. Future generations of old people may lack relatives to care for them, or they may have weak family ties.

Changes in the roles of women also affect how the old are treated. Historically, tending the elderly was the task of daughters or daughters-in-law who were full-time homemakers. As more women work outside the home, they are less available to care for aged parents. Yet women who work full time are still more likely than men to be expected to care for elderly parents, a situation that can greatly increase the stress and physical burdens of working women.

Grandparents Raising Grandchildren. A growing number of elderly people in the United States are facing an unexpected new burden: raising their grand-children, who have become their responsibility because the children's parents are absent due to divorce, incarceration, or other reasons. Sociologists refer to this grow-ing phenomenon in child care as the "skipped-generation" household, one in which a grandparent and grandchild reside with no parent present. The 2000 census revealed that 5.8 million grandparents lived with grandchildren younger than age 18. Of these, 2.4 million served as the grandchildren's primary caregivers (see Table 9–6).

Census data also show the following:

Nearly 40 percent have been caring for their grandchildren for five years or more.

Most grandparent caregivers—60 percent—are under age 60.

About 64 percent are women.

About 20 percent live in poverty.

These data destroy the myth that this is an inner-city, minority phenomenon. More than half (1.3 million) of these caregivers are white, and an increasing number are liv-ing in rather well-off families (Simmons and Dye, 2003). All these grandparents who are primary child-care givers have the effect of saving U.S. taxpayers the cost of care for about twelve times as many children as are cared for by the nation's foster care sys-tem, the government's safety net for these youngsters. Their work saves the nation more than $6.5 billion a year, but it represents a major departure from the ideal of "golden age retirement" for the elderly (Dervarics, 2004).

RETIREMENT

Retirement is a fairly recent concept. Before the advent of Social Security and pension plans, few workers could afford to stop working. As a result, people worked into old age, often modifying the nature of their work to match their diminished strength.

From the point of view of society as a whole, retirement creates problems because those who are no longer in the labor force are dependent on the wealth produced by those who are still working. Figure 9–6 on page 312 shows that over the next twenty-five years there will be major increases in the ratio of retirement-age people to working-age adults. In fact, the United States will fare rather better than nations like Japan, Austria, and Germany, where the number of retirees may severely tax the ability of the working

TABLE 9–6	Grandparent Responsibilities, 2000		
	Total	Male	Female
All grandparents living with grandchildren	5,771,671	2,054,842	3,716,829
Grandparent responsible for grandchildren	2,426,730	905,675	1,521,055
Grandparent not responsible	3,344,941	1,149,167	2,195,774

Source: Simmons & Dye, 2003. (Grandparents Living with Grandchildren: 2000 Census Brief)

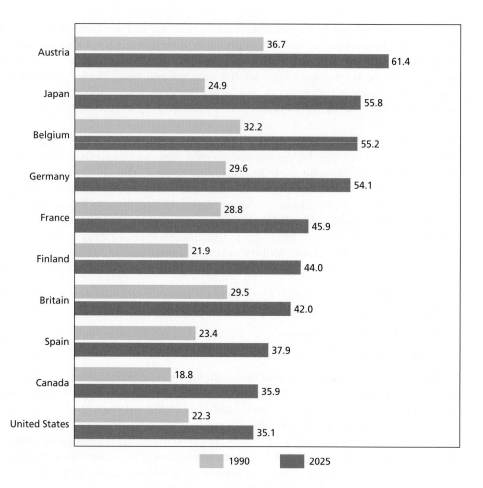

**Figure 9–6 Ratio
of Retirement-Age People
to 100 Working-Age Adults,
1990 and 2025**

Source: Nicholas D. Kristof, "Aging
World, New Wrinkles," *The New
York Times,* September 22, 1996,
pp. 1, 5. Data from Organization
for Economic Cooperation and
Development. © 1996 by The
New York Times. Reprinted
by permission of The New York
Times Graphics.

population to produce adequate surpluses. But even in the United States, the problem of increasing dependency ratios poses a threat to the Social Security and Medicare systems, a problem to which we return in the Social Policy section of the chapter.

One measure that might reduce the rate of increase in economic dependency is to extend the average working years of older workers. Such measures are more popular than one might imagine. Significant numbers of workers would prefer to continue working as long as possible even if they could be assured of financial security in retirement. Even when people have retired from jobs they disliked, they have trouble adjusting to their new status. Part of the difficulty lies in the lack of role models and reference groups. As noted earlier in the chapter, this is a problem that all older people must cope with, even the fortunate few who have financial security and good health.

DEATH

Death and age have always been closely linked, but today death is almost exclusively the fate of the old. This association has some significant implications. Although the old have always died, the dying have not always been old. Only in recent decades has death occurred mainly among the elderly. Because of the link between old age and death in modern industrial societies, the social issues related to death involve aging as well. In fact, one reason that the old are avoided and isolated is their association with death.

Social scientists study death in terms of its psychological and social impact. Their research indicates that the old, perhaps because of a natural process of disengagement, have less fear of death than the young. There are also indications that during the process of dying a distinct pattern of feelings and behavior emerges. This *dying trajectory* differs from one person to another and from one situation to another.

The best-known description of the dying trajectory was proposed in the now-classic work of Elisabeth Kübler-Ross (1969, 1975). Kübler-Ross believes that the dying process is characterized by five stages: (1) denial and isolation, (2) anger and resentment, (3) bargaining and an attempt to postpone death, (4) depression and a sense of loss, and (5) acceptance. Some social scientists have pointed out that Kübler-Ross's research involved primarily young people with terminal illnesses and that the stages she identified may not always apply to the elderly—especially the very old, who sometimes claim to be ready for death well before it is clear that they are dying (Retsinas, 1988).

By understanding the dying process, physicians, caretakers, friends, and family members can make the experience easier for the dying person. Being informed of one's true condition is very important to the terminally ill (Callahan, Meulen, & Topinkova, 1995). Several studies suggest, however, that current practices in hospitals and nursing homes offer almost no possibility of a good and meaningful death. Critically ill patients are usually treated as though they were already dead. Their autopsies are planned; they are sometimes kept in hallways or supply closets; their relatives may be approached for a donation of organs. In contrast, **hospices**—special institutions designed for the terminally ill—are as comfortable and homelike as possible and are staffed by personnel who are trained in working with the dying. A hospice may be a place, a set of services, or both. Hospices increasingly emphasize home health services for the dying, including visiting nurses, on-call physicians, and counselors. Home care enables many people to live their final days in familiar surroundings close to their loved ones (Hastings Center, 2003).

The underlying problem addressed by the hospice movement is discussed in Chapter 2: Today, because of the availability of life-prolonging medical technology, people are increasingly faced with choices about how to die. Surveys indicate that most people would prefer to die at home. Being at home with one's family seems to provide a greater chance for "death with dignity"; being institutionalized implies loss of control and individuality.

Federal laws that allow Medicare reimbursement for home hospice care went into effect in 1983. This policy encouraged more people to choose home care for the dying. In consequence, the number of hospice patients has increased dramatically, from about 100,000 in the early 1980s to more than 500,000 today (Hospice Foundation of America, 2002). Although this figure indicates the increasing popularity of dying at home, it masks the extreme stress many individuals and families may experience as they attempt to provide around-the-clock care in their homes (Pipher, 1999).

Death with Dignity. "Death with dignity" has become a popular phrase as people confront the issues of relegating the old and the terminally ill to institutions and to a life sustained by machines. Often, the use of these technologies prolongs the dying process rather than maintaining life. Widespread concern about these problems is further evidence of the need for hospices and home health care for the aged.

One of the most unusual episodes in the sociology of old age is the story of Brandeis University professor Morris Schwartz. Much to his surprise, Schwartz became one of the most respected contemporary voices on issues of life and death. And it is all because a former student took the trouble to renew their friendship and to listen to what his former professor had to say.

The student, Mitch Albom (1998), visited the terminally ill Schwartz, whom everyone called Morrie, every Tuesday for several months. He recorded his insights about life and death, and compiled them into a book entitled *Tuesdays with Morrie,* which became a best-seller. It was featured on the *Oprah Winfrey Show,* and a television movie of the story was made. By now the book has reached millions of people with its message.

Morrie Schwartz.

Morrie Schwartz had many lessons to teach about confronting death. Chief among them is that death is part of life and must be experienced fully. It is not something to be ashamed of, to be whispered about, as is too often the case. For Schwartz, the end of life is a time to dwell on "love, responsibility, spirituality, awareness." To do so, despite his increasing weakness and pain, the former professor surrounded himself with the people and things he loved and, according to Albom, essentially wrapped himself in a cocoon of human activities, conversation, interaction, and affection. He even hosted his own "living funeral" to give his family and himself the rare opportunity to hear and say the things that they all felt needed to be said. Schwartz's criticism of the American way of death was thus countered by the offer of a loving and deeply personal example of how death can be dignified, spiritual, and enlightening.

Social Policy

The primary social-policy issues concerning the elderly are housing, health care (including controversies over the right to die), retirement, and Social Security.

Housing

From 1980 to the present, the proportion of elderly people living alone did not change significantly, but since the number of people over 65 in the population increased from about 24 million to more than 32 million, the total number of people living alone increased to almost 10 million. Of these, women constitute the vast majority (*Statistical Abstract*, 2006). Isolation and loneliness, and the depression these may engender, become serious problems for the solitary elderly, especially when their ability to get out and see others decreases.

Most elderly people who live with their children or other younger relatives do so for financial reasons or because of declining health. Most older people prefer to live in their own homes, but near family members. However, as they and their homes age, problems arise that are increasingly difficult to cope with. At the same time, their income tends to decrease and their health-care needs tend to increase, further reducing their ability to live independently.

Despite these problems, most older people want to continue living where they are. Not only do they view it as demeaning to move to a retirement community or an "old folks' home," but their housing choices may be limited by long waiting lists or lack of appropriate housing in a particular area. Among people aged 65 to 74, only about 2 percent are in nursing homes; of those aged 75 to 84, the figure is 6 percent. But according to federal surveys, 23 percent of those over 85 are in nursing homes. Because so many more people in the last group suffer from dementia or physical infirmities, an increasing proportion will require nursing-home or comparable care, which in turn will require an increase in public funds from the present level of about $18 billion.

The combination of federal budget cuts, the continuing war in Iraq, and the effects of Gulf Coast storms are likely to drastically reduce the ability of governments at all levels to provide housing subsidies for the elderly or low-income populations. The only major political initiative that may aid elderly people should come in the form of legislation on health care, particularly legislation affecting the costs of prescription drugs.

Health Care

The problem of providing health care for the aged must be viewed in the context of the rapid expansion of the elderly population. Between 1900 and 2000, the number of Americans over the age of 65 grew eightfold while the population as a whole tripled. By 2030, nearly one-quarter of the U.S. population will be over 65 (Altman & Shactman, 2002). Moreover, more than 3 million elderly people are among the oldest old—those over 85—currently the fastest growing age group in the nation. These people are most likely to be mentally or physically impaired and hence most in need of care that they cannot afford.

As a result of these trends, Medicare, the federal program that provides health care for the elderly, is in financial trouble. The basic problem is that Medicare payments to doctors, hospitals, and other health-care facilities are increasing at a faster rate than the revenues coming into the fund from payroll taxes (Medicare is part of the Social Security system). This accounts for proposals that would require elderly people in higher income brackets to pay taxes on the Medicare benefits they receive, to pay for a larger share of their medical care, and to obtain a second opinion before undergoing major surgery. These recommendations are opposed by representatives of the black elderly, who believe that blacks suffer disproportionately from cutbacks in Medicare and Medicaid coverage. They recommend instead that greater emphasis be placed on cost containment and preventive measures.

Some observers believe a more comprehensive policy toward health care for the elderly is needed. In the meantime, greater planning and steps to distribute income to living family members so that it is not absorbed by long-term care are becoming a ritual of aging in many families. Many elderly people fear that they will lose all their savings if they are placed in a residential care institution, be it a nursing home or a long-term-care facility. Recent changes in the Medicare laws protect elderly people from losing all of their savings if their spouse is institutionalized. Typically, however, the elderly person lives alone, and it is still common for insurance plans, including Medicare, to insist that an individual's assets be used to pay the costs of nursing-home or hospital care above Medicare's contribution. As a result, many elderly are creating "living trusts" in which they cede ownership of their assets to their children or beneficiaries but retain the right to use those assets to pay for their living expenses.

As the 2008 presidential election approaches, the nation's elderly voters are being heavily courted by all the potential candidates. As a major swing vote, they are capable of defeating or electing a candidate about whom they have strong feelings. This is one reason that issues related to Social Security and medical care, such as subsidies for prescription drugs, continue to play a major role in political campaigns at both the national and state levels. AARP, the largest single lobbying organization in the United States, exerted considerable influence over congressional elections in key states with high proportions of elderly residents, and AARP and other organizations will continue to exert a powerful influence on social policies that affect the elderly. It is equally likely, therefore, that generational conflict over who pays the bills for Social Security and Medicare will increase in years to come.

In 2003 President Bush signed the landmark Medicare Prescription Improvement and Modernization Act, after intense lobbying from major drug companies, a last-minute approval by AARP, and bitter partisan debate in Congress. In signing the bill, President Bush said,

> First and foremost, this new law will provide Medicare coverage for prescription drugs. Medicare was enacted to provide seniors with the latest in modern medicine. In 1965 that usually meant house calls, or operations, or long hospital stays. Today, modern medicine includes out-patient care, disease screenings, and prescription drugs.

The startup of the prescription drug benefit under Medicare encountered a variety of major problems, most of them associated with the difficulty of evaluating competing drug plans and deciding which one best meets the needs of a particular individual. And as expected, the plan has drawn a great deal of criticism, partly because many seniors do not find their drug costs lowered and a large proportion of the $400 billion that it is expected to cost over the next ten years will go to insurance companies that administer the benefit. Annual prescription drug costs for senior citizens covered by Medicare average about $3,200, of which seniors will still pay 66 percent, or about $2,100. Seniors who live below 135 percent of the poverty threshold and do not have assets (other than a car or home) worth $6,000 for a single person or $900 for a couple will have all their prescription costs covered, a major improvement for low-income seniors. Over two-thirds of seniors do not qualify, however (*Public Citizen*. 2004). The legislation is also controversial because it failed to adopt measures that would keep drug costs down by allowing imports of generic prescription medicines from other countries, such as Canada, where they are less expensive. But if the drug policy for seniors is controversial, it is far less so than Republican proposals to change the nation's Social Security system.

Retirement and Social Security

The Social Security system was not designed to be the main source of income for the elderly. It was originally intended as a form of insurance against unexpected reductions in income due to retirement, disability, or the death of a wage-earning spouse. However, the system has become a kind of government-administered public pension plan. Many people do not have pensions, investments, or sufficient savings to support them in retirement, and this, coupled with the practice of mandatory retirement, has made Social Security the main source of income for the elderly.

Perhaps the greatest flaw in the Social Security system is that its benefits are too small for the purpose they must serve. In 2007 the average monthly benefit was $1,049.40 for retired workers, $978.50 for disabled workers, and $993.10 for widows and widowers (U.S. Social Security Administration, 2007). This is far from an adequate income. When it was created seventy years ago, Social Security was intended to provide an income supplement for elderly Americans. In fact, with the number of Americans receiving other pension funds declining rapidly, about 10.6 million people, or 22 percent of the 48 million who received Social Security benefits in 2005, live on that check alone, according to the Social Security Administration (Waggoner, 2005).

Social Security is financed by fixed wage and payroll taxes based on the first $90,600 of annual income. This means that lower-paid workers pay a higher proportion of their income in Social Security taxes than higher-paid workers do. Social Security benefits, however, are based on the amount of tax paid, not on a percentage of total income. Thus, the poorest workers will remain the poorest after retiring.

The Social Security system also discriminates against women. At age 65 a woman is entitled to benefits equal to half of those received by her husband, even if she has never worked outside the home. If she has been employed and has paid Social Security taxes, she can receive benefits on her own account or through her husband. But she cannot do both. Because most husbands work longer than their wives, most women can collect higher Social Security payments by drawing from their husbands' accounts.

After his reelection in 2004, President Bush made reform of the Social Security system his primary policy initiative. "As we fix Social Security," he stated,

> we must make it a better deal for our younger workers by allowing them to put part of their payroll taxes in personal retirement accounts. Personal accounts would be entirely voluntary. The money would go into a conservative mix of bond and stock funds that would have the opportunity to earn a higher rate of return than anything the current system could provide. A young person who earns an average of $35,000 a year over his or her career would have nearly a quarter million dollars saved in his or her own account upon retirement. That savings would provide a nest egg to supplement that worker's traditional Social Security check, or to pass on to his or her children.

The president calls this an "ownership" approach to Social Security reform because individuals and their families would no longer risk losing their Social Security benefits at death but would be able to pass them on to heirs like any other form of wealth. Critics note that this approach changes the Social Security system from a social insurance system to a privatized system of personal accounts. Among the prime beneficiaries of a privatized system would be financial institutions like banks and brokerage houses, which would receive large sums for managing private social security accounts. There is also widespread agreement, even among the president's supporters, that privatization does nothing to address the projected shortfalls in Social Security funds that will occur later in this century as more of the baby boom generation reaches retirement age. In any case, even before the disasters of the Gulf Coast storms in 2005, privatization of Social Security was becoming extremely unpopular, especially among older voters—who, as noted earlier, carry a great deal of weight in American politics. And Hurricanes Katrina and Rita forced the Social Security debate to be placed on a "back burner."

In what ways is the Social Security system a form of social insurance, and how would that change if the system were privatized? Who would be most likely to benefit and who most likely to lose out under a system of privatized social security?

Future Prospects

As the Baby Boom generation continues to age, government and the media will pay more attention to the problems of aging. There will likely be increased support for hospice care, Medicare, and related programs that address the health needs of the elderly, as well as ongoing debates over Social Security and even assisted suicide. But this does not mean that members of the baby boom generation will accept aging gracefully. A recent survey by the Yankelovich polling firm found that "people 60 years old today have an actuarial life expectancy of 82.3, but boomers don't consider themselves bound by the laws of statistics; they fully expect that advances in health care and genomics are going to enable them to live past 100" (Adler, 2005, p. 2). Yet while many members of this huge generation may be in denial about their age, enough of them are aware of the problems of aging so that they are placing increasing pressure on elected officials for legislation that will serve their needs. At the same time, it is clear that as life expectancy increases, so will the retirement age, so that larger numbers of seniors will remain in the labor force, both full time and part time. The decline of employer-based retirement plans is another major reason why elderly people are remaining in the paid labor force in growing numbers.

What implications does the aging of the baby boom population have for social policies directed at the problems of the aged?

Current Controversies

DO WE HAVE A RIGHT TO DIE?

Probably the most controversial doctor in the United States today is Jack Kevorkian, the so-called Michigan suicide doctor. It seems that whenever he uses his painless death apparatus to inject a willing patient with a lethal drug, he is featured in the national news and either imprisoned or threatened with imprisonment. Kevorkian's actions raise a larger issue for public debate: Do individuals have the right to kill themselves, and do doctors or other medical professionals have the right to allow them to do so or even to assist them? As more elderly people in this and other aging nations endure lingering and painful illnesses, these questions will be asked with increasing frequency.

The ancient Hippocratic norms of medical practice deny doctors the right to hasten death. But these norms are changing as a growing number of terminally ill patients plead with medical workers for alternatives to life-prolonging procedures that may actually increase their physical and mental suffering.

Those who believe in the sanctity of life are quick to argue that for the state to condone assisted suicide or the individual's right to commit suicide by any means is an abdication of the obligation to value human life, be it that of an unborn fetus or an aging, terminally ill individual (Wilson, 1994). Szasz (1992) and others who support the right to die admit that Kevorkian is performing a public service by raising the issue for public debate. They also believe that ultimately an individual of any age ought to have access to the drugs or other means that would allow death to be an individual choice, not one that must be assisted by a "death doctor."

In 1997 the Supreme Court ruled that the "right to die" is not a constitutional right. This decision allowed Congress to pass laws that effectively nullify Oregon's right-to-die statutes, even though Oregon had previously held referendums on the issue (Kaminer, 2000). In 1998 Dr. Jack Kevorkian administered a lethal injection to Thomas Youk, who was suffering from a painful terminal illness. For assisting in this suicide Kevorkian was convicted of second-degree murder and sentenced to 10 to 25 years in prison.

Both the sentencing of Dr. Kevorkian and the recent political battles over the right to die have also highlighted the pervasive problem of chronic pain and inadequate approaches to palliative care. Many health professionals point out that the greatest fear of terminally ill patients is the suffering their illness will cause for family members, but

Dr. Kevorkian leaving prison in 2007.

they also fear the extreme pain that often accompanies such illnesses. Until recently, patients did not have adequate access to pain-reducing drugs or to care oriented toward making their last days as comfortable as possible. Gradually, with the rise of hospice care and greater attention to pain and its treatment, this situation is changing.

GOING BEYOND LEFT AND RIGHT

What right do people have to take their own lives? What right do governments have to intervene in such a private decision? Today people on the right often ask the first question, usually out of a concern that suicide, doctor assisted or otherwise, represents yet another step toward the devaluation of life itself. People on the left are more prone to ask a version of the second question out of a desire to preserve the autonomy of the individual when faced with suffering. Curiously, however, the issues of the right to die and assisted suicide find people on the left arguing against government intervention and people with more conservative views arguing against individual autonomy. (See the Current Controversies box above.)

The majority of elderly people, many of whom are disturbingly close to the realities of these issues, tend to avoid these left–right ideological divisions. Their behavior in choosing living wills and "do not resuscitate" orders suggests that the desire to avoid needless suffering when faced with the inevitability of death is a normal and practical human response. Their behavior does not in itself argue for a right to die, but it does suggest that many would take the position that these matters are best resolved by individuals, their doctors, and their immediate family.

The tragic case of Terri Schiavo provides an example of how Americans are increasingly understanding end-of-life issues as private ones involving individuals and their families. Schiavo's case became a national issue as political leaders went all the way to the Supreme Court to prevent her doctors from withdrawing her from the life support systems that had prolonged her existence for many years. The Court refused to hear the case, and life support was withdrawn. An autopsy showed conclusively that Schiavo could never have recovered consciousness. The public's reaction to the effort to force her doctors to leave the breathing and feeding tubes in her body was fiercely negative, as the vast majority saw her as an innocent victim of political ideology.

Summary

- The United States is an aging society, and this fact has a major impact on social institutions as well as on the lives of individuals. The social problems of the aged are aggravated by three factors: labeling, the concept of work as the basis of personal value, and economic deprivation.

- From the functionalist perspective, aging is a social problem because the institutions of modern society are not meeting the needs of the dependent elderly. Interactionists believe that the elderly are stigmatized because they do not conform to the norms of a youth-oriented culture. Conflict theorists view the problems of the elderly as stemming from lack of power to shape social institutions to meet their needs.

- Many of the problems faced by the aged in America today arise from the nature of modern Western society, in which their productive and cultural functions have been disrupted by modernization.

- Age stratification is the segregation of people into different groups or strata on the basis of their age. It limits the kinds of roles that the members of each group can hold, and it can lead to conflict.

- The number of aged people in the United States is increasing, and so is the proportion of the population that is over the age of 65. Two-thirds of the elderly live in urban areas.

- Ageism is bias against the aged. It arises largely from the belief that the old are useless because they do not work and cannot reproduce, and it is common in government, business and industry, the medical profession, and the media.

- The aging process can be divided into primary aging and secondary aging. Primary aging is a result of molec-ular and cellular changes. Secondary aging is an accelerated version of normal aging caused by environmental factors like stress or poor diet.

- The psychological difficulties of the aged stem largely from the fact that their new status is poorly defined, and they therefore tend to accept the negative labels applied to them. For example, it is widely believed that intellectual ability declines with age, but this belief is incorrect. Intellectual capacity remains unchanged until very late in life, and senility affects only 1 percent of elderly people.

- The aged exhibit many characteristics of minority groups. In particular, they are victims of prejudice, stereotyping, and discrimination. They are also increasingly subject to mental and physical abuse. Among the popular stereotypes about the elderly are the portrayal of older women as hypochondriacs, the negative view of widowhood, the rocking-chair image, and the belief that the old are sexually inactive.

- The aged are more prone to chronic illnesses but less able to pay for medical care. Despite the passage of Medicare and Medicaid, many elderly people still lack adequate health care. A major geriatric health issue is unnecessary institutionalization.

- Older workers often experience economic discrimination, both in the form of mandatory retirement and when they seek new employment. Older women and members of minority groups face additional hardships.

- Most older people want to live near their children, and many live with them. Many families, however, are ill equipped to care for elderly parents, making institutionalization the only alternative for those who are unable or unwilling to live alone.

- Workers who retire have trouble adjusting to their new status. They lack role models and reference groups; many must also cope with reduced income.

- Social scientists have studied the dying trajectory—the pattern of feelings and behavior that emerges during the dying process. They have identified five stages: denial, anger, bargaining, depression, and acceptance. The hospice movement attempts to provide special institutions for the terminally ill as well as home health services for the dying.

- There is no coherent housing policy for the aged, and existing health-care programs are costly and inadequate. The Social Security system has also been a target of criticism because it discriminates against women and against elderly people who continue to work; moreover, the payments are too low to support those who lack other sources of income.

Key Terms

ageism, p. 296
modernization, p. 297
age stratification, p. 298

gerontology, p. 304
primary aging, p. 304

secondary aging, p. 304
hospices, p. 313

Social Problems Online

The U.S. Administration on Aging (AoA) has a Web site at **www.aoa.dhhs.gov/** with connections to the Internet and e-mail resources on aging. The resource topics range from Alzheimer's disease to consumer information, to legal services, to state and local agencies. Social scientists will be interested in the links to demographic centers, data sets, and statistical information. A short statistical profile of older Americans can be found on the U.S. Census Bureau's Web page, at **www.census.gov/population/www/socdemo/age.html**.

A branch of the AoA, the National Aging Information Center (**www.aoa.dhhs.gov/naic/dbs.html**), offers downloadable statistics from a searchable database. The Maxwell School of Syracuse University has a Center for Policy Research (**www-cpr.maxwell.syr.edu/links.htm**), which provides several links to other sites of interest, with brief summaries of the types of data sets included. The page is rich with connections to U.S. and western European research institutions.

One of the largest and most important nongovernment organizations in the United States is AARP, at **www.aarp.org/**. Counting the 35 million elderly Americans as its "constituents," AARP offers several services on its Web pages. Of interest to students of social problems are several short reports of survey data. In a partisan but not inaccurate manner, they track public opinion about issues that affect older Americans. As part of its education and mobilizing efforts, AARP posts up-to-the-minute news briefs on public policy questions such as Social Security. It also addresses consumer issues of interest to its members, such as fraud in telemarketing.

Research Navigator

Follow the instructions on pages 26–27 of this text to access the features of Research Navigator. Once at the Web site, enter your Login Name and Password. Then, to use the Content Select database, use keywords such as "gerontology," "age stratification," and "Social Security," and the search engine will supply relevant and recent scholarly and popular press publications. Use the *New York Times* search-by-subject archive to find recent news articles related to problems of aging, and the Link Library to find relevant Web sites organized by the key terms associated with this chapter.

In Research Navigator, go to the ebsco host and type in the terms *aging* and *public institutions*. You should find an article by Konrad M. Kressley about the impact of aging on different social institutions. What institutions are discussed? How will aging affect them, according to the article? What, in your opinion, is the significance that the article is in a journal called *The Futurist*?

16

THE CHANGING
Family

Dominant Trends

- *With an ever-increasing proportion of mothers with children in the labor force—slightly less than 30 percent of families now include a male wage earner and a homemaker mother—there is increased pressure on policymakers to address family and work issues such as better child-care institutions.*

- *Throughout the developed world, the proportion of children being raised in single-parent families is rising, and in the United States about one-third of children under 18 are living with a single parent.*

- *Divorce rates remain high in the Western world, where marriages are based more on individual choice than on interfamily arrangements, and in the United States there is about a 50 percent chance that a given marriage will end in divorce.*

- *Teenage birthrates continue to fall in the United States and elsewhere in the world due to better communications to teens about the risks and burdens of early parenthood.*

- *With resources for child support dwindling in the United States, less than half of single mothers with needy children receive help from federal, state, or local governments.*

The family is a vital institution in all societies, although the structure of families and what is expected of parents and children may vary widely across different cultures and societies. In India or Pakistan, for example, parents generally try to select their children's spouses, a practice that most people in Western cultures reject. As a central child-rearing institution of all societies, however, the family is not itself a social problem. It is when families encounter stresses—including stress caused by major social forces such as globalization—that they are likely to break apart, and children and parents may experience negative consequences that can pose problems for entire societies. Teenage pregnancy, juvenile delinquency, domestic violence, and isolation and loneliness are a few of the social problems related to issues affecting families.

In every recent presidential election campaign, "family values" has been a hot issue. Conservatives attack liberals for their tolerance of alternative family forms, especially gay marriage and single parenthood. Liberals assert that the conservatives' attacks are a smoke screen to divert attention from the relatively low levels of assistance given to struggling families by the institutions of government. These debates are not likely to disappear in the foreseeable future, especially as the diversity of family forms in the United States and throughout the world continues to increase. And the debate tends to emerge in a variety of situations. For example, the popular television show *The Simpsons* has been a target of much criticism by conservatives, but those who defend the show claim that despite their outrageous behavior, the Simpsons actually represent the contemporary nuclear family (Cantor, 2000).

No matter how they view the consequences of change in families, sociologists agree that the family is here to stay as a social institution (Mason, Skolnick, & Sugarman, 2003). They also agree that what Americans understand by "family" is becoming far more diverse. Alongside the more traditional two-parent nuclear families, there will be an increasing number of families with one parent or with stepparents, as well as gay and lesbian families. A major question, to which we will turn in the Social Policy section of the chapter, is to what extent laws and other government policies can help people in families of all kinds realize their full potential as human beings.

Marriages may end in divorce, and children may be raised by one parent or by other relatives, yet society continues to regard the nuclear family as the norm. In another society, an extended-family system might remain the norm despite the frequent dispersal of such families into nuclear units. A social problem arises only when the pressure for change can no longer be accommodated within the limits of existing social structures or when those who want to maintain those structures fear that they cannot do so. Often these pressures result in changes in the norms themselves. For example, as divorce rates rise, we no longer condemn couples whose marriages are about to break up; instead, we alter our norms for marriage. We encourage couples to work out their problems, but if divorce is inevitable, we accept it and sanction another, relatively new norm—remarriage (Turner, 2002).

As the social institution that organizes intimate relationships among adults and socializes new generations, the family is frequently singled out as the source of many social problems. Functionalist theorists argue that the inability of certain groups, especially the poor and immigrants, to maintain their traditional structures in new societies causes their children to seek alternative relationships—for example, in gangs, criminal groups, or other deviant peer groups. Interactionists study patterns of interaction within the family for clues to why some family members drift toward deviant careers. They often find that certain kinds of families, especially those headed by women or those in which the couple does not marry and conform to conventional norms of family formation, are stigmatized as the source of social problems like teenage pregnancy and welfare dependency. For conflict theorists, the family is a source of social problems when the values that are taught within it conflict with those of the larger society. But regardless of their theoretical perspective on the family, sociologists tend to focus on what can be done by other institutions in society, particularly social-welfare institutions, to maintain and reinforce family stability.

In this chapter we examine various types of problems and policy initiatives related to family structure. But first it is important to gain a clear understanding of the nature of families.

THE NATURE OF FAMILIES

A **kinship unit** is a group of individuals who are related to one another by blood, marriage, or adoption. Within the kinship group there is usually a division of authority, privilege, responsibility, and economic and sex roles. Definitions of kinship differ from one society to another. In some societies the basic kinship group is the **nuclear family**—a father, a mother, and their children, living apart from other kin (or, increasingly, a single parent and his or her children). In other societies a more common type of kinship group is the **extended family**—parents, children, grandparents, aunts, uncles, and others living together or in very close proximity. In the typical extended family, parents may retain authority over their married sons and daughters, who maintain their nuclear family units within the larger extended-family kinship structure. Increasingly, societies exhibit another type of kinship group, the **modified extended family,** in which the individual nuclear families live separately, but the extended family remains a strong kinship organization through a combination of interpersonal attachments and various forms of economic exchanges and mutual aid.

The nuclear family is the predominant kinship group in hunting-and-gathering societies and in industrial societies, whereas the extended family is more likely to be found in agrarian societies. However, almost all societies, regardless of their level of economic and political development, are organized around a system of modified extended kinship units within which the nuclear family is a more or less autonomous unit. In societies in which the extended-kin system is the dominant family type, married couples generally choose to live within the family network established by either the man's or the woman's kinship group. In societies in which the nuclear family is dominant, newly married couples are expected to set up a household that is relatively independent of both the maternal and the paternal kinship groups while maintaining ties to both extended families.

Industrialization seems to promote the development of smaller family units that are more mobile, both geographically and socially: Although extensive ties with relatives may be maintained, the nuclear family becomes the basic familial unit as the extended family loses its major functions. Functionalist theorists proposed that industrialization, the growth of cities, and modern technology and its demands for a highly

The nuclear family unit, consisting of mother, father, and children, is common not only in modern industrial nations but in many hunting-and-gathering societies as well. In fact, the traditional Eskimo family kinship system is organized in much the same way as the American nuclear family.

educated and mobile labor force brought about a decrease in the economic functions of the extended family and an increase in the functions of the nuclear family (Goode, 1959; Parsons, 1943). However, after years of empirical research on changing family structure in different types of societies, sociologists no longer believe there is a unilinear trend from extended to nuclear family forms that accompanies industrialization and urbanization (Casper, 2002). There is evidence that nuclear families predominated in preindustrial periods and that extended-family forms persist in some industrial societies even with increases in nuclear-family organization. Changes in family form and function in the United States and other large contemporary societies suggest that many different family forms are possible and will coexist under different economic and social conditions (Skolnick & Skolnick, 2007).

Regardless of type, all families are characterized by an organization of roles. If the family is to function adequately, its members must perform those roles in ways compatible both with the expectations of other family members and with the standards of their society.

How do major changes in the economy and in the composition of the labor force contribute to changes in the way families are organized and the way they budget their time?

Adequate Family Functioning

All families are continually undergoing change because they must constantly adapt to a family cycle of development in which the roles of all family members change (Popenoe, 2005; Williams, 2000). For example, most families go through the stages of early marriage, child rearing, the empty nest, and retirement. During each stage and in the periods of transition from one stage to the next, the family faces the challenge of maintaining stability and continuity, that is, functioning adequately.

Failure to function adequately could lead to problems within the family. Such failure is usually involuntary, resulting from either external or internal crises. External crises such as war and economic recession disrupt the family from the outside. The absence of a parent during military service changes both that parent's roles and those of the other parent; unemployment of a parent who usually works can be unsettling not only because other family members are likely to be anxious about their unexpected economic insecurity, but also because the unemployed parent suffers a loss of self-esteem and/or authority. It is extremely difficult to maintain loving relationships when the family is experiencing severe economic hardship; in surveys on divorce, the majority of respondents consistently list arguments over money as a major, if not the leading, cause of their divorce (Mason, Skolnick, & Sugarman, 2003).

Internal crises arise within the family—for example, when a family member suffers from a serious physical or mental disorder. Many families adjust to the need to take on the roles of the handicapped member and the responsibility of caring for him or her. However, this added burden may cause strain. Marital infidelity can be another source of internal crisis, particularly if it is seen as a threat to the family. The same can be said for a major change in the roles of family members. For example, a parent who suddenly decides to work outside the home instead of staying home with the children may cause other family members to feel threatened or confused.

These stresses and other interpersonal problems may reduce the family to an "empty shell," one that is held together not so much by feelings of warmth and attraction as by outside pressures. Within the shell, members of the family feel no strong attachment to one another; they neglect mutual obligations and in general keep communication to a minimum (Cuber & Haroff, 1965; Okun, 1996).

Several factors contribute to the continuation of empty-shell marriages. Habit and fear of change play a role, as do economic constraints. In addition, both partners may feel that divorce or separation would be wrong or might harm the children. There is also usually some social pressure to stay together; in many areas, social life for adults more or less presupposes married couples. Also, some marriage counselors assume that their job is to preserve the marriage, even though their clients might be happier unmarried (Turner, 2002).

Although about half of all marriages begun during the past two decades will end in divorce, another half will not. Because the breakup of marriages is more often associated with social problems, less attention is devoted to marriages that remain vital throughout the partners' lives. Indeed, with all the stresses and changes that couples must endure, and given the greater acceptance of divorce, it is almost miraculous that so many marriages remain satisfying, that is, that each partner feels fulfilled emotionally, sexually, and socially even with advancing age. Sociologists are only beginning to understand what makes marriages long-lasting and vital, but clearly economic influences on the married couple are of great importance (Cherlin, 1996; Skolnick & Skolnick, 2007).

Effects of Women's Employment

In the traditional concept of the American family, the husband worked in the paid labor force and the wife worked—unpaid—at home. In 1960, about 60 percent of American families still conformed to this model. By 2005, only about 30 percent did so (*Statistical*

All couples argue, but conflict is a daily routine for some, and their home life tends to be tense and unhappy. Family researchers are often surprised at how long such conflicted relationships may last.

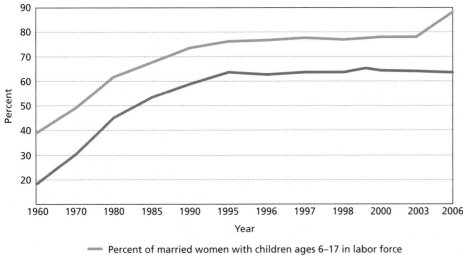

Figure 10–1 Employment Status of Married Women with Children, 1960–2006

Source: Data from U.S. Bureau of Labor Statistics, 2007.

Abstract, 2005). What had been accepted as the norm for generations has become an exception. Today about 71 percent of American women with children under the age of 18 work outside the home (U.S. Bureau of Labor Statistics, 2007). Figure 10–1 shows trends in the labor force participation rate (the percentage of a population actively working or seeking work) for married women in families in which the husband is present in the home. Note especially the dramatic increase in the proportion of women with children under age 6 who are now in the labor force (64.6 percent) from the level recorded in 1960 (18.6 percent). Much of the conflict over family issues and over the sharing of domestic and economic roles stems from this major change.

Many women entered the labor force to use the skills they had learned in college and out of a new sense of identity stimulated by the women's movement. Many others found jobs simply because they needed the money. For both groups, the reversals of economic trends that occurred in the late 1970s, early 1990s, and 2001–2002 were major blows. Economic opportunities became less abundant, and debt replaced savings. The cost of living outstripped disposable income, and people found themselves working harder than ever just to keep from falling behind. In many cases, women were hit hardest by these economic recessions. Often they were single parents, but even working wives experienced severe stress and anxiety. As Katherine Newman (1988) found in her extensive interviews of middle-class women, "Having experienced the benefits of middle-class life in their own childhoods, they felt they owed it to their kids to reciprocate across the generations. Downward mobility made it almost impossible to follow through" (p. 215).

Most sociologists agree that the movement of women out of the home and into the labor force is one of the most important social trends of the second half of the twentieth century (Furstenberg & Cherlin, 1991; Popenoe, 2005). It has caused an upheaval in traditional male and female roles in the family, as well as in other social institutions, as couples struggle to balance the demands of work and family life.

Despite this massive transformation, attitudes about working mothers have not changed as fast as the statistics. In her study of women who became mothers after the massive movement of American women into the labor force, sociologist Kathleen Gerson (1985) found that most expected or hoped to be able to stay home and care for their young children as their mothers had done. Those whose mothers had been full-time workers expected to be workers themselves and typically welcomed the challenges of work and motherhood. But for all working mothers, Gerson found that inequalities in the workplace, lack of support for their domestic roles (in the form of family sick leave, for example), and lack of support from their spouses made their decision to enter the labor force while their children were young a very difficult (but increasingly necessary) one (Jacobs & Gerson, 2004).

Several studies have concluded that if the wife works outside the home as a matter of choice, the marriage is as happy as or happier than it would be if she chose to remain at home; if she works out of necessity, marital happiness suffers. The relative value of working by choice and remaining at home varies at different stages of the family life cycle: When there are preschool children, happiness seems greater if the wife remains at home; when the children are in elementary school, working by choice seems to produce greater happiness; after the children enter high school, the value of the two choices seems about equal. However, when the wife works out of necessity, marital happiness is lower in all cases (Skolnick & Skolnick, 2007).

Most evidence does not support the traditional view that women are fulfilled by a domestic role. Surveys on this issue tend to show that the lives of both career women and full-time homemakers include a mixture of satisfactions and problems (NORC, 1999). Although many working women have a strong sense of independence and enjoy their work, they have more complicated, hectic lives than full-time homemakers, who have more time for themselves but may suffer from boredom, stagnation, and lack of independence and money.

In a landmark study of women's attitudes about work and marriage, Arlie Hochschild (1990) found that women who work have less time for themselves and often think of the work they do in the home as a kind of "second shift." Some women resent the extra work and the time spent juggling the responsibilities of job and home; others take the situation for granted. In a study of middle-class men's reactions to the problem of the "second shift," Kathleen Gerson (1993) found that many men are beginning to shoulder more of the responsibility for domestic tasks like child care. And recent statistics from the U.S. Census Bureau show that an increasing number of men are becoming "house husbands," at least in the sense that almost one out of five married men is minding preschool children at home—although these statistics do not reflect their feelings about the matter or the quality of their child care.

A more problematic finding of Gerson's study is that a significant proportion of the men she interviewed were becoming what she calls "autonomous males." They appear to have decided that it is too difficult to adjust to the demand for greater equality or to find wives with more traditional views; instead, they are choosing to avoid lasting relationships in favor of the single life. This is an international trend. Research on the Italian family, for example, finds that more men are choosing to marry later in life and remaining in their family of origin for more of their adult years. This is placing new strains on the family and resulting in a rapid decline in birthrates (Bohlen, 1996; Jacobs & Gerson, 2004).

Juggling Work and Family Responsibilities. A common theme in all urban industrial societies is the difficulty of juggling work and family responsibilities, especially for women (Jacobs & Gerson, 2004). Since 1970 there has been an increase in the numbers of women and men working more than 50 hours a week. This segment of the labor force is the most stressed, and those with children have the greatest difficulty in coping with domestic and work responsibilities. But the data also show that, on the average, women are working fewer hours a week than men, even though the percentage in the 50 hours or more category has doubled since 1970.

Polls often reveal that women with young children would prefer to stay home rather than work, but that economic conditions and the desire to achieve and maintain a middle-class lifestyle often oblige both parents to work, sometimes at more than one job (Lamanna, 1997). Although the traditional belief that young children suffer if their mothers work was shared by a strong majority as late as the 1970s, this consensus has declined rapidly as more women have actually experienced both work and mothering. Married women of childbearing age, many of whom always did work for a variety of reasons, never quite shared the traditional view; by the 1990s less than a third believed that preschool children suffer if their mothers work outside the home (Rindfuss, Brewster, & Kavee, 1996).

Because couples often delay marriage while seeking greater economic security, in some cases the woman may have advanced further in her career than her husband by

Studies show that married women with children have less leisure time than their husbands because, in addition to fulfilling their work obligations, they do more of the driving, shopping, and child rearing, including both physical and emotional nurturance.

the time they have children, and the father may stay home to care for them. This imbalance in the traditional norm—male as provider, woman as caregiver—has created stresses in some marriages and innovative role changes in others (Casper, 2002). It should be noted that new telecommunications technologies allow for flexible solutions to the problem of role juggling, permitting more husbands to spend time at home as caregivers. Even so, families are increasingly shifting work and family roles, especially in the early years of marriage and child rearing. For example, the husband may return to school to upgrade his skills while the wife works full time, creating a situation in which the husband becomes the primary parent during those years. These may not be dominant trends, but they are showing up in family statistics. However, more women than men still choose to sacrifice long-term career goals and take part-time jobs so that they can spend more time in child rearing.

Some observers believe that the increasing amount of part-time work helps employers rather than employees. Part-time work is not well paid and usually does not include fringe benefits. In service industries, it results in a low-paid, floating work force that is highly advantageous to employers (Spain, 1996). The employers are, in effect, exploiting the pressure placed on women by the conflicting demands of family responsibilities and economic need.

One consequence of the difficulties couples encounter in juggling work and family roles is that marital happiness often decreases when children are born. Contrary to the common belief that children bring joy to a household, the added stress of caring for a child and managing new financial burdens can be a shock to couples who are not prepared for the realities of parenthood. As a result, growing numbers of couples are postponing childbirth or deciding not to have children at all, as shown by the relatively low birthrates among middle-class couples in most industrial nations (Strong, DeVault, & Cohen, 2005). These trends also explain why social policies such as family leave are extremely popular among couples with young children, who are facing the stresses of work and family role conflicts, and desire some help from the larger society (Berns, 2007; Stone, 2007).

The Black Family

For most of the second half of the twentieth century, indicators of family well-being were alarmingly negative for African Americans (Jencks & Peterson, 1991; Moynihan, 1965). In fact, as recent research by William J. Wilson and others points out, many of the problems of African American families are concentrated in segregated inner-city communities. The drastic decline in husband–wife families in these economically and socially depressed communities is, however, "part of a process that now affects all racial and ethnic groups in the United States" (Wilson, 1996a).

TABLE 10–1	Percentage of Children Living in Single-Parent Families, 1980–2006

Children	Percent			
	1980	1990	2000	2006
Living with both parents				
All children	76.6	71.9	72.2	67.0
White, non-Hispanic	83.2	80.4	79.5	74.1
Black, non-Hispanic	46.9	37.0	41.1	35.0
Hispanic (of any race)	71.1	64.0	68.8	66.0
Living with mother only				
All children	16.3	20.0	23.4	23.0
White, non-Hispanic	11.4	13.4	16.1	18.2
Black, non-Hispanic	39.2	49.3	54.2	51.0
Hispanic (of any race)	19.8	24.0	26.6	25.0
Living with father only				
All children	2.0	3.9	4.4	5.0
White, non-Hispanic	2.0	3.3	4.4	5.0
Black, non-Hispanic	2.8	5.4	4.7	4.0
Hispanic (of any race)	1.6	5.9	4.6	4.0

Source: Data from U.S. Census Bureau.

Much of this variation is explained by differences in opportunities and behavior. In African American communities, rates of marriage vary positively with education; better-educated women are far more likely to marry than are less-educated women. Among whites, the relationship is reversed: White women with more education are less likely than those with less education to marry. "The positive association between education and marriage among African Americans," Wilson (1996a) observes, "is in part due to the extraordinarily low rate of marriage among less educated black Americans, many of whom are concentrated in inner-city neighborhoods" (p. 88).

Data on trends in single-parent families, shown in Table 10–1, indicate that, after some improvements in the late 1990s and the early years of the new century, the proportion of children living with both parents is again declining. This is particularly true of children in poor families, who tend to be members of racial minority groups. Note that from 2000 to 2006 there was a sharp decrease in the proportion of white children living in two-parent families. Today about one-third of children in U.S. households live with a single parent. African Americans have experienced the greatest decline in two-parent families and the greatest increases in single-parent families; the numbers of single-parent families among whites and Hispanics have risen rapidly over the past twenty-five years as well. The table also shows a rather surprising upward trend in the proportion of single-parent families in which the parent is the father. Although it represents only 4.4 percent of families with children, this proportion has more than doubled over the past two decades, making father-only families an important category for further analysis and research (Pinsof, 2002; Rogers, 2001).

Most social scientists agree that the single most important cause of these historic changes has been the sudden and almost complete disappearance of work in inner-city communities for less educated minority males (and, to a somewhat lesser extent, for white males as well). Unless they can reasonably be expected to help support a new family, young fathers are increasingly considered poor prospects for marriage, and marriage norms seem to be weakening as a result of these economic considerations. Especially true among African Americans, it is far less so among more recent arrivals to the inner city, such as Mexicans. The trend, however, is occurring to varying degrees in all population groups (Strong, DeVault, & Cohen, 2005).

The population of males of marriageable age who are not developing marketable skills and are at risk of becoming involved in illegal activities in their impoverished neighborhoods is a major source of the decline in family strength in the inner city (Oppenheimer, 1994; Wilson, 1996a). Table 10–2 shows that the proportion of African American males ages 18 to 24 who are not in school and have not finished high school ("dropouts") decreased during the economic good times of the 1990s and began rising again in the early years of the twenty-first century. With renewed emphasis at all levels of government and society on staying in school, this proportion is now slowly decreasing. This pattern probably reflects the availability of jobs for young minority workers, but it is disturbing because lack of education is a major contributor to single parenthood and family instability. (The table also shows the extremely high drop-out rates among Hispanic students, which mirror the situation among African American students earlier in the twentieth century. In contemporary America, large numbers of Hispanic students are dropping out of high school in favor of low-wage, entry-level jobs. Unfortunately, these jobs tend to severely limit their later economic mobility.)

We can infer, therefore, that income and education are major factors in explaining black–white differences in the marital status of men: "If, instead of their own income distribution, black men had the income distribution of white men, their marital status distribution would . . . be more like that of white men" (Jaynes & Williams, 1989, p. 530).

In sum, insofar as the black family is distinctive, it is probably a consequence, for the most part, of the special intensity and duration of the poverty and discrimination suffered by African Americans. (See Chapters 6 and 7.) In effect, the problems of the black family are symptomatic of larger social problems (Turner, 2002). Therefore, we will not undertake a detailed study of the black family as such but will consider the evidence and possible causes of problems among families in general, bearing in mind that some of these occur with particular frequency among poor blacks.

TABLE 10–2	High School Dropouts, by Race and Hispanic Origin: 1975–2005 (in percent, as of October)						
	1975	1980	1985	1990	1995	2000	2005
Total[a]	15.6	15.6	13.9	13.6	13.9	13.0	11.8
White	13.9	14.4	13.5	13.5	13.6	13.4	11.6
Male	13.5	15.7	14.7	14.2	14.3	15.3	13.3
Female	14.2	13.2	12.3	12.8	13.0	11.4	19.8
Black	27.3	23.5	17.6	15.1	14.4	13.8	14.2
Male	27.8	26.0	18.8	13.6	14.2	16.9	16.7
Female	26.9	21.5	16.6	16.2	14.6	11.0	12.0
Hispanic[b]	34.9	40.3	31.5	37.3	34.7	31.7	28.4
Male	32.6	42.6	35.8	39.8	34.2	37.1	31.7
Female	36.8	38.1	27.0	34.5	35.4	25.5	24.7

[a]Includes other races, not shown separately.

[b]Persons of Hispanic origin may be of any race.

Source: Adapted from *Statistical Abstract*, 2006.

Despite the dramatic rise in single-parent families, especially among African Americans, the extended family is still a thriving institution of African American life.

DIVORCE

All but unheard of in the nineteenth century and still rare before World War I, divorce and remarriage have become commonplace in American society. From the early 1930s until the late 1950s, divorce rates in the United States remained fairly constant—about 1.3 per 1,000 people. As late as 1966, the divorce rate was still only 2.5. But in 2005 half as many couples got divorced as married—about 1.2 million divorces and about 2.3 million marriages—representing a divorce rate of 3.9 per 1,000 people (U.S. Census Bureau, 2006). This trend is partially responsible for the significant increase in the proportion of female-headed and single-person households in the U.S. population. Some experts on the family argue that the divorce rate peaked at 5.3 per 1,000 people in 1981 and has declined significantly since then. But as we see in the On Further Analysis box on page 333, there may be less to cheer about than this trend suggests.

The traditional correlation between socioeconomic and educational levels and the frequency of divorce is no longer as true as it once was. For example, divorce used to be much more likely among people with a high-school education than among those who had completed college, and more frequent among the poor than among members of the middle and upper-middle classes. But in recent years the divorce rate has risen among college-educated couples and those in higher socioeconomic groups.

The highest rate of divorce, amounting to about one-third of all divorces, occurs in the first three years of marriage. This widely known fact leads many people to believe that having children "cements" a marriage and adds to marital happiness. Sociological research conducted in the 1950s documented this popular belief, but it also demonstrated that the facts are otherwise: Having babies early in a marriage does not make a couple happier and often makes them less happy (Skolnick & Skolnick, 2007). In subsequent decades, people still believed that children "cement" marriages, even though the empirical evidence showed that having children increases the strains on a couple's time, energy, money, and other resources; thus, couples who are not happy in their relationship often become less so when babies arrive (Ross & Huber, 1985). One implication of this research is that couples who can plan the arrival of their children have a better marriage and family prognosis than those who cannot.

On a global scale, research on changing patterns of marriage and divorce in 72 nations shows that the changes associated with modernization, especially the rapid growth of

On Further Analysis

LESS DIVORCE OR LESS MARRIAGE?

News that the divorce rate has diminished somewhat in the past two or three years seems to suggest that more married people are thinking long and hard before choosing divorce. But in reality most of the decline can be attributed to the fact that fewer people are getting married, which means that there are fewer divorces (Hacker, 2002). The average age at which people are marrying is rising, and the greatest decline in rates of marriage is occurring among younger people. Because divorce rates are highest among young married couples, it follows that divorce rates are declining, but that is not necessarily because marriages are more stable.

The divorce rate compares the number of divorces to the total population. But from 1980 to 2000, while the population grew by 28 percent, the number of marriages rose by somewhat less than 15 percent, with the largest drop, as we have noted, occurring among those in their early twenties. These early marriages have been replaced by cohabiting couples—young people living together—so there are fewer actual marriages. When people who are living together separate, their actions do not show up in the divorce statistics, even though what they experience on a social and emotional level may be equivalent to divorce.

Another factor in the lower divorce rate is the growing number of people who choose to live alone. The accompanying chart shows that there has been a large increase—from 13 percent in 1960 to 26 percent in 2000—in the proportion of men and women living alone. Much of this increase has occurred among elderly widows and widowers, but an important segment of this single population consists of unmarried and divorced individuals. The graph also shows that the largest decrease is in the proportion of married couples with children, from about 45 percent of U.S. households in 1960 to about 28 percent in 2000.

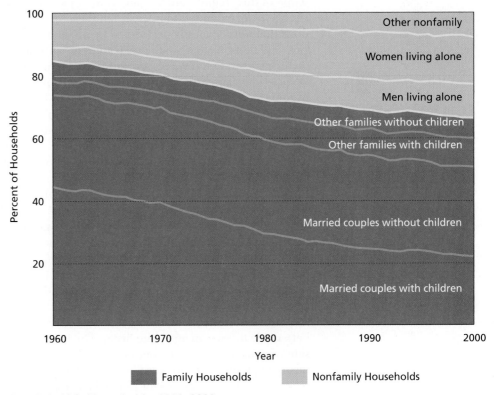

Trends in U.S. Households, 1960–2000

Source: U.S. Census Bureau.

urban populations (urbanization), increasing levels of employment in salaried and hourly wage positions, and increased levels of education, are also associated with higher divorce rates. The phenomenon of divorce appears to be closely linked to modernization, regardless of the particular religion that is dominant in a nation. Also, contrary to much speculation, global research indicates that women's increasing participation in the labor force is not associated with higher rates of divorce (Strong, DeVault, & Cohen, 2005).

The New "Divorce Divide"

Recent analysis of divorce rates in the United States and other highly industrialized nations indicates that there is a widening gap between divorce rates among people with high levels of education and those with less education. Sociologist Steven P. Martin describes a "divorce divide" in which "families with highly educated mothers and families with less educated mothers are clearly moving in opposite directions" (cited in Hurley, 2005, p. F7). For women in the United States with college degrees, divorce rates are about one-third lower than they are for women without college degrees. Indeed, much of the recent small but perceptible decline in divorce rates is accounted for by college graduate couples, while divorce rates among couples with less education remain at their historically high levels. This "divorce divide" is largely a consequence of the greater economic well-being of college-educated couples and the greater financial stress experienced by non-college-educated couples, which leads to greater marital instability (Conley, 2005).

What is the "divorce divide," and how is it related to men's and women's education?

Explanations of Trends in Divorce Rates

An examination of all the forces that put pressure on marriage would be beyond the scope of this chapter, but we can point out some of them. Most frequently cited is the change from extended to nuclear families. Another factor is the extent to which functions that were formerly performed by the family have been assumed by outside agencies. Still other factors are the relaxation of attitudes about divorce, the reformation of divorce laws so that divorces are easier to obtain, and the growing number of educated women who can earn a living independently of their husbands. (The general change in role expectations for women is discussed in Chapter 8.)

The change to a smaller family unit, coupled with the mobility of many modern families, places more responsibility on a husband and wife for the satisfaction of each other's emotional needs. Where once there were plenty of relatives or long-term neighbors at hand to whom the partners could turn for companionship, today spouses are more dependent on each other.

The decrease in family size has been accompanied by a decrease in family functions. Food production, education, entertainment, and other activities that were once centered in the home are now performed by outside agencies. This emotional satisfaction becomes increasingly important as the bond that holds a marriage together. If that emotional bond weakens and the couple feels incompatible, there are fewer economic and other social forces to take its place (Gelles, 1995).

Because of the greater social tolerance of divorce, partners who might once have resigned themselves to an unhappy marriage, or quarreled constantly yet stayed together, may now feel more inclined to get a divorce. Women—at least educated women—are better able to earn an adequate living. The increasing acceptance of sexual activity outside of marriage also contributes to the likelihood of divorce. In addition, a child of divorced parents is no longer likely to suffer embarrassment, pity, or discrimination in school. Finally, the chances for remarriage, especially for men, are fairly high.

The Impact of Divorce

Divorce, even when desired by both partners, is almost always accompanied by considerable emotional and financial strain. This is especially true for women, who often have to work and care for children without adequate economic and psychological help from their partners. Because more jobs are open to them, well-educated women are better able to cope with the effects of divorce and in fact may choose not to remarry. Other women have more limited options. Most husbands do not continue to support their families after divorce, although they are often legally required at least to pay child support. Divorced mothers, therefore, are frequently forced into poverty and dependence on public assistance; the leading cause of dependence on welfare (formerly known as Aid to Families with Dependent Children) is divorce or desertion (Ellwood, 1988). And because it is assumed that divorced people will soon remarry, adequate social supports are not provided to single parents.

There are about 1.2 million divorces in the United States each year. Of these, approximately 50 percent involve couples who have one or more children (*Statistical*

Abstract, 2005; Sweet & Bumpass, 1987). The majority of these divorces occur in marriages of less than ten years' duration; as a result, young children, who are most dependent and vulnerable, are especially likely to feel the impact of divorce. Although divorce has become a common event and children of divorced parents may no longer feel the stigma they once did, there is no question that in the vast majority of families in which divorce occurs it is an extremely difficult experience for children as well as for adults.

Children may experience divorce as the end of life as they knew it, as a falling apart and a severe disruption of their existence. They feel fear, anger, depression, and confusion. Often they blame themselves for contributing to their parents' difficulties. Over a longer period, children (and, typically, their mothers) experience divorce as a severe diminution in their material well-being; one of the leading causes of poverty among children is the dissolution of their parents' marriage. They may also become "latchkey children," far more responsible for their own care after school and for the care of their siblings than they might have been had there not been a divorce.

Much research focuses on families with preschool children in the period immediately following a divorce. The lifestyle of these families often becomes chaotic—meals are eaten at irregular times, the children's bedtimes are erratic, and so forth. The separated spouses experience anxiety, occasional depression, and personal disorganization, and the children tend to be bewildered and frightened. Other research has found that children whose parents are divorced are twice as likely as children from intact families to need professional help for an emotional, behavioral, mental, or learning problem (Berns, 2007).

In an important study of the effect of divorce on children, Wallerstein and Blakeslee (1989, 2000) tracked 60 families with a total of 93 children for twenty-five years after divorce. Although some of the children were better off than they would have been in an unhappy intact family, for most of them the divorce had serious consequences. A significant finding was that many divorced parents are unable to meet the challenges of parenting and instead depend on the children to help them cope with their own problems. The result is an "overburdened child" who must not only handle the normal stresses of childhood, but also help a parent avoid depression.

Divorce has a major psychological impact on adults as well. In research that challenges the findings of Wallerstein and Blakeslee's study, E. Mavis Heatherington and her associates argue that many adults find their lives enhanced after divorce. In fact, however, only one in four divorced women actually make this claim (Hacker, 2002; Heatherington & Kelly, 2002). In a classic study, Robert Weiss (1979) observed single parents for several years and identified three common sources of strain: (1) responsibility overload—single parents must make all the decisions and provide for all the needs of their families; (2) task overload—working, housekeeping, and parenting take up so much time that there is none left to meet unexpected demands; and (3) emotional overload—single parents must constantly give emotional support to their children regardless of how they feel themselves. This and other research suggests that the number of parents in the home is not as crucial to children's adjustment after divorce as the functioning of the member who is present (Lamanna, 1997; Skolnick & Skolnick, 2007).

Other consequences of divorce that can create problems include the increase in the number of single people in the population, more complicated family relationships when divorced people remarry, and the right of grandparents to see their grandchildren. The basic social problem created by the high divorce rate, however, is that the other institutions of society (e.g., schools and economic institutions) remain geared to the traditional family. These institutions are now under pressure to adapt to the needs of single people and single-parent families—for example, to provide more care for children of working parents, more flexible working hours, and more welfare services.

Stepfamilies

Nearly 50 percent of families in the United States are stepfamilies, and the number is growing continually. Today about 30 million children under age 13 are growing up in "blended" families. Because stepmothers typically bear much of the emotional burden in these families, research is focusing on their problems and how they manage relationships with their own children and their stepchildren. Recent studies indicate that stepmothers typically work quite hard to be good parents to their stepchildren while maintaining open lines of communication with the children's natural parents—not always an easy task (Orchard & Solberg, 1999). Although these findings attest to the strength of marriage and family norms, it is also true that combining children in a new family often adds conflict and tension to family life, and this in turn is sometimes seen as a cause of the relatively high divorce rate for such marriages (National Stepfamilies Resource Council, 2007).

Cohabiting Couples

Most common among people under the age of 25 and over the age of 65, cohabitation has been increasing at a rate of approximately 15 percent a year for the past decade or more. Among younger people, living together is most popular in college towns, where students may have more opportunities to experiment with intimate living arrangements (Wolf, 1996). There are more than 3.5 million cohabiting couples in the United States, and this arrangement is even more popular in some western European nations. Although some cohabiting couples may see living together as a form of trial marriage, others regard it as an alternative to conventional marriage; this is especially true of elderly unmarried couples (Strong, DeVault, & Cohen, 2005).

In the United States, in contrast to Europe, cohabitation seems to serve far more as a trial marriage than as a long-term family commitment. Recent data show that about half of all cohabiting relationships last less than a year, and that only 10 percent of cohabiting couples are still together after six years. In Europe, however, unmarried couples tend to stay together as long as married couples (Bumpass & Liu, 2000). On the other hand, about 37 percent of married women in a survey by the U.S. Department of Health and Human Services said that they had lived with their husband before marrying, which suggests that although cohabitation may be a relatively unstable bond, it is a common step toward eventual marriage (National Center for Health Statistics, 1997).

POSTPONEMENT OF MARRIAGE

Postponement of marriage became more common in the decades following World War II as young people chose to concentrate on education and careers. Today American women are postponing marriage longer than ever before. The median age of women who marry for the first time is 25.8 years. Men also are marrying later than at any time since 1900, with a median age at first marriage of 27.1 years. (See Figure 10–2, which

Figure 10–2 Median Age at First Marriage for Men and Women, 1890–2005

Source: Data from U.S. Census Bureau, 2007.

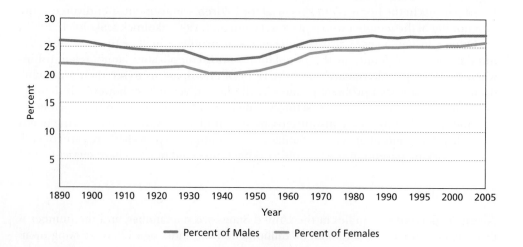

shows trends in age at first marriage from 1890 to 2005.) One result of this trend, coupled with the high divorce rate, is that more than one American adult in ten lives alone.

Postponement of marriage has a variety of implications for the family. One is a decrease in the average number of children per family—the longer marriage is postponed, the fewer children the couple is likely to have when they eventually do marry. Advances in reproductive technologies and medical care during pregnancy have made it possible for more women to have children while in their forties, and there has been an increase in the number of women who bear their first child late in their reproductive years. Even in such cases, however, the family is likely to have only one or at most two children.

When couples have children relatively late in life, they also become grandparents later and for a shorter time than those who marry and have children earlier. (This is especially true for men, who have a shorter life expectancy than women.) Postponement of marriage is also correlated with an increase in the proportion of childless couples because many people who marry late choose not to have children for personal or economic reasons or because the risk of birth defects increases with the age of the mother.

As a demographic trend, postponement of marriage has a significant effect on the population as a whole. A change of only two years in the median age at first marriage can make a vast difference in the number of married couples in the population in a given year. Moreover, because men tend to marry women who are younger than themselves, women who postpone marriage become caught in a "marriage squeeze": The number of women who would like to marry is greater than the number of available men (Biblarz & Raftery, 1999; Rossi & Rossi, 1990).

CHANGING NORMS OF PARENTHOOD

Births to Unmarried Women

Anthropologist Bronislaw Malinowski (1941) noted that in most so-called primitive societies there is a social dogma to the effect that "every family must have a father; a woman must marry before she may have children; there must be a male in every household" (p. 202). In other words, it is expected that every child will be provided with a legitimate father who will act as its protector and guardian.

Actually, there are societies in which marriage is not always a social prerequisite for parenthood. In parts of West Africa, for example, a woman may bear a child out of wedlock, and no stigma will be attached to her or to the child as long as the father's identity is reasonably certain. It is not sexual activity out of wedlock that is frowned on, but promiscuity.

In our society, many of the stigmas traditionally associated with premarital pregnancy have been reduced. Relatively few children of unmarried women are given up for adoption. Nevertheless, premarital pregnancy is still frowned on, generally because it indicates that sexual intercourse has occurred out of wedlock; the stigma is removed only if the couple is willing to marry before the child is born. Society still expects children to be provided with two recognized parents, and failure to meet this norm may result in various degrees of social condemnation. One form of condemnation is the legal classification of the child as illegitimate.

It is important to keep this legal aspect in mind when considering the social problem of illegitimacy. Granted that the one-parent family faces special problems—especially in a society in which the nuclear family is the norm—those problems are in themselves no different whether the single parent is unmarried, widowed, or divorced. Many of the distinctive difficulties of the unwed mother and her child, at least in the United States, are a matter of legal status.

In recent years there has been a growing trend toward enactment of stricter child-support laws and stronger enforcement of such laws. Single mothers do not often have the resources to pursue deadbeat fathers. In consequence, under the leadership of the federal government and some states, like Wisconsin, new efforts are being made to enforce compliance with court orders of child support for all children, regardless of the parents' marital status, a subject to which we will return shortly.

Many sociologists view the weakening of marital norms as one of the greatest and most negative changes in the family as a major institution of modern society. According to many experts, growing up fatherless is never a desirable condition (Popenoe, 2005). Others point out, however, that many nontraditional families provide children with a degree of love and nurturing that is lacking in families where the father is present but struggling with a problem such as alcoholism or unemployment. Thus, the controversy over "family values" continues in sociology as well as in the popular media (Crittenden, 2001).

Teenage Pregnancy

The very good news about teenage fertility and childbearing is that in the United States teenage birthrates have recently fallen to a level not witnessed in four decades. The lingering bad news is that teenagers are still having babies in greater numbers than their counterparts in other urban industrial nations.

Figure 10–3 shows that teenage birthrates have fallen by more than two-fifths in the past 15 years (Henshaw, 2001; National Center for Health Statistics, 2007). Births to minority teenagers, which were higher at the beginning of the period, are falling steadily. Birthrates are still high among all U.S. teenagers compared to rates in other nations. The United States ranks with Indonesia, the Phillippines, and Turkey as the nations with the highest teenage birthrates, whereas the rates in Japan, France, Germany, and Britain are significantly lower. These nations also provide their teenagers with far more sex education, more access to birth control, and superior health institutions.

The U.S. state with the lowest teenage birthrate has a rate about equal to the highest rate in the developed world outside the United States. Figure 10–4 shows that although no state stands up well in international comparisons, Vermont has a rate of about 27, whereas states in the South and Southwest have extremely high rates of teenage fertility.

A persistent issue in the United States today is whether young women who become pregnant should be allowed to have abortions. Data on abortions among young women ages 15 to 19 show that abortion rates declined from a peak of about 45 per 1,000 women in the mid-1980s to fewer than 30 per 1,000 in the late 1990s. But the impact of abortion on young women's lives remains an area of controversy and continued research. In 1990 the National Institute of Child Health and Human Development reported the results of a study of black teenagers who came to family planning clinics in Baltimore for pregnancy tests. The young women were divided into three groups: those who chose to have an abortion, those who bore the child, and those who turned out not to be pregnant. The groups were followed for two years. The researchers found that 90 percent of the group who had abortions and 79 percent of

Figure 10–3 Birthrates for Females Ages 15–17, by Race and Hispanic Origin: 1980–2005

Note: Data for 2005 are preliminary, Rates for 1980–1989 are calculated for all whites and all blacks. Rates for 1980–1989 are not shown for Hispanics; white, non-Hispanics; or black, non-Hispanics because information on the Hispanic origin of the mother was not reported on the birth certificates of most states.

Source: Centers for Disease Control and Prevention, National Center for Health Statistics, National Vital Statistics System.

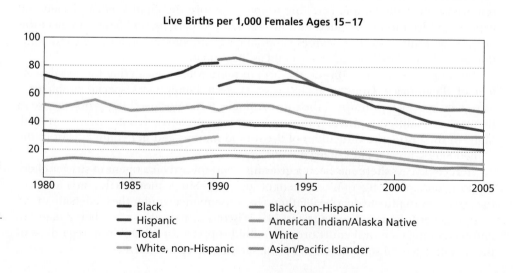

Live Births per 1,000 Females Ages 15–17

Black — Black, non-Hispanic — Hispanic — American Indian/Alaska Native — Total — White — White, non-Hispanic — Asian/Pacific Islander

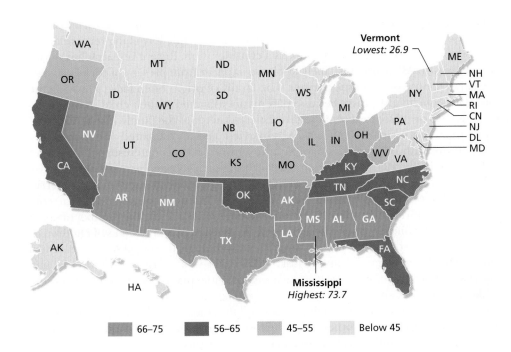

Figure 10–4 Birthrates by State for Ages 15 to 19 (per 1,000 women)

Source: Data from National Center for Health Statistics, 2005.

Map legend:
- 66–75
- 56–65
- 45–55
- Below 45

Vermont Lowest: 26.9

Mississippi Highest: 73.7

those whose pregnancy tests were negative graduated from high school or stayed in school. Among those who bore children, 68 percent dropped out of school. The study also found that 4.5 percent of those who chose abortion experienced an adverse psychological effect, compared to 5.5 percent of those who bore children. Opponents of abortion criticized the study, contending that two years was not a long enough period to produce meaningful results and that "postabortion stress syndrome" often does not show up until five years after the abortion.

Gay and Lesbian Families

Does marriage between same-sex partners threaten the institution of marriage? Is marriage an institution reserved for men and women, as President Bush and many other Americans insist it is, or should same-sex unions be granted the same legal status as heterosexual married couples, in which case the term *marriage* would be accorded to gay and lesbian as well as heterosexual marriages? Or should same-sex unions be considered "civil unions" rather than marriages, even if the same legal rights apply in both cases?

These are some of the extremely controversial questions being debated in the United States and many other democratic nations. How these questions are answered usually sorts people into either culturally conservative or culturally liberal camps. Most major religions do not condone homosexual marriages, but in 2005 the Spanish Parliament passed laws making same-sex marriages legal despite strong disapproval from the Catholic Church. Canada has passed similar legislation. But while the debate rages, the number of same-sex households and same-sex unions—whether called marriages or civil unions—is growing (Burns, 2005a; Spain, 2000). We do not know the exact number of such unions, but in 2005, when Massachusetts legalized marriage between people of the same sex, more than 6,000 couples came forward to become legally married.

Almost as controversial are the decisions by major corporations like Disney and Xerox to extend health and other insurance benefits to the domestic partners of gay and lesbian employees, causing some conservative groups to threaten boycotts against these corporations. In the context of the AIDS epidemic, these decisions represent an important moral stance because they could lead to high medical insurance costs. On the other hand, the policies require employees to declare their sexual preference and document their partnerships before benefits can be extended to their partners. This can have negative consequences if an employee faces homophobia in the workplace.

Discuss the pros and cons of same-sex marriage. Do you believe that laws allowing same-sex marriage threaten the institution of marriage? Defend your argument.

The AIDS epidemic has led gay couples to consider longer-term relationships and, in doing so, to desire children of their own. Of course, people form long-term relationships for many reasons, but clearly AIDS is a consideration. Recent research has shown that people with AIDS are most likely to obtain support from present or former lovers, especially a spouse or domestic partner. The family of origin often fails to provide the support that one might expect because parents are ashamed of their child's homosexuality and AIDS or refuse to accept the domestic partner into the family (Ayala, 1996).

Many gay couples consider themselves married, and an estimated one-third of lesbians and one-fifth of gay males have children from previous heterosexual marriages (Richmond-Abbott, 1992). As reproductive technologies become increasingly effective, more lesbian couples are able to have children through artificial insemination (Morris, 2005). In addition, although laws in many states make it difficult for gay and lesbian couples to adopt children, many have succeeded in doing so. As a result, the number of same-sex couples with children is steadily increasing. In a review of forty studies of children of same-sex couples sponsored by the American Psychological Association, researchers found that children of gay unions are just as likely to be well adjusted as children of heterosexual unions. The children of gay and lesbian couples play the same games, have similar likes and dislikes, and score equally well on intelligence tests. They do suffer, however, from a sense that society rejects their parents and that their friends may not understand their home situation. On the other hand, they are no more likely than children of heterosexual parents to be confused about sexual identity (Shapiro, 1996).

HOMELESS FAMILIES

Although homelessness has been recognized as a serious social problem since the early 1980s, only recently has it become evident that many of the homeless are families—usually mothers living on the streets with their children. No one knows exactly how many homeless families there are in the United States. The Harvard Joint Center for Housing Studies estimates that about 750,000 people are homeless on any given night in the United States. They base this estimate on extensive studies of the approximately 3 million people who live in highly precarious housing situations in which they must scrape together all their available resources just to pay rent. Martha Burt (1994) of the Urban Institute, the nation's leading expert on counting the homeless, estimates the total number of homeless people at over 40,000, depending on the time of year, the state of the economy, and the availability of low-cost housing. Christopher Jencks (1994) has pointed out, however, that the number could vary quite widely, depending on how one defines homelessness. For example, families that live in public housing projects, where the lease may be held by a mother or grandmother, are often at risk of becoming homeless as a result of family disputes or crackdowns by authorities. So on a given night, the number of homeless families who are seeking aid may vary according to the climate of enforcement in a community, and the total number of homeless families may vary according to how long families must live in shelters or on the streets before they are considered homeless (Burt, 1994).

The plight of homeless families is illustrated by a case described by sociologist Jonathan Kozol (1988): Laura, a Hispanic woman, lives with her four children in a welfare hotel in New York City. The plaster on the walls in the hotel is covered with a sweet-tasting, lead-based paint; Laura's 7-year-old son is suffering from lead poisoning. The bathroom plumbing has overflowed and left a pool of sewage on the floor, and a radiator valve periodically releases a spray of scalding steam. Laura's 4-month-old daughter has contracted scabies, a serious skin disease. Laura has taken her children to a clinic, but because she cannot read, she is unable to follow instructions about their care that have been sent to her through the mail. She also was unable to read a request for information from her welfare office, and her welfare payments have been cut off as a result.

The families who are most at risk of becoming homeless are those who have experienced a crisis such as divorce or desertion, resulting in a drastic reduction of income

This homeless family having their Thanksgiving dinner in the shadow of the Capitol symbolizes the plight of poor families who can no longer afford adequate shelter.

and hence inability to pay for shelter. Studies have indicated that a large majority of homeless families do not have relatives, parents, or close friends to whom they can turn for support (National Coalition for the Homeless, 2005). In addition, many homeless women with children are victims of family violence and may initially seek refuge in shelters for battered women. This suggests the need for more extensive public programs to provide emergency shelter for adults with children. These and related issues are discussed more fully in Chapter 13.

Shelter Poverty and Homelessness. When families must pay more than 30 percent of their monthly income for rent or other housing payments, social scientists refer to them as "shelter poor." Figure 10–5 shows that the nation's essential

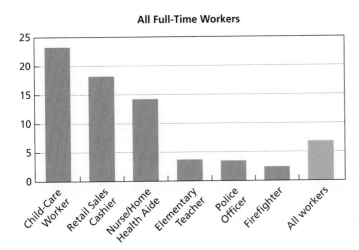

Figure 10–5 Percentage of Low-Paid Essential Workers Facing Severe Housing Cost Burdens

Source: Harvard Joint Center for Housing Studies, 2007.

but low-paid workers, especially those working in child care and retail establishments and as aides in nursing homes and hospitals, often face **shelter poverty.** The lack of affordable housing affects them most directly, although the figure also shows that about 6 percent of all full-time workers face the same problem. At present, the problem of shelter poverty is growing. The 2007 report of the Harvard Joint Center for Housing Studies notes that "in just one year the number of households spending more than half their income increased by a startling 1.2 million, to 17 million in 2005."

FAMILY VIOLENCE

Child Abuse

Child abuse is a serious problem in the United States. At least 750,000 children are physically abused each year, and many die as a result. Between 15 percent and 18 percent of mothers and between 6 percent and 10 percent of fathers interviewed in random sample surveys say that they were physically abused as children (Jaffe, Lemon, & Poisson, 2003). One important survey compared two-parent families in the mid-1970s, when child abuse became a national issue, and similar families in 1985, after ten years of publicity and efforts to prevent violence directed at children. In the earlier sample, 14 percent reported incidents of severe violence worse than slapping or spanking, including beating with an object, kicking, and hitting with fists; ten years later about 11 percent reported such behavior. This is an extremely small reduction, given the increased attention to the problem, and recent studies indicate that child abuse has not declined appreciably since the mid-1980s, if at all (Berry, 1995).

Child abuse may be defined as a deliberate attack on a child by a parent or other caregiver that results in physical injury. A major obstacle to research on this topic is concern for the traditional rights of parents, who have the right to inflict physical violence on their children. The most universal type of physical violence is spanking and other kinds of corporal punishment by parents (Tower, 2002).

If parents are to be responsible for raising and training children, they need to exercise a certain degree of authority, including the right to punish. Our culture strongly defends the right of parents to govern their children as they see fit, and it has traditionally approved of corporal punishment for this purpose ("Spare the rod and spoil the child"). Thus, one of the first court cases in which an outside agency successfully intervened to protect an abused child was the 1874 *Mary Ellen* case, in which the plaintiff was the Society for the Prevention of Cruelty to Animals.

Increased concern with children's rights has changed this picture somewhat. Child labor laws, actions of the Society for the Prevention of Cruelty to Children, and changes in the handling of juvenile delinquents have helped reinforce these rights. However, the rights of parents and the preservation of the family unit are still regarded as primary concerns, even when in any other situation the nature of the injury would warrant criminal investigation and possible prosecution. Indeed, the traditional autonomy of the family unit prevents the authorities from even learning about many cases of abuse, let alone intervening. Some researchers estimate that only one case in three is ever discovered (Reiss & Roth, 1993; Strong, DeVault, & Cohen, 2005).

The victims of child abuse appear to be fairly evenly distributed over all age groups and between the sexes, although there are some changes in sex distribution during different stages of childhood and adolescence. At least half the victims have been abused prior to a reported incident. A significant proportion of children seem to invite abuse through provocative behavior, although this plays a much smaller role in explaining attacks on children than the cultural norms discussed earlier. Of all cases of abuse, almost 90 percent are committed by the child's parent or guardian (National Clearinghouse on Child Abuse and Neglect Information, 2005).

A family in which there is child abuse typically has one or more of the following characteristics:

1. There is only one parent.
2. The parent's socioeconomic status and level of education are low.
3. The parent is highly authoritarian.
4. The family includes four or more children and has received some kind of public assistance within a year of the abuse.
5. The family changes its place of residence frequently.

Although these characteristics are found in many poor families, it is important to note that any correlation between abuse and poverty is biased by the fact that the behavior of the poor is more likely to be reported in official records than that of members of other classes, who are better equipped to conceal their activities. However, some specific problems, such as stress, anxiety, and alcohol abuse, are particularly prevalent in poor families.

Because studies based on official statistics have an inherent bias against the poor, the findings of a classic longitudinal study by Brandt Steele and Carl Pollock (1974) are of interest. For five and a half years the researchers, both psychiatrists, studied sixty families in which significant child abuse had occurred. These families were not chosen by any valid sampling technique and therefore cannot be regarded as statistically representative; they were merely families that happened to come to the attention of the investigators. They did, however, span a wide range of socioeconomic and educational levels, and they included urban, rural, and suburban residents. The information the researchers obtained led them to conclude that poverty, alcoholism, unemployment, broken marriages, and similar social and demographic factors are less significant than previous studies had seemed to indicate. Instead, Steele and Pollock found a typical personality pattern among abusive parents: The parent demands a high level of performance from the child at an age when the child is unable to understand what is wanted and unable to comply; and the parent expects to receive from the child a degree of comfort, reassurance, and love that a child would ordinarily receive from a parent. When the expected performance and nurturance are not forthcoming, the parent retaliates the way a small child might, with violence; but in this case the violence is not by the weak against the strong, but by the strong parent against the weak, defenseless child.

It is important to note that in every case studied, Steele and Pollock found that the abusive parents had themselves been subject to similar unreasonable demands in childhood, and in a few cases they found evidence of the same experience among the grandparents. More recent research confirms that child abuse is far more likely in families in which one or both parents have a history of abuse as children and there are other symptoms of family dysfunction, including alcohol and substance abuse (National Clearinghouse on Child Abuse and Neglect Information, 2005).

Spouse Abuse

On a rainy day in March 1992, Shirley Lowery, a Milwaukee bus driver, was stabbed to death by the man from whom she had fled a few days before. She was attacked as she hurried into the county courthouse to seek an injunction against her former companion, whom she accused of beating and raping her and threatening her life. Like many abusive husbands and boyfriends, her companion could not tolerate the idea of her leaving him. Lying in wait for her in the courthouse hallway, he stabbed her nineteen times with an eight-inch butcher knife.

Violence between spouses has long been acknowledged and even tolerated as part of domestic life. Wives are the most frequent victims, although cases of battered husbands are sometimes reported. Very often the victims are seriously injured, yet, as with violence directed against children, the traditional autonomy of the family, together with the traditional subordination of women within the family, has made the authorities reluctant to intervene. Only recently has spouse abuse become an issue of social concern, and it is still difficult to assess its frequency and its impact on American family life.

Spouse abuse is a form of violence that actually demands the use of profiling by the police. The FBI's most recent research reports on family violence and police responses points out that in the vast majority of cases the dispute is not two-sided:

> Domestic abuse is about one person dominating and controlling another by force, threats, or physical violence. The long-term effects of domestic violence on victims and children can be profound. A son who witnesses his father abuse his mother is more likely to become a delinquent or batterer himself. A daughter sees abuse as an integral part of a close relationship. Thus, an abusive relationship between father and mother can perpetuate future abusive relationships.
>
> Battering in a relationship will not improve on its own. Intervention is essential to stop the reign of terror. When intervention is lacking, the results can be dire: An average of 1,500 American women are killed each year by husbands, ex-husbands, or boyfriends.

Yet, until fairly recently, the FBI report continues,

> police officers rarely ventured into the private domain of the marital relationship. At most, officers responding to calls for help attempted to calm things down and arrange for one party to leave the home for the evening. While such an approach provided a short-term solution, it rarely helped bring about an end to the violence.

During the 1980s this response began to change as communities implemented more aggressive strategies to address domestic abuse. Many law enforcement agencies began to explore new ways for officers to respond to domestic violence calls. Gradually, the focus shifted from merely "maintaining the peace" to arresting offenders, protecting victims, and referring battered women to shelters and other community resources available to help victims of domestic violence. (Marvin, 1997, p. 13)

Even when faced with constant violence, a surprising number of women make no attempt to leave the men who abuse them. Lenore Walker (1977) has suggested that this passivity is a form of fatalism. A pattern of dependency, of "learned helplessness," is established early in many women's lives:

> It seems highly probable that girls, through their socialization in learning the traditional woman's role, also learn that they have little direct control over their lives no matter what they do. . . . They learn that their voluntary responses really don't make that much difference in what happens to them. Thus, it becomes extremely difficult for such women to believe their cognitive actions can change their life situation. (pp. 528–529)

Other experts have described wife abuse as "a complicated and cumulative cycle of tension, belittlement, violence, remorse, and reconciliation that can lead to a paralysis of will and extinction of self-respect" (Erlanger, 1987, p. 1). This "battered women's syndrome," they claim, is a result of the deliberate undermining of a woman's sense of independence and self-worth by a possessive, overly critical man. "There is a sense of being trapped," one victim reports. "You live in terror and your thinking is altered" (quoted in Erlanger, 1987, p. 44).

In testimony before Congress in 2005, Diane Stuart, director of the U.S. Department of Justice's Office on Violence Against Women, reported that about 50,000 victims of spouse abuse are treated every six months and more than 2,400 arrests are made in every six-month period for violations of protective orders (Stuart, 2005). Unfortunately, this last is a low number compared to the number of such orders issued, and too many women are left unprotected despite orders of protection. Many battered women remain with their husbands in an attempt to protect their children. Conversely, the children may try to intervene and defend their mother, thereby causing the father to turn on them.

Family violence is a concern of law enforcement officers throughout the world because they are frequently called upon to intervene in family disputes. Women who are endangered by violent marriages can appeal to the courts for orders of protection, and children and mothers can seek shelter from batterers in safe houses and family violence centers, but these and other measures to cope with family violence require supportive social policies and funding, as we see in the following discussion of politics and policies relating to the family in America.

Social Policy

In every national political campaign for the past twenty years the contending parties and candidates have devoted attention and resources to issues of the family. We hear endless debates about how to restore faltering "family values" or about which policies will best support and enhance the family as a social institution. Sociologists, too, align themselves differently on issues of the family, with some, such as David Popenoe, focusing their research on the dangers and consequences of fatherless families, and others, such as Arlene Skolnick and Daphne Spain, choosing to present data on how the diversity of family types today confirms the adaptability of the family as a social institution. There is not a great deal of evidence, however, to support the claim that social policies intended to bolster family values and morality make a great deal of difference (Hacker, 2002). On the other hand, policies that improve the economic situation of families, allowing married couples to avoid the intense stress of poverty and unemployment, or debt and bankruptcy, do help decrease rates of marital breakup and divorce, especially since the one issue that most commonly leads to family quarrels and stress is money. There are also many policies—especially those dealing with day care for children of working parents, shelters for battered spouses and children, improvements in enforcement of orders of protection and collection of child support, improved services to needy children and families, and health care and education for low-income families—that can be shown to help specific families cope with difficult situations.

Social policies related to problems of families can be divided into four major categories: divorce law and alimony, efforts to reduce teenage pregnancy, programs to assist low-income families, and child care and family support.

Divorce Law

In the 1950s and 1960s, as attitudes toward divorce became more liberal, there was a growing demand for changes in state divorce laws. Laws that permitted divorce only in extreme cases—adultery, for example—were challenged in many states. Beginning with California in 1970, many states liberalized their divorce laws and moved toward the concept of no-fault divorce. No-fault divorce laws allow judges to decide on such issues as child custody and division of property without blaming one partner or the other; this eliminates the need for children to testify about parental behavior and thus be dragged into a bitter court battle in addition to the pain they are already suffering. Many states followed California's lead, instituting no-fault laws and allowing couples to petition for divorce under compatible (previously agreed-on) terms.

The no-fault approach does not entirely eliminate strife. In many instances the courts must still adjudicate conflicting claims and settle rancorous custody battles. However, contrary to the claims of critics who believed that no-fault policies would lead to an increase in divorce rates, comparative research shows that divorce rates have not increased disproportionately in states with liberal divorce laws (Cherlin, 2003).

The Ongoing Debate over Divorce Law. Several states are considering measures that would make it more difficult, rather than easier, for couples to divorce, especially if they have children. Leaders of this movement argue that no-fault laws in most states have not produced lower divorce rates, happier families, or less suffering for children of divorced parents. Louisiana, Arkansas, and Arizona, for example, have taken the lead in passing laws that create a voluntary "covenant" form of marriage. Couples in this type of marriage sign a contract that requires them to seek counseling when they experience marital difficulties and forbids them to invoke no-fault reasons for divorce, such as incompatibility or loss of affection. Only adultery, felony conviction, or physical or sexual abuse are grounds for breaking the marital pledge. In its first few years of operation, the Louisiana "covenant" enlisted 3 percent of all marriage licenses, but it is far too early to know how well such policies are working to prevent divorce. It should be noted, however, that divorce rates in the three states just mentioned are far higher than the national mean, as is the case in the South and Southwest in general; this is what prompted "family values" lobbying groups to urge passage of "covenant" marriage legislation in the first place (Hacker, 2002).

Compare and contrast no-fault divorce and covenant marriage from the standpoint of child welfare.

Alimony. Alimony—the money paid by one partner for the support of the other, usually by the husband to the wife—has been closely tied to the concept of fault in divorce proceedings. In the absence of no-fault provisions, the main purpose of a divorce trial has been to fix blame on one party or the other and to make the guilty party (usually the husband) pay a certain amount over and above that which would ordinarily have been paid; if the fault rested with the wife, she would receive less than the ordinary amount. However, when a decree of divorce can be granted without the need to punish either partner, alimony can be awarded on the more realistic basis of financial need and ability to provide. Theoretically, this means that it would no longer be unusual for a man to receive alimony from his ex-wife if she has greater earning power; also, a woman with no children would not necessarily be granted alimony, or would receive alimony only temporarily, to give her time to become self-supporting.

Child Support. Children often suffer economically as a result of divorce. This fact, along with the growth of female-headed households, has led policymakers to focus on the child-support system as a way to reduce high poverty rates among children in single-parent families and the public cost of supporting those families (Laakso, 2000). As a result of this focus, child-support collections from divorced parents have been increasing steadily. Still, one-third of eligible children are receiving no child-support payments (Winter, 2005). Approximately 12 million mothers are legal custodians of their children, but only about 4.5 million receive child support in a given year. An estimated 2 million fathers are either very slow to pay or are not paying child support at all in any given year. In view of statistics like these, a high priority of family courts is to track down ex-husbands who fail to pay for the support of their children. In a 1988 decision, the United States Supreme Court ruled that fathers who fail to make payments because of financial problems must prove to authorities that they indeed lack adequate funds. Since then, the federal government and many states have instituted tougher policies on enforcement of child-support payments.

In recent years, much government effort has been centered on getting "deadbeat dads" to pay the child-care bills they owe. Despite a steady improvement in the amount of child support from absent parents to the custodial parent, the amount due continues to be much greater than the amount received. Approximately $36 billion in child-support payments is currently overdue (Laakso, 2000). However, if full payment were made, experts estimate that only about 10 percent of families currently living in poverty would be lifted above the official threshold—an important segment of the poor population, but a small one. In many states, child-support payments to women receiving TANF benefits go to the state to offset her family assistance. Students of child-support systems fear that this policy can actually create disincentives for mothers to report nonpayment of child support.

Stepped-up efforts to collect child support are important at all social class levels, but among the nation's poorest families there are clearly other policies—day-care subsidies, Medicaid, employment training, Head Start, and others—that are necessary parts of the social safety net.

Efforts to Reduce Teenage Pregnancy

One motivation for the passage of the 1996 Welfare Reform Act was the desire to change policies that seemed to reward early childbearing by single mothers. By withdrawing the entitlement provisions from the welfare program, for example, conservative lawmakers hoped to allow states to deny payments to teenage mothers or to provide them only under certain conditions. The underlying reasoning was that welfare payments encourage women, especially teenagers, to have babies that they might not otherwise have. Most sociologists who study this issue believe this reasoning is flawed. Before the passage of the 1996 law, welfare benefits varied widely from one state to another. Under the "welfare incentive" theory, one would expect to find higher teenage birthrates in the states with the highest welfare payments, but this was never true (Luker, 1996; Turner, 2002).

Sex education and access to birth control have been shown to reduce rates of teenage pregnancy. As we saw earlier, these rates have fallen to their lowest levels in forty years in the United States but are still far higher than those in European countries. Sexually active women clearly are using more birth control more effectively over time, but the reverse seems to be true for women who are not sexually active. And whereas the pregnancy rates are almost twice as high for sexually active teenagers, the level of sexual activity has actually tripled over a generation; thus, were it not for the effects of birth control and sex education, the pregnancy rates would be even higher than they are.

Abstinence Only, Abstinence Not. At this writing, Congress is preparing to cut the funding for so-called **abstinence only programs,** which are favored by the Bush administration. For the past few years, with the support of a Republican-dominated Congress, the Department of Health and Human Services has invested about $140 million a year in matching grants to states and private agencies that agreed to teach teenagers that they should remain celibate until marriage. But a study ordered by the Government Accountability Office, and another commissioned by Congress in 2007, revealed that abstinence programs did not influence sexual behavior. The findings showed that young people who attend the programs have the same number of sexual partners as those who do not attend. The research also revealed that some of the programs were actually teaching medically incorrect facts, such as the notion that the AIDS virus can pass through condoms or that condoms break at far higher rates than is actually the case. With these new findings at its disposal, it is highly unlikely that Congress will agree to continue such programs.

Despite the substantial social-scientific evidence, it is unlikely that there will be federal support for increased access to birth control or sex education directed toward teenagers. These issues are deadlocked by ideological differences in Congress and in many state legislatures. It is likely, however, that there will be new policy initiatives to make unmarried fathers more responsible for the support of their offspring. It is also possible that the cuts in aid for poor families, including those headed by teenage or young adult women, may begin to produce lower rates of teenage pregnancy. Some observers believe that even if previous welfare laws did not actually create incentives, society is becoming less tolerant of teenage pregnancy, and this change itself may lead to lower rates of pregnancy among teenage girls (Popenoe, 2005). On the other hand, some fear that new, more restrictive welfare laws may result in higher teen abortion rates and less support for children in single-parent families (Abramowitz, 1996; Strong, DeVault, & Cohen, 2005).

Child Care and Family Support

Samuel Preston (1984), a well-known sociologist and demographer, has made an eloquent plea for a coherent public policy to assist low-income families with children:

> If we care about our collective future rather than simply about our futures as individuals, we are faced with the question of how best to safeguard the human and material resources represented by children. . . . Rather than assuming collective responsibility, as has been done in the case of the elderly, U.S. society has chosen to place almost exclusive responsibility for the care of children on the nuclear family. Marital instability, however, has much reduced the capacity of the family to care for its own children. Hence insisting that families alone care for the young would seem to be an evasion of collective responsibility rather than a conscious decision about the best way to provide for the future. (p. 44)

Preston's (1984) comments are echoed in Hillary Clinton's book *It Takes a Village,* which applies the African adage "It takes a village to raise a child" to issues of child care and family life. The point here is that communities and governments need to assist parents in caring for their children. Such assistance might include medical care, day care for the children of working parents, early childhood education, after-school learning programs, summer recreation, and so on. Family expert David Popenoe (1995) observes that if communities are to provide such support, they, too, must be strengthened. "The seedbed of social virtue is childhood," he writes. "Social virtue is in decline in the United States for two main reasons—a decline in family functioning and a decline in community functioning." But, echoing what many conservative leaders say about these issues, Popenoe adds that it is not clear how communities can be strengthened; however, it is clear that individual men and women bear the responsibility for becoming good parents. "As individuals," he states, "we should seek to stay married, stay accessible to our children, stay active in our local communities, and stay put" (p. 98).

Future Prospects

While the debates about family values and community responsibility for raising children continue to engage pundits and political leaders throughout the United States, the fact remains that for more and more families child-care services in the community are becoming a necessity of family life (Casper, 2002). Today 30 percent of working mothers are placing preschool children in organized day care, an all-time high. The "workfare" demand incorporated into the 1996 Welfare Reform Act will send increasing numbers of mothers with young children into the labor force in coming years, and that, too, will swell the demand for day care. Thus, there is little question that day-care funding and day-care policies (e.g., licensing and regulation) will become an increasingly important area of social policy at all levels of government. These issues are discussed further in the Current Controversies box on page 349.

One of the brightest areas of change is the Family Leave Act, which was passed by Congress during President Clinton's first term in office. This measure requires businesses to allow leaves, with or without pay, to mothers and fathers of newborn children. Before the passage of the act there was no national policy that mandated specific family-related benefits for all workers (*Congressional Digest,* 1993). Vast changes in the composition of the work force, especially the dramatic increase in the number of women with young children, have clearly spurred interest in policies like family leave. In 2002 California became the first state in the United States to offer actual paid leave to its public employees, setting a precedent that will be highly influential in the state and federal elections of 2008.

On the downside, the crisis in affordable housing worsened in 2007 as thousands of low-income homeowners who had purchased variable-rate mortgages saw their interest rates soar as the housing market weakened. Unfortunately, the federal government and most state governments are spending lower proportions of their budgets on affordable housing, making it extremely difficult for low-income families to avoid shelter poverty.

FAMILY SUPPORT AND DAY CARE

About 80 percent of American infants and school-age children have working mothers. The rapid increase in the number of working mothers adds to the urgency finding high-quality child care during working hours. About 50 percent of working mothers report that they are unable to find satisfactory child care (Ford Foundation, 1990). At the same time, deep divisions in government about how best to establish and fund child care present major obstacles to new policies.

The 1996 Welfare Reform Act, which shifted the primary responsibility for welfare policy to the states, has resulted in cuts in food stamps and medical benefits, as well as in direct aid to single-parent families with young children. At the same time, there are increased demands for participation in work or training programs in lieu of welfare payments to reduce longer-term dependency on dole systems. The catch here, of course, is that welfare recipients need adequate day-care services or after-school programs if they are to join

the labor force without leaving their children unattended. Indeed, many fear that this problem will increase the incidence of child neglect and abuse in poor families that cannot afford adequate day care (Jaffe, Lemon, & Poisson, 2003; Luker, 1996). Moreover, the pressure to fund day care in communities throughout the nation is placing unprecedented burdens on private charities as well as state and federal budgets (Salter, 1996). For example, the Mission Day Care Center in San Francisco, which served about 300 poor children, was forced to close because it lost its annual $50,000 grant from the United Way. Most of the children are now cared for in less secure and less reliable situations. Although it is too soon to tell what the policy response to this situation will be, it may be that a number of ghastly events must occur before a climate of support for adequate child care can develop (Crittenden, 2001).

The Ford Foundation and other private philanthropic organizations have also called atten-

tion to the urgent need to improve existing day-care services. In California, for example, the California Child Care Resource and Referral Network has found that training new workers in the basics of child development and child care is an extremely high-priority need. There is also a serious problem of frustration and burnout among child-care workers, many of whom work 12-hour days with few breaks and have little contact with other practitioners and professionals. The network estimates that "every year some 60 percent of home-based providers [in California] close their operations" (Ford Foundation, 1990, p. 8). The network is seeking to develop a system of peer support, training, and assistance from local resources to improve this situation. Throughout the nation the problem of adequate funding and training of day-care providers and centers is becoming a growing social problem and an increasing challenge to policymakers.

GOING BEYOND LEFT AND RIGHT

Few issues arouse more passionate debate than those bearing on families and family responsibilities. People on the liberal side of the political spectrum tend to worry about the fate of single parents and their children, especially in poor families with evident unmet needs. People on the right may be equally concerned about poor mothers and their children, but they tend to believe that if more people took responsibility for their own actions, there would be fewer such cases. And so the debate over individual versus social responsibility continues without much resolution.

A sociological view of the issue is more pragmatic. What does the research show? If there are children with serious unmet needs for day care, early education, and protection against abuse, where will the resources come from? This may sound like a liberal approach, since it directs attention toward the children in need and does not necessarily speak to issues of responsibility, but eventually all of society's leaders, whether they are in universities or in legislatures, are called on to "do something" about social problems. When social policies are discussed, the facts often make a big difference in cutting through the ideological barriers. No one wants to see children suffer. On the other hand, no one wants policies that make problems worse. Thus, whenever practical solutions to problems of the family are discussed, sociologists and other social scientists attempt to provide facts, evaluations of existing approaches, and unimpassioned answers to ease the tensions aroused by angry debates over values.

A sociological view of the current crisis in affordable housing, for example, would offer arguments to address the concerns of people on both sides of the political divide. Although conservatives often oppose the use of tax revenues to increase the supply of affordable housing, social-scientific research shows that making housing available to low-income workers actually benefits those who hire them. In the past, some liberals have urged government to build public housing rather than relying on the housing market to supply affordable housing. Again, social-scientific data show that by using public subsidies to stimulate housing markets—for example, through low-interest loans to builders of low-cost housing—cities and states can most efficiently increase the supply of housing for those facing shelter poverty.

Summary

- A kinship unit is a group of individuals who are related by blood, marriage, or adoption. It may be a nuclear family (a father, a mother, and their children living apart from other kin), an extended family (parents, children, grandparents, and others living together or in close proximity), or a modified extended family (nuclear families living separately but maintaining interpersonal attachments and economic exchanges within the extended family).

- Families must adapt to a cycle in which the roles of their members change from one stage of development to the next. During each stage the family faces the challenge of maintaining stability and continuity. External or internal crises may reduce the family to an empty shell, in which family members feel no strong attachment to one another and neglect mutual obligations.

- Among the most important social trends of the second half of this century is the movement of women out of the home and into the work force. As a result, only about one-fifth of all married couples are supported by the husband alone.

- Some studies have shown that a wife's job may enhance family well-being, especially if the wife works outside the home as a matter of choice. Some women resent their "second shift" of work at home after working at a job, but others take it for granted.

- Although there are certain fairly consistent differences between black and white families—in particular, a larger proportion of poor, female-headed families among blacks—most of these differences are probably due to poverty and discrimination.

- The divorce rate has risen dramatically since the mid-1960s, reflecting severe pressures on the institution of marriage. Among them are the change from extended to nuclear families and the reduction in the number of functions performed by the family. In addition, because of the increased social tolerance of divorce, more couples are willing to get a divorce rather than continue an unhappy marriage.

- The problems associated with divorce include emotional and financial strain, particularly for women. Divorced mothers are frequently forced to accept public assistance. Children often become bewildered and frightened and may need professional help for emotional and other problems.

- Postponement of marriage has become common in the United States and has a variety of implications for the family: fewer children per family, an increase in childlessness, and a shortage of available men for women who wish to marry.

- Rates of teenage pregnancy have fallen to their lowest levels in forty years. However, teenagers in the United States are still having babies in greater numbers than their counterparts in other urban industrial nations. Another sign of changing norms is the increasing number of gay and lesbian couples who are raising children, either their own or adopted.

- Child abuse, sometimes leading to death, is a serious problem in the United States. Many abusive parents were themselves abused in childhood. Spouse abuse is also common and appears to be highly correlated with child abuse.

- Social policy to address divorce has consisted chiefly of reforms in divorce laws. Since 1970 no-fault divorce laws have been adopted in a number of states. These have alleviated some of the problems associated with divorce, but others remain. In particular, the courts are unable to enforce alimony and child-support settlements, with the result that many divorced women and their children suffer economic hardship.

- The 1996 Welfare Reform Act includes provisions designed to discourage teenage pregnancy. Sex education and access to birth control have been shown to reduce rates of teenage pregnancy, but these approaches lack widespread public support.

- There is a growing need for child-care services for families in all social classes. The Family Leave Act is a step in that direction, but the future of policy in this area is unclear. Another area of concern is the growing number of low-income families facing shelter poverty because of the lack of affordable housing.

Key Terms

kinship unit, p. 324
nuclear family, p. 324
extended family, p. 324

modified extended family, p. 324
shelter poverty, p. 342
child abuse, p. 342

alimony, p. 346
abstinence only program p. 347

Social Problems Online

Resources for exploring the challenges to families and how they fit into the larger society are available at many sites on the Internet. For example, the communitarian movement places the strengthening of the traditional nuclear family at the forefront of its political and intellectual agenda. Representative and sophisticated analyses of the state of the family can be accessed from the Civic Practices Network's (CPN) homepage at **www.cpn.org**. A collaborative and nonpartisan project, CPN is dedicated to building a movement for "new citizenship" and "civic revitalization."

A more traditional approach to family problems is through the legal system. Resources on family law are provided by the University of Indiana's law school at **www.law.indiana.edu**. Those interested in adoption law and reforms can follow the latest changes in that field, as well as get practical advice on adoption at several sites. Adoptive Families of America is the "largest nonprofit organization in the United States bringing together people interested in adoption and resources to support adoption," and it has a homepage at **www.AdoptiveFam.com** that provides an online catalog of resources for adoption, children, parenting, and multicultural awareness. The AdoptioNetwork (**www.adoption.org**) has a number of links in addition to such features as statistical profiles of domestic and international adoptions. Included on its page are U.S. presidential policy statements on adoption and related issues.

Families have changed over time and are different across cultures. The University of Manitoba's anthropology department has an online and interactive tutorial, "Kinship and Social Organization," at **www.umanitoba.ca/faculties/arts/anthropology/kintitle .html** that is engaging and informative.

Research Navigator

Follow the instructions on pages 26–27 of this text to access the features of Research Navigator. Once at the Web site, enter your Login Name and Password. Then, to use the Content Select database, use keywords such as "nuclear family," "blended family," and "same-sex marriage," and the search engine will supply relevant and recent scholarly and popular press publications. Use the *New York Times* search-by-subject archive to find recent news articles related to problems of families, and the Link Library to find relevant Web sites organized by the key terms associated with this chapter.

In Research Navigator, go to ebsco and type in the terms "divorce" and "children." You should find an article titled "Children and Divorce" from the journal *American Family Physician*. Select the pdf full-text version. According to this short article, what should family health practitioners know about how divorce affects children? Why do the authors recommend early intervention strategies?

PROBLEMS *of Education*

Source: Vincent Laforet/The New York Times

Chapter Outline

Dominant Trends

- Constant advances in the economy and technology demand ever more highly trained workers with increasing levels of higher education. As a result, 99 percent of all American children between ages 5 and 19 are enrolled in school, and increasing proportions of them will be expected to complete at least four years of college.

- Throughout the world, people with limited schooling face increasing difficulty making ends meet. The estimated lifetime earnings of high school graduates are at least $200,000 higher than those of dropouts.

- Quality of education and social class background are highly correlated. Thus, in poor inner-city neighborhoods it is not uncommon for public schools to have more than thirty students per class, while in suburban schools more affluent parents seek far smaller classes for their children.

- As political leaders and some educators put pressure on school systems for greater accountability and higher student performance, the trend toward standardized tests for students of all ages will continue to grow. Such testing was mandated by the No Child Left Behind Act.

- Among U.S. classroom teachers in public schools, only about two in ten use computers daily with students, and about four in ten never use the machines in their classrooms at all.

The issues that affect schools in the United States are staggering. Almost every aspect of schooling is subject to controversy. At present there is a debate about national education standards, school choice, school privatization, prayer in school, weapons in schools, standards for teachers, the impact of technology, classroom and school size, and much more. School reform figured prominently in the 2004 presidential election and will no doubt be an issue in every state and local election for years to come. But one of the ironies in all of the controversies that swirl around the schools, including those in higher education, is that people tend to like their own schools and to place the blame for "educational failure" elsewhere (NORC, 1999).

The No Child Left Behind Act of 2001, a major legislative initiative of the Bush administration, was designed to improve education in four clearly defined ways: accountability for results; an emphasis on doing what works based on scientific research; expanded parental school choice options; and expanded local control and flexibility. According to the act's accountability provisions, states must describe how they will close achievement gaps and make sure all students, including those who are disadvantaged or in special education classes, achieve academic proficiency. Schools that do not make progress must provide supplemental services, such as free tutoring or after-school assistance; take

corrective actions; and, if still not making adequate yearly progress after five years, make dramatic changes in the way the school is run. But many educators complain that under these strict guidelines schools suffer unfairly by being labeled as failing when they really are not. We will consider this important legislation further later in the chapter.

The supposed "failure" of the American educational system is a complex issue that is defined differently by different groups in society, depending on the goals of the group in question. For example, parents at all social-class levels are demanding that the schools do a better job of preparing students to work and live in a technologically sophisticated society. Various minority groups want schools to prepare their children to compete in American society yet, at the same time, not strip them of their cultural identity—or, in the case of Hispanics, of the language they learn at home. Educational policymakers believe that schools must do more to increase the overall level of student achievement. Many teachers, on the other hand, believe that parents should play a greater role in their children's education. And an increasing minority of parents are choosing to teach their children at home, a trend known as *homeschooling*.

As in the 2004 presidential election, education and the push for national standards will figure prominently in the 2008 presidential election campaigns. So will the claim, originally made by Al Gore, that schools need to be "wired" into the Internet. As these issues illustrate, not only the goals of education but also the means of achieving them, are subjects of heated debate. Should schools be more open to new ideas and teaching methods, or should they focus on the traditional curriculum— "the basics"? Indeed, what are the basics? Do they consist simply of reading, writing, and arithmetic, or do they include learning how to get along with others and how to communicate effectively? Are the basics the same for all students? These are only some of the fundamental questions being asked about public education in the United States today. There are many others. Should more qualified and effective teachers receive merit pay? Should the school year be longer? Should there be a standardized national curriculum? There is even some question about whether education should be a public institution. Perhaps high-quality private schooling should be encouraged by means of a government-sponsored voucher system that would refund to households the amounts they spend on public education through taxes. Such refunds could take the form of educational vouchers that could be used to pay for private schooling (Irons, 2007).

The United States has led the world in establishing free public education for its people. Per capita public expenditures on education are higher in the United States than in any other nation. Education is compulsory in the United States; the requirements differ from one state to another, but usually children must attend school until age 16. As a result, over 99 percent of all American children between the ages of 5 and 19 are enrolled in school, and about 75 percent of American adolescents remain in class full time through the final year of secondary school (*Statistical Abstract*, 2006). Moreover, the number of students enrolled in higher education increased rapidly in the twentieth century.

So what is wrong? Why is the educational system under attack? How does this impressive record constitute a "failure"? These questions can be answered in different ways, depending on the sociological perspective from which they are viewed.

SOCIOLOGICAL PERSPECTIVES ON EDUCATION

In democratic nations, education is the primary means of addressing a host of social needs and problems. The schools are expected to prepare new generations to be good citizens and reliable, capable workers. Schooling is expected to produce young people who can enter the labor force with the necessary skills in literacy, computation, and written expression. Higher education in colleges, universities, and professional training institutions is expected to produce young adults who can become scientists, professionals, and leaders in business and other institutions of society.

But these ambitious expectations hardly exhaust the list of demands placed on educators. Schools and institutions of higher education are expected to address and solve problems of inequality. They are not expected to make everyone equal—all societies recognize that people are born with differing interests and abilities—but they are expected to provide equal opportunities to learn and to gain the skills and experiences that society requires. And as if these demands were not enough, the schools are also expected to address other social problems, such as racism, sexism, and violence.

As might be expected, there are vast differences in the analyses of public education by sociologists who approach the subject from different theoretical perspectives. Functionalists stress stability and consensus; in their view, education is, or should be, one of several interdependent parts that work together to create a smoothly functioning society whose members all share the same basic values and beliefs. Conflict theorists argue that schools reproduce the society's system of inequality and class stratification in new generations of children (McLeod, 1995; Moore, 2004). They focus on the coercive aspects of education; they see society as divided into dominant and subordinate groups, with education being used as a tool to promote the interests of the dominant group while teaching the subordinate groups to accept their situation. Interactionists take still another approach: They examine how expectations of students' performance actually determine that performance and how these expectations can result in labels that shape the students' future. Each of these perspectives gives rise to different approaches to the study of public education.

Functionalist Approaches

From a functionalist perspective, problems in the educational system are a symptom of social disorganization. The educational system is geared to students from stable homes and communities. It is not well equipped to handle the problems of students from disorganized homes—for example, where there is divorce or cultural conflict. Such students are often depressed and angry, have trouble concentrating on their schoolwork, and therefore have difficulty achieving in school (Ballantine, 1993). According to social-disorganization theorists, these students are more likely to join deviant peer groups, such as gangs, that reinforce their negative attitudes toward school.

Also related to functionalism is the theory that educational problems stem from deviance from generally accepted norms of achievement. In this view, schools are agents of social control whose tasks are to reinforce society's values and to control deviance through discipline. This perspective can also be applied to the question of whether schools themselves produce deviance by setting unreachable standards for many students. In a study of boys in a British secondary school, for example, the researcher found that working-class students were unable to understand or appreciate the middle-class value orientation of the school. The school, in turn, was unable to modify its middle-class bias and hence was unable to deal with the working-class students' attitudes. The result was the development of a deviant group of alienated working-class youths (Willis, 1983).

Another functionalist approach analyzes the difficulties experienced by schools when they attempt to change their organization and their procedures in order to improve student performance. How can schools organize themselves to meet the demands of students with special learning needs? How can schools with high levels of student failure on standardized tests recruit better teachers and administrators? How can school systems offer parents and children more choices of schools and educational approaches? These are all issues that hinge, to a great extent, on how schools, or entire school systems, are performing as they try to meet the demands placed on them. The Bush administration's No Child Left Behind initiative seeks to make schools accountable for student failure on nationally distributed standardized tests of reading and math achievement. It also imposes penalties on schools and school districts when they fail to meet minimum standards of achievement. This is a functionalist approach to improving the schools because it is based on performance measurements, but sociological critics of the program, also arguing from a functionalist perspective, point out that the initiative does not provide adequate resources to help schools improve teaching and student performance (Klenk, 2005; Riordan, 2004).

Conflict Approaches

Viewed from a conflict perspective, the problems of education stem from conflicting views of the goals of education. The dispute over whether the schools should teach a universal curriculum in a single language or, instead, help preserve the cultural identities of minority students through bilingual education is an example.

Conflict theory has two main currents—Marxian and non-Marxian. The Marxian view stresses the goal of reducing social stratification and increasing equality. It argues that schools reflect the values of groups in society that are content with the status quo or favor even less equality. In a classic statement of this position, Samuel Bowles wrote that compulsory education in the United States developed to meet the needs of a capitalist economy for skilled and disciplined workers and, while doing so, to justify the unequal social status of workers and capitalists (Bowles, Gintis, & Groves, 2005). Other investigators, who are not necessarily Marxian theorists but whose research confirms some aspects of Bowles's theory, point to unequal access to education, especially higher education, and inequalities in the resources available to schools in different states or districts (Lavin & Hyllegard, 1996).

The non-Marxian version of the conflict perspective, which is referred to as the *value conflict approach,* focuses on intergroup conflicts that arise out of the desire to maintain or defend a group's status in a particular community. This leads to conflicts over such issues as busing to achieve school desegregation (Orfield, 1999). A case in point is the intense conflict that developed in Boston over efforts to desegregate that city's public schools through busing. One study of this conflict (Buell, 1982) emphasized the concept of the "defended neighborhood," a community that actively resists abrupt change. In more recent research, Douglas Massey and colleagues attribute the failure of school desegregation to the persistent segregation of communities. Housing segregation contributes to the resegregation of schools through white flight and the exclusion of minority families from housing markets in better school districts (Fischer & Massey, 2004).

Interactionist Approaches

According to the interactionist perspective, schools label students "achievers," "underachievers," or "rebels," and these labels follow them throughout their lives (Johnson et al., 2005). For some students, schools are "factories for failure." A well-known study of ghetto education found, for example, that "a 'slow learner' had no option but to continue to be a slow learner, regardless of performance or potential" (Rist, 1973, p. 93). According to labeling theorists, teachers form expectations about students early in the school year, and in various ways these expectations are communicated to the students themselves. The students tend to perform in ways that meet the teacher's expectations, thereby reinforcing them.

What explanations do sociologists offer for why public education generates so many debates and conflicts in U.S. society?

Research by Stanford Dornbusch and his colleagues at Stanford University shows that students also use labels like "slacker" and "nerd" to categorize one another and to explain how they sort themselves into cliques that perform quite differently in social and academic settings (cited in Leslie, 1996).

The various perspectives on education as a social problem and the kinds of policy recommendations generated by each one are shown in Table 11–1.

TABLE 11–1 | Perspectives on Education

Basic Perspective	Research Approach	View of Education as a Social Problem	Policy Recommendations
Functionalism	Social disorganization	Schools cannot help students who come from disorganized backgrounds or have low IQs.	Requiring schools to work more closely with parents or guardians, or in some cases take their place.
	Deviant behavior	Problems stem from deviance by some groups from accepted norms of achievement.	Greater discipline; remedial education for nonachieving students; cracking down on weapons in school.
	Institutional	There are difficulties in shaping educational institutions to meet demands for better performance.	Allowing parents greater choice in schools.
Conflict theory	Class conflict	Those with wealth and power try to ensure that their children get high-quality education; those with little wealth and power cite evidence that their children are shortchanged.	Channeling adequate resources to the schools to improve the quality of education for the poor and educationally disadvantaged.
	Value conflict	Problems stem from tensions between different groups over the goals of education.	Allowing different groups to achieve their educational goals while also achieving basic competency.
Interactionism	Labeling	Schools label students as "achievers," "underachievers," or "rebels."	Elimination of labeling practices such as ability tracking.

Each time schoolchildren recite the Pledge of Allegiance, they are affirming the values of American citizenship. One of the primary functions of the educational system is to produce citizens who are aware of their rights and responsibilities in a democracy.

EDUCATIONAL ATTAINMENT AND ACHIEVEMENT

Today, ever-greater proportions of American students are finishing high school and going on to college. As shown in Figure 11–1, from 1940 to 2000 the nation underwent a transformation in which high-school completion, rather than school leaving (dropping out), became the norm. But there is clearly a long way to go in decreasing the number of students who drop out of high school and increasing the proportions who complete four years of college. For members of minority groups, these continue to be especially pressing educational issues.

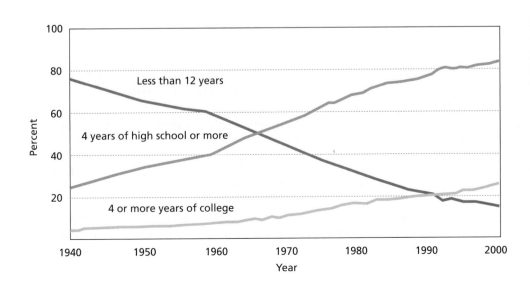

Figure 11–1 Years of School Completed by Persons Age 25 and Over, 1940–2000.

Source: National Center for Education Statistics, 2001.

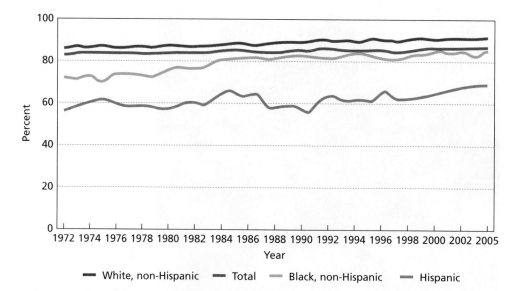

Figure 11-2 Rates of School "Status Completion," 1972–2005 (percent of 18–24-year-olds in U.S. population who have either graduated from high school or received equivalency degrees).

Source: Data from U.S. Census Bureau.

The gap in **educational attainment** (number of years of school completed) between blacks and whites has narrowed considerably since the turn of the century, mainly as a result of the increase in the minimum amount of education received by almost all Americans. In 2005, 85 percent of Americans over age 25 had completed four years of high school or more, but that proportion was 80 percent for African Americans and 57 percent for Latino students (*Statistical Abstract*, 2005). And the high-school dropout rate was about 7 percent for white students, 13 percent for African Americans, and 28 percent for Latinos. These figures, though still far too high, represent significant reductions over the past thirty years. In 1976, 12 percent of whites, 21 percent of African Americans, and 34 percent of Latinos dropped out of high school. (See Figure 11–2.)

Rates of school leaving remain higher among inner-city blacks and Hispanics than among whites, and alienation from school causes many minority teenagers and young adults to finish their schooling in high-school equivalency programs. Despite this serious problem, however, the educational gap between blacks and whites continues to narrow.

It is argued that the higher dropout rates among minority students are caused by the fact that they do not receive enough help at home. This is known as the cultural-disadvantage argument. Although minority enrollments are higher today than at any time in the past, the parents of these students have less education than the parents of white students and therefore are less able to assist their children.

Although the primary cause of dropping out is poor academic performance, students often drop out of high school because of the difficulties they encounter in trying to cope with school, family, and work roles at the same time. They may be married and/or pregnant or working at a regular job (this increases the likelihood of dropping out by more than one-third). Whatever the cause, dropping out has a number of serious consequences. The earnings of school dropouts are considerably lower than those of high-school graduates. This disadvantage continues throughout life: The estimated lifetime earnings of high-school graduates are at least $200,000 higher than those of dropouts. Most dropouts believe leaving school before graduating was a poor decision, and an estimated 40 percent eventually return to the educational system (Stringfield & Land, 2002).

At the college level, educational attainment for low-income members of minority groups is hindered by lack of financial aid as a result of cutbacks in federally funded student assistance. Cutbacks in federally funded assistance, particularly the emphasis on loans rather than outright grants, place a college education out of reach for many minority students. The disparities in educational attainment between white and minority students are a matter of concern to those who believe equality of educational attainment is basic to other kinds of social equality. For them, encouraging students to finish high school, developing systems of school financing that provide equal resources for all schools, and ending segregation are important policy goals.

In all the controversies surrounding public education, there is little agreement even among experts. From a social-scientific viewpoint, part of the problem of knowing whether U.S. schools are truly failing to produce well-educated students lies in the difficulty of conducting comparative research. Comparative studies must hold constant social variables such as language and social class, and this is never entirely possible. However, one recent study succeeded in administering standardized tests in different languages and in controlling for social class.

How U.S. Students Measure Up in International Comparisons. One of the issues underlying the clamor for educational reform in the United States is the fact that on many standardized tests administered throughout the world, the United States lag behind many other advanced industrialized nations. Figure 11–3 shows that the average score of fourth-grade students in the United States on combined reading and information scales is higher than the international average, but lower than that of students in Sweden and England. Note, however, that because of the great diversity of U.S. students and schools, there is a great deal of variation in the U.S. students' scores. Much of this variation is explained by whether the students are attending schools in which high proportions of students are eligible for free lunch in school, a measure of their family's financial need. The figure shows dramatically that the lower the income of fourth-graders, and the greater their concentration in the schools, the less well they do on standardized international tests. Similar results apply to tests of mathematics and science.

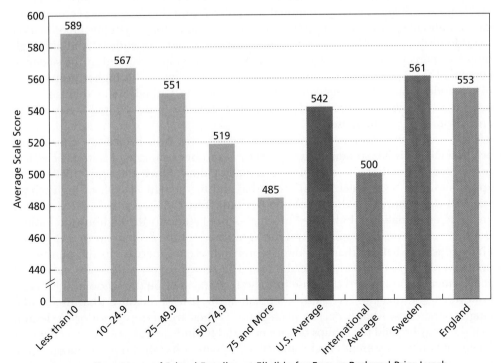

Figure 11–3 Fourth-graders' Average Scores on International Reading and Literacy Tests, by Rates of Student Poverty, 2004.

Source: Adapted from National Center for Education Statistics, 2004.

The No Child Left Behind initiative is designed in part to address the gap in reading and math scores between minority and nonminority students. How do problems like class inequalities and residential segregation contribute to these achievement gaps?

The Third International Mathematics and Science Study (TIMSS) is the largest and most rigorous international comparison of education ever undertaken. It has many components, including studies of student performance, extensive interviews with parents about their children's schools and their performance in them, analysis of teacher-training systems, comparisons of different nations' educational policies, and much more. In an earlier phase of the study, the primary researcher, Harold W. Stevenson (1992), and his team looked at differences in performance on standardized tests between students in the United States and Asia (China, Japan, and Taiwan). They found that "the test results confirm what has become common knowledge: schoolchildren in Asia perform better academically than do those in the U.S." (p. 71). In mathematics, for example, first-graders in U.S. schools did not perform as well as comparable children in Asian schools, although students in some of the better U.S. schools had scores similar to theirs. By the fifth grade, however, the U.S. students had fallen far behind their Asian counterparts; students at only one school in the U.S. sample scored as high as students at the worst school in the Asian sample. Interviews with parents in the different nations indicated that Asian parents are far more demanding of their children and far less likely to accept poor or mediocre school performance than American parents are.

Later phases of the TIMSS research centered on comparisons among the United States, Germany, and Japan. Among the many findings, the authors note that sorting students by ability (tracking) is far more prevalent and begins earlier in the United States than in Germany or Japan (where tracking is banned entirely in the primary grades). This may help account for differences in parents' acceptance of their children's school performance and the lower average standards set by U.S. parents (Stevenson, 1998).

Another study, which compared schools in the United States and selected European nations, found quite different results (Organization for Economic Cooperation and Development, cited in Celis, 1993). When test scores of U.S. students from sixteen public school systems in inner-city, suburban, and rural districts were compared to similar sets of scores from schools in sixteen European, Canadian, and Australian systems, the results showed that U.S. students outperformed students in twelve other nations. In math, U.S. students scored ahead of students in only two other nations, but in science they scored in the middle range, along with students in Canada, France, England, Scotland, and Spain. This international study also found that U.S. colleges, especially community colleges, do a better job of preparing students for a changing labor market than do institutions of higher education in the other nations studied. And although only 15.5 percent of U.S. college and university degrees are awarded in the sciences, compared to 32 percent in Germany and 26 percent in Japan, far higher proportions of all students attend colleges and universities in the United States than in those nations; hence, the absolute number of science students in the United States is high and is continuing to increase.

The controversy over scholastic achievement scores (which measure **educational achievement,** or what students have learned) is another example of how difficult it is to determine whether the schools are actually failing. Since the early 1960s there appears to have been a decline in the verbal and mathematical skills of high school students as measured by the Scholastic Aptitude Test (SAT), a standardized college entrance examination administered to high-school students throughout the nation. But there are conflicting opinions on the significance of the drop in mean SAT scores. Many educators believe that the lower scores indicate an increase in the number of underprepared students who take the test. The scores reflect a decrease in student achievement (and hence a decrease in the effectiveness of public schooling). Others, however, argue that the SAT and other standardized tests measure what used to be taught rather than what is currently taught, that they are unimportant or irrelevant, that they may be valid for groups but are not valid for individuals, and so on. The most recent national assessment of educational achievement has shown some encouraging improvement in students' math scores (Applebome, 1997). Nevertheless, the level of student achievement remains a subject of widespread debate.

EDUCATION AND EQUALITY: THE ISSUE OF EQUAL ACCESS

It is well known that educational attainment (number of years of school completed) is strongly correlated with socioeconomic status (Riordan, 2004). Educational researcher Robert Slavin (1997) notes,

> Among 4th graders whose parents graduated from college, 70 percent were reading at or above the basic level. This drops to 54 percent for children of high-school graduates and 32 percent for children of high school dropouts. Among children whose homes had magazines, newspapers, encyclopedias, and at least 25 books, about 70 percent scored at or above basic; among those without these resources, fewer than half scored this well. Differences in mathematics, writing, and science are similar. Further, performance differences increase as students get older. (p. 3)

An egalitarian society has a responsibility to provide equal access to high-quality education for all its citizens. Critics claim that American society has failed to meet this responsibility, particularly for minority groups. This criticism has become especially sharp as the composition of student populations has changed. Since the 1960s increasing numbers of blacks, Hispanics, and other minority groups have become concentrated in central cities, while whites have moved to the suburbs. In some metropolitan areas, as a result, over 90 percent of the students in public schools are black or Hispanic. And because central-city schools often have fewer resources than suburban schools, the quality of education available to black and Hispanic central-city residents tends to be lower than that available to white suburban residents.

Nor are urban minorities the only slighted populations. Native Americans and Alaskan Inuit have also suffered as a consequence of inadequate education and lack of access to high-quality educational institutions. Both groups live in remote rural areas, where educational choices are extremely limited. In addition, Native Americans have been forced to depend on reservation schools, which they consider inferior (Fischer & Massey, 2004; Fuller & Elmore, 1996).

In recent years Native Americans have become increasingly upset over what they perceive as a lack of commitment by the federal government to improving the quality of education on reservations, which are administered by the Federal Bureau of Indian Affairs. Educational attainment of Native Americans is among the lowest for any minority group in the nation.

Black Students

A major factor in the lower educational attainment of blacks than of whites is that before World War I about 90 percent of all blacks in the United States lived in the southern states (Orfield & Eaton, 1996). The South was then (and remains to some extent) less affluent than the North. The data in Figure 11–4 show that most southern

Figure 11–4 Average Expenditure per Pupil, by State.

Source: Data from Education Intelligence Agency, 2005.

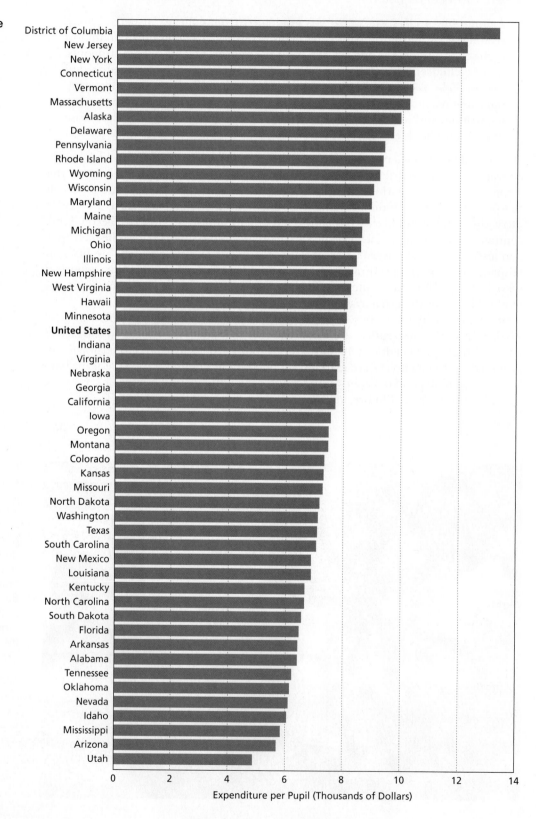

Expenditure per Pupil (Thousands of Dollars)

states and some western ones continue to spend far less per student than school systems in the Northeast. Because black students are disproportionately concentrated in the Deep South, one effect of this difference is that blacks (and poor southern whites) receive only about 70 percent of the amount of schooling received by whites in more advantaged areas of the nation.

In the North, educational opportunities for blacks and whites are more equal, but inequalities between schools in poor black communities and those in more affluent white suburbs tend to perpetuate differences in educational attainment. At the beginning of the twentieth century, northern-born blacks were rapidly closing the educational gap between themselves and whites, but the gap widened again after 1915. The reasons for this reversal are complex. An important factor was the competition between black children and the children of European immigrants, who tended to come from better-educated families and thus enjoyed an advantage over blacks, whose parents had migrated from the South. Another factor, beginning in the Great Depression and continuing to the present, was the higher rate of unemployment among blacks. The employment status of parents has a great deal to do with the educational attainment of their children because children of low-income parents are more likely to drop out of school (Slavin, 1997). A third factor was segregation. Segregation tends to increase disparities between groups, not only because minority schools, which are usually located in central cities, have fewer highly qualified teachers and other resources, but also because students in those schools do not learn the values, work habits, and skills they need to compete effectively in the larger society (Darling-Hammond, 1998; Orfield, 1999).

Hispanic Students

Another minority group that has faced difficulties in gaining equal access to education is Hispanic Americans. This large group (which accounts for over 10 percent of the U.S. population and is growing much faster than the population as a whole) is highly concentrated in metropolitan areas. The educational attainment of Hispanic students is lower than the average for all students. A significant factor in this difference is that Hispanic students who have recently arrived in the United States either do not speak English at all or do not speak it well enough to succeed in school. An especially important factor is that Hispanic students, like blacks, have experienced the effects of de facto segregation and poor schools, a problem particularly acute in large metropolitan areas (Carriuolo, Rodgers, & Stout, 2002; Orfield & Eaton, 1996).

Since the late 1960s a primary goal of education for Hispanic students has been to improve their ability to use English without allowing them to fall behind in other subjects. One technique for achieving this is bilingual/bicultural education, in which students are taught wholly or partly in their native language until they can function adequately in English, and in some cases longer. This approach has received the support of the federal Office of Civil Rights, which requires that schools take "affirmative steps" to correct minority students' deficiencies in the English language in order to receive federal funds.

Bilingual/Bicultural Education. The desirability of teaching young non-English-speaking pupils in any language other than English is a subject of intense debate, particularly in California and other states with large Hispanic populations (Colvin, 1996). On one side are those who believe that preserving the language and culture of minority groups is a worthwhile, even necessary, goal of public education. On the other are those who believe that minority students must be "immersed" in English-language instruction if they are to be prepared to compete effectively in American society. Minority parents themselves often disagree on which approach best serves their children.

The Bush administration's No Child Left Behind initiative does not ban special programs for English language learners in public schools, but it does insist that all students, regardless of their native language or the recency of their arrival in U.S. classrooms, must take the standardized proficiency tests and that their test scores must be included in calculating school performance scores. This has placed even more pressure on school districts, many of which have increasing numbers of non-English-speaking children registering each year, to create special programs, including bilingual classes and intensive English instruction for nonnative speakers.

Parents and teachers who believe bilingual education is helpful in keeping their children from falling behind in substantive fields such as math and science face intense pressure from supporters of the growing English Only movement. These opponents of bilingual education wish to eliminate any use of other languages in government, schools (other than specific foreign language classes), and other public institutions. They are active in many states, especially those in the Southwest with a large number of Spanish-speaking residents. However, recent careful research on how students with limited English proficiency can best learn English while keeping up with their other studies indicate that bilingual programs in the early grades, and instruction in English as a second language in the primary and middle grades, result in the highest levels of achievement by non-English-speaking students (Genesee et al., 2005).

In the war against terrorism, an extreme shortage of fluent speakers of Arabic among Americans offers new evidence that, contrary to the claims of the English Only movement, educators would be well advised to regard the language abilities of non-native English speakers as a major national resource that must be preserved rather than suppressed.

Asian Students. Students from Chinese, Korean, East Indian, and other Asian backgrounds face entirely different problems in U.S. schools. Due to their higher achievement on most measures of school performance, Asian students and their parents are proud of their scholastic achievements but often feel that they are treated as the "model minority" who are expected to be uniformly high achievers and extremely well behaved in schools (Abboud & Kim, 2005; Yu, 2006). Asian Americans make up 4 percent of the U.S. population but represent 20 percent of the students now attending America's elite Ivy League schools. But for Asian students who do not outperform their peers or do not behave according to cultural stereotypes, the extremely high expectations of their families and the larger society can present severe problems. At Cornell University, for example, Asian students do extremely well in science and engineering programs, but their high achievement comes at an extreme cost for some. Only 14 percent of the total Cornell student body are self-identified Asian Americans, but 13 (61%) of the 21 Cornell students who have committed suicide since 1996 have been Asian or Asian American. In consequence, Cornell and other universities have created special counseling programs to reach out to Asian students and help them deal with stress (Cornell University Online, 2006).

Preschool Programs

While ideological controversies have swirled around education in elementary and secondary schools, more pragmatic policies have been developed and tested at the preschool level. Head Start and other early-education programs have grown in importance, especially since evidence of their effectiveness in addressing the needs of children from low-income families has accumulated. Evaluations consistently show that children in such programs make gains that continue throughout their later school years and beyond. Head Start would probably not exist as a federally financed program had it not been for a modest but pioneering early-intervention project in Michigan known as the Perry Preschool Project, and the research that accompanied it.

The Perry Preschool Project studied 123 black children from low-income families in a neighborhood on the south side of Ypsilanti, Michigan. The children, all of whom had IQs between 60 and 90, were randomly divided into an experimental group that received a high-quality preschool program and a control group that received no

Among the most important goals of good preschools anywhere in the world are to help very young children feel comfortable in the classroom environment and to develop social skills, such as cooperation, attention, and sharing.

preschool program. Information about all the participants was collected and examined annually from the ages of 3 to 11 and again at the ages of 14, 15, and 19. The information included data on their families; their abilities, attitudes, and accomplishments; their involvement in delinquent and criminal behavior; and their patterns of employment and use of welfare assistance. Members of both groups were tested and interviewed; the testers and interviewers were not informed of the group membership of the participants in the study.

The preschool program to which 58 of the children were assigned was "an organized educational program directed at the intellectual and social development of young children" (Berrueta-Clement et al., 1984, p. 8). It was staffed by a team of four highly trained teachers. Most of the children participated in the program for two years, at the ages of 3 and 4.

The results of the Perry project were dramatic. Preschool education improved cognitive performance in early childhood; improved scholastic achievement during the school years; decreased rates of delinquency, crime, use of welfare services, and teenage pregnancy; and increased high-school graduation and college enrollment rates. According to the researchers, "These benefits considered in terms of their economic value make the preschool program a worthwhile investment for society" (p. 1).

Perhaps the most significant outcome of the Perry project was its effect on educational attainment: Two out of three of the students in the preschool group graduated from high school; the comparable rate for the non-preschool group was one out of two. As noted earlier, failure to graduate from high school is a major obstacle to later educational progress and an important factor in many job and vocational-training opportunities.

The Perry Preschool Project, and similar programs inspired by it, are outstanding examples of how social-scientific research can play a vital role in public policy. Conservative policymakers, who usually seek to curtail public spending for education and other government services, have been persuaded by this research to continue funding Head Start. In fact, continuing research on the Perry Preschool students has astonished both supporters and critics of the project, as explained in the On Further Analysis box on page 366. Unfortunately, however, at present only one in five preschool-age children in families below the poverty line attends a high-quality preschool program.

What are some of the arguments for investing in early-childhood education? Do the benefits outweigh the costs? How does the concept of human capital help explain the goals of such programs?

INVESTMENTS IN CHILDREN'S FUTURES: SOCIETY BENEFITS

Early-childhood education programs like Head Start are considered investments in **human capital.** In other words, when the society creates and pays for early-childhood education, or schools, or universities, it is spending public funds to build the skills and capabilities (i.e., the human capital) of its citizens. In so doing, it may be improving the entire society, not just the condition of those who happened to be in the program. The key word for social scientists is that the programs "may" have these beneficial effects. Unless we conduct rigorous social-scientific studies, we cannot actually know whether the funds invested produced any improvements in achievement. And even if research is pursued, only years later will it be possible to determine whether the individuals who participated in a program actually did better as adults than similar people who did not experience early-childhood education (or whatever program is under consideration). For these reasons, when we do have long-term research results, they tend to be highly significant from the standpoint of social policy. In the case of early-education programs, and especially the Perry Preschool Project and similar examples, the research is in and the results are stunning.

Participants in the Perry program "performed better than nonparticipants in almost every area of schooling and of work and social life—from lower rates of special education placement and greater rates of high school graduation, through greater likelihood of employment, higher earnings, more stable marriages, and less delinquency and adult criminal activity" (*Focus*, 2005, p. 7).

High-quality early-education programs like the Perry program can be successful, but can they remain successful in a permanent and larger-scale fashion? Evidence from Chicago, where there are many "child–parent centers" that operate like the Perry Preschool Program in Michigan, shows that even in a larger system the approach is extremely successful.

Critics of social programs often object to using public funds for such investments in human capital. Careful analysis of the costs and benefits of early-education programs shows, however, that such investments are profitable both for individuals and for the society as a whole because they return high gains for every dollar spent. The accompanying table offers strong evidence that investing in children's human capital pays off in the future. Note that the average costs per child for the Perry program are $16,514 while for the Chicago program they are $7,738. But the benefits of the two, once the participants reach adulthood, are far larger in both cases. Based on the higher earnings and savings and reduced rates of crime (and its high cost to society) of former preschool pupils, compared to people who did not attend a preschool class, it is unwise not to make such investments.

With such powerful proof of their lasting benefits to individuals and to society, one must ask why far more children in the United States who need high-quality preschool services are not getting them (Schweinhart, 2002). Unfortunately, with federal, state, and county budgets facing severe reductions, it is likely that preschool programs will also contract rather than grow.

Economic Benefits and Costs of Two Early Childhood Interventions

	Perry	Chicago CPC
Child-Care Benefit	986	1,916
Earnings Increase	40,537	32,099
K–12 Savings	9,184	5,634
College/Adult Costs from Extra Education	−782	−644
Reduced Crime	94,065	15,329
Reduced Welfare Use	355	546
Future Generation Earnings Effect	6,181	4,894
Reduced Abuse/Neglect	0	344
Total Benefits	150,525	60,117
Total Costs	16,514	7,738
Net Present Value	134,011	52,380
Benefits-to-Costs Ratio	9.11	7.77

Source: Barnett, 2004.

Desegregation

Efforts to alleviate some of the problems discussed in this section have centered on racial integration, or, more accurately, desegregation. Much of the pressure for change in this area has come from court rulings and legal mandates.

Desegregation effectively began with the Supreme Court's 1954 ruling in *Brown* v. *Board of Education of Topeka, Kansas,* which was based in part on the argument that segregation had negative effects on black students even when their school facilities were equal to those of white students. Black students in segregated schools knew that their schools were inferior and were likely to believe that they themselves were inferior as well.

To avoid the formation of such a negative self-concept, the Supreme Court decided that black children should associate with white children as early as possible and should be taught by both white and black teachers.

In the 1980s, the pace of desegregation slowed, especially in the Northeast. As noted in Chapter 7, there are a number of cities in which the distribution of the white and nonwhite populations places severe limits on the extent to which schools can be desegregated. Research by Douglas Massey and Judith Denton (1993) on the persistence of residential segregation suggests that without stronger enforcement of fair-housing laws and other measures to reduce racial segregation, it will be extremely difficult to accelerate the pace of school desegregation. The situation is aggravated by the tendency of middle-class urban residents to enroll their children in private schools. Nevertheless, many school systems throughout the country have adapted successfully to the demand for desegregated public schools.

In 1991, the Supreme Court held that the Oklahoma City schools could be permitted to cease busing children to meet the requirements of a 1972 desegregation order. The Court ruled that school systems could be released from busing orders once they have taken "all practicable steps" to eliminate segregation. The Harvard Project on School Desegregation notes that during the Reagan administration there was an explicit policy not to take legal action against school districts that failed to make progress toward desegregation. The administration also largely abandoned busing because it believed "compulsory busing of students in order to achieve racial balance in the public schools is not an acceptable remedy" (Orfield & Eaton, 1996, p. 17).

In 2007, the Court, in a bitterly divided 5–4 decision, reversed the landmark precedent set in the 1954 *Brown* v. *Board of Education* decision against school segregation. The 2007 decision ruled that voluntary policies designed to select students based on race in order to achieve more integrated classrooms are unconstitutional. The decision addressed cases involving schools in Seattle and Louisville, Kentucky, that used race when assigning some students to schools in an effort to end racial isolation and prevent resegregation. Conservatives called the ruling a clear blow to the concept of racial diversity as a vital public policy. Civil rights advocates worried that the ruling would obliterate the concept that race can be a factor in remedying societal discrimination of any kind. In a short time, they argued, there will be greater segregation in U.S. schools, which will adversely affect students from lower-income neighborhoods.

In its 1954 desegregation ruling, the Supreme Court overturned the "separate but equal" doctrine. What was that doctrine, and do you think the 2007 ruling revives that earlier justification for segregation?

SCHOOL REFORM: PROBLEMS OF INSTITUTIONAL CHANGE

The primary obstacle to significant changes in the educational system is that educational institutions have a built-in tendency to resist change. To some extent this is a useful quality: Schools tend to conserve society's values and do not yield easily to educational fads. Nevertheless, they must be able to change in response to changes in other major institutions. Such changes are highly visible, and several have been mentioned in other parts of this book. The family, for example, has changed dramatically as increasing numbers of women have entered the labor force. Economic institutions also are changing as jobs that require specialized skills replace jobs that require little training. These and other changes in American society call for adults with skills and outlooks different from those that were typical of their parents' generation. The schools are largely responsible for preparing students for these new adult roles (Moore, 2004).

The nature of schools themselves is a major barrier to change. Schools have been compared with "total" institutions—prisons, mental hospitals, and other institutions in which a large group of involuntary "clients" is serviced by a smaller group of employees (Ballantine, 1993). A central problem of such institutions is the maintenance of order and control, a concern that leads to the development of elaborate sets of rules and monitoring systems. Although schools are not total institutions in that not all the activities of their "clients" take place within their boundaries, they exhibit one of the key traits of total institutions: The administrators tend to place a high priority on maintaining their authority.

Schools as Bureaucracies

According to Daniel Bell (1973),

> It is a truism of sociology that the initial patterns of any social system, like the first tracks through a virgin forest, shape its future modes. Traditions become established, routines are set, vested interests develop, innovations either are resisted or must conform to the adaptive patterns laid down at the start, and an aura of legitimacy surrounds the existing ways and becomes in time the conventional wisdom of the institution. (p. 402)

This aptly describes the situation of education in what Bell calls "postindustrial" society.

Educational sociologists have documented the extent of bureaucratization in the American educational system. They point out that increases in bureaucratization are associated with increases in organizational size and complexity. This is certainly true of American school systems. The one-room schoolhouse has become a complex system characterized by an increasingly specialized division of labor. Today's schools have large administrative staffs that include a variety of specialists such as community relations experts and guidance counselors. Even the teachers are specialists—for example, in a certain age group or, at the high-school level, in a particular subject (Johnson et al., 2005).

Another bureaucratic characteristic of modern school systems is the development of an elaborate hierarchy of authority. (See Figure 11–5.) The relationships among

Figure 11–5 A Typical School District's Educational Bureaucracy.

Source: From *Encyclopedia of Education*, Vol. 8, ed. Lee C. Deighton, Macmillan Literary Reference. Copyright © 1971 by Macmillan Library Reference. Reprinted with permission of Gale, a division of Thomson Learning: www.thomsonrights.com. Fax 800-730-2215.

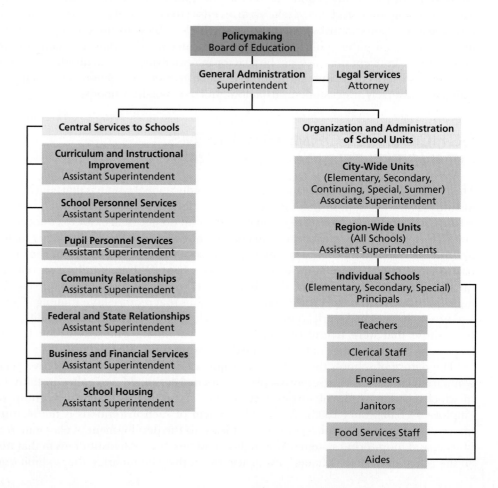

people at various levels of the hierarchy have an important effect on educational policy at the district and school levels. In big-city school systems, for example, there may be several administrative layers between the superintendent and the schools themselves. In such cases the superintendent may be unable to control the implementation of policies. A similar situation exists at the classroom level. Teachers have considerable autonomy in how they run their classrooms; if they choose to, they can resist innovation simply by not following the directives of school boards and principals. The imposition of national standards and increased emphasis on performance on standardized tests at all levels of education is designed, in part, to force teachers and local educational administrators to "teach to the tests" so that wide variations in what students experience in their classrooms will be diminished (Orfield, 1999).

Classroom and School Size

For teachers and their unions, especially in large cities and less affluent districts, a primary issue in school reform is classroom size. Teachers simply find it far easier to provide high-quality instruction in classrooms where there are no more than twenty-five students. Project Star, a systematic longitudinal study conducted in the Tennesee schools, confirmed that smaller classes yield better results (Bracey, 1995). Throughout the United States, the average class size is twenty-three in the primary grades. Over 80 percent of teachers and school administrators believe that a class size of seventeen is ideal. For many decades parents who could afford to do so have enrolled their children in private schools with small classes, especially where the alternative was urban public schools with large classes. In inner-city neighborhoods it is not uncommon for classes to include more than thirty students, with much crowding and inadequate learning materials like textbooks (Bell, 1998; Bracey, 1999). Educators argue that calls for reform that do not address declining learning environments in impoverished communities are useless (Drevitch, 1994; Meier, 2002a).

Another reform movement calls for smaller schools in order to address the problems of large, impersonal, bureaucratic schools (Meier, 2002a; Sizer, 1992). Veteran school reformers like Theodore Sizer of the Coalition for Essential Schools and Deborah Meier—an innovative and charismatic school principal who has achieved success in inner-city schools—argue that the reforms included in the Goals 2000: Educate America Act are motivated by a "top-down" desire to impose national standards, which will increase reliance on standardized testing and further reduce the educational responsibilities of teachers, parents, and students. They argue that educational reform should begin at the school level and that large, impersonal schools need to be divided into smaller schools, where administrators and teachers know every student and where parents and teachers can have a greater voice in decisions about how the school should operate.

Recent research on the relationship between high-school size and student performance shows that scores are higher in schools with fewer than 600 students and lowest in high schools with more than 900 students. Large schools are a particular problem in inner-city communities with high proportions of poor and minority students (Bracey, 1998).

School Choice

Efforts to create smaller schools, schools with special approaches to learning, or schools that promote a particular religious orientation invariably become enmeshed in the ongoing debate over school choice (Alexander, 1996; Meier, 2002a). People who are dissatisfied with the public schools or seek special educational opportunities for their children are often attracted to proposals for expanding the array of choices parents have, including parochial and secular private schools. Republican candidates at all levels of government often favor a system of vouchers that parents could "spend" in sending their children to any kind of academically accredited school they wish. This policy is especially controversial because conservative supporters of school choice also believe vouchers or other school-choice programs should allow families to choose private and parochial schools as well as public ones. In 2002, in a bitterly contested 5–4 ruling, the United States Supreme Court upheld a state-run school-choice program that provides vouchers worth up to $2,250 each to Cleveland students, who may use them to attend religious or secular private schools. As a result of the ruling, legal experts predict that there will be new court battles over school choice at the state level (Gehring, 2002).

Social-scientific research offers little support for the belief that school choice improves performance. After reviewing the evidence to date, educational researchers Salvatore Saporito and Annette Lareau (1999) concluded, "Indeed, if there is a single, consistent finding in the empirical literature on school choice, it is that students from poorer families or with less educated parents are less likely than middle class families to apply to—or participate in—public choice programs" (p. 1).

The Christian Coalition advocates a system such as the one used in Georgia, known as the Hope scholarship program, in which the state offers money to students with a B or better average to attend the college or university of their choice. Under this proposal, the successful Georgia model would be extended to the high-school and primary grades as a way of increasing the choices open to parents and thereby increasing enrollments in Christian schools as well as in other private schools.

Charter Schools. Other, more liberal educators often argue for greater choice in the selection of public schools. Members of the movement for smaller schools, for example, often advocate the creation of special schools, known as charter schools, which are innovative in their use of resources and yet are funded as public schools. As the array of choices within the public school system widens, they argue, there will be more pressure on the conventional schools to become more competitive and to improve their educational methods (Meier, 1991, 2002a).

In the decade since the first charter schools opened, the U.S. charter-school movement has produced about 800 schools in 29 states and the District of Columbia, enrolling more than 100,000 students. Each charter school reflects its founders' educational philosophies, programs, and organizational structures. Research by the federal government shows that these schools serve diverse student populations and are committed to improving public education, but their student populations do not include a proportionate number of students with special needs or with English language deficiencies.

Recent research sponsored by the federal government indicates that students in charter schools do not perform measurably better on reading and math tests in the fourth grade than do students in noncharter public schools with similar student populations. And among disadvantaged students—that is, students who are eligible for a free or reduced-price lunch—fourth-graders in charter schools did not score as high in reading or mathematics, on average, as fourth-graders in other public schools (National Center for Education Statistics, 2003).

These results are disappointing for advocates of charter schools, but the demand for greater school choice and parents' desire for alternatives to some of the public schools in their communities will continue to stimulate the growth of charter schools and other alternatives to public schooling, such as homeschooling.

Homeschooling. Homeschoolers are students whose parents report that their children are taught at home rather than in a public or private school. Although many parents in the homeschooling movement are motivated by religious principles and want to include specific religious instruction in their teaching, or wish to avoid the secular aspects of public schooling, many others simply believe that they can do a better job teaching their children than the schools can, or wish to emphasize specific language or other skills in their home teaching. In 2000, the latest year for which national survey data are available, 850,000 children, accounting for 1.7 percent of students nationally, were being homeschooled.

Students who are homeschooled perform as well, if not better, on average than those graduating from public schools. Critics of the movement often argue, however, that while withdrawing students from the public schools may be a good solution to what parents perceive as problems of those schools, homeschooling also takes students out of the school community, perhaps to the detriment of that community, which loses the talents of these students. For their part, homeschooling parents argue that their children should be allowed to play on local public-school teams and to use other school resources. (Some school districts have complied with these requests.) Homeschooling is facilitated by the wealth of educational materials and resources now available on the Internet (Clements, 2004).

The Technological Fix

Much of the pressure for change in the schools has developed out of the typically American belief in the value of technology. The "technological fix," it is widely believed, can solve any problem. Thus, it is commonplace to attempt to apply such techniques as cost accounting, systems analysis, closed-circuit television, and computer technology to educational problems. Although the evidence does not support the notion that technology can solve the problems of public education, some technological initiatives have had positive consequences. According to Parelius and Parelius (1987), "Students have more and better materials, a greater variety of courses, increased freedom to choose among diverse educational alternatives, and a less authoritarian relationship with teachers and administrators." However,

> there are some important ways in which the school has remained impervious to technological advances. . . . The basic classroom unit of the school has remained fundamentally unchanged. The role structure consisting of one teacher to a room full of students is still with us. . . . The teacher is still concerned with discipline . . . students are still expected to be obedient, punctual, and docile. . . . Blackboard and chalk, paper and pen remain the primary tools. . . . This mode of interaction has successfully resisted change for a long period of time. (p. 84)

The latest technological innovation to assume the dubious status of a "techno-fix" is the networked computer. At various times former Speaker of the House Newt Gingrich and former Vice President Al Gore have urged educational systems to add more computers and networks to their classrooms. But what is the basis for this strong advocacy of computers in education?

Part of the rush to wire classrooms for computers and Internet access comes from the fact that throughout the nation an estimated $4 billion per year is being spent doing just that—primarily in more affluent suburban schools (Dede, Honan, & Peters, 2005). Chris Whittle's Edison Project, which features the same kind of technological approach, has attracted a great deal of national and international attention (Mosle, 1993). The project has opened a chain of for-profit schools that use high-technology computers and satellite linkups to create schools that are more efficient and successful than public schools. Edison schools are now operating in 25 states, but there is little evidence that they are an improvement over public schools (Miron & Applegate, 2000).

Although there is a growing computer gap between wealthier and poorer school districts, many inner-city districts that lack computers and teachers trained to use them must deal with even greater problems, such as overcrowded classrooms, inadequate facilities, and lack of basic textbooks. Research in the United States shows that among classroom teachers in public schools only about two in ten use computers daily with students, and about four in ten never use the machines in their classrooms at all. And even when the computers are being used, it is most often for low-end applications and word processing. The most frequent explanation for this behavior is that teachers do not know how to use computers and that many are "technophobes," afraid of new technologies. But the research shows that seven out of ten of the same teachers routinely use computers at home to write to friends, search the Internet, and much more (Cuban, 1999). It appears to be far easier to interest legislators in buying unproven computer and telecommunications systems for schools than in training teachers to apply these technologies to learning (Dede, Honan, & Peters, 2005).

Teachers' Unions

Another factor that affects school operations is the increased popularity of teachers' unions. Membership in teachers' trade unions like the National Education Association and the American Federation of Teachers has risen significantly since midcentury—from less than 10 percent of all teachers in the early 1960s to over 30 percent at present. These unions seek to improve the status and material well-being of their members, but they also support a range of policies directed toward reform of the educational system. Among other things, they demand smaller classes, more resources for the handicapped and slow learners, and more funds for in-service training for teachers. On the other hand, they often oppose policies whose goal is to improve the competence and motivation of public school teachers (discussed in the next section). For this reason, critics of the unions claim that they are more interested in maintaining the status quo than in genuine educational reform.

Partly because of the unions' efforts to professionalize and partly as a result of economic factors, there is renewed interest in teaching as a career. Annual surveys of the occupational intentions of U.S. college students demonstrate a steadily growing interest in teaching careers, especially among women. (See Figure 11–6.) Among men, this interest leveled off during the economic boom of the 1990s, when more lucrative careers attracted them away from educational careers, but now that such alternatives are less abundant, men, too, are showing an increasing interest in teaching. The increase is attributed to widespread publicity about educational reforms, higher salaries for starting teachers, and awareness of an impending shortage of teachers. Education is now the third most popular undergraduate major (after business and the social sciences), and enrollments of education majors have been increasing.

School Violence

Television coverage of the 1999 killings and suicides at Columbine High School in Littleton, Colorado, brought school violence into homes throughout the world. But Columbine was only one of a series of tragic episodes of violence that have shaken Americans' confidence in the security of their children in schools once thought to be safe havens for learning and social development. The American public perceives fighting,

Figure 11–6 Growing Interest in Teaching Careers.

Source: Data from National Center for Education Statistics, 2005.

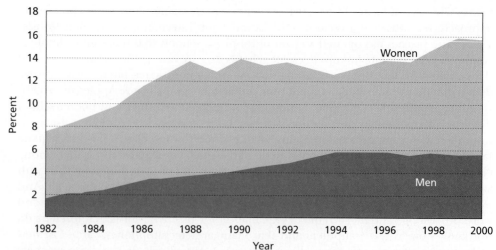

violence, and gangs as the three most serious problems of public schools. The facts, however, contradict these perceptions. The number of violent victimizations of any kind in schools decreased from 59 per 1,000 students in 1993 to a low of 26 per 1,000 in 2000 (Bureau of Justice Statistics, 2002). Unfortunately, it does not take many sensational incidents of school violence, combined with the more normal occurrences of bullying and petty theft, to expand fears of school violence beyond reasonable levels.

To explain why extremely violent episodes are occurring in schools, social scientists and others have often cited, among many possible causes,

> (a) failure of parents to supervise their children; (b) violence in the media; (c) access to guns and other lethal weapons; (d) harassment of students who are nonconformists; (e) the influence of religious cults and "outsider" groups; and (f) low self-esteem brought on by social isolation. Much attention has been focused on the influence of violent video games such as Doom that law enforcement agencies and the military use to desensitize recruits to killing and to sharpen their marksmanship skills. (Guetzloe, 1999, p. 21)

Many observers believe the underlying problem is that the role of the teacher no longer commands automatic respect because students do not care whether their teachers approve of their behavior. When large numbers of students are frustrated and alienated, and their parents are uninvolved in their education, only the most forceful, experienced teachers are able to remain in control of their classes.

Solutions such as installing metal detectors and hiring additional security guards have been attempted, and these measures may help prevent violence by outsiders, but they do not convey authority to teachers. Educators are searching for ways to empower teachers who are intimidated by violent students. Several possibilities have been suggested: creating smaller high schools or "schools within schools"; expecting more from students than mere attendance; and encouraging dropouts to return to school as adults. The last suggestion is especially attractive because adult high-school students often become role models for younger students, and their presence tends to reduce the amount of disorder in the schools they attend. More discouraging is the fact that, even by the most conservative estimates, 3.3 million children experience domestic violence each year. These individuals, in turn, are most likely to commit violent acts against their peers (Szyndrowski, 1999).

In an effort to prevent violence among students, many school systems have installed metal detectors and imposed severe punishments on students caught bringing weapons to school.

Efforts to prevent school violence are beginning to achieve some success, even though episodes of violence continue to make headlines. In Chicago schools, the frequency of violent incidents fell consistently and dramatically over four years because of the city's decision to increase funding for school security. Between 1989–1990 and 1993–1994, the schools employed more security officers to supplement those supplied by the Chicago Board of Education. According to school principals, the biggest deterrent to violence is the presence of adults, especially parents, in the schools. But Chicago school principals also instituted such changes as school uniforms, more student activities, and programs designed to change students' behavior, such as peer mediation and conflict resolution (Burns, 2005b).

Social Policy

The public school is the nation's largest educational institution, offering basic education to the greatest number of children. However, as noted earlier in the chapter, public education has been subject to criticism on a number of fronts. The policy recommendations arising out of such criticism take two main forms, depending on whether their proponents have conservative or liberal views on educational policy.

Of all American social institutions, education is most subject to intentional change through social policy. Schools and educational systems are also attractive targets for critics. Those who believe American society has become too secular may advocate prayer in the schools. Others, who believe the schools have a responsibility to steer children away from the dangers of AIDS or early pregnancy, may advocate more thorough sex education. Still others, who lament the supposed failure of the schools to produce adequately trained students, may come up with proposals for educational reform.

As mentioned earlier, a popular scheme among conservative critics is a plan to provide parents with vouchers that would allow them to choose among public and private schools that offer all kinds of educational options. The theory is that increased competition among schools to attract students would improve the schools' efficiency or cost-effectiveness while stimulating a more open market for educational practices. The main criticism of voucher plans is that they are likely to be used most effectively by more highly educated and affluent parents, leaving the poorer schools to less well-equipped parents; this would worsen the existing situation of stratification and inequality in education.

An alternative to school vouchers is reform of the property tax system for funding schools in the United States. Most public school systems are funded through a levy on residential property known as the school tax. In municipalities throughout the nation, property owners have become increasingly loath to pay higher taxes on their homes to fund increases in teachers' pay or improvements in the local schools. In large cities, where revenues from property taxes are lower, this system is largely responsible for inequities in funding between suburban and urban schools and explains why urban schools often lack the art, music, athletic, and science programs usually found in suburban schools. In the past, state education budgets were used to offset these differences, but as states cut back on public spending, the schools in poorer central-city communities suffer inordinately. Moreover, as homeowners age, they often become less favorable toward higher school taxes, especially because their own children are no longer in school. In consequence, school reform without reform of educational funding systems is not likely to progress very far.

There are some signs of change, however. Michigan, for example, is leading the way toward improving the quality of education in poor communities without increasing taxes in affluent communities. In 1994 voters in that state approved a new school-funding system based primarily on sales taxes rather than on property taxes. In the decade since Michigan changed its formula for funding public schools, the state has gone from a ranking of 32nd in inequities among schools to 17th, a major improvement in funding equity. Other states are adopting the Michigan model, but there is a problem: During peaks in the value of residential property, tax rolls increase, and so may school funding based on property assessments; at the same time, sales taxes may not increase or may even decrease, resulting in lower levels of school funding under the Michigan model (Mattoon, 2004).

Educational Conservatism and Back to Basics

Educational conservatives believe that the job of the school is to preserve the culture of the past and transmit it to successive generations. This means that schools must concentrate on "essentials"—that is, a set of fundamental subjects and skills—and that all students must be expected to master them. It also means that schools are agencies of social control and as such should stress order, discipline, and obedience.

This point of view has been expressed in a variety of ways since the 1930s, when the debate between "essentialists" and "progressivists" drew national attention. After World War II, it was alleged that the schools were failing to safeguard the values of "Americanism"; after the launching of the Sputnik I satellite by the former Soviet Union in 1957, American education was blamed for neglecting subjects that were vital to national survival. Critics claimed that instead of concentrating on mathematics, history, foreign languages, and other disciplines, high schools encouraged students to divert themselves with trivial subjects like ceramics, stagecraft, and table decorating.

The back-to-basics movement found support in the 1983 report of the National Commission on Excellence in Education (*A Nation at Risk*), which called for longer school hours, more homework, and more discipline. It also proposed that teachers receive salary increases based on merit rather than seniority, on the assumption that this would motivate teachers to do a better job in the classroom. The commission recommended that high schools concentrate on what it termed the "Five New Basics": English, mathematics, science, social studies, and computer science. It also recommended that schools and colleges adopt more rigorous standards and higher expectations for academic performance, on the theory that students will learn more in a more challenging environment.

This recommendation has spurred the trend toward experimentation with year-round schooling. After shifting almost half its high schools to a year-round schedule, in 2004–2005 the Los Angeles school district abandoned the experiment as too complicated and highly unpopular. As new schools were built, the need for year-round schools to accommodate a heavy influx of new students was eased (Hayasaki, 2005). New York and Miami are also experimenting with this approach in an effort to ease overcrowding in schools whose enrollments have been swollen by the arrival of many immigrant families in the past two decades. In 2002 the powerful United Federation of Teachers agreed to a contract that expanded the school day. But year-round schooling is not especially popular in parts of the nation where overcrowding is not an issue. An even more widespread response to the demand for more challenging school environments is the push for national standards (Barnes, 2002; Hirsch, 1996).

Testing for Educational Excellence, or Drill and Kill? The federal No Child Left Behind Act places heavy stress on achieving its goals through standardized tests in the primary grades. Schools that fall behind national or state averages can be penalized by losing motivated parents, who may be offered voucher incentives to choose other schools. And school districts can risk losing their federal funding if they do not comply with the federal requirements. Three years after the law went into effect, the results of the first nationwide test of fourth- and eighth-graders were disappointing. Test scores had improved slightly in math but declined in reading. Minority students also made some gains, but these were less than the gains being made before the passage of the law. Fourth-grade minority students showed the greatest improvements in math scores, but according to testing experts who analyzed the results, at the small rate of improvement recorded so far, it would take 200 years to close the existing gap between minority and nonminority students in math (Dillon, 2005).

Although they may support the goals of greater accountability and higher achievement, state educational leaders are having difficulty funding new programs to meet the federal standards for test results. Testing has the advantage of providing simple measures of achievement, and the emphasis on improving test scores has called attention to the need to require students and teachers to achieve at higher levels. Critics observe, however, that under the law, failure to improve reading and math scores often results in cuts in other curriculum areas, such as art, music, science, and social studies. And classroom teachers frequently experience what they call the "drill and kill" aspects of a heavy emphasis on testing as the major criterion of educational success. When they feel that they must "teach to the test," they risk losing the "teachable moments" when children are inspired to explore new areas of learning and develop their imagination.

What are the pros and cons of the No Child Left Behind Act?

The "Texas Miracle." The No Child Left Behind Act, a cornerstone of President Bush's first term in office, was inspired by what was called the Texas Miracle. In the late 1990s the Houston school district instituted a program of mandatory testing. After a few years the district began reporting results that indicated that the testing was having extremely beneficial effects. Many high schools that had been considered failures were reporting much higher graduation rates. The program gained national attention, and President Bush appointed the Houston school superintendent, Rod Paige, as Secretary of Education. The administration presented the No Child Left Behind Act to Congress as an initiative that had already been successfully tested. But in 2003 investigators discovered that instead of having a high-school dropout rate of 1.5 percent, as claimed, the Houston schools actually had much higher rates of 24 to 25 percent. In fact, students who had dropped out were systematically erased from the books or counted as transfers to another district, so schools where a quarter or more of the students never graduated were listed as having graduation rates of 98 percent. In sum, as a model for what became federal education policy, the so-called Texas Miracle points to a significant problem with this approach: Because it relies on a single measure of educational outcomes, it creates incentives for unethical practices (Dobbs, 2003).

"Reading First" and Social-Scientific Evaluation. The No Child Left Behind legislation emphasized the use of teaching methods backed by "scientifically based research" instead of instinct and fad. The centerpiece of the new research-based approach was Reading First, a $1 billion-a-year effort to help low-income schools adopt strategies "that have been proven to prevent or remediate reading failure" through rigorous peer-reviewed studies. According to materials distributed by the U.S. Department of Education (2007), the Reading First program

> focuses on putting proven methods of early reading instruction in classrooms. Through Reading First, states and districts receive support to apply scientifically based reading research—and the proven instructional and assessment tools consistent with this research—to ensure that all children learn to read well by the end of third grade. The program provides formula grants to states that submit an approved application.

By 2007 the Reading First program was mired in scandal and charges of widespread corruption. The Department of Education never presented systematic research findings on the materials and methods it subsidized and promoted. However, independent

President Bush's No Child Left Behind initiative seeks to make schools more accountable by rating them according to how well students do on standardized math and reading tests, and penalizing school districts with failing schools. Growing numbers of educators are finding that the emphasis on just two measures of school success is decreasing students' opportunities to study science, history, art, and music, and to go on school trips.

research agencies that monitor federal education spending concluded that the vast majority of the 4,800 Reading First schools had adopted one of the five or six top-selling commercial textbooks recommended by the Education Deptartment even though none of them has been evaluated in a peer-reviewed study. A high official in the Department of Education faced charges of corruption and of coercing school districts to adopt a particular textbook and the curriculum it promoted.

The Bush administration believes in phonics, which emphasizes repetitive drills that teach children to "sound out" words. Critics of this approach say that it is important to teach the meaning and context of words as well, an alternative known as the "whole language approach." Reading First money has been steered toward states and school districts that rely on phonics in teaching children to read. At this writing, Congress is beginning investigations of the Reading First program and the charges of cronyism behind the distribution of billions of federal dollars for an entirely untested and unproven initiative (Grunwald, 2006).

Humanism and Open Education

Another view of educational policy is based on the intellectual tradition known as **humanism.** In this view, the basic aim of education is to promote the maximum self-development of each individual learner, paying specific attention to differences among individuals' interests, needs, abilities, and values. Learning should be as "open" and meaningful as possible, with each learner establishing the goals of his or her own education.

In the United States, this approach gave rise to the movement that came to be known as *progressivism*. **Progressivism,** which began in the early 1900s and gathered momentum in the 1920s and 1930s, is associated with the educational philosophy of John Dewey. Dewey believed education should stress the expression of individuality and learning through experience. It should not be imposed from outside but should originate with the needs and interests of the learner. As Dewey (1916) defined it, education is "that reconstruction or reorganization of experience which adds to the meaning of experience, and which increases ability to direct the course of subsequent experience" (p. 126).

Dewey's views were central to the development of progressivism, which emphasized vocational training, "daily-living skills," and a "child-centered curriculum." They fell into some disfavor in the 1950s, but interest in humanistic education reappeared in the 1960s. In the course of the decade, numerous critiques of mainstream educational thought appeared—books with titles like *How Children Fail* (Holt, 1965), *The Way It Spozed to Be* (Herndon, 1968), *An Empty Spoon* (Decker, 1969), and *Death at an Early Age* (Kozol, 1967). In differing ways, each attacked what its author saw as rigid authoritarianism and systematic suppression of genuine learning in American schools.

The outgrowth of this criticism was a call for **open education,** or individualized instruction, based on the approach used in British elementary schools. The goal was independent, self-paced learning. Interest in open education became widespread in the 1970s; it was seen as the best way to make use of children's natural curiosity and to give them individualized attention. However, there is little evidence that open education improved students' intellectual achievement, and it has not proven to be a useful approach at the high-school level.

Access to Higher Education

Another area of education in which significant policy innovations have been made in recent decades is the public university. The public two-year (or community) college is assuming a central role in current educational policy. In the 1990s President Clinton and many state governors emphasized the need to create more opportunities for students to gain access to higher education even after they have been out of high school for some years (Applebome, 1996). The community colleges continue to be primary training and retraining institutions, helping people adapt to rapid economic changes in many regions of the United States. As opposed to many other nations, where apprenticeship programs are a primary route to careers for young people who do not attend universities, in the United States the community college and the four-year public university provide training and transition to adult careers.

Privatization of Public Higher Education. Privatization and the rising cost of tuition threaten access to state universities. Figures released in 2005 show that taxpayer support for public universities has fallen more precipitously since 2001 than at any time in two decades. Several presidents of important state universities have stated that the decline amounts to privatization of the institutions that played a crucial role in the creation of the American middle class.

During the years after World War II, America built the world's greatest system of public higher education. "We're now in the process of dismantling all that," said John D. Wiley, chancellor of the University of Wisconsin—Madison. The share of all public universities' revenues derived from state and local taxes declined to 64 percent in 2004 from 74 percent in 1991. At many of the nation's major public research and teaching universities, the percentages are far smaller. For example, about 25 percent of the University of Illinois's budget comes from the state. The taxpayer share of revenues at the University of Virginia is about 8 percent. These changes translate into higher tuition costs for students and less access by students from lower-income homes. Figure 11–7 shows that as levels of state funding have decreased, the share of funding paid for by tuition has increased. The average in-state tuition nationwide for students attending four-year public colleges increased by 36 percent from 2000–2001 through 2004–2005, according to the College Board, while consumer prices overall rose about 11 percent.

On a more positive note, Georgia's much-publicized Hope scholarship program, which provides higher-education funds for students who maintain a B or better average, is becoming a policy model that may be replicated elsewhere in the nation. More controversial, but perhaps of greater long-term importance, is the open-admissions

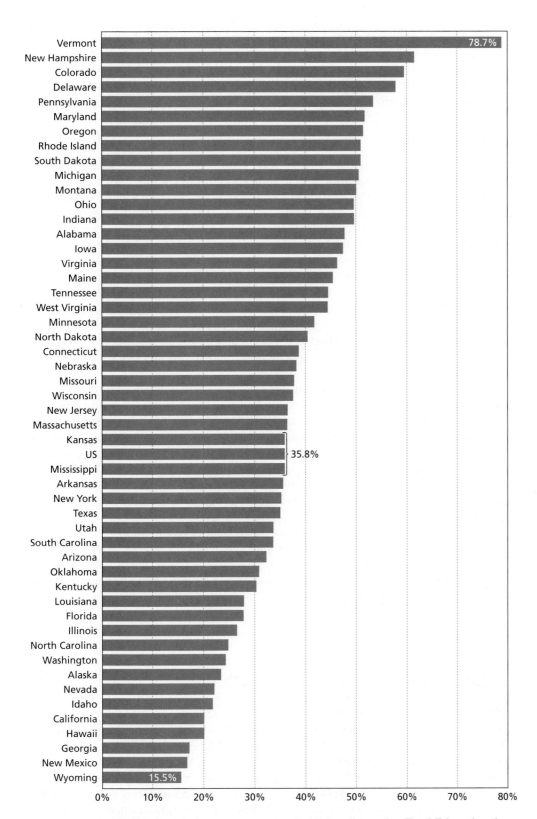

Figure 11–7 Net Tuition as a Percentage of Public Higher Education Total Educational Revenues, by State, 2004.

Source: State Higher Education Executive Officers, 2005.

program pioneered by the City University of New York (CUNY). Research has shown that students who gain access to higher education through open admissions make lasting gains in their jobs and incomes, which more than repay the expense of their education through the taxes they contribute over their working lives (Lavin, Alba, & Silberstein, 1981; Lavin & Hyllegard, 1996).

Future Prospects

Current trends in educational policy include efforts to improve the quality of public school teaching, a longer school year in some communities, and school choice.

The need to provide more incentives for teachers has received widespread recognition, and teachers' salaries have increased in recent years; the average salary for elementary and secondary school teachers is now about $40,000. There have also been demands that teachers receive higher pay and promotions based on merit, but with few exceptions there has been little progress toward this goal at either the federal or the state level. On the other hand, it is generally agreed that the quality of teachers must be improved, and there has been a great deal of discussion of such issues as improved education courses, standardized testing of teachers, and establishment of more rigorous requirements for certification. It has been suggested that a "master teacher" rank could be created that would recognize and reward outstanding teachers; however, teachers' unions fear that criteria other than ability and dedication might be used in designating master teachers.

On a more general level, although there has been much debate about the need to devote more resources to public education, the prospects are not bright. As mentioned, federal support for higher education (especially financial aid for students) has been greatly reduced. At the same time, the idea of a voucher system has not generated much support. As the administration's Leave No Child Behind program proceeds, districts with failing schools will come under increasing pressure to offer alternatives in the form of school choice, through vouchers or transfers to other schools, and this policy will undoubtedly fuel further controversy over whether public funds should be used to subsidize private and parochial schools.

Throughout this book we have seen many instances of the importance of education in a technologically advanced and rapidly changing society. We have also noted that teaching is becoming more attractive as a career choice. But if education is to meet the challenges facing it and if young people are to seriously consider teaching as a vocation, increased funding is necessary.

GOING BEYOND LEFT AND RIGHT

So many hopes are pinned on education, and schools are asked to do so many things to assist in the socialization of the young—from teaching them the "basics" to providing physical and moral education of all kinds—that it is little wonder that education is such a contested area of life in democratic societies. There are, however, some areas of convergence between people on the left and right sides of the debate over school reform. For example, there is increasing consensus that schools need to raise their standards, although as yet there is little consensus about whether the federal and state governments should be the proper enforcers and monitors of these standards. Also, those on the left and the right generally agree that more universal access to higher education is necessary if Americans are to cope with changing economic and technological conditions. But again, as yet there is no consensus on how to fund either elementary education or public colleges and universities. People of all ideological persuasions are seeking alternatives to the inadequate property tax system for funding the schools, and in time we may indeed see political, if not ideological, agreement on pragmatic means to fund the education that our society's students will need in coming decades.

Classroom size is an example of an educational issue that must be addressed through funding, which, in turn, depends on a consensus that the problem needs to be addressed in the first place. In the United States, suburban schools average about 19 students per classroom in the early high school years, while inner-city schools average about 30 students per classroom. Once they become aware of these disparities, people of all political persuasions tend to conclude that this inequality is unfair and are more willing to agree that funds should be invested to balance classroom size in all the nation's schools.

Summary

- The American educational system is subject to criticism for failing to produce competent, educated adults and for failing to reduce or eliminate inequality.

- Functionalist theorists believe that problems of public education arise because schools are not equipped to deal with students who come from disorganized homes. Also related to functionalism is the belief that the educational problems of certain groups stem from deviance from generally accepted norms of achievement. The institutional approach focuses on the problems of shaping educational institutions to meet the needs of changing economies and cultures.

- The conflict perspective sees educational problems as stemming from conflicting views about the goals of education. The class conflict approach argues that schools reflect the values of the dominant groups in society. This approach focuses on intergroup conflicts over such issues as busing to achieve desegregation.

- According to labeling theorists, schools attach labels such as "achiever" or "rebel" to students, and those labels follow them throughout their lives.

- Because educational attainment is strongly correlated with socioeconomic status, an egalitarian society has a responsibility to provide equal access to education for all its citizens. Although the educational gap between whites and minority groups has narrowed considerably, inequalities of access remain, especially in higher education.

- It has been shown that a high-quality preschool program can significantly affect subsequent educational achievement and attainment. As a result, the national Head Start program has been continued.

- The American educational system is highly bureaucratized, a fact that acts as a major barrier to educational change. Even the typically American belief in the "technological fix" encounters obstacles in the bureaucratic organization of school systems. Research has shown that smaller school and class size improves students' performance, but that school-choice programs do not.

- Educational policy recommendations take two main forms. Educational conservatives believe schools should focus on "essentials" or "the basics." They recommend increased attention to academic subjects, more homework and testing, and firmer discipline; some call for a national curriculum and standards. Liberal, or "humanist," educators believe schools should promote the maximum self-development of each individual learner. They call for individualized instruction, greater flexibility in curriculum planning, and increased opportunities for educational innovation.

- The federal No Child Left Behind Act places heavy stress on achieving its goals through standardized tests in the primary grades. Schools that fall behind national or state averages can be penalized by losing motivated parents, who may be offered voucher incentives to choose other schools.

- There is growing recognition of the need to improve the quality of public school teaching, but as yet there has been little progress toward this goal. Other current trends in educational policy include lengthening the school year in some communities and increasing opportunities for school choice.

Key Terms

Social Problems Online

For information about education on the Internet, a good place to start is Education Week on the Web (**www.edweek.org**/). It contains weekly updates and news articles, *Teacher Magazine* online, and special reports of interest to policymakers, all of which are archived.

The Putnam Valley (New York) school system (**www.pnwboces.org/links.htm**) has a host of links to other Internet sites concerned with K–12 education. They include U.S. government resources at the White House and the Department of Education (**www.ed.gov/index.jhtml**) and the Developing Educational Standards site at **http://edstandards.org**.

For higher education resources there are Web pages devoted to community colleges and traditional four-year institutions. The American Association of Community Colleges has a homepage at **www.aacc.nche.edu** that provides historical overviews of community colleges and brief statistical profiles of the institutions, students, and curricula. The Western Interstate Commission for Higher Education (**www.wiche.edu**) promotes educational resources in the western states. Its "Policy Analysis and Research" pages analyze educational attainment and inequality issues, with an emphasis on data that would be useful to policymakers.

The National Education Association (NEA), at **www.nea.org/index.html**, and the American Federation of Teachers (AFT), at **www.aft.org**, both represent the interests of teachers and have Web pages targeted to their members. Both Web sites contain membership information such as model labor contracts, but they also look at debates on educational policy and provide links to other education sites.

The National Parent Teachers Association (PTA) has its homepage at **www.pta.org**, where researchers can find programs and publications related to policy questions. Reports on current topics such as national standards are available for downloading. The American Prospect (**www.movingideas.org/content/en/issue_items/education/reform.htm**) has an online series on educational reform and computer technology, with articles and conference speeches. Under "Public Education," People for the American Way (**www.pfaw.org/pfaw/general**) features reports on school library censorship, efforts to introduce creationism in public schools, and opinion pieces on school voucher programs. On the conservative side of the spectrum is the Center for Education Reform (**http://www.edreform.com**), which advocates school voucher plans. It offers a sample of editorials and reports.

Research Navigator

Follow the instructions on pages 26–27 of this text to access the features of Research Navigator. Once at the Web site, enter your Login Name and Password. Then, to use the Content Select database, use keywords such as "No Child Left Behind," "charter schools," and "bilingual education," and the search engine will supply relevant and recent scholarly and popular press publications. Use the *New York Times* search-by-subject archive to find recent news articles related to problems of education, and the Link Library to find relevant Web sites organized by the key terms associated with this chapter.

Use the following keywords to find articles or research papers on "educational achievement," "home schooling," "human capital," or "residential segregation." Why did you select these articles or papers? What is their relevance to current problems of education?

12

PROBLEMS OF WORK
and the Economy

Dominant Trends

- Now about halfway through its economic transformation from an agrarian to an industrial society, China already manufactures a large proportion of the lower-cost consumer goods purchased in the United States and has become the fourth most important importer of U.S. goods. Total trade between the two nations has increased from about $4 billion in 1980 to $343 billion in 2006.

- Global corporations that produce goods and services in many different nations have a financial value, as measured by the overall value of their stock (capitalization) that is greater than the annual gross domestic product of entire nations.

- The United States continues to lose manufacturing jobs to rapidly growing regions of the world, especially China and India, and this trend also applies to manufacturing in Europe and other mature industrial regions of the world.

- As families in the United States and other advanced industrial nations struggle to make ends meet, mothers spend more time in the paid labor force. Between 1940 and 2007 the proportion of women in the U.S. labor force rose by 10 percentage points per decade.

- Economic globalization and the intense competition it engenders create strong incentives for managers and owners of companies to cut corners and avoid regulations, especially during federal administrations that avoid enforcement of existing laws. As a result, at least 100,000 Americans die of job-related diseases and accidents each year.

Before Hurricane Katrina swept through the Mississippi Gulf region, the St. Bernard School District employed 1,200 people. Now, with the region's economy still struggling to recover, the district can scarcely afford to pay its twelve remaining employees, and the town faces the prospect of layoffs among its firefighters and police officers. New Orleans is in similarly dire straits, with a larger deficit and immense losses to its economic base. Overall, Louisiana lost about $3.3 billion in lost taxes and fees, which added to the severe difficulties it is experiencing in attempting to rebuild its shattered economy. Few events in recent memory have so clearly revealed the close connections among work, the economy, and all the other institutions of the public sector (schools, hospitals, security forces, etc.). The storms that destroyed so much also brought to national attention the central issues of work and the economy (Dewan, 2007).

While governments and businesses in the Gulf region struggled to rebuild their economies, American automakers announced deep losses in profits and demanded concessions from their unionized employees. General Motors opened its books to the United Auto Workers to explain why rising health-care costs and global competition were eating into company revenues. Reluctantly, the union agreed to historic cuts in the health-care benefits that workers had won over many years of collective bargaining. In this case, as in many others considered in this chapter, workers and their families are feeling the effects of the current period of dramatic economic and environmental change.

THE AMERICAN FREE-ENTERPRISE SYSTEM: KEY TRENDS

While the U.S. economy remains by many measures the strongest on earth, its institutions are undergoing rapid and dramatic changes that can be grouped into a few master trends:

- Globalization of markets and the rise of major multinational corporations that compete for power on the world stage.

- Growth in service-sector jobs in the advanced economies and continued export of manufacturing jobs to regions with lower wage rates.

- Increasing reliance of families on the incomes of multiple workers, especially of women and formerly retired people.

- Increased reliance on innovations in technology and specialization to increase the productivity and competitiveness of companies and their employees.

These master trends shaping the economies of the United States and other nations are presented and explained in later sections of this chapter. We turn first, however, to a brief discussion of the basic principles underlying the system of corporate capitalism as it exists in the United States today.

When people refer to the American free-enterprise system, they are talking about an economic system known as **capitalism** (Dobbin, 2004; Friedman, 1962). The central social institutions of capitalism are **markets,** which regulate the worldwide flow of an almost infinite array of goods and services. Markets in a pure free-enterprise system are regulated by the demand for specific goods and services, and by the competition among suppliers to furnish them at a price that is attractive to buyers. In fact, however, almost all markets in nations throughout the world are regulated by acts of governments. These regulations usually attempt to protect buyers in such areas as the safety of products (e.g., rules about food and drug purity and airline maintenance). Other regulations seek to ensure that markets remain competitive and are not dominated by a handful of giant companies known as monopolies.

In other cases governments may try to affect the prices charged for various goods by imposing import taxes. These levies usually seek to give locally made products a price advantage over products imported from outside the nation. The North American Free Trade Agreement of 1993 (NAFTA), for example, is essentially an arrangement in which the United States, Mexico, and Canada agree not to impose import taxes on goods and services flowing among these countries. The protests in Seattle during the 1999 meetings of the World Trade Organization and similar protests in Genoa in 2002 brought many of the controversies surrounding the attempt to regulate world trade to national and international television audiences. Despite the protests, Congress and the Bush administration have continued to negotiate free-trade agreements, most notably the Central American Free Trade Agreement (Colvin, 2005). Unfortunately, enforcement of the environmental and labor clauses of these agreements remains quite weak (Wells, 2003).

Capital refers to equipment of all kinds and to hourly or salaried labor. Capitalists are people who use capital to produce goods and services in the hope of making a profit—that is, by selling their product at a market price somewhat higher than the costs of the equipment and labor used to create it. A capitalist who creates a new business venture is known as an **entrepreneur.** In the pure form of free-enterprise capitalism, the entrepreneur assumes all the risks and expects to make as much profit as possible with as little regulation as possible. In actual practice, most entrepreneurs try to minimize their risks in many different ways.

Formation of a corporation is one major way of minimizing risk. Corporations are chartered by governments to conduct business with limited liability to the owners of the business. **Limited liability** means that only the assets of the corporation are liable to seizure in the case of economic failure or wrongdoing. The entrepreneur's personal assets are not liable if the corporation fails. This protection is vital to the existence of corporations and makes it possible for them to raise funds for expansion by selling shares of their business in the financial markets (stocks and bonds). As they become part owners of the corporation, the shareholders are not liable for what the corporation does beyond the risk of losing their investment in the business. The fact that governments grant limited liability to corporations is one way in which the public, through its elected representatives, can try to make corporations responsible for their actions: Governments can revoke their charters if they violate federal or state laws.

Not all corporations sell shares to the public, but those that do are among the largest and most powerful economic entities in the world. Indeed, the global reach of large corporations, as well as their increasing power throughout the world, is often associated with social problems like environmental pollution, sudden unemployment in specific regions, the use of child labor in poor nations, and many others. It is also true that corporations often create opportunities for economic development and new jobs in formerly impoverished regions.

Inspired by the Marxian dream of a classless society in which everyone owns the means of production (i.e., capital), Communist nations like the former Soviet Union attempted to abolish free enterprise, competitive markets, and profits and to replace them with a planned economy in which government commands determined the flow of goods and services. The decline of the Soviet Union is attributed primarily to the failure of this "command" economic system, which created untold opportunities for corruption and waste.

Capitalist business practices are by no means free of problems, including ruthless dealings, exploitation of the powerless, and their own forms of corruption. Even when they are successful in generating economic growth and new employment opportunities, in a global marketplace success in one region may come at the expense of workers in another, a subject we introduce in the next section.

What are the key trends affecting the U.S. economy today?

GLOBAL MARKETS AND CORPORATE POWER

We hear a great deal about the effects of globalization, but the term and its meanings are often not defined. By **economic globalization,** social scientists refer to the growing tendency for goods and services to be produced in one nation or region and consumed in another, and for the companies that produce those goods and services to engage in business activities in many different regions of the world. This trend is not new, but it is accelerating. Commodities like sugar, coffee, tobacco, and tea were early entrants in the global marketplace of the eighteenth and nineteenth centuries. Sugarcane, for example, was produced on slave plantations in the Caribbean, made into raw sugar and rum, and traded in the northern colonies of what is now the United States and Canada for lumber and other products, which were brought back to the rapidly industrializing nations of Europe. Much of the early economic growth of England, France, and Holland, as well as their competition to establish colonies, was stimulated by this global trade.

In today's global economy, the major changes from older patterns of worldwide economic activity are due to the far greater speed of modern communications and transport. Fish produced in massive salmon farms in Chile, for example, can be on American dinner tables the next day. Information about prices and investment opportunities can travel with electronic speed over computer networks. Television can make a corporation like Coca-Cola, which has ventures everywhere, lose vast sums of money when there is a health scare about its products in one European nation (Belgium). Many of the social problems that globalization entails are due to the overwhelming influence of multinational corporations, both in the less developed nations, where they increasingly do business, and in their home nations (Frieden, 2007).

Multinational Corporations

Few aspects of globalization are more controversial than the operations and even the existence of **multinational corporations** (or transnational corporations). The definition of these entities is extremely broad. They may produce many different kinds of goods and services, but they are all large corporations (often with many subsidiary corporations) that have their headquarters in one country but pursue business activities and profits in one or more foreign nations (Gordon, 1996; Smelser & Swedberg, 2005). In this sense, multinationals have existed at least since the international banking houses of the Italian Renaissance. American firms like Singer, United Fruit, and Firestone have had extensive foreign operations—and political influence—since the late nineteenth century. For the most part, however, these were national companies with secondary foreign operations.

The sharp rise in foreign investments and the concentration of financial resources that followed World War II led to the development of transnational corporations. These companies are international organizations that operate across national

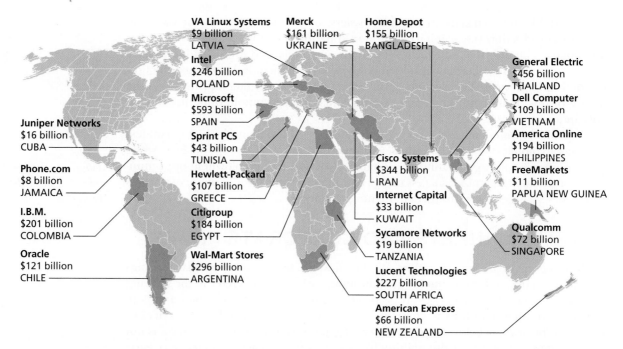

Figure 12–1 Gross Domestic Products of Selected Countries and Companies Whose Market Capitalizations Are About Equal to Them

Source: Gross Domestic Products of Selected Countries and Companies Whose Market Capitalizations Are About Equal to Them, from the article "A Company Worth More Than Spain?" by G. Morgenson. Copyright © 1999 by *The New York Times.* Reprinted by permission of The New York Times Graphics.

boundaries, whatever their country of origin may be. Their size, wealth, influence, and diversity of operations have grown enormously. The annual sales of companies like General Motors, IBM, and the major petroleum corporations exceed the gross national product of many nations—not just the poorer countries of the third world, but highly industrialized countries like Switzerland and South Africa as well. (See Figure 12–1.) Increasingly, therefore, the term *multinational* is used to emphasize the fact that these corporations operate outside national boundaries almost as if they were nations unto themselves.

For decades, the multinational auto companies, such as General Motors and Ford, have been producing thousands of cars in Europe for sale in the expanding European markets. They have had less success in the growing Asian markets, which are dominated by Japanese manufacturers. Now the Japanese multinational manufacturers, especially Toyota, Nissan, and Honda, are increasing the production of cars in the United States, using Japanese methods and parts. These and other multinational companies try to create an image of themselves not as Japanese or American, but as world companies that are above nationalistic sentiments. Although the multinationals will certainly continue to grow and to account for an increasing share of the world's production of goods and services, they are widely criticized for operating outside the control of any nation. One way in which multinational corporations are a source of social problems is that they tend to move quickly to areas where labor costs are lowest, often to the detriment of workers left behind in the nations where they began their operations.

Global Factory, Global Sweatshops

Multinational corporations are transforming the world's economy by focusing on rapidly developing markets and on labor forces in the less-developed nations, which have an oversupply of workers in their manufacturing sectors and an undersupply of highly skilled workers with technological training. No longer confined to producing their products in just one country, the multinationals have created a "global factory" that is made possible by two kinds of technology: high-speed transportation and component production (Martin & Torres, 2004). The first enables companies to get raw materials, finished products, communications, and so on from one point to another anywhere in the world. The second divides the production process into component operations that can be carried out anywhere, thereby allowing multinational companies to take advantage of the worldwide supply of cheap labor. For example, U.S. baseball manufacturers send the materials for their product—leather covers, yarn, thread, and cement—to Haiti, where the baseballs are assembled for wages far below those paid for similar work anywhere in the United States (Galbraith, 1998).

Critics of U.S. multinationals have been especially vocal in condemning the practice known as **outsourcing**—locating plants that produce goods for American markets in third-world nations where the firm can take advantage of lower wage rates. This practice in effect "exports" manufacturing jobs from the United States to the third world, greatly reducing the number of industrial jobs available for American workers. In recent years, however, a countertrend has become evident: Multinational firms are increasing their investments in the United States. Sony of Japan has purchased CBS Records; Japanese and German automobile manufacturers have opened plants in the United States to assemble their cars, often using parts manufactured abroad. These arrangements are considered preferable to outsourcing because they keep jobs in the United States. But many foreign-based multinationals resist union contracts and the resulting higher wages and benefits (Martin & Torres, 2004).

In addition to engaging in outsourcing, multinational corporations attempt to sell their products in third-world markets. As the populations of those nations increase and their standard of living also rises (albeit much more slowly), they represent a vast untapped source of profits. However, multinationals increasingly produce high-technology products and services intended for markets with much greater buying power. Accordingly, many observers (e.g., Rohatyn, 1987) argue that it is necessary to develop more buying power in the third world. This in turn requires that workers in those nations be paid higher wages and not have to work in "sweatshops," in which they are essentially forced to endure conditions that would not be tolerated in affluent nations.

Many of the protesters in Seattle in 1999 were responding to revelations that major multinational corporations, or local companies under contract to them, hire child labor at extremely low wages. For example, the Nike Corporation subcontracts with local employers for about 75,000 Asian workers to make Nike shoes. In some cases 11-year-old workers, who earn about $2.20 a day, are producing sneakers at a cost of about $6 a pair. The sneakers are then sold in the United States for $80.00 or more and are advertised by celebrities like Tiger Woods. Revelations that Nike, McDonald's, and other major global corporations were purchasing goods made by sweatshop labor stimulated the antisweatshop movement and forced these powerful corporations to take strong positions against the use of such labor (Wells, 2003).

Those who argue that the United States should apply trade sanctions, such as import duties, against nations that exploit their workers believe that wages in Latin America, Asia, and the Middle East will increase only if the rights of workers are protected from repression by their governments and powerful businesses. Workers must have the right to bargain collectively for wages, pensions, and health and other benefits. But representatives of China, Pakistan, India, and many other less developed nations where multinationals are active argue that insistence on workers' rights and other protections would drive labor costs up and diminish one of the few advantages poor nations have in the global marketplace. They claim that proponents of labor standards are protectionists who "stand against the trading interests of the developing countries" in order to "advance their own economic interests" (Bhagwati, 1999; Colvin, 2005).

EFFECTS ON AMERICAN WORKERS

For the American worker, the growth of multinationals and global markets means that a steadily decreasing number of employers have come to dominate the labor market. This has had several effects. Chief among them is that as unions cope with increasingly large and centralized corporations, they, too, tend to become large and centralized, and their leadership tends to become oligopolistic (Gordon, 1996). The growth of multinationals is also associated with the tendency to export capital and jobs overseas, where labor is cheaper and more plentiful. American manufacturing workers have been most seriously affected by this trend. In 1960, over 28 percent of all U.S. workers were employed in manufacturing jobs. By 2005, this figure had dropped to 11.3 percent (Bureau of Labor Statistics, 2005).

During the 1970s and 1980s U.S. plants, factories, mills, and other industrial facilities suffered as capital was diverted abroad. Unable to maintain their competitive edge, many manufacturing facilities closed. Especially hard hit were plants in the nation's older, single-industry cities and towns, most of which were located in the manufacturing belt of the Midwest. When rubber mills in Akron, Ohio, and steel mills in Youngstown, Ohio, and the Pittsburgh area shut their doors, the local economies were devastated. With few secondary industries to fall back on, these cities experienced severe economic and social upheavals during the recessions of the mid-1970s and early 1980s and 1990s.

The biggest losers in the decline in manufacturing have been industrial towns and cities in the Northeast and Midwest. Manufacturing cities like Gary, Indiana, once the nation's most important producer of steel, have been hit hardest. In the 1970s the Gary steel mills employed almost 28,000 workers in relatively well-paid jobs with good benefits. Today, fewer than 8,000 workers are employed in the Gary mills. Nevertheless, modernization of the steel industry, leading to greater efficiency and quality control, may produce a turnaround. Steel exports are rising, and steel companies' profits are improving.

Over the past generation or so there have been three unprecedented changes in the American labor force, largely because of transformations in the global economy. First is the shift from manufacturing to service employment. Second is the enormous increase in the number of women working outside the home—women of all ages and from all kinds of family backgrounds. Third is the emergence of new technologies and unprecedented economic growth in the past ten years, much of it related to the global influence of the U.S. economy.

From Manufacturing to Services

Because people work for so much of their lives, it is important to understand the social problems related to work. Later in the chapter we discuss four: unemployment, automation, alienation, and occupational safety and health. In this section we explore four patterns of change in the nature of work in the United States that have accompanied the shift from a manufacturing-based to a service-based economy. These trends are reflected in Figure 12–2, which projects out to 2014 the changes economists and sociologist expect to see in the U.S. labor force. These predictions do not carry good news for the future of employment in production (manufacturing) and farming, fishing, and forestry, which is likely to experience continued declines. But they do show that jobs in the professions, services, construction, management, maintenance, and transportation will continue to grow in number. However, a large proportion of service jobs and jobs in sales are low-paying and do not provide benefits. These trends go a long way in explaining why political and educational leaders constantly emphasize the importance of staying in school and gaining the educational credentials required for the better-paying positions that will open up in the future.

The impact of the transition from an agricultural economy to an industrial one dominated by large corporations and government organizations can be gauged from a

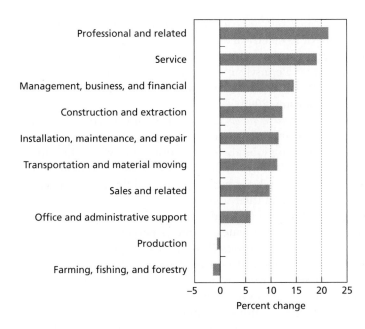

Figure 12–2 Percent Change in Total Employment, by Major Occupational Group: Projected 2004–2014

Source: U.S. Bureau of Labor Statistics, 2005.

few figures. In 1900, 27 percent of the total labor force consisted of farm workers and 18 percent of white-collar workers. By 2007, only about 2.2 percent of the labor force consisted of farming, forestry, and fishing workers, whereas about 60 percent were white-collar workers (U.S. Department of Labor, 2007).

White-collar workers—professional, managerial, clerical, and sales personnel—are the largest occupational category in the nation, surpassing the blue-collar group since 1956. Most of the new white-collar jobs are professional and clerical. The number of clerical personnel has increased by more than 500 percent since 1900 and now accounts for about 17 percent of all employed people (*Statistical Abstract*, 2006). Clerical workers now vie with skilled and semiskilled workers as the largest occupational group in the labor force.

The decline in farm employment since the turn of the century has been as dramatic as the rise in white-collar employment. Farm workers—farmers, managers, and farmhands—once the largest occupational category in the United States, are now the smallest.

Blue-collar workers have witnessed enormous changes in the nature of their work. A declining proportion of the overall labor force, manual workers still constitute a very large segment of the work force but are employed in a changing array of jobs. The proportion of unskilled laborers has decreased. Similarly, the slight overall net gain in service occupations masks some important changes within that category. People employed as private household workers now account for less than 1 percent of the total labor force; in 1900 they accounted for 5 percent. In contrast, the proportion of other service personnel—hotel workers, waiters, barbers, and others—has risen to about 15 percent of all employed people; in 1990 it was 4 percent.

The momentous shift from an economy dominated by manufacturing employment to one dominated by jobs in services of all kinds results in improvements in some work-related social problems and at the same time creates new ones. For example, accidents and deaths on the job are far more prevalent in an economy dominated by agriculture and extractive industries, such as mining and lumbering, or one in which there are large numbers of workers in heavy industries, such as metals production and auto and truck manufacturing. The rate of accidental deaths at work in 1960 was 21 per 100,000 workers, but by 2000, with the rise of service work as the leading form of employment, that rate had declined to 4 per 100,000 workers. Mining and agriculture remain the most dangerous work environments in the United States, with about 30 and 20 deaths per 100,000 workers, respectively. In service work, on the other hand, the rate of accidental deaths is 2 per 100,000 each year (*Statistical Abstract*, 2006). As the United States produces more of its electrical energy with coal mined within its borders, there is a continuing need to enforce mine safety regulations. Senator Arlen Specter, from the coal-mining state of Pennsylvania, cites cuts in the number of federal mine safety inspectors between 2000 and 2006 as one of the reasons for the dramatic increase in fatal mine accidents (Watson, 2006).

Note also that societies with a *service economy* or *postindustrial economy* (terms that social scientists often use to refer to the labor market of mature industrial societies that export many of their manufacturing jobs abroad) do not entirely lose their manufacturing infrastructure. There are still mines, railroads, auto plants, and many other sources of blue-collar work, but they are a declining proportion of the total and are no longer setting the pace of social change in their societies.

The decline in union membership is a good indication of this change. In 1960, at the height of union influence in the United States, about 27 percent of employees in the private sector were members of trade unions. Today, about 9 percent are union members, a reflection of the shift from manufacturing work, which was always more heavily unionized, to white-collar service work, which, with the exception of government work, is less unionized. This rate varies from one state to another. In Michigan, Illinois, and Ohio, states with higher proportions of manufacturing jobs, at least 18 percent of private-sector employees are union members, whereas in Georgia, Utah, and Mississippi, states with so-called "right to work" laws that make it much harder for unions to organize workers, less than 10 percent are union members. These differences are extremely important because unions help workers obtain not only higher pay but also health and other benefits that nonunion workers do not often have. Thus, the proportion of families with health insurance is higher for union families than for nonunion ones. Indeed, the loss of union jobs to global manufacturing sites outside the United States has resulted in more jobs with lower average pay and fewer benefits, a major cause of the growing gap between workers whose share of the national income is stagnant and those who benefited most from the economic boom of the 1990s.

Another aspect of the shift from manufacturing to services is the growing importance of what is known as "contingent" work, work that is not based on written employment contracts and regular hours. This problem is particularly serious for female workers.

Women in the Global Labor Market

The labor force, as defined by the federal government, consists of all people 16 years of age or over (excluding those in institutions[1]) who worked one hour for pay during one survey week (the employed) plus those who did not work during the survey week, do not have a job, and are actively seeking work (the unemployed). The most significant trend in the labor force is the inclusion of married women and the exclusion of older men.

Many social scientists argue that after the shift from manufacturing to service work, the single most significant trend in the labor force in the twentieth century was the enormous increase in women as paid workers. A century ago women and men rarely did the same work. Although there were always women in the labor force, much of the work they did was unpaid and in the home, usually involving extremely long hours. Married women were expected to remain at home. Between 1940 and 1990, however, the proportion of married women in the labor force—that is, the percentage working or looking for work—rose by 10 percentage points per decade. As we see in Figure 12–3, today the proportion of married women living with their spouse who work is 71.2 percent, and for women in other marital statuses (divorced, separated, widowed) it is almost 79 percent. Not shown in the figure is the fact that over 80 percent of women

---

[1]Prisons, asylums, and nursing homes.

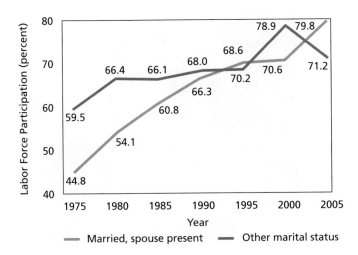

Figure 12–3 Labor Force Participation of Women with Own Children, by Marital Status, United States: 1975–2005

Source: Statistical Abstract, 2006.

who have bachelor's degrees are in the labor force, a rate that is rapidly approaching that of men (Tienda, 1999).

Among African American women, William J. Wilson notes,

> Noncollege black women had very little chance during the first half of this century to take a job other than as a domestic servant. After 1960, demand increased for clerical and service workers. Black women were able to take those positions, so much so that by 1980, only a small percentage of black women were domestic household servants. But, ironically, just as blacks and Hispanics started to move into those clerical positions, changing demand began to reduce opportunities as bank tellers, typists, and so on. Now, folks who don't have college degrees face a new challenge because the areas that were opening up are starting to close. Yet it's far better than it was. (Quoted in Tienda, 1999, p. 48)

Over the past 40 years the sheer number of people in the U.S. labor force has increased dramatically, again largely because of the rapid influx of women. In 1970 there were 78 million men and women in the labor force; now there are more than 130 million, of whom well over 40 percent are female. But for many of these workers, and especially for women, the costs of maintaining the home and raising children make it necessary to hold more than one job. About 6 percent of both women and men are multiple job holders. When asked why they must work two jobs, 31 percent of men say that they do so to pay regular household bills. But among women who maintain families themselves, over 40 percent say that they hold a second job to pay the bills, and the percentage rises to 53 percent of black female chief breadwinners and 40 percent of Hispanic women in the same situation (*Statistical Abstract*, 2006).

Some women who are second job holders need that job because the first job is part time and does not provide sufficient earnings to make ends meet. The majority of part-time workers are women. When questioned about why they were working part time, about 6.6 million men and women said that they were in school, but 5.5 million, again mostly women, said that they were part-timers because of family obligations, including problems with child care (*Statistical Abstract*, 2006). Here the problem is balancing work and family roles. As economist Juliet Shor concludes, "The major barrier is the structure of jobs. We have not been able to make good jobs compatible with child-rearing roles. The labor market is inflexible" (quoted in Tienda, 1999, p. 48). The massive entry of women into the labor market, sociologist Marta Tienda (1999) observes, is partly because of the need for child care: "Because we rely on other women to take care of our children, two women can enter the labor force for every one that takes on a new job. When women go to work, we buy child-care services, more takeout food and other services, all of which are driving economic growth in a profound way. It also means that we are fueling stratification [inequality]" (p. 48).

As the proportion of women in the labor force has increased, so has the frequency with which women with dependent children experience layoffs and unemployment.

How do sociologists explain the rapid rise in the proportion of women in the labor force in the past half-century?

Finally, it should be noted that even though women are employed in greater numbers than ever before, their jobs are vulnerable during economic recessions; and although many women are highly motivated to work, outside employment has not released most of them from household and family tasks. As we saw in Chapters 8 and 10, a married woman typically works many hours at home in addition to holding an outside job.

Technology and Specialization

Much of the growth in the U.S. economy in the 1990s was fueled by the rise of new technologies, especially in computers, telecommunications (including Internet applications), biotechnologies, and e-commerce. As noted earlier, improved coordination of global production systems through faster transport of materials, goods, and people makes it possible to export manufacturing jobs overseas while creating more managerial, information resources, and financial positions in the metropolitan centers of North America, Europe, and Asia. But even more significant is the rapid growth in applications of computer technologies. Every year the percentage of U.S. workers who use computers daily at their jobs increases dramatically. Between 1993 and 1998, this percentage rose from 46 percent to 50 percent, which translates into 12.5 million more computer users at work. In 2006, about 60 percent of women, who are more likely than men to have white-collar jobs, worked regularly with computers, far above the national average (*Statistical Abstract*, 2007). Although the most common application was word processing, increasing proportions of women and men are using computers for a wider variety of tasks, often involving the World Wide Web.

Technology. Computer and telecommunications have spawned an astounding array of new Internet-related businesses, such as Amazon.com and eBay. The growth of many of these was made possible by intense speculation in technology stocks at the end of the 1990s and well into 2000, but it is still too soon to know the many implications these new businesses will have for workers and consumers. One effect is clear, however: The number of self-employed people is growing rapidly. Much of this growth is made possible by the rise of new technology-based businesses (which require Web page designers, programmers, and other technical specialists). The telecommunications technologies also allow many more people to create and manage their own home businesses, and thus to make their living at home. In 2006, 10.5 million people reported that they were self-employed (*Statistical Abstract*, 2007).

In the next few decades, new technologies will continue to fundamentally change the character of work in America. Many people fear—not unrealistically—that the principal change will be a reduction in the number of jobs. In this regard, sociologists Stanley Aronowitz and William DiFazio argue that for many millions of people in the older Western industrial nations, which are experiencing a combination of high rates of job elimination through automation and extensive exportation of less skilled work to low-wage regions of the world, there will be a "jobless future." Increasingly, they and others predict, new entrants to the labor force who do not have essential skills will undergo long spells of unemployment and circulation through training programs, but their work histories will not enable them to become secure in a middle-class lifestyle (Aronowitz & DiFazio, 1994; Dobbin, 2004). Critics of this viewpoint note that the American economy has continued to produce millions of new jobs at all skill levels despite the undeniable displacement and change caused by automation (Kasarda, 1995; Wetzel, 1995).

Specialization. Specialization is a long-term trend in the labor market. The vast majority of people in the labor forces of urban industrial societies are employees of small or large companies or of public administrations. For them, too, computer and other technologies are changing the nature of their work and the types of jobs available to them. Specialization, however, began long before the advent of computers. As the number of goods and services increases, so does job specialization. As the complexity of production processes increases with product diversity, so does job specialization.

As mentioned earlier, there are four broad categories of employment (white-collar, blue-collar, service, and farmworkers). Within these categories, of course, there are literally thousands of jobs. The *Dictionary of Occupational Titles*, published by the Department of Labor, lists more than 22,000 jobs—a total that contrasts sharply with the 325 recorded by the 1850 census. The vast difference indicates the increasing specialization of labor and the complexity of its divisions.

Specialization has several important implications. First, lower-echelon workers who were trained only for a single, narrow job and who lose it may have difficulty in finding another like it. Second, these workers often feel they are merely adjuncts to a machine or a process, with little chance to develop and use more than minor skills or abilities. This feeling often leads to dissatisfaction with work. For high-level managers, the increase in specialization has created problems of coordination and cooperation that present great challenges (Braverman, 1974).

What are some of the beneficial and negative effects of economic globalization on American workers?

PROBLEM ASPECTS OF WORK

What are the effects of the new technologies? According to sociologist Shoshanna Zuboff (1982), managers and employees whose jobs are controlled by factory computer systems come to believe their effective "boss" is the computer. In some cases, unionized employees have protested the new forms of hidden computer supervision. Workers in regional telephone companies, for example, blamed computer technology for eroding the family culture of the old national telephone company known as "Ma Bell." They equated the computer with oversupervision, stress, and excessive discipline.

Computer control not only affects workers but also alters the structure of the organization. For one thing, most computer-based operations require a separate data-processing staff. Computer specialists are different from many of the other people in a factory. They have skills that the others do not understand, and their job is not actually to produce the product but to provide efficient means of producing it. Computer technology, therefore, creates a new interdependence between the workers directly concerned with the end product and those concerned with data processing, whose job is to help accomplish the other workers' goal. People with high status in the organization but no technical expertise must cooperate with the technical experts, such as programmers and systems analysts, who have no supervisory authority—a relationship unique to modern organizations (Smelser & Swedberg, 2005).

Such cooperation is not easy. Aronowitz and DiFazio (1994) note that technologies like computer-assisted design have eliminated highly skilled jobs in architecture and engineering because computers can now accomplish many drafting and design tasks that once employed thousands of technical workers who were gradually moving up through the ranks of the technological elite. They also note that the workers who remain after their colleagues have been replaced by technological systems are not necessarily more contented; they must live with the lingering fear that new technologies will eventually eliminate their jobs as well.

It seems that the new technologies may exacerbate some conditions that produce job dissatisfaction. Work will probably become increasingly demanding and precise. These changes will continue to increase demands by employers for a more highly educated and competent labor force. They also give rise to increased job insecurity and job stress.

In the past, economic downturns have caused the highest levels of unemployment among blue-collar workers—laborers and machine operators (operatives)—but the end of the high-tech investment bubble and the declines in aerospace and other high-tech industries have caused far more economic insecurity in the ranks of managers and skilled professionals than was previously the case. Unemployment rates decreased for all workers between 1992 and 2000 but rose dramatically between 2000 and 2002. These shifts were most precipitous for blue-collar operators and laborers, but the graphs also show that after 2000, unemployment among managers and professionals increased by an unprecedented 76 percent. Since 2001, managers and professionals have also spent far more time unemployed than they typically did during the boom years. Note in the graph that before the recession of 2000–2001, the percentage of unemployed managers and professionals who were out of work for more than six months had declined to almost 10 percent, but by 2002 it had shot up to about 27 percent, almost attaining the level of the severe recession at the beginning of the 1990s, before the high-tech boom.

The Changing Nature of Employment

A striking feature of the years from 2000 to 2006 was relatively high employment rates and consistently low unemployment. Because people change jobs and spend some time looking for new ones for a variety of reasons, not just because of economic downturns and layoffs, some unemployment is considered normal. Economists argue about the precise meaning of "full employment," but the consensus is that an unemployment rate between 4 percent and 4.5 percent is to be expected in a thriving economy. From this perspective, it appears that the U.S. economy is thriving; in 2007 the unemployment rate was 4.8 percent. Why, then, in one poll after another, do the majority of American workers express fears about their economic future? Globalization, the export of high-paying manufacturing jobs overseas, and the increase in the proportion of lower-paying jobs in the U.S. economy are some of the reasons. But the increasing numbers of jobs that do not pay adequate benefits raise more immediate concerns for millions of workers and their families.

Insecurity about Declines in "Good Jobs." If you were offered a full-time job in the private sector with relatively low wages, without health benefits, without an employer-paid pension plan, and with no sick leave or disability policy, would you consider it a good job? Probably not, yet employers are offering workers more jobs like that one every year, according to data from the most recent U.S. Department of Labor survey of employee benefits. They show that worker (and thus family) benefits are on the wane. Only 52 percent of jobs in the United States come with medical benefits, down from 53 percent in 1999. Yet the medical insurance system depends heavily on employment-based medical benefits. Employers are also moving away from defined-benefit pension plans—which they pay into—in favor of defined-contribution plans, the most common of which are so-called 401k plans, which the employee pays into and must pay taxes on once he or she retires. Only 37 percent of private-sector jobs provide short-term disability benefits, just 57 percent offer any paid sick leave, and a mere 15 percent offer employees any child care (although this proportion has actually increased since the family-friendly legislation of the late 1990s).

As a consequence of these negative trends, an increasing number of workers in lower-paying jobs, especially in service sectors like home health care and retail sales, do not have any of these benefits, and many workers in other private-sector jobs fear that they will lose theirs. Only 45 percent of workers in jobs paying less than $45,000 a year have employment-based health insurance (Robert Woods Johnson Foundation, 2007). Thus, while workers still fear the loss of their jobs and long bouts of unemployment, in the current period of "full employment" but declining employer-provided benefits, they are experiencing new forms of insecurity and economic stress as they struggle to find ways to obtain adequate health insurance and worry about their lack of pension savings (Hacker, 2006). And as they grow older, they must begin to worry about whether they will have adequate health-care coverage if they retire or must stop working for other reasons. Figure 12–4 shows that even large employers are steadily cutting back on health benefits for their retirees, causing many individual to continue working until they qualify for federal health insurance (Medicare).

How can it be that while the U.S. economy continues to produce new jobs and unemployment remains low, many American workers feel economically insecure?

Unemployment. In the past, economic downturns have caused the highest levels of unemployment among blue-collar workers—laborers and machine operators—but the end of the high-tech investment bubble in 2002 and the rash of mergers and acquisitions in many industries have caused far more economic insecurity in the ranks of managers and skilled professionals than was previously the case. At the end of 2002 Congress voted not to extend unemployment benefits to those who were out of work for lengthy periods, thus further increasing the economic insecurity experienced by the unemployed at all social-class levels (DePalma, 2002). In an extensive study of the impact of the 2001 terrorist attack on the World Trade Center on workers in the airline industry, William Kornblum and Steve Lang found that although Congress spent

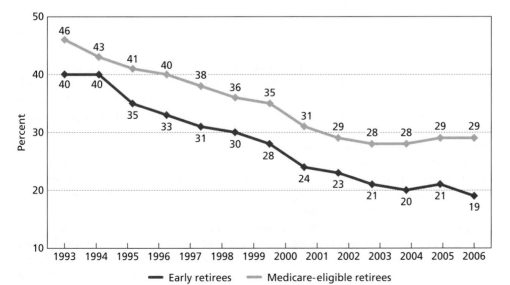

Figure 12–4 Percentage of Private-Sector Employees Receiving Selected Types of Employee Benefits

Source: Data from U.S. Bureau of Labor Statistics, 2007.

billions of dollars to offset the industry's losses, its refusal to extend unemployment benefits greatly increased the difficulties experienced by 10,000 workers in the New York–New Jersey metropolitan region. These workers had faced severe layoffs due to airline mergers and bankruptcies before 9/11 and were either being recalled to former jobs or starting new ones when the terrorist attack occurred. Since most of them did not live in the vicinity of the towers, they were excluded from direct aid, and many experienced extremely long periods of unemployment, loss of medical benefits, and in many cases, severe psychological stress (Kornblum & Lang, 2005).

Prolonged joblessness causes serious psychological and social damage. A significant part of today's work force has been denied not only the benefits of a regular and sufficient income, but also the emotional rewards of a steady job: the sense of self-worth that comes from doing a job well and having others value that performance; the sense of community fostered by daily association with colleagues—in sum, the feeling that one is participating in society and contributing to it. The unemployed person, whether involuntarily retired, partially or intermittently out of work, or chronically unemployed, is denied many of these rewards. (For problems of the involuntarily retired person, see Chapter 9.)

The Intermittently and Chronically Unemployed. In a competitive society, job insecurity is common. Even when the unemployment rate is low, many people are unemployed for part of the year, and others are underemployed. More serious, however, is chronic unemployment. In general, the unemployment rate for blacks and other minority groups is twice as high as the rate for whites. The chronically unemployed and their children rarely acquire the capacity to break out of the unemployment pattern without some state or federal help. Many of them are high-school dropouts, and their low educational attainment equips them only for low-skilled jobs. These young men and women may not yet have family obligations, but they are nonetheless reluctant to take dead-end jobs as domestics or kitchen workers. (See Chapters 6, 7, and 8 for fuller discussions of the relationships among discrimination, unemployment, and poverty.)

Frictional Unemployment and Permanent Displacement. Many workers undergo short spells of unemployment; they may be temporarily laid off from a factory job or may leave one job to search for another that is different or better. Economists call this *frictional unemployment* because it is a normal consequence of labor force mobility or brief economic changes in local labor markets. But a great deal of unemployment results in the permanent displacement of workers. Permanent displacement is extremely serious because often the employee must find work in an entirely different industry or field, which often necessitates retraining of some kind.

The "Invisible" Unemployed and the "Discouraged" Worker. As stated earlier, the labor force is made up of people age 16 and over (excluding those in institutions) who worked one hour for pay during the survey week plus those who did not work during the survey week, do not have a job, and are actively seeking work. By definition, all other people over the age of 16 are not in the labor force and therefore are not included in government unemployment reports. This definition persistently understates the size of the labor force and the volume of unemployment. First, it excludes unemployed people who, though able and willing to work, did not actively seek work during the survey week. A second factor is the failure of the official data to reflect adequately the underemployment of people with part-time jobs. Numerous studies by sociologists and economists have estimated that a more accurate measure of unemployment would be about double the official rate.

The problem of "invisible" unemployment becomes more serious in recessions, when the average duration of unemployment increases; many people eventually stop looking for jobs altogether because they think it will be impossible to find one. These are known as "discouraged" workers, people who are out of work not because of personal disadvantages, such as being too old or too young, untrained, or overeducated, but because industries and manufacturers have cut back production and eliminated a large number of jobs. For example, the Bureau of Labor Statistics estimates that the recession of the early 1990s caused about 1 million people to drop out of the labor force in a single year (Rackham, 1991).

Consequences of Unemployment. What are the consequences of being without work? A classic study of 105 unemployed men in Detroit showed that the chief characteristic is extreme isolation (Wilensky, 1966; see also Kornblum & Lang, 2005). Half the men in the study had no close friends, half never visited neighbors, and few belonged to organizations or engaged in organized activities. These findings were in sharp contrast to the social life of an equal-sized sample of employed men. Such data tend to support the thesis that work is necessary if one is to be, in a full sense, "among the living." When work ties are cut, participation in community life declines and the sense of isolation grows. Thus, those with the most tenuous work connections—the retired, the elderly, those who have been squeezed out of the labor market, and those who seldom get into it—are often isolated from their communities and from society at large (Hamrick, 2001).

Further studies on the emotional and social effects of long-term unemployment were conducted by D. D. Braginsky and B. M. Braginsky in 1975. This research was confined to high-status unemployed men who had been thrown out of work in the recession of the mid-1970s. The subjects consisted of two groups, one a control group of employed white-collar men and the other a group of jobless men between the ages of 23 and 59. Almost half of the jobless men were college graduates; many had been engineers and company managers. The researchers found that such men undergo a "social transformation"; the trauma of unemployment causes a change of attitude that persists even after they are reemployed. Loss of one's job is commonly interpreted as a judgment of incompetence and worthlessness. In the Braginsky study the unemployed men expressed these feelings. Their self-esteem was lowered, and they felt alienated from society. They experienced depression, a common reaction to loss. Most suffered deep shame and avoided their friends. Many of those who did find new jobs did not fully recover their self-esteem.

As more and more women have entered the labor force, the consequences of unemployment for women have become more important, particularly for women who are single parents, who are divorced or separated, and whose families are dependent on their earnings. Katherine S. Newman (1988) found that middle-class women who are divorced "typically have to make do with 29 to 39 percent of the family income they had before divorce" (p. 202). When these women are in the labor force and experience layoffs and unemployment, it is often difficult for them to support their families while looking for new jobs. Typically they had interrupted their careers for marriage and child rearing, and they are less competitive in the labor market than men, who have been working more or less continuously. In this regard it is worthwhile to point out that the single greatest reason that women go on welfare is the "double jeopardy" situation of loss of spouse and loss of job (Reskin & Hartman, 1986; Smelser & Swedberg, 2005).

Job Stress

As more people work multiple jobs, are employed on a contingent basis, or experience the sometimes frantic environment of high-tech companies, their physical and mental lives are often negatively affected (Ross, 2000). A 1999 survey of workers' problems conducted by the National Institute for Occupational Safety and Health (NIOSH) found that job stress, because of irregular workloads, uncertain work expectations, loss of control over the pace of work because of increased computerization, poor social environments, and overall job insecurity, was reaching alarming levels. "We've identified this as a top priority issue," Linda Rosenstock, the institute's director, said. "The

U.S. public is reporting very high levels of stress at work, and often reporting it's the largest source of stress they face. Shifting work patterns due to the global economy are aggravating these issues" (quoted in Grimsley, 1999, p. 1D).

Gary Namie, an organizational psychologist who operates a Web site for workers with job stress, said that in one month fourteen people who contacted the site said that they were considering suicide. "Stress is not to be taken lightly," Namie said. "Stress can kill. Stress is real. It's not imaginary. It has a biological basis. It's unconscionable that someone should sacrifice their health for the sake of a paycheck" (quoted in Grimsley, 1999, p. 1D). According to NIOSH, stress can be alleviated by ensuring that workloads are appropriate for workers' capabilities, clearly defining workers' roles and responsibilities, improving communication, providing opportunities for social interaction, and establishing work schedules that are compatible with other life responsibilities (cited in Grimsley, 1999).

Alienation

When people go to work, they sacrifice some personal freedom and assume some risk. A job demands that a person put his or her time at another's disposal. It may also mean spending money and time on commuting and enduring physical hazards and discomforts, psychological traumas, boredom, and frustration. In return, workers can expect varying amounts of pay and fringe benefits, job security, meaningful work, opportunities for advancement, flexibility in work time, decent surroundings, and positive interactions with peers and supervisors. Each of these factors affects job satisfaction.

The concept of **flexitime,** or sliding work hours, is very appealing to workers—so appealing, in fact, that one survey showed that many workers are willing to remain in jobs they dislike because their schedules are flexible (Kenworthy, 2004). But although flexitime and other creative approaches are appealing and have shown some success, it is more usual for workers in the United States and Europe to feel squeezed between the fear of displacement and the demand that they work longer hours under greater stress. Critics of the automated, postindustrial society argue that these conditions are likely to cause new outbreaks of industrial strife and to stimulate alienated workers to form unions (Gordon, 1996; Martin & Torres, 2004).

Marx and other nineteenth-century social critics attacked the assignment of people to activities that have no meaning for them. Factory workers, they charged, are merely part of a productive process, lacking control over either the process or the product. Workers who lose the capacity to express themselves in their work will experience **alienation.**

In modern work situations, several elements combine to produce a sense of alienation. The primary source today is the clash between a person's self-image and the requirements of his or her job. Those who believe they need the companionship of others may feel stifled by a job that does not allow them to socialize with fellow workers. Some people may be alienated by jobs that offer little opportunity for personal judgment. Others may see themselves as independent and decisive but find that their bosses are constantly and closely supervising them. The symptoms of alienation are not necessarily confined to blue-collar workers. Alienation may occur in any hierarchy that limits autonomy and the chance to use individual skills. Thus, white-collar workers often feel estranged from their employers and the long-term interests of their companies.

Are the causes of alienation different for different types of workers? Are white-collar workers, such as accountants or engineers, affected by the same factors as blue-collar workers, such as assemblers or welders? A study of nearly 800 workers by the Survey Research Center at the University of Michigan (cited in Gruenberg, 1980) found that although intrinsic sources of job satisfaction are important to all workers regardless of their educational background, such external satisfactions as wages and vacation time are more important for blue-collar workers. This emphasis on what they get out of the job rather than on what they put into it may reflect the low level of job satisfaction felt by most blue-collar workers.

The "underground economy" includes many types of businesses that do not report their transactions or pay taxes. An example is the peddler who buys wholesale merchandise and resells it on the street.

Occupational Safety and Health

People have long been concerned about the physical toll exacted by work. Medical writings reveal that even in ancient Rome physicians recognized an unusually high frequency of lung disease among metalworkers, miners, and weavers of asbestos cloth. During the Renaissance each craft was known to have its unique maladies. But the industrial revolution created a new wave of deadly occupational hazards. From the beginning, the American labor movement, at the urging of rank-and-file workers and union activists, made safety one of its top priorities. Yet despite this long history of concern and awareness, occupational health remains a serious problem. Figure 12–5 presents the most dangerous occupational categories, some of which have fatality rates ten or twenty times the average. These tend to be male-dominated occupations, which explains why about 90 percent of those killed on the job are men (Nordheimer, 1996). As the graph shows, mining; agriculture, forestry, and fishing; construction; and transportation have the highest fatality rates.

Industrial accidents are only part of the problem. Proponents of occupational health have widened their focus to include illnesses as well as accidents, and they have concentrated on preventing work-related diseases rather than merely treating or

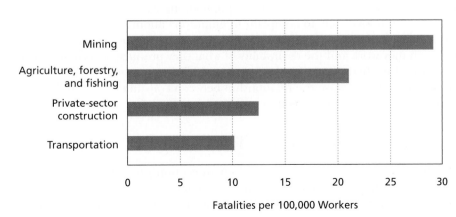

Figure 12–5 Fatality Rates for the Most Dangerous Occupational Categories

Source: Statistical Abstract, 2006.

Health scandals and extremely high rates of injury in the meatpacking industry at the turn of the last century helped convince Americans of the need for government health and safety regulations. Shown here is a "dressing room" in a meatpacking plant in 1882.

compensating workers for them. The situation is grim: At least 100,000 Americans die of job-related diseases each year.

Perhaps the greatest health hazards come from the chemicals industry. Chemicals, which are involved in the manufacture of almost every product we use, can also produce cancer. Workers who are exposed to certain chemicals have an unusually high rate of malignancies. They frequently suffer from other health problems as well, such as nervous disorders and sterility; their children may suffer from birth defects.

Occupational health is an issue loaded with moral, medical, and economic questions. Industries cite the enormous impact that needed changes will have on the entire economy as the cost of occupational health is passed along to consumers in the form of higher prices. Others argue that compulsory adherence to proposed health regulations will put them out of business or force them to relocate to other countries. Many workers, more fearful of imminent unemployment than of future illness, agree with their employers and take their chances in the workplace. Others, realizing that their interests as consumers and citizens may outweigh their economic stake, join the ranks of consumer activists.

As workers in the United States and other industrialized nations organize to deal with occupational safety issues, there is more incentive for industries to locate in low-wage regions of the world, whose impoverished populations are far less capable of recognizing dangers and less likely to complain to employers about dangerous working conditions (Alli, 2001; Rifkin, 1995). That even more workers do not question the conditions in which they work and the desirability of what they produce is perhaps attributable in part to their high level of indebtedness, which has resulted from extensive use of consumer credit. Because the relationship between consumers and credit is an important one, we devote the next section to this subject.

CONSUMERS AND CREDIT

The United States is a consumer society, one with an economy based on the activities of numerous corporations that depend on the disposable income, or buying power, of consumers. A consumer society requires a large middle and upper class with enough leisure time to enjoy the use of many goods and services that are not strictly necessary (although they may be perceived as such). Americans are proud of their access to an abundance of consumer goods and often contrast that abundance with the scarcities common in many other nations, especially those in less developed regions of the world.

There are several drawbacks to a consumer-based economy, however. Among these are the dominance of large corporations and franchise operations, and the unplanned spread of shopping malls. Smaller businesses find it extremely difficult to compete with better financed, more efficient, highly profitable businesses. Indeed, franchise chains like McDonald's and Burger King have come close to wiping out the mom-and-pop restaurant and the roadside stand, traditional symbols of business independence.

The activities of franchise operations and major corporations like General Motors and IBM are accompanied by massive advertising campaigns. "Early to bed, Early to rise, Advertise, Advertise, Advertise" is the advice of McDonald's former advertising director. The communications media are inundated by advertising messages, so much so that advertising slogans have become part of our everyday conversation. ("Getting there is half the fun," an executive may comment ruefully as she arrives late for a meeting. "Don't leave home without it," a father may say to his son as he hands him an umbrella.) It cannot be denied that advertising plays a crucial role in a consumer society (Ritzer, 1993), but some observers are concerned about its effects on other aspects of social life. For example, the growth and development of television and radio stations have been based primarily on their effectiveness as vehicles for advertising, which is their main source of income. To what extent does the dependence of the media on advertisers influence the content of the news and other information they broadcast? These are areas of active social-scientific research (Gans, 1979).

Problems of Debt Entanglement

The effects of a consumer society on other aspects of cultural and social life are a matter of concern to social scientists and others who caution that it leads to excessive materialism, a tendency to judge people by their possessions, and other negative consequences like waste and planned obsolescence. But perhaps the most serious flaw of a consumer society is that it requires the ready availability of credit. Large-scale production of consumer goods depends on a steady flow of profits, which in turn requires that purchases be made constantly, not just whenever the consumer has a windfall or can accumulate enough through savings—hence the widespread use of consumer credit in the United States.

Since the 1950s the United States has been transformed from a cash to a credit society. As credit companies compete fiercely to lend money to credit seekers, they grant more and more loans to individuals from low-income households. Figure 12–6 shows that the total debt held by low-income families is approaching $700 billion— more than the $650 billion of total income earned by the 40 million U.S. households

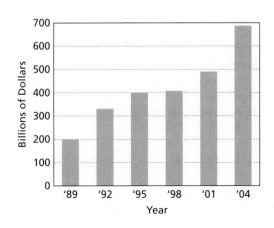

Figure 12–6 Total Debt Held by Low-Income Families*

*Those earning $30,000 or less a year, in 2004 dollars.

Source: Grow & Epstein, 2007.

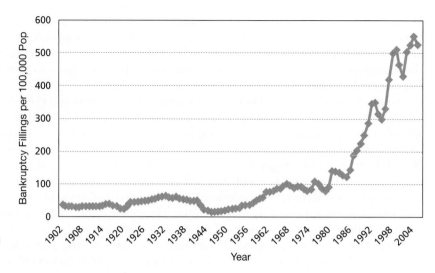

Figure 12–7 Bankruptcy
Filings per 100,000 Population

Source: Zywicki, 2005.

earning $30,000 or less (Grow & Epstein, 2007). Although the enormous increase in consumer credit has been a boon to the U.S. economy, it has given rise to a new and pervasive social problem: debt entanglement and bankruptcy. This problem has received little attention either from social scientists or from policymakers, yet it is one of massive proportions. Each year more than 10 million workers have their wages garnisheed to meet their unpaid debts; many others are sued by their creditors for defaulting. The problem is particularly severe for low-income unskilled workers, who are predominantly black and Hispanic.

Figure 12–7 shows the dramatic increase in individual bankruptcies since 1990. Researchers have found that half of all bankruptcies are due to financial failure on the part of average homeowners, particularly female heads of households. A study of bankruptcies in the United States (Sullivan, Warren, & Westbrook, 2000) disproved a number of common myths. Using records of 1,529 consumer bankruptcy filings in three states, the researchers showed that contrary to the popular notion that "credit card junkies" are abusing the credit system, these people account for less than 2 percent of bankruptcies. Most people who go bankrupt are homeowners who can no longer pay their debts, often because of family dissolution or medical emergencies. About 10 percent are individuals who invested in risky financial ventures. However, these account for about 25 percent of the total debt of bankrupt individuals because often they were quite rich and defaulted on large loans. Rising consumer debt, coupled with economic recession, can spell financial ruin for even more families than one might expect, especially when medical expenses pile up, as described in the On Further Analysis box on page 406.

In 2005, as the nation was reeling from the impact of Hurricanes Katrina, Rita, and Wilma, a new law making it more difficult for families to erase their debts through bankruptcy went into effect. After years of intense pressure from banks and credit card companies, Congress passed legislation that requires a number of steps, including mandatory counseling and agreements to repay some proportion of debts according to a specific schedule, before judges could grant bankruptcy protection. In the House, the Republican leadership allowed no amendments or real debate; in the Senate, one proposed amendment would have protected families declaring bankruptcy for medical reasons, but it failed (Alter, 2005). In the days before the law went into effect, courts and legal offices throughout the nation were swamped with last-minute requests from families and individuals seeking to declare bankruptcy (Dash, 2005).

How do recent changes in bankruptcy laws affect people who have taken on too much credit card or other consumer debt?

Corporate Crime and Business Failure

The spectacular failure of the Enron Corporation, followed by revelations of innumerable illegal and amoral dealings by some of the nation's richest and most powerful business leaders, created a major economic crisis for American corporations in the early years of the new millennium. From 1999 to 2005, senior executives and directors of major American corporations siphoned off for their own personal gain about $5 billion in salary, bonuses, and the proceeds from sales of stocks and stock options, knowing that their companies were about to lose much of their value and that employees and stockholders would suffer serious financial losses. Global Crossing's Gary Winnick received $512.4 million; Enron's Kenneth Lay, $246.7 million; and WorldCom's Scott Sullivan, $49.4 million. Lesser-known corporate leaders did not receive as much public attention, but they also engaged in corporate banditry. Clark McLeod and Richard Lumpkin, the former chairman and vice-chairman of McLeodUSA, a telecommunications company based in Cedar Rapids, Iowa, quietly sold stock worth $99 million and $116 million, respectively, before the rest of the company's stockholders were wiped out. Even veteran observers have been taken aback by recent events. "It became a competitive game to see how much money you could get," Paul Volcker, the former chairman of the Federal Reserve Board, said to a reporter for *The New Yorker* in 2002. One of the nation's most respected financial leaders, Volcker tried and failed to rescue Arthur Andersen, Enron's accounting firm, which ended up going out of business. "Corporate greed exploded beyond anything that could have been imagined in 1990," Volcker went on. "Traditional norms didn't exist. You had this whole culture where the only sign of worth was how much money you made" (quoted in Cassiday, 2002).

Many analysts blame the system of corporate compensation, which made it possible for a few top executives to be awarded huge sums in company stocks or options to buy stocks in the corporation. Having accumulated millions of dollars' worth of stocks and bonds in their companies, some executives could not restrain themselves from cashing in on these securities even when they knew that public disclosure of their companies' earnings records were being falsified and that once this knowledge became public, the value of the companies' stocks would fall to almost nothing, which is what happened in the case of Enron and many others. But other major corporate leaders, such as

When a bank forecloses on a mortgage, the property owners lose their rights to the property and must vacate it or be evicted. More than 400,000 people lost their homes in this way in 2007 because of the mortgage crisis caused by reckless lending practices.

On Further Analysis

MEDICAL BANKRUPTCIES

The continuing crisis of health-care coverage in the United States accounts for about half of all household bankruptcies. This is the finding of a study by Elisabeth Warren and her colleagues at the Harvard School of Public Health. Shortly after this study was published, the new federal law making it more difficult for families to declare bankruptcy went into effect. General Motors announced that it was cutting back on retirees' health benefits, and Wal-Mart, the nation's largest employer, announced that it was finally going to offer its employees a low-cost health insurance policy, for about $12 a month. Unfortunately, the policy would have at least a $1,000 deductible clause, meaning that the individual or family would be required to pay that amount in medical bills before the insurance coverage took over. This was another reminder that the lack of adequate health insurance remains a social problem that has implications and effects throughout U.S. society.

The Harvard bankruptcy study found that average out-of-pocket medical debt for those who filed for bankruptcy is $12,000. Sixty-eight percent of those who filed for bankruptcy had health insurance, but the study found that 50 percent of all bankruptcy filings were partly the result of medical expenses. Before the new bankruptcy legislation went into effect in 2005, every 30 seconds someone filed for bankruptcy in the aftermath of a serious health problem.

Half of all workers in the lowest paid jobs, such as those offered by Wal-Mart, and half of all workers in jobs in the middle pay range either had problems with medical bills in the past twelve months or were paying off accrued debt. One-quarter of workers in higher-paid positions also reported problems with medical bills or were paying off accrued debt. Additional findings from the Harvard study are presented in the accompanying table. They show that the majority of bankruptcies occur in households with two or more people, so many children are included. The majority of those filing for bankruptcy have some college education and are homeowners. The median income of filers is about $25,000. Remember that the median is a number that falls exactly in the middle of a distribution of measures, so although $25,000 is a rather low annual family income, many of those filing had incomes well above this figure. Regular and "medical" bankruptcies are most frequent among people in the bottom and in the middle of the income distribution. Warren and her colleagues point out that "medical bankruptcy is a particularly American phenomenon since almost all the other economically advanced nations have systems of universal health insurance that prevent such indebtedness" (Himmelstein et al., 2005).

Demographic Characteristics of Primary Debtors in Bankruptcy Filings, 2001

	All Bankruptcies	Major Medical Bankruptcies[a]
Median age (years)	41	42
Percent male[b]	45.1%	44.2%
Percent of households filing under chapter 7	62.2%	62.3%
Average number of debtors and dependents per bankruptcy	2.65	2.75
Percent with at least some college education	53.5%	55.8%
Percent current homeowners or lost home in past 5 years	55.3%	56.5%
Median income in year prior to bankruptcy filing	$25,000	$24,500

Note: $p > 0.05$ for all comparisons between debtors with a major medical cause and other debtors.
[a]Bankruptcies meeting at least one of the following criteria: illness or injury listed as specific reason, uncovered medical bills exceeding $1,000, lost at least two weeks of work-related income because of illness/injury, or mortgaged home to pay medical bills.
[b]Data are for primary and secondary debtors combined.
Source: Himmelstein et al., 2005.

Martha Stewart and Jack Welch, were involved in the scandals without taking their entire corporate empires down with them. Welch, the former chief executive officer of General Electric, one of the world's largest and most successful corporations, was found, as a result of public divorce proceedings, to have enjoyed corporate benefits that amounted to many millions of dollars per year and were guaranteed to him long after his retirement. Thus, in this period of corporate scandal, even the most respected and powerful business leaders were tarnished.

Examples of lavish spending and lack of concern for employees contributed to the frenzy of spending and debt entanglement that marked the end of the boom years and the beginning of the new millennium. At this writing, observers of American social policy are waiting to see what specific reforms will come out of these scandals and how many of the most powerful individuals involved will actually be forced to give up some of their questionable but immense wealth.

The threat of terrorism has altered the world economic system in ways that were completely unanticipated before the 2001 attacks. With the end of the cold war in 1989, the United States had begun to reduce the proportion of the federal budget devoted to military spending and divert some public funds to addressing social problems like health care, crime, and education. In the new climate of the war on terrorism, however, the military is once again the largest, perhaps the only, growth area of public spending, and along with homeland security is likely to be so for the foreseeable future.

A second major change in economic affairs is often termed *globalization* and refers to the ever greater economic interdependence of nations. This trend led to the passage of NAFTA in 1993 and the emergence of the European Union in the 1990s. NAFTA is intended to move the nations of North America (Canada, the United States, and Mexico) closer to a condition of free trade—trade that is not hampered by tariffs and import or export quotas. Free trade can stimulate economic growth, but as we saw earlier, it can also have grave consequences for companies and workers in industries that undergo rapid change as a result. For example, Mexican peasants who grow corn fear that they will be wiped out by competition from U.S. agribusinesses, while U.S. autoworkers fear that their jobs will be lost to Mexican workers whose wages average less than half of theirs.

Congress recently voted to grant Most Favored Nation trading status to China, a policy that the administration supported but many prolabor members of Congress opposed. The major labor unions, especially those of the autoworkers and steelworkers, vigorously oppose this and related policies because they believe China violates workers' rights and does not permit workers to join democratic labor unions. They also claim that child labor and forced prison labor are tolerated in China.

A third major area of economic policy in which heated debates are likely in the next few years is the issue of regulation versus deregulation of businesses in the United States. With an administration that is extremely favorable toward business and business leaders, deregulation of business activities in such areas as environmental impacts, labor relations, and taxation is highly likely. Whether there will be any significant reform of corporate compensation to avoid the scandals that shook confidence in American corporate affairs in 2001 and 2002 is still not clear. President Bush finally called for the resignation of the chairman of the Securities and Exchange Commission, a chief monitor of the financial markets and finance-related corporations, but at this writing it does not seem likely that his new appointments to this and other relevant positions will usher in a new climate of corporate responsibility. By firing his treasury secretary in late 2002 and replacing him with a tougher corporate leader, the president signaled his desire for a tougher attitude toward business wrongdoing.

In 2005 Congress passed the Sarbanes-Oxley bill, which imposes strict reporting requirements on corporate leaders and members of corporate boards. The bill makes it mandatory for corporate leaders to sign off on company audits so that if there has been any form of corrupt or illegal accounting, corporate leaders cannot simply blame faulty accounting practices. By 2005, however, business lobbyists were complaining that the law was too harsh and was imposing new and costly requirements on businesses. On the other hand, continuing corporate crime, failures of major financial houses on Wall Street, and the indictment of House majority leader Tom DeLay for illegal campaign fund-raising contributed to a continued climate of support for legislation like the Sarbanes-Oxley bill.

Future Prospects

In the future the U.S. administration, whether Democratic or Republican, is likely to push for more free trade and fewer international tariffs. At the same time, it will be under continuing pressure from those most likely to be hurt by this policy: unions, farmers, and businesses with strong investments in domestic markets (Yang & Satchell, 1999).

Increasing the availability of health insurance and other benefits for workers in part-time and temporary working situations would be an enormous policy change in the United States. This is not currently on the agenda of congressional leaders or leaders of either party. The lack of health insurance for workers at the lower end of the income hierarchy remains a glaring social policy issue and a major problem for those who wish to continue reforming welfare regulations. As he toured the ruined neighborhoods of Louisiana and Mississippi after the hurricanes of 2005, President Bush promised speedy relief and assistance to people who would be rebuilding their homes and communities. But neither the administration nor Congress showed any interest in extending health-care benefits to the hurricane victims, nor were there any efforts to grant them extended unemployment benefits, supplemental food stamps, or other "social safety net" measures.

Congress did take up proposals to cut Medicare and food stamp eligibility, a signal that reform of the welfare laws continues to be the most important aspect of economic and social policy in the United States. These major social policy changes were part of the Republican party's agenda and were included in the Democratic party's platform during the 1996 presidential election campaign. They were motivated by a desire to reduce federal spending and debt as well as to encourage welfare recipients to enter the labor force. As we have seen in earlier chapters, the effects of the reforms are beginning to be felt throughout the nation. There will be enormous changes in the lives of poor Americans and many others because of the elimination of Aid to Families with Dependent Children and changes in home relief, food stamps, and Medicaid. In most major cities people are being obliged to work in order to continue receiving welfare benefits. As long as the economy remains strong, there will be few protests about the policy changes. But in a recession or in the aftermath of natural disasters like Hurricane Katrina, welfare reform in the absence of job-creating strategies is likely to cause many economic and social hardships, which in turn are likely to stimulate attempts to revise the welfare reform law passed in 1996.

GOING BEYOND LEFT AND RIGHT

Economic affairs often divide people in ways related to their own pocketbooks. On the right, there is a tendency to favor social policies that cost as little as possible, rely on the forces of supply and demand, and insist on individual initiative. On the left, there is a tendency to support policies that use the power of government to shape economic outcomes. The desire to create jobs for the poor, for example, is a liberal one, whereas the desire to cut welfare grants and oblige people to work for their incomes is a more conservative policy stance. During recessions, when the poor compete for low-skill job opportunities, it is likely that people on the left and the right will arrive at a compromise over the need for job-creating policies, both in private business and in the public or civic voluntary sectors of the economy (schools, parks, hospitals, etc.). Such a compromise will not settle the ideological dispute over market forces versus government initiatives, but in the practical effort to ease suffering and give more people meaningful work, it is likely that some middle ground will be found. Not to do so is to invite great social unrest.

The passage in 2007 of a new minimum wage bill, with support from both Republicans and Democrats, is an example of how perceptions of fairness cut across ideological lines. In the face of a widening gap between the haves and the have-nots, Congress was unwilling to allow a huge segment of the low-wage labor force to sink into poverty. It raised the minimum wage from $5.15 to $7.15 per hour (to go into full effect in two years), fully realizing that this advance would not lift many poor households out of poverty but would at least indicate that the nation's leaders cared about the plight of those at the bottom of the economic ladder.

Summary

- When people refer to the free-enterprise system, they are talking about an economic system known as *market capitalism*. Markets regulate the worldwide flow of goods and services. Almost all markets are regulated by acts of governments that attempt to protect buyers and ensure that markets remain competitive.

- *Capital* refers to equipment and labor; *capitalists*, or *entrepreneurs*, invest in labor and equipment to produce goods and services in the hope of making a profit. Corporations are a means of reducing the risk to entrepreneurs by limiting their personal liability in the event of a business failure.

- By *economic globalization* social scientists refer to the growing tendency for goods and services to be produced in one nation or region and consumed in another, and for the companies that produce them to engage in business activities in many different regions of the world.

- A controversial aspect of globalization is the growth of multinational corporations—international organizations that operate across national boundaries. Multinational corporations are widely criticized for operating outside the limits of any nation's ability to control their conduct. They have contributed to the emergence of a global factory in which the production process is divided into component operations that can be carried out anywhere in the world.

- For the American worker, the growth of corporate power means a decreasing number of employers and a growing tendency to export capital and jobs overseas. Many U.S. manufacturing facilities have closed, especially in the nation's older cities and towns.

- Work in the United States underwent major changes in the twentieth century. The greatest change was the transition from an agricultural economy to an industrial one, with the result that today white-collar workers are the largest occupational category in the nation.

- With respect to the age and sex composition of the labor force, the most significant trend is the inclusion of married women and the exclusion of older men. Older men are being eliminated from the labor force primarily because of educational and occupational obsolescence.

- Another significant trend is the increasing specialization of labor. The total number of jobs in the American economy has increased steadily, but in the past decade low-wage jobs were created at a much higher rate than high-wage jobs.

- New technologies have had a variety of effects on the workplace. Managers and employees whose jobs are controlled by computers sometimes feel that the computer is their boss. Computer control can also alter the structure of the organization. Some analysts believe these trends will lead to a jobless future for many new entrants into the labor force who lack essential skills.

- Since the end of the economic boom of the 1990s, increasing numbers of workers, both blue-collar workers and managers and professionals, have experienced significant job insecurity and unusually long periods of unemployment.

- Official definitions underestimate the size of the labor force and the volume of unemployment. They exclude unemployed people who did not actively seek work during a particular week, and they fail to reflect the underemployment of part-time workers who would like to work full time. A disproportionate number of the unemployed are young, nonwhite, or both. Among the consequences of unemployment is a sense of isolation, which produces depression.

- The chief sources of job satisfaction, in addition to monetary compensation, are individuality, independence, and a sense of accomplishment. The absence of these factors can lead to dissatisfaction and alienation. Blue-collar workers place more emphasis on external satisfactions than do white-collar workers.

- The problem of occupational health involves industrial accidents and job-related diseases; perhaps the greatest health hazards are found in the chemicals industry.

- The United States is a consumer society; its economy is based on the activities of numerous corporations that depend on the buying power of consumers. A serious flaw of a consumer society is that it requires the ready availability of credit. The enormous increase in consumer credit has created serious debt entanglement.

- The failures of major corporations and misdeeds by business leaders have created a major economic crisis for American corporations. Many analysts blame the system of corporate compensation that provides temptations for executives to benefit themselves at the expense of employees and stockholders.

- Economic policies must respond to several major changes in the United States and in the rest of the world, the most significant of which is the globalization of economic activity. These changes have led to reductions in military spending and the passage of NAFTA. The welfare reform act of 1996 is having a major impact on debates over economic policy and may lead to renewed efforts to create jobs for workers with low skill levels. In coming years a major area of debate will center on whether business activities should be subject to stricter government regulation.

Key Terms

capitalism, p. 386
markets, p. 386
capital, p. 386
entrepreneur, p. 386

limited liability, p. 386
economic globalization, p. 387
multinational corporations, p. 387

outsourcing, p. 389
flexitime, p. 400
alienation, p. 400

Social Problems Online

For those who wish to investigate the state of the U.S. economy, the federal government provides several indispensable resources. The Bureau of Labor Statistics's Web site (**www.bls.gov**) displays several boxes that provide a window on the world of work. Click on Economy at a Glance to view statistics on current employment trends. More sophisticated data are available, as are links to other statistical sites. Research papers, many in downloadable form, are accessible through Publications and Research Papers.

The Department of Labor's Web page (**www.dol.gov**) supplies other labor-related data, including reports on occupational injury and illness rates. The Economics and Statistics Administration, at **https://www.esa.doc.gov**, is the source of much of the statistical, economic, and demographic information collected by the federal government.

Information on how the nation's banking system works is available from the Federal Reserve's homepage at **www.federalreserve.gov**. The page provides an informative and easy-to-understand guide to the Federal Reserve, along with congressional testimony, press releases, statistics, research papers, and the all-important minutes of the Federal Open Market Committee. International financial data are featured on the Web pages of the International Monetary Fund (**www.imf.org/**) and the World Bank (**www.worldbank.org/**). The Organization for Economic Cooperation and Development (OECD) at **www.oecd.org/** has extensive data on social indicators such as health and education. It also provides downloadable reports on various aspects of economic development.

Virtually the entire gamut of subjects covered by the academic discipline of economics is just a click away at the WWW Virtual Library on Economics (**www.helsinki.fi/WebEc/EconVLib.html**). Besides sections on the nuts and bolts of the discipline, such as micro- and macroeconomics, there are online courses and a Reference Shelf. One of the best resources for demystifying the "dismal science" can be found at the homepage of the Left Business Observer (**www.leftbusinessobserver. com**). There, current debates and news stories are explained in plain and often witty prose. The site also offers numerous links to resources from the business, financial, academic, and political worlds. Economic policy debates take center stage at the Web pages of the Electronic Policy Network (**www.movingideas.org**). They emphasize how government programs affect low- and middle-income people and offer reports on such topics as the federal budget, the minimum wage, and welfare reform. The American Enterprise Institute (**http://www.aei.org/**) advocates restricting government involvement in business affairs.

Research Navigator

Follow the instructions on pages 26–27 of this text to access the features of Research Navigator. Once at the Web site, enter your Login Name and Password. Then, to use the Content Select database, use keywords such as "free-enterprise system," "multinational corporations," and "sweatshop labor," and the search engine will supply relevant and recent scholarly and popular press publications. Use the *New York Times* search-by-subject archive to find recent news articles related to problems of education, and the Link Library to find relevant Web sites organized by the key terms associated with this chapter.

Using the terms "consumer debt," "bankruptcy," and "employment insecurity," use Research Navigator to find articles on these topics. Choose the one that appeals to you most and write a one-paragraph summary of its contents. What is the importance of the article for the future of workers in the United States?

13

URBAN
Problems

Chapter Outline

Dominant Trends

- The movement of the world's people from rural to urban areas is accelerating. In the first decade of this century, the urban population has exceeded that of its rural areas, with the most rapid growth occurring in cities with fewer than 500,000 people, mainly in third-world nations.

- Major cities in the developing world are growing more rapidly than the huge cities of the West. Tokyo remains the largest city in the world, but the New York metropolitan region, the largest in the United States, has slipped to eleventh place. By 2015, the five largest cities will be Tokyo, with 36.2 million residents, Mumbai with 22.6 million, Delhi with 20.9 million, Mexico City with 20.6 million, and São Paulo with 20 million.

- Throughout American history, no population group has experienced such persistent residential segregation in urban areas as African Americans, and recent changes in the U.S. economy and the legal system offer little hope this trend will change in the near future.

- The fastest growing urban communities in the United States will continue to be found on the edges of older cities and their rapidly aging suburbs.

- As housing becomes ever more expensive and more Americans experience "shelter poverty," homelessness will continue to plague cities and towns. On any given day, at least 800,000 people are homeless in the United States, including about 200,000 children in homeless families.

Many of the social problems we have discussed so far—poverty, mental illness, AIDS, drug abuse, violence, and others—are especially serious in the nation's cities, not because city people are less moral than rural people, but because cities, especially large cities, act as magnets for those who deviate from the norm and seek the company of others like themselves. Often this deviance is what makes cities so fascinating and creative, and it helps explain the attraction of city life for musicians, actors, artists, and people who wish to escape from what they see as the stultifying sameness of rural areas or suburban communities. But the attraction of the city for people who are different and who seek the greater tolerance and anonymity of urban life also increases the concentration of people who are ill and need help. The legacy of racism and racial and class segregation also leaves the cities with much higher concentrations of poor people than would be expected if these social problems were evenly distributed through the population.

In 2005, in the aftermath of Hurricane Katrina, President Bush referred to the convergence between urban inequalities and racial discrimination in a speech at the National Cathedral in Washington, D.C. "Americans of every race and religion were touched by this storm," he said, "yet the greatest hardship fell upon citizens already facing lives of struggle—the elderly, the vulnerable, and the poor. And this poverty has roots in generations of discrimination and segregation that closed many doors of opportunity." Yet New Orleans is hardly alone in having a large proportion of its minority residents living in dire poverty. As many cities become de facto poorhouses, they require additional help from states and from the federal government. To better appreciate why this is so and why the policies that have been suggested to address this situation are controversial, it is worthwhile first to step back and consider what we understand by cities and by such terms as **rural** and **urban.**

The U.S. Bureau of the Census defines the **urban population** as all persons living in places with 2,500 or more inhabitants that are legally incorporated as cities, villages, boroughs, and towns (*Statistical Abstract*, 2007). An **urbanized area,** in the official census definition, "comprises one or more places [e.g., incorporated cities or towns] and the adjacent densely settled surrounding territory that together have a minimum population of 50,000 persons" (p. 4). Metropolitan regions usually include a number of urbanized areas as well as less densely settled areas on their fringes. Rural areas are those that are not classified as urban.

Although it is not difficult to define the words *urban* and *rural* in abstract terms, such definitions are not readily applicable to the real world. Today there is no longer a clear distinction between rural and urban life. **Urbanism**—a way of life that depends on industry, mass communication, a mobile population, and mass consumer markets—has penetrated even to rural places. For example, whereas the farm was once considered the epitome of rural life, today an increasing proportion of farms are large-scale agribusinesses and the small farm is an endangered species. Farming communities are linked to major metropolitan regions by interstate highways, and the residents watch the same TV shows as people in the densely settled inner cities. In other words, it is not a question of whether a place is rural or urban, but of the extent to which urbanism has influenced it.

AN URBANIZING WORLD

The urban revolution is a worldwide phenomenon, as can be seen in the changing ranking of cities. In 1950 the New York metropolitan area was the largest in the world. It was the third largest in 1995, although still the largest in the United States. But according to U.N. population projections, it will be in about eleventh place by 2015, outstripped by Tokyo, Mumbai, Lagos, Shanghai, Jakarta, São Paulo, Karachi, Beijing, Dhaka, and Mexico City (UN-Habitat, 2005).

In the developing world, people are leaving rural villages to seek their futures in cities. In sociological terms, this is a dominant trend of the modern era. In the more affluent regions of the world, as already noted, the majority of the population are city dwellers. But in much of Latin America, Asia, and Africa, the wrenching shift from country to city life is still occurring. Cities are growing at astounding rates, their populations doubling in a generation or less. Many Latin American cities are quite old, often older than the oldest U.S. cities, but the urbanization of rural populations is continuing. In Africa, many cities are only beginning to experience explosive growth. The rural-to-urban transition in Africa will be a major trend of the twenty-first century (Dugger, 2007).

Figure 13–1 highlights the shift toward a predominantly urban world: By 2025 the vast majority of people will live in cities. The rural–urban transformation was largely completed in Europe and North America before 1975 but is now occurring rapidly in Latin America. The population projections shown in Figure 13–1 suggest that a similar transformation will occur in Asia and Africa in the next two decades. Not shown in the figure is the fact that China's urban population jumped from 19 percent to 28 percent between 1960 and 1992 and has been growing at 4.8 percent each year since that time. This means that the urban population of China today is probably almost half the entire Chinese population of 1.2 billion. Sub-Saharan Africa is also experiencing explosive urban growth. Its urban population is increasing by 4.5 percent per year, which means that soon Africa, too, will be a continent dominated by cities rather than by agricultural and pastoral populations (Palen, 2005).

This rapid urban growth presents enormous problems for developing nations, which are still struggling to address the persistent poverty of their rural villages. Urban populations are extremely dependent on investments in transportation, education, and health-care institutions, as well as in the basic infrastructure of vital services (water, sewage, electricity, communications, and the like). When people are moving to cities in search of jobs and other types of economic opportunity (in education or expanding markets, for example), the resulting growth in person-power helps alleviate some social problems. In many of the developing nations, however, urban newcomers have great difficulty in finding work and making ends meet. The city beckons with the opportunity for escape from rural poverty, but once in the city many find that they lack the skills required to survive in the new and entirely strange urban social world (United Nations Population Fund, 2007).

Thus, although many of the consequences of this urban transformation are positive, in that people who can no longer earn a living on the land are finding new

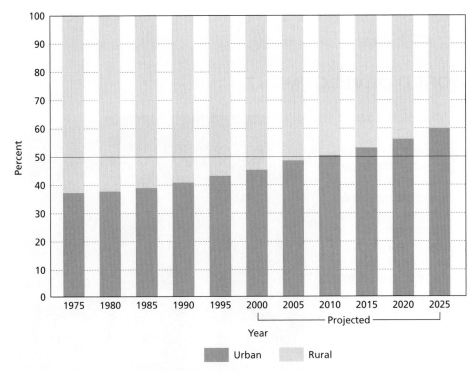

The figures below show urban population growth in five major regions, projected to 2025.

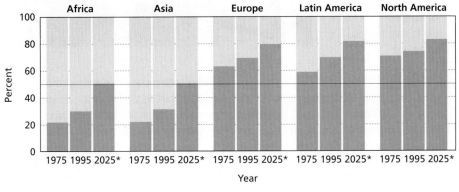

*Projections.

Figure 13–1 Percentage of World's Population Living in Urban Areas

Source: "Percentage of World's Population Living in Urban Areas," from the article *Hope and Pragmatism for U.N. Cities Conference.* Copyright © 1996 by The New York Times. Reprinted by permission of The New York Times Graphics.

opportunities for education and work in the cities, many other consequences are negative. Crowding, poverty, lack of adequate housing, and the threat of gangs and violence are only some of the social problems new urban migrants experience in very rapidly growing cities. And the cities themselves are often overwhelmed by the sheer mass of the new arrivals. Urban infrastructures—water, sewage, transportation, lighting, and medical-care facilities, to name a few—are often inadequate to meet the new demands. India, for example, is the world's second most populous country and has more than 3,000 cities and towns, but only eight of them have sewage treatment plants. Nor is this problem unique to India. The World Resources Institute estimates that 90 percent of the raw sewage from urban areas in developing nations is seeping into streams and oceans. The World Bank estimates that by 2010, 1.4 billion people will not have safe drinking water or sanitation (cited in United Nations Population Fund, 2007).

In a world where social, economic, and environmental interconnections are ever more apparent, the conditions of life in metropolitan regions are an important issue for the developing and more affluent nations alike. In the more affluent industrial nations, older cities are also undergoing rapid change as jobs are lost to lower-wage

Social Problems: A Global View

CITIES AND WORLD DEVELOPMENT

The earth's human population is rapidly becoming urban. By 2015 almost two-thirds of the world's people will live in densely settled urban places rather than in agricultural villages (Abrahamson, 2004). If you take a moment to study the accompanying map, you should be able to locate the cities listed in the chart below it. Notice how many of the major cities of Asia, Africa, and Latin America are experiencing explosive growth now and will do so well into the future.

Foremost among the beneficial effects for most migrants to cities are increased freedom and opportunity, but with these advantages come the problems of poverty, violence, and insecurity. Let us consider these positive aspects of urbanization along with their attendant social problems, focusing on the condition of women and children in developing regions of the world.

Freedom and Opportunity

The majority of migrants to cities seek release from the restrictions and poverty of rural villages and small towns. Women especially find release from the gender norms that often prevent them from developing their full potential. In the cities they have a better chance to control their reproductive lives and therefore to have fewer children. With smaller families, they can invest more in their own personal growth and, where resources are limited, do a better job of ensuring that their children gain the education they will need if they are to succeed in the contemporary urban world. As urbanization proceeds, fertility rates fall. Women in the less developed regions of the world, where less than half of all families live in cities, now average 3.0 children per household. In 2050, population estimates predict that almost 60 percent of families will live in cities and the average number of

children will have fallen to 2.1 (Cohen, 2000).

As rates of urbanization increase, so does the proportion of elderly people. Because there are somewhat fewer children and because health care in cities is often far better than in villages, people in cities tend to live longer. But do these new elderly populations actually have better lives than the elderly in more rural settings? Much depends on the success of particular societies, and their cities, in addressing the needs of the elderly, and to date the record is quite mixed.

Poverty, Violence, Insecurity

Many cities in the developing regions of the world, such as Cairo, Egypt; Lagos, Nigeria; and Mumbai, India, are growing at extremely rapid rates, as can be seen in the accompanying chart. They are expected to experience even faster rates of growth over the next decades, until they are as large or even far larger than the New York metropolitan region and other major metropolitan regions in the developed nations. Cities like Mumbai and Mexico City are producing educated, middle-class families at far higher rates than are rural villages and small towns (Palen, 2005), but along with this rapid growth come severe social problems. People in these cities often live in makeshift shelters on the streets or in huge

squatter settlements. Crime and violence in the squalid migrant neighborhoods may severely limit the actual freedom and opportunity experienced by newcomers, especially women and children. The dream of escape to the city can become a nightmare of dire poverty and loneliness if women and children are afraid to venture outside or if grinding poverty forces them to scavenge and beg. And since so many rapidly growing cities are also located along earthquake faults or in low-lying oceanfront areas, the effects of natural disasters, as seen in the effects of earthquakes in Pakistan in 2005 or the East Asian tsunami in 2004, can wipe out families before they have had a chance to gain a decent foothold in the new urban environment.

How will cities in the United States and other economically advanced nations compare in size and rates of growth to cities in Asia and Africa in coming decades?

areas and new populations with new needs demand attention, while budgets for services and infrastructure investment are cut. In addition, in the United States, as in other nations where cities are no longer the centers of industrial production, vast changes are occurring in the nature of the social problems these cities must face as they attempt to cope with rapid social change. Some of the most important changes occurring throughout the world are discussed in the Social Problems: A Global View box above.

Size of Urban Population
○ 5 million and over since 1950
● 5 million and over since 2000
◉ 5 million and over in 2015 (projected)

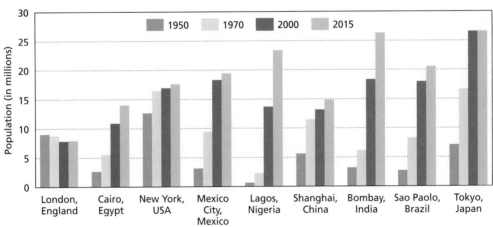

Source: UN-Habitat, 2005.

THE AMERICAN CITY

Until the nineteenth century the United States was an agrarian country; the few existing cities were scarcely more than market towns. Increasingly efficient transportation and communication and the effects of industrialization caused the bulk of urban growth. Just as technological innovations, such as the use of cast iron in building construction and the invention of the elevator, made it possible for a city to expand vertically, more efficient modes of transportation, such as horse-drawn buses and rail-roads, made it possible for cities to expand horizontally as well. Railway lines and tele-graph wires crossed the continent, closely tying cities to the nation's agricultural heartland. In turn, these improved methods of communication promoted westward expansion and the development of new cities. Many towns were built around railroad lines. Urban growth provided a larger market for agricultural products, which motivat-ed farmers to invent new ways of growing and harvesting crops in order to increase efficiency and minimize expense. The resultant technological advances contributed to the development of the city.

As cities grew, however, the existence of large populations within limited amounts of space began to present special problems. Living in a concentrated community focuses attention on matters of mutual concern and need, matters that even the indi-vidualistic American was unable to ignore. Lighting, fire protection, the care of streets, crime prevention, sewage disposal, water, community health, and marketing facilities all became part of the community consciousness and hence the concerns of municipal governments.

Urban Growth and Social Problems

It was not until the twentieth century that adequate water supply and waste disposal systems were finally developed. Before then, cities were notorious for death rates that were substantially higher than those in rural areas, with larger cities suffering higher rates than smaller ones. Writing in 1899, Arnold Weber (1968) attributed this "exces-sive urban mortality . . . to lack of pure air, water, and sunlight, together with unclean-ly habits of life induced thereby." He went on to say, however, that there was "no inherent external reason why men should die faster in larger communities than in small hamlets, provided they are not too ignorant, too stupid, or too individualistic to cooperate in the securing of common benefits" (p. 348). In fact, innovations in medi-cine and sanitation did improve the conditions of early urban life.

Antiurban Bias

Perhaps as a result of the congestion and corruption just described, antiurban senti-ment became a tradition in American culture. Public sentiment against cities has gen-erally echoed the antiurban bias of Thomas Jefferson, who compared "the mobs of great cities" to sores on the human body (Kennedy, 2000).

American literature, particularly in the nineteenth century, extolled the virtues of the self-sufficient farmer in an agricultural paradise, evoking memories of simpler, happier, more innocent times. The city has often been perceived as contrary to the "natural" relationship between the person and the environment. Although the image of a sacred city—Jerusalem or Rome—occasionally appears, it is the image of the sin-ful city—Sodom and Gomorrah or "Gay Paree"—that predominates. Heresy and vice are associated with the city; virtue and justice live in the country. This is true in litera-ture throughout the world, and it remains a common theme in North America.

In recent years the spread of AIDS and highly addictive drugs like crack have rein-forced the negative image of the nation's largest cities, especially New York, Los Angeles, and Miami. It is very likely that the negative view of large central-city areas reflects the continuing tradition of antiurban thought, which is only reinforced by current prob-lems that are concentrated in the cities. To make matters worse, the city is often viewed as a temporary place of settlement, a central place of concentration for immigrants and rural newcomers where one attempts to gain a foothold in society before moving to the suburbs, where there is a bit of greenery and one can visit the city but is not obliged to live there.

Respondents to polls about quality of life and preferred place of residence consis-tently voice the opinion that life in central cities is less attractive for most people than life in suburbs and small cities (NORC, 2005). One consequence of these negative opinions about central-city life is the continual growth of suburbs and the gradual loss of population in the nation's older cities. As a result, according to Eli Ginzberg (1993), one of the nation's foremost analysts of urban social policy, "The core of urban life has shifted dramatically from the city center to the metropolitan area, with a growing proportion of the population living and working in the suburbs and in the outlying metropolitan areas" (p. 36). But Ginzberg notes that this change can be overstated because almost one-third of the nation's citizens continue to reside in communities and neighborhoods in the inner city.

The Composition of Urban Populations

The majority of Americans live in large metropolitan areas. There they encounter a very different environment from that provided by small towns or rural communities. Urban life gives rise to subcultures, social institutions, and personality traits that are not found in rural settings (Fischer, 1984); sociologists who study urbanism seek to explain these phenomena. In our discussion of urbanism, we stress the special consequences of life in cities both for individuals and for their communities.

Minority Migration. Today's cities are populated largely by the descendants of rural Americans and immigrants from other countries who came in search of better jobs, higher wages, improved schooling for their children, cultural and political freedom, and a generally higher level of living. The migration to the cities began in colonial times but accelerated in the 1920s, when the drop in foreign immigration forced America's cities to look to the rural heartland for cheap labor. Attracted by the prospect of ready employment in the industrial cities of the Northeast, Midwest, and South, large numbers of rural blacks moved to urban areas.

This migration considerably altered settlement conditions in the larger urban communities. Unlike the foreign migrants, who had settled in mixed urban enclaves and begun to intermarry and disperse, the blacks who moved to northern cities settled in neighborhoods that quickly became, and remained, all black. Whereas earlier foreign immigrants gradually increased their incomes and moved out of the immigrant neighborhoods, the black settlements were more permanent, creating cities within cities. The tendency of the wealthy to move to the suburbs had already been established among the cities' white populations, and it was increased by the urban segregation of blacks. Although today blacks are moving into suburban communities in record numbers, they remain disproportionately represented in the central cities. As a result, their upward mobility has been severely limited, and the precedent has been set for the increased economic and cultural segregation found in the cities. (See Chapter 7.)

Many U.S. cities have seen a continual influx of foreign immigrants over the past four decades. Miami, Los Angeles, New York, and Houston now have large concentrations of immigrants, many of whom have come from Latin America, the Caribbean, and Asia. At present about 800,000 legal immigrants from these regions are admitted to the United States each year, and an uncounted number of illegal entrants arrive as well. In cities with older segregated ghettos adjacent to newer immigrant neighborhoods, there are increasingly frequent episodes of conflict between the newcomers and established residents. On the other hand, there are also many instances of intergroup cooperation and renewed economic growth in these rapidly changing urban communities (Kotkin, 2005). We will return to this subject in Chapter 14.

What aspects of urban social environments make city life so attractive to migrants from less urbanized regions?

Voluntary and Involuntary Segregation. Residential segregation may take either of two forms: (1) voluntary segregation, in which people choose to live with others similar to themselves (e.g., the ethnic, artistic, or homosexual neighborhoods of large cities), and (2) involuntary segregation, which occurs when various segments of the population (e.g., blacks, Jews, or the aged) are forced by social or economic circumstances to live in specific areas of the city. Although at first most immigrant groups chose to live together in urban enclaves, the situation of urban blacks and other minorities today is largely one of involuntary segregation.

Throughout American history no population group has experienced such persistent residential segregation in urban areas as African Americans (Massey & Denton, 1993). Although white immigrant groups such as the Irish, Italians, and Poles were segregated in earlier periods, only African Americans have experienced high rates of segregation throughout the nation's history.

For most city dwellers, residential segregation means a limited choice of lifestyles. This is especially true for minority groups and poor whites—particularly the elderly—and is caused as much by a negative self-image as by racial and economic segregation. It is difficult for the poor, the aged, and others to escape from undesirable or dangerous urban areas. As a consequence, these people cannot be described as entirely voluntary residents of a particular neighborhood. As neighborhoods decline, all people whose daily activities take them into these areas face the hardships brought about by loss of capital and lack of support facilities and community services.

Douglas Massey, the foremost U.S. expert on urban racial segregation, argues that residential segregation of African Americans contributes to unemployment, educational inequality, high rates of criminal victimization, and drug addiction. He advocates much stronger enforcement of the antidiscrimination clauses of the Fair Housing Act as a way to attack persistent segregation (Massey & Anderson, 2001). We return to this point in the Social Policy section of the chapter.

As noted in Chapter 7, residential segregation is measured by using census data that list the racial and ethnic composition of small areas (blocks or groups of blocks known as census tracts) within metropolitan regions. Table 13–1 presents data on the racial and ethnic composition of neighborhoods in metropolitan areas, their inner-city regions, and their suburbs. We see, for example, that in U.S. metropolitan areas in 2000, African Americans lived in neighborhoods in which 33 percent of the residents were white and 51.4 percent were black. These figures represent an improvement since 1980, when almost 62 percent of an average African American's neighbors were black and 30 percent were white. The table shows that central-city neighborhoods are more racially segregated than their larger metropolitan regions and that suburban areas are distinctly less segregated—although there, too, separation of racial and ethnic groups remains widespread. Hispanics are slightly less segregated than African Americans, but for both groups, while there has been slow improvement since 1980, segregation persists throughout metropolitan regions. Asians represent an exception to the general pattern of racial segregation in American cities. With more buying power than other racial minorities, many Asian American families can afford to purchase homes in more affluent white neighborhoods. For each population group, however, there is a gradual trend toward increased diversity in inner-city and suburban neighborhoods, an encouraging sign for the future of racial integration in other American institutions, such as public schools (Logan, 2001).

Muslim Newcomers in U.S. Cities. People of Muslim background from North Africa, the Middle East, Iran, and South Asia (Pakistan in particular) constitute a relatively small minority in the United States, with about 2.8 million people reported in the 2000 Census (see Table 13–2), but their numbers increased by 8 percent between 1990 and 2000. Like most other immigrant groups arriving in the United States, people of Muslim origins tend to settle in regions where they can find others who speak their languages and share their religion. In consequence, Muslims in the United States tend to be most numerous in a few metropolitan regions: Los Angeles–Long Beach, New York–New Jersey, Detroit, and Chicago. These metropolitan regions are home to over 80 percent of the nation's Muslims (Logan and Deane, 2003). Although they add important new cultural and linguistic resources to these urban regions, the ongoing war on terror, which has led to increased scrutiny of Muslim newcomers, also adds to the insecurity that many Muslim immigrant families have experienced since 9/11 (Bryan, 2005).

TABLE 13–1	Segregation and Isolation Weighted Averages, 1980–2000

	Total Metro Area			Central Cities			Suburbs		
	1980	1990	2000	1980	1990	2000	1980	1990	2000
Whites									
Dissimilarity with blacks	69.9	64.4	59.9	66.9	59.8	53.7	61.1	56.6	52.5
Dissimilarity with Hispanics	41.9	41.7	45.1	42.2	40.5	43.3	33.2	34.4	37.5
Dissimilarity with Asians	38.4	39.9	38.9	36.2	36.8	33.8	37.2	38.1	37.6
The average white lives in a neighborhood with									
a % white of	88.4	85.3	80.2	83.6	78.9	71.6	91.2	88.4	83.8
a % black of	4.9	5.7	6.7	7.2	8.6	10.3	3.5	4.3	5.3
a % Hispanic of	4.6	5.9	7.9	6.4	8.3	11.3	3.6	4.7	6.5
a % Asian of	1.5	2.7	3.9	1.9	3.7	5.2	1.2	2.3	3.4
Blacks									
Dissimilarity with whites	73.8	68.8	65.0	74.9	69.8	64.9	63.1	58.7	56.6
Dissimilarity with Hispanics	61.4	58.8	52.8	60.0	59.0	53.3	55.5	52.4	47.7
Dissimilarity with Asians	73.1	67.5	61.8	72.1	67.9	62.8	66.0	60.6	55.3
The average black lives in a neighborhood with									
a % white of	30.4	33.1	33.0	22.6	24.4	24.3	51.2	50.9	46.6
a % black of	61.8	55.9	51.4	69.3	64.4	60.2	41.6	38.6	37.7
a % Hispanic of	6.1	8.4	11.4	6.4	8.7	11.6	5.3	7.7	11.1
a % Asian of	1.1	2.2	3.3	1.0	2.1	3.0	1.2	2.4	3.7
Hispanics									
Dissimilarity with whites	50.7	50.6	51.5	53.5	53.0	52.7	42.7	44.0	46.5
Dissimilarity with blacks	60.6	54.0	49.2	59.0	52.5	47.7	58.9	51.9	48.0
Dissimilarity with Asians	50.3	48.4	49.5	51.1	48.2	49.5	46.0	45.1	46.8
The average Hispanic lives in a neighborhood with									
a % white of	47.3	41.8	36.5	40.3	35.0	30.0	57.5	50.2	43.3
a % black of	10.2	10.2	10.8	13.0	12.9	13.1	5.9	6.9	8.4
a % Hispanic of	38.4	42.4	45.5	42.4	46.2	49.3	32.6	37.6	41.4
a % Asian of	3.0	5.2	5.9	3.1	5.5	6.1	2.9	4.9	5.7
Asians									
Dissimilarity with whites	41.2	42.0	42.1	40.7	41.7	39.9	37.5	38.6	40.5
Dissimilarity with blacks	65.3	58.2	54.4	64.9	57.3	54.0	59.6	54.7	51.0
Dissimilarity with Hispanics	46.1	45.1	47.2	46.4	44.0	46.3	41.7	42.6	45.0
The average Asian lives in a neighborhood with									
a % white of	67.5	60.4	54.0	59.8	52.5	46.2	76.7	68.5	60.6
a % black of	8.2	8.5	9.2	10.6	10.8	11.4	5.4	6.1	7.4
a % Hispanic of	13.1	16.3	17.4	15.2	19.0	20.3	10.6	13.5	14.9
a % Asian of	10.0	14.7	17.9	13.0	17.6	20.6	6.5	11.8	15.9

Source: John R. Logan, 2001. "Ethnic Diversity Grows, Neighborhood Integration Lags Behind." Lewis Mumford Center, December 18. Accessed at http://www.s2.brown.edu/cen2000/reports.html

TABLE 13–2	Composition and Growth of Muslim-Origin Populations of the United States, 1990–2000

	Population		Percent of Muslim-Origin Population		Percent of Total Population		Growth
	1990	2000	1990	2000	1990	2000	1990–2000
North African	200,498	420,711	12.9%	14.7%	0.08%	0.15%	109.8%
Middle Eastern	799,924	1,410,363	51.6	49.2	0.32	0.50	76.3
Iranian	270,236	384,731	17.4	13.4	0.11	0.14	42.4
South Asian	280,043	652,328	18.1	22.7	0.11	0.23	132.9
Muslim-origin total	1,550,671	2,868,133	100.0	100.0	0.62	1.02	85.0
Non-Hispanic white	188,013,404	194,433,424			75.6	69.1	3.4
Non-Hispanic black	29,188,456	35,203,538			11.7	12.5	20.6
Hispanic	21,836,851	35,241,468			8.8	12.5	61.4
Asian	6,977,447	10,050,579			2.8	3.6	44.0
Total U.S.	248,709,873	281,421,906			100.0	100.0	13.2

Source: Logan & Deane, 2003.

THEORIES OF URBANISM

As mentioned earlier, the propensity for large numbers of people to live in cities and for urban ways of life to become dominant throughout a society is known as *urbanism*. In rapidly changing regions of the world, such as large portions of Africa and Latin America, cities are growing at even greater rates than they are in North America and Europe. Does life in cities and the spread of urban areas over the globe account for other social problems, such as crime, the breakup of families, and intergroup conflict? Do urban people differ in some fundamental way from those who live in rural areas? Such questions have been the subject of much research and theory and are summarized in the three theories of urbanism to which we now turn.

Wirth's Theory

Several theories of urbanism have been proposed. The oldest and most influential is that of Louis Wirth, whose basic argument is that cities increase the incidence of both social and personality disorders. He described the city as "a relatively large, dense, and permanent settlement of socially heterogeneous individuals" (quoted in Fischer, 1984, p. 29). Borrowing extensively from the teachings of another sociologist, Georg Simmel, Wirth argued that the urban environment literally assaults the city dweller with multiple and intense stimuli. The pressures of this overabundance of stimulation force urban dwellers to adapt in order to maintain their mental equilibrium. Wirth contended that the resultant adaptation has negative effects. The mechanisms that permit the city dweller to withstand the shock of multiple stimuli also cause him or her to become insulated from other people. As a result, the typical city dweller "becomes aloof, brusque, impersonal in his dealings with others, and emotionally buffered in his human relationships" (p. 31). When such withdrawal fails to counter the effects of overstimulation, people experience "psychic overload," which produces irritation and anxiety.

The effects of psychic overload are illustrated by the following remarks of a frustrated urban resident: "You must understand this is a cramped place. Sometimes it feels like, well, like everything has been put through a trash compactor. Density like this annuls certain clauses in the social contract; it begets those dull, middle-distance stares, a defense mechanism. Some of us don't even acknowledge our next-door neighbors" (Jaynes, 1988, p. 29). Wirth asserted that this interpersonal estrangement loosens the bonds that unite people. In some cases, these bonds are completely severed, and the result is antisocial and alienated behavior. When people are left without emotional support or societal restraint, they begin to act out their fantasies. According to Wirth, this explains the intense creativity and technological advancement, as well as the psychopathic and criminal behavior, that are prevalent in cities. Each extreme is a result of looser social restraints and interpersonal relationships (Abbott, 2000).

Another by-product of city life is the economic process of competition and specialization, which results in community differentiation. Usually this differentiation is most visible in the division of labor, although it exists in other forms as well—for example, in separate districts for businesses, residences, and entertainment. In urban environments people often assume many different roles during an average day, roles that involve social interaction with coworkers, neighbors, close friends, and family. According to Wirth, the very multiplicity of people and places that compete for an urban dweller's time and attention weakens social bonds. As people continue to enter into primary relationships outside the family, the family becomes less important. Because many of these relationships are scattered across the city, neighbors also play a less significant role. In Wirth's opinion, such loosening of social ties produces an alienated condition, or anomie, a weakening of the norms that govern acceptable social behavior (Palen, 2005).

Once the personal approach to preserving societal norms has been weakened, other attempts to control social behavior must be made. Most often, these take the form of complaints to impersonal government authorities. Wirth believed such impersonal control can never fully replace the power and moral strength of small primary groups. Therefore, he considered cities—with their inclination toward individualism, estrangement, stress, and especially social disorganization—as societies in which social relationships are weak. Such weakness may indeed provide more freedom for individuals, but it also leads to social disruption and personality disorders.

Compositionalism

Wirth's theory is not accepted by all urban sociologists. Herbert Gans, among others, has challenged Wirth's ideas about the effects of urbanism on personal behavior. *The Urban Villagers*, Gans's (1984) classic study, is a closeup view of life in the Italian neighborhoods of the West End of Boston shortly before they were torn down in the name of "urban renewal." Gans shows that many families were deeply committed to a life spent largely within the neighborhood. That is, they were immersed in the life of the Italian American community and were not at all like the disorganized slum dwellers of Wirthian theory. The forms of deviance found in the neighborhood—gang activity and some organized crime—did not result from social disorganization. Nor were these neighborhoods dominated by impersonal institutions such as housing authorities, as Wirthian theory would predict.

Gans (1984) used these findings and those from similar community studies in immigrant neighborhoods to conclude that personal behavior is shaped by the social life of specific neighborhoods and communities, not by the larger social forces described by Wirth under the heading of urbanism. Fischer (1984) called this a *compositional theory* of urbanism. The difference between the two theories rests on opposing views of how the city affects the existence of small groups. Compositionalists see the city as a mosaic of social worlds—intimate social circles with their roots in kinship, ethnicity, neighborhoods, occupations, and lifestyles. Whereas Wirth believed that the pressures of the city disrupt these worlds, drawing people away from close associations with family and neighbors, compositionalists believe that these worlds persist undiminished in an urban setting. Gans contends, in fact, that the closeness of these social worlds envelops individuals and protects them from the pressures of city life. Compositionalists cite economic position, cultural characteristics, and marital and family status as the determinants of personal behavior. The strength of these attributes, rather than the size or density of the community at large, molds a person's social and psychological experience.

Subcultural Theory

Fischer's (1976, 1995) own theory of urbanism agrees with the Wirthian theory in acknowledging that cities produce major social-psychological effects. Fischer, however, believes that these effects occur not because existing social groups break down but because cities foster new ones. Known as the *subcultural theory,* Fischer's argument suggests that the most socially significant consequence of an urban community is the promotion of diverse subcultures—culturally distinct groups such as college students, Chinese Americans, artists, and homosexuals. In New York's Greenwich Village and San Francisco's Castro district, for example, communities of gay men and women create a local culture of tolerance for homosexuality. In addition, they create institutions of homosexual thought and expression—newspapers, theater, cabarets—in which the norms of the straight world are suspended to a degree and other sexual norms are encouraged or discussed. People who are homosexual feel more free to express themselves in such communities and to form close relationships with one another.

In contrast to Wirth, who held that no significant primary social relationships can be achieved in an urban environment, Fischer (1984, 1995) believes that people in cities live in meaningful social worlds. More important, subculturists contend that large communities attract immigrants precisely because of this distinctively urban phenomenon. In Fischer's view, urbanism intensifies subcultures, partly through critical mass: A large city is more likely than a small community to attract a sizable proportion of a given subculture. This process operates for artists, academics, bohemians, corporate executives, criminals, and computer programmers, as well as for ethnic or racial minority groups. Subcultural intensification also occurs through multigroup contact. In a densely populated environment, subcultures are constantly bumping into one another. Sometimes these groups coexist; in other instances tensions mount. When one subculture finds another annoying, threatening, or both, a common reaction is to embrace one's own social world even more firmly.

Critical Urban Theory and the Los Angeles School

Throughout the world, especially in cities that experienced major growth in the twentieth century, sociologists are increasingly critical of the lack of regulation of that

Large cities promote the emergence of diverse subcultures, which add to the enjoyment of life for many city people.

growth, which has benefited a small number of rich and powerful owners of real estate and capital but has had detrimental effects on much of the rest of the urban population. They point out that runaway, largely unregulated urban growth has been marked by avoidable environmental disasters and widening gaps between the haves and the have-nots. Because Los Angeles is the city most often used as an example of such unrestrained growth, this critical theory of recent urban growth (or *sprawl,* as some prefer to call it) is sometimes identified as the "Los Angeles School" of critical urban theory (Scott, 1999).

Mike Davis, the most widely known member of the Los Angeles School, is extremely critical of the way Los Angeles's boosters and real estate speculators have disregarded severe environmental conditions in their efforts to stimulate growth and profits. In his view, the building of new communities on fire- and earthquake-prone desert landscapes, where water is piped from hundreds of miles away, illustrates how a greedy business elite has disregarded good urban planning practices in the interest of huge profits (Davis, 1998). Davis and other members of this informal academic school also emphasize how Los Angeles's "widening extremes of wealth and poverty, its blend of first- and third-world cultures, its deeply rooted political conservatism, and its peculiar spatial organization," completely dependent on the automobile and subsidies for highway construction, present a strong contrast to the older "Chicago School" models of urban growth and other urban theories. Those theories do not directly criticize the role of powerful owners of capital and their political allies, who have knowingly shaped the growth patterns of metropolitan regions in the postindustrial period (Scott, 1999, p. 3). Because the desert metropolitan regions of Arizona, Nevada, Utah, along with Southern California, are among the most rapidly growing areas of the United States, the Los Angeles School of critical urban research is particularly important for understanding how such growth occurs.

Compare and contrast "urbanism" and "urbanization," using examples to illustrate your points.

METROPOLITAN GROWTH

The mass migration from the farms to the cities in the nineteenth century has been described as a rural–urban flow. But in the twentieth century, with most of the U.S. population living in or near urban areas, the pattern of flow has changed from rural–urban to intermetropolitan. In 1910 the Bureau of the Census identified twenty-five **metropolitan districts.** This term was designed to assist in the measurement of urban populations, which even then could no longer be contained within the traditional urban political boundaries. These districts varied in size from the largest (New York, with 616,927 acres of land and 6,474,568 people) to the smallest (Portland, Oregon, with a population of 215,048 and a land area of 43,538 acres). Through this approach, the unity of such urban areas as the Twin Cities of Minnesota, the cities of San Francisco Bay, and the two Kansas Cities along the Missouri–Kansas border was recognized. The importance of the urban clusters around Philadelphia, New York, and Boston also became apparent.

Since 1983 the U.S. Bureau of the Census has defined the urban population according to residence in three categories of urban settlement. The largest of the three, the **consolidated metropolitan statistical area (CMSA),** refers to large metropolitan complexes within which are recognized subcenters that may themselves have large core areas, called **primary metropolitan statistical areas (PMSAs).** Dallas and Fort Worth and the urban areas surrounding them, for example, are classified as a CMSA, but statistics are also published separately for the Dallas and Forth Worth PMSAs. **Metropolitan statistical areas (MSAs)** have a large urban nucleus (a city of 500,000) and surrounding communities that are closely linked to it through economic and social activities. Indianapolis, Indiana, is an MSA, as is Little Rock–North Little Rock, Arkansas.

How do "metropolitan" and "urban" areas differ? An urban area usually contains a large population within a limited area. A metropolitan area contains several urban

TABLE 13–3	Metropolitan and Nonmetropolitan Area Population: United States, 1960–2000				
	1960	**1970**	**1980**	**1990**	**2000**
Metropolitan areas					
Number of areas	212	243	268	268	276
Population (1,000)	112,885	139,480	177,505	198,407	225,968
Nonmetropolitan areas, population (1,000)	66,438	63,822	49,037	50,311	55,453

Source: Statistical Abstract, 2005.

communities, all of which are located in close proximity to one another. For example, the greater New York metropolitan area contains not only New York City but also Long Island, Westchester County, and parts of New Jersey (including Newark) and Connecticut. Metropolitan regions also include suburban communities.

Table 13–3 shows how many new metropolitan areas have emerged since 1960, as well as the enormous increase in the amount of land included in such areas. Some of these areas have become socially and economically interrelated, forming urbanized regions or in some cases an urban corridor such as Boston–New York– Philadelphia–Washington. Figure 13–2 shows the growth patterns of metropolitan regions in the United States. Although it is not indicated in the figure, the most rapidly growing metropolitan region in the western United States is Las Vegas, whose population almost doubled, from 697,000 in 1990 to 1.3 million in 2000, despite the city's location in one of the most arid regions of the nation.

Note the dramatic growth of regions in the South and West, in marked contrast to those in the Midwest and Northeast. With the exception of Minneapolis–St. Paul, many of the latter experienced population declines in the 1970s and modest increases, often due to the influence of immigration, in the 1980s. Although they are not growing rapidly, metropolitan regions in the Northeast remain the largest on the continent. Social scientists often use the term **megalopolis** to refer to these large areas (Garreau, 1991, 1996; Gottmann, 1978).

Figure 13–2 Growth of Metropolitan Regions (Percentage Growth in Population Between 1990 and 2000)

Source: Statistical Abstract, 2005.

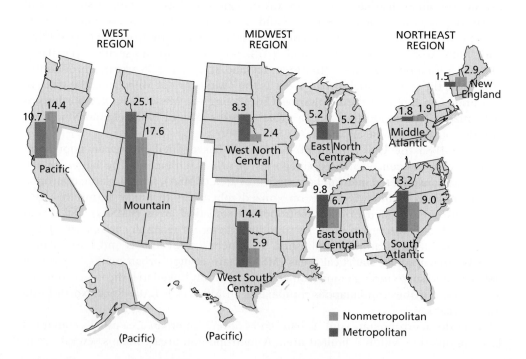

The problem of brush fires raging through suburban developments is likely to increase in severity as population growth in arid regions of the United States far outpaces growth in the rest of the nation.

The development of megalopolitan areas has large-scale environmental effects. The energy consumed in the major megalopolitan regions of the United States, especially the BosWash (Boston-to-Washington) corridor, contributes enormously to acid rain and other problems in the Northeast and elsewhere. Air pollution and the demand for shrinking supplies of water in the SanSan (San Diego–San Francisco) megalopolitan strip are reaching emergency proportions. Development along major auto routes between urban areas within the megalopolitan regions is also a growing problem as urban growth threatens to choke out green space and result in unplanned urban sprawl.

Rural Depopulation and Its Consequences

A major consequence of the explosive growth of metropolitan regions has been the depopulation of rural areas outside these sprawling regions. The more productive rural areas continue to achieve economic growth and manage to sustain their farming economies; this is the case in states like Iowa, Ohio, and Wisconsin, where farming is vital to the sustenance of urban and metropolitan regions. However, in less densely settled areas of the nation, such as Nebraska, the Dakotas, and other western prairie states, the decline of family farming and the continued migration of younger people to cities and metropolitan regions cause major social problems.

The 2000 U.S. Census reveals that while the population of the nation as a whole grew by 13 percent over the decade, the population of many rural counties in the Northeast, the South, and the Plains states fell by 9 percent or more during the 1990s (Egan, 2002). All told, the population of nonmetropolitan counties grew by 5.3 million, or 10.3 percent, from April 1990 to April 2000. This is in sharp contrast to the increase of just 1.3 million, or 2.7 percent, that took place over the decade from 1980 to 1990. Although this recent growth seems to represent a population rebound for rural America, in fact much of it is occurring in areas on the edges of nearby metropolitan regions. In rural counties that are not adjacent to metropolitan areas, growth in the decade was only 5.5 percent, well below the national average (U.S. Census Bureau, 2000). But in more isolated rural counties with declining numbers of family farms and decreases in other types of jobs, net population losses have left people and communities with little hope for positive change in the near future.

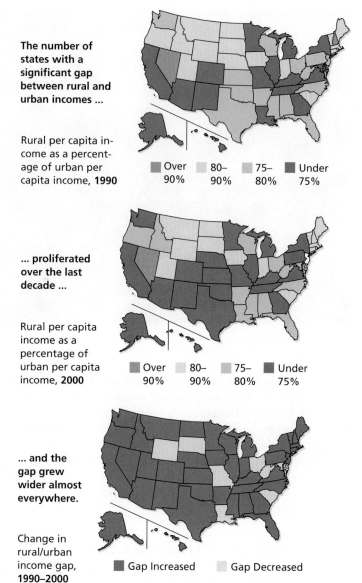

The number of states with a significant gap between rural and urban incomes ...

Rural per capita income as a percentage of urban per capita income, **1990**

◼ Over 90% ◼ 80–90% ◼ 75–80% ◼ Under 75%

... proliferated over the last decade ...

Rural per capita income as a percentage of urban per capita income, **2000**

◼ Over 90% ◼ 80–90% ◼ 75–80% ◼ Under 75%

... and the gap grew wider almost everywhere.

Change in rural/urban income gap, **1990–2000**

◼ Gap Increased ◼ Gap Decreased

Figure 13–3 Rural America's Downward Spiral, 1990–2000

Note: The terms *urban* and *rural* here refer to each state's metropolitan and nonmetropolitan counties. New Jersey and Washington, D.C., do not have any nonmetropolitan counties.

Source: "Rural Poverty and Rural-Urban Income Gaps: A Troubling Snapshot of the Prosperous 1990s" by Thomas Rowley and Kathleen Miller, published by the Rural Policy Research Institute.

With population decline and the loss of farms and small industrial shops have come increased poverty, crime, and drug addiction. Problems once most associated with the densely populated and impoverished communities of older manufacturing cities are now appearing in rural areas that have lost their vitality as their populations migrated to seek opportunities in the rapidly growing metropolitan regions. The maps in Figure 13–3 compare rural per capita income as a percentage of urban per capita income in 1990 and 2000. They show that the number of states with a significant gap between rural and urban incomes increased markedly during that decade. Closely related to this relative decrease in rural incomes has been an increase in crime in rural areas. Figure 13–4 compares crime rates in two very urban states, New York and New Jersey, with those in seven rural states where many counties have experienced negative growth. It shows that crime rates in those states now exceed those in the highly urbanized ones.

Most economic aid to farm states comes in the form of agricultural subsidies, the majority of which go to the largest agricultural producers, not to the smaller farmers who still fight to remain in their rural counties. About 1.2 million of the nation's 2 million farms make less than $10,000 in sales annually. But an estimated 70 percent of the

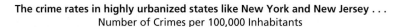

The crime rates in highly urbanized states like New York and New Jersey . . .

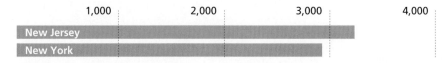

. . . **are lower than in many of the nation's rural states.**

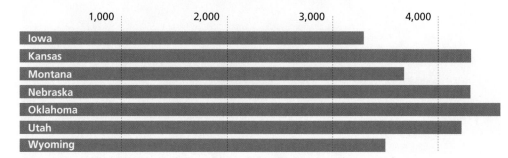

Figure 13–4 Crime Rates in Selected Urban and Rural Areas
Source: UCR, 2002.

$125 billion in federal farm supports and subsidies goes to 10 percent of farms, most of which are owned by agribusiness corporations rather than individual families. Most jobs in rural areas are nonagricultural, and about 25 percent of them pay wages that are insufficient to raise a family above the official poverty level. These conditions, which contribute to the social problems of declining rural areas, are only likely to worsen in coming years (Egan, 2002). Steep increases in fuel prices in 2005 threatened to make rural communities even more isolated, especially in the absence of adequate public transportation in rural areas and small towns.

The Transportation Boom

In the leading nations of Western Europe, especially Holland, France, Germany, and Denmark, investment in rail transport, high-speed trains, and improved bus transportation promises to limit the unplanned effects of megalopolitan development, but similar investments in the urban transportation infrastructure have not been made in the United States. On the other hand, as we will see in Chapter 15, the United States has succeeded in implementing air pollution controls that are more stringent than those of European nations, and these controls have had highly positive effects, although air pollution remains a serious problem in major urban regions.

Relatively primitive communication and transportation facilities and the need for defensive fortifications forced ancient and medieval cities to be compact, and the movement of their inhabitants was restricted to a relatively small area. This was also true for cities in the United States throughout most of the nineteenth century, when walking was the chief mode of transportation. After 1870, however, several major advances, beginning with the horse-drawn streetcar, allowed urban residents the luxury of living up to five miles from their places of business. The day of the commuter had dawned. Electric trolley lines and streetcars were introduced in the 1880s and 1890s, extending the commuting distance to about ten miles. When rapid-transit electric trains were introduced around the turn of the century, the distance doubled once again. The movement to the suburbs had begun.

The trend toward suburbanization began in earnest with the introduction of commuter railways. As wealthy third- and fourth-generation urbanites retreated from the central city, putting ever larger distances between their residences and their places of business, the separation between low-income and high-income neighborhoods increased markedly. Quick to follow the trend, commercial institutions began their

High-speed trains are increasingly common in Europe and Japan, but not in the United States, where investments in air and highway travel have been seen as more important than investment in rail transit.

own redistribution process. The first to vacate the central city were convenience-goods and service establishments, the businesses most dependent on the type of customer who was rapidly moving to suburbia. As these businesses and various manufacturing concerns were leaving the central city, professional service organizations were moving in, creating a central business district made up of administrative, communications, financial, and other businesses that serviced the entire metropolitan region.

By the 1930s the automobile had made suburban development a major factor in the economic, social, and political life of the United States. Motor vehicle registration increased from 8,000 in 1900 to 26,352,000 in 1930, representing an increase from approximately one automobile for every 10,000 people to one per household (Flink, 1976; Kimes, 2004). The automobile altered the shape of urban expansion. Whereas previous suburban growth had developed along railroad lines and other public transport systems, the automobile permitted much more dispersed growth. By 1930 urban sprawl was well under way.

Edge Cities. In the 1980s and 1990s urban growth entered a new stage. On the perimeters of metropolitan areas, large urban clusters emerged, dense and more focused than the conventional suburb. Sometimes referred to as "edge cities," these new developments rival downtown areas in size and surpass them as sources of jobs. An example of this trend is Tysons Corner. Once a crossroads village in rural northern Virginia, Tysons Corner is now a burgeoning business and shopping center on the edge of the Washington, D.C., metropolitan area. More than 70,000 people work in Tysons Corner, but little else happens there; community life and institutions are almost entirely lacking (Stevens, 1987). Nevertheless, as shown in Figure 13–5, there are many existing edge cities in the Washington, D.C., area, as well as some emerging ones. These new centers for office buildings, shopping malls, and in some cases light manufacturing are surrounded by suburban and exurban communities and are often located near major transportation nodes like Dulles International Airport.

Many other metropolitan regions, notably Los Angeles, Phoenix, Atlanta, Dallas, and northern New Jersey, are experiencing an explosive growth of edge cities as well. Because many of these new areas of economic growth are relatively inaccessible to poor inner-city residents, the mismatch between jobs and population is becoming a pressing urban social policy issue (Garreau, 1996; Low, 2003).

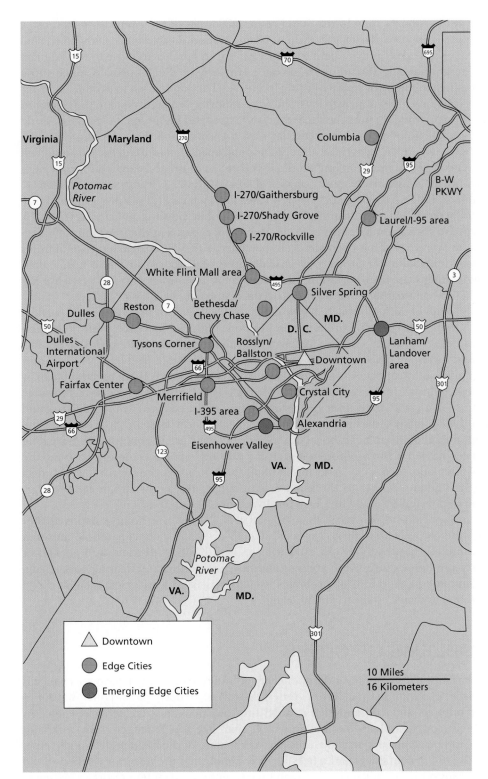

Figure 13–5 Edge Cities in the Washington, D.C., Area

Source: From *Edge City* by Joel Garreau, copyright © 1991 by Joel Garreau. Used by permission of Doubleday, a division of Random House, Inc. Electronic rights by permission of Raphael Sagalyn, Inc.

The Impact of Suburban Growth

Public policy, especially in the areas of urban renewal and highway construction, has encouraged suburbanization, often to the detriment and/or destruction of central-city neighborhoods. Financial opportunities—particularly Federal Housing Authority or Veterans Administration mortgages—make buying a house more attractive and easier in the suburbs than in the aging residential areas of the central city. Because a large proportion of a mortgage payment is interest and therefore tax deductible, simple economics makes it expedient for many American families to move to the suburbs.

Federal financing for home ownership, primarily in the suburbs, is much more accessible than funds for rental housing in the city. This has tended to produce increasing social-class segregation, with lower-income minorities concentrated in the cities and more affluent whites in the suburbs. Explicit efforts to add higher-quality rental housing to the stock of inner-city housing have had mixed results. Public housing, almost all of it built before the 1980s, has added about 1.3 million apartment units to the existing stock of lower-cost rental housing, but about 15 percent of those units are troubled by high rates of drug abuse, crime, and violence (Liebman, Katz, & Kling, 2004; Williams & Kornblum, 1994). Except in the very few cases in which careful planning made it possible to achieve successfully integrated projects, public housing policies have merely managed to keep lower-income people in the city, thereby strengthening patterns of segregation. Moreover, it has been almost impossible for the cities to obtain federal funds for mass transportation projects. By encouraging highway construction rather than strengthening mass transportation, the government encourages industry to leave the city, thereby eliminating a major portion of the central city's tax base.

The steady growth of suburbs has posed many problems for the older cities, particularly in their internal structure and composition. With the increasing differentiation between the central city and the suburban ring, and the subsequent outflow of population and industry, America's cities face social and economic problems of seemingly insurmountable proportions. As urban history shows, the steady flight to the suburbs by business, industry, and residents—all eager for less expensive and more comfortable quarters—has made renovation and rehabilitation of the central city both difficult and expensive. In many older metropolitan areas, particularly those in the Northeast, the abandonment of urban neighborhoods to the poor, who are ill equipped to move long distances, has led to the proliferation of slums, causing both the economic base and the actual population of the city to decline. Although the suburbs, the nearby towns, and all of their residents belong to the same metropolitan area as the urban centers, they escape responsibility for the financial burdens they place on the cities.

It is important to recognize that suburbs are no longer as homogeneous as they once were (or were thought to be; see Table 13–1). Long characterized as bedroom communities, suburbs today mix rural villages with business districts, and pockets of poverty and homelessness with areas of middle-class comfort and wealth. Nor are suburbs immune to the kinds of problems usually associated with cities, such as traffic congestion and lack of affordable housing.

What is urban sprawl, and why is it so difficult to control in major metropolitan regions?

PROBLEMS OF CITIES

Modern cities are constantly undergoing change and restructuring. Economic change is especially significant in urban areas. As new industries are born and old ones die, entire neighborhoods and communities may be lost and new ones created elsewhere. In the 1950s, for example, economic growth in cities like San Francisco, New York, and Seattle was based on seaport industries. But automation in the handling of goods (especially the use of containers and trucks) greatly diminished the need for workers in the ports. Many port cities still serve as transshipment centers, but far fewer workers are needed to perform this function. Some cities have made up for the loss in seaport employment by building major jetports. Still, economic and social change is so rapid that cities are continually racing to adapt and to attract new industries. In the meantime they continue to attract newcomers, many of whom bring more than their share of troubles.

These major social changes affect urban centers more drastically than they do other communities, and they often create a variety of urban problems. Among these are decentralization, relocation of manufacturing, and financial problems, all of which are complicated by the division of government responsibility between cities and suburbs.

These problems are discussed in this section. Two other serious problems, the lack of affordable housing and the increase in homelessness, are discussed in the next section.

Decentralization

A primary cause of central-city decay is **decentralization:** the flight to the suburbs of middle- and upper-middle-class families; the influx of poor minority groups, the chronically unemployed, the aged, and others who tend to be more of a liability than an asset to central-city budgets; the retreat of commerce and industry from the taxing jurisdiction of central cities; the disparity between the requirements of available jobs in the central city and the skills of the resident labor force; and the daily flow into the city of suburban residents, who utilize public facilities without paying for their upkeep. All these circumstances strain the budgets of the central cities at a time when their revenues are decreasing and their public service obligations have increased substantially.

The decade between 1920 and 1930 was a period of pronounced decentralization, or suburbanization, in the United States. In subsequent decades the population within the suburban rings increased significantly more than the population of the central cities. By the 1960s suburbanization accounted for almost all the growth within metropolitan areas, and today the growth of central cities is still smaller than that of the outer fringes. But this does not mean that there is no population change inside the cities. On the contrary, as more affluent households move from inner cities to suburban areas, new populations are constantly arriving, especially from other nations. Thus, although population figures may not show them as growing, the inner cities are in fact subject to major population shifts (Logan, 2001).

The 2000 census confirmed that the fastest growing urban communities are on the fringes of metropolitan areas. During the 1980s and 1990s there was a significant shift of jobs and people to the outer counties of metropolitan regions. In many metropolitan regions the rapid growth of suburban communities attracts jobs that were formerly located in the urban core.

In addition to the movement to the suburbs, there has been a tremendous shift of population from the Snowbelt cities of the North and East to the Sunbelt cities of the South and West—Houston, San Antonio, Phoenix, and others. As the population has moved, so have jobs, adding to the problems of the older, larger cities in the northern industrial states. But life is not always sunny in the Sunbelt cities either. In California, for example, severe drought and increasing overpopulation, lack of affordable housing, and earthquakes have tarnished the image of Southern California as the embodiment of the American Dream. Although the large-scale influx of immigrants continues to produce growth in the Los Angeles metropolitan area, it is likely that the region will experience continuing economic problems because of the end of the cold war and the decline in defense production, as well as the effects of environmental catastrophes ranging from earthquakes to brush fires and mud slides (Davis, 2003).

In the 1990s there were numerous natural calamities such as flooding in cities and towns of the Mississippi, Ohio, and Missouri valleys; earthquakes and brush fires in California; and hurricanes in the Gulf states. These added to the burden of financing the repair and maintenance of urban infrastructures. Because the majority of the nation's metropolitan population lives in disaster-prone regions, it is likely that natural disasters and their consequences will become more frequent in coming years as both the population and the surface area of these metropolitan centers continue to grow. The devastation of cities and communities after Hurricanes Katrina and Wilma struck the Gulf Coast in 2005 called worldwide attention to how precarious many metropolitan areas are in a time of rapid climate change, a subject that will be discussed in more detail in Chapter 14.

Relocation of Manufacturing

Manufacturers benefit from suburban relocation because they can minimize their transportation and freight costs by locating near suburban highway systems. Accordingly, manufacturing firms have left the inner cities in large numbers. To a certain extent, their departure has been balanced by an influx of new types of business establishments that offer specialized goods and services. Legal, government, and professional complexes and service organizations such as travel agencies, advertising firms, and brokerage houses have all become more numerous in recent decades. Yet although the percentage of white-collar jobs has increased in the central cities, it has increased much faster in the outlying suburban areas.

Especially dramatic has been the rise of high-tech manufacturing centers like Silicon Valley in California and the Route 128 region near Boston. Among the industries that have found it advantageous to operate in these areas are manufacturers of office and computing machines, communication equipment, electronic components and accessories, and engineering and scientific instruments, as well as computer and data-processing services and research and development labs. These industries are dependent on intensive, sophisticated technical research, and hence the new manufacturing zones are almost always located near major universities like the Massachusetts Institute of Technology. High-tech firms have created large numbers of new jobs, especially high-paying jobs in science, engineering, and management. One result is a growing demand for expensive housing in the surrounding communities, which tends to increase the average price of housing in the area and displace lower-income residents (Kasarda, 1995).

How has deindustrialization affected the prospects of many cities in the United States?

Financial Problems

Property assessments are the primary source of tax revenues for city governments. As a result of the exodus of industry to the suburbs, the real estate tax base of most central cities has been greatly reduced. Population shifts within the boundaries of metropolitan areas have further increased the financial pressures on central cities. For the larger metropolitan areas, the increased concentration of low-income groups in the inner cities demands a larger investment in welfare and other social programs. Many cities, fearful of losing residents and businesses to the suburbs, also need to invest in large-scale physical rehabilitation and redevelopment projects.

The economic gap between healthy suburbs and distressed cities has worsened in recent years, despite signs of improvement in some areas. Many urban specialists fear that cities with financial difficulties will channel funds away from essential services, such as streets, water and sewage systems, and mass transportation facilities, to finance their debts and meet operating costs.

Related to the problem of finances is the poor condition of the infrastructure (i.e., physical facilities) of many cities. Most American cities grew rapidly after World War II, especially in the 1950s. Large investments were made in public transportation, bridges, and highway systems to serve rapidly growing and increasingly affluent urban populations. But by the 1980s much of this infrastructure had begun to wear out. Estimates made by the federal government in the early 1980s indicated that billions of dollars would be needed to repair and rebuild crumbling city facilities. In the mid-1980s many observers warned that the decay of the country's roads, bridges, sewers, and rail and water systems had reached alarming proportions. These warnings were reinforced by an increase in the frequency of accidents caused by train derailments and collapsing bridges and overpasses. At the same time, however, the federal budget deficit rose to record levels, precluding large-scale federal investment in infrastructure projects.

Government

A major cause of the problems of cities today is the inequitable distribution of economic resources and costs of public services between the cities and higher levels of government. Of every $100 the U.S. government collects in taxes, it spends about $18 on national defense, $23 on Social Security, $14 on income security (federal pensions, unemployment insurance, food and nutrition assistance, etc.), and $20 on interest on the national debt. It spends less than $1 to run the federal government, $8 on health-care services and

Large tracts of urban real estate have been abandoned because of high crime rates or the inability of tenants to make rent payments. Public–private partnerships using federal housing funds have provided these formerly homeless families with their first decent, affordable housing.

research (not including Medicare), $2 on transportation (especially highways), and a little less than $1 on criminal-justice assistance to states and cities (*Statistical Abstract*, 2006). Although residents of metropolitan regions consider crime and overcrowded prisons to be major social problems, one can see from these figures that very little of the tax revenue collected at the federal level is returned to municipalities to help them cope with these problems. In consequence, suburbs with affluent residents who pay high property taxes can afford adequate protection, whereas inner cities with poorer residents, which have much less revenue from property taxes, must depend on the meager return from federal taxes to tackle not only crime but also poor education, inadequate health care, and other major problems.

In addition, many urban social problems extend beyond the jurisdiction of any single local government and often cross state boundaries as well. Such concerns as air and water pollution require control over entire areas rather than strict observance of municipal boundaries. This is also true for major waterways, mass transit, and water supplies. The situation for recreational facilities, public institutions like libraries and museums, and public services like police and fire protection is less clear. The benefits of all these services are not restricted to a single municipal jurisdiction. On the other hand, they are not equally distributed throughout the entire metropolitan area. Who, then, is to pay how much for these necessary services?

City governments have been forced to bear the financial burden for municipal services even though those services are extensively utilized by suburban residents. Thousands of visitors flock to city museums and parks every day, placing additional burdens on sanitation and public-health facilities and transportation systems, all of which must be paid for out of municipal funds. In this way, city residents assume the tax burden for their suburban neighbors. Numerous social scientists have pointed out that regardless of its political boundaries, a metropolitan area is in fact a single economic entity, with an integrated labor market, a unified transportation system, and a closely interrelated set of housing markets. Dividing this entity into separate local economies results in inefficiency and duplication of services.

In extreme cases the discrepancies between municipal boundaries and social needs can have dire consequences. This is illustrated by East St. Louis, Illinois, which has been described as "a textbook case of everything that can go wrong in an American city." Once a prosperous blue-collar town of stockyards and meat-packing plants beside the Mississippi River, in the 1990s East St. Louis was "a city at rock bottom, a partly inhabited ghost town whose factories and theaters and hotels and auto dealerships and gas stations and half its schools are mostly burned-out shells" (Wilkerson, 1991, p. A16). Although riverboat gambling has brought some new jobs and income, the city remains mired in poverty. The causes of this situation include a rapidly declining tax base and the fact that even though East St. Louis borders on St. Louis, it is a separate municipality in another state. Camden, New Jersey, across the river from Philadelphia, is another example of a city that suffers because it is dominated by a "sister city" in another state. Throughout the world there are many other examples of cities that are disadvantaged by their location near a far more dominant neighbor (Brunn, Williams, & Zeigler, 2003).

SHELTER POVERTY, HOMELESSNESS, AND NEIGHBORHOOD DISTRESS

Shelter Poverty

As noted in Chapter 6, the majority of America's poor live in substandard, deteriorated housing that has been rejected by people who can afford better. This is especially true of poor members of minority groups, who inhabit substandard housing either because they cannot afford anything better or because discrimination keeps them where they are. As a result, people with higher incomes live in new housing in the suburbs, while the poor live in older central-city housing. Shelter poverty, it should be noted, also occurs among affluent families when sudden unemployment decreases their income while mortgages and other housing costs remain the same. But shelter poverty is most prevalent among families at or below the poverty line.

Some experts argue that many sections of cities that are severely run down can be rehabilitated. Others claim that this does nothing to solve social problems. The standard procedure in most urban renewal or redevelopment programs involves the mass removal of slum housing. To accomplish this, the residents of the area must be removed first. Because most urban renewal projects result in more expensive housing, the residents are for the most part unable to return to their former neighborhoods. Those who can afford to return find that the characteristics that made the neighborhood their own—churches, schools, family, and friends—are no longer there. The majority of those who are dislocated as a result of urban renewal move to nearby areas that will probably be cleared in future renewal projects.

Instead of providing adequate housing at a low cost, most urban renewal drives the poor out of rehabilitated areas because too often the redeveloped housing is intended for people with high incomes. Low-cost housing for low-income residents has never been financially feasible. Meanwhile, federal public housing policy often ensures the development of a "federal slum." By preventing the working poor from living in the housing projects, the government restricts the projects to the very poor, people on welfare, broken families, and the disabled.

It should be noted that much public housing is far better than the dilapidated, decaying buildings it replaced. However, the problem of segregation of the poor remains; in addition, the quality of the neighborhoods in which the housing projects are located is often substandard. Critics of public housing point out that "even when dwelling units occupied by the poor are not overcrowded, contain their own kitchens and bathrooms, and may even be in somewhat decent repair, they are set in a dismal environment. They are surrounded by abandoned buildings and located on streets that are unsafe and littered with trash" (Salins, 1986, pp. 24–25). A major reason for this situation is that more affluent communities tend to oppose even small additions of low-income housing to their neighborhoods.

Homelessness

A frequent consequence of shelter poverty is homelessness. People become homeless for a variety of personal reasons, including mental illness, drug and alcohol addiction, and the severe post-traumatic shock that many returning war veterans have experienced. But the chief cause of homeless is poverty and the resultant inability to afford the cost of housing. People who cannot afford rent increases, for example, may end up among the large number of homeless people in the nation's big cities. Moreover, many young families who would have purchased a house a decade ago are forced to stay in rental housing. This development has tended to push rents up and squeeze lower-income people out of the rental market; because of the lack of space in public housing, the result, for many, is homelessness.

Another trend that has contributed to the housing problem is *gentrification,* the return of affluent, single people and childless couples to selected central-city neighborhoods. As these new urban residents restore and renovate buildings and upgrade apartments in decaying neighborhoods, poor residents are forced to seek living space in other parts of the city. If they are unable to find housing they can afford, they, too, may end up among the homeless.

We have noted at several points in this book that homelessness has become a major social problem in recent decades. As a result of numerous factors, including deinstitutionalization of mental patients, the increasing concentration of poor people in central cities, the lack of low-cost housing, and the displacement of poor families by urban renewal and gentrification, there has been a large and visible increase in the number of homeless people who wander through public places in central cities. The size of the homeless population is extremely difficult to assess: Homeless people are virtually impossible to keep track of; moreover, estimates of their numbers tend to reflect the interests of the organizations that provide them.

According to Martha Burt of the Urban Instutute, the nation's leading expert on the size of the homeless population,

> On any given day, at least 800,000 people are homeless in the United States, including about 200,000 children in homeless families. These startling statistics, however, do not tell the whole story. Homelessness in America is a "revolving-door" crisis. Many people exit homelessness quickly, but many more individuals become homeless every day. During a year's time, four or five times as many people experience homelessness as are homeless on any particular day. Calculations from different sources show that . . . at least 2.3 million, and perhaps as many as 3.5 million, people experienced homelessness at some time during an average year. Because more families with children than unpartnered people enter and leave homelessness during a year, families represent a relatively large share of the annual population. As a result, during a typical year, between 900,000 and 1.4 million children are homeless with their families. (Burt, 2001, p. 1)

The severe hurricanes of 2004 and 2005 have created thousands of additional homeless families. But among the poor who are not victims of natural catastrophes, major changes in the economy and other institutions have also produced higher rates of homelessness. As Burt writes,

> Structural, personal, and political factors influence the level of homelessness and determine where it will occur most often. Structural factors in the United States that have fueled the problem include
>
> - Changing housing markets for extremely low-income families and single adults are pricing more and more people with below-poverty incomes out of the market.
> - Dwindling employment opportunities for people with a high school education or less are contributing to the widening gap between rich and poor.

Technically, this mother and her children may not be homeless, as they have a place to sleep, but how long can they live in a dingy motel? As affordable housing becomes scarcer, scenes like this one become more common.

- The removal of institutional supports for people with severe mental illness, epitomized by drastic reductions in the use of long-term hospitalization for the mentally ill, are leaving many individuals with few housing options.

- Racial, ethnic, and class discrimination in housing, along with local zoning restrictions that exclude affordable housing alternatives, persists in many areas.

"If housing were inexpensive," Burt observes, "or people could earn enough to afford housing, very few individuals would face homelessness. Increasingly, however, there is a dearth of affordable housing, not only in major metropolitan areas but throughout the nation" (Burt, 2001).

There have always been homeless groups in the United States: hoboes, unemployed migrants, and the like. For them, homelessness was either a chosen lifestyle or a more or less temporary condition. Today's homeless people are a more serious problem. Not only is the homeless population larger than ever before, but it includes a much wider range of groups—deinstitutionalized mental patients and displaced families, chronic alcoholics, destitute drug addicts, Vietnam veterans, unemployed laborers, and others. This large population has placed a heavy burden on the public and private shelters and other social services of American cities. In some cities, existing shelters and other facilities are woefully inadequate, and as a result homeless people have sought refuge in bus terminals and train stations. Policies for dealing with homelessness are discussed further in the Social Policy section of the chapter.

Distressed Neighborhoods

As a consequence of the flight of more secure middle-class people from the central cities over the past thirty years or more, there has been an increase in what social scientists call **neighborhood distress.** In discussing this problem, it is important to note that it is extremely difficult to define precisely what constitutes a neighborhood. The Census Bureau divides urban regions into **census tracts,** areas that are relatively homogeneous in population, socioeconomic status, and living conditions. Census tracts, which have an average population of 4,000 people, are equivalent to urban neighborhoods for analytical purposes.

In the largest central cities of the United States, there are slightly over 14,000 census tracts. Analyses of the characteristics of inner-city tracts reveal that in many there

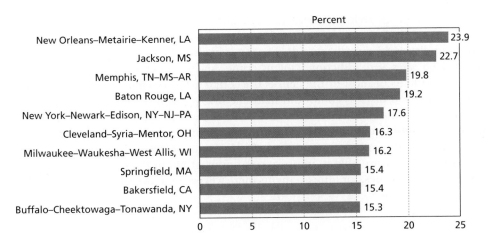

Figure 13–6 Large Metropolitan Areas with the Highest Share of Children in Severely Distressed Neighborhoods, 2000

Source: William O'Hare and Mark Mather, "The Growing Number of Kids in Severely Distressed Neighborhoods: Evidence from the 2000 Census." Kids Count/PRB Report on Census 2000. Annie E. Casey Foundation, Baltimore and Population Reference Bureau, Washington, DC. October, 2003.

have been sharp increases in the degree of neighborhood distress. According to social scientists such as Paul Jargoswky (1998), severely distressed neighborhoods with at least three of the following four characteristics are defined as census tracts:

1. A high percentage of people (27.4 percent or more) living in poverty

2. A high percentage of families with related children headed by women with no husband present (37 percent or more)

3. A high percentage of 16- to 19-year-olds who are not enrolled in school and not high-school graduates (23 percent or more)

4. A high percentage of civilian, noninstutionalized men ages 16 to 64 who are unemployed or not in the labor force (34 percent or more)

The cutoff values for these criteria are one standard deviation above the mean census tract values from the U.S. Census. In other words, these are census tracts with levels of economic and social distress that are far above average. We do not have detailed census tract data for periods between the decennial census, but poverty statistics indicate that rates of neighborhoods distress have climbed in the first five years of the new millennium. In Figure 13–6 we see that the New Orleans metropolitan area had by far the highest percentage (almost 24 percent) of these distressed census tracts in 2000, a fact that became painfully evident in the 2005 hurricane season. But Baton Rouge, where so many people from the New Orleans area fled after Hurricane Katrina, was fourth on the list, followed by major metropolitan areas such as New York and Cleveland.

Growing up in distressed neighborhoods has lasting negative effects on children. Table 13–4 shows that between 1990 and 2000, despite a booming economy, the number

TABLE 13–4	Children and Adults Living in Severely Distressed Neighborhoods, 1990 and 2000				
	1990		2000		Change 1990 to 2000	Percent Change
Population	Number (thousands)	Percent	Number (thousands)	Percent	Number (thousands)	Percent Change
Total	15,196	6.1	18,129	6.4	2,932	19.3
Under age 18	4,747	7.5	5,599	7.7	852	18.0
Age 18 and over	10,450	5.6	12,530	6.0	2,080	19.9

Source: O'Hare & Mather, 2003. (Data from Population Reference Bureau)

of children under age 18 living in distressed neighborhoods rose by 852,000, an increase of 18 percent. It is difficult to overstate the consequences of this concentration of poor children in distressed neighborhoods. These are likely to be the areas with the highest rates of drug sales and addiction, violent crime, and housing abandonment. Twenty years ago residents of most of the census tracts that are now characterized by poverty and neighborhood distress could find manufacturing jobs nearby. Today the jobs are gone, and the economic future of these areas is extremely uncertain. Although some communities outside central cities also suffer from high rates of poverty and related social problems, the most important test of policies to address urban social problems will be whether they are able to improve conditions of life in the distressed neighborhoods of the inner cities, for improvements there will result in overall improvements for all residents of urban areas.

Social Policy

Intentionally or unintentionally, social policies instituted by governments at all levels, and especially by the federal government, have encouraged suburban sprawl and contributed to the problems of rural areas and inner cities (Brown, 1997; Lofland, 1998). Policies that subsidize mortgages for buyers of private homes favor the suburbs over denser apartment neighborhoods. Policies that favor highway and road construction over mass transit encourage the growth of communities at the edges of metropolitan areas but make it more difficult for people without adequate personal transportation to reach jobs and educational opportunities. To correct these biases, recent administrations have developed policies that encourage economic development, housing construction, and transportation alternatives in inner-city areas and the older suburbs that surround them. In larger cities like Chicago, New York, St. Louis, Atlanta, and many others, these policies have helped spur economic and social revitalization of the city center.

Throughout the nation, residential land values in cities are significantly higher than in the suburbs, indicating that a central location is desirable to many people. Housing in the central cities, particularly in high-rise apartment complexes, is very expensive. The fact that a central location still has a high economic value is the best evidence that the central city can be restored. Indeed, many urban sociologists view restoration projects in central-city neighborhoods—such as Capitol Hill in Washington, D.C.; Old Town and New Town in Chicago; Pioneer Square in Seattle; and Olympic Park in Atlanta—as indications of a revival of central-city life. Others are encouraged by the growth of luxury apartments and condominiums in and around the business districts of urban centers.

However, as noted earlier, the revitalization of neighborhoods by the upper-middle class is not always beneficial to all concerned. In particular, the poor and the elderly are often victims of this trend as their apartment buildings are converted into condominiums or cooperatives and they come under intense pressure to leave homes and neighborhoods that they can no longer afford. In addition to the return of the middle class, therefore, if today's cities are to be fully revitalized, some of the businesses that moved to the suburbs will have to return.

To some extent, this has happened already. Large regional capitals like New York, Boston, Louisville, Philadelphia, and Baltimore have undergone a transition to new industries based on light manufacturing of high-technology goods and the provision of new services, especially in finance, insurance, international trade, air freight, and research and development. The influx of new workers, often in higher-paying jobs, has stimulated leisure industries in these cities as well (Garreau, 1991).

An example of the kind of redevelopment that is occurring in some urban centers is the Times Square project in New York City. This project pooled funds from public and private sources to redevelop the Times Square area as a combined entertainment, wholesale marketing, and office complex. The project was controversial, however, because it had the potential to drive up rents in the area, thereby displacing low-income residents. Moreover, the plan called for the preservation of the historic theaters on Forty-second Street, even though public support of the arts, including the theater, had decreased significantly in recent years. In 1994 the Disney Corporation announced that it would open a major cultural development center in Times Square, a sign of the project's potential for eventual success. This announcement quieted some critics of the project, who argued that, like many other urban redevelopment plans, it emphasized the building of structures at the expense of the building of institutions such as theater companies or musical production organizations (Goldberger, 1996; Zukin, 1991). Today the new Times Square is attracting millions of domestic and foreign visitors annually and has become a focus of economic growth in the central city.

Housing

During the 1980s the federal government eliminated or drastically reduced many programs that had provided housing assistance to American families for fifty years. The Reagan administration believed that the forces of supply and demand, operating independently of government incentives and subsidies, would meet the need for moderate- and low-income housing. In effect, this amounted to the lack of a housing policy at the federal level.

At the state and local levels, in contrast, some new initiatives emerged in the late 1980s and early 1990s. Local governments began setting up funds to provide housing assistance to low- and moderate-income families, encouraging private and public partnerships to develop low-cost housing, and earmarking certain taxes (e.g., offshore oil taxes or real estate transfer taxes) for financing housing programs. These policies can be seen as part of the increased emphasis of many state governments on economic revitalization.

At the federal level, the public housing properties controlled by the U.S. Department of Housing and Urban Development, in cooperation with local managing authorities, are continually subject to changes in policy. The Clinton administration pursued a policy of tearing down dangerous and deteriorated high-rise housing in favor of low-rise garden apartments or single homes. It hoped to demolish some 100,000 units of the old housing and sought funding to cover the costs of replacing it. Unless replacement housing becomes available quite soon, however, this policy runs the risk of contributing still further to the problem of homelessness if there is a serious downturn in the economy.

The Bush administration's efforts to increase domestic security and fight international terrorism, along with massive cuts in federal taxes, continue to increase federal deficits. These shifts in policy and taxation in turn will inevitably result in cuts in available funds for spending on social issues like low-income housing and programs to combat homelessness (Stevenson, 2002). On the other hand, the administration's emphasis on allowing and encouraging "faith-based" agencies to use federal funds to conduct their social programs may result in more varied local programs to deal with severe shortages in lower-cost housing and aid to the indigent and homeless, but current evidence suggests that reductions in public funds during a time of increasing homelessness and stress are compounding the problems of many communities.

How is the 2007 Supreme Court decision on segregation likely to affect urban social policies?

Homelessness

Long-term changes in urban centers, particularly the influx of wealthy people into poorer communities (gentrification) and the replacement of manufacturing jobs with lower-paid service-sector jobs, have produced a serious lack of adequate housing for the poor. Shelters and temporary quarters need to be augmented; but without

Current Controversies

REINSTITUTIONALIZATION VERSUS COMMUNITY CARE

Oliver Sacks, the award-winning psychiatrist and author whose research with the mentally ill is the basis for the movie *Awakenings,* is a firm believer in the need to reopen state hospital wards for the mentally ill homeless who now sleep on city streets, in parks and rail terminals, and in temporary shelters. These troubled people are supposed to be cared for in community mental-health centers, halfway houses, and group homes, but in too many cases they are not. To alleviate their suffering, he proposes making room for them in state hospitals, where they can obtain proper treatment.

On a related front, William J. Bennett, former director of the Bush administration's antidrug programs, advocates the creation of orphanages for children in drug-infested neighborhoods. "We may just have to . . . find some way to get children out of the environment which they're in, to go to orphanages, to go to Boys Town, to expand institutions like that, where they will be raised and nurtured," he declared in a speech to an antidrug organization (quoted in Kosterlitz, 1990, p. 2120).

Many sociologists support Bennett's view. Joyce A. Ladner, for example, has conducted extensive studies of foster care and adoption, and notes that "we're seeing increasing numbers of children who are not getting adequate care and for whom adequate care is not an imminent possibility" (quoted in Kosterlitz, 1990, p. 2120). Society, she says, must cease to believe blindly in an ideal family life that often does not match reality and must put more children in group settings that offer safety and stability.

Those who oppose the movement toward reinstitutionalization warn of a return to the era of the "snake pit" and the grim, underfunded, understaffed orphanage. They point out that many mental hospitals and orphanages were shut down because they had become dumping grounds for society's most troubled and neglected members. The ideals of community care, patients' rights, and the mainstreaming of people with mental disabilities or histories of neglect may be threatened if society again resorts to "warehousing" its most problematic citizens. Advocates of community-based care believe

that cities and towns need more support in their efforts to add to the insufficient number of small, local care programs and facilities. They see the reinstitutionalization movement as a return to the past.

What is a concerned citizen to think? On the one hand, respected medical professionals such as Sacks advocate a return to institutionalization. On the other hand, many experts continue to hold out hope for community-based care and mainstreaming. Yet these are not necessarily mutually exclusive policies. One could advocate an increase in well-funded and well-staffed orphanages and mental hospitals while at the same time pressing for more community-based facilities. The problem, of course, is that mental hospitals and community care facilities are competing for public and private funds. For the care of dependent children without parents, for example, the federal government now makes available about $256 million a year, but an estimated $1 billion a year is needed if real progress is to be made toward providing adequate care. Competing budget demands make it unlikely that such funds will be provided.

---

increased investment in low- and moderate-income housing, it is likely that gentrification, along with the "normal" calamities of arson and urban blight, will continue to add to the homeless population.

In addition to the need for shelter, there are special needs among the homeless that have only recently been recognized and addressed by policymakers. Foremost among these is the spread of AIDS. It is estimated that between 15 and 20 percent of shelter residents are infected with the AIDS virus and have such symptoms as diarrhea, weight loss, chronic fevers, and pneumonia. Although they account for a small proportion of the homeless population, they present a major problem because they need hospice care and cannot be integrated with the residents of public shelters. A similar situation exists with respect to the mentally ill, as we saw in Chapter 3. (Some experts believe the mentally ill and homeless children should be cared for in institutions, a proposal that is discussed in the Current Controversies box above.)

A survey conducted in 2001 by the U.S. Conference of Mayors found significant increases in homelessness and in the demand for emergency food supplies in twenty-seven major American cities as a result of diversion of funds for the war on terrorism. Requests for emergency food assistance climbed an average of 23 percent and requests for emergency shelter assistance increased an average of 13 percent. Food supplies for the indigent increased by about 12 percent, not enough to meet the increased demand. Only one-third of the cities surveyed reported that they were able to feed their hungry populations adequately. Increasing poverty rates reported by the U.S. Census Bureau in 2005 point to an increase in hunger in America.

Future Prospects

Debates about the future of urban and rural poverty, about how to provide urgently needed health insurance for people without access to preventive medical care (who use emergency rooms as their family doctors) will continue no matter who is elected president in 2008. Any improvements in addressing these issues will have beneficial impacts on urban neighborhoods as well as on depressed rural areas and Native American reservations. But the initiatives taken in recent years by creative local governments with progressive mayors will also figure prominently in policy discussions. The example set by Mayor Michael Bloomberg of New York City in providing thousands of new low-cost housing units for homeless and potentially homeless families will no doubt gain national attention. So will the initiative taken by Mayor Corey Booker in impoverished Newark to turn that beleaguered city's economy around and improve the lives of minority people living in distressed neighborhoods. More attention to environmental issues by federal officials and a new president is also likely to result in new funding for urban mass transit, better air and water quality, and more attention to the health problems of urban residents.

GOING BEYOND LEFT AND RIGHT

Dislike of city life is not a monopoly of people on the conservative end of the political continuum, who typically live in suburban or small-town residential environments. Many people on the liberal side also dislike urban life, preferring to live in exurban or rural areas such as Vermont or the Pacific Northwest. Although those on the left are more likely to support efforts to improve conditions of life in the inner cities, they often send their children to private schools and buy vacation homes far from the stresses of the central city.

There are many important exceptions to these observations, but this behavior illustrates one of the main problems of the inner city: Its neighborhoods, often racially segregated, are not seen as desirable living environments. Increasingly, therefore, policymakers on both sides of the ideological divide recognize society's pressing need to address the plight of inner-city communities. The strategy of creating empowerment zones to attract new businesses is popular with policymakers on both the left and the right, but these zones have yet to prove their worth in the difficult task of revitalizing economically depressed communities in the inner cities.

Summary

- The U.S. Census Bureau defines the urban population as all persons who are living in places with 2,500 or more inhabitants that are legally incorporated as cities, villages, boroughs, and towns. Many social problems, such as poverty, mental illness, drug abuse, and violence, are especially serious in the nation's cities.

- The urban revolution is a worldwide phenomenon. Throughout the world, rapidly growing cities are experiencing social problems such as crowding, poverty, lack of adequate housing, and the threat of gangs and violence.

- Most urban growth has been caused by increasingly efficient transportation and communication and the effects

of industrialization. Urban growth has stimulated technological advances, but it has also created various social problems as well as a strong antiurban bias among a large proportion of the American public.

- The population of U.S. cities today consists largely of descendants of immigrants from other countries and from rural areas of the nation. Cities continue to receive large numbers of immigrants from other countries, and conflict between the newcomers and residents of older ghettos is frequent.

- Residential segregation, both voluntary and involuntary, is common in urban areas. African Americans have been subject to the highest and most persistent rates of segregation throughout the nation's history.

- The three main theories of urbanism are the Wirthian theory, the compositional theory, and the subcultural theory. The Wirthian theory holds that cities increase the incidence of social and personality disorders because city dwellers must adapt to a multitude of intense stimuli. The compositional theory views the city as a mosaic of social worlds that protect individuals from the pressures of city life. The subcultural theory suggests that urban life promotes diverse subcultures.

- Some sociologists, who have come to be known as the Los Angeles School, are increasingly critical of unregulated urban growth. They point to the undue influence of real estate developers and speculators on growth patterns of metropolitan regions.

- Many urban areas are not single cities but what the Census Bureau terms *metropolitan statistical areas* and *consolidated metropolitan statistical areas*. The core areas of these urban centers are primary metropolitan statistical areas. The term *megalopolis* is often applied to a region that contains several metropolitan areas.

- The growth of metropolitan areas has been associated with the development of new forms of transportation, including the streetcar, the commuter railway, and especially the automobile. These hastened the trend toward suburbanization, which was also encouraged by urban renewal and highway construction programs and by federal programs that encourage home ownership.

- In the 1980s urban growth entered a new stage. On the perimeters of metropolitan areas, large urban clusters emerged, denser and more focused than the conventional suburb. Sometimes referred to as edge cities, these new developments rival downtown areas in size and surpass them as sources of jobs.

- Many rural areas have been depopulated as metropolitan regions have grown and younger people have migrated to cities. Population decline and the loss of farms and small industrial shops have led to increased poverty, crime, and drug addiction.

- As suburbs and edge cities have grown, the central cities have decayed. A primary cause of decay is decentralization, the flight of middle-class families to the suburbs coupled with the influx of poor minority groups, the unemployed, and the aged to the central cities. Business and industry have also moved to the suburbs; in the cities, manufacturers have been replaced by establishments that offer specialized goods and services.

- Unskilled or semiskilled jobs have been transferred to the suburbs, and white-collar jobs in the cities are filled by skilled personnel, leaving unskilled central-city residents with fewer opportunities for employment.

- The exodus of industry to the suburbs has significantly reduced the real estate tax base of most central cities. At the same time, the increase in the low-income population of the cities creates additional financial burdens. This situation has resulted in serious financial problems for large cities. Related to this problem is the deterioration of the infrastructure, or physical facilities, of many cities, which has been made even worse by natural calamities like hurricanes, brush fires, and earthquakes. The financial problems of cities are exacerbated by the inequitable distribution of economic resources and costs between the cities and higher levels of government.

- Housing is a major problem in the central cities. Many urban residents are shelter poor, meaning that they must pay so much for housing that they no longer have enough money for other necessities. Shelter poverty is most prevalent among the poor, who are forced to live in substandard, deteriorated housing. Urban renewal or redevelopment programs involve removing such housing, thereby displacing the poor, and replacing it with housing for people with higher incomes. Housing projects for the poor, on the other hand, quickly turn into slums.

- Gentrification, the renovation of decaying neighborhoods by affluent residents, has displaced poor city dwellers and added to the homeless population. This large population has placed a heavy burden on public and private shelters and other social services in American cities.

- Over the past thirty years there has been an increase in what social scientists call neighborhood distress. Distressed neighborhoods are characterized by high rates of poverty, joblessness, female-headed families, and teenage school dropouts. Such areas are also likely to have the highest rates of drug sales and addiction, violent crime, and housing abandonment.

- Many of America's oldest cities are undergoing a process of revitalization as members of the upper-middle class return, together with new industries. Nevertheless, there is still an urgent need for social policies to improve conditions of life in the inner cities. Such policies are unlikely as an increasing proportion of the federal budget is devoted to combating terrorism at home and abroad.

Key Terms

rural, p. 413
urban, p. 413
urban population, p. 413
urbanized area, p. 413
urbanism, p. 414

metropolitan districts, p. 425
consolidated metropolitan statistical area
(CMSA), p. 425
primary metropolitan statistical areas
(PMSAs), p. 425

metropolitan statistical areas (MSAs), p. 425
megalopolis, p. 426
decentralization, p. 433
neighborhood distress, p. 438
census tracts, p. 438

Social Problems Online

The problems of cities are addressed at several sites on the Internet. The Center for Urban Studies at Wayne State University in Detroit (**www.cus.wayne.edu/**) has a Web page that features programs concerning a variety of topics such as evaluation research, community development, and intervention services for children, and information about demographics and mapping. Its Urban Safety Program highlights the problems of crime and safety. Statistics and technical reports, as well as tips on safety and crime prevention, are available for downloading.

A good source for housing information is CHAPA, the Citizens' Housing and Planning Association, of Boston. Its Web page, at **www.chapa.org**/, has selections on the latest federal and state housing news, updates on legislation, and research reports and handbooks. For a look at European policies on housing and homelessness, York University in Britain provides a Web page for its Centre for Housing Policy (**www.york.ac.uk/inst/chp/**). Newsletters from the Centre provide an overview of some of the ways in which British and U.S. policies differ.

Research Navigator

Follow the instructions on pages 26–27 of this text to access the features of Research Navigator. Once at the Web site, enter your Login Name and Password. Then, to use the Content Select database, use keywords such as "urbanization," "residential segregation," and "homelessness," and the search engine will supply relevant and recent scholarly and popular press publications. Use the *New York Times* search-by-subject archive to find recent news articles related to urban problems, and the Link Library to find relevant Web sites organized by the key terms associated with this chapter.

Go to Research Navigator and search for articles about urban poverty. You should find an article titled "Cities Tackle Day Labor Dilemma." What is the day labor dilemma, and how is it related to high rates of immigration to American cities? Why do you think "day labor markets" have flourished in so many U.S. cities?

14

POPULATION
and Immigration

Dominant Trends

- Although its growth is decelerating in most regions, the world's population continues to grow beyond the 6.6 billion it reached in 2007.

- At present growth rates, the world's population will double in about 45 years, with the bulk of the growth occurring in less-developed nations that already have difficulty providing jobs and social services to their young populations.

- As scientific warnings of accelerating global warming convince more national leaders to take action against greenhouse gasses, increased pressure is exerted on the United States, which uses more energy than any other nation.

- China and India are taking steps to reduce abortions and infanticides of female babies. An estimated 500,000 females are missing from China's annual birth statistics because of these practices.

- The United States receives an estimated 800,000 immigrants and refugees per year, along with an untold number of illegal immigrants. These trends are fueling rancorous debates about appropriate immigration policies and how to deal with the approximately 8 to 12 million illegal residents, many of whom are already hard at work in the nation's labor force.

In many parts of the United States, and in other nations as well, changes in population because of alterations in rates of births or deaths or patterns of immigration lead to major social problems. In the United States there is a low rate of natural population increase, but a high rate of immigration. Immigration thus accounts for much (but by no means all) of the overall growth of the U.S. population. It is often difficult to assimilate new immigrants into American society. The newcomers require education, health care, and other services that may strain already tight municipal budgets. Yet, were it not for immigration, nations like the United States would have growing labor shortages. Immigration also helps alleviate the effects of severe population pressure in other parts of the world. Indeed, in most nations the problem is not low rates of natural growth, but high rates of reproduction and population increase.

THE WORLD'S POPULATION

Although humanity has flourished for more than 2 million years, the rapid and problematic rise in population that concerns us in this chapter is a feature of the last 300 years. The average population growth rate before 1650 is thought to have been about two-thousandths of a percent per year, and the world's population in that year is estimated to have been 500 million. Thereafter, the rates and numbers leap: By 1900 the annual growth rate had reached fully half of 1 percent, and a billion people had been added to the world's population. Between 1900 and 1940 the rate rose to 1 percent; by 1960, to 2 percent. The numerical total reached 2.5 billion in 1950 and 6 billion in 1999. (See Figure 14–1 on page 448.) At this writing, population experts at the United Nations estimate the world's population at about 6,602,000,000, which means that in the five years since the population reached 6 billion, a number of people greater than the combined populations of Canada and the United States was added to the world total. If the world's population continues to grow at the current rate, it will double in a mere forty-five years. This doubling is not likely to happen, because there is already evidence of a deceleration in the rate of world population growth. If it did occur, however, it would create far worse pressures on the world's resources than are experienced today.

Figure 14–2 on page 448 presents what demographers believe will be the actual curve of world population growth between now and 2050. Due largely to continued development of poorer nations and increasing empowerment of women throughout the world, population growth rates are expected to continue to moderate so that the rate of growth of the world population will slow. Many people still

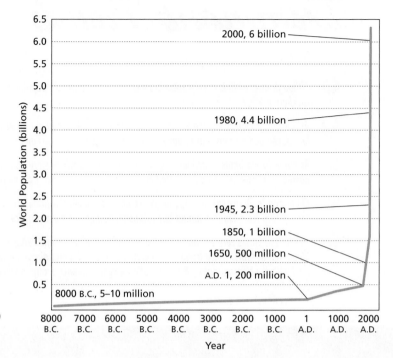

**Figure 14–1 World Population
Growth from 8000 B.C. to A.D. 2000**

Source: Data from Office of Technology
Assessment.

believe that the world is experiencing a continuing population explosion. This is not
the case. In fact, the peak population growth rate, 2.04 percent a year, occurred in the
late 1960s. Since then the growth rate has fallen to 1.35 percent, and it is expected to
fall further, to 1.1 percent, in the period from 2010 to 2015 and to 0.8 percent from
2025 to 2030. There will be a corresponding slowdown in the growth of demand for
food. Nevertheless, adding another 3 billion people to the world population by 2050
will create major problems of migration, environmental pressure, and resource management (Food and Agriculture Organization, 2005).

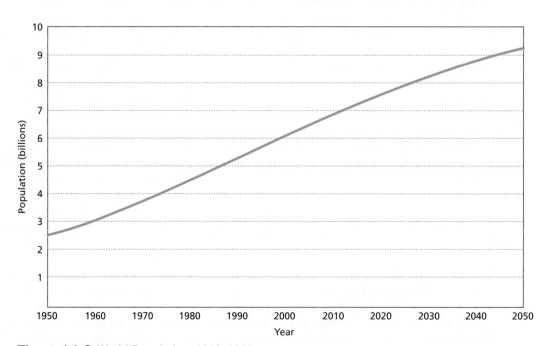

Figure 14–2 World Population, 1950–2050

Source: U.S. Census Bureau, 2005.

Measures of Population Growth

Before we discuss the significance of these figures, a few definitions are in order. A commonly used measure of population growth is the **crude birthrate,** or the number of births per 1,000 population. A crude birthrate of 20, for example, means that each year a given group of 1,000 people will produce 20 babies. This does not tell us what percentage of the population is of childbearing age or how many people can afford to raise children. It also does not tell us how long these 20 babies are likely to live—in particular, whether or not they will live long enough to produce children. Similarly, a crude death rate of 10 indicates only that among a group of 1,000 people, 10 will die every year. Again, this figure tells us nothing about the distribution of deaths—whether they occurred among old people or among those of childbearing age.

The differential between the (crude) birthrate and the death rate is called the **rate of population growth (natural increase)** and is usually expressed as a percentage. (Population growth is also affected by migration to and from the particular unit, a factor that can be ignored for the purposes of this discussion.) In our hypothetical 1,000-person group, in which 20 people were added by birth and 10 removed by death, the total population at the end of the year is 1,010—a growth rate of 1 percent.

Taken as a whole, the peoples of the world are not reproducing at a higher rate than in the past, but more people are living to the age of fertility and beyond. In effect, more babies are surviving to produce babies themselves. This change is traceable to several causes: enormous advances in sanitation, disease control, and public health; our increased ability to compensate for excessive cold, heat, and other dangers to life in our environment; and our greater power to prevent or quickly counteract the effects of famine, drought, flood, and similar natural disasters.

Most nations have population growth rates of 0.1 percent to 3.0 percent, with the older, more industrialized nations grouped at the low end and the less developed nations at the high end. (See Table 14–1.) If a nation's population growth rate is negative, more

TABLE 14–1	Changes in Population, Selected Countries, 1998 and 2002

Country	Rate of Natural Increase (Percentage)	
	1998	2002
China	1.0	0.7
South Korea	1.0	0.8
Japan	0.2	0.2
India	1.9	1.7
United States	0.6	0.6
United Kingdom	0.2	0.1
France	0.3	0.4
Nigeria	3.0	2.7
Argentina	1.1	1.5
Philippines	2.3	2.3
Peru	2.2	2.0
Kenya	2.0	2.0
Mexico	2.2	2.1
Sudan	2.1	2.1
Brazil	1.4	1.3

Source: Population Reference Bureau, World Population Data Sheet, 1998 and 2002.

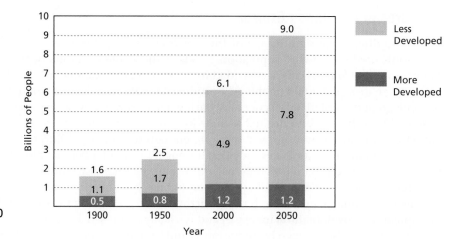

Figure 14–3 Population in More Developed and Less Developed Regions, 1900–2050

Source: Gelbard et al., 1999.

people are lost through death than are gained through birth and immigration, and the total population can be expected to decline over time. When a nation's population growth rate is 2 percent or more, as is true for many of the less developed nations, this is considered "explosive" population growth. If it were to continue unabated, such a rate would cause the population to double in thirty-five years or less. (A growth rate of 1 percent will cause a population to double in seventy years.) There is, however, evidence from some sub-Saharan nations of a decline in fertility because of greater availability of contraceptives and increased education of women (Ashford, 2001).

For the less developed nations, growth rates of 1 percent are unlikely to occur in the near future. Growth in the developing regions of the world is expected to taper off in coming decades, but in these populations the momentum of growth caused by large numbers of young people who will be attaining childbearing age is expected to result in large numerical increases. Figure 14–3 shows that populations in the developing nations may almost double, from about 4.19 billion today to 7.8 billion at midcentury. We will see shortly, however, that the experience of the industrialized nations indicates that fertility can be controlled even without large-scale use of contraception and that in many of the wealthier nations of the world fertility rates have actually declined to levels below that required to replace the population (Ashford, 2001).

Population Decline and World Migrations. Russia and many other European nations have been experiencing extremely slow or even negative rates of natural population increase. According to estimates by the United Nations, these nations have such low birthrates—below the average of 2.1 children per woman needed to maintain equilibrium—that they are experiencing population declines. Italy, once one of Europe's most fertile nations, is projected to lose almost a quarter of its current population by 2050. A consequence of the European "baby bust" is an increased flow of migrants into Europe from southern Europe, the Middle East, and Asia, where populations are growing rapidly. Similarly, as the natural growth rate of the U.S. population slows, demand for labor is increasingly filled by Latino migrants from countries with far higher birthrates. These are aspects of the global patterns of migration that we will consider in greater depth shortly (Kupchan, 2005). To understand why populations grow or decline, however, it helps to have an understanding of the process of demographic transition.

What are some of the main social forces that influence population growth?

The Demographic Transition

Lower death rates are closely associated with the spread of technological change and higher living standards, which constitute part of a process known as the **demographic transition.** In this process, a population shifts from an original equilibrium in which a high birthrate is more or less canceled out by a high death rate, through a stage in

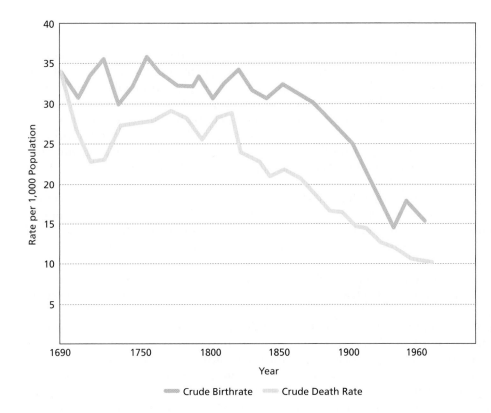

Figure 14–4 Crude Birth and Death Rates for Sweden, 1690–1960

Note: This chart exemplifies the classic demographic transition, in which death rates and birthrates eventually become more or less equal and the rate of population growth stabilizes. Many less developed nations have birth and death rates similar to those in the center of the chart, where crude death rates are declining and birthrates remain high—a formula for population explosion.

Source: Matras, 1973. Armand Colin Editeur, Paris.

which the birthrate remains high, but the death rate declines, to a final equilibrium in which the birth and death rates are lower, but the population is much larger. The first stage is characteristic of peasant and primitive populations before large-scale improvement in sanitation, health care, and the like. This is followed by a period of rapid population growth as traditional values about family size, together with the lack of birth control techniques, keep the birthrate high while technological advances produce a steady decrease in the death rate, especially of infants. In the final stage, which is characteristic of industrialized societies, values change, the birthrate declines, and rates of natural increase slow.

The demographic transition first occurred in northwestern Europe. During a period of about 100 years in the eighteenth and nineteenth centuries, death rates decreased by about 60 percent while birthrates remained at their traditional high levels. Then, toward the end of the nineteenth century, fertility began a long-term decline. Figure 14–4 illustrates this process in the case of Sweden.

Wherever industrial technology has taken hold on a local level, the third stage of the demographic transition has followed—from northwestern Europe to North America, Australia, and New Zealand and later through the rest of Europe. Today the populations of Japan, Singapore, Taiwan, Hong Kong, and two or three other such areas have reached the final phase, and they have tended to reach it much more quickly (in about thirty years) than the northern European nations did.

On the other hand, large areas of Asia, Africa, and Latin America remain in the middle phase, with sustained high birthrates and reduced death rates. In this century, and very dramatically since World War II, the amazingly effective adoption of Western methods in medicine and public health on a massive scale, usually involving international aid programs, has resulted in a rapid decline in mortality. Within a span of about twenty-five years, death rates fell from approximately 40 per 1,000 to 20 or less. But fertility remains high, often over 40 per 1,000, and the growth rate reaches 3 percent in some places. Adults live longer, and more of the young survive to have children; there are no new frontier lands to draw off excess population. In these societies, population growth often outstrips economic and social development, producing poverty and social unrest.

Several nations that are still in the middle phase of the demographic transition border the United States to the south. Among them are the countries of the Caribbean and Central America: Mexico, Haiti, the Dominican Republic, and Puerto Rico. Their inhabitants are subject both to the stresses of overpopulation and to the influence of American popular culture through television and mass consumer markets. These countries are poor, and many are ruled by violent and repressive regimes—both factors that produce migration to the United States. Currently the United States admits about 800,000 immigrants annually, an increase from about 600,000 in the late 1980s and a direct result of the 1986 Immigration Reform and Control Act, which established higher immigration quotas. (The implications of this increase are discussed later in the chapter.) The United States remains a land of opportunity for immigrants because of its slow rate of population growth. Here, except for the baby boom during and after World War II, births have outpaced deaths only to a modest degree.

The birthrate in the industrialized nations had begun to drop before the institution of organized family planning programs. The organized programs have certainly accelerated the process, however, especially in the United States: They have made information and contraceptives more widely available, led to the repeal of laws against the use of contraceptives, and influenced opinion in favor of birth control. Thus, in contrast to the 1800 figure of about 55, the crude birthrate in the United States stood at 14.1 in 2005. In the 1970s the total fertility rate (the average number of children born per woman throughout the childbearing years) fell below 2.1, the rate required to maintain the population at the same level. In 1800 the total fertility rate was 7.0, an extremely high rate that reflected the demand for farm labor and the high value placed on having many children (Preston, 1987; U.S. Census Bureau, 2005).

In his thorough analysis of low population growth rates in the non-European industrialized nations (Canada, United States, Japan, Australia, and New Zealand), demographer Samuel Preston (1987, 2005) concludes that "the recent fall in fertility is related to declining proportions married, increased use of contraception and abortion, and a reduction in family size desires" (1987, p. 44). Of these factors, Preston identifies delay or indefinite postponement of marriage as the most important. He finds, for example, that fertility decreased in Japan well before the widespread use of contraception and well before the large-scale entry of women into the labor market. The critical factor was postponement of marriage—Japanese parents were requiring their grown children to delay marriage until they had accumulated the resources to support a child or two.

What does the women's rights movement have to do with changes in fertility rates throughout the world?

Rising Expectations

In the less developed countries (LDCs) themselves, there has been considerable improvement in the living standards of a portion of the population. This improvement has led to a state of mind known as *rising expectations,* the belief that if conditions have already begun to improve, the trend will continue and a larger portion of the population should be able to share in its benefits.

This process began in the late 1950s and early 1960s, when many LDCs, particularly in sub-Saharan Africa and Southeast Asia, gained independence from the former colonial powers (Geertz, 2005). Turning their attention to efforts to improve the lives of their generally isolated, rural populations, governments embarked on campaigns for favorable terms of trade and direct aid from the developed nations. Ever greater sums were invested in education, health care, transportation, and communication. These investments ultimately resulted in changing expectations among the populations of the LDCs as newly educated and healthier multitudes were exposed to the media and all the information about culture and standards of living that they convey (Martine, 1996).

In many rural parts of the world, a single communal television set contributes to the villagers' rising expectations for material well-being.

It is important to distinguish between the **standard of living** of a population, which is what people want or expect in the way of material well-being, and the **level of living,** which is what people actually obtain. In many less developed countries and nations of the former Soviet bloc, there is a wide gap between the two, and this produces frustration and political instability. These problems make economic and social development in the poor regions of the world even more problematic.

Literacy rates are a good indicator of the likelihood that poor and powerless populations may be rapidly gaining a new perspective on their situation. Illiteracy has been decreasing steadily, from an estimated 32.5 percent of the total world population in 1970 to 20.3 percent in 2000 (United Nations Development Programme, 2002). These figures, of course, do not show the tremendous disparities in literacy that persist. For example, Cuba enjoys a 96 percent literacy rate and Chile's literacy rate is 94.5 percent, whereas the figure for Egypt is 49.2 percent, for India 53.4 percent, and for Pakistan 36.2 percent.

More recent literacy figures are encouraging, especially because they show that although women make up two-thirds of the world's illiterate adult population, in all regions they are gaining access to education and literacy at faster rates than are men. Worldwide, the proportion of illiterate women age 15 and over decreased from 28.5 percent to 25.8 percent. This trend is most evident in Africa. The percentage of illiterate African women fell by 6.4 percentage points, to 49.2 percent, so that for the first time, the majority of women in Africa are literate. Although these figures clearly show that the world's population is increasingly literate, they also show that much improvement is needed, as one adult in five remains illiterate. The World Education Forum held in Dakar in April 2000 set a goal of halving adult illiteracy by 2015, but meeting that goal will require more resources than are currently available. Unless extraordinary efforts are made, the proportion of illiterate adults will have decreased by only another five percentage points by that date (UNESCO, 2002).

Energy Consumption and Quality of Life. While literacy and the wide-ranging awareness that it fosters have increased, mushrooming populations have tended to more than absorb the sums devoted to their well-being, creating a significant lag in the fulfillment of their rising expectations. Per capita energy consumption is a good indication of the quality of life of a population, and by this measure stark disparities remain: The United States, by far the world's largest consumer of energy, uses about 343 million Btu's of energy per person per year, compared to France (186), Mexico (63), the United Kingdom (167), Colombia (28), and India (15) (*Statistical Abstract,* 2007). The extremely high U.S. rate reflects the nature of American industry, transportation, and housing. The typical middle-class, generally suburban American lifestyle presumes considerable use of gasoline as well as the consumption of extremely large quantities of paper, steel, synthetic chemicals, aluminum, and so forth, all of which require high levels of energy for their production.

The fact is that the gaps in living standards between the have and have-not societies have actually widened. In such a situation, rising expectations are associated with a wide spectrum of social problems, including political instability and backwardness, neocolonialism, and terrorism, as well as renewed international migrations by the poor. This is especially true in the heavily indebted nations of Asia, Africa, and Latin America.

Food and Hunger

Almost three-quarters of a billion people are hungry in a world where there is plenty to eat. Every 3.6 seconds someone somewhere dies of hunger; children account for 75 percent of these deaths (*Population Today,* 2000). The irony of this situation is that although there may not be much food in their villages or enough food to go around in a particular region, food is actually plentiful in the world today. The fundamental problem is the maldistribution of available food (World Bank, 2007). In Western Europe and North America, the average person's diet supplies about 3,500 calories a day. In much of Africa south of the Sahara and in South Asia, average caloric intake is less than two-thirds of this total. (See Figure 14–5.) An adult working at heavy labor, as

Figure 14–5 Undernourishment, Selected Nations

Source: Food and Agricultural Organization, 2002.

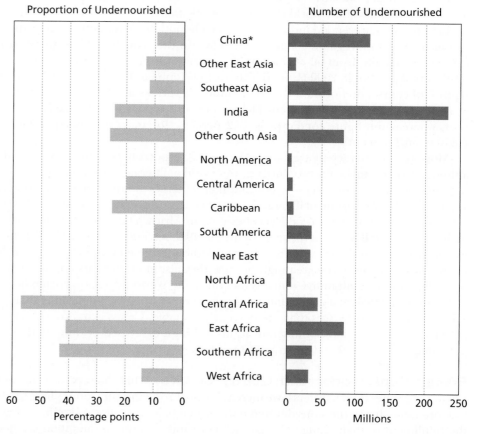

*Including Taiwan

many agricultural workers in developing nations do, needs over 3,500 calories a day, but this total is relatively rare in those nations. Thirty-five countries, including almost half the nations of Africa, have food supplies that afford their populations an average of less than 2,200 calories a day. According to estimates by the Food and Agriculture Organization (2002), an affiliate of the United Nations, about 800 million people, almost 15 percent of the world population, eat less than 2,000 calories a day. This hungry population is chronically undernourished and experiences the lowered resistance to diseases that comes with semistarvation.

Starvation in the Midst of Plenty. Amartya Sen, 1998 Nobel prizewinner in economics, has conducted research that contributes to saving millions of lives in the impoverished regions of the world. Sen's research on the causes of famines in the world shows that nations that neglect the poor often do so in the midst of economic good times. Societies that attend to the poorest of the poor can save their lives, promote their longevity, and increase their opportunities through education and productive work. Societies that neglect the poor, on the other hand, may inadvertently allow millions to die of famine—even in the middle of an economic boom, as occurred during the great famine in Bengal, India, in 1943, the subject of Sen's most famous case study. Sen demonstrated that the Bengal famine was caused by an urban economic boom that raised food prices, thereby causing millions of rural workers to starve to death when their wages did not keep up. And why didn't the government react by dispensing emergency food relief? Sen's answer was enlightening. Because colonial India was not a democracy, he said, the British rulers had little interest in listening to the poor, even in the midst of famine. This political observation gave rise to what might be called Sen's Law: Shortfalls in food supply do not cause widespread deaths in a democracy because vote-seeking politicians will undertake relief efforts; but even modest food shortfalls can create deadly famines in authoritarian societies.

One of the paradoxes of world hunger is that food supplies have been increasing over the past twenty years while the cost of food has been decreasing. There are adequate supplies of food at relatively low prices, but the poorest segments of many populations in the developing nations cannot afford it. Their wages have fallen too low to enable them to buy available food, or at least the combinations of foods that would

Amartya Sen, a scholar from India whose work has produced a new understanding of the catastrophes that plague people, won a Nobel Prize in economics in 1998.

How do you think current patterns of population growth are likely to influence world hunger in coming decades?

prevent malnutrition and related illnesses (Conway, 1997). Changes in the technologies of food production, some of which are extremely controversial (see Chapter 15), have been increasing world food production and promise to do so well into the future. As populations in the poorest nations continue to grow rapidly, it becomes especially difficult for these nations to feed their poor children, but often political violence, civil strife, and corruption, which divert food aid, are more responsible for malnutrition than absolute shortages.

POPULATION CONTROL

Efforts to control population growth can take any of three basic approaches: (1) Reduce the rate of growth of the population, (2) control fertility to achieve a zero rate of population growth, or (3) achieve a negative rate of growth and thus reduce the size of the population. Obviously, all three of these approaches involve reduction of the birthrate. However, even when it is agreed that births should be limited, there is much less agreement on how fast and to what extent limits should be imposed—indeed, on whether or not they should be imposed at all (i.e., whether limits on family size should be voluntary or involuntary). Efforts to limit births raise a number of moral and ethical questions, but the costs of not making such efforts could be catastrophic.

Family Planning

Voluntary efforts to limit births customarily take the form of family planning. Essentially, a family planning program allows couples to have the number of children they want. Although this policy usually entails helping couples limit childbearing, it can also involve helping couples who want children and have been unable to have them. The stress is usually placed on the good of the family—especially the health of the mother and children and the ability to provide education and other desired advantages.

In the United States, the family planning movement owes much to the energy and dedication of a nurse named Margaret Sanger, who hoped to free women from the burdens of unlimited childbearing. In 1916 she opened the nation's first birth control clinic (and was jailed for doing so). Later court decisions permitted physicians to prescribe birth control for health reasons; these were the first in a series of decisions that permitted the sale and advertisement of contraceptive materials and the dissemination of information about birth control. By 1965, some 85 percent of married women in the United States had used some method of birth control (Ehrlich, Ehrlich, & Holdmen, 1977). By 2004, 98 percent of women who had ever been sexually active used at least one contraceptive method (Mosher et al., 2004).

Zero Population Growth (ZPG)

In 1968, in response to widespread concern about population growth, an organization known as Zero Population Growth (ZPG) was founded. Its goal was to promote an end to population growth as soon as possible through lowered birthrates, both in the United States and in other nations. It would achieve this goal by educating the public about the dangers of uncontrolled population growth and by taking political action to encourage policies that reduce growth rates.

The organization has been active in promoting access to birth control and legalized abortion, and it has had a definite effect on attitudes toward family size and population control. However, ZPG has encountered some opposition on social and economic grounds. It is argued, for example, that halting population growth would greatly change the age composition of the population, creating a larger proportion of older people and thereby adding to the problems of an already overburdened society. Moreover, a nongrowing population implies a nongrowing economy, and it is often assumed that a continually growing economy is necessary for the maintenance of a high standard of living.

It should be noted that family planning and population control are not synonymous. Family planning has historically dealt with the needs of individuals and families, not those of societies. Kingsley Davis (1971) has pointed out some fundamental weaknesses of the family planning approach as a means of large-scale population control. Chief among them is its basic assumption that the number of children couples want is the number they should have. In a poor country with a growth rate of 3 percent per year, a family of five or six children, which is probably desired by most couples, will be anything but desirable for the economic health of the country—or for the family's own chances of economic betterment. In addition, the strongly medical emphasis of the usual family planning program can limit its large-scale effectiveness, particularly in developing countries, where doctors and nurses are usually scarce (Smil, 1997).

Population Control in LDCs

In less developed countries, efforts at population control have, in a few rare but instructive cases, used compulsory methods of birth control. One such method is sterilization of parents who have had a specified number of children. India adopted such a plan in 1976, with financial incentives to encourage volunteers and, in some states, fines and other penalties for births after the third child. In one year more than 8 million sterilizations were performed. As might be expected, this program met with great resistance. Although no one disputed the need to curb the rate of population growth, the Indian government was severely criticized for what was considered a compulsory rather than a strictly voluntary policy; in fact, the policy contributed to the defeat of the government of Indira Gandhi.

China's population program differs in some important ways from that of any other country. China, whose population is now 1.3 billion, has adopted a policy of one child per family for urban dwellers; the goal is a 40 percent reduction in population size by 2050. Couples are strongly urged not to have more than one child unless both parents were only children themselves, and birth control information and materials are readily available. At the same time, the bearing and rearing of children are supported through such policies as paid maternity leave, time off for breast-feeding, free nursery care, and all needed medical attention (Li, 1995).

This far-reaching policy has already slowed China's population growth significantly, but not without enormous social consequences. Political unrest has increased in the cities, where the policy is far more easily implemented than in the countryside. Far

Many Asian nations have entered the low-growth phase of the demographic transition. In China, however, strict measures designed to discourage couples from having more than one child are highly controversial.

worse, recent studies of the policy's effects indicate that couples are seeking ways to determine the gender of unborn infants so that they can abort female fetuses. The traditional culture of China favors boys over girls to such a degree that many couples believe they must have a male child at all costs. Although no one knows exactly how many female infants are aborted or killed, and some Chinese authorities dispute Western analyses of the situation, the fact remains that the excess of recorded live male births over female births is far greater in China than in any other society. This suggests that various forms of abortion, infanticide, and secret adoptions are occurring. Demographers who have studied the situation closely believe that about half of the estimated 500,000 females missing from the annual birth statistics may have been secretly adopted by foreigners through illicit adoption agencies, but no one knows the fate of the others. Clearly, these are serious, even if unintended, consequences of China's drastic population reduction policy (Ashford, 2001; Johannson & Nygren, 1991).

Nothing as drastic as China's population control policy has ever been attempted before (except in cases of war or genocide), and only a nation with a very authoritarian and highly controlled population can successfully implement such a policy. Thus, for the time being, voluntary birth control seems to be a more realistic—and more desirable—approach in LDCs. Indeed, family planning programs are the primary form of population control in most of these countries, sometimes supplemented by other social and economic policies. The main thrust of these programs is the provision of birth control information along with educational programs that demonstrate the economic benefits of smaller families. Many programs are directed toward women who have already borne three or more children.

Fertility control in Brazil stands in marked contrast to China's experience (Martine, 1996). As shown in Table 14–2, Brazil's population growth, as measured by the fertility rate, was extremely high in the 1960s but has fallen precipitously in recent years and is now similar to the slower growth rates of the European industrial nations. This decrease in fertility is not solely a consequence of economic development and greater affluence. Northeast Brazil is by far the poorest region of the nation, yet even here there have been dramatic decreases. Experts on the demography of Brazil concur that there is no single explanation for these momentous changes.

Brazil has no government fertility control policy like that of China, nor does it have a national policy for making contraception widely available. Studies show that the contraceptive choices made by people in Brazil are similar to those made by people in the United States, but with some important exceptions. Women bear most of the responsibility for contraception and tend to rely on birth control pills or, once they have had the desired number of children, on sterilization. An extremely small proportion of couples

TABLE 14–2	Total Fertility Rate, Brazil and Northeast Region of Brazil, 1960–1995	
Years	Brazil	Northeast
1960–65	6.00	7.44
1965–70	5.75	7.11
1970–75	4.97	6.77
1975–80	4.17	5.97
1980–85	3.37	4.76
1985–90	2.82	3.97
1990–95	2.48	3.50

Source: Martine, 1996.

report that they rely on condoms. Abortion is not legal, except in cases of rape or risk to the mother's life, and is not reported in official statistics, but research in urban areas has found high rates of illegal abortions. Most important, however, is the desire to limit births. Where does this desire originate? In Brazil, as elsewhere, people's aspirations for a lifestyle in which they can afford consumer goods and raise fewer children with a decent level of education, health care, and material comfort seem to be a major factor. Contributing to these aspirations are the increased education of women and the influence of the mass media, especially television (Martine, 1996).

In the 1960s and 1970s it appeared that nations like Brazil were doomed to experience a population explosion, leading to drastic overpopulation. These recent changes and the research that explains their causes highlight some of the ways in which population growth may be controlled in other areas of the world, without the kinds of drastic and authoritarian measures that have been undertaken in China.

THE U.S. POPULATION

The U.S. population is growing at a rate of about 1 percent per year, far slower than those of the less developed nations, but faster than those of most other highly developed nations. The most important source of U.S. population growth is natural increase (just over 60%), owing to more births than deaths, and growth owing to net migration (about 40%), because more people are immigrating to the United States than leaving it. Figure 14–6 below and Table 14–3 on page 460 present estimates of likely population growth at current rates of natural increase and net migration. By 2050 the populations of most other developed nations are likely to be slowly decreasing while that of the United States continues to increase, perhaps to as many as 420 million residents. This estimate assumes that high rates of immigration to the United States will continue over the next two or three decades and that these immigrant populations will have higher birthrates than older, native-born populations (Kent & Mather, 2002).

Steady population growth means that people are continuing to settle in new communities to raise their families, and many migrate in search of new opportunities. Recent decades have seen increased migration to the Sunbelt and western states. In 1950, for example, 26 percent of the population lived in the Northeast and 13 percent lived in the West. By 2000 these percentages had shifted to 19 and 22.5 percent, respectively. Figure 14–7 on page 460 shows that many of the fastest-growing states—that is, those with the highest rates of net migration—are located in the Southwest and West. Although the map shows that California ranks high among states with a high net migration, in fact California is no longer growing at the boom rates it experienced in the 1960s and 1970s; however, Nevada has taken up much of the slack. Note that the

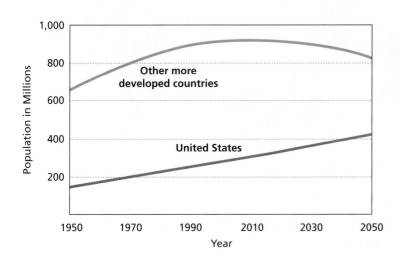

Figure 14–6 Population Growth in the United States and Other More Developed Countries, 1950–2050

Note: Other more developed countries include all European countries, Australia, Canada, Japan, and New Zealand.

Source: Kent & Mather, 2002. Copyright © 2002. Reprinted by permission of The Population Reference Bureau.

TABLE 14–3	Population of the United States and Selected More Developed Countries, 2002 and 2050 (Projected)

	Population (millions)		
	2002	2050	Percent change
United States	287.7	420.1	46.0
Russia	145.0	118.2	–18.5
Japan	127.1	99.9	–21.4
Germany	82.4	73.6	–10.7
France	59.9	61.0	1.8
United Kingdom	59.9	64.0	6.8
Italy	57.9	50.4	–13.0
Ukraine	48.4	37.7	–22.0
Spain	40.2	35.6	–11.4
Poland	38.6	33.8	–12.4
Canada	31.9	41.4	29.8
Australia	19.5	24.3	24.6

Source: Kent & Mather, 2002. Copyright © 2002. Reprinted by permission of The Population Reference Bureau.

Pacific Northwest, with its rapidly growing technology industries, is experiencing quite rapid growth even though it is not in the Sunbelt.

Another significant change in the U.S. population in recent years is the increase in age and income disparities between old and new ethnic groups. The median incomes of Russian, Polish, and Italian Americans are among the highest in the nation, whereas those of Spanish-speaking groups, especially Puerto Ricans, are the lowest. Conversely,

Figure 14–7 Net International and Interstate Migration, by State: 2000–2001

Source: U.S. Census Bureau, 2002.

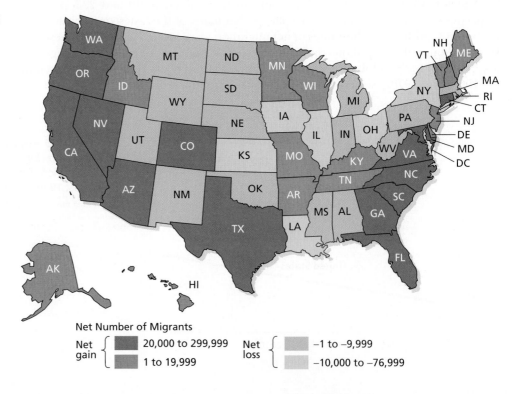

Net Number of Migrants

Net gain: 20,000 to 299,999 / 1 to 19,999

Net loss: –1 to –9,999 / –10,000 to –76,999

the proportion of people under 18 years of age is lowest among the old ethnic groups, whereas the Spanish-speaking groups include the highest proportion. This means that the fastest growing ethnic minorities in the United States are also among the poorest segments of the population.

Finally, slow growth has been a factor in the dramatic persistence of immigration to the United States, and differences in fertility between old and new ethnic groups have a significant impact on the composition of the population. Immigration also raises a number of complex policy issues, as will become clear later in the chapter.

IMMIGRATION AND ITS CONSEQUENCES

Throughout the world, people in poor nations dream of moving to richer ones. Most often they do not wish to uproot themselves entirely but hope to be temporary sojourners, working at better-paying jobs. If they can save and send money home, they may some day be able to return to a better life in their homeland.

Immigration to the United States has reached levels unmatched since early in the twentieth century. But the movement of people from poor to richer lands is occurring elsewhere as well. There has been an influx of people into Germany and France from poorer areas to the south, especially Turkey and northern Africa. In the Middle East there has been a great movement of temporary workers from Egypt to the richer and underpopulated nations of Saudi Arabia and Kuwait. Before the 1991 war in that region, many of the immigrant workers were Palestinians or Yemenites. In Japan there are Korean immigrants, and in Australia there are immigrants from many Asian nations. But the United States leads the world in total number of immigrants.

In fact, it is often said that the United States is a nation of immigrants. Since the earliest days of European settlement, North America has attracted people from all over the world. Some, like the black slaves from Africa, were brought against their will. Many other groups came in search of new opportunities and freedom from oppression. Over two centuries the tides of immigration brought people of different races, different religions, different cultures, and different political views to these shores. This diversity of peoples has become one of the most important aspects of American culture. Tolerance of differences, struggles against racial oppression, arguments about the assimilation of immigrants, the variety of diet and dress and music—all can be traced to the unique contributions of people of many different national origins and cultures.

But immigration has also contributed to some of the problems that plague American society. Beginning with the exclusion of Native Americans from their original lands, immigration has led to ethnic and racial conflict; competition among nationality groups for a piece of the pie; debates about immigration policy, illegal immigration, and the exploitation of illegal aliens; and the stresses and costs associated with educating and caring for newcomers. These and other issues can become severe social problems when they are not addressed in a timely fashion. To better understand why this is so, we will begin with a summary of the major periods of immigration to the United States.

Immigration to the United States: A Brief History

The Early Colonial Period (to 1790). During the colonial period, the major population groups in North America other than Native Americans had come from Great Britain and accounted for 77 percent of the total population. African and native-born slaves of African origin accounted for 19 percent, German immigrants for 4 percent, Irish immigrants for 3 percent, and Dutch immigrants for 2 percent (Bogue, 1985; Portes, 2001). There were many other immigrant groups in the population, but their numbers were much smaller.

Old Northwest European Migration (1820–1885). Large-scale immigration to the new nation known as the United States began again in 1820 and was dominated by people from England and other areas of northwestern Europe until about 1885. In this wave of immigrants, the largest groups came from northern and Western Europe, especially Germany, Ireland, and England. The proportion of immigrants from Ireland reached high levels in the 1840s and 1850s as a result of severe famine and economic catastrophe in Ireland. German immigration reached a peak in the years after 1848, when popular revolutions in Germany failed and many Germans sought asylum or greater political freedom in the United States.

The most significant nonwhite immigrant group during this period was the Chinese, many of whom settled on the West Coast or in the Rocky Mountain states, along with a smaller number of Japanese. Many of the Chinese immigrants were brought in by labor contractors who were seeking low-wage workers for the construction of railroads.

The Intermediate Migration from Southern and Eastern Europe (1885–1940). Because of the breakup of the Austro-Hungarian and Ottoman empires and the resulting political upheavals, many thousands of people from southern and eastern Europe found their way to the United States. The major immigrant groups during this period were Italians, Poles, Hungarians, Serbians, Croatians, Greeks, and Jews from all of these nations and from Russia. During this period, waves of nativist feeling (anti-immigrant or antiforeigner sentiment) swept across sections of the United States. Among other things, nativism gave rise to the oriental exclusion movement, which flourished between 1882 and 1907 and resulted in sporadic violence against Chinese and Japanese Americans and the passage of legislation in some states that stopped further immigration of Asians.

At the same time, large numbers of Mexican immigrants began streaming into the Southwest, the West, and portions of the Midwest. These immigrants often joined relatives and friends in parts of California and the Southwest, where Mexicans had been living long before these regions became part of the United States.

During this period Congress passed the Immigration Act of 1921, which for the first time in American history established quotas and strict controls over the admission of new immigrants, imposing an overall quota of 150,000 per year. Before 1921 there had been no specific limits on immigration to the United States, and well over 20 million immigrants had arrived since the early nineteenth century.

The Post–World War II Refugee Period (to 1968). By the end of World War II, hundreds of thousands of Europeans had lost their homes and property, and many were refugees. Some, like Jews and Roman Catholic activists, were fleeing religious persecution. In 1945 Congress agreed to admit 185,000 immigrants per year, many of whom would be European refugees.

The New Immigration (1968–Present). In 1968 Congress again voted to increase immigration quotas, establishing totals of 170,000 per year from the Eastern Hemisphere and 120,000 from the Western Hemisphere. Priority would be given to immigrants who were political or religious refugees or who had close relatives living in the United States. (This is known as the principle of family unification.) In 1980 Congress increased the overall quota to 280,000 per year, not including additional refugees and special categories that might be designated in the future (e.g., the *marielitos,* former political prisoners from Cuba). The increases in immigration quotas in recent decades have given rise to a new pattern of immigration to the United States, with the largest flows of people coming from Asia and Latin America (Zolberg, 2006).

Once Again a Nation of Immigrants. In the past few years the United States has been turning once again into a nation of immigrants. According to Aristide Zolberg (2003), "In 1970 less than 5 percent of the U.S. population was foreign-born, the lowest proportion since records began to be kept in 1850. But by the turn of the millennium they made up 11 percent of the population—their number had nearly tripled, from 9.6 million to 30 million, and showed no sign of abating" (p. 1).

The upper photo, taken about 1900, shows immigrants waiting to leave Ellis Island after many hours of screening and processing. In an effort to modernize its procedures, the U.S. Citizenship and Immigration Service is testing a new system in which processing takes place before arrival in the United States, and each new immigrant is issued a pass that resembles a credit card.

Recent Trends in Immigration to the United States

The U.S. Citizenship and Immigration Service (USCIS) estimates that about 30 million people come across the borders of the United States each year. Most of these are temporary visitors. However, between 2000 and 2004 about 4.6 million immigrants came to live and work in the United States, continuing a tradition of immigration and eventual citizenship that goes back to the nation's founding. But because of the fear of

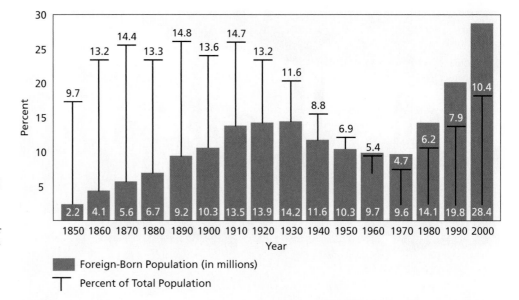

Figure 14–8 Foreign-Born Population and Percent of Total Population for the United States: 1850–2000

(For 1850–1990, resident population. For 2000, civilian noninstitutional population plus Armed Forces living off post or with their families on post.)

Source: U.S. Census Bureau.

terrorism, the nation's relatively open borders and lack of restrictions on internal migration have become severe problems for the authorities who must try to keep track of those who are temporary visitors and those who intend to become permanent residents. We return to this subject in the Social Policy section of the chapter.

Rates of immigration to the United States declined during much of the twentieth century after the period of massive immigration in the late 1800s (see Figure 14–8). By 2000, however, liberalized immigration laws once again made the United States, along with Canada and Australia, among the world's leading immigrant-receiving nations. Today slightly over 10 percent of the U.S. population is foreign born, but since the population is far larger than it was at the peak of European immigration at the turn of the twentieth century, there are far more foreign-born residents than ever before. Of these, the largest share came from the Americas (Mexico, Canada, the Caribbean, and Latin America). Asia—especially the Philippines, Korea, and China—contributed the next largest share, and Europe, which accounted for the bulk of earlier immigration to the United States, was a distant third (U.S. Department of Homeland Security, 2004).

Neither the increase in immigration nor the specific composition of the immigrant population is a social problem in itself. But there are groups in American society that oppose immigration and are hostile toward immigrants, and the resulting conflicts and tensions can be a problem for immigrants and for the regions or cities that receive them. Because new immigrants tend to settle near other immigrants, these tensions can run especially high in regions with large immigrant populations. Also, not all immigrants enter legally. The presence of illegal aliens, or undocumented immigrants, is one of the most severe social problems associated with immigration. In the remainder of this section, therefore, we consider the social problems caused by the uneven distribution of immigrants in the United States and the special problems of undocumented immigrants. (See the Social Problems: A Global View box on pages 466–467.)

In what ways does immigration to the United States today differ from immigration in the late nineteenth century?

Urban Concentration of Immigrants

The vast majority of the immigrants who arrive in the United States tend to remain in only a few cities and regions. New York, Los Angeles, Miami, Chicago, and their metropolitan regions are the preferred destinations of almost half of the nation's immigrants. Mexicans tend to congregate in the Southwest and Vietnamese in Texas, but the major urban centers of the West and East Coasts absorb far more than their proportional share of new immigrants.

The concentration of new immigrants in a few metropolitan regions greatly adds to the problems of both immigrants and nonimmigrants in those areas. This concentration, especially of Spanish-speaking and Chinese-speaking newcomers, leads to the formation of large non-English-speaking enclaves, where education becomes a problem and the economic and social assimilation of the newcomers may create difficulties for native-born citizens. Increasingly frequent attacks against immigrants and members of minority groups and the rise of nativist and anti-immigrant feelings in many parts of the United States are another consequence of the concentration of immigrants in certain localities (Brimelow, 1995).

The phenomenon of **chain migration,** the primary cause of this urban concentration, refers to the tendency of immigrants to migrate to areas where they have kin and others from their home communities. Although there may be opportunities for them in nearby cities and towns, they often remain in the place of original settlement because of the presence of people who share their culture and language and can help them adjust to their new social environment. There are wide differences in sources of immigrants to various regions of the United States. New Jersey, for example, receives its highest numbers of immigrants from Italy and Cuba, whereas California receives most of its immigrants from Mexico and the Philippines.

The uneven distribution of immigrants greatly adds to the costs of education and health care in the cities in which they become concentrated. Because many immigrants arrive without any form of health insurance and do not speak English well enough to qualify for employment, schools and adult education programs are taxed to the maximum. These expenses of the cities are not usually compensated for by the federal government, even though the entry of immigrants is regulated by federal legislation.

A problem that affects the immigrants in these urban centers is the intense competition and, at times, direct hostility they encounter from nonimmigrants or immigrants who have lived there for long periods. For example, Koreans tend to establish businesses (especially wig stores, fruit and vegetable stores, and other retail businesses) in segregated minority communities, where costs are lower. They thus become a new ethnic and racial group in those communities. Often they encounter anger and hostility from residents who believe the Koreans are not sensitive to their needs and their local culture (Kim, 2003). This is a theme explored by the African American filmmaker Spike Lee in his movie *Do the Right Thing.* Elsewhere in the nation—along the Gulf Coast of Texas, where Vietnamese shrimp fishermen have come into conflict with native-born fishermen, or in the Southwest, where Mexican immigrants are often discriminated against by earlier settlers—the difficulties of life as a stranger in a strange land are amplified by prejudice and violence.

In response to the hostility they often encounter, children and adolescents in the new groups often form defensive gangs. Those who do not wish to join gangs may be considered deviant and isolated by their peers. But some immigrant groups, notably the Chinese and Koreans, attempt to shelter their children from the problems of urban street life by imposing a strict set of values and high expectations for achievement in school (Caplan, Whitmore, & Choy, 1989). Children of Asian immigrants make rapid strides in American schools, often achieving the highest honors in their high schools and on standardized achievement tests. Indeed, the school achievement of Asian Americans is now so high that many of the brightest Asian students have come to believe they are subject to admission quotas in private universities, an experience exactly analogous to that of high-achieving children of Jewish immigrants two generations ago (Kim, 2003).

Undocumented Immigrants

No one knows with great accuracy how many undocumented immigrants actually arrive. Every year the USCIS locates more than 1.2 million illegal immigrants, many of whom are deported. The USCIS estimates that there are over 11 million illegal immigrants now residing in the United States. By far the largest percentage are

Social Problems: A Global View

THE WORLDWIDE REFUGEE PROBLEM

Millions of people throughout the world find themselves suddenly without homes. In 2005, for example, a severe earthquake in Kashmir made hundreds of thousands of people homeless, and many became refugees in nearby India or Pakistan. There are also millions of **political refugees**, especially people who are fleeing wars, ethnic cleansing, and predatory gangs controlled by local warlords. (See the accompanying map and tables.) The United Nations High Commission for Refugees is the agency most directly responsible for addressing the needs of some 20 million refugees around the world. The term *refugee* is defined as "a person who is outside his/her country of nationality or habitual residence; has a well-founded fear of persecution because of his/her race, religion, nationality, membership in a particular social group or political opinion; and is unable or unwilling to avail himself/herself of the protection of that country, or to return there, for fear of persecution." The United Nations Commission also recognizes the international scope of refugee crises and the need for international cooperation in tackling the problem.

Wars and warlordism have the greatest influence in creating refugee populations. War in Afghanistan, from the conflict initiated by the former Soviet Union in the 1980s to the contemporary U.S.-led war against terrorists, has created over 2 million political refugees in neighboring Iran and Pakistan. The ethnic hostilities in the former Yugoslavia (Bosnia, Croatia, Kosovo) have produced over 1 million refugees, as have the ethnic violence and civil wars in Chechnya and the Caucasus Mountains.

Canada and the United States are among the world's most welcoming nations for refugees. Canada accepts a far larger number of refugees in proportion to its population, but that nation has historically needed to "import" people to augment its labor force. In the United States, the largest refugee populations are usually those whose countries of origin have experienced wars in which the United States has played a part, such as Vietnam, Cambodia, and Iraq, or whose native country is located close to the United States, as in the case of Haiti.

Iraq: Four Million Refugees, and Counting

International refugee agencies are experiencing a far greater refugee crisis in Iraq than they anticipated in 2003, at the beginning of the U.S.-led invasion and largely unplanned occupation of that country. The violence among sectarian factions and by insurgents fighting the U.S. presence there has produced more than 4 million refugees, according to estimates by the United Nations High Commission for Refugees (2007). The accompanying chart and tables show that the vast majority of displaced Iraqis are in camps or on the streets of other Iraqi cities to which they have fled to escape violence and "ethnic cleansing." Others are in camps and crowded refugee neighborhoods of nearby nations, especially Syria, Jordan, Egypt, and Iran. Less than 1 percent have reached nations outside the Middle East. Of these, far more have found asylum in Germany and Sweden than in the United States.

Although many thousands of Iraqis have applied for political asylum in the United States, thousands of others have been kidnapped and killed in the most brutal fashion simply because they have worked for the United States and its interests in Iraq—as translators, as assistants of various kinds, and in many other capacities. It is especially ironic that before the invasion of 2003, while Saddam Hussein was still in power,

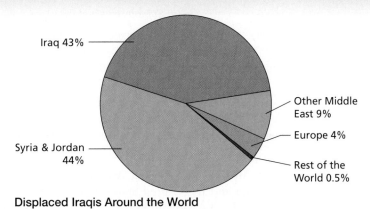

Displaced Iraqis Around the World

Source: United Nations High Commission for Refugees, 2007.

the United States was a world leader in acceptance of Iraqi refugees. But as shown in Table C, beginning in 2002 it became far more difficult for Iraqis to enter the United States. Under intense pressure from other nations, as well as domestic critics, to increase the flow of refugees from Iraq into the United States, in 2007 the State Department agreed to speed up its visa processing and seek to admit at least 6,000 a year, and more if possible, in recognition of the assistance the applications have given to the U.S. cause. However, at this writing the administration has made few efforts to make sure that its Iraqi refugee goals are actually met (Raghavan, 2007; Shelby, 2007).

Table A: Displaced Iraqis in the Region

Syria	1,200,000
Jordan	750,000
Egypt	100,000
Iran	54,000
Lebanon	40,000
Turkey	10,000
Gulf States	200,000

Table B: Iraqi Refugees Elsewhere in the World, 2006–2007

Germany	52,900	U.S.	6,000	Bulgaria	1,200
U.K.	22,300	Switzerland	5,000	Austria	1,200
Netherlands	21,800	Canada	4,000	Greece	820
Sweden	21,100	Finland	1,600	New Zealand	820
Australia	11,100	Italy	1,300	Armenia	460
Denmark	10,700	France	1,300	Romania	450
Norway	8,500	Hungary	1,200	Ireland	340

Table C: Resettlement of Iraqi Refugees, 1992–2005 (Government Figures)

	1992	1993	1994	1995	1996	1997	1998	1999	2000	2001	2002	2003	2004	2005	2006[*]
United States[†]	3,440	4,610	4,980	3,480	2,530	2,680	1,410	1,960	3,150	2,470	460	300	70	200	200
Canada	1,170	2,230	1,340	1,160	1,140	1,150	780	690	1,160	1,130	920	530	720	520	90
Australia	—	1,330	950	2,880	1,680	1,360	1,730	1,750	950	620	2,140	1,940	1,560	1,850	120
Sweden	1,580	110	650	540	—	330	270	150	340	250	250	90	30	60	80
Netherlands	230	220	460	470	390	120	30	10	10	10	20	10	—	—	—
Denmark	160	250	170	330	250	290	200	130	60	70	210	—	—	—	—
New Zealand	100	10	220	320	140	270	240	170	50	80	220	300	30	120	—
Norway	—	200	20	—	—	620	220	180	90	130	170	60	—	—	10
Finland	—	—	—	—	—	340	—	120	150	90	110	20	10	—	—

[*]UNHCR referred cases only. Final figures for some countries will be higher.
[†]Figures for U.S. fiscal year. Data includes families members resettled for the purposes of family reunion.

Source: United Nations High Commission for Refugees, 2007.

TABLE 14–4	Modes of Entry for the Unauthorized Migrant Population	
Entered legally with inspection	Nonimmigrant visa overstayers	4 to 5.5 million
	Border-crossing card violators	250,000 to 500,000
	Subtotal legal entries	*4.5 to 6 million*
Entered illegally without inspection	Evaded the Immigration Inspectors and Border Patrol	6 to 7 million
Estimated total unauthorized population in 2006		11.5 to 12 million

Source: Pew Hispanic Center Estimates based on the March 2005 Current Population Survey and Department of Homeland Security Homeland Security Reports. Table excerpted from Pew Hispanic Center fact sheet, "Modes of Entry for the Unauthorized Immigrant Population," http://pewhispanic.org. © 2006.

people from Mexico and Central America who have illegally crossed the border between Mexico and the United States, but recent alien arrest statistics suggest that the number of illegal Asian and European immigrants is also increasing.

Modes of Entry to the United States. Nearly half of all undocumented immigrants arrive legally as visitors to the United States, passing through ports of entry where they are processed by the U.S. Citizenship and Immigration Service. As Table 14–4 shows, they become illegal immigrants when they exceed the time allocated to them to visit or reside in the United States. As much as 45 percent of the unauthorized immigrant population falls into this category of **overstayers.** But an even larger proportion, from 6 to 7 million people according to estimates by the Department of Homeland Security, have entered the country illegally by evading immigration inspectors and border control agents. These are the most notorious illegal immigrants, especially visible and controversial in the southwestern border states, but untold numbers of evaders also arrive over the Canadian border and through ports like New York City through other forms of human smuggling. Authorities in New York City estimate that there are at least 30,000 undocumented immigrants there.

Undocumented immigrants are easily exploited by ruthless individuals who know that these immigrants cannot readily go to the authorities when they have been victimized. But illegal aliens from China have an especially difficult time. To be transported the great distance from China to the United States and to be smuggled into the New York area, many promise to pay as much as $50,000 to professional smuggling rings. Once in New York, they often have no means of repaying this debt, and because they cannot qualify for regular work or any social benefits, they are at the mercy of the people who brought them into the city. The smugglers often insist that the immigrants work at illegal activities, such as collecting gambling debts, or that they work in local restaurants at extremely low wages. If they attempt to leave in search of better opportunities elsewhere, they may be killed. In essence, this practice has created a new form of slavery (Foner, 2000; Kwong, 1997).

Nor is the situation much easier for illegal immigrants from Mexico and Central America. It is not unusual for them to pay large sums to smugglers, known as coyotes, who attempt to direct them across the border. Very often they are captured and lose both their chance to work in the United States and the hard-earned funds they gave to the smugglers. If they do gain entry into California or Texas and manage to find work, their status is quite precarious because employers must report them if they are discovered not to have proper documents. Thus, employers who continue to hire them or disregard the evident forgery of their documents also tend to exploit them by paying pitifully low wages and expecting inordinate amounts of work.

It is not clear exactly what effect illegal residents have on the U.S. economy. They may take some jobs away from native-born residents, but they also perform functions

Increased immigration results in the creation of new ethnic communities in the cities where immigrants arrive in large numbers. Shown here is "Little Hong Kong" in Flushing, New York, a point of entry for many immigrants from the Far East.

that citizens are reluctant to do—"dirty work" or stoop labor on row crops, for example—and they help maintain some industries by accepting lower wages and inferior working conditions. This may hold back progress on wages and working conditions for others, but the survival of such industries stimulates growth in associated services, actually creating more jobs. Indeed, it appears that migrants—who can generally be laid off or discharged more easily than citizens—play a vital, if equivocal, role in many advanced nations, cushioning the native-born population from economic uncertainty (Piore, 1979). And when an increasing proportion of adults are retired—as an estimated 20 percent of U.S. adults will be in 2035—the taxes paid by employed legal immigrants become extremely important.

In a study of rural Mexican communities that typically send many immigrants, legal and illegal, to the southwestern United States, Wayne A. Cornelius (1989) found that people there are knowledgeable about changes in U.S. immigration laws and how they affect their chances of finding work and of being apprehended by the authorities. In his extensive interviews, Cornelius found no evidence that immigrants or likely immigrants were changing their behavior, despite the knowledge that it has become more difficult to gain entry to the United States. He did find that more people were planning to become documented temporary farmworkers, but he found no decrease in the number who intended to immigrate illegally. He also found that more women intended to enter the United States, a fact that is confirmed in the statistics of immigration authorities, which show a steady increase in the number of undocumented Mexican women who attempt to cross the border.

What are the major components of illegal immigration to the United States?

Social Policy

Terrorist attacks and the continuing wars in the Middle East and elsewhere have created immense problems both for immigrants and for those responsible for controlling the nation's borders (Martin & Martin, 2001). In Colorado, Arab students have been jailed even though there is little evidence that they have been involved in terrorism-related groups or organizations. Heightened vigilance on roads and at airports has made it far more difficult for immigrants and foreign-born residents of the United States to move around the country.

According to Maria Jimenez (2001), an expert on immigration policy and an advocate of immigrant rights for the American Friends Service, there has been a backlash against immigrants since the terrorist attacks of September 11, 2001. "We had advanced to where we were challenging a lot of the restrictive immigration legislation passed in 1996," she says.

> We were on our way in terms of a very strong social movement. But with the fact that many of the people who perpetrated this tragedy were foreign born, and were immigrants who lived in the United States—people are equating immigration with terrorism, which is not the case. Immigration is always a good political scapegoat for certain groups. We had, I think, gotten a lot of the anti-immigrant groups in the background as to their positions, but they are on the front burner now.

Opponents of liberal immigration policies, on the other hand, are redoubling their efforts to challenge current U.S. immigration policies. The Center for Immigration Studies, a "think tank" devoted to research on the effects of immigration in the United States, believes that immigrants compete with U.S. citizens for jobs and help drive down wages. It also represents the viewpoint that liberal immigration policies led to inadequate enforcement of immigration laws, which in turn facilitated the terrorist attacks.

Neither of the major political parties in the United States can openly oppose immigration for fear of alienating potential voters, although there are factions within both parties that question current immigration policies (Zolberg, 2006). Population policy, on the other hand, brings the major parties into direct conflict, with Republicans calling for strong restrictions on programs to control population growth, while Democrats support such programs. The Bush administration, for example, recently reversed a policy of funding U.N. population programs that included education on contraception and family planning.

On the world stage, population policies are often hammered out at world congresses such as the historic International Conference on Population and Development, held in Cairo in 1994 (McIntosh & Finkle, 1995). Individual nations are, of course, free to pursue their own population policies, as we have seen in China, but nations like the United States and England, agencies of the United Nations, and international development agencies like the World Bank all send delegates to world congresses in an effort to develop a broader policy consensus. Increasingly, therefore, these conferences are marked by lively debates about the sensitive issues of population growth and its control.

The 1994 Cairo conference was unusual for the role played by women in its deliberations. Although there was not always a consensus among the women delegates themselves on family planning issues, there was wide agreement that empowering women through increased literacy, grassroots economic development, and political rights would have a profound impact on population trends. The more women can control their fertility, the conference decided, the more they will be able to make choices that benefit themselves and their children, including limiting the number of children they choose to bear.

The United States and other major participants in these conferences take such recommendations quite seriously. Although they continue to promote contraception and family planning, the new policies of local development and female empowerment are also shaping the actions of aid agencies throughout the world.

Immigration Reform?

At this writing, Congress has been debating immigration reform for at least two years, but in the summer of 2007 it failed to pass a comprehensive immigration reform bill that had the backing of President Bush and congressional leaders from both parties. The bill included a temporary worker program to allow agricultural workers into the country for limited periods and a system for granting legal permanent status to illegal immigrants already residing in the country (a step toward eventual citizenship). Both programs were supported by the president but were highly controversial. Billed as a form of "amnesty" for illegal immigrants, the proposal for granting legal status to illegal residents was forcefully opposed by conservative Republicans, whose fierce opposition alienated the vast majority of Latinos. The result of the debate is a stalemate. Supporters of immigration reform argue that the United States will never deport over 11 million illegal immigrants, especially as their labor is clearly vital to the continuing success of the U.S. economy. Opponents have pressed state and local governments, as well as the federal government, to crack down on employers who hire undocumented workers. They have led some highly visible crackdowns, in one of which—at a large maker of wooden shipping pallets—1,900 illegal workers and seven company executives were arrested.

Until recently, it was not against the law to employ illegal immigrants. This situation changed in 1986, when Congress passed the Immigration Reform and Control Act. Under the new law, employers are subject to civil penalties that range from $250 to $10,000 for each illegal alien they hire. Concerning people who are already living in the United States illegally, it is generally agreed that mass deportation is not feasible. Thus, the 1986 law offered legal status to illegal aliens who entered the United States before January 1, 1982, and have lived here continuously ever since. These undocumented aliens may qualify for permanent status (a green card), which in turn allows them to apply for U.S. citizenship and also allows them to freely leave and reenter the country.

The Immigration Reform and Control Act sought to stem the flow of illegal immigrants from Mexico and elsewhere through a number of reforms in existing laws. The bill included the employer sanctions just noted. It also sought to discourage illegal immigration by measures that would reduce the chances of finding work in the United States. In particular, it offered legal status to immigrants who claimed three months of prior agricultural work, thereby increasing the supply of legal labor for the big farms of southern California and decreasing the need for more casual, often illegal labor.

The continuing flow of illegal immigrants, especially across the U.S. border with Mexico, has prompted some political leaders in the Southwest to advocate the construction of a fence along the entire 1,275-mile U.S.–Mexican border. Although this idea appeals to those who want the U.S. government to make a greater effort to prevent illegal immigration, there is no assurance that such a fence would be effective, aside from having a negative effect on international relations (Goldsborough, 2004).

The extent to which immigration cuts across racial, ethnic, and class lines results in broad-based popular support for pro-immigration policy. The principle of family unification—long a basic element of immigration policy—also explains why immigration legislation has public support. So many people are directly affected or have friends who are affected by efforts to unite families separated by immigration that opposition to the abstract idea of population growth is blunted by human concerns.

Unintended Consequences

MAKING FAMILY UNIFICATION MORE DIFFICULT

In 1996 Congress failed to win adequate support, even from some conservative members, for placing strict lower quotas on legal immigration to the United States. But in a less publicized piece of legislation, Congress imposed income requirements on sponsors of new immigrants that could make it far more difficult for poor immigrants already in the country to help members of their families immigrate under the terms of family unification.

Under the new law, the sponsor of an immigrant or an immigrant family must show that she or he is earning at least 125 percent of the poverty level ($20,500 for a family of four). Under the old law, there was no such requirement. The law's proponents argue that the measure will cut down on the number of new immigrants who apply for welfare benefits. But research by the Urban Institute on a random sample of immigrants shows that 40 percent did not earn enough in the previous year to sponsor an immigrant family member, compared to 26 percent of native-born Americans—who might also be of immigrant stock (Dugger, 1997).

Another clause in the new law permits immigrants to sue their sponsor for support until they either obtain U.S. citizenship or have worked and paid taxes for ten years. Again, the law's intent is to prevent immigrants from applying for welfare, but it also forces individuals to choose between attempting to unite their families and facing unknown future consequences. Some immigration experts believe the law will actually encourage illegal immigration and at the same time discourage family unification for many legal immigrants and naturalized U.S. citizens, who previously would have been able to arrange for their parents and children to join them. And as the federal government and many states begin to crack down on illegal immigrants and bar legal immigrants from certain forms of welfare eligibility, another consequence of the new anti-immigrant attitude is increased political mobilization of immigrants, who are becoming U.S. citizens in record numbers.

Why do opponents of immigration reform reject any form of "amnesty" for undocumented workers and their families?

But as shown in the Unintended Consequences box above, recent changes in immigration laws make family reunification far more difficult for immigrants who are poor. Indeed, alterations in the U.S. welfare laws, as well as seemingly minor ones in the immigration laws, are creating enormous changes and some chaos among immigrant populations in the United States.

Welfare reform has hit legal immigrants especially hard. Laws passed by Congress in 1996 deny welfare benefits (including Medicaid and food stamps) to legal immigrants who are not citizens, many of whom are too old to work and rely on minimal welfare and health benefits. And to make matters more difficult for some immigrant families, new regulations announced by the federal government require immigrants to recite the citizenship oath even if they are disabled by Alzheimer's disease, severe mental retardation, or other mental disabilities. These regulations are being challenged in the courts, but they are in effect in some states.

Future Prospects

It is very likely that the next Congress, to be elected along with a new President in 2008, will be able to pass an immigration bill with many of the features of the one that was defeated in 2007. That bill would have offered illegal immigrants who have been living in the United States for a certain length of time, and have paid taxes and not been arrested, a chance to pay a fine and eventually gain permanent status (a "green card"). Another feature of the defeated bill would have placed far greater emphasis on the skills of individuals who seek to immigrate to the United States than on whether they have family members already in the country. The latter policy, known as **family reconciliation,** is highly popular among immigrants and strongly opposed by conservatives. A new version of the reform bill is likely to offer a compromise between the two selection criteria (skills and family reconciliation). Staunch opponents of illegal border crossings will still support the huge system of fences proposed for the U.S.-Mexican border, but this project, though under construction in some places, is unlikely to gain widespread support in a new Congress.

GOING BEYOND LEFT AND RIGHT

There are no clear left and right viewpoints on immigration, but there are some people with strong views on the issues involved. Those on the right may be of the opinion that the United States is threatened by hordes of newcomers, some of whom will become burdens on the welfare rolls. But many other people with conservative views argue that immigrants are needed to provide low-wage workers, to compete with workers in other regions of the world, to do the work that people born here do not want to do. On the left there are also divisions. Some liberals argue that immigrants add new vitality to the society and its culture and that they are living reminders of the traditions of American democracy. But others on the left side of the political spectrum may voice concern about the possibility that immigrants drive down wages for native-born workers and compete with poor Americans for entry-level jobs, especially as welfare reform pushes more poor people into the job market.

Clearly, there are subdivisions within the major ideological divisions. In deciding where you stand, these disputes will help you realize that there are no easy solutions. Because immigrants are encouraged in a variety of ways to work in the United States and to strive to become U.S. citizens, it is reasonable to argue that people who are already citizens have some responsibility for helping the newcomers achieve a better life, regardless of one's political ideology.

Many aspects of immigration reform are not highly controversial. We have seen, for example, that 45 percent of illegal immigrants are overstayers. The USCIS, now a branch of the Department of Homeland Security, requests funding for continued development of its US-Visit computer system, which will match computer records of arrivals with records of individual departures. Such a system is likely to appeal to most voters, regardless of ideology.

Summary

- A common measure of population growth is the crude birthrate, or the number of births per 1,000 population. The differential between the crude birthrate and the death rate is the rate of population growth, or natural increase. Today, more people are living to childbearing age, so the world's population is growing faster than in the past and putting increased pressure on resources and the environment.

- The demographic transition is a process that consists of three stages: (a) a high birthrate canceled out by a high death rate, (b) a high birthrate coupled with a declining death rate, and (c) low birth and death rates. The process began in northern Europe in the eighteenth century and has occurred in all areas where industrial technology has taken hold on a local level. Today large areas of Asia, Africa, and Latin America remain in the middle phase of the demographic transition.

- An unintended effect of population growth, coupled with awareness of higher living standards, is the revolution of rising expectations, in which people develop higher expectations for their own future and that of

their children. Literacy rates serve as an indicator of rising expectations. Although literacy rates have increased in many countries, the gaps in living standards between rich and poor societies have widened. Hunger and malnutrition are persistent problems in the less developed regions of the world.

- The population of the industrialized nations is growing at a relatively slow rate, and it appears likely that this rate can be maintained through voluntary population control (e.g., family planning). ZPG and other organizations have been active in promoting access to birth control and legalized abortion.

- In some less developed countries, compulsory birth control has been attempted and has met with considerable resistance. In these countries the most effective policies provide not only birth control devices, but also economic and social incentives to limit family size.

- The main trends in the U.S. population are slow growth, population redistribution, and increasing immigration. Among the effects of these trends are the disproportionate representation of minority groups in the older central cities and increased age and income disparities between old and new ethnic groups.

- The United States is often described as a nation of immigrants; since the earliest years of European settlement, it has attracted people from all over the world. And since the 1970s the rate of legal immigration to the United States has accelerated. The largest numbers of immigrants have come from Asia and Latin America.

- A problem related to immigration is the uneven distribution of immigrants among cities and regions in the United States. Large numbers settle in New York, Los Angeles, Miami, and Chicago, greatly adding to the costs of education and health care in those cities.

- Immigrants in urban centers encounter intense competition and, at times, direct hostility. Their children may form defensive gangs or be isolated by their peers. Some immigrant groups shelter their children from street life and encourage them to achieve in school.

- Millions of undocumented immigrants are currently residing in the United States, and more arrive each year. Undocumented immigrants are easily exploited by employers and others. Their effect on the U.S. economy is not clear, but it appears that they cushion the native-born population from economic uncertainty.

- Population-related policies in the United States focus mainly on immigration. It is illegal to transport or employ undocumented immigrants. Illegal aliens who entered the country before 1982 and have lived here continuously ever since may qualify for permanent status. The principle of family unification is a basic element of immigration policy, but recent changes in immigration laws have made it more difficult for low-income immigrants to bring other members of their family to the United States. Efforts to reform immigration policy have been unsuccessful because of strong opposition to proposals that would grant legal status to illegal immigrants already residing in the United States.

Key Terms

crude birthrate, p. 449
rate of population growth (natural increase), p. 449
demographic transition, p. 450

standard of living, p. 453
level of living, p. 453
chain migration, p. 465
political refugee, p. 466

overstayer, p. 468
family reconciliation, p. 472

Social Problems Online

The Internet provides considerable data on population, migration, and other areas of interest to demographers. A search might begin at the United Nations Population Fund (**www.unfpa.org**/), where the annual *State of World Population* reports are available. The United Nations Development Programme at **www.undp.org**/ has links to statistical sources and other features.

An online bibliographic resource is maintained by the Princeton University Office of Population Research. Browsable versions of its publication *Population Index* are available for issues since 1986 at **http://popindex.princeton.edu**/. A user-friendly search interface makes it easy to locate specific citations or to do free-text searches. The U.S. government provides data and reports about demographic trends in the United States on the Census Bureau Web page (**www.census.gov**/).

The Population Council is one of the largest international nongovernmental organizations (NGOs) involved in research and advocacy about issues affecting the world's population. Its homepage is located at **www.popcouncil.org**/. It contains recent publications and working papers, news releases, and links to development and population resources as well as to other international NGOs.

Migration and the social problems associated with it are addressed by the European Research Centre on Migration and Ethnic Relations (ERCOMER) in the Netherlands. ERCOMER publications, reports on conferences, and links to numerous other research and advocacy groups are available at its Web site at **www.ercomer.org**.

Population Connection, formerly Zero Population Growth, disseminates its views at **www.populationconnection.org**.

Research Navigator

Follow the instructions on pages 26–27 of this text to access the features of Research Navigator. Once at the Web site, enter your Login Name and Password. Then, to use the Content Select database, use keywords such as "world population growth," "illegal immigrants," and "refugees," and the search engine will supply relevant and recent scholarly and popular press publications. Use the *New York Times* search-by-subject archive to find recent news articles related to problems of population and immigration, and the Link Library to find relevant Web sites organized by the key terms associated with this chapter.

In the EBSCO host, enter the term "demographic transition." You will find an article by George Musser titled "The Climax of Humanity." In addition to the demographic transition, what other related transitions does the author discuss? Why does the author contend that "demographically and economically, our era is unique in human history. Depending on how we manage the next few decades, we could usher in environmental sustainability—or collapse"?

15

TECHNOLOGY
and the Environment

Dominant Trends

- *Global warming, now recognized as a technology-based social problem, will assume ever greater urgency as nations struggle to agree on policies to reduce emission of carbon dioxide and other greenhouse gases.*

- *On a per capita basis, the United States is by far the world's leader in carbon dioxide emissions, with an annual average of 5.4 tons per person. In 2006 China's total carbon dioxide emissions were higher, but they remain far lower on a per capita basis. Neither the United States nor China has yet to adequately respond to pressure to take the lead in cutting carbon dioxide emissions.*

- *Automation, in which machines replace human labor, continues to increase the productivity of the U.S. economy but also accounts for the loss of high-quality jobs.*

- *About 55 percent of U.S. households are equipped with computers and Internet service, a technology that will continue to revolutionize how people communicate and do business but will also contribute to a wide variety of "cyber crimes" such as identity theft.*

Of all the many ways in which technology has changed our lives, probably none has more far-reaching consequences than its impact on the earth's environment. The problems of global warming, acid rain, toxic waste disposal, and water and air pollution are direct consequences of technological advances. The way we use energy has an enormous impact on the earth's ecological systems. The technologies of production, climate control, transportation, and agriculture transform the physical shape of the planet and lead to environmental stress. The United States is the world's greatest consumer of natural resources, especially carbon-based energy from fossil fuels (coal, oil, and natural gas). It is also the world's leader in the production and use of technological systems of all kinds. The U.S. government and the nation's citizens therefore bear much of the responsibility for seeking ways to reduce the negative effects of pollution due to energy consumption.

Environmentalists claim that in recent years the United States has shifted its concerns away from environmental protection—especially in relation to such crucial issues as global warming—in favor of deregulation and pro-growth policies that have the effect of increasing pollution. They view with alarm the Bush administration's refusal to sign the Kyoto Accords on emissions of carbon dioxide and other greenhouse gases, which cause atmospheric warming.

Responding to critics of its environmental policies, the administration has proposed a series of guidelines and voluntary measures to reduce the nation's greenhouse gas emissions and encourage energy conservation (Purvis, 2004). As in any other dispute, there are arguments on both sides of this debate; these are discussed in detail later in the chapter.

Energy technologies, including petrochemicals, electricity, nuclear power, hydroelectricity, and others, are basic to everyday life throughout the world, so much so that we often take their availability for granted. But we do that to our peril. The contemporary world has become entirely dependent on energy technologies, but we cannot assume that they will always be at our disposal or that we can recover them after disasters such as earthquakes and hurricanes. To better understand the meanings of technologies and their relation to modern science, we turn to some basic social-scientific definitions.

THE NATURE OF TECHNOLOGY

The dictionary definition of **technology** is "the totality of means employed by a people to provide itself with the objects of material culture." In this sense, technology is a way of solving practical problems; indeed, it is often viewed as the application of scientific knowledge to the problems of everyday life. But neither the dictionary definition nor the view of technology as applied science places enough emphasis on its organizational aspects. Langdon Winner (1977, 2004) has provided a useful set of dimensions for understanding the broader meaning of technology:

1. Technological tools, instruments, machines, gadgets, which are used in accomplishing a variety of tasks. These material objects are best referred to as *apparatus,* the physical devices of technical performance.

2. The body of technical skills, procedures, routines—all *activities* or behaviors that employ a purposive, step-by-step, rational method of doing things.

3. The *organizational* networks associated with activities and apparatus (Winner, 1977, pp. 11–12).

Technological change refers to changes in any or all of the major dimensions of technology listed here. Some technological changes have revolutionary significance in that they alter the basic institutions of society. Thus, the industrial revolution—that is, the development of factories and mass production—has drastically altered the organization of a number of noneconomic institutions, including the family, religion, the military, and science itself.

Not all technological change is revolutionary, however. Some innovations spur minor adjustments in other sectors of society or among small numbers of people. Nor does technological change always consist of a single major invention. Daniel Bell (1973), perhaps the most prominent sociologist in this field, defines technological change as "the combination of all methods [apparatus, activities, organization] for increasing the productivity of labor and capital" (p. 188). This is a valuable definition because it stresses the combination of methods that alter production rather than single innovations. After all, the technological revolution that took place in American agriculture from the end of the nineteenth century to World War II involved hundreds of major inventions and the skills and organization to support them. The combination of all these factors allowed the United States to make the transition from an agrarian society to an urban industrial society in less than one century.

What is the relationship between science and technology?

Technological Dualism

The term **technological dualism** refers to the fact that advances in technology can have both positive and negative impacts. This is not a new idea; the ancient Greeks believed the god Apollo embodied this dualism because he could bring them new techniques of healing but could also use those techniques to cause death. In our own time, the problem of the good and evil consequences of technologies is ever present. Think of the controversy over guns: Larger numbers of guns in a population are associated with higher rates of violence, but their defenders claim that the violence is not caused by guns but by those who use them for bad purposes. In the case of television, this revolutionary communication technology has the power to disseminate vast amounts of news and other information to ever greater numbers of people. But television is also associated with negative consequences such as a decline in newspaper readership and an increase in "infotainment" rather than less entertaining political and economic news. Automotive technology, like television, has changed almost every aspect of how we live, but it has also contributed immensely to the problem of global climate change. And nothing illustrates the dual nature of technologies better than nuclear power, which on the one hand has many peaceful uses but on the other hand is used in nuclear weapons that could someday destroy entire human societies (Clarke, 2005).

Technology and Global Inequality

Are new technologies increasing the gap between haves and have-nots throughout the world? The potential consequences of lack of access to technologies are a subject of

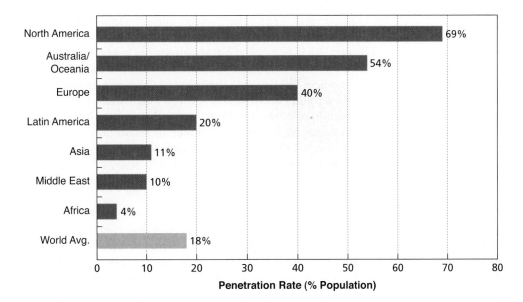

Figure 15–1 Internet Penetration, by World Region
Source: Internetworldstats, 2007.

lively debate and new research. *The Human Development Report* of the United Nations Development Programme (1999), which focuses on these issues, notes that "the fusion of computing and communications—especially through the Internet—has broken the bounds of cost, time, and distance, launching an era of global information networking. In biotechnology the ability to identify and move genetic materials across species types has broken the bounds of nature, creating totally new organisms with enormous but unknown implications" (p. 57). These technologies are creating new markets and new fortunes, many of which are dominated by individuals and corporations in the wealthier nations, especially the United States.

Figures 15–1 and 15–2 show that Asia accounts for the largest absolute number of Internet users, while Africa lags far behind. However, Internet access as a proportion of the population (i.e., "penetration") is highest in North America and Europe, leaving enormous potential for growth in the less developed regions of the world. On a global basis, only 18 percent of possible users currently have Internet access.

Information and the technologies that convey it can be a positive force for social change, but too often they are not delivering on their potential. Existing patterns of inequality prevent more equal access to computers and even to telephones. People in

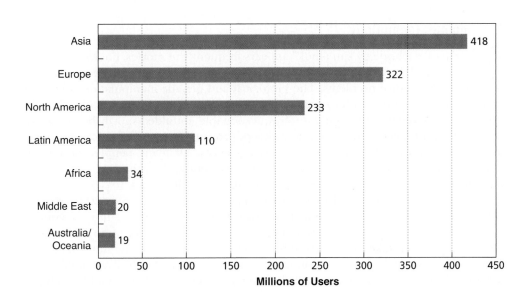

Figure 15–2 Internet Usage, by World Region
Source: Internetworldstats, 2007.

developing nations, for example, suffer from the most serious infectious diseases. Yet medical personnel in those nations often lack access to the information they need to combat those diseases. The average U.S. medical library subscribes to about 5,000 journals, many of which are also available online to people with computers and Internet access. Nairobi University's medical library, long regarded as the best medical school library in East Africa, has only 40 medical books and a dozen journals, and students at the university have extremely limited access to the Internet, with its online journals and technical discussions. This one example could be multiplied by hundreds of other situations in which people in the third world suffer because of their limited access to new technologies that hold so much promise for the betterment of their lives.

The Digital Divide

In the United States, the gap between those with access to computers and the Internet and those without such access is often referred to as the **digital divide.** Poor families are far less likely to be among the two-thirds of American households that are active on the Internet. But this divide, still immense in the third world, is narrowing quickly in the United States. Efforts to give children time on computers in schools have greatly reduced the gap. In 2000 approximately 98 percent of U.S. schools gave their students Internet access. That figure was 65 percent in 1996. For schools in which two-thirds or more of the students are eligible for a free school lunch (a measure of attendance by poor children), 94 percent had Internet access, compared to 53 percent in 1996 (*Statistical Abstract,* 2002).

These are extremely encouraging statistics, but one might reasonably ask how important the Internet is in students' overall education. In fact, there are few hard data on this subject. Many parents and political leaders believe Internet access is a sort of passkey to success in the global economy, but research on this issue lags behind speculation. It is clear, however, that students who master the more technical aspects of computers and their applications have more career options than those who do not. From that perspective, narrowing the digital divide is a significant accomplishment (Williams-Harold, 2000).

CONTROLLING TECHNOLOGY

Some critics of technology are convinced that it has become an autonomous force in society—one that is less and less subject to the control of democratic political institutions. A more hopeful view stresses social adaptation to technological innovation. In this section we explore these contrasting views of technology.

Autonomous Technology

The theme of "technology run amok" appears frequently in movies, books, and other fictional works. But these fictional nightmares are based on real experiences or real possibilities for future problems. The biological and genetic manipulations depicted in the immensely popular film *Jurassic Park,* with its lesson that fooling Mother Nature can be extremely dangerous and morally questionable, unfolded shortly before scientists in Scotland succeeded in cloning a sheep, proving that the technology to reproduce exact replicas of human beings already exists. To many people, cloning of humans as a scientific possibility is even more frightening than the more far-fetched but equally possible (in theory) idea of producing living dinosaurs.

The computer named Hal that ran the space mission in the film *2001: A Space Odyssey* malfunctioned and had to be taken over by its human crew. This is, of course, a satirical view of computers' domination of human life, but how often do we read about computer mistakes that result in bureaucratic disasters affecting hundreds, even thousands, of people? We depend on machines, which are all too frail and fallible, yet we know that machines do not literally have lives of their own. People make machines and operate them, not vice versa. How can it be, then, that technology has achieved a seeming independence from human control, as many critics argue?

The answer, according to Winner (1986, 1997) and others, is not that individual machines exercise tyranny over human subjects but that the technological order—the complex web that connects the various sectors of technology, such as communication, transportation, energy, manufacturing, and defense—has enmeshed us in a web of dependency. People who live in simple societies meet their basic survival needs with a fairly small number of tools and a simple division of labor. To accomplish such goals as building a shelter, gathering and growing food, and warding off enemies, they have evolved a set of tools that families and other groups manufacture and use as the need arises. The lives of these people are dominated by the need to survive, and technology simply provides the means for doing so. In modern industrial societies, however, most people spend most of their productive hours working to meet the quotas, deadlines, and other goals of large organizations. Each of the corporations, government bureaucracies, and other organizations that together make up the technological order produces goods and services that people want or need. These organizations do so not with a few tools, but with a complex array of machines and skills. As a whole, the technological order supplies the basic necessities of life, along with innumerable extras. But in the process, much of the life of society has been diverted from meeting the needs of survival to meeting the requirements of technology.

We have seen elsewhere in this book that military technology accounts for a large proportion of the federal budget. The devastating bombing of the Taliban and Al Qaeda forces in Afghanistan in 2001 demonstrated to many Americans that this technology was worth the expense. But the allied victory and the evident effectiveness of the weapons systems inspired many observers to ask why the nation could not use its technological know-how to improve schools and health care and solve other social problems. In attempting to answer such questions, Daniel Bell (1991) notes that smart bombs and computer-assisted weapons are technologies designed to meet well-defined and very narrow objectives. He warns that " 'solutions' to the social problems (if solutions are possible) spring from the different values people hold" (p. 23).

Most sociologists do not see technology as autonomous. They argue that we have been drawn into the momentum of technological change but are not sure where it is taking us. In the following pages, we discuss this theme as it applies to particular technologies.

Automation

A classic example of the difficulty of understanding the interaction between technology and human values is automation, the replacement of workers by a nonhuman means of producing the same product. People may lose jobs because of automation, but should we fight to keep these jobs, many of which may be among the dirtiest and most dangerous ones in industrial facilities? On the other hand, the greatly feared displacement of workers by machines may or may not increase productivity and thus create new wealth, which could be channeled into the "higher" work of humans: health care, education, caring for the aged, and so on.

In fact, the stereotypical image of automation, in which a worker is replaced by a mechanical robot, is actually occurring throughout the industrialized world. Each of these machines replaces at least three workers because it can work continuously, whereas human workers must be replaced every eight hours. But most robots replace more than three workers, even though they must be tended by highly trained maintenance personnel. Thus, automation increases the productivity of the economy because a constant or decreasing number of workers can turn out more of a desired product. The question remains, however, of whether the new wealth generated by higher productivity will be used to benefit the entire society or only individuals who are already wealthy.

The direct replacement of workers by machines is the most dramatic and perhaps the most widely held image of automation. Evidence suggests, however, that the contemporary effects of automation as measured by increasing productivity, defined as output per hour of labor, have been much less than the stereotypical image of robots replacing workers would suggest. According to one estimate, productivity due to machines (as opposed to organization) improved at a fairly consistent annual rate of about 2.5 percent between 1919 and 1953 (Solow, 1959; cited in Bell, 1973). In the 1960s the pace of automation increased somewhat, but no major change occurred in the 1970s. In the 1980s and 1990s, although the U.S. economy continued to create new jobs, the impact of automation reduced the number of new jobs in the manufacturing sector, especially automobiles and steel. (See Chapter 12.) In the 1990s, however, employment in the production of computing equipment and other digital technology grew rapidly until the "dot-com bubble" burst and many new high-tech companies went out of business.

Whistle-Blowers

So many of the proposed solutions to technological problems are themselves new technologies that opportunities abound for abuse and personal profit through their application. People who see abuses of new technological systems often run grave personal risks when they attempt to expose them. These individuals are known as **whistle-blowers.**

Within any organization, certain ways of doing things, beliefs about the environment in which the group operates, and ideas about how individuals should behave become established. Whistle-blowers challenge some element of this body of procedures, beliefs, and norms in an effort to bring about change. At the least, they must endure snubs or ostracism by fellow workers. At the worst, they may be fired or even subjected to physical violence.

The difficulty of succeeding in such a situation can be appreciated by reviewing the experience of Peter Faulkner (1981), an engineer for a private nuclear engineering firm, who in 1974 publicized certain hazardous deficiencies in the design of nuclear power systems. Early in the 1970s Faulkner had become concerned because many systems contained design flaws that posed grave threats to the public and to the natural environment: "Overconfident engineering, the failure to test nuclear systems fully in intermediate states, and competitive pressures that forced reactor manufacturers to . . . sell first, test later" (pp. 40, 41) contributed to the persistence of these flaws.

Curious about whether his fellow engineers shared his concerns, Faulkner (1981) discussed his perceptions with them. From these discussions, he realized that many of them shared his view that poor management had led to the marketing of defective reactors. But most of his colleagues preferred to leave management problems to the executives, even though this resignation of responsibility contributed to the design flaws with which they were already familiar from their daily experience. Senior engineers informed him that utility executives "didn't want management advice—only technical assistance to get them over the next hill."

Frustrated by the indifference of his colleagues, Faulkner made the difficult and costly decision to present articles that criticized the industry to a Senate subcommittee and a scientific institute. Dissemination of critical papers clearly violated the ethics of the nuclear industry and of the engineers within it, but Faulkner acted to further what he considered a higher goal—public safety. Within two weeks he had been interviewed by the company psychiatrist, who wanted to learn whether Faulkner had been motivated by some deep-seated hostility to embarrass his firm. A week later he was fired.

The explosion of the space shuttle *Challenger* in January 1986 is sometimes attributed to a similar situation: failure to listen to whistle-blowers in the company that manufactured the shuttle's solid-fuel booster rockets. It is true that engineers repeatedly warned of the danger of engine seal failure in very cold weather, that they were overruled by their superiors, and that when they testified at congressional hearings on the disaster they were either fired or "promoted" to meaningless positions. However, the situation was much more complex than these facts suggest. The pressure to go ahead with the fatal launch was enormous, and subsequent investigations revealed that other aspects of the shuttle program, particularly safety procedures, were seriously deficient. As Lee Clarke (2005) points out in his book *Worst Cases,* modern technological systems are extremely complex, and despite the best intentions of managers and employees, information is often lost or suppressed because of lack of coordination between different parts of the system. The tragic example of the two space shuttle disasters illustrates the need for more thorough technology assessment, which is discussed in the Social Policy section of the chapter.

Identity Theft—A Global Crime Wave in Cyberspace

In 2005 ChoicePoint, Inc., one of the largest providers of consumer information in the United States, discovered that a ring of identity thieves had broken into their computer system and obtained the driving, banking, Social Security, and other personal records of more than 145,000 clients. The thieves then began changing the addresses of some of the names as a way of obtaining credit cards for these stolen records. Although the scam was intercepted before individual clients suffered grave losses, the company's reputation was badly damaged. In the same year, serious breaches of security leading to identity theft at Lexis Nexis, a worldwide leader in global business and legal data, and at the Bank of America revealed how extensive the problem of identity theft can be for both individuals and corporations.

Identity theft refers to the illegal possession of another person's private account numbers and the use of those numbers for fraudulent purposes. No one knows exactly how widespread this form of theft is, but recent estimates indicate that one in four American adults has been affected by identity theft and that the overall value of losses due to this form of crime is over $4 billion. The average victim must spend about 600 hours and $1,400 clearing his or her name and credit records after the crime has been committed (Lynch, 2005). The widespread use of online databases has given computer hackers an incentive to work with conventional criminals to "phish" through millions of online computers in search of openings that will enable them to invade private and corporate computers and steal identity data. As widespread as this computer "phishing" has become, however, experts on identity theft point out that even more identity information is obtained through old-fashioned means like stolen wallets, lost

This advertisement offers some practical suggestions for avoiding identity theft. The growing frequency of such ads is an indication that the problem is becoming widespread and is extremely costly both to the victims and to society.

identification cards, and fishing through trash bins. Nevertheless, much of the effort to develop ways of fighting identity theft focuses on increasing security for critical databases in government and the corporate sector (Lynch, 2005).

Bureaucracy and Morality

As noted earlier, technology consists not only of machines, but also of procedures and organizations. Today much of the productive activity that occurs in complex societies takes place in large bureaucratic organizations. With their orientation toward specified goals, their division of labor into narrowly defined roles, and their hierarchical authority structures, such organizations are supremely efficient. But like technology in general, some of the qualities of large organizations that make them so productive and valuable can also cause harm. For example, individuals in a hierarchical system may commit immoral acts because they are not personally responsible for the consequences of those acts, which are carried out under the direction of superiors.

The list of immoral acts committed on the instructions of superiors in large organizations is long. Writing as London was being pounded by Nazi bombs during World War II, George Orwell (quoted in Milgram, 1974) described the irony of one such situation:

> As I write, highly civilized human beings are flying overhead, trying to kill me. They do not feel any enmity against me as an individual, nor I against them. They are only "doing their duty," as the saying goes. Most of them are kind-hearted law abiding men who would never dream of committing murder in private life. On the other hand, if one of them succeeds in blowing me to pieces with a well-placed bomb, he will never sleep any the worse for it. (pp. 11–12)

Stanley Milgram called attention to the fact that when an immoral task is divided up among a number of people in a large organization like an air force or a bomb factory, no one person, acting as an individual, actually decides to commit the act, perceives its consequences, or takes responsibility for it. It is easy for each participant to become absorbed in the effort to perform his or her role competently. It is also psychologically easy to reduce guilt with the rationalization that one's duty requires the immoral behavior and that one's superior is responsible in the end (Blass, 2004).

In a famous series of experiments conducted at Yale University, Milgram (1974) studied the conditions under which people forsake the universally shared moral injunction against doing harm to another person in order to obey the instructions of someone in a position of authority. Subjects entered the laboratory assuming that they were to take part in a study of learning and memory. One person was designated a "learner" and the other a "teacher." The experimenter explained that the purpose of the study was to observe the effect of punishment on learning, and then the learner was strapped into a chair and electrodes were attached to his wrist. Next, the learner was told that the task was to learn a list of word pairs and that for every error he would receive an electric shock of progressively greater intensity. The teacher, who had been present for this interchange, was escorted to another room and seated at the controls of a large shock generator. Each time the learner gave a wrong answer, the teacher was to flip the next in a series of thirty switches designed to deliver shocks in 15-volt increments, from 15 to 450, starting at the lowest level. (See Figure 15–3a.)

In reality, the learner was an actor who received no shock but registered greater discomfort as the supposed intensity of the shocks increased. Grunts gave way to verbal complaints, to demands for release from the experiment, and then to screams. The true purpose of the experiment was to study the behavior of the teachers. They were affected by the cries and suffering of the learners—especially in high-proximity situations—but whenever they hesitated to deliver a shock, the experimenter ordered them to continue. In one form of the experiment, almost two-thirds of the subjects administered the maximum shock of 450 volts. (See Figure 15–3b.) Interviews with these subjects (who had been carefully selected to represent a cross section of society) revealed that they tended to adjust to their task by absorbing themselves in its technical

(a)

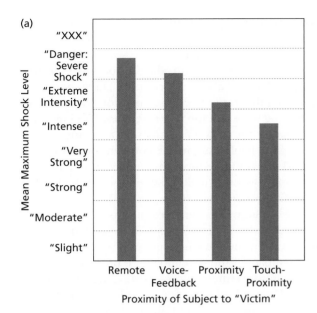

(b)

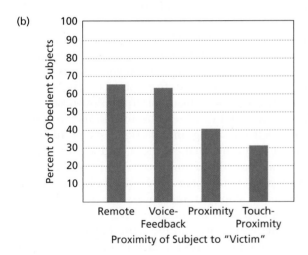

Figure 15–3 Results of Milgram's Experiments on Willingness to Obey People in Authority *Part (a) shows the extent to which proximity to the "victim" affected the subject's willingness to administer the maximum shock. Part (b) shows the percentage of obedient subjects under varying degrees of proximity to the "victim." The subject is the person administering the shock; the "victim" is an accomplice to the experimenter. The voltage levels indicated in (a) ranged from 15 for "slight shock" to a maximum of 450 for "XXX." No actual shocks were administered.*

Source: Maximum Shocks Administered in Experiments 1, 2, 3 and 4, p. 35 & Fig. 6 Mean Maximum, p. 36 from Obedience to Authority: An Experimental View by Stanley Milgram. Copyright © 1974 by Stanley Milgram. Reprinted by permission of HarperCollins Publishers.

details, transferring responsibility to the experimenter, and justifying their actions in the name of scientific truth (Milgram, 1974).

Milgram's experiments generated a great deal of controversy and contributed to the establishment of rules for governing federally funded social-science research that uses human subjects. At the same time, there has not been any significant debate about the implications of his findings for society. Should people be taught that disobedience to authority under some conditions is necessary? This is the situation faced by whistle-blowers, who actually overcome their feelings of subservience to technologically oriented bureaucratic hierarchies (Blass, 2004).

TECHNOLOGY AND INSTITUTIONS

Sociologists who study technology and the effects of technological change most often concern themselves with the adaptation of social institutions to changing technology or, conversely, the adaptation of technology to changing social institutions. The best known statement of these relationships is William F. Ogburn's **cultural lag** theory, first stated in the 1920s. According to Ogburn (1957), a founder of the study of technology in the United States, "A cultural lag occurs when one of two parts of culture which are correlated changes before or in greater degree than the other part does, thereby causing less adjustment between the two parts than existed previously" (p. 167).

A classic example of cultural lag involves the failure of social-welfare legislation over a period of thirty or forty years to adjust to the introduction of new industrial machinery in the United States at the end of the nineteenth century. The frequency of industrial accidents was increasing during that period because operators were not adequately protected from the rapidly moving wheels of the new machines. The loss of life and limb generally meant financial disaster for workers' families because under existing law, employers could not easily be held liable. As a result, compensation was meager and slow to come. Only when worker's compensation and employer liability were introduced early in the twentieth century was this maladjustment, which had led to much impoverishment and suffering, finally corrected (Ogburn, 1957).

Typically, social institutions and technology adjust and readjust to each other in a process that approaches equilibrium, unless one or the other alters so radically that a lag develops. In the history of transportation technology, radical changes have occurred relatively often. Witness the impact of the steamboat, the railroad, the automobile, and the airplane. Sometimes mere refinements in existing technology can devastate the social arrangements that had evolved in response to older machines and procedures. This is what occurred in the railroad town of Caliente (not its real name) when diesel power replaced steam in the 1940s. A classic study by Cottrell (1951) describes the results.

Caliente had been settled at the turn of the century, when the railroad was built, and it owed its existence almost entirely to the railroad. When the line was put through, the boiler of a steam engine could withstand high pressures and temperatures for only short periods. A locomotive had to be disconnected from service roughly every 100 miles, and Caliente was located in the middle of the desert for this purpose.

Over the years the community had invested considerable sums in its own future. Railroad workers and others had put their life savings into mortgages; merchants had built stores; and the town had constructed a hospital, a school, and a park. But the diesel engine undermined the economic base of the town, saddling its residents with devalued property and no means of supporting themselves. Diesel engines require much less maintenance and many fewer stops for fuel and water than do steam engines. Thus, the railroad employees who lived in Caliente either lost their jobs or were transferred; the town had become irrelevant from the point of view of the railroad. In the American free-enterprise system, the profitability of the railroad determined the fate of the town. The railroad was under no obligation to cushion the social impact of its move and the state did not offer any assistance—so the town died.

The construction of interstate highways after World War II had the opposite effect. The width, straightness, and limited access of interstates permit greater traffic flow and higher speeds than possible on conventional roads. The highways therefore expanded the potential markets of retail and service businesses located near them. Improved markets, in turn, tend to increase employment in retail and service businesses. The promise of new jobs attracts new residents from areas with less opportunity. Thus, a study of the impact of interstate highways on nonmetropolitan counties between 1950 and 1975 was able to establish an association between highway construction and population and economic growth along the interstate corridor (Lichter & Fuguitt, 1980).

Ogburn's (1957) theory of cultural lag and other sociological research on adaptation to technological change are often considered examples of technological determinism, the crude theory that technological innovation dictates changes in social institutions and culture (Winner, 2004). But Ogburn demonstrated that in many instances cultural change occurs long before technological change. Such technological lags are major challenges to modern science and engineering. For example, American culture has come to depend on the availability of relatively cheap fossil fuels. As supplies dwindle or become more difficult to secure for political reasons, technological breakthroughs are needed to maintain the supply of low-cost energy. Thus, if physicists and engineers could control the nuclear fusion reaction (in which hydrogen atoms are fused into helium, releasing vast amounts of energy) so that its energy could be captured, Americans might once again have a source of plentiful, cheap fuel.

Fusion research is still in its early stages, however. Upon completion, the most powerful fusion reactor yet designed will be able to generate only about 3 percent as much wattage as the best fission reactors (Riley & McLaughlin, 2001). If economically feasible fusion reactors are to be built, the nation must invest in the training of additional physicists and technicians as well as research facilities and equipment. But because fusion research drains huge sums from the pool of money available for energy research, many critics argue that the federal government should diversify its research grants. They believe other technologies, such as solar energy, may become much more economical than fusion as researchers solve the problems that contribute to their cost. Public debate of this nature is an important part of the process of overcoming technological lag (Baillie & Casey, 2005).

The pressure to discover cheap and efficient routes to the control of nuclear fusion has led scientists to either falsify data or almost entirely neglect the rules of scientific inquiry. This seems to have occurred in the late 1980s in the case of two chemists, one in Utah and the other in England, who shocked the scientific world with the announcement that they had discovered a fusion reaction that did not require immense quantities of energy. While the team was garnering lucrative research contracts from firms that were hoping to profit from the discovery, efforts to replicate the cold fusion experiment were made in laboratories throughout the world. None of those efforts was successful. In a study of this scientific scandal, the research physicist Frank Close (1991) warns that the pressure to make discoveries and to bring in profits for universities and research institutes can create an incentive for unscientific manipulations of data or serious lapses in scientific judgment. The cold fusion fiasco illustrates why the norms of science are valuable and need to be protected (Lynch, 2005).

Transhumanism. Transhumanism is the very small but growing social movement that advocates the ethical use of technologies to enhance human capabilities. A combination of science fiction fantasy and serious applications of science, transhumanism is interested in how advances in genetics, biological methods, or the development of transplantable devices may extend human memory, sight, or strength. Transhumanists are fascinated by the idea of the **cyborg,** a creature that is part human and part technological systems, as represented in countless adventure films.

At this writing, examples of transhumanism are quite limited, but advances in creating artificial limbs and in transplant technologies suggest a bright future for advocates of these ideas. Voice recognition systems, genetic engineering of individual-specific

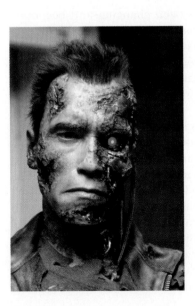

If cyborgs fascinate audiences in movie theatres, could it be because applications of cybernetic and biotechnical technologies are coming ever closer to creating them in reality?

drugs to fight cancer, and the use of stem cells to grow new limbs or organs for transplantation are technologies that already exist or are likely to in the near future. But there is much in transhumanism that generates lively debate. For example, it is similar in some ways to eugenics, the idea that "unfit" individuals should not be allowed to have children and that human selection to breed superior individuals should be encouraged. This discredited idea was actually put into effect in some of the sadistic and bizarre medical and population experiments conducted during the Nazi regime. According to their own official statements, however, transhumanists roundly reject eugenics and uphold the

> principles of bodily autonomy and procreative liberty. Parents must be allowed to choose for themselves whether to reproduce, how to reproduce, and what technological methods they use in their reproduction. The use of genetic medicine or embryonic screening to increase the probability of a healthy, happy, and multiply talented child is a responsible and justifiable application of parental reproductive freedom.
>
> Beyond this, one can argue that parents have a moral responsibility to make use of these methods, assuming they are safe and effective. Just as it would be wrong for parents to fail in their duty to procure the best available medical care for their sick child, it would be wrong not to take reasonable precautions to ensure that a child-to-be will be as healthy as possible. This, however, is a moral judgment that is best left to individual conscience rather than imposed by law. (www.transhumanism.org)

No doubt these ideas will raise many ethical and personal issues for sociologists and all members of society. But they are also likely to be with us as social issues well into the future.

TECHNOLOGY AND THE NATURAL ENVIRONMENT

In recent decades the American public has been increasingly concerned about the impact of pollution on its air and water (Brown, 2001). This concern has led to research and speculation about our ability to control the sometimes harmful effects of certain technologies on the natural environment. Barry Commoner (1992), one of the best known authorities on this subject, has described the fundamental problem in terms of a clash between the speed of change in human civilization and the pace of change in the cycles of the natural environment; he has also noted that most vital natural resources are rapidly being exhausted.

According to Commoner, human civilization has been changing and becoming more complex at an accelerating rate. The ideas, facts, and procedures that make up science and technology at any given time serve as a platform for future progress. A single technological advance such as the wheel, the internal-combustion engine, or the semiconductor may form the basis of an enormous range of inventions. As the ability of humans to exploit the resources of the earth has grown, so has the size of human populations (Commoner, 1992; Egan, 2007).

These two developments—accelerated technological and scientific change and rapid population growth—are causing pollution and depletion of the natural environment as never before. Natural cycles of purification can absorb only a limited amount of certain artificial substances before ecological damage is done. Water pollution occurs when streams, rivers, lakes, and oceans can no longer purify themselves. When wind, rain, and snow can no longer remove the particles deposited in the air by machines of various kinds, pollution is the result (Commoner, 1992; Toolan, 1998). In these cases, the speed at which technology creates pollutants exceeds the pace at which nature can absorb them. The spectacular fires and pollution that spewed from Kuwait's burning oil wells after the Persian Gulf war were stark reminders of the destructive forces unleashed by humans and the urgent need to control them.

Sometimes technologies that seem benign and that we take for granted as part of everyday life have unanticipated consequences. Earlier in this century pesticides and herbicides revolutionized agriculture, making it much more productive. Subsequent research has linked many of these chemicals to the destruction of fish and birds and to certain cancers in humans. Along the same lines, for years we used aerosol containers for purposes ranging from personal hygiene to applying whipped cream to ice-cream sundaes. In the mid-1970s the suspicion that a propellant used in aerosol cans was eroding the atmospheric ozone layer, which protects us from harmful radiation, led to the use of different propellants.

Perhaps the central question is this: Can we control such harmful effects before it is too late? In many cases the technology exists to control environmental damage, but powerful interests do not wish to shoulder the cost of doing so. Here the problem becomes one of creating a political consensus around a solution. In other cases, the technology needed to get us out of jams that earlier inventions have helped put us into does not yet exist. Thus, advanced economies around the world are consuming energy in the form of oil, which is becoming depleted and for which an adequate substitute has not yet been found. Any technological solution to this and other problems will almost inevitably contribute to a whole new generation of crises.

ENVIRONMENTAL STRESS

An investigation of winter fish kills in Wisconsin lakes led to the unexpected conclusion that they were caused by snowmobiles. Heavy snowmobile use on a lake during the winter compacts the snow and makes the ice opaque. This reduces the amount of sunlight that reaches underwater plants, which need it for photosynthesis. As the plants' oxygen production declines, they die, and their decomposition consumes considerable amounts of the oxygen left in the water. As a result, the fish are asphyxiated.

As this example suggests, we can best understand environmental stress as the interaction of three systems: the natural environment, the technological system, and the social system. The fish, ice, oxygen, and plants are all elements of the natural system. The snowmobile is an element of the technological system. That this vehicle is produced, marketed, and used is a product of the social system—as is the fact that no one is held responsible for the fish kills.

As recreational vehicles take more people off the roads and onto deserts, dunes, and frozen lakes, the negative impacts multiply.

Taking a broader perspective, we can define the natural system as containing these elements and their interrelationships: air, water, earth, solar energy, plants, animals, and mineral resources. Our technological system includes transportation, farming, electricity-generating facilities, manufacturing processes and plants, various methods for extracting mineral resources, and the actual consumption and disposal of the products of these processes. Our social system includes attitudes, beliefs and values, and institutional structures. And as with the fish and the snowmobiles, so in larger matters we must look to our social and technological processes for the origins of the problems in the natural system.

Origins of the Problem

The term **environmental stress** refers to what society does to the environment. Examples include discharging substances into the air, water, and soil; producing heat, noise, and radiation; removing plants and animals; and physically transforming the environment through drilling, damming, dredging, mining, pumping, and so on (Brown, 2001). Environmental stress is not synonymous with pollution, although pollution is perhaps its most familiar form. Webster's dictionary defines *pollution* as "a state of being impure or unclean, or the process of producing that state." **Environmental pollution,** therefore, is the presence of toxic agents added to the environment by society in quantities that are potentially damaging to humans and other organisms. (Ehrlich & Ehrlich, 2004).

Four concepts are basic to understanding environmental stress: interdependence, diversity, limits, and complexity (Ophuls, 1977). *Interdependence* literally means that everything is related to and depends on everything else; there is no beginning or end to the web of life. *Diversity* refers to the existence of many different life and life-support forms. A basic principle of ecology is that the greater the diversity of species, the greater the probability of survival of any given one. *Limits* are of several kinds. First, there is a finite limit to the growth of any organism. Second, there is a limit to the numbers of a given species that an environment—including other organisms—can support. Finally, there is a finite limit to the amount of materials available in the earth's ecosystem.

Complexity refers to the intricacy of the relationships that constitute the web. Because of this complexity, interventions in the environment frequently lead to unanticipated and undesired consequences. For example, DDT (dichloro-diphenyl-trichloro-ethane) was once repeatedly sprayed over large areas of land to eliminate various disease-carrying or crop-destroying insects. To an impressive degree, it succeeded. But DDT is a long-lasting chemical, and its effects are not limited to insects. Much of it was washed from farmlands and forests into rivers and oceans, where it was taken up by smaller organisms at the bottom of the food chain. Eventually, as small creatures consumed tiny plants and larger creatures consumed smaller ones, several species of fish-eating birds accumulated so much of the poison that their eggs developed very thin shells, which consistently broke before hatching. These species were in grave danger of extinction, although the users of DDT never intended such a result (Ehrlich & Ehrlich, 2004). Only federal restrictions on the use of DDT prevented the elimination of these bird species.

One of the major difficulties in dealing with environmental stress, therefore, is the number of problems involved and the extent to which they are interrelated. This will become clear as we explore the specific problems and the efforts that have been made to combat them.

Air Pollution

If the atmosphere is not overburdened, natural processes will cleanse it and preserve its composition. Through photosynthesis, for example, green plants combine water with the carbon dioxide that we and other organisms exhale, and they produce oxygen and carbohydrates. But these natural processes, like other resources, have limits. They can remove only a limited quantity of harmful substances from the air; if pollution exceeds their capacity to do so, the air will become progressively more dangerous to those who breathe it.

Human activities are overtaxing the atmosphere. Although the specific nature of air pollution varies from one locality to another (as a function of geography, climate, and type and concentration of industry), we can identify some of the common components. These include organic compounds (hydrocarbons); oxides of carbon, nitrogen, and sulfur; lead and other metals; and particulate matter (soot and fly ash).

In urban areas, almost half of the carbon monoxide in the air comes from motor vehicles. The remainder comes from the burning of fossil fuels (oil and coal) in power-generating plants, airplanes, and homes; airborne wastes from manufacturing processes; and the burning of municipal trash. Certain chemical processes frequently render these pollutants more dangerous after they reach the atmosphere. In the presence of sunlight, the emission of hydrocarbons and nitrogen oxides (primarily from cars) produces the photochemical soup, called smog, that envelops many of our cities; and various oxides combine with water vapor in the atmosphere to produce corrosive acids that eat away the surfaces of many buildings.

Pollution is particularly severe in parts of the world where regulations still permit the use of leaded gasoline and where large populations still rely on firewood or other combustibles for cooking. Over parts of China and Southeast Asia, for example, there is an atmospheric layer of ash and aerosol pollutants almost two miles thick extending for hundreds of miles that is disrupting weather systems and causing droughts in much of the region. This extreme air pollution may endanger continued growth in this rapidly developing part of the world as well as the health of millions of people (*Environment*, 2002).

Effects on Human Health. The effects of chronic air pollution are of great significance for human health in the long run. Continued exposure to air pollutants and their accumulation in the body—essentially a slow poisoning process—increases the incidence of such illnesses as bronchitis, emphysema, and lung cancer (Calhoun, 2005). Air pollution also causes severe eye, nose, and throat irritations, and poor visibility as a result of smog has been cited as a factor in both automobile and airplane accidents.

Well before the outbreak of SARS (severe acute respiratory syndrome), people in many Chinese cities were wearing masks in an effort to protect their lungs from high levels of dust and pollution.

Economic Effects. Air pollution has economic effects as well. Accelerated deterioration of property increases maintenance and cleaning costs; blighted crops mean lost income for farmers and higher food prices for consumers; pollution-caused illnesses erode productivity, reduce workers' earnings, and raise the cost of medical care for everyone. The sulfur emitted from the smokestacks of factories and power plants in the United States would be worth millions of dollars if it could be recovered.

Ecological Effects. Finally, air pollution may have a dangerous long-term effect on the earth's ecosystem. For example, several studies suggest that fluorocarbon gases, commonly used in spray cans and refrigeration systems, may be breaking down the earth's protective ozone layer (Yoon, 1994). (The ozone layer surrounds the earth from an altitude of eight to thirty miles above sea level; it screens out many of the sun's harmful rays.) Fluorocarbon molecules, according to these studies, are not broken down in the earth's lower atmosphere but continue to rise to a much higher altitude. Here they are broken up by high-intensity radiation and begin to chemically destroy ozone molecules. Destruction of the ozone layer would lead to a much higher worldwide incidence of skin cancer and crop failure; there would also be changes in the world's climate.

Concern about ozone depletion was heightened by the finding that the ozone layer above Antarctica decreases by roughly 40 percent each October, shortly after sunlight reappears following the Southern Hemisphere's winter months. The atmosphere's ozone layer screens out a portion of the sun's ultraviolet rays, exposure to which can cause skin cancers. But in areas of the earth where the ozone layer is depleted, especially southern Chile and Argentina, the risks associated with exposure to the sun increase dramatically. Release of chlorine gases into the air (from spray cans, for example) had been a major cause of the recent decline in atmospheric ozone. Since spray cans with chlorine gas propellants were banned in the United States and most other parts of the world in the 1990s, scientists have observed improvements in ozone levels, and further improvement is expected if chlorine and other pollutants can be regulated (Glausiusz, 2002). Recent reductions in the size of the ozone hole over Antarctica are an outstanding example of how action to reduce emissions of a particular pollutant can result in huge improvements in climate systems (Gore, 2006).

A particularly troublesome form of air pollution, and one that has attracted increasing attention in recent years, is **acid rain.** This term refers to rainfall that contains large concentrations of sulfur dioxide, which is emitted by utility and industrial plants in many parts of the nation. Acid rain has a highly detrimental effect on forests and lakes, causing severe damage to trees and to fish and other forms of aquatic life and polluting water supplies.

The Global-Warming Controversy. Of all the many aspects of pollution and environmental stress, perhaps none alarms scientists and environmental groups as much at present as **global warming**—the dangerous warming of the planet because of continued high levels of carbon emissions into the atmosphere. Created primarily by the burning of fuel by humans, the amount of carbon dioxide in the atmosphere is estimated to have increased by 15 to 25 percent since 1800 and is expected—assuming that we do nothing to prevent it—to reach twice the preindustrial level by 2050 (Union of Concerned Scientists, 2002).

Figure 15–4 shows the steady increase in average global temperatures since the industrial revolution, with the rate of increase accelerating over the past three decades. The United States, which consumes one-third of the world's energy, is the largest contributor to the production of greenhouse gases. Third-world countries burn fossil fuels at far lower rates than industrialized nations, but many of the former meet their energy needs by burning wood, straw, and similar fuels, which also emit carbon. And as countries such as South Korea become more industrialized, they increase their use of fossil fuels. At the same time, the felling and burning of forests in tropical countries adds between 1 billion and 2 billion tons of carbon emissions to the worldwide total. Growing populations and the associated demand for energy, land, and

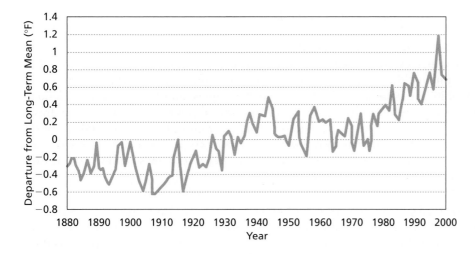

Figure 15–4 Global Temperature Changes, 1880–2000

Source: U.S. National Climate Data Center, 2001.

other resources mean that carbon emissions—and hence the amount of carbon dioxide in the atmosphere—are likely to increase for the foreseeable future. Some scientists are concerned that the buildup of carbon dioxide in the atmosphere could produce a "greenhouse effect." That is, the carbon dioxide would trap heat near the earth's surface, raising the average temperature of the atmosphere. Such overheating, even by a few degrees, could melt the polar ice caps, with calamitous results.

At present, there is widespread consensus among scientists that global warming is a real and present danger (Hesman, 2000). Still, there is continued debate about its implications. In 2005, for example, scientists reported that the Arctic ice cap had melted to an unprecedented degree (see Figure 15–5). Professor Liz Morris of the British Antarctic Survey, a world-renowned expert on the Arctic, noted,

> All data goes through cycles, and so you have to be careful, but it's also true to say that we wouldn't expect to have four years in a row of shrinkage. That, combined with rising temperatures in the Arctic, suggests a human impact; and I would also bet my mortgage on it, because if you change the radiation absorption process of the atmosphere (through increased production of greenhouse gases) so there is more heating of the lower atmosphere, sooner or later you are going to melt ice. (Quoted in Black, 2005)

The chief danger posed by shrinking sea ice is that it can accelerate the rise in sea levels, resulting in more dangerous coastal flooding like that which occurred during

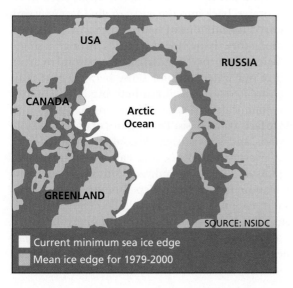

Figure 15–5 Arctic Ice in Retreat

Source: Reprinted by permission of the National Snow and Ice Data Center.

the severe hurricanes of 2005. It can also threaten the stability of massive ocean currents like the Gulf Stream, which could have catastrophic effects on the climate of the United States and other regions of the world. Still, the Bush administration and major energy companies are not convinced that these and similar changes are more than periodic fluctuations. Nor are they convinced that even if climate change is accelerating, all of its consequences will be negative. They question whether there is adequate scientific evidence to justify expensive retrofitting of power plants and more drastic measures to conserve energy. The administration, therefore, has proposed a series of voluntary guidelines and conservation measures that corporations can apply to reduce greenhouse gas emissions. This infuriates those who accept the scientific findings and fear imminent catastrophe (Purvis, 2004).

What is the main cause of global warming, and why is it a major social problem?

Radioactivity. The two large explosions that occurred on April 26, 1986, at the nuclear power plant in Chernobyl in the former Soviet Union released a cloud of radioactive gases over central and northern Europe. People in these regions experienced the highest levels of radioactive fallout ever recorded there. Two weeks later, minor airborne radioactivity was detected throughout the Northern Hemisphere (Flavin, 1987).

Many environmental scientists fear that the health of people in the former Soviet Union and Europe could be severely affected by this event for decades. Radioactivity is the most dangerous form of air pollution because it increases the probability that people will develop various kinds of cancer. Moreover, in the Chernobyl accident, 135,000 people had to be evacuated from populated areas within 20 miles of the plant. Thus, the problems of airborne radioactivity, together with the need to evacuate huge populations when accidents occur, have raised severe problems for the nuclear power industry throughout the world. Nor are such problems limited to recent years. Thousands of U.S. military personnel and civilians were exposed to high levels of radiation during the 1950s, when tests of nuclear explosions were conducted. The Clinton administration adopted a policy of making these events public so that the injured parties may seek compensation and so that confidence in the government's ability to control hazardous technologies can be restored.

Water Pollution

Water is constantly moving through what is known as the hydrologic cycle. It is found in the atmosphere as vapor; it condenses and falls to the earth as rain, snow, or dew; it percolates underground or runs off the surface as streams, rivers, and finally oceans; it evaporates into the atmosphere as vapor once again; and the cycle continues. While on the ground, water may be absorbed into the roots of plants and, through the leaves, eventually evaporate back into the atmosphere; or it may be drunk from streams by animals or people and excreted or evaporated back into the earth or air. Or it may sink into underground reservoirs and be stored for millions of years.

It is quite possible for water to be used more than once as it passes through a single round of the hydrologic cycle if it is sufficiently purified between uses by natural or artificial means. However, we render much of our water unfit for reuse because of various kinds of pollutants: raw and inadequately treated sewage, oil, synthetic organic chemicals (detergents and pesticides), inorganic chemicals and mineral substances, plant nutrients, radioactivity, and heat. We therefore face a dual crisis: The amount of water available to us could be insufficient for our demands, and what is available could be polluted.

Just as air can cleanse itself if not overburdened, so, too, can rivers, lakes, and oceans. But we have been discharging wastes, directly or indirectly, into our waterways in amounts that prohibit natural purification. In fact, some 25 percent of the U.S. population is not served by sewage treatment facilities (IBISWorld, 2005). The bacteria in untreated sewage render the water unfit for drinking, swimming, and many industrial uses. Finally, the use of oxygen to decompose the waste reduces the life-support capacity of the water, with a consequent decline in the number and variety of fish. As the population grows, the problem of waste disposal will become even more acute.

Current farming practices, such as extensive use of nitrate and phosphate fertilizers, also seriously impair water quality. Rain and irrigation cause the runoff of large quantities of these materials into rivers and lakes. The fertilizers work in water much as they do on land, producing algae "blooms"—huge masses of algae that grow very quickly and then die. As with the decomposition of sewage, the decay of these blooms consumes oxygen, thereby killing fish and other animals that have high oxygen requirements. As the algae decay, they settle at the bottom of the water, along with various compounds of nitrogen and phosphorus. At one time the bottom of Lake Erie was covered by a layer of muck from 20 to 125 feet thick. Only intensive efforts by environmentalists to stop pollutants from being discharged into the lake and adjoining waterways saved Lake Erie from total destruction.

Long-lasting pesticides and radioactive substances are especially dangerous because they accumulate in the tissues of animals that eat food contaminated with them. One reason this poses such a serious problem is the process known as biological magnification, whereby the concentration of a given substance increases as it ascends the food chain. This can be an especially serious danger in the vicinity of nuclear plants, where safe levels of radioactivity in the surrounding waters may still produce high levels of radioactivity in plankton. Those levels, in turn, can multiply to produce extremely high levels of radioactive contamination in birds and fish that eat these microorganisms (Ehrlich & Ehrlich, 1991).

Another form of water pollution is thermal pollution. The effluents of many factories and generating plants—especially nuclear power plants—are warmer than the rivers and lakes into which they flow, and when discharged in quantity they may raise the water temperature by as much as 10 to 30 degrees Fahrenheit. Such thermal pollution can be ecologically devastating. Because most aquatic animals are cold-blooded, they are at the mercy of the surrounding water temperature. If the temperature rises beyond an organism's capacity for metabolic adjustment, the animal will die. Because larvae and young animals are far more susceptible than mature organisms to slight temperature variations and because increases in temperature also interfere with the spawning and migratory patterns of many organisms, thermal pollution may exterminate some aquatic populations through reproductive failure.

Solid-Waste Disposal

We do not really "consume" most products, despite our reputation as a consumer society. It is more accurate to say that we buy things, use them, and then throw them away. Thus, we had over 410 million tons of solid wastes to dispose of in 2005 (an increase of 30 million tons from 2000), including food, paper, glass, plastic, wood, abandoned cars, cans, metals, paints, dead animals, and a host of other things (*BioCycle World*, 2005). The annual cost of disposing of such waste amounts to billions of dollars.

The two principal methods of solid-waste disposal are landfills and incineration. Although landfills are supposed to meet certain sanitary standards, violations are common. Improperly designed municipal incinerators are major contributors to urban air pollution. In 2005 the United States recycled approximately 30 percent of its solid-waste garbage; about 8 percent was incinerated and 62 percent placed in landfills (*BioCycle*, 2005).

The large-scale introduction of plastics and other synthetics has produced a new waste disposal problem: Whereas organic substances are eventually decomposed through bacterial action, plastics are generally immune to biological decomposition and remain in their original state when they are buried or dumped. If they are burned, they become air pollutants in the form of hydrocarbons and nitrogen oxides.

In the 1980s and 1990s the waste disposal problem took on new urgency as many landfill sites filled up and fears of groundwater contamination caused many communities to forbid the opening of new sites on their land. In 1987, in a notorious illustration of the seriousness of the problem, a barge filled with garbage from Long Island spent several weeks searching the East Coast for a site that would accept its load of waste.

The United States lags behind other industrial nations in efforts to deal with the problem of solid-waste disposal. The accumulation of garbage in landfills, like this site in Alaska, is becoming one of the nation's most critical environmental problems.

Currently, many states are trying to export their solid wastes elsewhere, primarily to states that are attempting to develop commercial landfill operations. In the meantime, however, there is a growing shortage of disposal sites as older ones are filled or closed as a result of community protests (Melosi, 2005).

Environmental Racism, Environmental Justice. Solid-waste dump sites are often located near low-income neighborhoods on the outskirts of metropolitan regions or in rural areas (Board, 1996). Because these neighborhoods are also quite likely to be home to members of minority groups, there is a growing tendency for solid-waste dumping to be a particular problem for African Americans and Latinos. Many local activists and residents of these neighborhoods term such dumping *environmental racism.* This issue is increasingly recognized, especially among African Americans, as a serious social problem that they experience to a far greater extent than would be expected if the dumping sites were located on a more equitable basis (Kenny, 1996). Low-income people—especially poor African Americans and Mexicans—have far higher levels of illnesses because of contamination of their water and gardens by toxic runoff from these dump sites.

The destruction of much of the U.S. Gulf Coast by severe hurricanes in 2005 exposed the consequences of years of environmental racism, as the most vulnerable households were those of poor people. Those who experienced the worst aspects of the environmental pollution caused by the storms were also disproportionately African Americans and other members of racial or ethnic minorities (especially Latinos and Vietnamese fishermen). Reponses to these and similar disasters are contributing to the growth of a global movement for environmental justice. Dorceta E. Taylor, an environmental sociologist at the University of Michigan, described the movement for environmental justice as "a well developed environmental ideological framework that explicitly links ecological concerns with labor and social justice concerns" (Taylor, 2000, p. 508). Robert Bullard, one of the movement's founders, has studied transportation policies in the United States and other nations and found that policies favoring private forms of transportation, especially the automobile, to the disadvantage of public mass transit—buses, subways, regional rail systems—contribute heavily to the disadvantage experienced by poor communities. At the same time, residents of those communities bear far more than their fair share of the burden of living near major oil refineries and chemical plants (Bullard, 2005).

Toxic Wastes. There is, in addition, the problem of toxic wastes or residues from the production of plastics, pesticides, and other products. These residues have typically been buried in ditches or pits. The famous case of Love Canal, near Niagara Falls, arose when toxic residues that had been dumped into the unfinished canal seeped into the surrounding area and contaminated both the soil and the water, creating severe health hazards for local residents. In 1978 Love Canal was declared an environmental disaster area, and more than 200 families were evacuated from the neighborhood. In early 1985, after more than six years of litigation, 1,300 former residents were awarded payments totaling $20 million in compensation for health problems (including birth defects and cancers) suffered as a result of the contamination of their neighborhood by toxic wastes. In 1991, thirteen years after the discovery of the contamination and the beginning of cleanup efforts, some houses in the Love Canal area were declared habitable again.

The problem of waste disposal is not limited to industrialized nations; it is becoming a worldwide concern, as described in the Social Problems: A Global View box on pages 498–499.

Radioactive Wastes. The United States currently produces about 20 percent of its electricity in nuclear power plants. These plants pose a special problem because the radioactive fuel in the reactor's core must be replaced periodically. The spent fuel must be deposited somewhere under extremely well-protected conditions because it is highly dangerous and can contaminate surrounding water and lands. In the last two decades, as tons of nuclear waste have accumulated in temporary storage sites, the U.S. government has spent over $4 billion on efforts to create a system for permanent storage. The United States currently has 77,000 tons of spent nuclear fuel and other nuclear wastes (*Ecologist*, 2002).

Radioactive wastes must be stored safely for up to 1,000 years before they become harmless. During that time, any alteration in the seismological conditions of the burial site could disturb the radioactive material and contaminate the area. A large facility under Yucca Mountain in Nevada is now ready, but disputes about its safety (e.g., in an earthquake) have cast some doubt on whether the facility will be used. There is also a major controversy over how the radioactive wastes would be transported to the site. Most people who think about the problem want the wastes to be disposed of properly, but few are willing to have trucks or trains carry these hazardous materials through their communities (*Ecologist*, 2002). In 2007, when an earthquake damaged significant quantities of radioactive waste material stored at a Japanese nuclear plant, people around the world were reminded of the growing danger posed by these wastes in a world hungry for energy. The incident was also a reminder of how much radioactive material is stored at locations throughout the world, from decommissioned nuclear weapons as well as existing weapons, a subject to which we return in the next chapter.

Other Hazards

Besides the environmental problems just noted, other threats to our well-being arise from the indiscriminate use of technological knowledge. These include land degradation, noise pollution, chemical hazards, and the undesirable consequences of certain large-scale engineering projects.

Land Degradation. Any local ecosystem, such as a forest, swamp, or prairie, is a complex matrix of interrelated and interacting organisms and processes, one that

GLOBAL CORPORATIONS AND ENVIRONMENTAL JUSTICE

As the disposal of toxic chemical wastes and other pollutants becomes an increasing problem in the United States and other developed nations, the corporations and governments that produce the waste are turning to impoverished nations for waste disposal. This practice often meets with resistance from indigenous peoples—Indians in Central and Latin America, Africans in Nigeria, and others. Too often, this resistance is crushed by authoritarian regimes in the areas targeted for waste disposal because lucrative dumping contracts represent new sources of money for corrupt officials far from the areas where dumping will take place.

The accompanying table lists countries that have recently been targeted for hazardous-waste dumping by companies based in the United States or other developed nations. The table also shows what kind of waste is involved in each case, along with its source.

Frances Adeola, a sociologist who studies global trends in environmental injustice and racism, notes that in Nigeria and the Amazon there have been killings of environmental activists who opposed the pollution of vast areas of land and the massive deforestation of their native habitats. Her research demonstrates the need for stronger international norms protecting human rights to a safe and sound environment. But in nations led by corrupt regimes such legislation is not likely without increased pressure from world agencies like the United Nations. Adeola and other social scientists argue forcefully that environmental justice must be included as a component of human rights proposals.

In the industrial region on the U.S.–Mexican border, pollution of local water runoff is often caused by American corporations doing business in Mexico. Environmental regulations contained in treaties like NAFTA (North American Free Trade Agreement) are not adequately enforced outside the United States.

both supports its own patterns of life and contributes to those of the larger regional, continental, and planetary ecosystems. Serious alteration of a local ecosystem, therefore, can affect the balance of life in a larger area. Yet through greed and/or ignorance of ecological principles, we have diminished or destroyed the capacity of large land areas to support life. We are only beginning to recognize the possible consequences.

Huge deserts can be created by misuse of the environment. In 1952, 23 percent of the earth's total land area was classified as desert or wasteland; by 2000, an estimated 36 percent of the earth's land area was threatened by desertification. In arid northwestern China, efforts to plow highly erodable land for increased grain production

Proposed Toxic Waste Dumping in Selected Third-World Countries by Multinational Corporations (MNCs)

Target Country	Waste Product	Amount	Source Country
Argentina	Sewage sludge	10,000 tons/month	U.S.
Bangladesh	Municipal waste	60,000 tons	U.S.
Belize	Sewage sludge	10,000 tons/month	U.S.
Brazil	Toxic industrial wastes	(unspecified volume)	U.S.
Colombia	Incinerator ash	1 million tons/year	MNC
Costa Rica	Incinerator ash, coal ash	200,000 tons/month, 3–4 million tons	U.S.
Dominican Republic	Incinerator ash	1 million tons/year	MNC
El Salvador	Incinerator ash, coal ash	200,000 tons/month, 3–4 million tons	U.S.
Equatorial Guinea	Radioactive material, radon, and dioxin	(unspecified volume)	MNC
Guatemala	Lead slag, incinerator ash	245,000 tons, 1 million tons/year	U.S.
Indonesia	Ash and residue waste, plastic waste	20,843 kg, 6,406,992 kg	MNC
Jamaica	Incinerator ash, garbage	1 million tons/year, 3,600 tons/day	MNC
Mexico	Chemical solvents and paint thinners, toxic waste	34 barrels, 6,500 drums	U.S.
Morocco	Toxic waste	2,000 metric tons	U.K.
Namibia	Sludge, plastic, infectious nuclear wastes	7 million tons/year	U.S.
Nicaragua	Incinerator ash, municipal waste	200,000 tons/month, 1,700 tons/day	U.S.
Panama	Incinerator ash	30 million tons	U.S.
Papua New Guinea	Toxic waste	over 600,000 metric tons/month	MNC
Paraguay	Garbage	100,000–200,000 tons/month	U.S.
Philippines	Lead acid battery waste; plastic waste	(unspecified volume)	MNC
Sri Lanka	Plastic waste and scrap	over 425 tons	MNC
Thailand	Uranium and thorium	over 13,000 tons	U.S.
Uruguay	Industrial waste; toxic waste	(unspecified quantity)	MNC
Venezuela	Industry-contaminated sewage sludge, dissolved air flotation from the petroleum refining industry	40,000 tons/year, (unspecified volume)	MNC

Source: Proposed Toxic Waste Dumping in Selected Third-World Countries by Multinational Corporations (MNCs) from the article "Environmental Justice Human Rights–Social Aspects," by F.O. Adeola. Copyright © 2000 by *American Behavioral Scientist* 43 (4). Reprinted by permission of Sage Publications, Inc.

have resulted in huge dust storms that are contributing to desertification (Brown, 2001). Recent research on the expansion of arid lands and deserts shows that overgrazing by domesticated animals, dependence on wood for fuel, and depletion of soil nutrients by crops produce desertification. When natural cycles of drought and wet seasons interact with human overuse, the rate of desertification can increase drastically (Herrmann & Hutchinson, 2005). It takes from 300 to 1,000 years to produce one inch of topsoil under the most favorable conditions. Many areas of the earth are now losing topsoil at the rate of several inches per year because of management techniques that expose the soil to wind and water erosion. Such irreparable losses are intolerable in view of the world's increased need for arable land.

Shorelines like this one in Turkey are fouled with garbage, a global environmental problem.

Noise Pollution. Noise is a dysfunctional consequence of technology. It is produced by airplanes, cars, buses, trucks, motorcycles, motorboats, factory machinery, dishwashers, garbage disposals, vacuum cleaners, television, radio, phonographs, air conditioners, jackhammers, bulldozers, and much else. Noise, which can be harmful even when it is not consciously heard, directly affects physical and emotional well-being. Studies have shown that people today suffer from greater hearing losses with increasing age than in the past and that noise contributes significantly to the tension of daily life, sometimes even precipitating stress-related illnesses like peptic ulcer and hypertension (O'Neil, 2002). Hearing loss caused by excessive noise now affects about 10 million people in the United States, especially those who work in loud environments or who listen to extremely loud music on earphones. There is also evidence from recent studies that noise from nearby airports can adversely affect the reading scores of schoolchildren (Maxwell & Evans, 1997).

Chemical Contamination and Globalization of the Food Supply. Pressure to get new products on the market has resulted in the widespread use of various pesticides and herbicides without adequate testing of their long-run cumulative effects. It has also led to the massive use of plastics and other synthetics, which create serious problems of disposal, and untested industrial chemicals like vinyl chloride gas. Moreover, there has been a proliferation in the variety and amount of food additives—chemicals that are used in processing food and sometimes cause allergic reactions. Little is known about the long-term effects of continual ingestion of these substances, either alone or in combination.

Chemical contamination of the global food supply is a growing social problem. In 2007 hundreds of people in Panama were sickened by contaminated toothpaste imported from China. Pets died in a number of countries, including the United States, because a Chinese factory had illegally substituted a toxic chemical for glycerine. The crisis, which continues at this writing, threatens the Chinese economy and the reputation of its products. In the United States, the scandals revealed how difficult it is to prevent the importation of contaminated products. Cuts in funding reduced the number of field inspectors employed by the Food and Drug Administration by almost 30 percent

This river has been "liberated," in that a dam that once impeded the migration of fish upriver has been demolished. Part of a growing trend in the United States and Canada, the removal of dams, while often desirable for environmental reasons, may conflict with the need for electricity generated by hydroelectric power.

between 2000 and 2003, reducing the agency's regulatory effectiveness and increasing the risks to consumers (Barboza, 2007).

Large-Scale Engineering Projects. Humans have always taken immense pride in their ability to change the face of the earth in ways that are deemed beneficial. However, they frequently fail to anticipate and assess the associated costs. Thus, a new dam is hailed both as an engineering masterpiece and as an improvement to the surrounding area because it opens up new lands for agriculture, settlement, and recreation. Less often recognized is that although a dam may permit the controlled distribution of water to desired locations, it also results in water loss through evaporation. Moreover, large dams have caused earthquakes because of the tremendous pressure exerted by the billions of gallons of water they store.

Strip mining also poses hazards to the environment. Much of the coal in the United States lies deep within the earth and must be obtained by underground mining. However, there is also a great deal of coal lying close enough to the surface for strip mining, in which the top layers of soil are removed so that the coal can be excavated. Although strip mining is cheaper and safer than underground mining, it causes much greater harm to the environment. Vast areas of land are denuded of all living things and scarred by huge, ugly trenches. Because the topsoil is removed during the strip-mining process, healthy plant life cannot return for centuries. And because the soil balance is disturbed, water supplies in the area may be irreparably damaged; increased erosion at the mining site can cause both local and distant water sources to become contaminated by sediment, dissolved acids, and other pollutants.

THE UNITED STATES AND THE WORLD ENVIRONMENT

William C. Clark (1989) has written, "Our ability to look back on ourselves from outer space symbolizes the unique perspective we have on our environment and on where we are headed as a species. With this knowledge comes a responsibility not borne by the bacteria: the responsibility to manage the human use of planet earth" (p. 47). Because Americans are among the wealthiest, the most educated, and the most polluting of the earth's peoples, environmental scientists often argue that they bear a large share of the responsibility for wise management of the planet.

The difference in living standards between the United States and most other countries is enormous. In stark contrast to the hunger that prevails in many poor nations, the increased affluence of the United States and other developed countries has made possible a steady increase in per capita consumption of meat and other nutritious foods. In fact, Americans consume, on the average, four times as much food per person as people in poor nations. This is not to say that all Americans are overfed. The poor in the United States, like those in poor countries, are plagued by hunger, malnutrition, and disease (Brown, 2004).

The food consumed by Americans includes a much larger proportion of meat than of grain. By contrast, three-fourths or more of the food energy in the diet of Asians comes directly from grain (Ehrlich & Ehrlich, 1991). Vast quantities of grain—one-third of total world production—are fed to livestock in the United States and other developed countries to produce meat. It is sometimes claimed that this practice is immoral because the grain fed to livestock in the United States could be used to nourish hungry people elsewhere in the world.

It is true that the United States exports large amounts of grain to all parts of the world. Some of these exports are part of international aid programs that help alleviate the problem of hunger in the poorer nations; in fact, some of the world's least developed nations depend heavily on this aid. But it remains true that the developed nations consume a disproportionate share of the world's food resources.

Figure 15–6 compares energy and resource consumption in major regions of the world. It shows that with only 5 percent of the world's population, the United States consumes 25 percent of the world's fossil fuel and produces 72 percent of its hazardous waste. Because the high-consumption American lifestyle is emulated in many developing nations, it is difficult to imagine how conservation can become a stronger value than it is today (Bender & Smith, 1997).

The significance of these facts is twofold. The industrialized nations consume a disproportionate share of total food and energy resources, leaving comparatively little for the majority of the world's population. This is one explanation—though by no means the only one—for the desperate plight of people in the least developed nations. The other major effect of the dominant position of the United States in the world economy is that it contributes to environmental problems both at home and abroad. As the

Figure 15–6 Share of Population, Resource Consumption, and Waste Production

Source: Natural Resources Defense Council, 2007.

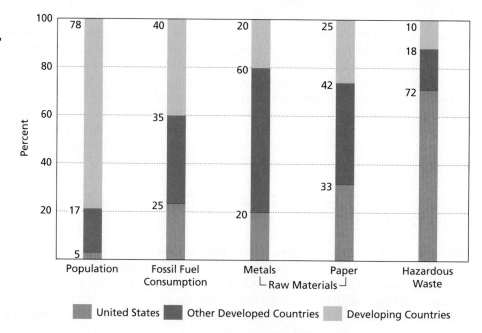

| TABLE 15–1 | Annual Water Availability Per Capita for Seven Regions with Water Problems (Annual Water Availability Per Capita of Less Than 1 Million Liters Per Year) and for the United States |

A	B
Egypt	40
West Bank	126
Jordan	255
Saudi Arabia	300
Israel	376
Syria	440
Kenya	610
United States	1862

A: region; B: water availability per capita (thousands of liters per year).

Source: Water Resources: Agricultural and Environmental Issues. DAVID PIMENTEL, BONNIE BERGER, DAVID FILIBERTO, MICHELLE NEWTON, BENJAMIN WOLFE, ELIZABETH KARABINAKIS, STEVEN CLARK, ELAINE POON, ELIZABETH ABBETT, and SUDHA NANDAGOPAL. BioScience, Vol. 54, Issue 10, pp. 909–918, October 2004. Copyright, American Institute of Biological Sciences.

world's most industrialized nation, the United States "exports" technologies that can contribute substantially to the environmental problems of other nations. A vivid example is the disaster that occurred in Bhopal, India, in December 1984, in which a deadly gas, methyl isocyanate, escaped from a Union Carbide storage tank, killing more than 2,000 people and injuring about 100,000 others.

In sum, as populations increase in size and affluence, the complexity of social organization, the imbalances in energy and food budgets, the depletion of resources, and the difficulty of correcting these problems also increase. If the United States is to maintain its position as a world leader, it must take the lead in developing a way to control environmental problems.

The United States and other affluent nations can use their resources to help control the growth of the world's population. Through their own aid and through cooperation with agencies of the United Nations and the World Bank, they can help poorer nations develop more adequate and sustainable water supplies. The severe shortage of water in the arid Middle East and many parts of Africa contributes to the political problems of these regions, as shown in Table 15–1. Ecologists estimate that unless continued action is taken, water shortages in arid areas of the world may produce serious regional conflicts and even warfare (Pimentel et al., 2004).

What does the U.S. share of world energy consumption have to do with the controversy over global warming?

Social Policy

The administration of George W. Bush came to office in January 2001 ready to fulfill its campaign promise to review and revise all environmental actions of the Clinton–Gore administration that it believed placed undue regulatory burdens on industry and commerce and thus represented obstacles to economic growth. In consequence, in one of its first and most controversial environmental rulings, the administration refused to sign the international treaty to establish goals for reductions in emissions of carbon dioxide and other greenhouse gases (known as the Kyoto Protocol). Since

A herd of musk oxen graze inside one of the proposed oil exploration sites in the Arctic National Wildlife Refuge, in Alaska.

then, it has rolled back environmental regulations for national forests, mining in national parks, wetland preservation, and much more. At this writing, it is continuing to pursue an extremely controversial plan for oil drilling in the Arctic National Wildlife Refuge, arguing that the oil that may be available there could help offset domestic energy shortages. Opponents of the plan argue that the amount of oil potentially available in the refuge does not justify the impacts of drilling and pipeline construction in one of the last great wilderness regions in the nation.

On what may be a more positive front, though it is also highly political, the administration has issued the first regulations that place limits on California's ability to siphon water from the Colorado River. With an extremely conservative coalition dominating Congress, environmental activist groups consider the prospects for any positive environmental legislation to be extremely bleak, and with the continued threat of terrorism and conflict in the Middle East, the environmental situation at the global level is also quite uncertain.

Policy on Global Warming

In 2002 the Bush administration announced a policy of funding additional studies of global warming, a decision that was denounced by environmental groups in the United States and throughout the world. The consensus among earth scientists is that global warming poses a genuine threat and needs to be addressed immediately through increased efforts to curb emissions of greenhouse gases. They argue that further study of the situation is always needed, but that in this instance it represents a cynical effort to delay the responsibility to do anything about the crisis. Most experts agree that without U.S. support, efforts to reduce emissions will be ineffective. Despite these fears, in 2002 negotiators from 165 countries agreed on a set of rules for implementing the 1997 Kyoto Protocol, which calls on about forty industrialized nations to limit their carbon emissions or reduce them below 1990 levels.

The United States and Australia, the two major nations that refused to sign the Kyoto accords, argue that developing nations, especially China and India, are now emitting a great deal of carbon dioxide and other greenhouse gases. The Bush administration's policy, as noted earlier, is to urge the developing nations to voluntarily control their emissions, just as it is urging energy suppliers and automakers in the

United States to voluntarily restrict domestic greenhouse gas emissions. Few experts on energy policy expect that voluntary compliance will yield significant reductions in the coming years. They are far more positive about the administration's ideas concerning the creation of markets for emission credits (*International Debates*, 2005).

Pollution Credits. The creation of markets to buy and sell pollution credits is a more conservative antipollution policy favored by the Bush administration and by many experts on global pollution problems. Companies that pollute could acquire credits from the agency in charge of regulating their particular industry by reducing their emissions below the levels set by the agency. They could then sell the credits to other companies whose emissions exceed regulatory maximums. The market in credits rewards industries that clean up their act while allowing those that cannot reduce emissions to continue to operate without society as a whole exceeding global limits on greenhouse gases. This market approach was included in the Kyoto program, and on a global scale the total value of pollution trading markets is now over $2.2 billion a year. But the Bush administration and its allies in Congress have failed to establish the regulatory levels for greenhouse gasses that would permit a full-scale market for pollution credits to develop in the United States. On the other hand, they have proposed a pollution trading system for mercury emissions, a proposal that is highly problematic because some pollutants, such as mercury and sulfur dioxide, are so toxic and dangerous that companies should not be permitted to release them into the environment (Bowen, 2002).

How do pollution credit systems promise to reduce global carbon dioxide emissions?

Science and Policy Making. The refusal to accept the recommendations of innumerable scientific commissions, and especially those of the National Academy of Sciences on global warming, has created a great deal of conflict between the nation's scientists and the Bush administration. The conflict between conservative policymakers and scientists goes far beyond energy and pollution policies, however. In 2004 more than 60 leading scientists—Nobel laureates, leading medical experts, former federal agency directors, and university chairs and presidents—voiced their concern over the misuse of science by the Bush administration, starting with global warming:

> The administration has consistently misrepresented the findings of the National Academy of Sciences, government scientists, and the expert community at large. Thus in June 2003, the White House demanded extensive changes in the treatment of climate change in a major report by the Environmental Protection Agency (EPA). To avoid issuing a scientifically indefensible report, EPA officials eviscerated the discussion of climate change and its consequences.

Scientists who have worked on policy evaluations of birth control medications (e.g., the plan B contraceptive), on basic biological research (e.g., stem cells), on environmental impacts (e.g., lead and mercury poisoning), and many other issues joined in stating that

> When scientific knowledge has been found to be in conflict with its political goals, the administration has often manipulated the process through which science enters into its decisions. This has been done by placing people who are professionally unqualified or who have clear conflicts of interest in official posts and on scientific advisory committees; by disbanding existing advisory committees; by censoring and suppressing reports by the government's own scientists; and by simply not seeking independent scientific advice. Other administrations have, on occasion, engaged in such practices, but not so systematically nor on so wide a front. Furthermore, in advocating policies that are not scientifically sound, the administration has sometimes misrepresented scientific knowledge and misled the public about the implications of its policies. (Union of Concerned Scientists, 2002)

For its part, the administration has answered its critics in the scientific community by claiming that it values science but often finds scientists to be ideologically biased or to fail to understand that their findings are often inconclusive and that elected officials have the final say about major social policies. Thus, the administration prefers to speak of global climate change, a more neutral term in its view, rather than the more alarming term *global warming*, because it believes the scientific community has not fully established whether the planet's climate is actually warming due to greenhouse gases. This further angers many natural and social scientists, who see the president's statements about intelligent design, global climate change, stem cell research, and many other controversial scientific issues as fundamentally antiscience. In assessing the conflict, Nobel laureate David Baltimore (2004) concluded that

> Either religious conservatism or economically based political caution has played a determining role in administration policy. However, it looks as though the criticism from individual scientists and from the Union of Concerned Scientists has been influential in causing the administration to be more honest about the underlying science. We should welcome this new posture. Nevertheless, although the realities of the science may be better accepted, the policy implications are still being ignored. Our goal now should be to have the policies track the science.

Appropriate Technology

As is evident from much of the discussion in this chapter, issues of environmental control and restoration often overlap with policies designed to reduce the negative effects of new technologies. The growing fields of technology assessment and risk assessment, for example, contributed to the sensational debates that culminated in the defeat of legislation to fund research and development of a commercial supersonic passenger airplane in the United States (Hall, 1982; Ormes, 1973). Public fears about the effects of sonic booms were not allayed by the results of scientific assessments, and the proposal was defeated. England and France went on to produce a supersonic jet, the Concorde, which has shown that sonic boom effects can be controlled. Social policies that deal with technologies and their environmental consequences are extremely controversial—especially when potentially lucrative products are involved—making scientific assessment of the environmental impact of proposed technologies even more important.

Appropriate technologists advocate major changes in technology itself. In most cases **appropriate technology** is smaller-scale technology. Thus, Amory Lovins (1977, 1986) argues that we need to reexamine our basic way of life and the energy needs that accompany it. Renewable energy sources such as wind and solar energy, which can be harnessed by families and communities, are preferable to such sources as nuclear power, which is polluting, requires massive amounts of capital, and is controlled by large corporations.

The appropriate technologists are often accused of advocating an impractical retreat to a simpler way of life. In answer to this charge, they argue that their alternatives sound impractical because most people assume that continued economic and institutional expansion is necessary. A closer examination of social needs would make smaller-scale technology seem more appropriate. Appropriate technologists also point out that they do not oppose all technology, only large-scale technology that has unfavorable social consequences (Clifford, 2005).

Future Prospects

Facing intense pressure from nations that have taken the lead in addressing the problem of global warming, in 2007 the U.S. Congress began taking steps to establish the basic regulatory mechanisms necessary for a "cap and trade" approach to the reduction of greenhouse gases. Under such a system, Congress and the president would agree on upper limits for carbon dioxide emissions by energy producers. Companies whose emissions exceeded those limits could buy credits that would allow them to exceed the carbon cap by a specified amount. The credits would be purchased from companies that had reduced their emissions and received credits for those reductions. Note, however, that such a market is based on a regulatory regime that imposes emission limits and penalties for those who exceed them. Such regulation is opposed by the Bush administration, which favors voluntary controls on emissions. Since such voluntary controls have proven ineffective, after 2008 a new Congress and president are very likely to fall into step with other nations in accepting regulation that leads to a carbon trading system. The urgency of the global warming crisis will no doubt encourage this change, as well as others on a broad range of environmental issues.

GOING BEYOND LEFT AND RIGHT

Do companies have the right to pollute or exterminate endangered species to save jobs? People on the ideological right often answer this question with a qualified yes. Those on the left often say no, arguing instead that environmental restoration will add new, less damaging jobs to the economy. In some parts of the world these debates are extremely rancorous; the same is true of disputes over timber cutting in the western part of the United States.

Another view of environmental problems suggests that no matter what our politics are, we are the problem. Most people who live in affluent nations consume large quantities of gasoline and other consumer goods. Unless we begin to understand the global consequences of our consumption, it is argued, we will never reduce the level of stress on the environment. This is an argument based on facts. However, although it goes beyond left–right debates, it is not very popular with large segments of the American public.

A good example of social policy that goes beyond the traditional divisions between conservatives and liberals is the growing demand for "cap and trade" markets for carbon dioxide and other greenhouse gas emissions. Such a market would enable companies that cannot reduce their emissions of these gases to buy credits that would allow them to exceed the limits. Companies that reduced their emissions would earn credits that they could sell to companies that need them. While this market system is based on regulations designed to reduce greenhouse gas emissions, it relies on market principles for enforcement. Thus, it is a mixed policy of regulation (caps on emissions) and free market trading.

Summary

- Technology has three dimensions: the apparatus, or physical devices, used in accomplishing a variety of tasks; the activities involved in performing these tasks; and the organizational networks associated with activities and apparatus.

- Existing patterns of inequality in different regions of the world prevent more equal access to new technologies. In the United States, the gap between those with access to computers and those who lack such access is referred to as the digital divide.

- Advances in technology can have both positive and negative effects. When technology has adverse side effects,

people tend to blame the technology itself rather than the combination of economic, social, and technical factors.

- The concept of autonomous technology is a recurrent one in American social thought. One element in this concept is the idea that technology has become independent of human control. Most writers on the subject do not believe this is the case. Instead, they argue that the social order has become interwoven with the technological order to such an extent that we have become enmeshed in a web of dependency.

- In bureaucratic organizations, individuals may commit immoral acts because they are not personally responsible for the consequences of those acts, which are carried out under the direction of superiors. Whistle-blowers are individuals who place their personal moral concerns in opposition to the activities of an organization. They often suffer as a result of their efforts.

- The best known statement about the relationship between technology and institutions is Ogburn's theory of cultural lag. According to Ogburn, a cultural lag occurs when one of two correlated parts of a culture changes before or in greater degree than the other, thereby causing less adjustment between the two parts than existed previously. Typically, social institutions and technology readily adjust and readjust to each other, but sometimes one or the other changes radically and a lag develops.

- Environmental stress results from the interaction of the environment, the technological system, and the social system. This interaction produces air and water pollution, problems of solid-waste disposal, and other hazards. A difficulty in dealing with environmental stress is the number of problems involved and the extent to which they are interrelated.

- Americans consume, on the average, four times as much food per person as people in less developed countries. Energy resources and consumption are also distributed unevenly throughout the world, with energy use in the United States amounting to about one-third of the worldwide total. To satisfy their high standard of living, Americans put enormous stress on the environment. Many observers believe that the United States should take the lead in efforts to reverse the effects of environmental stress throughout the world.

- A number of laws designed to control or reduce the harm being done to the environment have been passed since the 1960s, and some progress has been made. The 1997 U.N. conference on global warming drafted an international agreement—the Kyoto Protocol—on reducing the emission of greenhouse gases. The Clinton administration took steps to tighten regulations concerning air pollution, solid-waste disposal, and drainage of wetlands; and it invoked the 1965 Civil Rights Act to combat excessive exposure to pollution hazards in minority communities. However, the Bush administration has refused to sign the Kyoto Protocol and has rolled back environmental regulations in many areas.

- Appropriate technologists advocate changes in large-scale technologies that have unfavorable social consequences. Technology assessment and risk assessment use both physical and social-scientific methods in studying the social consequences of existing and proposed technologies.

Key Terms

technology, p. 477
technological dualism, p. 478
digital divide, p. 480
whistle-blowers, p. 482

cultural lag, p. 485
cyborg, p. 487
environmental stress, p. 490
environmental pollution, p. 490

acid rain, p. 492
global warming, p. 492
appropriate technology, p. 506

Social Problems Online

Organizations that seek to conserve and protect the environment are well represented on the Internet. The oldest environmental group in the United States, the National Audubon Society, can be accessed at **www.audubon.org**/. Its Web page provides legislative updates, information about the organization, and educational campaigns. Virtual nature walks feature text and graphics about local flora and fauna from the society's sanctuaries, such as Florida's Corkscrew Swamp.

The Sierra Club "promotes conservation of the natural environment by influencing public policy decisions." Its Web site at **www.sierraclub.org**/offers online copies of its magazines, *Planet* and *Sierra,* that inform the reader about urban ecology as well as endangered species and natural wonders. The Web page also addresses momentous issues such as global warming.

The activist group Earth First! (**www.earthfirst.org**) defines its mission as working to save "the earth's remaining sacred natural land and its inhabitants from the destructive greed of corporations."

The Nature Conservancy (**www.tnc.org**/) preserves wetlands and other environmentally sensitive and threatened areas by purchasing them or controlling their use. Its Web page provides links to a library, the magazine *Nature Conservancy,* and descriptions of programs in the United States, the Caribbean, and South America.

Envirolink, at **www.envirolink.org**/, is an Internet site with links to other environmental groups throughout the English-speaking world. It includes a daily update of news stories about ecological issues. Organizations critical of the mainstream environmental movement on the grounds that it overestimates ecological damage or encourages unwarranted government involvement include the Science & Environmental Policy Project (SEPP) (**www.sepp.org**/) and the Heartland Institute (**www.heartland. org**/), which both offer downloadable reports. SEPP targets its publications toward the scientific community and the media.

Research Navigator

Follow the instructions on pages 26–27 of this text to access the features of Research Navigator. Once at the Web site, enter your Login Name and Password. Then, to use the Content Select database, use keywords such as "global warming," "identity theft," and "environmental justice," and the search engine will supply relevant and recent scholarly and popular press publications. Use the *New York Times* search-by-subject archive to find recent news articles related to problems of technology and the environment, and the Link Library to find relevant Web sites organized by the key terms associated with this chapter.

In Research Navigator, go to the EBSCO host and type in "energy independence." Among the first entries you should find is an article by Philip J. Deutch entitled "Energy Independence." What does the author tell us about limiting our reliance on foreign sources of oil? What does the author think about alternative sources of energy such as wind power, coal as a replacement for foreign imports, and nuclear power? Do you agree or disagree with his arguments?

16

WAR AND GLOBAL *Insecurity*

Dominant Trends

- Terrorism will remain a major global concern as groups with little military power attempt to use the techniques of "asymmetrical warfare," such as suicide bombings, to terrify civilian populations and weaken the regimes they oppose.

- Warfare will remain a global scourge, accounting for the loss of millions of lives each decade. During World War II, for example, almost 17 million soldiers and 35 million civilians were killed.

- People who have been displaced by warfare and terrorism will continue to crowd makeshift refugee camps and refugee neighborhoods. In Iraq there are at least 4 million displaced people within the country and in camps in nearby nations.

- The war in Iraq will add many thousands of disabled veterans to the roster of those receiving compensation from the U.S. government for war-related disabilities (more than 2 million in 2007).

- Efforts to prevent nations like Iran and North Korea from producing nuclear weapons and efforts to keep nuclear materials and weapons from terrorist groups will remain a central concern for the United Nations and most of the world's nations.

Terrorism was a serious social problem in the United States and many other regions of the world before the suicide bombing of the World Trade Center and the Pentagon on September 11, 2001. One need only think of the years of terrorist bombings in Northern Ireland or Sri Lanka, the deadly bombing in Oklahoma City, sniper attacks against abortion clinic doctors, the episodes of terror attacks in Israel and elsewhere in the Middle East, or on the Indian subcontinent, or in Russia and Chechnya. But since 9/11 and the declaration by the U.S. government of a "war against terrorism," the world has entered a new era in which terrorism and armed responses against suspected terrorists have become dominant issues. Terrorism in the post-9/11 world and the American and British invasion and occupation of Iraq in 2003 have had enormous impacts on global economic conditions, on the ability to travel and maintain open borders, on civil rights and the protection of basic freedoms, and much else, as we will see in this chapter.

The new century and millennium began on a note of great hope for world peace. The sudden fall of the Soviet Empire and the destruction of the Berlin Wall ended the long period of superpower conflict known as the cold war. Indeed, the twentieth century had been called the Century of Total War, both because of the vast increase in the human capacity for waging war and because the possibility of wars that involve the entire globe is inherent in the rise of nations with global political ambitions (Aron, 1955). Although the end of the cold war has somewhat lessened the threat of global war and nuclear holocaust, the spread of advanced weapons around the globe, the rise of smaller nuclear powers such as North Korea and Iran, and the worsening of environmental and ethnic problems have increased the threat of wars of all kinds in many parts of the world. At this writing, the crisis over nuclear arms production in Iran is worsening just as the United States and Britain attempt to bring about a new and more democratic regime in Iraq and end their occupation of that country.

What can be done to reduce the likelihood of terrorism and war? No one can answer this question with certainty. Much may depend on how well individual citizens understand the causes and consequences of terrorism and war, and on how effectively they participate in debates over policies designed to control and limit the use of force in settling national differences.

TERRORISM, GLOBAL AND DOMESTIC

The FBI (2007) defines **terrorism** as "the unlawful use of force or violence against persons or property to intimidate or coerce a government, the civilian population, or any segment thereof, in furtherance of political or social objectives." Violent terrorist acts—kidnapping, torture, bombings, and the like—are often committed by a nation or by a political movement to call attention to its cause and to shake people's faith in the ability of their government to eliminate the threat. The movement may be a revolutionary one that seeks far-reaching change in the government or hopes to gain control over the state. But not all terrorism is revolutionary in nature. The terrorism of cocaine barons in Colombia (known as **narcoterrorism**) is designed to take revenge on the authorities and to intimidate them into lax enforcement of the law. The terrorism of governments like that of Nigeria against their own people (known as repressive terrorism or **state terrorism**) is also not associated with revolutionary movements (Mazrui, 1996).

But **revolutionary terrorism** is the most common form, and it often leads to the other types. In Peru, for example, the revolutionary terrorist group Túpac Amaru opposes the government but also protects cocaine traffickers in return for funds to support the movement. In the Middle East, revolutionary Arab terrorist groups like Hammas and Hezbollah have been enlisted by heads of state, such as Saddam Hussein and Muammar Qaddafi, to conduct repressive terrorist acts. In Northern Ireland, terrorism was motivated by the desire of the Irish Republican Army and its nonmilitary civil party, Sinn Fein, to achieve independence from England, but the Protestant minority fears independence, and the resulting political stalemate still erupts in terrorist violence from time to time.

Since 9/11, terrorism has become the most dangerous threat to world order. In its effects, and sometimes in its causes, terrorism is comparable to more traditional forms of war. It destabilizes governments, preys on innocent victims, and involves large amounts of financial and human resources. Yet unlike war, which openly pits opponents against each other in a recognized trial of strength, terrorism is covert. It seeks to sway the masses through intimidation.

The bombings of the federal office building in Oklahoma City, the World Trade Center in New York City, and the Pentagon; the letter bombs mailed by the so-called

This photo captures the shock and terror experienced by people who witnessed the 9/11 terrorist attacks, both as the attacks occurred and later, as they stood before the smoldering wreckage and watched rescue workers frantically combing through the rubble.

Although, as of 2007, there have been no major acts of terrorism in the United States since 2001, bombings in Madrid, London, Jordan, Indonesia, Pakistan, and other nations indicate that terrorism remains a serious threat to world peace and international security.

Unabomber; the still unresolved acts of bioterrorism in which deadly anthrax spores were released in Senate offices and elsewhere in the United States; the nightclub bombing in Bali, Indonesia; the bombing in the London Underground in 2005; and the attempted bombings in Scotland in 2007 are only a few recent examples of terrorism. These acts suggest that terrorism is increasing not just in the United States but throughout the world.

Measuring Terrorism in the United States

Well before the destruction of the World Trade Center, the FBI was engaged in efforts to track trends in terrorist acts against civilians within U.S. territorial boundaries. This is a difficult task, because many acts of violence may not be perpetrated by people or groups seeking to further their political aims. And some groups that advocate violence may not actually be responsible for violence committed in their names. Much depends on careful investigation and meticulous tracking of groups that do advocate violence. At any given moment, the FBI may be conducting investigations of hundreds of cases of suspected terrorism. When the crimes committed indicate a pattern that seems to involve the continued threat of political violence from an individual or group, the Bureau opens a special "domestic security/terrorism investigation."

Even before 9/11, during the 1990s, the FBI was routinely conducting eight to twelve such investigations simultaneously. Groups charged and indicted for acts of terrorism during the ten-year period from 1988 to 1998 included members of both domestic and international terrorist groups. Among the domestic groups, the analysis included domestic left-wing groups, many of which espouse revolutionary Marxist ideologies. Domestic environmental terrorist groups and domestic right-wing terrorist groups espouse a wide range of racist-white-supremicist, fundamantalist-antiabortion, or extreme fascist-Nazi ideologies. Three times as many domestic right-wing terror groups as left-wing ones were identified in the analysis (Smith et al., 2002). Among the international terror groups, Al Qaeda, led by Osama bin Laden, had not yet been identified but was operating in the United States, as is now evident from investigations of terrorist groups since September 11, 2001.

TABLE 16-1	Incidents of Terrorism Worldwide and in Iraq and Afghanistan		
		2005	**2006**
Incidents of Terrorism Worldwide		11,153	14,338
Incidents resulting in death, injury, or kidnapping of at least one individual		8,028	11,170
Incidents resulting in death of at least one individual		5,135	7,332
Incidents resulting in the death of zero individuals		6,018	7,007
Incidents resulting in the death of only one individual		2,881	4,091
Incidents resulting in the death of at least 10 individuals		228	291
Incidents resulting in the injury of at least one individual		3,838	5,718
Incidents resulting in the kidnapping of at least one individual		1,152	1,334
Individuals worldwide killed, injured, or kidnapped as a result of incidents of terrorism		74,217	74,543
Individuals worldwide killed as a result of incidents of terrorism		14,618	20,498
Individuals worldwide injured as a result of incidents of terrorism		24,761	38,191
Individuals worldwide kidnapped as a result of incidents of terrorism		34,838	15,854
Incidents of Terrorism in Iraq and Afghanistan			
Incidents of terrorism in Iraq		3,468	6,630
Incidents in Iraq resulting in death, injury, or kidnapping of at least one individual		2,834	6,026
Individuals in Iraq killed, injured, or kidnapped as a result of incidents of terrorism		20,685	38,813
Incidents of terrorism in Afghanistan		491	749
Incidents in Afghanistan resulting in death, injury, or kidnapping of at least one individual		366	555
Individuals in Afghanistan killed, injured, or kidnapped as a result of incidents of terrorism		1,540	2,943

Source: U.S. Department of Homeland Security, 2007.

Patterns of Global Terrorism. In a recent analysis of patterns of global terrorism, the U.S. Department of Homeland Security (2007), along with hundreds of cooperating law enforcement agencies from nations throughout the world, compiled and analyzed incidents of terrorism. The data presented in Table 16–1 show that between 2005 and 2006 the number of terrorist incidents increased dramatically, although much of the increase was accounted for by increased acts of terrorism in Iraq and Afghanistan. The Bush administration responded to the report with the following statement:

> Five years after 9/11, the international community's conflict with transnational terrorists continues. Cooperative international efforts have produced genuine security improvements—particularly in securing borders and transportation, enhancing document security, disrupting terrorist financing, and restricting the movement of terrorists. The international community has also achieved significant success in dismantling terrorist organizations and disrupting their leadership. This has contributed to reduced terrorist operational capabilities and the detention or death of numerous key terrorist leaders.

Critics claim that the U.S. invasion of Iraq has stimulated the growth of Al Qaeda and other terrorist groups, while the administration claims that its policies allow U.S. and allied forces to fight terrorism abroad instead of waiting for its perpetrators to attack the United States again. This is a highly complex matter of intelligence assessment and political judgment that goes beyond the scope of this text, but it is clear from the data in the table that terrorism continues to be a major obstacle to security in Iraq and Afghanistan, as well as elsewhere in the world where terrorist groups exist.

Origins of Terrorist Groups

Fluctuations in the number of terrorist acts can be caused by many factors. Chief among these are events in the more troubled areas of the world. The prospect of lasting peace in the Middle East or a resolution of the conflict in Northern Ireland could produce major decreases in the total number of terrorist acts; conversely, any worsening of conditions in these and similar areas could lead to higher rates of terrorism (Henderson, 2001; U.S. Congress, 1993).

In addition to its origins in political radicalism, terrorism may spring from various kinds of cults that have much in common despite differing ideologies. In March 1997 Americans were shocked when thirty-nine members of the cult known as Heaven's Gate were discovered in a mass suicide in an affluent San Diego suburb (Bruni, 1997). As in earlier instances of mass murder and suicide, these were linked to the charismatic appeal of deranged leaders believed to possess supernatural powers. The history of David Koresh and the Branch Davidians in Waco, Texas, follows the same pattern. The more convinced members were of the leader's power, the more isolated they felt from the rest of society. A collective paranoia developed as they perceived themselves to be targets of society's hate. In both cases, these feelings led to acts of irrational violence (Niebuhr, 1995).

As noted earlier, terrorism can be perpetrated by agencies of the state. Adolf Hitler and Josef Stalin practiced state terrorism, using brutality, fear, and legalized murder on an overwhelming scale to subjugate the masses. The attack and fire that destroyed the Branch Davidian compound in Waco, Texas, suggest that this tragedy may also be considered an episode of state terrorism. Whereas victims of other forms of terrorism may hope to be rescued by government or police forces, victims of state terrorism can have no such hope. Indeed, the extreme nature of state terrorism has led many people to argue that violent rebellion is a justifiable reaction.

The terrorist recruit is often well educated and young, with an upper-middle- or middle-class background. Although it is true that poverty and a sense of hopelessness can motivate many people to join terrorist groups, we learned quickly in the case of Mohammed Atta and others involved in the suicide attack on the World Trade Center that the leaders of complex terrorist operations are often highly educated people with many opportunities open to them. The leaders of Al Qaeda, bin Laden and Dr. Ayman al-Zawahiri, come from wealthy, educated families, and they are not scheming against the West out of isolation and ignorance. Recent research shows that they are instead motivated by failed or futile attempts to adopt Western ways. Atta and others among bin Laden's followers, for example, had hoped to succeed in Western nations, but after failing there they were open to recruitment for terrorist training by Al Qaeda. Other Al Qaeda terrorists came to the West with a political agenda and lived a double life as members of what are called "sleeper cells" until they were mobilized by their Al Qaeda masters. It appears that their exposure to Western culture and societies was somehow a damaging experience. Those who were religious by upbringing felt compromised by the looser mores of the West, while others tried to fit in but were rebuffed.

As individuals, terrorists want to save the world, although their concept of salvation is based on a limited set of inflexible beliefs. The terrorist believes that purity of motive justifies whatever methods are employed. In this detachment from reality, coupled with total willingness to surrender life itself for the cause, terrorists become dehumanized. They see themselves as catalysts, worthless in themselves, through which social change can be accomplished (Dershowitz, 2002).

Terrorism and Religion

That so many terrorist individuals and groups are motivated by extreme religious beliefs and feelings is one of the chief ironies of the present war on terrorism. All the major religions seek peace and understanding among people throughout the world. Yet we see in the case of domestic terrorists that many are members of radical Christian groups and that Al Qaeda and other contemporary Islamic terrorist groups espouse various forms of fundamentalist Islam—even though, as numerous Islamic leaders have pointed out, terrorism violates the basic foundations of Islamic law. But in his analysis of the contribution of religious radicalism to contemporary terrorism, sociologist Amitai Etzioni notes that

> The sad but unavoidable fact is that Islam, like Christianity and Judaism, has both temperate and virulent strands. Christianity in earlier ages not only had an Inquisition but also those who justified it in religious terms. The Church supported the mass torture and murder that took place during military dictatorship in Argentina, deeming them necessary to "excise the cancer of communism." The terrorism in Northern Ireland has religious roots, and Operation Rescue claims religious justifications. Militant Judaism not merely claims a right to the West Bank and finds scriptural support for a still Greater Israel, but also blessed those who assassinated Yitzhak Rabin, the peacemaker.
>
> So, like other world religions, Islam has its aggressive and subjugating forms. Perhaps the most important of these is Wahabism, the version of Islam that is most dominant in Saudi Arabia and a leading influence on Muslim fundamentalists elsewhere. Wahabism was first practiced by an eighteenth-century scholar, Mohammad ibn Abd al-Wahhab, who lived in central Arabia. Claiming to return to original Islam, like fundamentalists in other religions, Wahabism rejects all innovations, stresses literal belief in the Qu'ran and the Hadith (the sayings or traditions of Mohammad), and calls for the formation of states to be governed strictly according to Islamic law. It rejects all notions of human rights and democratic forms of government as secular and Western notions. (2002, p. 3)

Like many fundamentalist belief systems, extreme forms of Islam tend to be totalitarian in that they seek to control the person's total life: what she or he eats, listens to, wears, and reads. They seek to achieve these goals through coercion and the use of fear rather than by persuasion or democratic decision making. Thus, in trying to distance the U.S. war on terrorism from conflict with Islamic civilization itself, President Bush was correct in stating, "The face of terror is not the true faith of Islam. Islam is peace." Yet it is also true that true believers of Islam or any other religion can become persuaded that the "ends justifies the means" and then may resort to terror or other illegitimate uses of force against innocent civilians (Lewis, 2001).

In this process, the victim, who in the terrorist's mind is merely a pawn in the struggle for societal reform, is stripped of human rights and identity. The terrorist wants to punish society, to force it to accept his or her demands. The terrorist preys on both known and unknown victims, assured that—as representatives of an abhorrent society—the victims are responsible for society's wrongs and are unworthy of compassion. Because any society is the combined achievement of thousands of individuals and many generations, the injustice of terrorist thinking is obvious. Terrorists' victims are innocent people whose lives are destroyed by fanatical intolerance.

Those who suffer as a result of terrorist acts can be divided into two groups. The first are random victims, people who are simply in the wrong place at the wrong time. Bombings, hijackings, and the spontaneous seizure of hostages victimize whoever happens to be available. Other members of society are intimidated by the casualness of this kind of terror, and the terrorist hopes that they will pressure their government to meet his or her demands. The other category of victims includes individuals who are singled out because of their prominence. They, too, become dehumanized symbols: All politicians bear the blame for whatever political injustices the terrorist perceives; all businesspeople are held personally responsible for commercial waste and greed. The civilians who have been killed or injured in bombings by terrorist groups as part of the Palestinian–Israeli conflict are an example of the first category; the prominent computer scientists targeted by the Unabomber and the murdered Israeli leader Yitzhak Rabin are examples of the second.

Terrorism's Impact on Society

Terrorism can be extremely effective. As a form of warfare waged by the relatively powerless against powerful states, contemporary global terrorism as practiced by Al Qaeda and the regional organizations allied with it has had significant effects on world trade and on the institutions of the United States and other nations. The effects of recent terrorist activity include the following:

- Increased fear of attack and heightened security at airports, ports, and major landmarks and federal buildings.

- Erosion of civil liberties, including heightened government secrecy, limitations of habeas corpus, and curtailments of freedom of speech in the interests of security.

- Economic consequences: Especially due to attacks on airlines, there have been drastic curtailments in international tourism and trade.

- Health consequences: Fear of bioterrorism is likely to put more civilians at risk as more people are vaccinated against diseases like smallpox, which before 9/11 was no longer considered a threat to world health.

- Political consequences: Terrorism threatens to polarize the world between Islamic and Christian civilizations, has placed the United States on a war footing, and has increased the chances of war not just in Iraq but elsewhere in the Middle East and on the Korean peninsula. Tensions between the United States and its European allies have worsened as the United States, the world's only superpower, is increasingly seen as seeking to extend its power over the Middle East and other regions of the world. (Pew Research Center, 2002)

It is far too early to fully understand or assess the potential consequences of terrorism or the war on terrorism for people in the United States and elsewhere in the world. While war clouds gather and threats of major terrorist attacks continue, it is difficult to find anything positive in the current situation. But if the current world crisis

After the attacks on the Pentagon and the World Trade Center, the Bush administration and Congress created the Department of Homeland Security and made inspections at the nation's airports the responsibility of federal marshals and personnel who work under their supervision. For many Americans, these inspections are their only encounters with the ongoing "war on terrorism."

yields improvements in the ability of nations to cooperate in combating terrorism, and if the Islamic nations begin to solve some of their problems of poverty and political instability, the war against terrorism will have had some positive consequences together with the negative ones. At the same time, the world's major powers, and especially the United States, find their military and logistical resources stretched thin as they struggle to confront threats of terrorism. This leaves them less inclined to intervene in genocidal wars in Africa like the one occurring at this writing in the Darfur region of the Sudan (Kristof, 2005).

WAR AND ITS EFFECTS

For those who experience its tragic devastation, war is the most serious social problem one can imagine. Over the centuries warfare has taken millions of lives. According to one estimate (Sorokin, 1937), between 1100 and 1925 about 35 million soldiers were killed in some 862 wars in Europe. Other investigators have calculated that between 1816 and 1965 alone, about 29 million soldiers were killed in thirty-three major European conflicts (Singer & Small, 1972). These figures do not include the untold millions of civilians who perished as well. By any standard, the twentieth century was the deadliest in human history. During World War I, 8 million soldiers and another 1 million civilians died. The casualties of World War II were even higher: Almost 17 million soldiers and 35 million civilians were killed. In the Soviet Union, the generation of men old enough to fight in World War II was decimated. In the Persian Gulf War, it is estimated that between 75,000 and 100,000 Iraqi soldiers died, but the impossibility of knowing exact casualty figures is a reminder of how devastating that war—and the ensuing boycotts—was for Iraq. In 2005 the U.S military announced the loss of its 2000th soldier in Iraq, but at this writing it has not publicized any data about the far larger number of U.S. personnel who have returned with serious and lasting injuries, nor are there any reliable data about the thousands of Iraqi casualties.

Long after peace is declared, many soldiers bear the scars of their battlefield experiences. For every American soldier who died in battle in the major wars of this century, between two and four others received nonfatal wounds. Many of the wounded have required medical care for months or years, and many have been so badly injured that they have not been able to hold a job or return to a normal way of life. In 2006 about 2 million veterans were receiving compensation from the U.S. government for war-related disabilities. Of these, about 160,000 were totally disabled (*Statistical Abstract,* 2007). The poor are especially likely to be recruited into dangerous military roles. Several studies have shown that during the Vietnam War, battle deaths and injuries were more common among lower-class soldiers than among those from the middle and upper classes (Janowitz, 1978; Moskos, 2005).

Not all war-related disabilities are physical. War takes a psychological toll as well. During and after World War II, Harvard sociologist Samuel Stouffer and his colleagues (1949) conducted the first major study of war stress. They found correlations between psychological stress and several types of combat experience. For example, soldiers stationed close to the front lines—who were constantly exposed to the threat of injury or death to themselves and their friends, the hardships of life on the battlefield, the value conflicts involved in killing others, and inability to control their own actions—suffered psychological stress to a greater extent than others. In the decades since Stouffer's research, mental-health experts have identified post-traumatic stress disorder (PTSD) as a common aftereffect of battle. People suffering from PTSD feel generally irritable, depressed, and unhappy and have nightmares and flashbacks of war experiences. One study of Vietnam War veterans found that 36 percent of all men exposed to heavy combat during the war displayed PTSD for an average of ten years after their tour of duty (Kadushin, 1983; Quindlen, 2005).

The psychological impact of the Vietnam War may have differed from that of earlier American wars because it was a guerrilla war. That is, the enemy blended with the

This family belongs to the southern Iraq population of "marsh Arabs" who were forced from their homes when the regime of Saddam Hussein drained thousands of acres of wetlands and destroyed their way of life. They are seen here passing a remnant of the old regime, a large poster of Hussein depicting him as the protector of their homeland. The photo captures the stark realities facing many Iraqi families since the fall of the dictator.

civilian population and therefore seemed to be everywhere and nowhere at the same time. These conditions may have been responsible for the unusually high levels of violence against civilians that characterized the war as well as for the mistreatment of prisoners and the use of such weapons as napalm, which killed civilians and the enemy indiscriminately. Soldiers who saw or engaged in these forms of violence suffered from psychological disorders to a greater extent than those who did not.

Indirect Effects of War

In addition to the killing and the wounding, war disrupts the lives of the civilians whose homeland has become a battleground. Often it leads to mass migrations of people trying to escape from danger or persecution or looking for new opportunities. Between 1986 and 1999, for example, 1.3 million political refugees were granted refuge and the opportunity to become U.S. citizens (U.S. Committee on Refugees, 2002). Of these, about 382,000 came from Vietnam and about 106,000 from Bosnia, both nations in which the United States was directly involved in warfare and its aftermath. Of course, thousands of refugees were accepted by other nations as well. When refugees arrive in a new country, their problems are not over. As we noted in Chapter 7, they often encounter prejudice, unemployment, and difficulty in adjusting to a new culture.

The Bush administration's "war on terror" has made it much more difficult for political refugees and asylum seekers to gain admission to the United States. Iraqis who face severe danger and death threats because they have helped the Coalition forces have not been able to gain political refugee status. In 2007 the U.S. ambassador to Iraq called for all Iraqis working for the U.S. government to be granted refugee status in recognition of the dangers they face (Pilkington, 2007).

Finally brought to trial in 2005, the former Iraqi dictator, Saddam Hussein, attempted to disrupt his trial in every way possible, while outside the courtroom those still loyal to him or his former political party continued to lead the insurgency against the U.S.-led occupation and the rebuilding of the war-torn nation.

Another major cause of wartime migration is government policy. During and after World War II, a number of European states forced whole populations to move. During the war, the German government ordered hundreds of thousands of ethnic Germans to move back to Germany from the eastern European nations that Germany had invaded. After the war, under the terms of the Potsdam Treaty, many more Germans were required to move from various eastern European nations to areas within the redrawn borders of Germany.

Some of the indirect effects of war are not as easy to calculate as the numbers of refugees. For example, it is impossible to measure the economic damage caused by war. Billions of dollars must be diverted from productive uses, first into arms and then into the effort to repair the damage caused by arms. Even less quantifiable is the impact of war on how people think. World War I left in its wake widespread disillusionment with traditional values. To the men in the trenches, patriotism lost much of its appeal. After the war many people were pessimistic about the future of civilization and were alienated from their former way of life.

Liberated Iraq is a good example of the longer-term political and social effects of even a "successful" war. The nation's people remain badly divided in their feelings about what kind of government—secular or religious—should be established, but they are unified in their desire that the Americans and the British leave as soon as possible. But this will not happen as long as the many ethnic and religious factions of the Iraqi population cannot work together to ensure peace and the rule of law on their own. Similarly, in the former Yugoslavia, uneasy truces cannot heal the hatreds caused by ethnic expulsions and intergroup brutality.

Effects of Nuclear War

In the past 100 years, wars have become less frequent but more intense as military technology has become more lethal. The development of nuclear weapons in the

1940s contributed to peace among the major powers, but if peace breaks down, a war of almost unimaginable destructiveness could ensue. Some idea of the nature of that destruction is provided by accounts of the bombing of Hiroshima, Japan, during World War II.

On the morning of August 6, 1945, as the people of Hiroshima were preparing to go to work, an American aircraft flew over the city. Seconds later, a nuclear bomb exploded 2,000 feet above the center of the city. Even though the 12.5-kiloton device was tiny by modern standards, its effect was devastating. The force and heat of the blast annihilated tens of thousands of people almost instantly and delivered a deadly dose of radiation to thousands of others; within three months, some 130,000 would be dead.

Many of those who survived were burned and maimed. One woman, who had been with some junior high school boys about a mile from the center of the blast, was knocked unconscious. "When I came to, I looked around," she said in a recent interview. "The boys had been so cute before, but now their clothes were burned off and they were nearly naked. Their skin was cut up and ripped off. Their faces were peeling off as well." She herself was so hideously deformed that her own parents urged her to show mercy to her husband and leave him. "At that time, I cried every day, wishing that I had died immediately," she said. She added that she did not seek compensation from the United States. "I just want [Americans] to feel sorry and to try to abolish nuclear weapons" (quoted in Kristof, 1995, pp. 1, 12).

Nuclear bombs more than 1,600 times more powerful than the one that destroyed Hiroshima have now become standard in the weapons systems of the major world powers. In 2001, for example, the Natural Resource Defense Council reported that the 192 missile warheads on one U.S. Trident submarine—constituting less than 3 percent of the existing U.S. arsenal—could cause more than 50 million casualties if programmed to hit major urban areas of a nation (Barry & Thomas, 2001).

Rogue States and Weapons of Mass Destruction

The possibility that Iran and North Korea could produce nuclear bombs and missiles, and the fear that these and other weapons of mass destruction, such as biological agents like the smallpox virus, could be sold to terrorist organizations, have become part of the fearful post-9/11 global scene. North Korea, Sudan ruled by tribal warlords, and Zimbabwe under Robert Mugabe have become what are now known as *rogue states*. These are nations whose governments refuse to adhere to the rule of law either on the domestic or the international stage, and routinely threaten their own citizens and those of other nations with violence and terror. In the nations of the former Soviet Union, including Russia, there is concern that controls over existing stockpiles of nuclear weapons may not be adequate to prevent dangerous fissionable materials from falling into the hands of terrorists or leaders of rogue states.

Vladimir Orlov, a Russian expert on nuclear weapons material and its security, finds that protection of nuclear warheads in Russia is on a par with that of the United States. But he notes that security in the facilities that store or produce materials used to create nuclear weapons "is about 50/50" (quoted in Coleman, 2003, p. 25). Moreover, Russia has sold fissionable materials to North Korea for its nuclear energy plants, even though these materials can also be used in making bombs. But Orlov believes the worst threats come from zones of instability such as Afghanistan, Pakistan, and some of the easternmost regions of the former Soviet empire, where extreme political instability and poverty create weak or nonexistent government controls. "Such instability," he says, "provides opportunities for radical political groups as well as organized crime. Billions of dollars are pumped through these zones; they are epicenters of the world's black market of arms, drugs, forged money, documents, and people" (quoted in Coleman, 2003, p. 27). Such nonstate—or failed-state—regions of the world are surely the most dangerous places on earth because they are often cradles of terrorism and hold the potential for the proliferation of weapons of mass destruction.

The specter of global nuclear war has lessened since the fall of the Soviet empire. The United States, Russia, and Ukraine have agreed to dismantle or otherwise disable their missiles, but vast destructive nuclear capabilities remain in place around the globe. The possibility that nuclear bombs will be obtained by nations in unstable areas of the world such as Southeast Asia, North Korea, and the Middle East keeps the threat of nuclear war alive. Even a limited nuclear war would create human catastrophes on a scale not hitherto experienced, to say nothing of the environmental damage and destruction such wars would cause for years afterward, even in regions beyond the boundaries of the original conflict. These concerns, as well as the possibility that nuclear weapons could be used by terrorists, suggest that it is premature to celebrate the end of the threat of nuclear war. Experts in the field agree that efforts to control the proliferation of nuclear weapons are as vital today as they ever were (Cirincione, 2005).

What are rogue states, and why are they such a danger to the rest of the world?

CONTROLLING WARFARE

Can warfare be controlled to decrease or prevent its worst ravages and abuses? This is an age-old dilemma, but it is much in the news today in connection with the "war on terrorism" and the genocidal war in Sudan, the separatist terrorism in Chechnya, and violent civil strife in Nepal and other nations.

War on Terrorists and the Rule of Law

Controversies over the possible use of torture in prisons run by American forces in Iraq, in Guantanamo, Cuba, and perhaps in secret locations elsewhere in the world also raise many questions about whether nations can protect their citizens from terrorist attacks without resorting to inhumane practices such as those revealed in the notorious case of Abu Ghraib in Iraq. Allegations that American forces used deadly phosphorous bombs in Iraq while they attacked civilian neighborhoods of Fallujah and other cities also point to the difficulty of controlling the actual conduct of warfare.

Arguing that a war on terrorism allows the president to invoke special executive powers, the Bush administration claims that rules of conventional warfare, especially the Geneva Accords and international agreements on the treatment of enemy combatants, do not apply. Opponents of the president's position argue that failure to honor the traditional rules for treating prisoners and for conducting warfare risk the kinds of abuses that led to a catastrophic loss of American credibility and respect on the world stage during the second Iraq War. Representatives of the administration and the military deny that explicit directives from high levels of command were the cause of prisoner abuse in Iraq and Guantanamo, and at this writing, only low-level military personnel have been disciplined in the aftermath of the enormous international scandal that followed revelations of the abuses.

What are some of the pros and cons of applying the rule of law—particularly the rules governing the treatment of prisoners of war—to individuals suspected of engaging in terrorism?

In 2004 the Supreme Court rejected the U.S. government's attempts to detain an American citizen indefinitely without trial. The Court cited principles of individual liberty that in its view had been threatened by policies enacted in the aftermath of the September 11, 2001, attacks. In her decision for the majority in this case, Justice Sandra Day O'Conner wrote, "It is during our most challenging and uncertain moments that our nation's commitment to due process is most severely tested; and it is in those times that we must preserve our commitment at home to the principles for which we fight abroad." Justice O'Connor added, "We have long since made clear that a state of war is not a blank check for the president when it comes to the rights of the nation's citizens." Nevertheless, the administration continues to pursue aggressive and controversial tactics in detaining terror suspects and combating insurgents in Iraq, and the global debate over the control of war and prisoners of war intensifies as well (Lelyveld, 2005). At the same time, new technologies of warfare, such as unmanned bombers and global positioning systems installed in "smart bombs," make possible pinpoint

Few events during the war in Iraq did as much to inflame anti-American sentiments in the Islamic world than the revelations of abuses and torture in the Abu Ghraib and Guantanamo prisons. The crude drawing on this wall calls attention to what many Muslims view as a grave contradiction between the United States' stated purpose of bringing freedom and democracy to Iraq and its abuse of Iraqi prisoners.

attacks on suspected enemy positions. But these and other new technologies have not prevented very high numbers of civilian casualties in Iraq.

"Just Wars" and War Crimes

Despite the increasing scale, sophistication, and destructiveness of modern warfare, there has been some progress toward controlling the conduct of war. As evident in the U.N. and congressional debates before the Persian Gulf War, a body of international law deals with armed conflicts. It includes a complex set of rules that defines the rights and privileges of those who fight and that attempt to protect noncombatants. Table 16–2 on page 524 lists some of the specific actions that have been declared war crimes under international law.

Underlying this body of law is the ancient concept of the "just war." This doctrine, which developed out of the shared culture of Greek and Roman civilization, has two major branches: justification for going to war (*jus ad bellum*) and justifiable acts in wartime (*jus in bello*). *Jus in bello* is concerned with whether or not a particular war is being fought "justly." It sets limits on the means of violence (e.g., the use of particularly inhumane weapons) and on the injury or damage done to civilians.

The rules of *jus in bello* are difficult to enforce and are frequently violated. In the Vietnam War, for example, the United States used chemical defoliants that harmed human, animal, and plant life. American planes bombed North Vietnamese population centers, and both sides tortured and assassinated civilians. The most notorious American attack on civilians was the massacre of between 175 and 400 noncombatants, including infants, at the hamlet of My Lai in March 1968. For this crime, one American officer was convicted and sentenced to life imprisonment, but he was released after serving two years in prison (Beer, 1981).

Further instances of disregard for international law were seen in Kosovo, Bosnia, and the Persian Gulf War. In Kuwait, for example, the Iraqi invaders used torture and terrorism. In addition, by pouring crude oil into the Gulf and setting fire to the Kuwaiti oil fields, they added an extremely ominous form of violence, environmental terrorism, to the arsenal of war tactics.

TABLE 16-2 | War Crimes

1. Making use of poisoned or otherwise forbidden arms or munitions.
2. Treachery in asking for quarter or simulating sickness or wounds.
3. Maltreatment of corpses.
4. Firing on localities which are undefended or without military significance.
5. Abuse of or firing on a flag of truce.
6. Misuse of the Red Cross or similar emblems.
7. Wearing of civilian clothes by troops to conceal their identity during the commission of combat acts.
8. Improper utilization of privileged (exempt, immune) buildings for military purposes.
9. Poisoning of streams or wells.
10. Pillage.
11. Purposeless destruction.
12. Compelling prisoners of war to engage in prohibited types of labor.
13. Forcing civilians to perform prohibited labor.
14. Violation of surrender terms.
15. Killing or wounding military personnel who have laid down arms, surrendered or are disabled by wounds or sickness.
16. Assassination, and the hiring of assassins.
17. Ill-treatment of prisoners of war, or of the wounded and sick—including despoiling them of possessions not classifiable as public property.
18. Killing or attacking harmless civilians.
19. Compelling the inhabitants of occupied enemy territory to furnish information about the armed forces of the enemy or his means of defense.
20. Appropriation or destruction of privileged buildings.
21. Bombardment from the air for the exclusive purpose of terrorizing or attacking civilian populations.
22. Attack on enemy vessels which have indicated their surrender by lowering their flag.
23. Attack or seizure of hospitals and all other violations of the Hague Convention for the Adaptation of Maritime Warfare of the Principles of the Geneva Convention.
24. Unjustified destruction of enemy prizes.
25. Use of enemy uniforms during combat and use of the enemy flag during attack by a belligerent vessel.
26. Attack on individuals supplied with safe-conducts, and other violations of safeguards provided.
27. Breach of parole.
28. Grave breaches of Article 50 of the Geneva Convention for the Amelioration of the Condition of the Wounded and Sick in Armed Forces in the Field, of 1949, and Article 51 of the Geneva Convention of 1949 Applicable to Armed Forces at Sea: "wilful killing, torture or inhuman treatment, including biological experiments, wilfully causing great suffering or serious injury to body or health, and extensive destruction and appropriation of property not justified by military necessity and carried out unlawfully and wantonly."
29. Grave breaches of the Geneva Convention Relative to the Treatment of Prisoners of War, of 1949, as listed in Article 130: "wilful killing, torture or inhuman treatment, including biological experiments, wilfully causing great suffering or serious injury to body or health, compelling a prisoner of war to serve in the forces of the hostile Power, or wilfully depriving a prisoner of war of the rights of fair and regular trial prescribed" in the Convention.
30. Grave breaches of the Fourth Geneva Convention of 1949, as detailed in Article 147: "wilful killing, torture or inhuman treatment, including biological experiments, wilfully causing great suffering or serious injury to body or health, unlawful deportation or transfer or unlawful confinement of a protected person, compelling a protected person to serve in the forces of a hostile Power, or wilfully depriving a protected person of the rights of fair and regular trial prescribed in the present Convention, taking of hostages and extensive destruction and appropriation of property, not justified by military necessity and carried out unlawfully and wantonly." In addition, conspiracy, direct incitement, and attempts to commit, as well as complicity in the commission of crimes against the laws of war are punishable.
31. Any person commits an offence within the meaning of this Convention if that person unlawfully and intentionally delivers, places, discharges or detonates an explosive or other lethal device in, into or against a place of public use, a State or government facility, a public transportation system or an infrastructure facility:
    (a) With the intent to cause death or serious bodily injury; or
    (b) With the intent to cause extensive destruction of such a place, facility or system, where such destruction results in or is likely to result in major economic loss.

Source: Excerpt from pp. 669–701 from *Law Among Nations,* 7th ed. by Gerhard von Glahn. Copyright © 1996 by Allyn & Bacon. Reprinted by permission of Pearson Education, Inc.

THEORIES ABOUT WAR AND ITS ORIGINS

In the years since nuclear weapons were developed in the mid-twentieth century, war has become a much riskier policy than ever before, because local wars fought with conventional weapons could escalate into destruction on a vast scale. Just because the stakes have risen so high, however, does not mean that the chances of a nuclear holocaust are remote. The United States, still the only nation that has ever used nuclear bombs in war, has threatened to use nuclear weapons at least eleven times since 1946. These instances include the Berlin crisis of 1961, the Cuban missile crisis of 1962, and twice during the Vietnam War. Because warfare has become so dangerous and the world's military powers have built up huge stockpiles of both conventional and nuclear arms, many people have begun to study the causes of war in the hope of promoting peace. We turn now to a discussion of some of the theories that have been proposed to account for war.

No single theory can fully explain any given war. Nevertheless, a number of theories have shed light on some of the forces that contribute to war. For the purposes of this discussion, we will not consider rebellions, riots, and other forms of violence that take place within the borders of nations. Instead, we will adopt a narrow definition of war as a violent conflict between nations. We first consider the view that human beings are aggressive by nature.

Ethological and Sociobiological Theories

According to some scientists, humans have their primate ancestors to thank, at least in part, for the existence of war. During earlier phases of human evolution, aggressive behavior may have improved the odds of survival and become encoded in the genes of a growing number of individuals. Ethologists and sociobiologists believe that a predisposition to aggression may have been transmitted genetically from one generation to the next. One of the best-known proponents of this view is the ethologist Konrad Lorenz (1981). Like other ethologists, Lorenz has focused his research on the behavior of animals other than humans. From this work he has concluded that aggression is an instinct in humans, as it is in lower animals. Lorenz links aggression with territoriality. Just as animals defend their nests, burrows, and ranges, humans fight wars to defend their nations. It follows from this explanation that because war results from a natural urge, it is probably inevitable.

Many sociobiologists (scientists who study genetic influences on human behavior) also believe that humans have inherited a predisposition to engage in warfare. However, they are also well aware of the influence exerted by culture. In the view of the noted sociobiologist Edward O. Wilson, learned ways of doing things guide much of human behavior, but genetic tendencies also have a persistent influence. Although aggression may have been adaptive for humans thousands of years ago, Wilson (1975) believes that aggressive tendencies must be controlled if humans are to avoid global suicide.

Lorenz, Wilson, and their followers have been attacked by critics who argue that comparisons of human behavior with that of lower animals are suspect. Among humans, the motivation to fight is a learned response to symbols, such as speeches, flags, propaganda, and other stimuli. Thus, human warfare is far more complex than fighting among animals. Moreover, there is no evidence that instinct plays any role in human aggression (Montagu, 1973). In sum, the critics deny that genes influence human behavior in general and warfare in particular; instead, they explain behavior in terms of learned responses (Tremblay, 2000).

Clausewitz: War as State Policy

In seeking to account for war in terms of genetically influenced tendencies, Lorenz and Wilson have viewed humans who make war as individuals independently motivated by their biological nature. In fact, however, soldiers fight in a social context, and their actions are governed largely by the dictates of military organizations. The freedom of military leaders to direct their armies is constrained by other institutions in society, such as the government, industry, the press, and religious organizations. Finally, even if the leaders of a nation's institutions were to agree among themselves, they would not have a free hand. Political and economic forces that cross national boundaries determine what strategies are available to win a war and whether war itself is a practical tactic in a given situation.

One of the most influential theories of war, proposed in 1832 by the Prussian general and military philosopher Carl von Clausewitz, took into account some of these aspects of the social context of war. During the century before Clausewitz wrote, most of the nations in Europe had been governed by monarchs who had the power to wage war if the use of military force would serve their interests. For this reason, Clausewitz focused on the role of the monarch and described war as an alternative to diplomacy, engaged in for the purpose of gaining land, prestige, and other benefits. According to Clausewitz, war is strictly a means to an end, to be used only if its benefits outweigh its costs. The resources of the whole nation should be mobilized for just one purpose: victory (Rapoport, 1968). Thus, Clausewitz explained war in terms of the rational decisions of monarchs rather than irrational elements of human nature like a predisposition for aggression.

To support his claim that monarchs were the key actors in wars, Clausewitz adopted a fairly simple view of how societies function. He assumed, for instance, that the job of the military was to serve the monarch, regardless of the ambitions of military leaders. Thus, the interests of the military and the monarch were the same. In addition, Clausewitz did not foresee that by the end of the nineteenth century wealthy merchants and industrialists would be able to exert a strong influence on military policy. His functionalist approach to war and politics (i.e., the assumption that the military would always perform its function and serve the monarch) was weakened by the conflict inherent in the rise of powerful elites who could afford to marshal their own armed forces and challenge the power of the monarchy.

In the contemporary world, the social control of the armed forces remains a serious problem in many nations. It is encouraging in this regard to note that in Latin America, a region that for decades was dominated by military dictatorships, there has been a drastic decline in the prevalence of military rule. In 1979, at least seven Latin American nations, including Brazil, Argentina, and Chile, were ruled by military dictators; in 1989, there was only one military dictatorship—in Suriname (Brookes, 1991). At present the worst effects of war and violence in Latin America are being experienced in Colombia. The civil war there is complicated by the warring factions' involvement in the international drug trade. The United States has been sending technical and military support to help the embattled Colombian government combat the drug factions, but many observers fear that U.S. involvement will escalate the conflict and drag American forces into a deepening civil war (Guillermoprieto, 2000).

Critics of the war in Iraq also use Clausewitz's theory. Clausewitz taught that military power cannot operate effectively in a political vacuum or without the reinforcement of diplomacy. The political chaos and factional civil war in Iraq could involve the United States and Great Britain in a situation in which diplomacy and state-building cannot be effective without the power to back it up. This, in turn, could mean a very long period of occupation and the commitment of armed forces and vast resources over a far longer period than has been suggested as likely. The same critics point to Afghanistan, where an immediately successful military operation deposed a rogue state, the Taliban, but continued stability depends on the presence of outside military forces and relief operations (Powaski, 2003).

How did some critics of the war in Iraq use Clausewitz's theory of warfare to argue against the invasion?

Marx and Lenin on War

Early in the twentieth century Vladimir Ilyich Lenin built on the ideas of Karl Marx to propose a new theory of war, one that took into account some of the social changes that had transformed European societies since Clausewitz's time. According to Marx, two competing social classes were developing in all industrializing societies. The bourgeoisie owned the means of production—that is, land, factories, and other resources needed to produce the necessities of life. The other class, the proletariat, sold its labor to the bourgeoisie in return for wages that barely enabled its members to survive. Marx believed that political leaders acted as the agents of the bourgeoisie in their struggle to improve business conditions and keep the proletariat under control.

Marx predicted that as capitalist economies grew, their need for raw materials, labor, and new markets in which to sell finished goods would increase as well. Lenin claimed that the competition among Britain, France, Germany, and other major powers to establish colonies around the world during the nineteenth and early twentieth centuries was evidence that Marx's prediction was correct. Acting in the interests of the bourgeoisie—rather than in those of the monarch or nation, as Clausewitz had argued—the major powers were locked in a fierce competition for colonies. It was this competition that led to World War I, according to Lenin. In essence, the war pitted the national ruling classes against one another; the workers had nothing to gain by taking up arms (Rapoport, 1968). The basis of war, then, is economic competition among national ruling classes. Lenin contended that the violent overthrow of the bourgeoisie by the proletariat would eventually remove this motivation for warfare.

Institutional and International Perspectives

Marx and Lenin believed that economic interests shape most social phenomena, including warfare, but a number of social scientists have argued that noneconomic factors must also be considered. These explanations can be grouped into two types. The first takes the individual nation as the unit of analysis and looks inside societies at the relationships among institutions like the military, government, and business. The second group of explanations focuses on institutions and patterns of behavior that cut across national boundaries. According to this perspective, organizations such as the United Nations, as well as international treaties and trade networks, are among the factors that influence the likelihood of war or peace. We begin with the first set of explanations, looking within nations at the institutional forces that may be responsible for war.

Institutional Forces within Nations. Most social scientists believe that during much of the twentieth century the influence of military leaders on government policy has grown in the United States and many other nations. Many also view that growth as a threat to peace. They maintain that keeping a large, well-equipped military force at the ready makes it easier for political leaders to choose war rather than negotiation as a tactic for handling international conflicts (Barton, 1981). Supporters of military interests, on the other hand, argue that a powerful military discourages other nations from starting wars.

With the rise of aggressive totalitarian societies in Europe during the 1930s, social scientists began to analyze the growing influence of the military on domestic affairs. Harold Lasswell (1941) predicted the rise of "garrison states," in which military leaders impose dictatorial power on society, channel a growing share of the nation's resources into weapons production, and win public support through propaganda.

After World War II, a few critics voiced alarm at the newly won power of the military in the United States. In *The Power Elite,* C. Wright Mills (1956) argued that by the mid-1950s military leaders were

> more powerful than they have ever been in the history of the American elite; they have now more means of exercising power in many areas of American life which were previously civilian domains; they now have more connections; and they are now operating in a nation whose elite and whose underlying population have accepted what can only be called a military definition of reality. (p. 198)

During the war, military officers had met with heads of corporations to coordinate industrial output with military needs. America's political leaders were weak partners in this collaboration because they did not have the expertise to challenge the decisions of corporate and military leaders. Since then, according to Mills, military institutions had "come to shape much of the economic life of the United States" (p. 222). In effect, the U.S. economy never returned to its pre-World World II production patterns. Military and industrial leaders have ensured that a significant portion of the national budget is allocated to preparation for war. Today the United States is by far the world's most powerful military force, with weapons that no other nation possesses. With an administration that intends to maintain this military superiority and use it wherever it believes U.S. security is threatened, defense budgets in the United States are likely to remain extremely high for the foreseeable future, despite tax cuts and increasing levels of federal debt.

Although Mills doubted the ability of political leaders to control corporate and military elites, others have argued that government officials are indeed a powerful force in defining defense policy. In fact, according to Seymour Melman (1974), the president and top officials of the Pentagon and other federal agencies have the final say in most military decisions that are important to them. Melman has challenged the Marxist explanation of war as a tool used by the rich to solve certain problems of capitalist economies. In his view, managers at the top of the federal government have often made decisions that served their own interests but damaged the economy and the interests of the rich. Pentagon policy during the Vietnam War, for example, resulted in high rates of inflation and diverted money that corporate executives could have invested for other purposes.

In addition to military, political, and economic elites, there is another actor that affects the likelihood of war—the public. When Clausewitz wrote about warfare, public opinion did not matter much. Monarchs and ministers conducted diplomacy and war without interference from the populace. In the twentieth century, however, many states have become much more democratic. As a result, political leaders must take public opinion into account in setting foreign policy. In some cases public opinion actually favors war, especially when sentiments of **nationalism**—identification with the idea of nationhood and exaltation of the nation's culture and interests above those of all other states—are strong. In the early years of this century, powerful nationalistic feelings in Germany, a number of eastern European countries, Great Britain, and other nations helped make peace seem dishonorable and war a feasible option.

Today renewed nationalism in Southeast Asia, Taiwan and China, the former Soviet Union, and the Middle East poses a serious threat to prospects for world peace because the possibility of civil wars and nationalist movements leads to increased fear of terrorism and greater political instability. Moreover, local wars can draw in the larger nations, as occurred during World War I and could occur again in the Middle East.

The International Context of War and Peace. So far, we have limited our discussion to national institutions and domestic forces that tend to preserve or threaten peace. However, no discussion of the causes of war would be complete without some attention to the international context. The world is composed largely of independent sovereign states, each with its own interests. Because the supply of natural resources, power, prestige, and other valued commodities is limited, nations inevitably compete with one another. There is no central authority powerful enough to resolve all international conflicts peacefully. Nevertheless, a number of forces do reduce incentives to wage war. (See the Social Problems: A Global View box on page 529.)

One such force is international cooperation. The League of Nations and later the United Nations are examples of international institutions designed to promote cooperation among nations. A key function of these organizations is the settlement of disputes. The United Nations, for example, has helped restore peace in three wars between Israel and its neighbors, in the Korean conflict, in the Greek civil war, in Bosnia, and in a number of other conflicts. It has often failed to resolve clashes that involve the superpowers, however. The United States, Russia, and other major nations are often unwilling to give up some of their power to arbitrators, especially on issues of

Social Problems: A Global View

GLOBALIZATION AND THE HOPE OF WORLD PEACE

As Secretary General of the United Nations, Kofi Annan commissioned extensive research on U.N. interventions to stop the slaughter of innocent victims. This research has been subjected to harsh criticism, particularly for the failures of peacekeeping missions in Kosovo and Rwanda. But criticism is what the U.N. leader asked for. No social organization, especially a world body as fraught with problems as the United Nations, can improve its effectiveness without sound evaluations of its actions. One aspect of globalization is that the world has shrunk as a result of the instant flow of television and other images from one nation to another. When innocent populations are threatened with disaster, either from wars or from natural causes, there is an outcry from all directions to "do something" to help. Many other political considerations also come into play, but it is clear that world events now take place with far greater public awareness than ever before. In consequence, the United Nations has intervened in Iraq, Bosnia, Cambodia, Somalia, Rwanda, Haiti, the Great Lakes region of East Africa, Nigeria, Sierra Leone, East Timor, Liberia, and many other places (Urquhart, 2000).

The research Annan commissioned at the United Nations takes a hard look at these interventions. It faults not only the United Nations but many of the leading nations of the world as well. The two most extensive research reports evaluate U.N. operations in Kosovo in 1998 and in Rwanda during the 1994 genocide (United Nations, 1999a, 1999b). The Rwanda report notes that the genocidal violence began only four months after the disastrous intervention of U.S. Rangers in Somalia, and there was little or no enthusiasm in the United States or elsewhere for substantial military intervention in Rwanda. Annan, then head of the United Nations' peacekeeping department, approached more than 100 governments around the world in a vain attempt to gather troops to head off the looming genocide. The evaluation report concludes that with 5,000 troops, the genocide that cost the lives of more than 400,000 people, the majority women and children, could have been avoided. In Kosovo, too, intervention came too late to prevent ethnic cleansing and the destruction of many cities and countless lives.

The research points to one basic problem facing the United Nations and the world's nations as they consider intervention in potential disasters. The problem is that the United Nations has no constitutional authority to gather troops and enforce measures to bring about peace. No nation wishes to give up its sovereignty: "No government wants to set up a system which may, at some point in the future, be invoked against itself" (Urquhart, 2000, p. 19). Opponents of the United Nations are willing to consider participation in peacekeeping missions on an individual basis but are far from willing to work out anything that begins to look like a world government with its own military resources. While this attitude prevails, Annan's research concludes, the prospects of guaranteeing human security around the world remain rather dim.

Ellen Johnson-Sirleaf, president of Liberia, is the first female president of an African nation. A highly educated economist, she offers the Liberian population a chance to rebuild their lives after years of bloody civil strife.

vital national interest. Moreover, research on international organizations has cast doubt on their value as peacekeepers in general.

Although the United States and other nations are often drawn into global conflicts in the role of peacekeepers, recent research indicates that such third-party intervention has been largely unsuccessful. Almost invariably, the peacekeeping force has been unable to withdraw after successfully restoring peace between the combatants. This pattern does not appear due to personal or organizational failure on the part of the peacekeepers. Instead, it stems from the explosiveness of the conflicts themselves, the problems faced by peacekeepers in attempting to maintain neutrality, the difficulty of

Former leaders of the Irish Republican Army announce the signing of a peace accord that ended years of violence between Protestant and Catholic terrorist factions in Northern Ireland. This peaceful resolution of a bitter religious conflict shows that diplomacy and negotiations can be effective in leading warring factions away from the use of terror.

coordinating in-the-field mediation with diplomacy, and the lack of a workable model for peacekeeping. All these problems were encountered in Bosnia, Rwanda, Somalia, and Sierra Leone. But the desire to do something to ease bloody conflicts and to provide humanitarian aid continues to motivate third-party peacekeeping efforts and to improve their effectiveness in some instances (Rudolph, 1995; Walker, 1996).

International trade is another force that tends to promote peace. When influential citizens benefit economically from peaceful relations, support for war is diminished. Moreover, trade promotes a common outlook as well as common interests; trading partners are usually political partners. Today world trade is dominated by market economies like those of Japan, Europe, and the industrialized nations of the West. As the former communist nations of Eastern Europe develop market economies and economic growth transforms more of the nations of the Pacific Rim into economic competitors of the advanced nations, global competition is likely to increase, making it even more necessary to have international peacekeeping institutions and effective international law. This is especially true as the renewed influence of nationalism throughout the world threatens to produce greater instability and terrorism.

Social Policy

The war in Iraq, the resurgence of the Taliban in Afghanistan, and Iran's threats to renew their production of nuclear weapons, heightened tensions between India and Pakistan (both nuclear powers), continuing violence and terrorism elsewhere in the Middle East, fears of bioterrorism and attacks on airliners—these and other threats to peace make the world situation at this writing extremely gloomy. Following an outpouring of sympathy and support for the United States and its people after the attacks of 9/11, the perception is strong in Europe and elsewhere that the United States is pursuing a unilateralist set of policies with a "go-it-alone" attitude that subverts international bodies like the United Nations and seeks to enhance U.S. control of oil resources in the Middle East. The decision by the U.S. government to build an antimissile shield, and its refusal to sign international accords on war crimes, nuclear proliferation, and biological weapons, only reinforce the belief that the United States is not exerting positive leadership in seeking world peace.

The rise of negative feelings about the United States is quite evident from State Department and Pew Research Center survey results, as shown in Table 16–3. In many nations, the percentage of citizens with favorable views of the United States has declined dramatically. Worldwide opinion polls conducted in 2007 found few people,

TABLE 16–3	U.S. Image Slips (Percent Favorable View of United States)		
	1999/2000	2002	2007
West Europe			
Germany	78	61	30
Great Britain	83	75	51
Italy	76	70	53
France	62	63	39
East Europe			
Slovak Republic	74	60	41
Poland	86	79	61
Czech Republic	77	71	45
Bulgaria	76	72	51
Ukraine	70	80	54
Russia	37	61	41
Turkey	52	30	9
Americas			
Argentina	50	34	16
Bolivia	66	57	42
Peru	74	67	61
Venezuela	89	82	56
Brazil	56	52	44
Mexico	68	64	56
Canada	71	72	55
Asia			
Pakistan	23	10	15
Indonesia	75	61	29
South Korea	58	53	58
Japan	77	72	61
Africa			
Kenya	94	80	87
Nigeria	46	77	70

Source: From *What the World Thinks in 2002,* Pew Research Center for the People and the Press. Courtesy of Pew Global Attitudes Project, Pew Research Center, 2002.

even among the United States' closest allies, who were very favorable toward American policies, and there are sizable minorities in Western Europe and Canada with an unfavorable view. The most common negative attitude is the belief that the United States does not take into account the interests of others outside its borders when making international policies. In most countries where the surveys were conducted, majorities see U.S. policies as contributing to the growing gap between rich and poor nations. U.S. reluctance to intervene forcefully in the AIDS crisis, along with feelings that the war on terrorism and against Iraq masks U.S. economic and political ambitions, convince large numbers of people that the United States is not doing enough to solve global problems (Pew Research Center, 2007).

By 2005 Americans also began turning against the Bush administration's policy of pursuing largely unilateral strategies, such as the war in Iraq, to counter global terrorism. Poll data revealed that a large majority of Americans did not believe President Bush was doing a good job, and almost two-thirds of those surveyed thought the United States should play a shared role in international leadership, whereas only 25 percent thought the United States should be the most active nation in international leadership (Pew Research Center, 2005). These shifts in voter attitudes resulted in a landslide defeat for the Republican Congress in 2006 and seem to account for the continuing erosion of public support for the Bush administration and many Republican leaders as the nation heads toward the 2008 elections.

What are some explanations for the precipitous decline in favorable opinions of the United States among people in other countries?

Arms Control: A Promise Unfulfilled

The history of disarmament since nuclear weapons were invented consists of a series of limited agreements that have, until very recently, allowed the arms race to continue almost unabated. This is not to say that negotiations to achieve total disarmament have not been attempted. In August 1945 the first resolution passed by the United Nations set up the International Atomic Energy Commission and instructed it to propose plans for the complete elimination of nuclear weapons. Because the Soviet Union had not yet built a bomb, it vetoed the commission's proposal, which called for arms control first and prohibition at some time in the future. (Control would permit certain levels of weapons; prohibition would ban them entirely.)

In the early 1950s France, Great Britain, Canada, the United States, and the Soviet Union again tried to reach a general arms control agreement. In talks that lasted for several years, these nations reached a consensus on several issues, including the date at which total prohibition of nuclear weapons should take effect and how they should inspect one another's defense sites. However, disagreements on verification led to a deadlock that could not be resolved.

Despite their failure to ban nuclear weapons, the major powers have succeeded in formulating a number of treaties that limit certain weapons and regulate the spread of others. The first of these accords was the Nuclear Testban Treaty, which was signed in 1963. This agreement forbade all nuclear tests under water, in outer space, and on the ground, but it did not prohibit underground tests.

In addition to the testban treaty, agreements prohibiting the spread of nuclear weapons to Antarctica, Latin America, Mexico, and outer space were signed between 1959 and 1967. In 1968 the Nuclear Nonproliferation Treaty was ratified by the U.N. General Assembly. This treaty was designed to stop the flow of nuclear weapons to nations that did not already have them. However, the agreement did nothing to slow the production of nuclear weapons by nations that did have them.

Since the nonproliferation treaty was signed, the United States has entered into a series of negotiations with the former Soviet Union to limit strategic arms, that is, weapons considered essential to a nation's offense or defense. Two agreements emerged from the Strategic Arms Limitation Talks (SALT). The SALT treaties were flawed in a number of ways. First, they did not bind any nuclear powers except the Soviet Union and the United States. Other nations that possess the bomb, such as France and Great Britain, were not obligated by the terms of these treaties. Second, the limits on offensive weapons were set above existing levels, thus allowing for continued expansion of both nations' arsenals. Third, and even more detrimental to arms control, was the total lack of restrictions on improvements to existing weapons. Both nations were free to build greater accuracy, speed, and range into their missiles. Finally, the agreements did not prevent the two superpowers from developing new weapons like the cruise missile.

The Bush administration has revived a Reagan-era policy of developing an antimissile shield over U.S. airspace, a policy in violation of existing antimissile agreements. The announcement in 2002 that the United States would reserve the right to take unilateral action to protect its interests in the Middle East and elsewhere in the world, and that it would continue to act aggressively against nations that harbor terrorists or support terrorist groups, is defended on the grounds that in order to foster the values of freedom and democracy, the United States as the only remaining superpower needs to exert its influence throughout the world. But other nations, especially those already critical of U.S. politics in the Middle East, consider these policies further evidence of what they see as a dangerous shift toward unilateralism in international policy. And because the United States is the leading supplier of weapons on the world market, it is also accused of renewing arms races in regional "hot spots." (See the On Further Analysis box on page 534.)

A serious problem created by smaller regional wars and arms sales to poor nations is the legacy they leave behind in the form of unexploded ammunition and buried land mines. Rich nations like Kuwait have professional demolition experts to clear the land of thousands of buried mines. Poor nations like Somalia and Angola must endure unpredictable explosions that take the lives and limbs of thousands of poor farmers. In Afghanistan, the Soviets laid 12 million mines during the war in the 1980s. Similar situations exist in Cambodia and in many African nations. Because many of the land mines were made in the United States, this nation bears much of the responsibility for establishing better control over the sale of deadly military technology (Donovan, 1994).

Dealing with Terrorism

Terrorist acts, especially suicide bombings, kidnappings, and the holding of hostages, often attract worldwide attention. Indeed, terrorists use violence and drastic actions to attract media attention to their cause as well as to intimidate civilians and show governments that they can exert power. Although public sentiment often favors negotiating with terrorists to win the release of captives, the usual official policy is not to give in to terrorist demands (Clawson, 1988; Spector, 2003). Policies that have proven somewhat effective include the following: Governments should use boycotts and other measures to put pressure on states that sponsor terrorism; negotiators may promise anything to terrorists but not keep the promises after the captives have been released because promises made under threat are not valid; terrorists should be treated as criminals; the cooperation of journalists and media personnel should be enlisted to deprive terrorists of media attention; substantial rewards should be offered for information about and capture of terrorists; and an international campaign against terrorists should be undertaken with the help of a network of experts on the subject.

An informed public that will cooperate with antiterrorist policies is extremely important in combating this social problem. Since 9/11, for example, there have been predictions of widespread terrorism, especially against air travelers; and although the traffic on commercial flights was drastically reduced because of this fear, the cooperation of the public with searches and stringent antiterrorist measures at airports was credited with preventing more violence than actually occurred. However, although these policies help diminish the spread and effectiveness of terrorism, much larger forces are at work that seem to be increasing the likelihood of terrorist acts. (See the Unintended Consequences box on page 535.)

On Further Analysis

THE WORLD'S LEADING ARMS MERCHANT

The United States is the world's leader in the international sale of weapons, according to an annual report by the Congressional Research Service, a branch of the Library of Congress. In 2000 about half of all weapons sold on the global market were sold by American companies. Of these, about two-thirds were sold to developing countries in the Middle East, Africa, and Asia.

Arms sales are an extremely important segment of the U.S. world trade picture, so much so that the U.S. government regularly uses incentives to induce foreign governments to purchase American weapons systems. In 2002, for example, the Lockheed Martin Corporation, America's leading arms producer, was locked in fierce competition with European arms companies for the largest weapons deal, a $3.5 billion contract to replace Poland's obsolete jet fighter fleet. Lockheed, the eventual winner in the bidding, was about to lose out to a European contender when the U.S. government stepped in and offered Poland a loan of $3.8 billion to make the purchase from the American firm (Reuters, 2002).

The accompanying table documents the actual volume of international arms sales. It shows that between 1993 and 2000 the United States sold $124.2 billion worth of armaments on the world market, three times more than the next competitor, the United Kingdom. Note that China, the only Asian nation with significant arms sales, is only beginning to realize its potential as a player on the international arms scene; this is likely to change as China continues to develop its weapons production capabilities.

The United States is also the leading supplier of weapons of all kinds to developing nations, often in regions of political instability where weapons can also fall into the hands of terrorist groups. Russia is the leader in arms sales in Africa, where unstable regimes are a major concern, but the United States leads all other nations in weapons sales in the Middle East, Asia, and Latin America.

Arms Deliveries to the World, by Supplier: 1993–2000 (in millions of current U.S. dollars)

	1993	1994	1995	1996	1997	1998	1999	2000	Total 1993–2000
United States	15,172	13,345	15,991	14,820	16,274	16,482	17,935	14,187	124,206
Russia	3,400	1,700	3,500	3,100	2,600	2,200	3,100	3,500	23,100
France	1,500	1,300	2,800	3,600	6,300	6,800	3,100	1,500	26,900
United Kingdom	4,600	5,200	5,300	6,500	6,800	3,800	5,100	5,100	42,400
China	1,200	600	700	600	1,000	600	300	500	5,500
Germany	1,700	1,700	2,000	1,900	1,200	1,400	1,900	800	12,600
Italy	400	200	200	100	700	200	300	300	2,400
All Other European	2,300	3,400	3,500	3,400	4,400	3,200	2,700	2,000	24,900
All Others	1,900	2,000	2,000	1,800	2,300	1,600	2,100	1,500	15,200
TOTAL	32,172	29,445	35,991	35,820	41,574	36,282	36,535	29,387	277,206

Source: Grimmett, 2001. (Congressional Research Service)

The Oklahoma City terrorism trial raised questions about why the United States does not pass laws that require tagging explosives with an identifying chemical that would make it far more difficult to use commonplace materials like fertilizer as explosives for mass destruction. The National Rifle Association and other pro-weapons groups oppose such laws on grounds of individual freedom and self-protection (Guterl, 1996). Other experts on domestic terrorism argue that the United States should ban private armies and militias, but given the fierce lobbying that accompanies any effort to control sales of personal weapons, it is doubtful that the nation has the political will to accomplish this goal, even since 9/11.

The passage of the Homeland Security Act in 2002 represents the largest reorganization of the federal government in over fifty years. The Department of Homeland Security's mission is to prevent terrorist attacks within the United States, reduce America's vulnerability to terrorism, minimize the damage from attacks that do occur, and aid in the recovery from such attacks. The director of homeland security has jurisdiction over airport security, port security, border surveillance and management, and a wide variety of antiterror initiatives. The Coast Guard, the Federal Emergency Management Agency, the U.S. Customs Service, and the U.S. Citizenship and Naturalization Service are included in the department. The Bush administration also hopes that creation of the department will help solve persistent problems of lack of cooperation between the FBI and the CIA, but the department does not actually include these separate and extremely powerful investigative agencies.

Future Prospects

Reacting to increased criticism at home and abroad, the Bush administration has renewed its efforts at global diplomacy. In 2007 it achieved significant reductions in the threat of nuclear arms production in Korea, opened a new diplomatic channel with Iran to discuss security issues in Iraq, and stepped up its efforts to broker a solution to the conflicts between Israel and the Palestinians. With the United States international reputation at a low point, it is certain that whatever administration takes over the reins of government in 2008, international diplomacy will be a matter of continuing urgency.

It is also quite clear that as they face the continuing threat of international terrorist groups, the United States and other Western targets of terrorist attacks will continue to improve their intelligence capabilities. This entails developing more effective undercover operations, hiring agents with language skills, improving international cooperation, upgrading computer tracking systems, and gaining a more sophisticated understanding of why individuals become motivated to commit acts of suicidal violence.

Why does it matter what people outside the United States think of its policies and actions?

Unintended Consequences

TERRORISM AND THE INTERNET

The 1995 bombing in Oklahoma City and the 1997 Heaven's Gate mass suicide are tragic events that also cast a negative light on the Internet. The Oklahoma City bombing called attention to the proliferation of explicitly racist, anti-Semitic, white power, and terrorist-related sites on the World Wide Web. The Heaven's Gate suicides called attention to the equally robust growth of fringe religious groups, UFO enthusiasts, and many other seemingly apocalyptic or doomsday groups whose messages are easily accessible on the Internet. After 9/11, the revelation that Al Qaeda also uses the Internet to broadcast secret messages and recruit new adherents was a warning about misuses of the Internet (Tsfati & Weimann, 2002).

For those who are intent on keeping cyberspace as free from censorship as possible, these are problems that threaten the future of this exciting new communication channel. For those con-

cerned about exerting social control, however, the Internet is an increasingly problematic communications medium. In 1997, for example, the U.S. Parole Commission ruled that in certain cases federal parolees can be barred from using a computer to access the Internet (Johnson, 1997). But for every Web site that represents a potential threat to social order, there are at least ten times as many others that deal with benign subjects, from news of new allergy treatments to the latest weather report. Still, these recent events, as well as the problem of protecting minors from indecent advances by adults, have tarnished the Internet's image.

David Gelernter (1997), a noted Yale University computer scientist who was one of the Unabomber's victims, observes that the connection between the Internet and terrorism, the appeal of cults, and other social problems is not unusual or unexpected. He notes that since the

Heaven's Gate cult "ran a Web-page design business, they may have trolled for new members by sending e-mail to likely targets. They believed an alien spaceship was hiding behind the Hale-Bopp comet; they may have got the news over the Net, where rumors spread fast." But before they used the Internet, they recruited people into the cult through posters and other old-fashioned techniques. It is tempting to blame technology, Gelernter notes, but if people are confused about what to believe about good and evil, or God and humanity, why blame that on the Internet rather than face the real problem? It is clear, however, that as with all other technologies that expand the possibilities for human communication and persuasion (especially movies, radio, and television), the subject of how and whether to control some forms of activity and speech on the Internet will continue to be a social policy issue for the foreseeable future.

GOING BEYOND LEFT AND RIGHT

Should the United States be more forceful in banning the kinds of weapons used in domestic terrorism, such as assault rifles and unidentifiable explosives? Most people on the liberal side of American politics would agree that they should. Many on the conservative side would not. They may not believe in the spread of arms and private armies any more than others do, but they often fear the growing power of the federal government. How can this stalemate be resolved? The answer seems to be on a case-by-case basis. First, ban assault weapons, then pass laws calling for the addition of "taggants" to fertilizers and other materials that can be used as deadly explosives. Perhaps it takes tragedies like the Oklahoma City bombing to gain a consensus across the political spectrum, and even that consensus will not last long. Each victory in the effort to check the spread of weapons of terror needs to be gained when the "right" conditions are present. Such victories require the assent of people of all political persuasions—all, of course, except those who would resort to terror themselves.

In the aftermath of the Virginia Tech shootings in 2007, when it was revealed that the shooter, a man with diagnosed mental illness, had been sold a rifle without the mandatory background check, Congress, with the cooperation of gun control advocates and the National Rifle Association, passed stricter enforcement measures. This action is a sign that when confronted with the stark facts of negligence or greed leading to tragic violence, all the conflicting parties can reach important compromise agreements.

Summary

- Terrorism has reached alarming proportions in recent decades. Terrorist acts may be spurred by revolutionary fervor, the collective paranoia of followers of a deranged leader, or the attempts of a state to repress its citizens. Transnational terrorism is committed by independent agents who are essentially autonomous.

- Victims of terrorist acts are of two types: random victims and individuals who are singled out because of their prominence. In both cases, the victim is dehumanized in the eyes of the terrorist and used as a symbol of political or other injustice.

- Much contemporary terrorism is motivated by extreme religious beliefs, even though all the major religions seek peace and understanding among the world's people.

- Terrorism can be extremely effective in a number of areas. It can result in increased fear of attack and erosion of civil liberties as well as serious economic and political consequences.

- The direct effects of war include extensive death and destruction. In addition, many soldiers suffer lasting physical and psychological injuries.

- Indirect effects of war include disruption of the lives of people whose homeland has become a battleground. War also leads to mass migrations of people who are trying to escape persecution or seeking new opportunities. In addition, war causes immeasurable economic damage.

- The development of nuclear weapons has contributed to peace among the major powers. However, if peace breaks down, a war of unprecedented destructiveness could ensue. The presence of *rogue states* that refuse to adhere to the rule of law and may have access to nuclear weapons is a source of particular concern in the contemporary world.

- There has been some progress toward controlling the conduct of war. A body of international law that deals with armed conflicts includes rules that define the rights and privileges of those who fight and that attempt to protect noncombatants. However, these rules are difficult to enforce and are frequently violated.

- Among the theories that have been proposed to account for war is the view that humans have a predisposition for aggression that has been transmitted genetically from one generation to the next. This view is challenged by those who believe that the motivation to fight is a learned response to symbols.

- According to the nineteenth-century military philosopher Carl von Clausewitz, war is used by monarchs as an alternative to diplomacy to gain land, prestige, and other benefits. Marx and Lenin, on the other hand, believed that economic competition leads national ruling classes (as opposed to workers) to wage war on one another.

- Noneconomic explanations of war are of two basic types: those that look at relations among institutions within a society and those that focus on relations among nations. In the former category is the belief that a strong, influential military affects the likelihood that a nation will go to war. This view is expressed in Lasswell's prediction of the rise of "garrison states," in which military leaders have dictatorial power, and in Mills's warning of the power of the "industrial-military complex." An opposing view holds that government officials do indeed define military policy. In modern times, public opinion has also been an important factor in military policy decisions.

- Among the forces that reduce incentives to wage war are international organizations and international trade. As international economic competition increases, the need for international peacekeeping institutions will also increase.

- Policies aimed at reducing the buildup of arms have focused on international arms control treaties. These agreements have limited certain weapons and regulated the spread of others, reducing the chance that a minor incident will lead to a full-scale war. However, the arms race will continue in regions where nationalism and conflicts over borders threaten peace.

- The usual official policy toward terrorism is not to give in to terrorist demands and to treat terrorists as criminals. However, although this policy may diminish the spread and effectiveness of terrorism, other forces seem to be increasing the likelihood of terrorist acts.

- In 2002 Congress passed the Homeland Security Act, which created the Department of Homeland Security. The department's mission is to prevent terrorist acts within the United States, reduce the nation's vulnerability to terrorism, and minimize the damage and recover from attacks that do occur.

Key Terms

terrorism, p. 511
narcoterrorism, p. 512

state terrorism, p. 512
revolutionary terrorism, p. 512

nationalism, p. 528

Social Problems Online

War, revolution, and terrorism garner considerable attention on the Internet. For a current look at international violence, start with the daily newspaper. The daily edition of the *New York Times* (**www.nytimes.com**) can be accessed by following a simple registration procedure. The site also maintains an archive of past stories. Most of the other major national newspapers can be found by entering their names on any one of the major search engines. Foreign newspapers often offer a slightly different slant than U.S. papers. Because it serves the international business community, the *Financial Times* offers wide-ranging coverage of trouble spots throughout the world; it can be accessed at **www.ft.com/home/us**.

The Central Intelligence Agency (CIA) does more than engage in cloak-and-dagger activities. Its Web pages (**www.odci.gov**) offer lists of online publications, including its *World Factbook*, which provide basic information about geography, population, demographics, and governments (including names of chiefs of state and cabinet members).

Stanford University's Hoover Institution on War, Revolution and Peace at **www.hoover.org** analyzes social, political, and economic change from a largely conservative viewpoint. Selections from its *Hoover Digest* are available for reading or downloading and cover both domestic and international issues related to "principles of statecraft, the art of government, and relations among nations during war, revolution, and peace." From a more liberal perspective, the Carnegie Endowment for International Peace seeks to "invigorate and extend both expert and public discussion on a wide range of international issues," including worldwide migration, nuclear nonproliferation, regional conflicts, multilateralism, and the use of force. It provides a catalog of publications and an index of its magazine *Foreign Policy*, with articles from several issues. It can be accessed at **www.carnegieendownment.org/**.

The Center for Democracy and Technology (**www.cdt.org**) features resources that are critical of U.S. and other government efforts to restrict free speech and the flow of information in the name of countering terrorism. It disseminates information about Internet censorship and privacy issues and offers interesting scenarios on how the Internet can and cannot be used to further terrorism.

Peace Brigades International has a Web page at **www.peacebrigades.org** that offers links to humanitarian, human rights, and peace and justice organizations in the Caribbean, Latin America, North America, Europe, Australia, and New Zealand. Most of the organizations offer newsletters and publications that describe political, economic, and social conditions in specific countries or regions. Several groups provide opportunities for becoming active in human rights campaigns or other activities that promote peace and justice.

Those interested in research on feeding the world's hungry and relieving international poverty may access InterAction, "a coalition of more than 150 nonprofit organizations advocating for humanitarian assistance to the world's poor." Its Web page is located at **www.interaction.org**/. It offers an informative set of background briefing papers on the crisis in central Africa, as well as links to the United Nations' "ReliefWeb." Further information about Africa that places its various crises in historical and geopolitical context can be accessed at the University of Pennsylvania's African Studies Web page (**www.sas.upenn.edu/African_Studies/AS.html**).

Research Navigator

Follow the instructions on pages 26–27 of this text to access the features of Research Navigator. Once at the Web site, enter your Login Name and Password. Then, to use the Content Select database, use keywords such as "war on terrorism," "war crimes," and "arms control," and the search engine will supply relevant and recent scholarly and popular press publications. Use the *New York Times* Search-by-subject archive to find recent news articles related to problems of war and global insecurity, and the Link Library to find relevant Web sites organized by the key terms associated with this chapter.

Go to the EBSCO host and type in "international arms sales." Scroll down to the article entitled "The Arms Code of Conduct," by Gar Smith. What is the International Code of Conduct for arms sales? What is the current status of this code—where has it been ratified, and what nations mentioned in the article have not ratified it? Why would such a code help people in poor nations?

Glossary

abstinence only program A program designed to teach teenagers the value of remaining celibate until marriage.

acid rain A form of air pollution that is detrimental to forests and lakes; rainfall that contains large concentrations of sulfur dioxide, which is emitted by utility and industrial plants.

addiction Physical dependence on a drug.

affirmative action Programs that systematically increase opportunities for women and members of minority groups that have been the victims of past economic and social discrimination.

ageism Devaluation of the aged and the resultant bias against older people.

age stratification The process by which people are segregated into different groups or strata on the basis of age.

alcoholic A person who is addicted to alcohol.

alienation A condition experienced by workers who lose the capacity to express themselves in their work.

alimony The money paid by one partner for the support of the other after they have obtained a divorce.

anomie A weakening of the norms that govern acceptable social behavior; a disparity between approved goals and the approved means of obtaining them.

appropriate technology A policy perspective that advocates less complex and smaller-scale technological solutions than those offered by large-scale corporate and government institutions.

assimilation The process by which members of a racial or ethnic minority group take on the characteristics of the mainstream culture by adapting their cultural patterns to those of the majority group and by intermarrying.

aversion therapy A treatment program that employs nausea-producing drugs or electric shock to condition a patient against alcohol.

behavior conditioning See *aversion therapy.*

capital Equipment of all kinds and hourly or salaried labor. Used to produce goods and services.

capitalism A system for organizing the production of goods and services that is based on markets, private property, and the business firm or company.

census tract A relatively homogenous area with respect to population, socioeconomic status, and living conditions.

chain migration The tendency of immigrants to migrate to areas where they have kin and others from their home communities.

child abuse A deliberate attack on a child by a parent or other caregiver that results in physical injury.

civil law Laws that deal with noncriminal acts in which one individual injures another.

class stratification The stratification of individuals and groups according to their access to various occupations, income, and skills; see *social stratification.*

codependency A pattern in which members of a problem drinker's family participate in a pattern of interactions designed to excuse the problematic behavior.

community psychology An approach to the treatment of mental disorders that makes use of easily accessible, locally controlled facilities that can care for people in their own communities.

comparable worth The idea that the pay levels of certain jobs should be adjusted so that they reflect the intrinsic value of the job; holders of jobs of comparable value would then be paid at comparable rates.

conflict perspective A sociological perspective based on the belief that social problems arise out of major contradictions in the way societies are organized, which create conflict between those who have access to the "good life" and those who do not.

consolidated metropolitan statistical area (CMSA) The largest urban areas in the United States, comprising two or more closely linked major cities or primary metropolitan statistical areas, such as Dallas–Fort Worth or New York City–northern New Jersey–Long Island.

control group The subjects who do not receive the "treatment" in an experiment.

cost shifting The tendency for the costs of treating people with serious illnesses to be transferred from one insurance system to another.

crime An act or omission of an act for which the state can apply sanctions.

crime index A set of data on the most serious, frequently occurring crimes: murder and nonnegligent manslaughter, forcible rape, robbery, aggravated assault, burglary, larceny-theft, motor vehicle theft, and arson.

criminal law A subdivision of the rules governing society that prohibits certain acts and prescribes punishments to be meted out to violators.

cross-sectional data Data based on a questionnaire given to a sample on a single occasion.

crude birthrate The number of births per 1,000 population.

cultural lag A condition in which one of two correlated parts of a culture changes before or in greater degree than the other, thereby causing less adjustment between the two parts than existed previously.

cyborg A creature that is partly human and partly composed of technological systems.

decentralization The situation created by the flight of middle-class families from the central city to the suburbs, together with the influx of poor minority groups, the unemployed, and the aged to those areas.

de facto segregation Segregation that is a result of housing patterns, economic patterns, and other factors.

deinstitutionalization The discharge of patients from mental hospitals directly into the community.

de jure segregation Segregation that is required by law.

demographic transition The process in which a population shifts from an original equilibrium in which a high birthrate is canceled out by a high death rate, through a stage in which the birthrate remains high but the death rate declines, to a final equilibrium in which the birth and death rates are lower but the population is much larger.

demography The subfield of sociology that studies how social conditions are distributed in human populations and how those populations are changing.

detoxification A treatment in which an alcoholic is kept off alcohol until none shows in blood samples.

differential association An explanation of crime that holds that criminal behavior is a result of a learning process that occurs chiefly within small, intimate groups that value such behavior.

digital divide   The gap between those with access to computers and the Internet and those without such access.

discrimination   The differential treatment of individuals who are considered to belong to a particular social group.

drift hypothesis   See *social-selection (drift) hypothesis.*

drug   A chemical substance that affects body function, mood, perception, or consciousness; has a potential for misuse; and may be harmful to the user or to society.

drug abuse   The use of unacceptable drugs, and excessive or inappropriate use of acceptable drugs, so that physical, psychological, or social harm can result.

economic globalization   The growing tendency for goods and services to be produced in one nation or region and consumed in another, and for the companies that produce those goods and services to engage in business activities in many different regions of the world.

educational achievement   How much a student actually learns, measured by mastery of reading, writing, and mathematical skills.

educational attainment   The number of years of school an individual has completed.

embezzlement   Theft from an employer by an employee with privileged access to company finances.

endogamy   A norm stating that a person brought up in a particular culture should marry within the cultural group.

entrepreneur   A capitalist who creates a new business venture.

environmental pollution   The presence of substances added to the environment that are potentially damaging to people and other life.

environmental stress   What society does to the environment, for example, discharging substances into the air, water, and soil.

ethnic minority   A minority group made up of people who may share certain cultural features and who regard themselves as a unified group.

ethnography   The close observation of interactions among people in a social group or organization.

experimental group   The subjects who receive the "treatment" in an experiment.

extended family   A kinship unit that consists of parents, children, grandparents, and other related individuals who are living together.

family reconciliation   A policy in which applicants for immigration who have family members already legally residing in the United States are given priority over other applicants.

field research   See *participant observation.*

flexitime   An approach to work hours that allows employees to arrive and depart from the job when they choose, as long as they work during specific core hours and for a certain amount of time per week.

fraud   Obtaining money or property under false pretenses.

gender identity   A person's sexual self-image, as distinguished from physiological gender.

gerontology   The study of the physical causes and effects of the aging process.

global warming   The increase in average global temperatures caused by higher levels of carbon dioxide in the atmosphere.

habituation   Psychological dependence on a drug.

halfway house   A small residential community, usually under private auspices and most often in an urban area, in which for a period of weeks or months ex-patients are helped to adjust from hospital to normal life.

Head Start   A blanket term that refers to federally funded preschool programs aimed at preparing disadvantaged children for school.

health maintenance organization (HMO)   A prepaid group practice that provides complete medical services to subscribers in a specific region.

homogamy   The requirement that one must marry a person similar to oneself in religion, social class, and race or ethnicity.

homophobia   Hostility, violence, or discrimination directed at people because they are homosexual, or are suspected to be homosexual.

homosexuality   A sexual preference for members of one's own sex.

hospice   An institution designed for terminally ill patients.

human capital   The skills and capabilities of a nation's citizens.

humanism   Intellectual tradition that is concerned for the welfare of man; in education, this tradition emphasizes the maximum self-development of the individual learner; see *open education.*

institution   A more or less stable structure of statuses and roles devoted to meeting the basic needs of people in a society.

institution building   Research that attempts to show how people reorganize their lives to cope with new conditions, often creating new kinds of organizations and, sometimes, whole new institutions.

institutional discrimination   Discrimination that occurs as a result of the structure and functioning of public institutions and policies.

kinship unit   A group of individuals who are related to one another either by bloodlines or by some convention equivalent to marriage.

level of living   What people actually obtain in the way of material well-being.

limited liability   Term meaning that only the assets of a corporation, not the entrepreneur's personal assets, are liable to seizure in the case of economic failure or wrongdoing.

longitudinal data   Data derived from comparisons of matched samples over time.

lumpenproleteriat   A term used by Karl Marx to refer to the segment of the poor in a capitalist society who are not part of the labor force but are on the margins of the society, often subsisting through criminal and black-market activities.

managed care   A health-care program in which individual medical visits or treatments are limited to specific providers and services.

manslaughter   Unlawful killing of a human being without malice aforethought.

market   An economic institution that regulates exchange behavior through the establishment of different values for particular goods and services.

megalopolis   See *standard consolidated statistical area.*

mental disorder   Psychological or organic problems in the mental functioning of an individual that may require medical treatment but do not require hospitalization.

mental illness   Psychological or organic problems in the mental functioning of an individual that are considered serious enough to require hospitalization.

metropolitan district   An area that contains several urban communities, all of which are in close proximity to one another.

metropolitan statistical area (MSA)   An urban area that comprises a medium-sized city or two or more closely linked smaller cities, for example, Indianapolis, Indiana, or Little Rock–North Little Rock, Arkansas.

modernization   The transformation of societies to urbanized and industrialized ways of life based on scientific technologies, individualized rather than communal or collective roles, and a cosmopolitan outlook that values efficiency and progress.

modified extended family   A family structure in which the individual nuclear families live separately but the extended family remains as a strong kinship organization through a combination of interpersonal attachments among its members and various forms of economic exchanges and mutual aid.

multinational corporation An economic enterprise that is based in one country and pursues business activities in one or more foreign countries.

murder Unlawful killing of a human being with malice aforethought.

narcoterrorism The terrorism of cocaine barons in Colombia, designed to take revenge on the authorities and to intimidate them into lax enforcement of the law.

narcotic antagonist A substance that negates the effects produced by opiates.

nationalism Identification of the masses with the nation and exaltation of its culture and interests above those of all other states.

neighborhood distress A condition in which a neighborhood is characterized by high rates of poverty, joblessness, female-headed families, welfare recipiency, and teenage school dropouts.

nuclear family A kinship unit that consists of a father, a mother, and their children, living apart from other kin.

obesity A condition of significant overweight, in which the individual has a body mass index of 30 or higher.

open education Individualized instruction in schools; the goal is independent, self-paced learning.

organized crime A system in which illegal activities are carried out as part of a rational plan devised by a large organization that is attempting to maximize its overall profit.

outsourcing Locating of American manufacturing plants that produce goods for American markets in third-world nations, where the manufacturing firm can take advantage of lower wage rates.

overstayers Illegal immigrants who have exceeded the time allocated to them to visit or reside in the United States.

parole Supervision of people who have been released from prison.

participant observation A research technique in which the sociologist participates directly in the social life of the individuals or groups under study.

plea bargaining An arrangement in which an offender agrees to plead guilty to a lesser charge than that of which he or she was originally accused in return for a lighter sentence.

political refugees Refugees displaced by conditions such as war or genocide in their home countries.

prejudice An emotional, rigid attitude toward members of a particular group that is maintained despite evidence that it is wrong.

prevalence The extent to which a behavior appears in the population to any degree at all.

primary aging Age-related physical changes due to molecular and cellular changes in the body.

primary metropolitan statistical area (PMSA) Urban areas that comprise one major city and the adjacent, closely linked suburbs; for example, New York City.

probation Supervision of offenders who have not been sentenced to jail or prison.

progressivism A movement begun in the United States in the early 1900s; in education, this movement emphasized vocational training, "daily-living skills," and a "child-centered curriculum."

projection A means of releasing tension that involves attributing one's own undesirable traits to some other individual or group.

psychological dependence A condition in which a user needs a drug for the feeling of well-being that it produces.

psychotropic drugs Pharmaceutical drugs used in the management of stress, mental disorders, and mental illness.

racial minority A minority group made up of people who share certain inherited characteristics.

racial steering The deliberate refusal of real estate brokers to show houses to minority buyers outside specific areas.

racism Behavior, in word or deed, that is motivated by the belief that human races have distinctive characteristics that determine abilities and cultures.

rate of population growth (natural increase) The differential between the crude birthrate and the death rate.

recidivism The probability that a former inmate will break the law after release and be arrested again.

residual deviance Deviance from social conventions that are so completely taken for granted that they are assumed to be part of human nature.

revolutionary terrorism The most common form of terrorism; terrorism practiced by revolutionary groups.

role A certain set of behaviors that are expected of and performed by an individual on the basis of his or her status or position in society.

rural A term used to describe a sparsely populated area that is mostly used for agriculture, forestry, or other exploitation of resources.

sample A number of people who represent the behavior and attitudes of the larger population from which they are selected.

scapegoat A person or group that becomes a target of aggression displaced from the real source of the aggressor's frustration.

secondary aging Accelerated age-related physical changes caused by environmental factors such as lack of exercise and poor diet.

secondary deviance A term applied to behavior that elaborates on a deviant act in order to reinforce the role of deviant.

sexism Behaviors and beliefs that discriminate against women (or men) on the basis of gender.

sexual harassment Physical and nonphysical harassment of a sexual nature, including but not limited to graphic comments on the victim's body, propositions of a sexual nature, and the threat of adverse effects on the victim's employment or livelihood for lack of submission to sexual advances.

sexual identity A sense of one's attractiveness to others and of comfort with one's body and with feelings of sexual arousal.

shelter poverty A condition in which a family must pay more than 30 percent of its monthly income for rent or other housing payments.

social control The capacity of a society or social group to regulate itself according to a set of higher moral principles beyond those of self-interest.

social disorganization The condition that results when the expectations or rules by which society is organized fail to function effectively.

socialization The process by which individuals develop into social beings.

social norm A social standard that specifies the kind of behavior that is appropriate in a given situation.

social pathology A term applied to the "illness" of individuals or social institutions that fail to keep pace with changing conditions and thereby disrupt the healthy functioning of the social "organism."

social policy A formal procedure designed to remedy a social problem.

social problem Behavior that departs from established norms and social structures because individual and collective goals are not being achieved; a condition that a significant number of people believe should be remedied through collective action.

social stratification A pattern in which individuals and groups are assigned to different positions in the social order, with varying amounts of access to the desirable things in the society.

social-selection (drift) hypothesis The view that social class is not a cause but a consequence of mental disorder.

standard of living What people want or expect in the way of material well-being.

state terrorism Terrorism of governments against their own people; also known as repressive terrorism.

status A socially defined position in a group or organization.

status offense An act that is illegal if it is performed by a person under 18 years of age.

stereotyping Attributing a fixed and usually unfavorable or inaccurate conception to a category of people.

survey research A method for gathering information from a number of people, known as a *sample*, who represent the behavior and attitudes of the larger population from which they are selected.

technological dualism Term that refers to the fact that advances in technology can have both positive and negative impacts.

technology The apparatus or physical devices used in accomplishing a variety of tasks, together with the activities involved in performing those tasks and the organizational networks associated with them.

terrorism Use of violence or force against property or people in order to further political or social objectives through intimidation or coercion.

total institution A place where a large number of individuals, cut off from the wider society for an appreciable period, together lead an enclosed, formally administered round of life.

urban A term used to describe a densely settled area where manufacturing, commerce, administration, and a great variety of specialized services are available.

urbanism A way of life that depends on heavy industry, mass communication, a mobile population, and other characteristics generally associated with life in urban areas.

urbanized area According to the Census Bureau, a city (or cities) of 50,000 or more inhabitants plus the surrounding suburbs.

urban population According to the Census Bureau, all persons in places of 2,500 inhabitants or more that are incorporated as cities, villages, boroughs, or towns.

victimization report A Census Bureau survey that collects information from a representative sample of crime victims.

wealthfare The opportunities provided by government that enable the rich to become richer.

welfare state A nation in which a significant proportion of the gross domestic product is taken by the state to provide minimal social welfare for the poor, the aged, the disabled, and others who would not be able to survive under conditions of market competition.

whistle-blower A person who risks his or her reputation to reveal dangers in technology or in the application of technology.

working poor People with full-time jobs whose wages are insufficient to raise their incomes above the official poverty line.

Bibliography

ABBOTT, A. 2000. *Deportment and Discipline: Chicago Sociology at One Hundred.* Chicago: University of Chicago Press.

ABBOUD, S. K., & J. Y. KIM. 2005. *Top of the Class: How Asian Parents Raise High Achievers—And How You Can Too.* Berkeley, CA: Berkeley Trade.

ABRAHAMSON, M. 2004. *Global Cities.* New York: Oxford University Press.

ABRAMOWITZ, M. 1996. *Regulating the Lives of Women: Social Welfare Policy from Colonial Times to the Present,* rev. ed. Boston: South End Press.

ACLU (AMERICAN CIVIL LIBERTIES UNION). 2005, August 30. *ACLU Says Stealth Racial Profiling Report Shows Need for Federal Legislation.* www.aclu.org.

ADEOLA, F. O. 2000. "Environmental Justice; Human Rights—Social Aspects." *American Behavioral Scientist,* 43: 686.

ADLER, F., G. O. W. MUELLER, & W. S. LAUFER. 1995. *Criminology,* 2nd ed. New York: McGrawHill.

ADLER, J. 2005, November 6. "The Baby Boom: Suddenly 60." *Newsweek,* p. 2.

AGENCY FOR HEALTHCARE RESEARCH AND QUALITY. 2000. *Addressing Racial and Ethnic Disparities in Health Care.* Rockville, MD: Agency for Healthcare Research and Quality.

AGOUSTINOS, M., & K. J. REYNOLDS, eds. 2001. *Understanding Prejudice, Racism, and Social Conflict.* Thousand Oaks, CA: Sage.

AITKEN, P. V., JR. 1999. "Incorporating Advance Care Planning into Family Practice." *American Family Physician,* 59: 605.

ALBERNAZ, A. 2005, May. "Assessments Slated for Returning Soldiers." www.nepsy .com/leading/0505_ne_assessments.html.

ALBOM, M. 1998. *Tuesdays with Morrie.* Garden City, NY: Doubleday.

Alcoholism & Drug Abuse Weekly. 1998, August 17. "Federal, State Leaders Take Closer Look at Date-rape Drugs," p. 6.

ALEXANDER, A., & K. JACOBSEN. 1999. "Affirmative Action: A Critical Reconnaissance." *International Journal of Urban and Regional Research,* 23: 593.

ALEXANDER, K. 1996, January 5. "Christian Coalition Pushes for School Choice." *Atlanta Constitution,* p. F2.

ALLEN, B. 1999. "The Social Construction of What?" *Science,* 285: 205.

ALLEN, J. E. 2002, May 13. "Nearly 25% of Women Missed Care Because of Cost." *Los Angeles Times,* p. 1.

ALLI, B. O. 2001. *Fundamental Principles of Occupational Health and Safety.* Geneva, Switzerland: International Labor Organization.

ALTER, J. 2005, April 25. "A Bankrupt Way to Do Business." *Newsweek.*

ALTMAN, D. 1987. *AIDS in the Mind of America.* Garden City, NY: Doubleday Anchor Books.

ALTMAN, S. H., & D. I. SHACTMAN, eds. 2002. *Policies for an Aging Society.* Baltimore, MD: Johns Hopkins University Press.

AMERICAN ASSOCIATION OF UNIVERSITY WOMEN. 2001. *Hostile Hallways: Bullying, Teasing, and Sexual Harassment in School.* www.aauw.org.

AMERICAN PSYCHIATRIC ASSOCIATION. 1994. *Diagnostic and Statistical Manual of Mental Disorders,* 4th ed. Washington, DC: American Psychiatric Association.

AMNESTY INTERNATIONAL. 2005. www.amnestyusa.org/refugee/index.doc.

ANDERSEN, M. L., & P. H. COLLINS, eds. 2007. *Race, Class, and Gender: An Anthology,* 6th ed. Belmont, CA: Thomson/Wadsworth.

ANDERSON, E. 1992. *Streetwise.* Chicago: University of Chicago Press.

ANDERSON, E. 1999. *Code of the Street.* New York: Norton.

APPLEBOME, P. 1992, November 14. "Jailers Charged with Sex Abuse of 119 Women." *New York Times,* pp. 1, 7.

APPLEBOME, P. 1996, February 21. "Governors Want New Focus on Education." *New York Times,* p. B7.

APPLEBOME, P. 1997, February 28. "National Tests Show Students Have Improved in Math." *New York Times,* p. A15.

ARON, R. 1955. *The Century of Total War.* Boston: Beacon Press.

ARONOWITZ, S., & W. DIFAZIO. 1994. *The Jobless Future: Sci-tech and the Dogma of Work.* Minneapolis: University of Minnesota Press.

ASHFORD, L. S. 2001. *New Population Policies: Advancing Women's Health and Rights.* Washington, DC: Population Reference Bureau.

ATKINS, R. M. 1999. "Controlling Costs Without Mismanagement." *Behavioral Health Management,* 19: 12.

AULETTA, K. 1987. *Greed and Glory on Wall Street.* New York: Warner Books.

AUTISMINFO. 2007. autisminfo.com.

AYALA, V. 1996. *Falling Through the Cracks: AIDS and the Urban Poor.* Bayside, NY: Social Change Press.

BAILLIE, H. W., & T. K. CASEY, eds. 2005. *Is Human Nature Obsolete? Genetics, Bioengineering, and the Future of the Human Condition.* Cambridge, MA: MIT Press.

BALLANTINE, J. H. 1993. *The Sociology of Education: A Systematic Analysis,* 3rd ed. Upper Saddle River, NJ: Prentice Hall.

BANASZAK, L. A., ed. 2006. *The U.S. Women's Movement in Global Perspective.* Lanham, MD: Rowman & Littlefield.

BARBANEL, J. 1987, November 13. "Homeless Woman Sent to Hospital Under Koch Plan Is Ordered Freed." *New York Times,* pp. A1, A21.

BARBOZA, D. 2007, May 17. "China Grapples with Food Contamination Credibility Crisis." *International Herald Tribune.*

BARINAGA, M. 1996. "Backlash Strikes at Affirmative Action Programs." *Science,* 271: 1908–1910.

BARKER, P. R., G. MANDERSCHEID, & I. G. GENDERSHOT. 1992. "Serious Mental Illness and Disability in the Adult Household Population: United States, 1989." In R. W. Manderscheid & M. A. Sonnenschein, eds., *Mental Health, United States, 1992.* Washington, DC: Center for Mental Health Services and National Institute of Mental Health.

BARLOW, H. D., & D. KAUZLARICH. 2002. *Introduction to Criminology,* 6th ed. Upper Saddle River, NJ: Prentice Hall.

BARNES, J. E. 2002, November 25. "Off to a Slow Start." *U.S. News & World Report,* p. 47.

BARNETT, S. 2004. "Cost-Benefit Analysis of Preschool Education." National Institute for Early Education Research, http://nieer. org/resources/files/BarnettBenefits.ppt.

BARRETTE, C. 2007. "Juvenile Adults". Unpublished doctoral dissertation, Graduate Center, City University of New York.

BARRY, J., & E. THOMAS. 2001, June 25. "Dropping the Bomb." *Newsweek,* pp. 28–30.

BARRY, P. 2002. *Mental Health and Mental Illness.* Philadelphia: Lippencott.

BARTON, J. H. 1981. *The Politics of Peace: An Evaluation of Arms Control.* Stanford, CA: Stanford University Press.

BASSUK, E. L. 1984, July. "The Homelessness Problem." *Scientific American,* pp. 40–45.

BASSUK, E. L., A. BROWNE, & J. C. BRUCKNER. 1996. "Single Mothers and Welfare." *Scientific American,* 275: 60–68.

BECKER, H. S. 1963. "Becoming a Marijuana User." In *Outsiders: Studies in the Sociology of Deviance.* New York: Free Press.

BECKMAN, V. 1995, July/August. "Alcohol and Social Change." *World Health,* pp. 22–23.

BEER, F. A. 1981. *Peace Against War: The Ecology of International Violence.* San Francisco: Freeman.

BELL, D. 1973. *The Coming of Post-industrial Society: A Venture in Social Forecasting.* New York: Basic Books.

BELL, D. 1991, March 16. "The Myth of the Intelligent Society." *New York Times,* p. 23.

BELL, J. D. 1998, June. "Smaller = Better?" *State Legislatures,* pp. 14–19.

BELLUCK, P. 1996, November 17. "The Youngest Ex-cons: Facing a Difficult Road Out of Crime." *New York Times,* pp. 1, 40.

BENDER, W., & M. SMITH. 1997. "Population, Food and Nutrition." *Population Bulletin,* 51, no. 4. Washington, DC: Population Reference Bureau.

BENNETT, W. J., J. J. DIIULIO, JR., & J. P. WALTERS. 1996. *Body Count.* New York: Simon & Schuster.

BENOKRAITIS, N. V., & J. R. FEAGIN. 1986. *Modern Sexism: Blatant, Subtle and Covert Discrimination.* Upper Saddle River, NJ: Prentice Hall.

BERNARD, J. 1987. *The Female World from a Global Perspective.* Bloomington: Indiana University Press.

BERNS, R. 2007. *Child, Family, School, Community: Socialization and Support,* 7th ed. Belmont, CA: Thomson Higher Education.

BERNSTEIN, N. 2000, February 1. "Study Documents Homelessness in American Children Each Year." *New York Times,* p. A12.

BERRIOS, G. E. 1995. *The History of Mental Symptoms: Descriptive Psychopathology Since the Nineteenth Century.* New York: Cambridge University Press.

BERRUETA-CLEMENT, J. R., L. J. SCHWEINHART, W. S. BARNETT, A. S. EPSTEIN, & D. P. WEIKART. 1984. *Changed Lives: The Effects of the Perry Preschool Program on Youths Through Age 19.* Ypsilanti, MI: High/Scope.

BERRY, D. B. 1995. *The Domestic Violence Sourcebook: Everything You Need to Know.* Los Angeles: Lowell House.

BESHAROV, D. J., & P. GERMANIS, 1999. "Making Food Stamps Part of Welfare Reform." *Policy & Practice of Public Human Services,* 57: 6–12.

BHAGWATI, J. N. 1999, August 14. USNewswire.

BIBLARZ, T. J., & A. D. RAFTERY, 1999. "Family Structures, Educational Attainment, and Socioeconomic Success: Rethinking the 'Pathology of Matriarchy.'" *American Journal of Sociology,* 105: 321–365.

BILCHIK, S. 2003. "Sentencing Juveniles to Adult Facilities Fails Youths and Society." *Corrections Today,* 65: 21.

BINSTOCK, R. H., & L. K. GEORGE. 2001. *Handbook of Aging and the Social Sciences,* 5th ed. San Diego: Academic Press.

BioCycle World. 2005, April. "The State of Garbage in America," p. 6.

BIRENBAUM, A. 1995. *Putting Health Care on the National Agenda.* Westport, CT: Praeger.

BIRNBAUM, J. 1999, December 6. "Under the Gun." *Fortune,* pp. 211ff.

BLACK, D. 1984. *Toward a General Theory of Social Control.* Orlando, FL: Academic Press.

BLACK, R. 2005, September 28. "Arctic Ice 'Disappearing Quickly.'" BBC News, http://news.bbc.co.uk.

BLAKESLEE, S. 1994, April 20. "Poor and Black Patients Slighted, Study Says." New York Times, p. B9.

BLANCHARD, C. 1999, Winter. "Drugs, Crime, Prison and Treatment." Spectrum: The Journal of State Government, pp. 26–28.

BLASS, T. 2004. The Man Who Shocked the World: The Life and Legacy of Stanley Milgram. New York: Basic Books.

BLOOM, S. 2001. The Word as Scalpel. New York: Oxford University Press.

BLUMBERG, P. 1980. Inequality in an Age of Decline. New York: Oxford University Press.

BLUMSTEIN, A. 1982. "On the Racial Disproportionality of the United States' Prison Population." Journal of Criminal Law and Criminology, 73: 1259–1281.

BOARD, P. 1996. "Contaminated Lands." New Scientist, 152: 44–45.

BOGUE, D. J. 1985. The Population of the United States: Historical Trends and Future Projections. New York: Free Press.

BOHLEN, C. 1996, March 1. "At 30-something, Leave Home? Mamma Mia, No! Italian Men Choosing to Live with Their Parents." New York Times, p. A4.

BOND, J., P. COLEMAN, & S. PEACE, eds. 2007. Ageing in Society: An Introduction to Social Gerontology, 3rd ed. Los Angeles: Sage Publications.

BOOTH, A., D. R. JOHNSON, & J. EDWARDS. 1980. "In Pursuit of Pathology: The Effects of Human Crowding." American Sociological Review, 45: 873–878.

BORENSTEIN, S. 2007, February 27. "40 Percent of Army, Navy Psych Jobs Vacant." Associated Press.

BOURGOIS, P. 1995. In Search of Respect: Selling Crack in El Barrio. Cambridge: Cambridge University Press.

BOWEN, T. S. 2002, October. "Pollution Bills Could Push Emissions Markets Skyward." Red Herring, p. 22.

BOWES, M. P. 2005. "The Etiology of Alcohol Abuse and Dependence: What Happens in the Brain?" Psychiatric Times, 22, 3–6.

BOWLES, S., H. GINTIS, & M. O. GROVES, eds. 2005. Unequal Chances: Family Background and Economic Success. New York: Russell Sage.

BOZETTE, S. A. 1998. "The Care of HIV-infected Adults in the United States." New England Journal of Medicine, 339: 1897–1904.

BRACEY, G. W. 1995, September. "Research Oozes into Practice: The Case of Class Size. Project STAR in Tennessee." Phi Delta Kappan, pp. 89–90.

BRACEY, G. W. 1998, January. "An Optimal Size for High Schools?" Phi Delta Kappan, p. 406.

BRACEY, G. W. 1999, November. "Reducing Class Size: The Findings, the Controversy." Phi Delta Kappan, p. 246.

BRADBURY, B., & M. JANTTI. 1999, September. Child Poverty Across Industrialized Nations. UNICEF International Child Development Centre.

BRAGINSKY, D. D., & B. M. BRAGINSKY. 1975, August. "Surplus People: Their Lost Faith in Self and System." Psychology Today, pp. 68–72.

BRAVERMAN, H. 1974. Labor and Monopoly Capital: The Degradation of Work in the Twentieth Century. New York: Monthly Review Press.

BRICK, J., ed. 2004. Handbook of the Medical Consequences of Alcohol and Drug Abuse. New York: Haworth Press.

BRIGGS, K. A. 1984, November 12. "Catholic Bishops Ask Vast Changes in Economy of U.S." New York Times, p. 1.

BRIMELOW, P. 1995. Alien Nation: Common Sense About America's Immigration Disaster. New York: Random House.

BRITISH HOME OFFICE. 2002. Annual Reports.

BRONFENBRENNER, U. 1981. "Children and Families." Society, 18: 38–41.

BROOK, J. S., L. RICHTER, M. WHITEMAN, & P. COHEN. 1999. "Consequences of Adolescent Marijuana Use; Incompatibility with the Assumption of Adult Roles." Genetic, Social, & General Psychology Monographs, 125: 193.

BROOKES, J. 1991, March 24. "Latin American Armies Looking for Work." New York Times, p. E2.

BROWN, D. I. 1997. "Enhancing the Spatial Framework with Ecological Analysis." In M. Micklin & D. L. Poston, Jr., eds., Continuities in Sociological Human Ecology. New York: Plenum Press.

BROWN, L. R. 2001. Eco-Economy. New York: Norton.

BROWN, M. K. 1988. Working the Street: Police Discretion and the Dilemmas of Reform. New York: Russell Sage.

BROWN, T. L., G. S. PARKS, R. C. ZIMMERMAN, & C. M. PHILLIPS. 2001. "The Role of Religion in Protecting Adolescent Alcohol Use and Problem Drinking." Journal of Studies on Alcohol, 62: 696–705.

BRUNDTLAND, G. H. 2001. The World Health Report, 2001: Mental Health, New Understanding, New Hope. www.who.int/whr/.

BRUNI, F. 1997, March 29. "A Cult's 2-decade Odyssey of Regimentation." New York Times, p. A1.

BRUNN, S. D., J. F. WILLIAMS, & D. J. ZEIGLER, eds. 2003. Cities of the World: World Regional Urban Development, 3rd ed. Lanham, MD: Rowman & Littlefield.

BRYAN, J. L. 2005. "Constructing the 'True Islam' in Hostile Times: The Impact of 9/11 on Arab Muslims in Jersey City." In N. Foner, ed., Wounded City. New York: Russell Sage.

BRZEZINSKI, M. 2002, June 23. "Re-Engineering the Drug Business." New York Times Magazine, pp. 23–28.

BUCKLEY, W. F., JR. 1997, December 8. "Marijuana Myths/Marijuana Facts" (book review). National Review, p. 63.

BUELL, E. H. 1982. School Desegregation and Defended Neighborhoods: The Boston Controversy. Lexington, MA: Lexington Books.

BULLARD, R. D. 2005, January–February. "Transportation Policies Leave Blacks on the Side of the Road." The Crisis.

BUMPASS, L., & H-H. LIU. 2000, March. "Trends in Cohabitation and Implications for Children's Family Contexts in the United States." Population Studies, pp. 29–41.

BUNNELL, J. E. 1995. "Global Crime Calls for Global Partnerships." FBI Law Enforcement Bulletin, 64: 6–7.

BURBANK, P. M., ed. 2006. Vulnerable Older Adults: Health Care Needs and Interventions. New York: Springer.

BUREAU OF JUSTICE STATISTICS. 2002. Special Report: Substance Dependence, Abuse, and Treatment of Jail Inmates. Washington, D.C. U.S. Department of Justice.

BUREAU OF JUSTICE STATISTICS. 2006. Crime Victimization Survey, 2005. www.ojp.usdoj.gov.

BUREAU OF LABOR STATISTICS. 2005. Quarterly Census of Employment and Wages. Washington, DC: U.S. Department of Labor.

BUREAU OF LABOR STATISTICS. 2007. "Median Weekly Earnings by Employment Characteristics." Current Population Survey.

BURNS, K., ed. 2005a. Gay Marriage. Detroit: Glenhaven Press.

BURNS, K., ed. 2005b. School Violence. Detroit: Glenhaven Press.

BURT, M. 1994. Methods for Counting the Homeless. Washington, DC: Urban Institute Press.

BURT, M. 2001. What Will It Take to End Homelessness? Washington, DC: Urban Institute.

Business Week. 1999, October 18. "What Price Pollution? Leave That to a Global Market," p. 26.

BUSSEY, K., & A. BANDURA. 1999. "Social Cognitive Theory of Gender Development and Differentiation." Psychological Review, 106: 676–713.

CALHOUN, Y., ed. 2005. Air Quality. Philadelphia: Chelsea House.

CALIFANO, J. A. 1998, February 21. "A Punishment-only Prison Policy." America, pp. 3–6.

CALLAHAN, D. 1994. "From Explosion to Implosion: Transforming Healthcare." In W. Kornblum & C. D. Smith, eds., The Healing Experience: Readings on the Social Context of Health Care. Upper Saddle River, NJ: Prentice Hall.

CALLAHAN, D. 1995. "Once Again, Reality: Now Where Do We Go?" Hastings Center Report, 25: 33–37.

CALLAHAN, D. 1997. "Dying Well in the Hospital: The Lessons of SUPPORT (Study to Understand Prognosis and Preferences for Outcomes and Risks of Treatment)." Journal of Applied Gerontology, 16: 267–270.

CALLAHAN, D. 2003, March–April. "Too Much of a Good Thing: How Splendid Technologies Can Go Wrong." Hastings Center Report, pp. 19–22.

CALLAHAN, D., R. T. MEULEN, & E. TOPINKOVA. 1995. "Introduction: Special Issue on Resource Allocation and Societal Responses to Old Age." Ageing and Society, 15: 157–161.

CAMPBELL, E. 2005. "Injection Drug Use, Global HIV/AIDS, and Human Rights." Journal of Ambulatory Care Management, 28: 286–287.

CANNON, A. 1999, January 18. "Settling Up Old Debts." U.S. News & World Report, p. 29.

CANTOR, P. A. 2000. "The Simpsons: Atomistic Politics and the Nuclear Family." In Political Theory. Thousand Oaks, CA: Sage.

CAPLAN, N., J. K. WHITMORE, & M. H. CHOY. 1989. The Boat People and Achievement in America: A Study of Family Life, Hard Work, and Cultural Values. Ann Arbor: University of Michigan Press.

CAREY, M. A., & S. GOLDREICH. 2002, September 28. "House Abortion Bill Provides Both Sides of Issue with Stage for Pre-Election Debate." CQ Weekly, p. 2.

CAREY, M. A., & R. NARESH. 2002, August 3. CQ Weekly, pp. 2111–2114.

CARMODY, D. 1992, January 30. "Coverage of Smoking Linked to Tobacco Ads." New York Times, p. D22.

CARRIUOLO, N. E., A. RODGERS, & C. M. STOUT. 2002. "Valuing and Building from Strengths of Hispanic Students: An Interview with Juliet Garcia." Journal of Developmental Education, 25, 20–24.

CARSON-DEWITT, R. S. 1999. "Alcoholism." Gale Encyclopedia of Medicine, p. 79.

CARTER GOBLE ASSOCIATES. 2005. www.aclu.org/prison/medical/14699prs2003049.html.

CASPER, L. M. 2002. Continuity and Change in the American Family. Thousand Oaks, CA: Sage Publications.

CASSIDAY, J. 2002, September 23. "The Greed Cycle: How the Financial System Encouraged Corporations to Go Crazy." New Yorker, p. 64.

CELIS, W., III. 1993, December 9. "International Report Card Shows U.S. Schools Work." New York Times, pp. A1, A26.

CHAMBLISS, W. 1973. "The Saints and the Roughnecks." Society, 2: 24–31.

CHAMBLISS, W. J. 2000. Power, Politics and Crime. Boulder, CO: Westview Press.

CHERLIN, A. J. 1996. Public and Private Families: An Introduction. New York: McGraw-Hill.

CHERLIN, A. J. 2003. "Should the Government Promote Marriage?" Contexts, 2.

CHESLER, A. 1972. Women and Madness. New York: Avon.

CHESLER, P. 2005. Women and Madness, rev ed. New York: Macmillan.

CHODOROW, N. 1999. Testimony to the American Psychoanalytic Foundation. www.cyberpsych.org/homophobia/all.htm.

CHUDACOFF, H. P. 1989. How Old Are You? Princeton, NJ: Princeton University Press.

CIRINCIONE, J. 2005, November–December. "Lessons Lost." Bulletin of the Atomic Scientists, pp. 42–53.

CLAMPET-LUNDQUIST, S., K. EDIN, J. R. KLING, & G. J. DUNCAN. 2006, March. "Moving At-Risk Teenagers Out of High-Risk Neighborhoods: Why Girls Fare Better Than Boys." Working Paper no. 509, Industrial Relations Section. Princeton, NJ: Princeton University.

CLARK, W. C. 1989, September. "Managing Planet Earth." Scientific American, p. 47.

CLARKE, L. 2005. *Worst Cases: Terror and Catastrophe in the Popular Imagination.* Chicago: University of Chicago Press.

CLAWSON, P. 1988. "Terrorism in Decline?" *Orbis*, 32: 263–276.

CLEMENTS, A. D. 2004. *Homeschooling: A Research-based How-To Manual.* Lanham, MD: ScarecrowEducation.

CLIFFORD, M. J. 2005, April. "Appropriate Technology: The Poetry of Science." *Science and Christian Belief*, 17: 71–82.

CLOSE, F. 1991. *Too Hot to Handle.* Princeton, NJ: Princeton University Press.

COCKERHAM, W. C. 2006. *Medical Sociology*, 9th ed. Upper Saddle River, NJ: Prentice Hall.

COHEN, A. K. 1971. *Delinquent Boys.* New York: Free Press.

COHEN, J. E. 2000, November. "Population Problems: Recent Developments and Their Impact." *Asia-Pacific Review.*

COLE, D. 2000. *No Equal Justice.* New York: New Press.

COLE, J., & D. DURHAM, eds. 2007. *Generations and Globalization: Youth, Age, and Family in the New World Economy.* Bloomington: Indiana University Press.

COLEMAN, E. 2003, Winter. "It's Vladimir Orlov's Job to Come Up with Worst-Case Scenarios." *Ford Foundation Report*, pp. 24–27.

COLES, R. 1968. *Children of Crisis.* New York: Dell.

COLVIN, G. 2002, September 16. "Liar, Liar, Pants on Fire." *Fortune*, p. 160.

COLVIN, G. 2005, August 22. "Saving America's Socks—But Killing Free Trade." *Fortune.*

COLVIN, R. L. 1996, April 8. "Battle Heats Up Over Bilingual Education." *Los Angeles Times*, p. A1.

COMMONER, B. 1992. *Making Peace with the Planet.* New York: New Press.

CONFERENCE OF MAYORS. 2001. http://usmayors.org/uscm/news/press_releases/documents/hunger.

Congressional Digest. 1993. "Current Family Leave Policies," p. 72.

CONKLIN, J. E. 2007. *Criminology*, 9th ed. Boston: Pearson/Allyn and Bacon.

CONLEY, D. 1999. *Being Black, Living in the Red: Race, Wealth and Social Policy in America.* Berkeley: University of California Press.

CONLEY, D. 2005. *The Pecking Order: A Bold New Look at How Family and Society Determine Who We Become.* New York: Vintage.

CONNELL, R. W. 1995. *Masculinities.* Berkeley: University of California Press.

CONWAY, G. 1997. *Food for All in the Twenty-first Century.* Ithaca, NY: Cornell University Press.

CONWAY, G. 1999. "Food for All in the 21st Century." *Social Research*, 66: 351.

CORNELIUS, W. A. 1989. "Impact of the 1986 U.S. Immigration Law on Emigration from Rural Mexican Sending Communities." *Population and Development Review*, 15: 689–705.

CORNELL UNIVERSITY ONLINE. 2006, April 19. www.news.ornell.edu.

COTTRELL, W. F. 1951. "Death by Dieselization: A Case Study in the Reaction to Technological Change." *American Sociological Review*, 16: 358–365.

COUNCIL OF GRADUATE SCHOOLS. 2007. *Graduate Enrollment and Degrees: 1986 to 2005.* www.cgsnet.org.

COX, W. M., & R. ALM. 2000, January 24. "Why Decry the Wealth Gap?" *New York Times*, pp. A25, A29.

CREIGHTON, J. 2002, August. "Lack of Insurance Linked to Health Disparities." *Nation's Health*, p. 1.

CRESSEY, D. R. 1953. *Other People's Money: A Study in the Social Psychology of Embezzlement.* Montclair, NJ: Patterson Smith.

CRITTENDEN, A. 2001. *The Price of Motherhood: Why the Most Important Job in the World Is Still the Least Valued.* New York: Metropolitan Books.

CRITTENDEN, D. 1999. *What Our Mothers Didn't Tell Us: Why Happiness Eludes the Modern Woman.* New York: Simon & Schuster.

CUBAN, L. 1999, August 4. "The Technology Puzzle." *Education Week*, p. 68.

CUBER, J. F., & P. HAROFF. 1965. *Sex and the Significant Americans.* Baltimore, MD: Penguin Books.

CUMELLA, E. J. 2005, July. "Eating Disorders in Children: What Parents Need to Know." *Brown University Child & Adolescent Behavior Letter*, pp. 9–10.

CURTIS, W. R. 1986, Fall. "The Deinstitutionalization Story." *Public Interest*, 85: 34–49.

CUTLER, D. M., E. L. GLAESER, & J. L. VIGDOR. 1999. "The Rise and Decline of the American Ghetto." *Journal of Political Economy*, 107: 455.

CYBERSOURCE CORP. 2006. *Seventh Annual Online Fraud Report.* www.cybersource.com.

DALY, M. 1970. "Woman and the Catholic Church." In R. Morgan, ed., *Sisterhood Is Powerful.* New York: Random House.

DARLING-HAMMOND, L. 1998, Spring. "Unequal Opportunity: Race and Education." *Brookings Review*, pp. 28–33.

DASH, E. 2005, October 15. "Debtors Throng to Bankruptcy as Clock Ticks." *New York Times*, p. A1.

DAVIS, K. 1971. "Population Policy: Will Current Programs Succeed?" In D. Callahan, ed., *American Popular Debate.* Garden City, NY: Doubleday.

DAVIS, M. 1998. *The Ecology of Fear: Los Angeles and the Imagination of Disaster.* New York: Metropolitan Books.

DAVIS, M. 2003. *Dead Cities.* New York: New Press.

DAY, S. 2002, July 3. "Nicotine-Laced Water Is a Drug, F.D.A. Rules." *New York Times*, p. C1.

DEAME, L. 2005. "Global AIDS Toll Bleak." http://earthtrends.wri.org.

DE BEAUVOIR, S. 1972. *The Second Sex.* New York: Penguin.

DECKER, S. 1969. *An Empty Spoon.* New York: Harper & Row.

DEDE, C., J. P. HONAN, & L. C. PETERS, eds. 2005. *Scaling Up Success: Lessons Learned from Technology-based Educational Improvement.* San Francisco: Jossey-Bass.

DEIGHTON, L. C., ed. 2002. *Encyclopedia of Education*, Vol. 8. Farmington Hills, MI: Gale.

DEJONG, W., C. K. ATKIN, & L. WALLACK. 1992. "A Critical Analysis of 'Moderation' Advertising Sponsored by the Beer Industry: Are 'Responsible Drinking' Commercials Done Responsibly?" *Milbank Quarterly*, 70: 661–677.

DELAMATER, J., & W. N. FRIEDRICH. 2002. "Human Sexual Development." *Journal of Sex Research*, 39.

DELINT, W. 2000. "Authority, Regulation and the Police Beat." *Social & Legal Studies*, 9: 55–83.

DENAVAS-WALK, C., B. D. PROCTOR, & C. H. LEE. 2006, August. *Income, Poverty, and Health Insurance Coverage in the United States: 2005.* Washington, DC: U.S. Census Bureau.

DEPALMA, A. 2002, December 5. "White-Collar Layoffs, Downsized Dreams." *New York Times*, pp. B1, B10.

DEPARLE, J. 2004. *The American Dream: Three Women, Ten Kids, and a Nation's Drive to End Welfare.* New York: Viking.

DERSHOWITZ, A. 2002. *Why Terrorism Works.* New Haven, CT: Yale University Press.

DERVARICS, C. 2004. *Grandparent Responsibilities on the Rise.* Population Reference Bureau.

DES JARLAIS, D. C. 1987, April 26. "Addicts Will Change if They Get the Word." *Newsday*, p. 8.

DEWAN, S. 2007, February 16. "New Orleans's New Setback: Fed-Up Residents Giving Up." *New York Times*, p. A1.

DEWEY, J. 1916. *Democracy and Education.* New York: Macmillan.

DICKEY, B., W. FISHER, C. SIEGEL, F. ALTAFFER, & H. AZENI. 1997. "The Cost and Outcomes of Community-based Care for the Seriously Mentally Ill." *Health Services Research*, 32: 599–615.

DILLON, S. 2005, October 20. "Education Law Gets First Test in U.S. Schools." *New York Times*, p. A10.

DLUGACZ, Y. D. 2006. *Measuring Health Care: Using Data for Operational, Financial, and Clinical Improvement.* San Francisco: Jossey-Bass.

DOBBIN, F., ed. 2004. *The Sociology of the Economy.* New York: Russell Sage.

DOBBS, M. 2003, November 8. "Education 'Miracle' Has a Math Problem." *Washington Post*, p. A1.

DOHRENWEND, B. P., & B. S. DOHRENWEND. 1975. "Sociocultural and Social-Psychological Factors in the Genesis of Mental Disorders." *Journal of Health and Social Behavior*, 16: 369.

DONOHEW, R. L., R. H. HOYLE, R. R. CLAYTON, W. F. SKINNER, S. E. COLON, & R. E. RICE. 1999. "Sensation Seeking and Drug Use by Adolescents and Their Friends: Models for Marijuana and Alcohol." *Journal of Studies on Alcohol*, 60: 622.

DONOVAN, W. 1994, January 23. "One Leg, One Life at a Time." *New York Times Magazine*, pp. 26–29.

DRAPER, D. A., R. E. HURLEY, & A. C. SHORT. 2004, March–April. "Medicaid Managed Care: The Last Bastion of the HMO?" *Health Affairs*, pp. 155–167.

DREVITCH, G. 1994. "Where Do You Stand?" *Scholastic Update*, 126: 13–14.

DUGGAN, L., & N. D. HUNTER. 2006. *Sex Wars: Sexual Dissent and Political Culture*, 10th ed. New York: Routledge.

DUGGER, C. W. 1997, March 16. "Immigrant Study Finds Many Below New Income Limit." *New York Times*, pp. 1, 39.

DUGGER, C. 2007, June 27. "Half the World Soon to Be Urban." *New York Times*, p. A1.

DUNCAN, G., J. BROOKS-GUNN, & L. MARX. 1998, Fall. "Making Welfare Reform Work for Our Youngest Children." *Spectrum*, pp. 28–39.

DUNEIER, M. 2002. *Sidewalk.* New York: Farrar, Straus and Giroux.

DUNHAM, R. S., & L. SALCZAK. 2002, September 23. "Can Team Bush Regain Momentum?" *Business Week*, p. 38.

DURKHEIM, É. 1895/1950. *Rules of the Sociological Method*, 8th ed. S. A. Solvay & J. H. Mueller, trans.; G. E. G. Catlin, ed. New York: Free Press.

DURKHEIM, É. 1897/1951. *Suicide, a Study in Sociology.* New York: Free Press.

DUSTER, T. 2003, July–August. "In Memoriam: Dorothy Nelkin." *Hastings Center Report*, p. 20.

DUSTER, T. 2004. "Selective Arrests, an Ever-Expanding DNA Forensic Database, and the Specter of an Early Twenty-First Century Equivalent of Phrenology." In D. Lazar (Ed.), *DNA and the Criminal Justice System: The Technology of Justice.* Cambridge, MA: MIT Press.

ECKHOLM, E. 1995, February 24. "Studies Find Death Penalty Tied to Race of Victims." *New York Times*, pp. B1, B4.

The Economist. 2002, August 24. "Half a Billion Americans?"

ECKLUND, E. H. 2003. "Catholic Women Negotiate Feminism: A Research Note." *Sociology of Religion*, 64: 515–525.

EDELHOCH, M. 1999. "Welfare Reform in South Carolina: 'Roughly Right' Social Policy." *Social Policy*, 29: 7–15.

EDIN, K., & L. LEIN. 1997. *Making Ends Meet: How Single Mothers Survive Welfare and Low Wage Work.* New York: Russell Sage.

EDUCATION INTELLIGENCE AGENCY. 2005. *State Rankings, Current Expenditure per Pupil, 2002–03.* www.eiaonline.com.

EDWARDS, L. P. 1927. *The Natural History of Revolution.* Chicago: University of Chicago Press.

EGAN, M. 2007. *Barry Commoner and the Science of Survival: The Remaking of American Environmentalism.* Cambridge, MA: MIT Press.

EGAN, T. 2002, December 8. "The Seeds of Decline." *New York Times*, sec. 4, pp. 1, 3.

EHRENREICH, B. 1992, February 17. "Stamping Out a Dread Scourge." *Time*, p. 88.

EHRENREICH, B. 2001. *Nickel and Dimed: On (Not) Getting By in America.* New York: Metropolitan Books.

EHRLICH, P. R., & A. H. EHRLICH. 1991. *Healing the Planet: Strategies for Resolving the Environmental Crisis.* Reading, MA: Addison Wesley.

EHRLICH, P. R., & A. H. EHRLICH. 2004. *One with Nineveh: Politics, Consumption, and the Human Future.* Washington, DC: Island Press.

EHRLICH, P. R., A. H. EHRLICH, & J. P. HOLDREN. 1977. *Ecoscience: Population, Resources, Environment.* San Francisco: Freeman.

EL-BASSEL, N., L. GILBERT, & R. F. SCHILLING. 1996. "Correlates of Crack Abuse Among Drug-using Incarcerated Women: Psychological Trauma, Social Support, and Coping Behavior." *American Journal of Drug and Alcohol Abuse,* 22: 41–56.

ELLWOOD, D. T. 1987. *Divide and Conquer: Responsible Security for America's Poor.* New York: Ford Foundation.

ELLWOOD, D. T. 1988. *Poor Support: Poverty in the American Family.* New York: Basic Books.

ELLWOOD, D. T. 1996. May–June. "Welfare Reform as I Knew It: When Bad Things Happen to Good Policies." *The American Prospect,* pp. 22–30.

ELVIN, J. 1999, October 4. "Road Rage, Stadium Rage, Work Rage; What Next?" *Insight on the News,* p. 35.

ENGLAND, P. 2000. "The Pay Gap Between Male and Female Jobs: Organizational and Legal Realities." *Law and Social Inquiry,* 25: 913–931.

ENGLAND, P., M. S. HERBERT, & B. S. KILBOURNE. 1994. "The Gendered Valuation of Occupations and Skills: Earnings in 1980 Census Occupations." *Social Forces,* 73: 65–100.

Environment. 2002, November. "How Now, Brown Cloud," p. 7.

ENTMAN, R. M., & A. ROJECKI. 2000. *The Black Image in the White Mind: Media and Race in America.* Chicago: University of Chicago Press.

EPPRECHT, M. 2004. *Hungochani: The History of a Dissident Sexuality in Southern Africa.* Montreal: McGill-Queen's University Press.

EPSTEIN, C. F. 1993. *Women in Law,* 2nd ed. Urbana: University of Illinois Press.

EPSTEIN, H. 2002, May 9. "The Hidden Cause of AIDS." *New York Review of Books,* pp. 43–49.

ERIKSON, K. T. 1972. *Everything in Its Path: Destruction of Community in the Buffalo Creek Flood.* New York: Simon & Schuster.

ERIKSON, K. T. 1995. *A New Species of Trouble.* New York: Norton.

ERLANGER, H. S. 1987, November 8. "A Widening Pattern of Abuse Exemplified in Steinberg Case." *New York Times,* p. 1.

ETZIONI, A. 2002, July–August. "Opening Islam." *Society,* pp. 29–35.

EVANGELAUF, J. 1992, January 22. "Minority-group Enrollment at Colleges Rose 10% from 1988 to 1990, Reaching Record Levels." *Chronicle of Higher Education,* pp. 70–71.

EVANS, G. W., S. J. LEPORE, B. R. SHEJWAL, & M. N. PALSANE. 1998. "Chronic Residential Crowding and Children's Well-being: An Ecological Perspective." *Child Development,* 69: 1514.

FALK, D. M. 1999, August 16. "ADA Rulings Look Good to Businesses." *National Law Journal,* 21: B9.

Family Practice Management. March 2004. "Physicians Support Single-Payer System, Less Paperwork, Says Survey." Vol. 11, p. 36.

FARIS, R. E. L., & H. W. DUNHAM. 1938. *Mental Disorders in Urban Areas.* Chicago: University of Chicago Press.

FARLEY, R. 1996. *The New American Reality.* New York: Russell Sage.

FARLEY, R., S. BIANCHI, & D. COLASSANTO. 1979. "Barriers to the Racial Integration of Neighborhoods: The Detroit Case." *Social Indicators Research,* 6: 439–443.

FASTEAU, M. F. 1974. *The Male Machine.* New York: McGraw-Hill.

FAULKNER, P. 1981. "Exposing Risks of Nuclear Disaster." In A. F. Westin, ed., *Whistle Blowing!* New York: McGraw-Hill.

FEAGIN, J. R. 1991. "The Continuing Significance of Race: Anti-black Discrimination in Public Places." *American Sociological Review,* 56: 101–117.

FEAGIN, J. R. 1996. *Racial and Ethnic Relations,* 5th ed. Upper Saddle River, NJ: Prentice Hall.

FEAGIN, J. R., & K. D. MCKINNEY. 2003. *The Many Costs of Racism.* Lanham, MD: Rowman & Littlefield.

FEDERAL BUREAU OF INVESTIGATION. 2007. *FBI Terrorism Report 2004.* Washington, DC: Federal Bureau of Investigation.

FENSTERMAKER, S., & C. WEST, eds. 2002. *Doing Gender, Doing Difference: Inequality, Power, and Institutional Change.* New York: Routledge.

FIELDS, S. 1999, October 4. "Deadly Heroin Makes a Comeback." *Insight on the News,* p. 48.

FINEMAN, H. 1996, June 3. "Dulling a Sharp Wedge." *Newsweek,* p. 30.

FINEMAN, H. 2002, August 19. "Anxious in Sioux Falls." *Newsweek,* p. 30.

FISCHER, C. S. 1976, 1984. *The Urban Experience,* 2nd ed. New York: Harcourt Brace Jovanovich.

FISCHER, C. S. 1995. "The Subcultural Theory of Urbanism: A Twentieth-year Assessment." *American Journal of Sociology,* 101: 543–578.

FISCHER, M. J., & D. S. MASSEY. 2004, September. "The Ecology of Racial Discrimination." *City and Community,* pp. 221–241.

FLAVIN, C. 1987. "Reassessing Nuclear Power." In L. R. Brown, ed., *State of the World 1987: A Worldwatch Institute Report on Progress Toward a Sustainable Society.* New York: Norton.

FLINK, J. 1976. *The Automobile and American Culture.* Cambridge, MA: MIT Press.

Focus. 2005, Spring. "Inequality in America: What Role for Human Capital Policies?" Pp. 1–9.

FONE, B. R. S. 2000. *Homophobia, a History.* New York: Metropolitan Books.

FONER, N. 2000. *From Ellis Island to JFK: New York's Two Great Waves of Immigration.* New Haven, CT: Yale University Press.

FONER, N. 2007. *Wounded City.* New York: Russell Sage.

FOOD AND AGRICULTURE ORGANIZATION. 2002. *The State of Food Insecurity.*

FOOD AND AGRICULTURE ORGANIZATION. 2005. *World Agriculture: Toward 2015/2030.*

FORD, J., & C. KADUSHIN. 2002. "Between Sacral Belief and Moral Community: A Multidimensional Approach to the Relationship Between Religion and Alcohol Among Whites and Blacks." *Sociological Forum,* 17, 255–279.

FORD FOUNDATION. 1990. "Increasing the Quantity and Quality of Child Care." *Ford Foundation Letter,* 121: 1–9.

FOUNTAIN, J., S. HOWES, J. MARSDEN, C. TAYLOR, & J. STRANG. 2003. "Drug and Alcohol Use and the Link with Homelessness: Results from a Survey of Homeless People in London." *Addiction Research and Theory,* 11, 245–256.

FOUST, D. 1993, March 8. "'Now They're Really Down to the Dregs.' Resolution Trust Corp.'s Remaining Properties." *Newsweek,* p. 80.

FOX, M. F. 2005. "Women in Science: Career Processes and Outcomes." *Contemporary Sociology,* 34: 361–362.

FOX, R. 1989. *The Sociology of Medicine.* Upper Saddle River, NJ: Prentice Hall.

FOX, R. 1997. *Experiment Perilous.* New Brunswick, NJ: Transaction.

FRANKENBERG, E., & C. LEE. 2002, August. "Race in American Public Schools: Rapidly Resegregating School Districts." Cambridge, MA: The Civil Rights Project, Harvard University.

FREEDMAN, S. G. 1987, April 8. "New AIDS Battlefield: Addicts' World." *New York Times,* pp. B1, B7.

FREUDENBERG, N. 2001. "Jails, Prisons, and the Health of Urban Populations: A Review of the Impact of the Correctional System on Community Health." *Journal of Urban Health,* 78.

FREUDENHEIM, M. 1999, April 9. "A New Strain on the Cost of Health Care." *New York Times,* Business, pp. 1, 17.

FRIEDAN, B. 1963. *The Feminine Mystique.* New York: Dell.

FRIEDAN, B. 1993. *The Fountain of Age.* New York: Simon & Schuster.

FRIEDEN, J. A. 2007. *Global Capitalism: Its Fall and Rise in the Twentieth Century.* New York: Norton.

FRIEDMAN, L. M. 1993. *Crime and Punishment in American History.* New York: Basic Books.

FRIEDMAN, L. N. 1978. *The Wildcat Experiment: An Early Test of Supported Work in Drug Abuse Rehabilitation.* Washington, DC: U.S. Government Printing Office.

FRIEDMAN, M. 1962. *Capitalism and Freedom.* Chicago: University of Chicago Press.

FRIEDMAN, T. L. 2005. *The World Is Flat: A Brief History of the Twenty-first Century.* New York: Farrar, Straus and Giroux.

FUCHS, V. 1956. "Toward a Theory of Poverty." In *Task Force on Economic Growth and Opportunity. The Concept of Poverty.* Washington, DC: U.S. Chamber of Commerce.

FULLER, B., & R. F. ELMORE, eds. 1996. *Who Chooses? Who Loses? Culture, Institutions, and the Unequal Effects of School Choice.* New York: Teachers College Press.

FULTON, A. S., R. L. GORSUCH, & E. A. MAYNARD. 1999. "Religious Orientation, Antihomosexual Sentiment, and Fundamentalism Among Christians." *Journal for the Scientific Study of Religion,* 38: 14–23.

FURSTENBERG, F., & A. CHERLIN. 1991. *Divided Families.* Cambridge, MA: Harvard University Press.

GABAY, M., & S. M. WOLFE. 1997, September–October. "Nurse-Midwifery: The Beneficial Alternative." *Public Health Reports,* pp. 386–395.

GAGNON, J. H., & W. SIMON. 1973. *Sexual Conduct: The Social Sources of Human Sexuality.* Hawthorne, NY: Aldine.

GALBRAITH, J. K. 1958. *The Affluent Society.* Boston: Houghton Mifflin.

GALBRAITH, J. K. 1998. *Created Unequal: The Crisis in American Pay.* New York: Free Press.

GALEWITZ, P. 1999, September 24. "Combined Worth of America's 400 Richest Surpasses $1 Trillion." *Journal News,* p. 1D.

GALLAGHER, J., & J. HAMMER. 1998, February 17. "Gay for the Thrill of It." *The Advocate,* pp. 32–37.

GALLUP POLL. 2004, October 11–14. *The Gallup Poll.*

GANS, H. 1979. *Deciding What's News.* New York: Pantheon Books.

GANS, H. 1984. *The Urban Villagers,* 2nd ed. New York: Free Press.

GANS, H. J. 1995. *The War Against the Poor.* New York: Basic Books.

GARDNER, A. M. 2005, May 15. "Boot Camp: No Pain, No Gain." *New York Times Style Magazine,* p. 70.

GARFINKEL, I., L. RAINWATER, & T. M. SMEEDING. 2005, Spring. "Equal Opportunities for Children: Social Welfare Expenditures in the English-Speaking Countries and Western Europe." *Focus,* p. 16.

GARLAND, D. 2005. "Cruel and Unusual: Punishment and U.S. Culture." *Social and Legal Studies,* 14: 299–302.

GARREAU, J. 1991. *Edge City: Life on the New Frontier.* New York: Doubleday.

GARREAU, J. 1996, Summer. "Civilization Comes to the Suburbs." *New Perspectives Quarterly,* pp. 23–26.

GARRETT, L. 2005, July–August. "The Next Pandemic?" *Foreign Affairs,* 84, 3–23.

GAW, A. C. 1993. *Culture, Ethnicity, and Mental Illness.* Washington, DC: Psychiatric Press.

GEERTZ, C. 2005, Winter. "What Was the Third World Revolution?" *Dissent,* pp. 35–45.

GEHRING, J. 2002, September 25. "Legal Battle Over School Vouchers Returns to Maine." *Education Week,* pp. 1–3.

GELBARD, A. 1999. "World Population Beyond 6 Billion." *Population Bulletin* (Population Reference Bureau), vol. 54.

GELERNTER, D. 1997, March 30. "A Religion of Special Effects." *New York Times,* p. E11.

GELLES, R. J. 1995. *Contemporary Families: A Sociological View.* Thousand Oaks, CA: Sage.

GENESEE, F., K. LINDHOLM-LEARY, W. SAUNDERS, & D. CHRISTIAN. 2005. "Language Learners in U.S. Schools: An Overview of Research Findings." *Journal of Education for Students Placed at Risk,* 10: 363–386.

GERSON, K. 1985. *Hard Choices: How Women Decide About Work, Career, and Motherhood.* Berkeley: University of California Press.

GERSON, K. 1993. *No Man's Land: Men's Changing Commitment to Family and Work.* New York: Basic Books.

GIBBS, N. 2006, January 23. "Abortion's Middle Ground." *Time.* www.time.com.

GIELE, J. Z. 1988. "Gender and Sex Roles." In N. J. Smelser, ed., *The Handbook of Sociology.* Newbury Park, CA: Sage.

GILBERT, D. L. 1993. *The American Class Structure: A New Synthesis,* 4th ed. Belmont, CA: Wadsworth.

GILDER, G. 1993. *Wealth and Poverty.* San Francisco: ICS Press.

GINZBERG, E. 1993. "The Changing Urban Scene: 1960–1990 and Beyond." In H. G. Cisneros, ed., *Interwoven Destinies: Cities and the Nation.* New York: Norton.

GINSBURG, F. 1989. *Contested Lives: The Abortion Debate in an American Community,* 2nd ed. Berkeley: University of California Press.

GIROUX, H. A. 2005. "The Passion of the Right: Religious Fundamentalism and the Crisis of Democracy." *Cultural Studies/Critical Methodologies,* 5: 309–317.

GITLIN, T. 1996. *The Twilight of Common Dreams.* New York: Henry Holt.

GLASSER, I., & ZYWIAK, W. H. 2003. "Homelessness and Substance Misuse: A Tale of Two Cities." *Substance Use and Misuse,* 38: 551–576.

GLASSNER, B. 2000. *Culture of Fear: The Assault of Optimism in America.* New York: Basic Books.

GLAUSIUSZ, J. 2002, November. "Ozone Glee and Gloom." *Discover,* p. 12.

GOCHMAN, D. S., ed. 1997. *Handbook of Health Behavior Research.* New York: Plenum.

GOFFMAN, E. 1961. *Asylums: Essays on the Social Situation of Mental Patients and Other Inmates.* Garden City, NY: Doubleday.

"*Going Global.*" 2005, February 26. *Economist.*

GOLDBERGER, P. 1996, October 15. "The New Times Square." *New York Times,* pp. C11–C12.

GOLDMAN, L. G. 2004, October 4. "Cybercon." *Forbes,* p. 1.

GOLDMAN, H. H., R. G. FRANK, & T. G. McGUIRE. 1994. "Mental Health Care." In E. Ginzberg, ed., *Critical Issues in U.S. Health Care Reform.* Boulder, CO: Westview.

GOLDSBOROUGH, J. O. 2004, February 19. "A Fence Won't Stem the Tide of Immigration." *San Diego Union-Tribune,* p. B11.

GOLEMAN, D. 1990, May 29. "As Bias Crime Seems to Rise, Scientists Study Roots of Racism." *New York Times,* pp. C1, C5.

GOLEMAN, D. 1992, April 21. "Black Scientists Study the 'Pose' of the Inner City." *New York Times,* pp. C1, C7.

GONDLES, J. A., JR. 1999, August. "Hate Crime: Not New, but Still Alarming." *Corrections Today,* p. 6.

GOODE, E. 1999, June 1. "For Good Health, It Helps to Be Rich and Important." *New York Times,* Science, pp. 1, 9.

GOODE, W. J. 1959. "The Sociology of the Family." In R. Merton, L. Broome, & L. Cottrell, eds., *Sociology Today.* New York: Free Press.

GOODIN, R. E., ed. 1995. *The Theory of Institutional Design.* Cambridge: Cambridge University Press.

GORDON, D. M. 1996. *Fat and Mean: The Corporate Squeeze of Working Americans and the Myth of Managerial "Downsizing."* New York: Martin Kessler Books.

GORE, A. 2006. *An Inconvenient Truth.*

GOTTFREDSON, M. R., & T. HIRSCHI. 1995. "National Crime Control Policies." *Society,* 32: 30–37.

GOTTMANN, J. 1978. "Megalopolitan Systems Around the World." In L. S. Bourne & J. W. Simmons, eds., *Systems of Cities: Readings on Structure, Growth, and Policy.* New York: Oxford University Press.

GOULD, R. E. 1974. "Measuring Masculinity by the Size of the Paycheck." In J. H. Pleck & J. Sawyer, eds., *Men and Masculinity.* Upper Saddle River, NJ: Prentice Hall.

GOULD, S. J. 1981. *The Mismeasure of Man.* New York: Norton.

GOULD, W. B. 1968. "Discrimination and the Unions." In J. Larner & I. Howe, eds., *Poverty: Views from the Left.* New York: Morrow.

GOVE, W. R., M. HUGHES, & O. R. GALLE. 1979. "Overcrowding in the Home: An Empirical Investigation of Its Possible Consequences." *American Sociological Review,* 44: 59–79.

GREEN, A. S. 2005, January 13. "Ruling Drops Mandatory Sentencing." *The Oregonian,* p. A01.

GREENBERG, J. A. 1998. "Defining Male and Female: Intersexuality and the Collision Between Law and Biology." *Arizona Law Review,* 41: 265–328.

GREENLEY, J. R. 1972. "Alternative Views of the Psychiatrist's Role." *Social Problems,* 20: 252–262.

GRIMSLEY, K. D. 1999, January 18. "Survey: 26% of Workers 'Burned Out or Stressed' by Jobs." *Journal News,* p. 1D.

GRISWOLD, W. 2004. *Cultures and Societies in a Changing World,* 2nd ed. Thousand Oaks, CA: Pine Forge Press.

GRONFEIN, W. 1985, June. "Psychotrophic Drugs and the Origins of Deinstitutionalization." *Social Problems,* 32: 437–454.

GROW, B., & J. BUSH. 2005, May 30. "Hacker Hunters." *Business Week.*

GROW, B., & K. EPSTEIN. 2007, May 21. "The Poverty Business." *Business Week,* pp. 57–64.

GRUENBERG, B. 1980. "The Happy Worker: An Analysis of Educational and Occupational Differences in Determinants of Job Satisfaction." *American Journal of Sociology,* 86: 247–271.

GRUNWALD, M. 2006, October 1. "Billions for an Inside Game on Reading." *Washington Post,* p. B1.

GUETZLOE, E. 1999. "Violence in Children and Adolescents—A Threat to Public Health and Safety: A Paradigm of Prevention." *Preventing School Failure,* 44: 21.

GUILLERMOPRIETO, A. 2000, April 27. "Colombia: Violence Without End?" *New York Review of Books,* pp. 31–39.

GUSFIELD, J. R. 1975. "The Futility of Knowledge?: The Relation of Social Science to Public Policy Toward Drugs." *Annals of the American Academy of Political and Social Sciences,* 417: 1–15.

GUTERL, F. 1996, January. "The Chemistry of Mass Murder." *Discover,* p. 7.

GUTNER, T. 2002, June 24. "How to Shrink the Pay Gap." *Business Week,* p. 151.

GWATKIN, D. R. 2000. "Health Inequalities and the Health of the Poor." *Bulletin of the World Health Organization,* 78: 1–18.

HACKER, A. 2002, December 5. "Gore Family Values." *New York Review of Books,* pp. 20–25.

HACKER, J. S. 2006. *The Great Risk Shift: The Assault on American Jobs, Families, Health Care, and Retirement and How You Can Fight Back.* New York: Oxford University Press.

HAGEDORN, J. M. 1988. *People and Folks: Gangs, Crime, and the Underclass in a Rustbelt City.* Chicago: Lake View Press.

HAGEDORN, J. M., J. TORRES, & G. GIGLIO. 1998. "Cocaine, Kicks, and Strain: Patterns of Substance Use in Milwaukee Gangs." *Contemporary Drug Problems,* 25: 113–145.

HALL, P. 1982. *Great Planning Disasters.* Berkeley: University of California Press.

HAMRICK, K. S. 2001. *Displaced Workers, Differences in Rural and Urban Experience.* Washington, DC: U.S. Government Printing Office.

HANLEY, R. 2002, September 28. "Rumors of Gang Rites Rattling Paterson." *New York Times,* p. B6.

HANSON, D. J. 2007. *Binge Drinking.* www2.potsdam.edu/hansondj/BingeDrinking.html.

HARKEY, J., D. L. MILES, & W. A. RUSHING. 1976. "The Relation Between Social Class and Functional Status: A New Look at the Drift Hypothesis." *Journal of Health and Social Behavior,* 17: 194–204.

HARRINGTON, M. 1987. *The New American Poverty.* New York: Henry Holt.

HARTMANN, H. 1994, December. "Women Working a Third Shift." *Working Woman,* p. 16.

HARTMANN, H. 1995, Spring. "Feminism After the Fall." *Dissent,* pp. 158–159.

HARVARD JOINT CENTER FOR HOUSING STUDIES. 2007. *The State of the Nation's Housing 2007.* www.jchs.harvard.edu.

Harvard Mental Health Letter. 2005, May. "The Homeless Mentally Ill."

HASTINGS CENTER. 2003. *Access to Hospice Care: Expanding Boundaries, Overcoming Barriers.* Garrison, NY: The Hastings Center.

HAYASHI, E. 2005, September 22. "Overflowing with Problems." *Los Angeles Times,* p. B1.

HAZLETT, S. B., McCARTHY, M. L. LONDNER, M. S., & ONYIKE, C. U. 2004. "Epidemiology of Adult Psychiatric Visits to U.S. Emergency Departments." *Academic Emergency Medicine,* 11, 193–195.

HEATHERINGTON, E. M., & J. KELLY. 2002. *For Better or For Worse: Divorce Reconsidered.* New York: Norton.

HEISLER, C. J. 2007. "Elder Abuse." In R. C. Davis, A. J. Lurigio, & S. Herman, eds. *Victims of Crime,* 3rd ed. Los Angeles: Sage Publications.

HENDERSON, H. 2001. *Terrorism.* New York: Facts On File.

HENDERSON, H. 2005. *Drug Abuse.* New York: Facts On File.

HENDERSON, Z. P. 1995, Summer. "Children Need Space." *Human Ecology Forum,* pp. 20–23.

HENSHAW, S. 2001, March 5. *U.S. Pregnancy Statistics.* New York: Alan Guttmacher Institute.

HERBERT B. 1999, May 16. "Haunted by Segregation." *New York Times,* p. 17.

HEREK, G. M. 2002. "Gender Gaps in Public Opinion About Lesbians and Gay Men." *Public Opinion Quarterly,* pp. 40–66.

HERNDON, J. 1968. *The Way It Spozed to Be.* New York: Simon & Schuster.

HERRMANN, S. M., & C. F. HUTCHINSON. 2005. "The Changing Contexts of the Desertification Debate." *Journal of Arid Environments,* 63: 538–555.

HESMAN, T. 2000, March 4. "Climate Change Record in Subsurface Temperatures: Recent Heat May Indicate Faster Warming." *Science News,* p. 148.

HESSE-BIBER, S. J. 1996. *Am I Thin Enough Yet?: The Cult of Thinness and the Commercialization of Identity.* New York: Oxford University Press.

HEUMANN, L. F., M. E. McCALL, & D. P. BOLDY. 2001. *Empowering Frail Elderly People: Opportunities and Impediments in Housing, Health, and Support Services Delivery.* Westport, CT: Praeger.

HIMMELSTEIN, D. U., E. WARREN, D. THORNE, & S. WOOLHANDLER. 2005, February 2. "MarketWatch: Illness and Injury as Contributors to Bankruptcy." Health Affairs, Harvard University.

HIMMELSTEIN, D. U., S. WOOLHANDLER, I. HELLANDER, & S. M. WOLFE. 1999. "Quality of Care in Investor-owned vs. Not-for-Profit HMOs." *Journal of the American Medical Association,* 282: 159.

HIPPENSTEELE, S., & T. C. PEARSON, 1999, January–February. "Responding Effectively to Sexual Harassment." *Change,* pp. 48–54.

HIRSCH, E. D., JR. 1996. *The Schools We Need: And Why We Don't Have Them.* New York: Doubleday.

HIRSCHI, T., & M. GOTTFREDSON. 1983. "Age and the Explanation of Crime." *American Journal of Sociology,* 89: 552–584.

HOBB, D. 1997. "Professional Crime: Change, Continuity and the Enduring Myth of the Underworld." *Sociology,* pp. 57–73.

HOCHSCHILD, A. R. 1990. *The Second Shift.* New York: Avon Books.

HOGAN, C., P. B. GINSBURG, & J. R. GABEL. 2000, November–December. "Inflation Is Back." *Health Affairs,* pp. 1–4.

HOGE, C. W., S. C. MESSER, & C. A CASTRO. 2004. "Combat Duty in Iraq and Afghanistan and Mental Health Problems." *New England Journal of Medicine,* 351: 1799.

HOLT, J. 1965. *How Children Fail.* New York: Dell.

HOOKER, E. 1966. "The Homosexual Community." In J. O. Palmer & M. J. Goldstein, eds., *Perspectives in Psychopathology: Readings in Abnormal Psychology.* New York: Oxford University Press.

HOOYMAN, N. R., & N. A. KIYAK. 2005. *Social Gerontology: A Multidisciplinary Approach,* 7th ed. Boston: Allyn & Bacon.

HORGAN, J. 1993, February. "Genes and Crime." *Scientific American,* pp. 24, 26, 29.

HORNER, M. 1970. "Femininity and Successful Achievement: A Basic Inconsistency." In J. M. Bardwick, ed., *Feminine Personality and Conflict.* Belmont, CA: Brooks/Cole.

HOROWITZ, A. V., & T. L. SCHEID, eds. 1999. *A Handbook for the Study of Mental Health.* New York: Cambridge University Press.

HOSPICE FOUNDATION OF AMERICA. 2002, November 5. *Hospice Foundation of America Offers Advice for Those Struggling with Grief During the Holiday.* www .hospicefoundation.org.

HOUGHTON, M. A., & W. HOUGHTON. 2002, February 22. "Going Crazy: Managed Care & Mental Health." *Commonweal,* p. 17.

HOVEN, C. W. 2002, June 10. *U.S. Senate Field Hearing Regarding the Unmet Mental Health Needs of New York City Public School Children as a Result of the September 11th Attacks on the World Trade Center.* United States Customs House, New York City.

HUNT, L. G., & C. D. CHAMBERS. 1976. *The Heroin Epidemic.* Holliswood, NY: Spectrum Books.

HUNT, L. G., & M. A. FORSLAND. 1980. "Epidemiology of Heroin Use in Cheyenne, Wyoming: 1960–1977." In R. Faulkinberry, ed., *Drug Problems of the 70's: Solutions for the 80's.* Lafayette, LA: Endac Enterprises/Print Media.

HURLEY, D. 2005, April 19. "Divorce Rate: It's Not as High as You Think." *New York Times,* p. F7.

IBISWORLD. 2005, August. *Sewage Treatment Facilities in the United States.*

INCIARDI, J. A. 1999. *Criminal Justice,* 6th ed. Fort Worth, TX: Harcourt.

INTERNATIONAL DEBATES. 2005, October. "Global Climate Change and International Action to Limit Greenhouse Gas Emissions." *International Debates,* p. 193.

INTER-PARLIAMENTARY UNION. 2007. "Women's Representation in Parliament." www .ipu.org.

INTERNATIONAL CENTRE FOR PRISON STUDIES. 2005. *World Prison Population List–2005.* www.prisonstudies.org.

IRONS, E. J. 2007. *The Challenges of No Child Left Behind: Understanding the Issues of Excellence, Accountability, and Choice.* Lanham, MD: Rowman & Littlefield.

IWATA, E. 2005, June 29. "White-collar Crime Cases Prove Difficult to Prosecute." *USA Today,* p. B2.

JACKMAN, M. R., & R. W. JACKMAN. 1983. *Class Awareness in the United States.* Berkeley: University of California Press.

JACOBS, J. A., & K. GERSON. 2004. *Time Divide: Work, Family and Gender Inequality.* Cambridge, MA: Harvard University Press.

JACOBS, M. D. 1990. *Screwing the System and Making It Work.* Chicago: University of Chicago Press.

JACOBY, T. 2002, September 16. "Immigration Reform and National Security." *New York Times,* p. A17.

JAFFE, P. G., N. K. D. LEMON, & S. POISSON, 2003. *Child Custody and Domestic Violence: A Call for Safety and Accountability.* Thousand Oaks, CA: Sage Publications.

JAMISON, K. R. 2000. *Night Falls Fast: Understanding Suicide.* New York: Knopf, Vintage.

JANOWITZ, M. 1978. *The Last Half Century: Societal Change and Politics in America.* Chicago: University of Chicago Press.

JAYNES, D. J., & R. M. WILLIAMS, JR., eds. 1989. *A Common Destiny: Blacks and American Society.* Washington, DC: National Academy Press.

JAYNES, G. 1988, February 13. "Where Are You? A Nameless Man in a Grim World." *New York Times,* p. 29.

JENCKS, C. 1994, April 21. "The Truth About Homelessness." *New York Review of Books,* pp. 20–27.

JENCKS, C. 1995. *The Homeless.* Cambridge, MA: Harvard University Press.

JENCKS, C., & P. E. PETERSON, eds. 1991. *The Urban Underclass.* Washington, DC: Brookings University.

JENCKS, C., & J. SWINGLE. 2000, January 3. "Without a Net." *The American Prospect,* p. 37.

JIMENEZ, M. 2001, November 11. "Interview with Maria Jimenez." *In Motion Magazine,* pp. 7–9.

JOHANNSON, S., & O. NYGREN. 1991. "The Missing Girls of China: A New Demographic Account." *Population and Development Review* 17: 35–52.

JOHNSON, G. 1997, March 30. "Old View of the Internet: Nerds. New View: Nuts." *New York Times,* sec. 4, p. 1.

JOHNSON, J. A., et al. 2005. *Introduction to the Foundations of American Education,* 13th ed.. Boston: Pearson/Allyn and Bacon.

JOHNSTON, D. C. 2007, March 29. "Income Gap Is Widening, Data Shows." *New York Times,* pp. C1, C10.

JOHNSTON, L. D., et al. 2002. *Monitoring the Future.* http://monitoringthefuture. org.

JONES, S. L. 1999, October 4. "The Incredibly Shrinking Gay Gene." *Christianity Today,* p. 53.

JUDSON, G. 1995, September 1. "Child of Courage Joins Her Biographer." *New York Times,* pp. B1, B5.

KADUSHIN, C. 1983. "Mental Health and the Interpersonal Environment: A Reexamination of Some Effects of Social Structure on Mental Health." *American Sociological Review,* 48: 188–198.

KAHLENBERG, R. D. 1996. *Class, Race, and Affirmative Action.* New York: Basic Books.

KAISER FAMILY FOUNDATION. 2005. *NPR/Kaiser Family Foundation/Harvard Kennedy School of Government Survey on Health Care, 2005.*

KALANT, H. 2001. "The Pharmacology and Toxicology of 'Ecstasy' (MDMA) and Related Drugs." *Canadian Medical Association Journal,* 165.

KAMINER, W. 1999, December 20. "The War on High Schools." *American Prospect,* p.11.

KAMINER, W. 1999. "Feminists, Puritans and Statistics." *Dissent,* 46: 14–15.

KAMINER, W. 2000, January 3. "When Congress Plays Doctor." *American Prospect,* p. 8.

KANDEL, D. B. 1991. "The Social Demography of Drug Use." *Milbank Quarterly,* 69: 365–414.

KANDEL, D. B. 2006. "Testing the Gateway Hypothesis." *Addiction,* 101: 470-476.

KAPLAN, T. 2002. "TANF Programs in Nine States: Incentives, Assistance and Obligation." *Focus,* 22: 36–41.

KASARDA, J. D. 1995. "Industrial Restructuring and the Changing Location of Jobs." In R. Farley, ed., *State of the Union: America in the 1990s,* Vol. 1: *Economic Trends.* New York: Russell Sage.

KASINITZ, P. 1989. "Three Books About the Homeless." *Dissent,* 36: 566–569.

KATZ, J. 1988. *Seductions of Crime: Moral and Sensual Attractions in Doing Evil.* New York: Basic Books.

KATZ ROTHMAN, B. 1994. *The Encyclopedia of Childrearing.* New York: Henry Holt.

KENNEDY, R. 2000. *Burr, Hamilton, and Jefferson: A Study in Character.* New York: Oxford University Press.

KENNY, C. 1996. "Black Environmentalism in the Local Community Context." *Environment and Behavior,* 28: 267–282.

KENT, M. M., & M. MATHER. 2002, April. "What Drives U.S. Population Growth?" *PRB Bulletin,* p. 1.

KENWORTHY, L. 2004. *Egalitarian Capitalism: Jobs, Incomes, and Growth in Affluent Countries.* New York: Russell Sage.

KERR, T., M. TYNDALL, K. LI, J. MONTANER, & E. WOOD. 2005. "Safer Injection Facility Use and Syringe Sharing in Injection Drug Users." *Lancet,* 366: 316–318.

KESSLER, R. C., O. DEMLER, R. G. FRANK, M. OLFSON, H. A. PINCUS, E. E. WALTERS, P. WANG, K. B. WELLS, & A. M. ZASLAVSKY. 2005. *Prevalence and Treatment of Mental Disorders, 1990 to 2003.* World Health Organization.

KESSLER-HAMS, A. 2002. *In Pursuit of Equity: Women, Men, and the Quest for Economic Citizenship in 20th-Century America.* New York: Oxford University Press.

KILBORN, P. T. 1990, May 31. "Wage Gap Between Sexes Is Cut in Test, but at a Price." *New York Times,* pp. A1, D22.

KILBOURNE, J. 1991, Spring–Summer. "Deadly Persuasion: Seven Myths Alcohol Advertisers Want You to Believe." *Media & Values,* pp. 10–12.

KIM, C. J. 2003. *Bitter Fruit: The Politics of Black-Korean Conflict in New York City.* New Haven, CT: Yale University Press.

KIM, I. 1983. *Urban Newcomers: The Koreans.* Princeton, NJ: Princeton University Press.

KIMES, B. R. 2004. *Pioneers, Engineers, and Scoundrels: The Dawn of the Automobile in America.* DSAE International.

KIMMEL, M. S., J. HEARN, & R. W. CONNEL., eds. 2005. *Handbook of Studies on Men and Masculinities.* Thousand Oaks, CA: Sage.

KIMMEL, M. S., & M. A. MESSNER. 1992. *Men's Lives.* New York: Macmillan.

KING, E. A. 1999, September. "15 Myths About Adolescent Suicide." *Education Digest,* pp. 68–71.

KING, R. S., & M. MAURER. 2002. *Distorted Priorities: Drug Offenders in State Prisons.* Washington, DC: The Sentencing Project.

KINSELLA, K., & D. R. PHILLIPS. 2005. "Global Aging: The Challenge of Success." *Population Bulletin* (Population Reference Bureau), Vol. 60.

KINSEY, A. C., W. B. POMEROY, & C. E. MARTIN. 1948. *Sexual Behavior in the Human Male.* Philadelphia: Saunders.

KLEIN, A. 2007, May 9. "House OKs Reauthorization of Head Start." *Education Week,* pp. 25–26.

KLENK, J. 2005. *Choosing a School for Your Child.* Washington, DC: Office of Innovation and Improvement, U.S. Department of Education.

KOBRIN, S. 1959. "The Chicago Area Project—A 25-year Assessment." *Annals of the American Academy of Political and Social Sciences,* 322: 20–29.

KOCHHAR, R. 2004, October. *The Wealth of Hispanic Households: 1966 to 2002.* Washington, DC: Pew Hispanic Center.

KORNBLUM, W. 1993. "Following the Action with Violence Research. Review of Albert J. Reiss, Jr. & Jeffrey A. Roth, eds., *Understanding and Preventing Violence.*" *Contemporary Sociology,* 22: 344–346.

KORNBLUM, W. 2008. *Sociology in a Changing World,* 7th ed. Belmont, CA: Wadsworth.

KORNBLUM, W., & V. BOGGS. 1984, Winter. "New Alternatives for Fighting Crime." *Social Policy,* pp. 24–28.

KORNBLUM, W., & S. LANG. 2005. In N. Foner, ed., *Wounded City: New York After 9/11.* New York: Russell Sage.

KOSTERLITZ, J. 1990, September 8. "No Home, No Help." *National Journal,* p. 2120.

KOTKIN, J. 2005. *The City: A Global History.* New York: Modern Library.

KOZOL, J. 1967. *Death at an Early Age.* Boston: Houghton Mifflin.

KOZOL, J. 1988. "The Homeless and Their Children." *The New Yorker,* January 25, pp. 65ff; February 1, pp. 36ff.

KRAUSS, C. 1996, January 28. "Now, How Long Can Crime Go?" *New York Times,* p. 5.

KRISTOF, N. D. 1995, August 6. "The Bomb: An Act That Haunts Japan and America." *New York Times,* pp. 1, 12.

KRISTOF, N. D. 1996, September 22. "Aging World, New Wrinkles." *New York Times,* pp. 1, 5.

KRISTOF, N. D. 2005, November 29. "What's to Be Done About Darfur? Plenty." *New York Times,* p. A27.

KÜBLER-ROSS, E. 1969. *On Death and Dying.* New York: Atheneum.

KÜBLER-ROSS, E. 1975. *Death: The Final Stage of Growth.* Upper Saddle River, NJ: Prentice Hall.

KUPCHAN, C. A. 2005, October 4. "Europe's Baby Bust." *Los Angeles Times.* www .atimes.com.

KWONG, P. 1997. *Forbidden Waters: Illegal Chinese Workers and American Labor.* New York: New Press.

LAAKSO, J. H. 2000. "Child Support Policy: Some Critical Issues and the Implications for Social Work." *Social Work,* 45.

LAMANNA, M. A. 1997. *Marriages and Families: Making Changes in a Diverse Society.* Belmont, CA: Wadsworth.

LAMBERTH, J. 2000. www.aclu.org/court/lamberth.html.

LARANA, E., H. JOHNSTON, & J. R. GUSFIELD, eds. 1994. *New Social Movements: From Ideology to Identity.* Philadelphia: Temple University Press.

LASSWELL, H. D. 1941. "The Garrison State." *American Journal of Sociology,* 46: 455–468.

LAUMANN, E. O., J. H. GAGNON, R. T. MICHAELS, & S. MICHAELS. 1994. *The Social Organization of Sexuality: Sexual Practices in the United States.* Chicago: University of Chicago Press.

LAVIN, D. E., R. D. ALBA, & R. A. SILBERSTEIN. 1981. *Right Versus Privilege: The Open Admissions Experiment at the City University of New York.* New York: Free Press.

LAVIN, D. E., & D. HYLLEGARD. 1996. *Changing the Odds: Open Admissions and Life Chances.* New Haven, CT: Yale University Press.

LEE, R. D. 2007. *Global Population Aging and Its Economic Consequences.* Washington, DC: AEI Press.

LEIFMAN, H., E. KUHLHORN, & P. ALLEBECK. 1995. "Abstinence in Late Adolescence— Antecedents to and Covariates of a Sober Lifestyle and Its Consequences." *Social Science and Medicine,* 41: 113–121.

LELYVELD, J. 2005, December 15. "The Strange Case of Chaplain Yee." *New York Review of Books,* pp. 8–13.

LEONHARDT, D. 2005, September 1. "Poverty in U.S. Grew in 2004, While Income Failed to Rise for 5th Straight Year." *New York Times,* p. 1A.

LESLIE, C. 1996, July 8. "Will Johnny Get A's?" *Newsweek,* p. 72.

LEVITAN, S. A. 1968. "Head Start: It Is Never Too Early to Fight Poverty." In *Federal Programs for the Development of Human Resources.* Washington, DC: U.S. Congress, Joint Economic Committee, Subcommittee on Economic Progress.

LEWIN, T. 2000, January 6. "Grandparents Play Big Part in Grandchildren's Lives, Survey Finds." *New York Times,* p. A16.

LEWIN, T. 2005, September 16. "Nationwide Survey Includes Data on Teenage Sex Habits." *New York Times,* p. A12.

LEWINE, R. R., D. BURBACH, & H. Y. MELTZER. 1984. "Effect of Diagnostic Criteria on the Ratio of Male to Female Schizophrenic Patients." *American Journal of Psychiatry,* 14: 84–87.

LEWIS, B. 2001. *What Went Wrong: Western Impact and Middle Eastern Response.* New York: Oxford University Press.

LEWIS MUMFORD CENTER FOR COMPARATIVE URBAN AND REGIONAL STATISTICS. 2005. http://mumfordlyndns. org

LEWIS, O. 1968. *The Study of Slum Cultures—Backgrounds for La Vida.* New York: Random House.

LI, J. 1995. "China's One-child Policy: A Case Study of Hebei Province, 1979–88." *Population and Development Review,* 21: 563–586.

LICHTER, D. T., & M. CROWLEY. 2002, June. *Poverty in America: Beyond Welfare Reform.* Washington, DC: Population Reference Bureau.

LICHTER, D. T., & G. V. FUGUITT. 1980. "Demographic Response to Transportation Innovation: The Case of the Interstate Highway." *Social Forces,* 59: 492–511.

LIEBERSON, S. 1990. *From Many Strands,* 2nd ed. New York: Russell Sage.

LIEBMAN, J. B., L. F. KATZ, & J. R. KLING. 2004. *Beyond Treatment Effects: Estimating the Relationship Between Neighborhood Poverty and Individual Outcomes in the MTO Experiment.* Princeton, NJ: Industrial Relations Section, Princeton University.

LIPSKY, M. 1980. *Street Level Bureaucracy: Dilemmas of the Individual in Public Services.* New York: Russell Sage Foundation.

LIPTON, D. S. 1996. *The Effectiveness of Treatment for Drug Abusers Under Criminal Justice Supervision.* Washington, DC: U.S. Department of Justice, Office of Justice Programs, National Institute of Justice.

LISKA, A. S., & W. BACCAGLINI. 1990. "Feeling Safe by Comparison: Crime in the Newspapers." *Social Problems,* 37: 328–337.

LISTER, R. 2004. *Poverty.* Malden, MA: Policy.

LOFLAND, L. 1998. *The Public Realm: Exploring the City's Quintessential Social Territory.* Chicago: Aldine.

LOGAN, J. R. 2001, April 3. "Ethnic Diversity Grows, Neighborhood Integration Lags Behind." Report by the Lewis Mumford Center, http://mumford1.dyndns.org.

LOGAN, J. R. 2004. "Segregation of Minorities in the Metropolis: Two Decades of Change." *Demography,* 41: 1–22.

LOGAN, J. R., & G. DEANE. 2003. *The Muslim World in Metropolitan America.* Albany, NY: Lewis Mumford Center for Comparative Urban and Regional Research, State University of New York at Albany.

LORBER, J. 1994. *Paradoxes of Gender.* New Haven, CT: Yale University Press.

LORENZ, K. Z. 1981. *The Foundations of Ethology.* New York: Springer-Verlag.

LOVINS, A. B. 1977. *Soft Energy Paths: Toward a Durable Peace.* San Francisco: Friends of the Earth.

LOVINS, A. B. 1986. *Energy Unbound: A Fable for America's Future.* San Francisco: Sierra Club.

LOW, S. 2003. *Behind the Gates: Life, Security and the Pursuit of Happiness in Fortress America.* New York: Routledge.

LUDWIG, J., & J. R. KLING. 2006, April. "Is Crime Contagious?" Journal of Law and Economics.

LUKER, K. 1996. *Dubious Conceptions: The Politics of Teenage Pregnancy.* Cambridge, MA: Harvard University Press.

LUNDE, D. T. 1975, July. "Our Murder Boom." *Psychology Today,* pp. 35–42.

LYALL, S. 2004, July 22. "British Worry That Drinking Has Gotten Out of Hand." *New York Times,* p. A3.

LYMAN, M. D. 1996. *Drugs in Society: Causes, Concepts, & Control,* 2nd ed. Cincinnati, OH: Andersen.

LYNCH, J. 2005. "Identity Theft in Cyberspace: Crime Control Methods and Their Effectiveness in Combating Phyishing Attacks." *Berkeley Technology Law Journal, Annual Review 2005,* 20: 259–300.

LYNCH, M. P. 2005. *True to Life: Why Truth Matters.* Cambridge, MA: MIT Press.

MACCOBY, E. E., & C. N. JACKLIN. 1977. "What We Should Know and Don't Know About Sex Differences." In E. S. Morrison and V. Borsage, eds., *Human Sexuality: Contemporary Perspectives.* Palo Alto, CA: Mayfield.

MACCOUN, R., & P. REUTER. 2002, June 3. "Cocaine, Marijuana and Heroin." *The American Prospect,* pp. 34–37.

MacDONALD, H. 2001, Spring. "The Myth of Racial Profiling." *City Journal.*

MacGREGOR, S. 1990. "Could Britain Inherit the American Nightmare?" *British Journal of Addiction,* 85: 863–872.

MALES, M. 1996, February. "Crackdown on Kids." *The Progressive,* pp. 24–26.

MALES, M. 1998, July–August. "Disowning the Future." *Tikkun,* pp. 22–25.

MALINOWSKI, B. 1941. *The Sexual Life of Savages in North-western Melanesia.* New York: Halcyon House.

MALTZ, M. D. 1999. *Bridging the Gap in Police Crime Statistics.* Washington, DC: Bureau of Justice Statistics.

MANZA, J., & C. UGGEN. 2006. *Locked Out: Felony Disenfranchisement and American Democracy.* New York: Oxford University Press.

MARGARONIS, M. 1999, December 27. "The Politics of Food." *The Nation,* p. 11.

MARMOT, M. G. 1998, Fall. "Contribution of Psychosocial Factors to Socioeconomic Differences in Health." *Milbank Quarterly,* pp. 403–449.

MARMOT, M. G., M. G. SHIPLEY, & G. ROSE. 1984. "Inequalities in Death: Specific Explanations of a General Pattern." *The Lancet,* 1: 1003–1006.

MARTIN, E., & R. D. TORRES. 2004. *Savage State: Welfare Capitalism and Inequality.* Lanham, MD: Rowman & Littlefield.

MARTIN, P., & S. MARTIN. 2001, October 8. "Immigration and Terrorism: Policy Reform Challenges." http://migration.ucdavis.edu/ols/martin_oct2001.html.

MARTINE, G. 1996. "Brazil's Fertility Decline, 1965–1995." *Population and Development Review,* 22: 47–76.

MARTINSON, R. 1972, April 29. "Planning for Public Safety." *New Republic,* pp. 21–23.

MARVELL, T. B., & C. E. MOODY. 1997. "Age Structure Trends and Prison Populations." *Journal of Criminal Justice,* 25: 115–124.

MARVIN, D. R. 1997, July. "The Dynamics of Domestic Abuse." *FBI Law Enforcement Bulletin,* pp. 13–19.

MARX, K. 1867/1962. *Capital: A Critique of Political Economy.* Moscow: Foreign Languages Publishing House.

MARX, K., & F. ENGELS. 1848/1969. *The Communist Manifesto.* New York: Penguin.

MASON, M. A., A. SKOLNICK, & S. D. SUGARMAN, eds. 2003. *All Our Families: New Policies for a New Century,* 2nd ed. New York: Oxford University Press.

MASSEY, D. S., & E. ANDERSON, eds. 2005. *Problem of the Century: Racial Stratification in the United States at Century's End.* New York: Russell Sage.

MASSEY, D. S., & N. A. DENTON. 1993. *American Apartheid: Segregation and the Making of the Underclass.* Cambridge, MA: Harvard University Press.

MASSEY, D. S., & M. J. FISCHER. 2003. "The Geography of Inequality in the United States, 1950–2000." *Brookings-Wharton Papers on Urban Affairs,* pp. 1–39.

MASSEY, D. S., & M. J. FISCHER. 2004. "The Ecology of Racial Discrimination." *City and Community,* 3: 221–241.

MATRAS, J. 1973. *Populations and Societies.* Upper Saddle River, NJ: Prentice Hall.

MATTOON, R. 2004, June. "School Funding Ten Years After Michigan's Proposal A: Does Equity Equal Adequacy?" *Chicago Fed Letter.*

MAXWELL, L. E., & G. W. EVANS. 1997. "Design of Child Care Centers and Effects of Noise on Young Children." www.designshare.com/Research/Lmaxwell/ NoiseChildren.htm.

MAZRUI, A. A. 1996. "The New Dynamics of Security: The United Nations and Africa." *World Policy Journal,* 13: 37–42.

MBERE, N. 1996. "The Beijing Conference: A South African Perspective." *SAIS Review,* 16: 167–178.

McEWEN, C. 1988. "Continuities in the Study of Total and Non-total Institutions." In *Annual Review of Sociology.* Newbury Park, CA: Sage.

McINTOSH, C. A., & J. S. FINKLE. 1995. "The Cairo Conference on Population and Development." *Population and Development Review,* 21: 223–260.

McKEOWN, R. E., K. L. JACKSON, & R. F. VALOIS. 1998. "The Frequence and Correlates of Violent Behaviors in a Statewide Sample of High School Students." *Family and Community Health,* 20: 38–54.

McKERNAN, S-M. & RATCLIFFE, C. 2002. *Transition Events in the Dynamics of Poverty.* http://aspe.hhs.gov/hsp/poverty-transitions02/.

McLEOD, J. 1995. *Ain't No Makin' It,* 2nd ed. Boulder, CO: Westview Press.

MEARS, B. 2007. April 18. "Justices Uphold Ban on Abortion Procedure." CNN Washington Bureau. www.cnn.com.

MECHANIC, D. 1990, September 16. "Promise Them Everything, Give Them the Streets." *New York Times Book Review,* p. 9.

MECHANIC, D. 2005. *The Truth About Health Care: Why Reform Is Not Working in America.* New Brunswick, NJ: Rutgers University Press.

MECKLER, L. 2002, October 1. "HIV Prevention Groups Say Bush Administration Is Targeting Their Work." www.actupny.org/reports/cdc-condoms.html.

MEIER, D. 1991, March 4. "Choice Can Save Public Education." *The Nation*, pp. 253ff.

MEIER, D. 2002a. *In Schools We Trust: Creating Communities of Learning in an Era of Testing and Standardization.* Boston: Beacon Press.

MELMAN, S. 1974. *The Permanent War Economy: American Capitalism in Decline.* New York: Simon & Schuster.

MELOSI, M. V. 2005. *Garbage in the Cities: Refuse, Reform, and the Environment,* rev. ed. Pittsburgh: University of Pittsburgh Press.

MERTON, R. K. 1949. *Social Theory and Social Structure.* New York: Free Press.

MERTON, R. K. 1968. *Social Theory and Social Structure,* 3rd ed. New York: Free Press.

MEYER, J. W. 1985, May–June. "Institutional and Organizational Rationalization in the Mental Health System." *American Behavioral Scientist,* 28: 587–600.

MEYER, S. G. 2000. *As Long as They Don't Move Next Door: Segregation and Racial Conflict in American Neighborhoods.* Lanham, MD: Rowman & Littlefield.

MEYERS, M. K., A. LUKEMEYER, & T. M. SMEEDING. 1997, Summer–Fall. "The Cost of Caring: Childhood Disability and Poor Families." *Focus,* p. 52.

MIECH, R. A., A. CASPI, T. E. MOFFITT, B. R. ENTNER WRIGHT, & P. A. SILVA. 1999. "Low Socioeconomic Status and Mental Disorders: A Longitudinal Study of Selection and Causation During Young Adulthood." *American Journal of Sociology,* 104: 1096.

MILGRAM, S. 1974. *Obedience to Authority: An Experimental View.* New York: HarperCollins.

MILITE, G. A. 2007. *Gun Control.* San Diego: ReferencePoint Press.

MILLER, E. M. 1986. *Street Women.* Philadelphia: Temple University Press.

MILLER, W. B. 1958. "Lower Class Culture as a Generating Milieu of Gang Delinquency." *Journal of Social Issues,* 14: 5–19.

MILLS, C. W. 1956. *The Power Elite.* New York: Oxford University Press.

MILLS, V. K. 1972. "The Status of Women in American Churches." *Churches and Society,* 63: 50–55.

MIRON, G., & B. APPLEGATE. 2000. *Achievement in Edison Schools Opened Between 1995 and 1996.* Kalamazoo: The Evaluation Center/Western Michigan University.

MIROWSKY, J. 1985. "Depression and Marital Power: An Equity Model." *American Journal of Sociology,* 87: 771–826.

MONTAGU, A. 1973. "The New Litany of 'Innate Depravity,' or Original Sin Revisited." In A. Montagu, ed., *Man and Aggression,* 2nd ed. New York: Oxford University Press.

MOORE, R. 2004. *Education and Society: Issues and Explanations in the Sociology of Education.* Malden, MA: Polity.

MORGENSON, G. 1999, December 26. "A Company Worth More Than Spain?" *New York Times,* sec. 3, p. 1.

MORRIS, B. J. 2005, May 6. "Gay and Lesbian Americans, Vilified Again." *Chronicle of Higher Education,* p. B13.

MOSHER, W. D., et al. 2004. *Use of Contraception and Use of Family Planning Services in the United States: 1982–2002, Advance Data from Vital and Health Statistics.* Alan Guttmacher Institute, National Center for Health Statistics on Contraceptive Technology.

MOSKOS, C. C. 2005, May–June. "Saving the All-Volunteer Force." *Military Review,* pp. 6–7.

MOSLE, S. 1993, January 18. "Dim Bulb." *New Republic,* pp. 16ff.

MOYNIHAN, D. 1965. *The Negro Family: The Case for National Action.* Washington, DC: U.S. Department of Labor.

MUNTI, D. 2007, March 5. "Empowering the Poor." *Fortune,* p. 10.

MURRAY, C. 1984. *Losing Ground: American Social Policy, 1950–1980.* New York: Basic Books.

MURRAY, J. B. 1998. "Psychophysiological Aspects of Amphetamine-Metamphetamine Abuse." *Journal of Psychology,* 132: 227–238.

NAGEL, J. 1996. *American Indian Ethnic Revival.* New York: Oxford University Press.

NAGYPAL, E. 2004, December 1. "The Evolution of U.S. Earnings Inequality: 1961–2002." *Federal Reserve Bank of Minneapolis Quarterly Review.*

NATIONAL ADVISORY COMMISSION ON CIVIL DISORDERS. 1968. *Report of the National Advisory Commission on Civil Disorders.* Washington, DC: U.S. Government Printing Office.

NATIONAL ADVISORY MENTAL HEALTH COUNCIL. 1993. "Health Care Reform for Americans with Severe Mental Illness." *American Journal of Psychiatry,* 150: 1447–1465.

NATIONAL CAUCUS ON BLACK AGED. 1987. *The Status of the Black Elderly in the United States.* Report for the Select Committee on Aging, House of Representatives, U.S. Congress. Washington, DC: U.S. Government Printing Office.

NATIONAL CENTER FOR EDUCATION STATISTICS. 2001. *Digest of Education Statistics, 2001.* www.nces.ed.gov.

NATIONAL CENTER FOR EDUCATION STATISTICS. 2003, November. *America's Charter Schools: Results from the NAEP Pilot Study.* www.nces.ed.gov.

NATIONAL CENTER FOR EDUCATION STATISTICS. 2004. *Percentage of School enrollment eligible for free or reduced-price lunch.* http://nces.ed.gov.

NATIONAL CENTER FOR EDUCATION STATISTICS. 2005, *Digest of Education Statistics.* www.nces.ed.gov.

NATIONAL CENTER FOR HEALTH STATISTICS. 2007. *Fertility, Family Planning, and Women's Health.* Hyattsville, MD: National Center for Health Statistics, U.S. Department of Health and Human Services.

NATIONAL CENTER FOR INJURY PREVENTION AND CONTROL. 2002, October 18. *Impaired Driving Fact Sheet.* www.cdc.gov/ncipc/factsheets/drving.htm.

NATIONAL CENTER FOR STATISTICS AND ANALYSIS. 2002. *Traffic Safety and Alcohol.* Washington, DC: NCSA.

NATIONAL CLEARINGHOUSE ON CHILD ABUSE AND NEGLECT INFORMATION. 2005. *Child Maltreatment 2003: Summary of Key Findings.* http://nccanch.acf.hhs.gov/pubs/can_info_packet.cfm.

NATIONAL COALITION FOR THE HOMELESS. 2001. *Homeless Families with Children.* www.nationalhomeless.org.

NATIONAL COALITION FOR THE HOMELESS. 2005, June. *Facts About Homelessness.* www.nationalhomeless. org.

NATIONAL COMMISSION ON EXCELLENCE IN EDUCATION. 1983. *A Nation at Risk: The Imperative for Educational Reform.* Washington, DC: U.S. Government Printing Office.

NATIONAL COALITION ON HEALTH CARE. 2007. *Health Insurance Coverage.* www.nchc.org.

NATIONAL COMMISSION ON MARIHUANA AND DRUG ABUSE. 1973. *Drug Use in America: Problem in Perspective,* 2nd Report. Washington, DC: U.S. Government Printing Office.

NATIONAL INSTITUTE OF JUSTICE. 2005. *International Crime.* www.ojp.usdoj.gov/nij.

NATIONAL INSTITUTE OF MENTAL HEALTH. 2001. *Attention Deficit Hyperactivity Disorder: A Brief Overview of the Symptoms, Treatments, and Research Findings.* www.nimh.nih.gov/publicat/helpchild.cfm.

NATIONAL INSTITUTE OF MENTAL HEALTH. 2005. *Annual Report.*

NATIONAL INSTITUTE OF MENTAL HEALTH. 2007. www.nimh.gov/healthinformation.

NATIONAL INSTITUTE ON ALCOHOL ABUSE AND ALCOHOLISM. 1995, October. *Diagnostic Criteria for Alcohol Abuse and Dependence.* Washington, DC: U.S. Government Printing Office.

NATIONAL INSTITUTE ON ALCOHOL ABUSE AND ALCOHOLISM. 2004. "Results from the 2001–2002 National Epidemiologic Survey on Alcohol and Related Conditions (NESARD)." *Drug and Alcohol Dependence,* 74: 223–234.

NATIONAL INSTITUTE ON DRUG ABUSE. 1980. *Highlights from the National Survey on Drug Abuse: 1979.* Washington, DC: U.S. Government Printing Office.

NATIONAL INSTITUTE ON DRUG ABUSE. 2003. *Drug Use Among Racial and Ethnic Minorities* (rev.). www.drugabuse.gov.

NATIONAL INSTITUTE ON DRUG ABUSE. 2004, June. *Epidemiologic Trends in Drug Abuse, Advance Report: Prescription Drugs: Abuse and Addiction.* www.drugabuse.gov.

NATIONAL INSTITUTE ON DRUG ABUSE. 2007. www.nida.nih.gov.

NATIONAL STEPFAMILIES RESEARCH COUNCIL. www.stepfamilies.info/.

NATIONAL SURVEY ON DRUG USE AND HEALTH. Annual. Washington, DC: Substance Abuse and Mental Health Services Administration, U.S. Department of Health and Human Services.

NATIONAL YOUTH GANG CENTER 2004. *National Youth Gang Survey Analysis.* www.iir.com/nygc.

NEFF, J. A., & A. M. DASSORI. 1998. "Age and Maturing Out of Heavy Drinking Among Anglo and Minority Male Drinkers: A Comparison of Cross-sectional Data and Retrospective Drinking History Techniques." *Hispanic Journal of Behavioral Sciences,* 20: 225–241.

NELKIN, D. 1995, September 28. "Biology Is Not Destiny." *New York Times,* p. A27.

NESS, R. B., & L. H. KULLER, eds. 1999. *Health and Disease Among Women: Biological and Environmental Influences.* New York: Oxford University Press.

NEWMAN, K. 1988. *Falling from Grace.* New York: Free Press.

NEWMAN, K. 1999. *No Shame in My Game.* New York: Knopf.

NIEBUHR, G. 1995, April 26. "Assault on Waco Sect Fuels Extremists' Rage." *New York Times,* p. A20.

NIGRO, L. G., & W. L. WAUGH. 1996. "Violence in the American Workplace: Challenges to the Public Employer." *Public Administration Review,* 56: 326–333.

NOCERA, J. 1999, September 27. "Sometimes, a Serial Killer Is Just a Serial Killer." *Fortune,* p. 60.

NORC (NATIONAL OPINION RESEARCH CENTER). Annual. *General Social Survey, Cumulative Codebook.* Chicago: University of Chicago Press.

NORDHEIMER, J. 1996, December 22. "One Day's Death Toll on the Job." *New York Times,* sec. 3, pp. 1, 10.

NUSSBAUM, K. 1999, February. "Bye Bye to Pinkie Rings." *Working USA,* pp. 54–64.

OBER, K., L. CARLSON, & P. ANDERSON. 1997. "Cardiovascular Risk Factors in Homeless Adults." *Journal of Cardiovascular Nursing,* 11: 50–60.

OETTING, E. R., & F. BEAUVAIS. 1987, Spring. "Common Elements in Youth Drug Abuse: Peer Clusters and Other Psychosocial Factors." *Journal of Drug Issues,* pp. 133–151.

O'FARRELL, A., S. ALLWRIGHT, & D. BEDFORD. 2004. "Trends in Hospital Admissions for Self Inflicted Injuries Among Residents from a Health Board Region in Ireland over a 5 Year Period: The Increasing Positive Association with Alcohol." *Journal of Epidemiology and Community Health,* 58: A107.

OFFICE OF JUVENILE JUSTICE AND DELINQUENCY PROTECTION. 2005. www.ojjdp.ncjrs. org/.

OFFICE OF JUVENILE JUSTICE AND DELINQUENCY PREVENTION, U.S. Department of Justice. 2006. *Arrests of Youths, 1980–2004.* http://llojjdp.ncjrs.org.

OGBURN, W. F. 1957. "Cultural Lag as Theory." *Sociology and Social Research,* 41: 167–174.

OGDEN, D. W. 2003, September. "American Psychological Association (APA) et al., Amici Curiae." *Supreme Court Debates,* pp. 182–183.

O'HARE, W. P. 1996. "A New Look at Poverty in America." *Population Bulletin* (Population Reference Bureau), vol. 51.

O'HARE, W. P., & M. MATHER. 2003. *The Growing Number of Kids in Severely Distressed Neighborhoods: Evidence from the 2000 Census.* Washington, DC: Annie E. Casey Foundation and Population Reference Bureau.

OKUN, B. F. 1996. *Understanding Diverse Families: What Practitioners Need to Know.* New York: Guilford Press.

OLIVE, M. F. 2004. *Designer Drugs.* Philadelphia: Chelsea House.

OLIVER, M. L., & T. M. SHAPIRO. 1995. *Black Wealth/White Wealth: A New Perspective on Racial Inequality.* New York: Routledge.

O'NEIL, J. 2002, February 5. "Airplane Noise Hurts More Than Ears." *New York Times.*

OPPENHEIMER, V. C. 1994. "Women's Rising Employment and the Future of the Family in Industrial Societies." *Population and Development Review,* 20: 293–342.

ORCHARD, A. L., & K. B. SOLBERG. 1999. "Expectations of the Stepmother's Role." *Journal of Divorce and Remarriage,* 31: 107–124.

ORE, T. E. 2006. *The Social Construction of Difference and Inequality: Race, Class, Gender, and Sexuality,* 3rd ed. Boston: McGraw-Hill.

ORFIELD, G. 1999, December. "Policy and Equity: A Third of a Century of Educational Reforms in the United States." *Prospects* (Paris, France), pp. 579–594.

ORFIELD, G. 2001, July 17. *Schools More Separate: Consequences of a Decade of Resegregation.* Cambridge, MA: Harvard Civil Rights Project.

ORFIELD, G., & S. E. EATON. 1996. *Dismantling Desegregation: The Quiet Reversal of Brown v. Board of Education.* New York: New Press.

ORMES, I. 1973. *Clipped Wings.* London: William Kimber.

OSSORIO, P., & T. DUSTER. 2005. "Race and Genetics: Controversies in Biomedical, Behavioral, and Forensic Sciences." *American Psychologist,* 60: 115–128.

PAGER, D. 2003. "The Mark of a Criminal Record." *American Journal of Sociology,* 108: 937–975.

PAKHOMOU, S-M. 2004. "Serial Killers: Offender's Relationship to the Victim and Selected Demographics." *International Journal of Police Science and Management,* 6: 219–233.

PALEN, J. J. 2005. *The Urban World,* 7th ed. Boston: McGraw-Hill

PAONE, D., D. C. DES JARLAIS, & S. CALOIR. 1995. "Operational Issues in Syringe Exchanges: The New York City Tagging Alternative Study." *Journal of Community Health,* 20: 111–123.

PARELIUS, A. P., & R. J. PARELIUS. 1987. *The Sociology of Education,* 2nd ed. Upper Saddle River, NJ: Prentice Hall.

PARK, A. 2001, September 10. "More Drugs to Treat Hyperactivity." *Time,* p. 63.

PARK, R. E. 1955. "The Natural History of the Newspaper." In *Society: The Collected Papers of Robert Ezra Park,* Vol. III. New York: Free Press.

PARROTT, A., et al. 2004. *Understanding Drugs and Behaviour.* Hoboken, NJ: Wiley.

PARSONS, T. 1943. "The Kinship System of the Contemporary United States." *American Anthropologist,* 45: 22–38.

PATANJALI, P. C. 2005. *Development of Women Education in India.* New Delhi: Shree.

PATTERSON, J. T. 2001. *Brown v. Board of Education: A Civil Rights Milestone and Its Troubled Legacy.* New York: Oxford University Press.

PAUL, A. M. 1998, May–June. "Where Bias Begins: The Truth About Stereotypes." *Psychology Today,* pp. 52–57.

PEAR, R. 1997, May 18. "Academy Report Says Immigration Benefits the U.S." *New York Times,* p. 1.

PEAR, R. 1998, August 9. "Government Lags in Steps to Widen Health Coverage." *New York Times,* pp. 1, 22.

PEELE, S. 1987. "A Moral Vision of Addiction: How People's Values Determine Whether They Become and Remain Addicts." *Journal of Drug Issues,* 17: 187–215.

PEPINSKY, H. E., & R. QUINNEY. 1991. *Criminology as Peacemaking.* Bloomington: Indiana University Press.

PEW FORUM ON RELIGION AND AMERICAN LIFE. 2006, August 3. *Pragmatic Americans Liberal and Conservative on Social Issues.* Washington, DC: Pew Research Center.

PEW RESEARCH CENTER. 2002, December 4. *What the World Thinks in 2002.* Washington, DC: Pew Research Center.

PEW RESEARCH CENTER. 2005, November 17. "Opinion Leaders Turn Cautious, Public Looks Homeward." Washington, DC: Pew Research Center.

PEW RESEARCH CENTER. 2007. *Pew Global Attitudes Project.* http://pewglobal.org.

PIFER, A., & L. BRONTE. 1986. *Our Aging Society, Paradox and Promise.* New York: Norton.

PHILLIPS, M. 1998, October 25. "Forget Psychiatry, Stop Psychopaths." *New York Times,* p. 19.

PILKINGTON, E. 2007, July 23. "U.S. Ambassador Says Iraqi Aides Will Quit Unless Granted Asylum." *The Guardian.* www.guardian.co.uk/usa.

PILLARD, R. C., & J. M. BAILEY. 1998. "Human Sexual Orientation Has a Heritable Component." *Human Biology,* 70: 347–366.

PIMENTEL, D., et al. 2004, October. "Water Resources: Agricultural and Environmental Issues." *Bioscience,* pp. 909–918.

PINSOF, W. M. 2002. "The Death of 'Till Death Us Do Part': The Transformation of Pair-Bonding in the 20th Century." *Family Process,* 41, 135–157.

PIORE, M. J. 1979. *Birds of Passage.* New York: Cambridge University Press.

PIPHER, M. 1999. *Another Country: Negotiating the Emotional Terrain of Our Elders.* New York: Riverhead Books.

PIVEN, F. F. 1999, September. "The Welfare State as Work Enforcer." *Dollars & Sense,* p. 32.

PIVEN, F. F. 2004. *The War at Home: The Domestic Costs of Bush's Militarism.* New York: New Press.

PIVEN, F. F., & R. A. CLOWARD. 1972. *Regulating the Poor: The Functions of Public Welfare.* New York: Random House.

PIVEN, F. F., & R. A. CLOWARD. 1977. *Poor People's Movements: Why They Succeed, How They Fail.* New York: Pantheon Books.

PIVEN, F. F., & R. A. CLOWARD. 1982. *The New Class War: Reagan's Attack on the Welfare State and Its Consequences.* New York: Pantheon Books.

PLANT, M. 2003. "The 2003 European School Survey." Centre for Research in Public Health and Primary Care Development, Project on Alcohol and Other Drugs. http://usc. uwe. ac. uk.

PLATE, T. 1975. "Crime Pays." In P. Wickman & P. Whitten, eds., *Readings in Criminology.* Lexington, MA: D. C. Heath.

PLOUS, S., ed. 2003. *Understanding Prejudice and Discrimination.* Boston: McGraw-Hill.

POPENOE, D. 1995. "The Roots of Declining Social Virtue: Family, Community, and the Need for a 'Natural Communities Policy.'" In M. A. Glendon & D. Blankenhorn, *Seedbeds of Virtue.* New York: Madison Books.

POPENOE, D. 2005. *War over the Family.* New Brunswick, NJ: Transaction.

PORTES, A. 1995. *The Economic Sociology of Immigration.* New York: Russell Sage.

PORTES, A. 2001. *Ethnicities: Children of Immigrants in America.* Berkeley: University of California Press.

PORTES, A., & R. G. RUMBAUT. 1990. *Immigrant America: A Portrait.* Berkeley: University of California Press.

POSTMAN, N., C. NYSTROM, L. STRATE, & C. WEINGARTNER. 1987. *Myth, Men, and Beer: An Analysis of Beer Commercials on Broadcast Television, 1987.* Falls Church, VA: AAA Foundation for Traffic Safety.

POWASKI, R. E. 2003. *Return to Armageddon: The United States and the Nuclear Arms Race.* New York: Oxford University Press.

PRESTON, S. H. 1984, December. "Children and the Elderly in the United States." *Scientific American,* p. 44.

PRESTON, S. H. 1987. "The Decline of Fertility in Non-European Industrialized Nations." *Population and Development Review,* 12 (Suppl. 5): 26–47.

PRESTON, S. H. 2005. "The Escape from Hunger and Premature Death, 1700–2100: Europe, America, and the Third World." *Population and Development Review,* 31: 165–166.

Public Citizen. 2004, June 22. www.citizen.org.

PURVIS, N. 2004. "The Perspective of the United States on Climate Change and the Kyoto Protocol." *International Review for Environmental Strategies,* 5: 169–177.

QUADAGNO, J. S. 2002. *Aging and the Life Course,* 2nd ed. New York: McGraw-Hill.

QUINDLEN, A. 2005, August 8. "Scrap Metal, Not Soldiers." *Newsweek,* p. 64.

QUINNEY, R. 1979. *Criminology,* 2nd ed. Boston: Little, Brown.

QUINNEY, R. 1986. *Providence, the Reconstruction of Social and Moral Order.* Cincinnati, OH: Anderson.

RACKHAM, A. 1991, January 7. "Economic Downturn Creates Growth in Ranks of Overqualified or Discouraged Job Seekers." *Los Angeles Business Journal,* p. 27.

RADZINOWICZ, L. R., & J. KING. 1977. *The Growth of Crime: The International Experience.* New York: Basic Books.

RAGAVAN, C. 2001, February 5. "Cracking Down on Ecstasy." *U.S. News & World Report.*

RAGHAVAN, S. 2007, July 7. "U.N. Decries Neglect of Iraqi Refugees." *Washington Post,* p. A11.

RAINWATER, L. 1974. "The Lower Class: Health, Illness, and Medical Institutions." In L. Rainwater, ed., *Inequality and Justice.* Hawthorne, NY: Aldine.

RAINWATER, L., & T. M. SMEEDING. 2003. *Poor Kids in a Rich Country: America's Children in Comparative Perspective.* New York: Russell Sage.

RANGEL, C. B. 1998. "Why Drug Legalization Should Be Opposed." *Criminal Justice Ethics,* 17: 2.

RAPOPORT, A. 1968. "Introduction." In Carl von Clausewitz, *On War.* Harmondsworth, England: Penguin Books.

RAY, O. S. 1996. *Drugs, Society and Human Behavior,* 7th ed. St. Louis: Mosby.

RECKLESS, W. C. 1973. *The Crime Problem,* 5th ed. Upper Saddle River, NJ: Prentice Hall.

REES, R. W. 2007. *Shades of Difference: A History of Ethnicity in America.* Lanham, MD: Rowman & Littlefield.

REGIER, D. 1991. *Psychiatric Disorders in America: The Epidemiological Catchment Area Study.* New York: Free Press.

REGIER, D., W. NARROW, D. RAE, R. MANDERSCHEID, B. LOCKE, & F. GOODWIN. 1993. "The De Facto U.S. Mental Health and Addictive Disorders Service System: Epidemiological Catchment Area Prospective One-year Prevalence Rates of Disorders and Services." *Archives of General Psychiatry,* 50: 85–94.

REICH, R. 1992. *The Work of Nations: Preparing Ourselves for 21st Century Capitalism.* New York: Knopf.

REICH, R. B. 1998, Winter. "Broken Faith: Why We Need to Renew the Social Compact." *Generations,* p. 19.

REID, S. T. 1991. *Crime and Criminology.* Fort Worth, TX: Harcourt Brace.

REID, S. T. 1993. *Criminal Justice,* 3rd ed. New York: Macmillan.

REISS, A. J., JR., & J. A. ROTH, eds. 1993. *Understanding and Preventing Violence.* Washington, DC: National Academy of Science Press.

RENSENBRINK, C. W. 2001. *All in Our Places.* Lanham, MD: Rowman & Littlefield.

RESKIN, B., & H. HARTMAN, eds. 1986. *Women's Work, Men's Work: Sex Segregation on the Job.* Washington, DC: National Academy of Sciences Press.

RETSINAS, J. 1988. "Are There Stages of Dying?" *Death Studies,* 12: 207–216.

REUTERS. 2002, November 12. "Three Firms Bid for $3.5 bln Polish Jet Contract."

RICH, E., & EVANS, J. 2005. "Discourse." *Studies in the Cultural Politics of Education,* 26: 247–262.

RICHARDSON, D., & H. MAY. 1999. "Deserving Victims? Sexual Status and the Social Construction of Violence." *Sociological Review,* 47: 308.

RICHMOND-ABBOTT, M. 1992. *Masculine and Feminine: Gender Roles Over the Life Cycle,* 2nd ed. New York: McGraw-Hill.

RIESMAN, D., N. GLAZER, & R. DENNEY. 1950. *The Lonely Crowd.* New Haven, CT: Yale University Press.

RIESSMAN, C. K. 1983, Summer. "Women and Medicalization." *Social Policy*, pp. 3–18.

RIFKIN, J. 1995. *The End of Work: The Decline of the Global Labor Force and the Dawn of the Post-market Era.* New York: Putnam.

RILEY, D., & M. McLAUGHLIN. 2001. *Turning the Corner: Energy Solutions for the 21st Century.* Tahoe City, CA: Alternative Energy Institute.

RILEY, M. W. 1987, February. "On the Significance of Age in Sociology." *American Sociological Review*, 52: 1–14.

RILEY, M. W. 1996. "Discussion: What Does It All Mean?" *The Gerontologist*, 36: 256–258.

RILEY, M. W., R. L. KAHN, & A. FONER. 1994. *Age and Structural Lag: Society's Failure to Provide Meaningful Opportunities in Work, Family, and Leisure.* New York: Wiley.

RILEY, M. W., & J. WARING. 1976. "Age and Aging." In R. K. Merton & R. Nisbet, eds., *Contemporary Social Problems*, 4th ed. New York: Harcourt Brace Jovanovich.

RINDFUSS, R. R., K. L. BREWSTER, & A. L. KAVEE. 1996. "Women, Work, and Children in the U.S." *Population and Development Review*, 22: 457–482.

RIORDAN, C. 2004. *Equality and Achievement: An Introduction to the Sociology of Education*, 2nd ed. Upper Saddle River, NJ: Pearson/Prentice Hall.

RIST, R. C. 1973. *The Urban School: A Factory for Failure.* Cambridge, MA: MIT Press.

RITZER, G. 1993. *The McDonaldization of Society: An Investigation Into the Changing Character of Contemporary Social Life.* Newbury Park, CA: Pine Forge Press.

ROBBINS, R. 2001. *Global Problems and the Culture of Capitalism.* Boston: Allyn & Bacon.

ROBERTSON, J. 2005. *Same-sex Cultures and Sexualities: An Anthropological Reader.* Malden, MA: Blackwell.

ROBINS, L. N., et al. 1984. "Lifetime Prevalence of Specific Psychiatric Disorders in Three Sites." *Archives of General Psychiatry*, 41: 949–958.

ROBINSON, J. P., & G. GODBEY. 1996. "The Great American Slowdown." *American Demographics*, 18: 42–46.

ROCHMAN, S. 1999, October 12. "Leaving Safety at the Bedroom Door." *The Advocate*, p. 18.

RODRIGUEZ, J. 1999, Summer. "Welfare Reform and Latinos: Immigration and Cultural Politics." *Nieman Reports*, p. 45.

ROGERS, C. C. 2001, May–August. "A Look at America's Children and Their Families." *Food Review*, pp. 2–7.

ROHATYN, F. 1987, December 3. "What Next?" *New York Review of Books*, pp. 3–5.

ROMICH, J. L., & T. S. WEISNER. 2004. "How Families View and Use Lump-Sum Payments from the Earned Income Tax Credit." In G. J. Duncan & P. L. Chase-Lansdale, eds., *For Better and for Worse: Welfare Reform and the Well-being of Children and Families.* New York: Russell Sage.

ROSARIO, V. A. 2002. *Homosexuality and Science.* Santa Barbara, CA: HBC-CLIO.

ROSENBAUM, J. E., N. FISHMAN, A. BRETT, & P. MEADEN. 1996. "Can the Kerner Commission's Housing Strategy Improve Employment, Education, and Social Integration for Low-income Blacks?" *North Carolina Law Review*, 71: 1519–1566.

ROSENHAN, D. L. 1973. "On Being Sane in Insane Places." *Science*, 179: 250–258.

ROSS, A. 2000, January. "Techno-Sweatshops." *Tikkun*, p. 57.

ROSS, C., & J. HUBER. 1985. "Hardship and Depression." *Health and Social Behavior*, 26: 312–327.

ROSSI, A. S., & P. H. ROSSI. 1990. *Of Human Bonding: Parent–Child Relations Across the Lifecourse.* New York: Aldine de Gruyter.

ROSSI, P. H. 1989a. *Down and Out in America: The Origins of Homelessness.* Chicago: University of Chicago Press.

ROWLAND, D. 1994. "Lessons from the Medicaid Experience." In E. Ginzberg, ed., *Critical Issues in U.S. Health Care Reform.* Boulder, CO: Westview.

RUBINGTON, E., & M. S. WEINBERG. 1987. *Deviance, the Interactionist Perspective: Text and Readings in the Sociology of Deviance*, 5th ed. New York: Macmillan.

RUBINGTON, E., & M. S. WEINBERG. 1995. *The Study of Social Problems: Seven Perspectives*, 5th ed. New York: Oxford University Press.

RUDOLPH, J. R. 1995. "Intervention in Communal Conflicts." *Orbis*, 39: 259–273.

RUGGLES, P. 1990. *Drawing the Line: Alternative Poverty Measures and Their Implications.* Washington, DC: Urban Institute.

RUSSELL, K. 1999, August. "Is Crime 'Profiling' a Reasonable Premise?" *USA Today Magazine*, p. 12.

RUSSELL, K. K. 1987, June 14. "Growing Up with Privilege and Prejudice." *New York Times Magazine*, pp. 22ff.

SADD, S., & R. M. GRINC. 1996. *Implementation Challenges in Community Policing: Innovative Neighborhood-oriented Policing in Eight Cities.* Washington, DC: National Institute of Justice, U.S. Department of Justice.

SAFILIOS-ROTHSCHILD, C. 1974. *Women and Social Policy.* Upper Saddle River, NJ: Prentice Hall.

SALINGER, L. M., ed. 2004. *Encyclopedia of White Collar and Corporate Crime.* Thousand Oaks, CA: Sage.

SALINGER, L. M. 2005. "Rethinking Corporate Crime." *Contemporary Sociology*, 34: 312–313.

SALINS, P. D. 1986, Fall. "Toward a Permanent Housing Problem." *Public Interest*, pp. 22–34.

SALTER, S. 1996, March 10. "More Kids About to Fall Through the Cracks." *San Francisco Chronicle*, p. B11.

SAMPSON, R. 2001. *Disorder in Urban Neighborhoods: Does It Lead to Crime?* Washington, DC: Department of Justice, Office of Justice Programs, National Institute of Justice.

SAMPSON, R. J., & S. RAUDENBUSH. 1999. "Systematic Social Observation of Public Spaces: A New Look at Disorder in Urban Neighborhoods." *American Journal of Sociology*, 105: 603–651.

SANCHEZ-JANKOWSKI, M. 1991. *Islands in the Street: Gangs and American Urban Society.* Berkeley: University of California Press.

SANDEFUR, G. 1996. *Changing Numbers, Changing Needs: American Indian Demography and Public Health.* Washington, DC: National Academy Press.

SANDEFUR, G. T., & M. TIENDA, eds. 1988. *Divided Opportunities: Minorities, Poverty, and Social Policy.* New York: Plenum Press.

SANFORD, W. C., J. McCORD, & E. A. McGEE. 1976. "Abortion." In Boston Women's Health Book Collective, eds., *Our Bodies, Ourselves.* New York: Simon & Schuster.

SAPOLSKY, R. M. 2004. "Your Personal Pathology." *Scientific American*, 24: 9–10.

SAPORITO, S., & A. LAREAU. 1999. "School Selection as a Process: The Multiple Dimensions of Race in Framing Educational Choice." *Social Problems*, 46: 418.

SATEL, S. 2005, August 16. "A Whiff of 'Reefer Madness' in U.S. Drug Policy." *New York Times*, p. F6.

SCHEFF, T. J. 1963. "The Role of the Mentally Ill and the Dynamics of Mental Disorder." *Sociometry*, 26: 436–453.

SCHMALLEGER, F. 2000. *Criminal Justice Today.* Upper Saddle River, NJ: Prentice Hall.

SCHMIDT, G. 1997. "The Social Organization of Sexuality: Sexual Practices in the United States." *Archives of Sexual Behavior*, 26: 327–333.

SCHUCKIT, M. A., & T. C. JEFFERSON. 1999. "New Findings in the Genetics of Alcoholism." *Journal of the American Medical Association*, 281: 1875.

SCHULTE, B., & C. L. JENKINS. 2007, May 7. "Cho Didn't Get Court-Ordered Treatment." *Washington Post*, p. A1.

SCHUR, E. M. 1973. *Radical Nonintervention: Rethinking the Delinquency Problem.* Upper Saddle River, NJ: Prentice Hall.

SCHWEINHART, L. J. 2002. "Recent Evidence on Preschool Programs." *ERIC Digest*, pp. 5–12.

SCOTT, A. J. 1999. "Los Angeles and the LA School: A Response to Curry and Kenney." *Antipode*, p. 31.

SCULL, A. T. 1988. "Deviance and Social Control." In N. J. Smelser, ed., *The Handbook of Sociology.* Newbury Park, CA: Sage.

SEAL, K. H., et al. 2007, March 12. "Bringing the War Back Home." *Archives of Internal Medicine*, pp. 476–482.

SEARS, D. O., J. SIDANIUS, & L. BOBO, eds. 2000. *Racialized Politics: The Debate About Racism in America.* Chicago: University of Chicago Press.

SEIDMAN, S., N. FISCHER, & C. MEEKS, eds. 2006. *Handbook of the New Sexuality Studies.* New York: Routledge.

THE SENTENCING PROJECT. 2003. *Felony Disenfranchisement.* www.sentencingproject.org.

SHAPIRO, J. P. 1996, September 16. "Kids with Gay Parents." *U.S. News & World Report*, pp. 75–79.

SHAW, C. R. 1929. *Delinquency Areas: A Study of the Geographic Distribution of School Truants, Juvenile Delinquents, and Adult Offenders in Chicago.* Chicago: University of Chicago Press.

SHAW, J. 1999, October–December. "Laundering Moscow's Money." *Europe Business Review*, p. 20.

SHEEHAN, S. 1982. *Is There No Place on Earth for Me?* New York: Scribner.

SHELBY, D. 2007, March 30. "United States Prepared to Accept Additional Iraqi Refugees." USINFO. http://usinfo.state.gov.

SHERMAN, L. W., J. W. SHAW, & D. P. ROGAN. 1995. *The Kansas City Gun Experiment.* Washington, DC: National Institute of Justice, U.S. Department of Justice.

SHERRILL, R. 1997, April 7. "A Year in Corporate Crime." *The Nation*, pp. 1–9.

SHOOP, J. G. 1998. "Gang Warfare: Legal Battle Pits Personal Liberty Against Public Safety." *Trial*, 34: 12–16.

SIEGEL, L. 1999. *Criminology.* Belmont, CA. Wadsworth.

SILBERMAN, C. 1980. *Criminal Violence, Criminal Justice.* New York: Random House.

SIMMONS, T., & J. L. DYE. 2003. *Grandparents Living with Grandchildren: 2000.* Washington, DC: U.S. Census Bureau.

SIMPSON, G. E., & J. M. YINGER. 1985. *Racial and Ethnic Minorities: An Analysis of Prejudice and Discrimination*, 5th ed. New York: Plenum.

SINGER, J. D., & M. SMALL. 1972. *The Wages of War, 1816–1965: A Statistical Handbook.* New York: Wiley.

SIZER, T. R. 1992, November. "School Reform: What's Missing." *World Monitor*, pp. 20–24.

SKOLNICK, A. S., & J. SKOLNICK. 2007. *Family in Tradition*, 14th ed. Boston: Allyn & Bacon.

SLAVIN, R. E. 1997, December. "Can Education Reduce Social Inequality?" *Educational Leadership*, pp. 6–11.

SLOBIN, S. 1999, December 12. "Homeless in America: A Statistical Profile." *New York Times*, p. 3.

SMALL, M. F. 2002, July. "What You Can Learn from a Drunk Monkey." *Discover*, pp. 41–45.

SMEAL, E. 2005. "Feminist Majority Opposes Nomination of John Roberts for Chief Justice." Feminist Majority Foundation, www.feminist.org.

SMELSER, N. J., & R. SWEDBERG, eds. 2005. *The Handbook of Economic Sociology*, 2nd ed. Princeton, NJ: Princeton University Press.

SMIL, V. 1997. *Cycles of Life: Civilization and the Biosphere.* New York: Freeman.

SMITH, B. L., K. R. DAMPHOUSE, F. JACKSON, & A. SELLERS. 2002. "The Prosecution and Punishment of International Terrorists in Federal Courts: 1980–1998." *Criminology and Public Policy*, 1: 311–337.

SMOLOWE, J. 1996, Fall. "Older, Longer." *Time*, pp. 76–80.

SNOW, D. A. 1993. *Down on Their Luck: A Study of Homeless Street People.* Berkeley: University of California Press.

SNYDER, H. W., & M. SICKMUND. 2006. *Juvenile Offenders and Victims: 2006 National Report.* Washington, DC: U.S. Department of Justice.

SONTAG, E. 2005, April 24. "Many Say End of Firearm Ban Changed Little." *New York Times*, p. 1.

SOROKIN, P. 1937. *Social and Cultural Dynamics: Vol. 3. Fluctuations of Social Relationships, War, and Revolution.* New York: American Book.

SOUDER, M., & L. ZIMMER. 1998, January 12. "Symposium." *Insight on the News*, pp. 24–28.

SPAIN, D. 1996. *Balancing Act: Motherhood, Marriage, and Employment Among American Women*. New York: Russell Sage.

SPAIN, D. 2000. "Governing Out of Order: Space, Law and the Politics of Belonging." *Contemporary Sociology*, 29: 666–667.

SPECTOR, B. I. 2003. "Negotiating with Villains Revisited: Research Note." *International Negotiation*, 8: 613–621.

SPECTOR, M., & J. KITSUSE. 1987. *Constructing Social Problems*. Hawthorne, NY: Aldine de Gruyter.

SPERRY, L. 1995. *Pharmacology and Psychotherapy: Strategies for Maximizing Treatment Outcomes*. New York: Brunner/Mazel.

SQUIRE, S. 1987, November 22. "Shock Therapy's Return to Respectability." *New York Times Magazine*, pp. 78ff.

SROLE, L., T. S. LANGNER, S. T. MICHAEL, P. KIRKPATRICK, M. K. OPLER, & T. A. C. RENNIE. 1978. *Mental Health in the Metropolis: The Midtown Manhattan Study*, rev. ed. New York: New York University Press.

STAPLES, B. 1999. "Affirmative Action." August 9. *New York Times*, p. A14.

STARES, P. B. 1996. *Global Habit: The Drug Problem in a Borderless World*. Washington, DC: Brookings Institution.

STARR, P. 1982. *The Social Transformation of American Medicine*. New York: Basic Books.

STARR, P. 1995, September 3. "Look Who's Talking Health Care Reform Now: Proposed Changes to Medicare and Medicaid." *New York Times Magazine*, pp. 42–43.

STATE HIGHER EDUCATION EXECUTIVE OFFICERS. 2005. *State Higher Education Finance FY2004*. Boulder, CO: State Higher Education Executive Officers.

Statistical Abstract of the United States. Annual. Washington, DC: U.S. Government Printing Office.

STEELE, B., & C. B. POLLOCK. 1974. "A Psychiatric Study of Parents Who Abuse Infants and Small Children." In R. Helfer & C. Kempe, eds., *The Battered Child*. Chicago: University of Chicago Press.

STEFFENSMEIER, D., & E. ALLAN. 1996. "Gender and Crime: Toward a Gendered Theory of Female Offending." *Annual Review of Sociology*, 22: 459.

STEIN, A. 2001. *The Stranger Next Door*. Boston: Beacon Press.

STEIN, L. 2003, June 23. "Sex Trafficking." *U.S. News & World Report*.

STEINBERG, S. 1996, March. "The Affirmative Action Debate." *UNESCO Courier*, pp. 17–21.

STEINHAUER, J. 1995, August 2. "Study Cites Adult Males for Most Teen-age Births." *New York Times*, p. A10.

STERK, C. 1988, May 7. "Cocaine and HIV Positivity." *The Lancet*, pp. 1052–1053.

STERK, C. E. 2000. *Tricking and Tripping: Prostitution in the Era of AIDS*. Putnam Valley, NY: Social Change Press.

STEVENS, W. K. 1987, October 12. "Defining the 'Outer City': For Now, Call It Hybrid." *New York Times*, p. A14.

STEVENSON, H. W. 1992, December. "Learning from Asian Schools." *Scientific American*, pp. 70–76.

STEVENSON, H. W. 1998, March. "A Study of Three Cultures: Germany, Japan, and the United States—An Overview of the TIMSS Case Study Project." *Phi Delta Kappan*, pp. 524–530.

STEVENSON, R. W. 2000, January 23. "In a Time of Plenty, the Poor Are Still Poor." *New York Times*, p. 3.

STEVENSON, R. W. 2002, December 8. "The Incredible Shrinking Government, Bush Style." *New York Times*, p. 4.

STIGLITZ, J. 2002. *Globalization and Its Discontents*. New York: Norton.

STONE, P. 2007. *Opting Out? Why Women Really Quit Careers and Head Home*. Berkeley: University of California Press.

STOUFFER, S. A., E. A. SUCHMAN, L. C. DEVINNEY, S. A. STARR, & R. M. WILLIAMS. 1949. *The American Soldier*. Princeton, NJ: Princeton University Press.

STOVER, P., & Y. GILLES. 1987, October 27. "Sexual Harassment in the Workplace." Conference report, Michigan Task Force on Sexual Harassment, Detroit.

STRINGFIELD, S., & D. LAND, eds. 2002. *Educational At Risk Children*. Chicago: University of Chicago Press.

STRONG, B., C. DEVAULT, & T. F. COHEN. 2005. *The Marriage and Family Experience: Intimate Relationships in a Changing Society*, 9th ed. Belmont, CA: Wadsworth.

STUART, D. 2005, July 19. *Statement before the Committee on the Judiciary, United States Senate, Concerning Reauthorization of the Violence Against Women Act*.

SULLIVAN, M. 1989. *Getting Paid*. Ithaca, NY: Cornell University Press.

SULLIVAN, T. A., E. WARREN, & J. WESTBROOK. 2000. *The Fragile Middle Class: Americans in Debt*. New Haven, CT: Yale University Press.

SUSMAN, T. 2005. "Justice Has Its Say." *Newsweek*.

SUSSER, I., & T. C. PATTERSON, eds. 2001. *Cultural Diversity in the United States: A Critical Reader*. Malden, MA: Blackwell.

SUTHERLAND, E. H. 1961. *White Collar Crime*. New York: Holt, Rinehart & Winston.

SUTHERLAND, E. H., & D. R. CRESSEY. 1960. *Principles of Criminology*. Philadelphia: Lippincott.

SUTTLES, G. 1970. *The Social Order of the Slum*. Chicago: University of Chicago Press.

SWEET, J. A., & L. L. BUMPASS. 1987. *American Families and Households*. New York: Russell Sage.

SZASZ, T. S. 1992, Summer. "The Fatal Temptation: Drug Prohibition and the Fear of Autonomy." *Daedalus*, pp. 161–165.

SZASZ, T. S. 1994. *Cruel Compassion: Psychiatric Control of Society's Unwanted*. New York: Wiley.

SZASZ, T. S. 2003. *The Myth of Mental Illness: Foundations of a Theory of Personal Conduct*, rev. ed. New York: Perennial.

SZYNDROWSKI, D. 1999. "The Impact of Domestic Violence on Adolescent Aggression in the Schools." *Preventing School Failure*, 44: 9.

TAYLOR, D. E. 2000. "The Rise of the Environmental Justice Paradigm: Injustice Framing and the Social Construction of Environmental Discourse." *American Behavioral Scientist*, 43: 508–580.

THERNSTROM, A., & S. THERNSTROM. 2002. *Beyond the Color Line: New Perspectives in Race and Ethnicity in America*. Stanford, CA: Hoover Institution.

THOMAS, W. I., & F. ZNANIECKI. 1922. *The Polish Peasant in Europe and America*. New York: Knopf.

THOMPSON, M. L. 2007. *Mental Illness*. Westport, CT: Greenwood Press.

THORNE, B. 1994. *Gender Play*. New Brunswick, NJ: Rutgers University Press.

TIENDA, M. 1999, May 16. "A Man's Place." *New York Times Magazine*, p. 48.

TITTLE, C. R., W. J. VILLEMEZ, & D. A. SMITH. 1978. "The Myth of Social Class and Criminality: An Empirical Assessment of the Empirical Evidence." *American Sociological Review*, 43: 643–656.

TOBIN, J. 1994. "Poverty in Relation to Macroeconomic Trends, Cycles and Policies." In S. H. Danziger & G. Sandefur, eds., *Poverty and Public Policy*. Cambridge, MA: Harvard University Press.

TONER, R., & S. G. STOLBERG. 2002, August 11. "Decade After Health Care Crisis, Soaring Costs Bring New Strains." *New York Times*, pp. 1, 24.

TOOLAN, D. S. 1998, May 13. "Earth Day with Bella, Barry and Friends." *America*, pp. 3–5.

TOWER, C. C. 2002. *Understanding Child Abuse and Neglect*. Boston: Allyn & Bacon.

TRAUB, J. 1996, November 4. "The Criminals of Tomorrow." *The New Yorker*, pp. 50–65.

TRAVIS, J., & J. PETERSILIA. 2001. "Reentry Reconsidered: A New Look at an Old Question." *Crime and Delinquency*, 47: 291–310.

TREMBLAY, R. E. 2000. "The Development of Aggressive Behaviour During Childhood: What Have We Learned in the Past Century?" *International Journal of Behavioral Development*, 24: 129–141.

TROIDEN, R. R. 1987. "Becoming Homosexual." In E. Rubington & M. S. Weinberg, eds., *Deviance: The Interactionist Perspective*, 5th ed. New York: Macmillan.

TSFATI, Y., & G. WEIMANN. 2002. "www.terrorism. com: Terror on the Internet." *Studies in Conflict and Terrorism*, 25: 317–332.

TUCKETT, D., ed. 2003. *An Introduction to Medical Sociology*. London: Tavistock.

TURNER, J. 2002. *Families in America: A Reference Handbook*. Santa Barbara, CA: ABC-CLIO.

TURNEY, K., S. CLAMPET-LUNDQUIST, K. EDIN, J. R. KLING, & G. J. DUNCAN. 2006, April. "Neighborhood Effects on Barriers to Employment: Results from a Randomized Housing Mobility Experiment in Baltimore." Working Paper no. 511, Industrial Relations Section. Princeton, NJ: Princeton University.

UCR (UNIFORM CRIME REPORTS, FEDERAL BUREAU OF INVESTIGATION). Annual. *Crime in the United States*. Washington, DC: U.S. Government Printing Office.

UNAIDS. 2004. *Report on the Global HIV/AIDS Epidemic 2004*. Geneva: Joint United Nations Programme on HIV/AIDS.

UNAIDS/UNICEF/USAID. 2002. *Children on the Brink 2002: A Joint Report on Orphan Estimates and Program Strategies*. www.unicef.org.

UNESCO. 2002. www.unesco.org/bangkok/news/press/2001/02literacy.htm.

UN-HABITAT. 2005. *The Global Report on Human Settlements*. www.unhabitat.org/.

UNION OF CONCERNED SCIENTISTS. 2002, October 31. *Restoring Scientific Integrity in Policymaking*. www.ucsusa.org/scientific_integrity/interference/scientists-signon-statement.html.

UNITED NATIONS. 1999a, December 15. Report of the Independent Inquiry Into the Actions of the United Nations During the 1994 Genocide in Rwanda.

UNITED NATIONS. 1999b, November 15. Report of the Secretary-General Pursuant to General Assembly Resolution 53/55 (1998). Srebenica Report.

UNITED NATIONS DEVELOPMENT PROGRAMME. Annual. *Human Development Report*. New York: Oxford University Press.

UNITED NATIONS HIGH COMMISSION FOR REFUGEES. 2007, April. "Statistics on Displaced Iraqis Around the World."

UNITED NATIONS POPULATION FUND. 2007. *State of the World Population, 2007*. www.unfpa.org.

URQUHART, B. 2000, April 27. "In the Name of Humanity." *New York Review of Books*, pp. 19–22.

U.S. BUREAU OF JUSTICE STATISTICS. 2007. *Capital Punishment 2005*. www.ojp.usdoj.gov/bjs.

U.S. CENSUS BUREAU. Decennial. *Census of Population*. Washington, DC: U.S. Government Printing Office.

U.S. CENSUS BUREAU. 2001. Profile of the Foreign Born Population in the United States: 2000. *Current Population Reports*.

U.S. CENSUS BUREAU. 2005. *Current Population Survey*. www.census.gov.

U.S. CENSUS BUREAU. 2005. *International Database*. www.census.gov/ipc/www/idbprint.html.

U.S. CENSUS BUREAU. 2006. *Income, Poverty, and Health Insurance Coverage in the United States: 2005*. www.census.gov.

U.S. CENTERS FOR DISEASE CONTROL 2004, January 9. "State-Specific Prevalence of Current Cigarette Smoking Among Adults—United States, 2002." *Morbidity and Mortality Weekly Report*. Atlanta: U.S. Centers for Disease Control.

U.S. CENTERS FOR DISEASE CONTROL. 2004, May 21. "Youth Risk Behavior, Surveillance Report, 2003." *Monthly Mortality and Morbidity Report*. Atlanta: U.S. Centers for Disease Control.

U.S. CENTERS FOR DISEASE CONTROL. 2005. *CDC Surveillance Report, 2005*. Atlanta: U.S. Centers for Disease Control.

U.S. COMMISSION ON CIVIL RIGHTS, OHIO ADVISORY COMMITTEE. 2001, November 14. *Briefing on Civil Rights Issues Facing Muslims and Arab Americans in Ohio Post-September 11*.

U.S. CONFERENCE OF MAYORS. 2000. *A Status Report on Hunger and Homelessness in America's Cities: 2000.* Washington, DC: U.S. Conference of Mayors.

U.S. CONGRESS. 1993. *Proliferation Threats of the 1990's.* Hearing before the Committee on Governmental Affairs, U.S. Senate, 103rd Cong., 1st sess., February 24. Washington, DC: U.S. Government Printing Office.

U.S. CONGRESS, HOUSE COMMITTEE ON HEALTH, EDUCATION, LABOR AND PENSIONS. 2001. *Achieving Parity for Mental Health Treatment.* Washington, DC: Government Printing Office.

U.S. DEPARTMENT OF EDUCATION. 2007. *Reading First.* www.ed.gov.

U.S. DEPARTMENT OF HOMELAND SECURITY. 2004. *Yearbook of Immigration Statistics: 2004.* Washington, DC: U.S. Department of Homeland Security.

U.S. DEPARTMENT OF HOMELAND SECURITY. 2007. *Patterns of Global Terrorism Report, 2007.* www.globalsecurity.org.

U.S. DEPARTMENT OF JUSTICE, OFFICE OF JUSTICE PROGRAMS. 2006, April. *Highlights of the 2004 National Youth Gang Survey.* Washington, DC: U.S. Department of Justice.

U.S. DEPARTMENT OF LABOR, BUREAU OF LABOR STATISTICS. 2005, March. *A Profile of the Working Poor, 2005.* Washington, DC: U.S. Department of Labor.

U.S. DEPARTMENT OF LABOR, BUREAU OF LABOR STATISTICS. 2007. *Occupational Outlook Handbook.* www.bls.gov.

U.S. DEPARTMENT OF TRANSPORT, NATIONAL HIGHWAY TRAFFIC SAFETY ADMINISTRATION. ANNUAL. *Federal Highway Administration Annual Highway Statistics.* Washington, DC: U.S. Department of Transportation.

U.S. DRUG ENFORCEMENT AGENCY. 2002. *Purity and Price Report.* www.usdoj.gov/dea.

U.S. SURGEON GENERAL. 2005. *Surgeon General's Report on Mental Illness.* www.surgeongeneral.gov.

VAILLANT, G. E. 1983. *The Natural History of Alcoholism.* Cambridge, MA: Harvard University Press.

VANKATESH, S. 2000. *American Project.* Cambridge, MA: Harvard University Press.

WACQUANT, L. 2001. "Deadly Symbiosis." *Punishment & Society*, 3: 95–133.

WACQUANT, L. 2003. "Toward a Dictatorship Over the Poor?" *Punishment and Society,* 5: 197–205.

WAGGONER, J. 2005, August 16. "Millions of Americans Get By on Social Security Alone." *USA Today.*

WALDINGER, R. 2001. "Perils of the Promised Land." *Journal of American Ethnic History,* 20: 136–142.

WALKER, H. B. 1996. "The United Nations: Peacekeeping and the Middle East." *Asian Affairs,* 27: 13–19.

WALKER, L. 1977. "Battered Women and Learned Helplessness." *Victimology,* 2: 525–534.

WALKER, L. 1987, June 21. "What Comforts AIDS Families." *New York Times Magazine,* pp. 16ff.

WALLERSTEIN, J., & S. BLAKESLEE. 1989. *Second Chances: Men, Women and Children a Decade After Divorce.* New York: Ticknor & Fields.

WALLERSTEIN, J., & S. BLAKESLEE. 2000. *The Unexpected Legacy of Divorce: A 25-Year Landmark Study.* New York: Hyperion.

WATSON, J. 2006, February 12. "After Safest Year on Record, Coal Mining Deaths Raise Concern." Voice of America. www.voanews.com.

WATSON, R., & N. HOWE. 2003. *The 2003 Aging Vulnerability Index.* Washington, DC: Center for Strategic and International Studies.

WEBER, A. 1968. "Labor Market and Perspectives of the New City." In S. F. Fava, ed., *Urbanism in World Perspective: A Reader.* New York: Crowell.

WECHSLER, H., G. W. DOWDALL, G. MAENNER, J. GLEDHILL-HOYT, & H. LEE. 1998. "Changes in Binge Drinking and Related Problems Among American College Students Between 1993 and 1997: Results of the Harvard School of Public Health College Alcohol Study." *Journal of American College Health,* 47: 57–68.

WECHSLER, H., J. E. LEE, M. KUO, & H. LEE. 2000. "College Binge Drinking in the 1990s: A Continuing Problem: Results of the Harvard School of Public Health 1999 College Alcohol Study." *Journal of American College Health,* 48: 199–210.

WEISS, R. S. 1979. *Going It Alone: The Family Life and Social Situation of the Single Parent.* New York: Basic Books.

WEINER, M. D., S. SUSSMAN, P. SUN, & C. DENT, 2005. "Explaining the Link Between Violence Perpetration, Victimization and Drug Use." *Addictive Behaviors,* 30: 1261–1266.

WELLNER, A. S. 1999. "The Young and the Uninsured." *American Demographics,* 21: 72.

WELLS, D. 2003, September–October. "Global Sweatshops and Ethical Buying Codes." *Canadian Dimension.*

WEST, C. 1994. *Race Matters.* New York: Vintage.

WETZEL, J. R. 1995. "Labor Force, Unemployment, and Earnings." In R. Farley, ed., *State of the Union: America in the 1990s,* Vol. 1: *Economic Trends.* New York: Russell Sage.

WHITBOURNE, S. K. 2005. *Adult Development and Aging: Biopsychosocial Perspectives,* 2nd ed. Hoboken, NJ: Wiley.

WHITE, F. 2007, March 27. "America's Health Care Conundrum." www.cnw.ca/fr/releases/archive.

WHITE, M. 1998, September 10. "Study Shows Care in the Community Is Working." *Community Care,* p. 4.

WHITENER, L. A., B. A. WEBER, & G. J. DUNCAN. 2001. "Reforming Welfare Implications for Rural America." *Rural America,* 16: 2–10.

WHO (WORLD HEALTH ORGANIZATION). 1994. *Women and AIDS: Agenda for Action.* Geneva: World Health Organization.

WHO (WORLD HEALTH ORGANIZATION). Annual. *World Health Report.* www.who.int./whr/en/.

WILENSKY, H. L. 1966. "Work as a Social Problem." In H. Becker, ed., *Social Problems.* New York: Wiley.

WILGOREN, J., M. PATES, K. PATTERSON, & G. REUTHLING. 2005, March 22. "Shooting Rampage by Student Leaves 10 Dead on Reservation." *New York Times,* p. A1.

WILKERSON, I. 1991, April 4. "Ravaged City on Mississippi Floundering at Rock Bottom." *New York Times,* pp. A1, A16.

WILLIAMS, J. 2000. *Unbending Gender: Why Families and Work Conflict and What to Do About It.* New York: Oxford University Press.

WILLIAMS, R. M., JR. 1947. *The Reduction of Intergroup Tensions.* New York: Social Science Research Council.

WILLIAMS, T. 1989. *The Cocaine Kids.* Reading, MA: Addison-Wesley.

WILLIAMS, T. 1992. *Crack House.* New York: Addison-Wesley.

WILLIAMS, T. M., & W. KORNBLUM. 1985. *Growing Up Poor.* Boston: D. C. Heath/Lexington Books.

WILLIAMS, T., & W. KORNBLUM. 1994. *The Uptown Kids: Struggle and Hope in the Projects.* New York: Putnam.

WILLIAMS-HAROLD, B. 2000, March. "Across the Great Divide." *Black Enterprise,* p. 30.

WILLIAMSON, C., & T. CLUSE-TOLAR. 2002. "Pimp-Controlled Prostitution: Still an Integral Part of Street Life." *Violence Against Women,* 8: 1074–1092.

WILLIS, P. 1983. "Cultural Production and Theories of Reproduction." In L. Barton & S. Walker, eds., *Race, Class and Education.* London: Croom-Helm.

WILSON, E. O. 1975. *Sociobiology: The New Synthesis.* Cambridge, MA: Belknap Press.

WILSON, J. Q. 1977. *Thinking About Crime.* New York: Vintage Books.

WILSON, J. Q. 1993. *The Moral Sense.* New York: Free Press.

WILSON, J. Q. 1994, Winter. "Abortion: A Moral Issue." *Commentary,* pp. 78–89.

WILSON, J. Q., & R. J. HERRNSTEIN. 1985. *Crime and Human Nature.* New York: Simon & Schuster.

WILSON, W. J. 1987. *The Truly Disadvantaged: The Inner City, the Underclass, and Public Policy.* Chicago: University of Chicago Press.

WILSON, W. J. 1996a. *When Work Disappears: The World of the New Urban Poor.* Chicago: University of Chicago Press.

WILSON, W. J. 1996b, August 18. "Work." *New York Times Magazine,* pp. 26ff.

WILTON, R. D., & J. R. WOLCH. 1996. "The World of Homelessness According to Jencks." *Economic Geography,* 72: 82–88.

WINNER, L. 1977. *Autonomous Technology: Technics-out-of-Control as a Theme in Political Thought.* Cambridge, MA: MIT Press.

WINNER, L. 2004. "Trust and Terror: the Vulnerability of Complex Socio-technical Systems." *Science as Culture,* 13: 155–172.

WINTER, M. 2005. "Fragile Families and Child Wellbeing." *Human Ecology,* 32.

WIRTH, L. 1927. "The Ghetto." *American Journal of Sociology,* 23: 57–71.

WIRTH, L. 2002. *Breaking Through the Glass Ceiling: Women in Management.* Geneva, Switzerland: International Labour Office.

WOLF, R. 1996. *Marriages and Families in a Diverse Society.* New York: HarperCollins.

WOLK, J. L., & S. SCHMAHL. 1999. "Child Support Enforcement: The Ignored Component of Welfare Reform." *Journal of Contemporary Human Services,* 80: 526.

WONDERS, N. A., & R. MICHALOWSKI. 2001. "Bodies, Borders, and Sex Tourism in a Globalized World: A Tale of Two Cities—Amsterdam and Havana." *Social Problems,* 48: 545–571.

WORLD BANK. 2007. *World Development Report 2007.* Washington, DC: World Bank.

WREN, C. S. 1996, February 20. "Marijuana Use by Youths Continues to Rise." *New York Times,* p. A11.

WUETHRICH, B. 2003, March 7. "Chasing the Fickle Swine Flu." *Science, 299:* 1502–1505.

YANG, D. J., & M. SATCHELL. 1999, November 1. "Hell, No. We Won't Trade." *U.S. News & World Report,* p. 54.

YARDLEY, J. 2000, October 7. "The Heat Is On in a Texas Town." *New York Times,* p. 1.

YINGER, M. 1987, Spring. "From Several Threads, Stronger Cords." *Oberlin Alumni Magazine,* pp. 10–13.

YOON, C. K. 1994, March 1. "Thinning Ozone Layer Implicated in Decline of Frogs and Toads." *New York Times,* p. C4.

YU, T. 2006. "Challenging the Politics of the 'Model Minority' Stereotype: A Case for Educational Equality." *Equity and Excellence in Education,* 39: 325–333.

ZIMBARDO, P. G. 1972, April. "Pathology of Imprisonment." *Society,* 9: 4–8.

ZIMRING, F. E. 1985. "Violence and Firearms Policy." In L. A. Curtis, ed., *American Violence and Public Policy.* New Haven, CT: Yale University Press.

ZIMRING, F. E., & G. HAWKINS. 1997. *Crime Is Not the Problem: Lethal Violence in America.* New York: Oxford University Press.

ZOLBERG, A. 2003, November-December. "Uneven Flow." *New Leader,* pp. 1–3.

ZOLBERG, A. 2006. *A Nation by Design: Immigration Policy in the Fashioning of America.* New York: Russell Sage.

ZUBOFF, S. 1982, Winter. "Problems of Symbolic Toil." *Dissent,* pp. 51–62.

ZUKIN, S. 1991. *Landscapes of Power: From Detroit to Disney World.* Berkeley: University of California Press.

ZYWICKI, T. J. 2005. "An Economic Analysis of the Consumer Bankruptcy Crisis." *Northwestern University Law Review,* 99: 1463–1541.

Photo Credits

Index

Page references in *Italic* refer to illustrations, figures and tables.

Name Index

Subject Index